The Polysynthesis Parameter

OXFORD STUDIES IN COMPARATIVE SYNTAX

RICHARD KAYNE, *General Editor*

Principles and Parameters of Syntactic Saturation
GERT WEBELHUTH

Verb Movement and the Expletive Subjects in the Germanic Languages
STEN VIKNER

Parameters and Functional Heads: Essays in Comparative Syntax
EDITED BY ADRIANA BELLETTI AND LUIGI RIZZI

Discourse Configurational Languages
EDITED BY KATALIN É. KISS

Clause Structure and Language Change
EDITED BY ADRIAN BATTYE AND IAN ROBERTS

Dialect Variation and Parameter Setting:
A Study of Belfast English and Standard English
ALISON HENRY

Parameters of Slavic Morphosyntax
STEVEN FRANKS

The Polysynthesis Parameter
MARK C. BAKER

The Polysynthesis Parameter

Mark C. Baker

New York Oxford
Oxford University Press
1996

Oxford University Press

Oxford   New York
Athens   Auckland   Bangkok
Calcutta   Cape Town   Dar es Salaam   Delhi
Florence   Hong Kong   Istanbul   Karachi
Kuala Lumpur   Madras   Madrid   Melbourne
Mexico City   Nairobi   Paris   Singapore
Taipei   Tokyo   Toronto

and associated companies in
Berlin   Ibadan

Copyright © 1996 by Mark C. Baker

Published by Oxford University Press, Inc.
198 Madison Avenue, New York, New York 10016

Oxford is a registered trademark of Oxford University Press, Inc.

Library of Congress Cataloging-in-Publication Data
Baker, Mark C.
The Polysynthesis parameter / Mark C. Baker.
p. cm. — (Oxford studies in comparative syntax)
Includes bibliographical references and index.
ISBN 0-19-509307-0. — ISBN 0-19-509308-9 (pbk.)
1. Grammar, Comparative and general—Syntax.
2. Grammar, Comparative and general—Verb.
3. Mohawk language—Grammar.
4. Typology (Linguistics)
I. Title.   II. Series.
P291.B293 1995   415—dc20
94-32344

1   3   5   7   9   8   6   4   2

Printed in the United States of America
on acid-free paper

This book is dedicated to Jesus, the Christ:

You are worthy to take the scroll
and to open its seals,
because you were slain,
and with your blood you purchased men for God
from every tribe and language and people and nation.
You have made them to be a kingdom and priests to serve our God,
and they will reign on the earth.

Rev. 5:9–10 (NIV)

Preface

Among the most fascinating questions about language to both specialists and non-specialists is: How different are languages and what do those differences mean? This book represents an effort to come to grips with the first part of this question by looking in detail at a type of language that has had relatively little impact on the formulation and development of contemporary linguistic theory. These are the polysynthetic languages, informally defined as those languages in which verbs are built up of many parts, such that a single verb often performs the same expressive function as a whole sentence in more familiar languages. It has been an open question whether the analytical techniques of syntax can be applied profitably to languages such as these. The thesis of this book is that, appearances notwithstanding, many of these techniques and concepts do shed considerable light on the structure of polysynthetic languages once they are applied in the proper way.

In order to establish this point, the exposition is presented on three levels: the descriptive, the theoretical, and the comparative. On the descriptive level, the book presents many detailed facts about the syntax and syntax-related morphology of the Mohawk language, a paradigm example of polysynthesis. These are the result of extensive new fieldwork by myself and my team, supplemented by some textual analysis. The description attempts to be wide-ranging. Thus, while the book is not organized as a grammar of Mohawk, it contains all the major (although not every detail) that I would have included in the syntax and morphology sections of a grammar if I had written one. It also maintains a balance between those topics that are typically noticed by people who write data-driven descriptions of polysynthetic languages and those that are typically of concern to theoreticians working in a universalistic framework. This balance helps to diminish the possibility that languages might seem more diverse from one another than they are because of the diverse interests of those who work on them.

On the theoretical level, this book is concerned with discovering a conception of Universal Grammar that is valid for both polysynthetic languages and nonpolysynthetic languages. A minor theme, in this regard, is the identification and formulation of principles of grammar that are supported by material from both kinds of language rather than only one. The major theme, however, is concerned with the kind of allowance that must be made for linguistic variation within the theory of Universal Grammar. This book explores a strong and interesting position on this question, namely, that the characteristic constructions of polysynthetic languages share a common property. This common property can be given a rather simple and precise formulation that distinguishes polysynthetic languages from other types. In other words, there is a single, well-defined "Polysynthesis Parameter." Thus, while the system of syntactic principles in, say, Mohawk is virtually identical to that of, say, English, the syntactic structure of most sentences is quite different because of the need to conform to this special condition. This view contrasts sharply with two popular views about language differences, the first holding that languages differ from one another in many arbitrary and unrelated ways, and the second holding that languages do not differ from one another in any syntactically significant way.

The comparative level of this book emerges from its descriptive and theoretical concerns. If it is true that the various structures of Mohawk have the character they do because they must all satisfy a single general condition, then these structures or something like them should coexist in other polysynthetic languages as well. Indeed, polysynthetic languages should be similar to one another in a variety of ways. To show that this is true, the structure of Mohawk is compared with that of six other languages historically and geographically distant from it: Wichita, Southern Tiwa, Nahuatl, Mayali (and other Gunwinjguan languages), Chukchee, and Ainu. This comparison also helps to identify certain respects in which Mohawk is not a prototypical polysynthetic language. It is hoped that this will provide a useful compendium of the general characteristics of polysynthetic languages and thus serve as a resource for future research.

This book is organized into three major parts, together with an introductory and a concluding chapter. The introduction sets forth the conceptual background, provides a short description of Mohawk, and formulates a preliminary statement of its central property. This is called the Morphological Visibility Condition (MVC); in essence, it says that every argument of a lexical head in Mohawk must correspond to a suitable morpheme in the word containing that head. Thus, polysynthetic languages are constrained to be pure "head-marking" languages. Most readers should read the introduction first, after which they will be equipped to focus on those parts of the book that interest them most.

Part I deals with the topic of nonconfigurationality, that is, the fact that polysynthetic languages seem not to have a rigid phrase structure. This part develops in detail the claim that because of the MVC noun phrases have the status of adjuncts in the polysynthetic languages. This provides the key for understanding the behavior of anaphora, coreference, quantification, question formation, ellipsis interpretation, and relative clause formation, as well as word order in polysynthetic languages. Most of the information about syntax and the syntax–semantics interface is contained in this part.

Part II takes up the topic of word structure. In contrast to the fluidity of their phrasal syntax, the polysynthetic languages have elaborate, fixed, and rigid word structure. In fact, two distinct but interacting morphological systems—the agreement system and the incorporation system—are at work, both of which are discussed in detail. Word structure also turns out to give the most fine-grained information about syntactic structure in these languages. Again, the influence of the MVC is pervasive, triggering noun incorporation, limiting verb incorporation, and molding the internal syntax of noun phrases in an unusual way. The fact that all polysynthetic languages have approximately the same word structure also has important implications for morphological theory and its relationship to syntax.

Whereas parts I and II concentrate mostly on verbs, the canonical predicates, and nouns, the canonical arguments, in part III the results are extended to adpositional phrases (PPs) and embedded clauses (CPs). The MVC requires that phrases of these types must be adjunct modifiers rather than arguments, with a few principled exceptions. The MVC also influences the internal structure of these phrases, giving them a somewhat different shape from that found in other languages.

Finally, the concluding chapter gives an overview of the ways that polysynthetic languages differ from other languages, summarizing the argument that a single parameter is involved. It also contains a brief reflection on the nature, origins, and meaning of this kind of linguistic diversity.

I feel that I have received much personal enrichment from my involvement in the research reported here. I have found it intriguing, challenging, broadening, enlightening, frustrating, and fun. By making the research available to the field at large in this form, I hope that it will give others at least a pale reflection of those rewards.

Montreal   M.C.B.
September 1994

Acknowledgments

A project of this (or any) size depends, to a considerable extent, on the help of others. It has been such a large part of my professional life over the last five years that I fear I will forget to mention people, thereby offending those who have helped me. But I have certainly not forgotten everyone, as the following paragraphs demonstrate.

First, funding for the research has been received from a number of sources. The original pilot study was supported by the Humanities Research Grants Committee of McGill University. The bulk of the research was then performed under grants 410–89–0207 and 410–90–0308 from the Social Sciences and Humanities Research Council of Canada and grant 91–ER–0578 from the FCAR of Quebec. Finally, this book was completed while the author was a fellow at the Center for Advanced Study in the Behavioral Sciences; I am grateful for financial support in the form of grant SES–9022192 from the U.S. National Science Foundation to that institution.

Next I wish to mention those members of the Mohawk nation without whose help this research would have been impossible. The following individuals showed me hospitality and answered my questions with patience, vigor, and insight: Grace Curotte, Carolee Jacobs, Frank Jacobs, Georgina Jacobs, Doreen Jacobs, and Margaret Lazore. Indirectly helpful have been leaders in Mohawk language programs, including Dorothy Lazore, Eddie Cross, Annette Jacobs and, more generally, the staffs of the Kahnawake Education Center and the Kahnawake Cultural Center. I hope these people succeed in their goal of passing on the heritage of their language in spite of the difficulties involved. If this research supports that effort in some indirect way, I will be pleased.

Third, I wish to give special thanks to the members of the syntax and acquisition research team at McGill University—led by Lisa Travis, Lydia White, and myself—which provided the immediate context in which this research was carried out. In particular, student members Edward Ikeda, Adriana Chamorro, Jennifer Ormston, José Bonneau, and Mihoko Zushi had the courage and initiative to face the Mohawk language with me. I have been fortunate to be able to have such stimulating teammates.

I have also been very fortunate to come into contact with researchers on other polysynthetic languages, who have been generous in sharing their unpublished materials, checking examples for me, and conveying their impressions of those polysynthetic languages they know better than I. Donald Frantz, in particular, has gone beyond the bounds of collegial duty in this respect. Special thanks are also due to Nicholas Evans, whose unpublished work on Mayali I have found invaluable, and to Kenneth Hale for his impressions of Jemez and his corrections of my Nahuatl (among other languages).

Kenneth Hale has also influenced my research in several other ways. He has served as a model of how to conduct research on minority languages and has also given special advice and encouragement concerning what research to undertake and how to present it. Thank you!

Karin Michelson gave me special assistance in the first phase of the project, introducing me to the Iroquoian literature and community, showing me around Kahnawake, and helping me to make my first connections with the Mohawks. Thank you!

I have heard that Paul Postal wanted to argue against one of my analyses of Mohawk, but when he realized that it would not be feasible for him to do further research in that area, he offered to send me all of his Iroquoian materials instead, including some that would have been difficult to get by any other means. Thank you!

When it comes time to thank fellow linguists in general, I am most in danger of forgetting people. Nevertheless, I wish to thank my colleagues at McGill University for providing a favorable research environment and for answering my uninformed questions in their areas of expertise; I mention, in particular, Nicole Domingue and Michel Paradise (the chairs), Glynne Piggot, Karina Wilkinson, and Brendan Gillon. I have had an opportunity to present this work to students in classes at McGill University and the University of Ottawa; I thank them as a group for helping me to clarify and test many points. In particular, I also wish to thank Jan Voskuil and Maire Noonan for their energetic input. I have received useful comments on parts of an earlier draft from Kenneth Hale, Margaret Speas, and Eloise Jelinek. While I always wanted to publish this book, Richard Kayne took the initiative in encouraging me to do so. I have also benefited from the opportunity, over the last five years, to present aspects of this work to audiences at conferences, workshops, and colloquia too numerous to name, some of which are mentioned in the context of specific references and endnotes. Finally, in addition to those named, I have benefited from the suggestions or other assistance provided by the following individuals (in relatively random order): Noam Chomsky, Morris Halle, Alec Marantz, Maria Bittner, Joan Bresnan, Peter Austin, William Foley, Mark Durie, Emmon Bach, Henry Davis, Dominique Sportiche, Hilda Koopman, Tim Stowell, David Pesetsky, Luigi Rizzi, Ian Roberts, Teresa Guasti, Arhonto Terzi, Marianne Mithun, Daniel Everett, Armin Von Stechow, Wolfgang Sternefeld, Stephen Lapointe, Stephen Anderson, Chris Collins, Colin Phillips, David Stampe, Sharon Inkelas, and others.

Although I have tried not to neglect my family while writing this book, I am sure they can think of times when flexibility and understanding have been required of them—perhaps more than I fully realize. I am delighted to thank my wife,

Linda, and my children, Catherine and Nicholas, for giving me something worth coming home to and for sending me back refreshed. I also thank my mother, Jean, for helping to get me started and for still being there.

Finally, I wish to thank my God, who gave me life, strength, and all the abilities that I possess. This research project has included many elements of good luck, in which I have seen his hand. I have also felt his company refreshing in the lonely hours of sifting data, struggling to express myself, and wondering what it all means. I have been challenged by his call to honesty, integrity, and service in all endeavors. The thought that I was writing this book for him has been very real to me, and I am glad that he at least will read it. I hope he will also be pleased with it, knowing that he has high standards but also that he has vast experience in forgiving faults and imperfections. I hope that my human readership will share the same sentiments.

Contents

PART III Nonnominal Categories

The Polysynthesis Parameter

1

Introduction: Of Parameters and Polysynthesis

Languages differ. There is no doubt that the morphological and syntactic structures of Mohawk, Nahuatl, and Nunggubuyu look quite unlike those of English, French, and German. However, the true nature and extent of these differences is an important and controversial question. This is arguably one of the most important empirical questions that linguists can address, the answer having a variety of philosophical, sociological, and practical implications.

A priori, there are two extreme positions one can take toward the superficial differences among languages. On the one hand, it could be that Mohawk, for example, actually differs from, say, English in many minor ways, and that it is the cumulative effect of all these little differences that makes Mohawk seem so alien to an English speaker. The other approach would be to say that Mohawk differs from English in one essential way, but this difference is so deeply embedded in the grammatical system that it affects all kinds of linguistic structures. Which view is the correct one—or perhaps what mixture or intermediate position between the two extremes—is a central concern of linguistic theory.

Edward Sapir apparently considered the answer to this question obvious. He began his well-known introduction to what would now be called linguistic typology with the following words (Sapir 1921:120):

> For it must be obvious to any one who has thought about the question at all or who has felt something of the spirit of a foreign language that there is such a thing as a basic plan, a certain cut, to each language. This type or plan or structural "genius" of the language is something much more fundamental, much more pervasive, than any single feature of it that we can mention, nor can we gain an adequate idea of its nature by a mere recital of the sundry facts that make up the grammar of the language.

In this passage, Sapir expresses the view that the distinctive properties of different languages have something in common: they are specific realizations of some overall "plan." By using such terminology, Sapir seems to have in mind something

3

that is both characteristic of the language in question and conceptually unified. Moreover, he assumes that this is clear to all who have adequate experience with language.

Interestingly, Sapir's view is not obvious to many contemporary linguists. On the contrary, it is implicitly or explicitly denied in much current work. This is particularly true of those who adopt some version of Chomsky's "Principles and Parameters" (P&P) framework (see Chomsky and Lasnik 1993), but it holds of others as well. Therefore, one of three logically possible conclusions can be drawn: (1) contemporary generative linguists have not thought about the question at all, (2) contemporary generative linguists have not felt anything of the spirit of a foreign language, or (3) Sapir was wrong. This book proposes to study this question in some detail, using as a case in point the class of polysynthetic languages (as defined below), with special emphasis on the Mohawk language.

Specifically, I defend the view that Mohawk and similar languages have a single property that distinguishes them from other language types and that influences the form of virtually every sentence of the language. Thus, I will argue that Sapir was right in an important sense in saying that languages have a "structural genius." To the extent that this has been missed by many linguists, we can be accused of not having "felt . . . the spirit of a foreign language"—even when we know a large number of important and intricate facts about the language. On the other hand, Sapir was wrong at least to the extent of saying that this is "obvious." Indeed, we will see that certain factors make the basic plan of a language far from obvious. Nevertheless, the tools and techniques of current generative linguistic theory allow us to be much more precise and explicit about the structural genius of polysynthetic languages than Sapir could be, and enable us to show how that genius shapes the sentences found in texts or conversations.

Why use Mohawk to study this question? A short answer is, simply, that if one wanted to pick a language whose morphosyntax seemed as different as possible from that of English (the most extensively studied language of the world, at least in generative terms), Mohawk would be as good a choice as any and better than most. A somewhat more sophisticated version of this answer comes from the informal typological terms that linguists often use in their preliminary characterizations of languages. First, there is a sense that some languages are syntactically oriented, whereas others are morphologically oriented. Within the more morphologically oriented languages, one can identify two types: *head-marking* languages and *dependent-marking* languages, to use Nichols' (1986) terms. Roughly speaking, head-marking languages make extensive use of agreement morphology on, say, the verb to express linguistic relationships, whereas dependent-marking languages use Case morphology on noun phrases to express comparable relationships. On the other hand, following Greenberg (1963), linguists often categorize languages as being *head initial* (i.e., SVO or VSO), *head final* (SOV), or having *free word order.*[1] Moreover, there are some rough correlations between these two typological schemes. It is well known that head-final languages generally have well-developed systems of grammatical Case, that is, they are dependent-marking languages. Head-marking languages, on the other hand, very often have free word order, with dependents either preceding or following the head (Nichols 1992:ch. 3). This leaves SVO languages as the most likely to not have well-developed Case or agreement morphology. Thus, the following crude three-way typology underlies much descriptive and/or analytical work:

(1)

	I	II	III
Morphological type	Isolating	Dependent marking	Head marking
Word order type	Head initial	Head final	Free
Exemplar	English	Japanese	Mohawk

One often gets a sense that the diversity found in human language from a morphosyntactic perspective falls within the boundaries of these three types. Although many mixtures of these types are attested, there are perhaps no genuinely new types. English is a reasonably pure example of a head-initial, isolating language, as are some languages of West Africa and Southeast Asia. Japanese is a good example of a head-final, dependent-marking language, as are the South Asian languages and Turkish. Mohawk enters the picture as a very pure example of the free word order, head-marking type. For unfortunate historical reasons, less detailed information is known about this type of language than the others. I believe that a deeper and more sophisticated understanding of type III languages is needed, not only because of its inherent interest but also because of the light that it can shed on the question of linguistic diversity and thus on the nature of human language as a whole. This book aspires to be a step toward this goal.

There are also two practical reasons why Mohawk is a good choice. One is that it has been relatively easy to find talented and willing native speakers to work with. (See appendix C for a brief description of my consultants, data-collecting techniques, and other materials used.) The other advantage is that the basic morphological structure and phonological patterns of Mohawk are reasonably well understood, thanks to extensive work on it and the related Northern Iroquoian languages by Floyd Lounsbury, his students, and others they have influenced. Their results are presented in Lounsbury 1953, Postal 1979, Chafe 1967, Chafe 1970, Bonvillain 1973, Michelson 1973, Woodbury 1975, Williams 1976b, Deering and Delisle, 1976, and Michelson 1989, among others. Marianne Mithun has also published an important series of articles over the last fifteen years on typologically interesting features of these languages in comparison with other polysynthetic languages. Thanks to this previous work, it has been possible to address questions of syntax and higher-level morphology relatively directly. It would be impossible for me to cite references in every place where I have profited from this literature, but I hereby acknowledge that what I have done would have been impossible were it not for all this previous research.

The remainder of this chapter lays some groundwork for the rest of the study in several ways. First, recent thought about the nature of linguistic diversity is reviewed in somewhat more detail, centering around the notion of a parameter. Then, some typical characteristics of polysynthetic languages are presented. I will show that a common theme can be discerned in many of these characteristics that is amenable to being stated in parametric terms. Some implications of the "polysynthesis parameter" that result from this are then briefly mapped out, outlining the topics that will be considered in detail in the rest of the book. Finally, some basic facts and assumptions about morphological and syntactic structure are introduced.

1.1 Geniuses and Parameters

If there is such a thing as a structural genius to a language in Sapir's sense, it will clearly have to fit into Principles and Parameters theory[2] as one of the "parameters," the "principles" being those properties that are common to all human languages. With this in mind, consider the following quotation from Chomsky (1981:6), where he introduces the classical P&P notion of a parameter:

> Each of the systems of [the grammar] is based on principles with certain possibilities of parametric variation. Through the interaction of these systems, many properties of particular languages can be accounted for. We will see that there are certain complexes of properties typical of particular types of languages; such collections of properties should be explained in terms of the choice of parameters in one or another subsystem. In a tightly integrated theory with fairly rich internal structure, change in a single parameter may have complex effects, with proliferating consequences in various parts of the grammar. Ideally, we hope to find that complexes of properties differentiating otherwise similar languages are reducible to a single parameter, fixed in one way or another.

In spite of the differences in terminology and conceptual background, there is a similarity between Chomsky's conception and that of Sapir. Thus, Chomsky's notion of a "parameter setting" as a single, conceptually unified feature of a language that has repercussions in different areas is comparable to Sapir's notion of a single "plan" with pervasive implications that go beyond a few listable constructions. In the era of Chomsky 1981, the paradigmatic example of a parameter was the "Pro-Drop Parameter," based on foundational work by Rizzi (see Rizzi 1982). Thus, Italian and Spanish share the following properties, each of which distinguishes them from closely related French (and English) (Chomsky 1981:240, 280):

(2)   (i) Subjects of simple tensed clauses can be missing.
      (ii) Subjects can appear optionally after the verb in simple sentences.
     (iii) Subjects can be extracted from embedded questions.
      (iv) Null (subject) resumptive pronouns are found in embedded clauses.
       (v) Subjects can be extracted even if there is a complementizer preceding.
      (vi) Copular verbs agree with the postverbal NP rather than the expletive.
     (vii) Two adjacent verbs can "restructure" and act like a single verb.

These (or at least (i)–(v)) were taken to constitute a cluster of related properties, all traceable to a single, well-defined difference between Spanish and Italian, on the one hand, and French, on the other.

There is, however, an important difference in "grain" between Chomsky's notion of parameter and Sapir's notion of structural genius. Chomsky clearly envisioned a number of distinct parameters that could be set independently. French and Spanish may differ in the Pro-Drop Parameter, but they presumably have many other parameter values in common. In contrast, Sapir only allowed one structural genius per language. Chomskian parameters may have "proliferating consequences," but they fall short of being "fundamental" and "pervasive" in the full sense that Sapir had in mind. The properties in (2) are not obviously related, but they do have a common theme: they all hinge on the fact that Spanish and

Italian permit null preverbal subjects. In contrast, Sapir says of a structural genius that it is so basic that "we [cannot] gain an adequate idea of its nature by a mere recital of the sundry facts that make up the grammar of the language." Sapir's notion clearly goes deeper than Chomsky's. Thus, we might rephrase the question inspired by Sapir this way: Are there "macroparameters"?

With this in mind, let us review the history of the idea of a parameter since about 1980. The idea has been very influential and has produced much varied work. What are the lessons of that work? One might expect that more and more parameters comparable to the Pro-Drop Parameter would be discovered, and that researchers would gradually notice that these parameters (each resulting in a cluster of properties) themselves clustered in nonarbitrary ways. This would mean that the settings of different parameters were somehow related, leading to the discovery of macroparameters.

It is obvious to anyone familiar with the field that this is not what has happened. On the contrary, parameters have tended to become smaller and more construction-specific, rather than larger and more general. Medium-sized parameters have split up into "microparameters," rather than merging into macroparameters. Again, the Pro-Drop Parameter is a prime example: as linguists began to pay attention to a wider range of languages (including northern Italian and southern French dialects), the properties in (2) were seen not to form such a neat cluster after all. Rather, there are languages that have some of the properties on the list, but not all. Hence more than one factor must be involved in analyzing the cluster; more than one parameter must be at work. This trend toward fragmentation rather than unification can be seen in many other cases as well, including word order parameters, movement parameters, and configurationality parameters.

This fragmentation of parameters has in many cases reached the point where the "cluster" of properties accounted for by each parameter includes only one member.[3] To the extent that this happens, the very idea of a parametric cluster is called into question, and microparameters become no more general than the constructions of traditional grammar. As such, they are not parameters in the original sense at all, in spite of the fact that the terminology is retained. Thus, although the P&P notion of a principle has proved very fruitful in many different settings, the notion of a parameter has not fulfilled its original promise.

This trend has not gone unnoticed. Indeed, there is a growing body of work that responds to it by radically paring back the idea of a parameter, to the point of near nonexistence. The first important reference in this connection is Borer 1984, where it is conjectured that all parameters involve the "inflectional system" (which she defines in a technical way). Borer writes (1984:29):

> The inventory of inflectional rules and of grammatical formatives in any given language is idiosyncratic and learned on the basis of input data. If all interlanguage variation is attributable to that system, the burden of learning is placed exactly on that component of grammar for which there is strong evidence of learning: the vocabulary and its idiosyncratic properties. We no longer have to assume that the data to which the child is exposed bear directly on universal principles, nor do we have to assume that the child actively selects between competing grammatical systems.

Similarly, Fukui (1986) claims that parameters typically involve functional categories only. Although Baker 1988a does not discuss the theory of parameters per se, the key driving force noted there behind differences in complex predicate formation across languages is whether a given morpheme is specified as an affix or not. This and similar work have combined with some of the earlier ideas to form the ill-defined but suggestive conjecture that all parameters are "morphological" in nature. Chomsky (1992:4–5) tentatively adopts a version of this view, pointing out that it implies that essentially "there is only one computational system and one lexicon."[4]

Against this background, the thesis that there is a macroparameter distinguishing polysynthetic languages from other language types goes against the grain. Nevertheless, there are methodological reasons why macroparameters might have been missed, in spite of all of the work done on the topic over the last decade and a half. First, many linguists interested in parametric issues have adopted the methodology of comparing closely related languages, dialects, and varieties, inspired by Richard Kayne and Luigi Rizzi's seminal work on the Romance languages (e.g., Rizzi 1982, Kayne 1984). By using the common history of the languages as a natural control, this methodology is effective at discovering microparameters; however, it is not appropriate for discovering macroparameters, because the languages it compares are too similar. Second, linguists still do not know enough about parametric clusters. Any high-level parameter will involve a correspondingly abstract property of language, so its impact on particular structures will be indirect, mediated by the influence of other principles, parameter values, and lexical properties. This is well known, but it has still not been fully internalized; linguists seem to long for a simple checklist of properties that they can mechanically run through in testing a parametric claim. Rather, in order to find valid macroparameters we must increase our ability to look beyond the effects of microparameters, using, for example, the sophistication that has been gained from comparative studies of the Germanic and Romance languages. Finally, while there has been a great increase in the diversity of languages considered from the P&P viewpoint, there are still remarkably few languages that have received attention sustained and comprehensive enough for the discovery of macroparameters. This is the result of many practical factors: the relative scarcity and inaccessibility of suitable speech communities, the inherent difficulty of learning the languages, the time limitations placed on theses and research grants, and the need to know about everything at once. When these factors are combined, they reveal why the research done so far may not be sufficient to show that macroparameters do not exist.

This study tries to overcome these methodological barriers to the discovery of macroparameters. It is the result of five years of focused work on a language very different from those previously analyzed within the generative framework and seeks to be as broad as possible in the area of syntax and related morphology. I have constantly kept in mind two questions: What exactly are the syntactic properties of Mohawk that give it its distinctive "Mohawkness"? Do these properties have anything in common? I also consider the question of whether there are other languages that share Mohawk's distinctive character, if not its detailed properties. I propose the very strong position that polysynthetic languages differ from other languages in exactly one macroparameter. Moreover, polysynthetic languages differ from one another only in microparameters, that is, only in features that can be attributed to idiosyncratic morpholexical properties of the kind envisioned by Borer (1984) and Chomsky (1992).

1.2 An Initial Acquaintance with Mohawk

It is time to look at a bona fide polysynthetic language. If such languages have a property that is as "fundamental and pervasive" as Sapir envisioned, it should be manifest in virtually any sample of the language larger than a sentence or two. The trick is knowing what to look for. With this in mind, consider the following section of a Mohawk narrative,[5] taken from Williams 1976a:198–199 (before this portion, the narrator has described how her father bought eight bullheads and put them in a shallow place in the river by his house):

(3) a. Tsyahyákshera tówa' Λtóhetste' kíkΛ rake-nuhá'a eh
         one-week   maybe it-passed this my-uncle   there

         t-a-ha-hrárho-'.
         CIS-FACT-MsS-pull.up-PUNC
         'After about a week passed, my uncle pulled up [to my father's dock].'

     b. Ro-nehrakó'-u   yákΛ' kíkΛ tsi   ni-ka-nahskw-íyo-'s
         MsO-surprise-STAT PRT   this how   PART-NsS-animal-good-HAB

         kíkΛ kΛ́-[i]tsy-u.
         this NsS-fish-NSF
         'He was surprised (it is said) at how good-looking the fish were.'

     c. Tánu' ki' ne sΛ́ha' ye-s-ho-nehrakó'-u   tsi kwáh akwéku
         and   that NE more TRANS-ITER-MsO-surprise-STAT that even all

         skáthne tsi núwe ni-kutí-[i]teru-'.
         together that where PART-ZpS-stay-IMPF
         'He was even more surprised that they stayed all together in one place.'

     d. Ok óni' yákΛ' ná'a y-a-ho-[a]hry-úti-'   akwéku
         so also PRT   PRT TRANS-FACT-MsO-hook-throw-PUNC all

         wa-hshako-yéna-'   ki rabahbót.
         FACT-MsS/3O-catch-PUNC this bullhead
         'So then he threw in a fishline and caught all the bullheads.'

     e. Sha'téku ni-kúti   wa-hó-naw-e'.
         eight   PART-ZpS FACT-MsO-catch-PUNC
         'He caught [all] eight of them.'

     f. Kwáh yákΛ' khé s-a-há-hket-e'   kíkΛ rake-nuhá'a
         right PRT   there ITER-FACT-MsS-turn.back-PUNC this my-uncle

         s-a-hΛ-[i]tsy-a-hseruny-á-hna-'.
         ITER-FACT-MsA-fish-Ø-prepare-Ø-PURP-PUNC
         'Immediately my uncle turned back to go and prepare the fish.'

One thing that stands out about Mohawk even from this short sample is its nonconfigurational properties. Hale (1983) described three properties as being characteristic of nonconfigurational languages in a pretheoretical sense[6]: relative freedom of word order, the pervasive dropping of noun phrase arguments, and the existence of discontinuous expressions. All three of these properties are seen in (3). Thus, in (3a) the subject 'my uncle' precedes the intransitive verb 'pull up', whereas in (3f) the same noun phrase follows the intransitive verb 'turn back'. Similar freedom is found with direct objects: in (3e) the numeral object of 'catch' precedes the verb, but in other examples the direct object follows the verb. Indeed, in a simple transitive sentence like (4), the subject, verb, and object can appear in any of the six logically possible orders.

(4)   a. Sak ra-núhwe'-s   ako-[a]tyá'tawi.
         Sak MsS-like-HAB FsP-dress
         'Sak likes her dress.'

      b. Ra-núhwe'-s Sak ako-[a]tyá'tawi.
         like   Sak her-dress

      c. Sak ako-[a]tyá'tawi ra-núhwe'-s.
         Sak her-dress   like

      d. Ra-núhwe'-s ako-[a]tyá'tawi ne Sak.
         like   her-dress   NE Sak

      e. Ako-[a]tyá'tawi ra-núhwe'-s ne Sak.
         her-dress   like   NE Sak

      f. Ako-[a]tyá'tawi Sak ra-núhwe'-s.
         her-dress   Sak like

This property was discussed by Postal (1979:410–11), among others.[7] Mithun (1987) discusses in some detail the pragmatic factors influencing word order choice in the related language Cayuga. She also considers at some length whether any word order should be singled out as more basic or underlying, and she concludes that there is no evidence for such a choice.

The phenomenon of "argument drop" is also nicely illustrated by the text in (3). Sentence (3c) implies reference to both the uncle and the fish, but neither is represented by any independent noun phrase within the sentence. Similarly, (3b), (3d), and (3e) all contain references to the uncle, without any overt NPs. Nor is this only a property of subjects; objects can also be freely omitted in Mohawk. There are no good examples of this in (3), but (5) provides one.

(5)   Ra-núhwe'-s.
      MsS-like-HAB
      'He likes it.'

Indeed, any properly inflected verb in Mohawk is considered to be a complete and proper sentence as long as it is within an appropriate context. Sentence (3a) even provides an example of a dropped possessor, since there is no overt NP corresponding to 'my' in the expression for 'my uncle'. This characteristic of Mohawk is also discussed in Postal 1979 and has been noticed by all who work on Iroquoian languages.

Finally, (3d) provides an example of a discontinuous expression. Thus, in the clause meaning 'he caught all the bullheads', the word meaning 'all' appears before the verb, whereas the word meaning 'bullhead' appears after it. These two words, although clearly associated with the same argument role, do not form an NP constituent of the usual kind, at least at a superficial level of representation. This property of Mohawk is much less common and has rarely been pointed out by other researchers. Nevertheless, examples are found in texts and are spontaneously produced, particularly when one of the elements is a quantifier or numeral. Speakers also accept some examples in which demonstratives or relative clauses are split from their heads, as in (6) and (7).

(6) Ne *kík*Λ wa-hi-yéna-' ne *kwéskwes.*
    NE this FACT-1sS/MsO-catch-PUNC NE pig
    'I caught this pig.'

(7) Uwári *ísk*a yakó-yΛ ne *yako-tsh*Λ*ry-u.*
    Mary one FsO-have/STAT NE FsO-find-STAT
    'Mary has one [a ball], which she found.'

Part of the reason that such examples are statistically less common is simply that, apart from particles such as *ne,* whose functions are unclear, the average number of words in a noun phrase in Mohawk is close to one (less, if one counts pro-dropped NPs). Thus, the possibilities for discontinuous expressions are inherently limited. In addition, special discourse factors are needed to allow split NPs, particularly those like (6). Nevertheless, discontinuous NPs of some kinds are clearly allowed.

Nonconfigurational languages pose well-known problems for linguistic theory in general and P&P theories in particular. The existence of free word order and discontinuous expressions challenges the idea of a fixed phrase structure marker over which syntactic relationships such as subject and object can be defined. Moreover, the fact that noun phrases can be omitted at will seems to challenge the Theta Criterion—the fundamental principle that for each argument position of the verb there must be one and only one NP (or other phrase) that expresses that argument. Thus, the basic syntax of Mohawk seems to be loose in a way that is very different from a language like English.

Intuitively, it is clear what makes this freedom possible in Mohawk. All Mohawk verbs are inflected to show the person, number, and gender features of both their subject and their object. Similarly, a Mohawk noun is inflected to show the features of its possessor, if it has one. These inflections are obligatory, fixed in position, and in a one-to-one correspondence with the arguments of the verb (or noun). Thus, it is natural to say that these inflections count as pronouns, and provide the true subject and object of the verb. Full NPs, when they appear, have the status of some kind of adjunct or modifier. This view is a traditional one, with a long history in Amerindian linguistics. Foley (1991:228) says that the idea goes back at least as far as Wilhelm von Humboldt's analysis of Aztec in the 1830s. This view is implicit in Lounsbury's (1953) choice of the term "pronominal prefixes" for the relevant morphemes in Oneida, a language closely related to Mohawk. The idea has been developed within a P&P framework by Jelinek (1984, 1988, 1989), who was the first to point out systematically how it reconciles the basic facts of agreement-oriented nonconfigurationality with the principles of the P&P framework. In these terms, (4e) can be represented informally as in (8).[8]

(8)

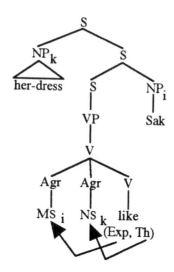

The same idea has been implemented in other current frameworks. Van Valin (1985) gives an analysis of Lakhota in these terms within Role and Reference Grammar. Bresnan and Mchombo (1987) do the same for Chichewa in the framework of Lexical Functional Grammar. Mithun (1987) explicitly adopts an informal version of this view for Northern Iroquoian languages, and a more technical version is found in Benger 1990 and Baker 1991a. Although many questions remain about how exactly to implement this basic intuition, something along these lines seems very likely.

Example (3) demonstrates other properties of Mohawk that do not fit under the nonconfigurationality rubric. Even if one factors out the agreement morphemes, it is obvious that much more can be expressed within the Mohawk verb than within the English verb. The most striking single example in the text is *sahʌtsyahseruny-áhna'* 'he went back to prepare the fish' in (3f). Here a single Mohawk word corresponds to a seven-word sentence in English. The direct object of the verb *hseruny* 'prepare' is the incorporated noun root *itsy* 'fish'. Such noun incorporation (NI) is very common in Mohawk. Two other examples of NI are contained in (3): *yahohryúti'* 'he threw a hook' in (3d), and *nikanahskwíyo's* 'they were such beautiful animals' in (3b). NI is quite productive, and speakers often consider incorporated and unincorporated versions of the same sentence to be essentially equivalent:

(9) a. Wa'-k-hnínu-'   ne ka-nákt-a'.
        FACT-1sS-buy-PUNC NE NsS-bed-NSF
        'I bought the/a bed.'

    b. Wa'-ke-nakt-a-hnínu-'.
        FACT-1sS-bed-Ø-buy-PUNC
        'I bought the/a bed.'

Furthermore, incorporated nouns (INs) in Mohawk can play a range of discourse roles. In (3f), *itsy* 'fish' is interpreted as a definite NP, referring to the bullheads that are the topic of the entire tale. On the other hand, *ahry* 'hook' in (3d) is interpreted as an indefinite NP that is not otherwise referred to in the story.[9] Finally, *nahskw* 'domestic animal' in (3b) is functioning as a kind of classifier; its reference is the same as the NP *kʌ́tsyu* 'fish' that appears in the same clause. Noun incorporation is one of the most striking properties of Mohawk; it has attracted considerable attention in many works (Postal 1979, Mithun 1984a, Baker 1988a, Hopkins 1988; see also Woodbury 1975 for Onondaga).

The word *sahʌtsyahserunyáhna'* 'he went back to prepare the fish' also contains two verbal elements: *hseruny* 'prepare', and *hna* 'go'. Although the second of these is a bound affix, its semantic contribution is roughly equivalent to that of a full lexical verb in English or Mohawk. Constructions of this type are not as characteristic of Mohawk as NI is; there is no free compounding of verb stems, for example. Nevertheless, they do constitute an important part of the language, and a range of concepts are expressed by, for example, inchoative, reversive, and causative affixes. Other polysynthetic languages are even richer in this regard, notably Nahuatl and Southern Tiwa.

In Baker 1988a, I proposed a leading idea about how complex predicates of this kind may be accounted for. There is an abstract similarity between NI examples such as (9b) and verbal suffixes such as *hna* 'go'. The verb *hninu* 'buy' is the kind of verb that is expected to select an NP complement, and the incorporated noun is interpreted as the head of that complement. Similarly, verbs meaning 'go' standardly select a verbal/clausal complement that expresses the purpose of going, and the verb root is interpreted as the head of this complement. Thus, the relationship between the parts of these two types of complex words is directly analogous. I argued (1988a) that these properties are to be explained by base generating ordinary (i.e., English-like) complementation structures and allowing the head of the selected phrase to undergo movement in the syntax. This can be represented informally as in (10).[10]

(10)　a.　　　　　　　　　　b.

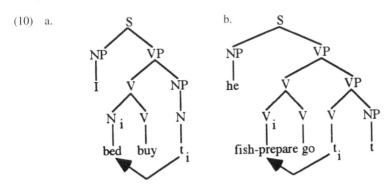

This analysis and the generalization it is based on also has a rather long history. It was inspired by work in generative semantics, in general, and by Williams' (1976b) analysis of Tuscarora, in particular. Indeed, Sapir (1911:265) stated the same generalization in pretheoretical terms for Paiute. This account goes a long way toward explaining which syntactic relationships can and cannot be expressed by productively formed morphologically complex words in Mohawk and other languages.

In (3) we can also see certain miscellaneous properties of Mohawk that do not fit in any obvious way under either the configurationality heading or the incorporation heading. For example, the independent nouns *rakenuhá'a* 'my uncle' and *kÁtsyu* 'fish' in (3) are inflected with prefixes that indicate the number and gender of the noun; these prefixes are cognate to the prefixes used to indicate the subject of verbs. The clearest instance of this is in (3b), where the noun *kÁtsyu* 'fish' has the same neuter subject prefix *ka* as the verbal predicate of the clause *nikanahs-kwíyo's* 'they are such nice animals'. Moreover, the Mohawk sample does not have various structures that are common in English texts, including infinitival verb forms, prepositional phrase arguments, and sentential subjects. These gaps are not just a result of the brevity of the sample; each of these constructions is, in fact, absent or severely restricted in Mohawk.

To summarize, many of our first impressions of Mohawk can be grouped under two broad headings: nonconfigurational phenomena and incorporation phenomena. In addition, there are various other properties such as inflection of nouns and restrictions on complementation. For each of the major groupings, there is a promising leading idea: Jelinek's pronominal argument hypothesis for nonconfigurationality and Baker's syntactic head movement hypothesis for incorporation. However, no positive theoretical link between these two ideas has been drawn in the literature. On the contrary, Jelinek (1989) draws a negative theoretical link: she argues that Baker-style incorporation is barred from nonconfigurational languages in general, in order to account for a cluster of properties that distinguish the Northern Athapaskan languages from the Southern Athapaskan languages (see also Benger 1990). If, however, a true relationship between these two ideas could be found, then we would have something that begins to be worthy of being called a macroparameter. This would be especially so if the property discovered also accounted for some of the "miscellaneous" properties of the language; the whole would then be more than the simple sum of the parts.

1.3 Toward a Macroparameter

There is an obvious common theme behind the two leading ideas discussed in section 1.2. Jelinek's approach to configurationality holds that the inflectional morphemes on a verb count as the subject and object of the verb. Baker's theory of incorporation holds that one part of a derived stem is the syntactic complement of the other part. In both cases, syntactic argument relationships are being expressed morphologically. Suppose that this is required to be so as a fundamental principle of certain languages. This idea can be stated informally as in (11).

(11)   *The Polysynthesis Parameter* (informal)
         Every argument of a head element must be related to a morpheme in the word
         containing that head.

where "head element" refers to an X^0 category in the X-bar system that is associated with an argument structure in the lexicon; the positions in an argument structure are called *θ-roles*. In order to make (11) more precise, however, we must specify what it means to be "related to a morpheme." To do this, we must define what kinds of morphemes count as fulfilling this condition, and what sort of relationship can hold between those morphemes and the arguments of the X^0 category.

For purposes of this work, it is sufficient to define the set of morphemes I am concerned with extensionally: they are agreement morphemes (also known as pronominal affixes) and incorporated roots. Intuitively, these are the kinds of morphemes on a verb that are suitable for expressing an argument of that verb. It has sometimes been suggested that agreement morphemes are, in fact, incorporated pronouns of some kind; one well-known example is Anderson's (1982) analysis of agreement in Breton. If this is true in general, then the two classes of argument-type morphemes could be unified under the rubric of "incorporated element." However, there are nontrivial problems facing such a unification, which I will not explore here (see Baker and Hale 1990 for some discussion). Instead, I treat "being related to an agreement morpheme" and "being related to an incorporated root" as two formally distinct ways of satisfying the Polysynthesis Parameter.

The other issue to resolve is the nature of the relationship that must hold between the argument-type morphemes and the θ-roles of the verb in question. There are two possibilities. The first is that the morpheme is itself the argument of the verb, receiving a θ-role from it directly. On this interpretation, the Polysynthesis Parameter becomes very similar to the Theta Criterion, which is usually stated more or less as in (12).

(12) *The Theta Criterion* (Chomsky 1981:36)
 For every θ-role there must be one and only one argument; for every argument there must be one and only one θ-role.

The Polysynthesis Parameter, then, would basically mean that in some languages the Theta Criterion is met morphologically rather than syntactically. This seems to capture the intentions of much of the traditional literature on these languages, inasmuch as the intuitions of the researchers can be usefully translated into generative terminology. It is quite explicitly the position of Jelinek (1984) for agreement morphemes.

The alternative understanding of (11) would be to say that the morphemes on the verb do not *replace* conventional argument phrases in these languages, but rather in some sense *reinforce* them. This is the position I adopt. The difference between this view and the previous one can be illustrated by comparing the syntactic structures in (14) that each would assign to a sentence like (9b), repeated here as (13)

(13) Wa'-ke-nakt-a-hnínu-'.
 FACT-1sS-bed-Ø-buy-PUNC
 'I bought the/a bed.'

Both (14a) and (14b) assume that tense and agreement morphology is associated with a distinct head position Infl(ection); this is discussed later. If the Theta Criterion applies word-internally rather than at the level of the sentence, then the syntactic structure of a form like this one is trivial, consisting of little more than the verb itself, as in (14a). In particular, there is no subject NP or object NP. On the

(14) a.   b.

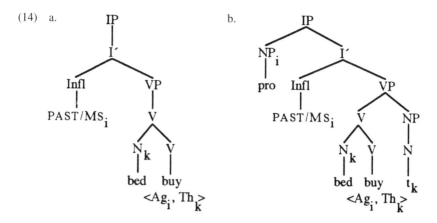

alternative interpretation, the Theta Criterion must still be met syntactically, and hence these NPs must exist, although they may be phonetically empty, as shown in (14b). On this interpretation, subject agreement on the verb does not render superfluous a null pronominal in subject position; nor does an incorporated direct object render superfluous a null, trace-headed NP in object position. Also, there is a much closer correspondence between the structure of the Mohawk sentence and that of its English gloss.

The (14b) analysis is consistent with my previous work (Baker 1988a, 1991a), but is in sharp contrast with the closely related ideas of Jelinek (1984) and Marantz (1984). Jelinek explicitly holds that θ-roles are assigned to agreement morphemes *instead of* to syntactic argument positions. Similarly, Marantz claims that (after merger) incorporated roots receive thematic roles *instead of* the phrases that they originally headed, which are no longer projected. However, (14b) has two advantages. First, one can capture restrictions on what a verb can agree with or incorporate by saying that the morpheme inside the verbal form must be in the proper structural relationship to an empty category outside it (i.e., the government relationship). This rationale for positing empty categories is parallel to Chomsky's (1976, 1981, 1982) well-known argument for traces and PROs, in which he claims that if these categories are posited, then the relationships between "gaps" and their antecedents reduce for the most part to independently motivated principles of anaphora. Second, (14b) allows one to apply linguistic principles such as those of Binding Theory and Weak Crossover in their standard forms to a language like Mohawk. It may be possible to rephrase most of my analyses so that they work over a structure like (14a), but there are no clear conceptual advantages to doing so. There would be a decrease in the abstractness of the syntactic representation, but there would be a corresponding increase in the abstractness of the conditions that are defined over syntactic representation. I do not know of anything that would be gained by doing this. There are also one or two places in the course of this work where it is particularly important to adopt (14b) rather than (14a).

How then do we develop (11) into a precise principle? The most natural way is to understand it not as a parameterized version of the Theta Criterion, but rather as a condition on argument relationships (i.e., θ-role assignment) that holds in some languages. Standard P&P theory includes a condition of this type as a way of deriving the Case Filter. Thus, Chomsky (1981:ch. 6), developing an idea attributed to Joseph Aoun, proposes the so-called Visibility Condition, which says that a phrase is "visible" (i.e., eligible) for θ-role assignment only if it is assigned abstract Case. Inspired by this, I propose (15) as the distinctive property of Mohawk and typologically similar languages.

(15)   *The Morphological Visibility Condition* (MVC)
       A phrase X is visible for θ-role assignment from a head Y only if it is coindexed
       with a morpheme in the word containing Y via:
       (i) an agreement relationship, or
       (ii) a movement relationship
             Yes: Mohawk, Nahuatl, Mayali, . . .
             No: English, French, Chichewa, ...

This means that although there must be a relationship between each θ-role of, say, a verb and a morpheme attached to that verb, this relationship is not direct. Rather, it is mediated by an NP or an argument of some other category. Thus, the verb's θ-role must be assigned to an appropriate phrase by the (conventional) Theta Criterion, and that phrase must be coindexed with a morpheme on the verb by the MVC. The types of coindexing relationships allowed are two that are standardly permitted in P&P theory: the coindexing that holds between an NP and an agreeing category and the coindexing that holds between a moved element and the trace left behind by movement. Arguably, these are the only two syntactic dependencies that are relevant to zero-level lexical categories; other relationships such as referential dependency are defined for maximal projections only. I represent both relationships by coindexing for convenience, but do not by this make any claims about the actual role of indices in syntactic structure. Throughout this work I refer to (15) as both the Polysynthesis Parameter and the Morphological Visibility Condition (MVC). The two terms differ in sense but not in reference: calling (15) the Polysynthesis Parameter emphasizes its status in the grammar and its observed effects on a language; calling it the MVC emphasizes its conceptual content.

It is worth considering the possibility of breaking the MVC into two separate parameters: one that stipulates that agreement makes a phrase visible for θ-role assignment and one that stipulates that incorporation makes a phrase visible for θ-role assignment. This would define at least three types of languages. First, there is the Mohawk type, in which both agreement morphemes and lexical roots count as rendering an argument visible. Languages with this property I call *polysynthetic*, thereby giving a technical sense to a word that Boas (1911) and Sapir (1921) use rather impressionistically in their typologies. Sapir characterizes polysynthetic languages as follows (Sapir 1921:128):

> A polysynthetic language, as its name implies, is more than ordinarily synthetic. The elaboration of the word is extreme. Concepts which we should never dream of treating in a subordinate fashion are symbolized by derivational affixes or "symbolic" changes in the radical element, while the more abstract notions, including the syntactic relations, may also be conveyed by the word.

For both Boas and Sapir, polysynthetic languages make the most use of morphology to represent grammatical notions; thus, it is natural to associate this label with the broadest setting of (15). Notice also that Sapir's notion of polysynthesis explicitly includes *both* combinations of radical plus derivational affix (many of which are a result of incorporation in my sense) and indications of "abstract notions including the syntactic relations" (i.e., inflectional morphology, such as agreement). Thus, my technical use of the term "polysynthetic" seems to be in the spirit of the word's original pretheoretical sense. However, it must be emphasized that many languages that Sapir and Boas would have called polysynthetic are not polysynthetic in my narrower and more technical sense. Some languages with quite impressive amounts of morphological complexity may not use that complexity to *systematically* represent *argument* relationships, as we shall see later. My claim is that these languages are of a fundamentally different type from Mohawk.[11]

The second type of language that breaking (15) into two parameters allows for is a language in which arguments must be agreed with, but incorporated roots are not permitted to make arguments visible. This would include languages for which Jelinek's theory of nonconfigurationality holds, but which either do not have incorporation phenomena at all or have only sporadic incorporation that does not interact with agreement. These can be called "nonconfigurational head-marking languages," where the term "head-marking" is taken from Nichols (1986). Many of the languages that Jelinek has investigated may be of this type: Warlpiri, Navajo, Salish, Choctaw, and perhaps the Algonquian languages. This class of languages is not a primary focus of study in this work; its existence seems likely, but remains to be proven conclusively.

Third, there are languages for which neither part of (15) holds. These will be of a wide variety of types, since their "structural genius" lies elsewhere. Certainly they include configurational, isolating languages like English, Yoruba, and Chinese, as well as head-final languages—both those that are configurational and those like Japanese, Hindi, and German where the nonconfigurational characteristics seem to be due to Case marking rather than agreement.[12] They will even include languages that have some pronominal affixes and/or incorporation phenomena, but where this is not systematic for all argument types. Examples are Bantu languages, such as Chichewa (Bresnan and Mchombo 1987, Baker 1988a); Northern Athapaskan languages, such as Slave (Rice 1989); Haisla (Bach 1993); and Papuan languages, such as Alamblak (Bruce 1984) and Yimas (Foley 1991). Such languages *may* make use of the same constructions as Mohawk, but they are not forced to do so by the MVC. These languages can and do have a considerable degree of morphological complexity; for example, Haisla and Slave are not strikingly less "polysynthetic" than Mohawk in the pretheoretical sense. Nevertheless, in Haisla there is no incorporation, no true agreement, and the affixes (of which there are approximately 500) "never seem to encode the primary arguments of stems" (Bach 1993:6). Thus, I claim that even these languages have a fundamentally different parameter setting from that of Mohawk.

In principle, this system would seem to allow a fourth type of language: one in which argument relationships must be represented by some type of head marking, but agreement does not suffice. In fact, such a language could not exist on general principles. The reason is simply that incorporation is not flexible enough to satisfy the MVC by itself. NI is typically limited to (underlying) direct objects. This is seen overtly across languages and has a plausible theoretical account: only move-ment from a direct object is consistent with the standard properties of Move α (see Baker 1988a:chs. 2 and 3, as well as chapter 7 in the present volume, for extensive discussion). Thus, any verb that took a subject argument would violate the MVC in such a language. But presumably all languages have such verbs. Therefore, no such language could exist.

1.4 Preliminary Evidence for the MVC

As acknowledged earlier, no part of the Polysynthesis Parameter is really new. The statement that agreement morphemes can represent arguments is found in Jelinek 1984; the fact that lexical roots and affixes can represent arguments is found in Marantz 1984 and Baker 1988a. What originality the proposal has comes from putting both types of morphology under the same principle. The key idea of the Polysynthesis Parameter is that agreement morphemes and incorporated noun roots are part of the same system. If this is so, we would expect there to be interactions between the two. In fact, such interactions can be seen at three differ-ent levels, which encourages us to believe we are on the right track:

(i) Across languages and language families. It is plausible heuristically to sup-pose that the presence of robust noun incorporation is a reasonably reliable indica-tion that incorporated nouns count for the MVC, and hence that the value of (15) for the language in question is "Yes." The reasoning given at the end of the last section implies that the language must also have pronominal agreement mor-phemes.

For these purposes, we may consider noun incorporation to be "robust" in a language if: (a) it is reasonably productive, (b) the noun root is fully integrated with the verb morphologically, (c) the noun is referentially active in the discourse (see Mithun 1984a and chapter 7 in the present volume), and (d) both the noun root and the verb root can, in general, be used independently. The rationale for these criteria is as follows. Criteria (a) and (c) exclude languages where NI is only a matter of lexicalizations and historical residues. Criterion (b) avoids the question of caseless/determinerless NPs adjacent to the V in verb-final languages. These constructions have been analyzed as noun incorporation in, for example, Turkish (Knecht 1985) and Hindi (Mohanan 1991). However, Lamontagne and Travis (1987) provide another approach to this sort of phenomenon. Criterion (c) elimi-nates languages with productive N–V compounding in the lexicon, such as various Oceanic languages, as described by Rosen (1989b). Criterion (d) excludes lan-guages like those of the Eskimoan family, where NI is obligatory with some verbs and forbidden with the rest (Sadock 1980, Fortescue 1984; see also Sapir 1911).

Languages with NI that meets all four criteria include [13]: Mohawk and the other Northern Iroquoian languages (e.g., Seneca (Chafe 1967), Tuscarora (Williams 1976b)), Wichita (Rood 1976), Kiowa (Watkins 1984), Southern Tiwa (Allen et al. 1984), Huauhtla Nahuatl (Merlan 1976; see also Andrews 1975 for Classical Nahuatl), the Gunwinjguan languages of Northern Australia,[14] Chukchee (see Spencer 1993 and references cited therein), and perhaps Classical Ainu (Shibatani

1990). This list includes at least one member of every language family considered to have type III or IV NI (NI that is discourse relevant) in Mithun's (1984a) survey article, plus two others in which significant information has become available only since Mithun's article (the Tanoan languages, where Mithun's criteria clearly apply, and Ainu, where data are inconclusive).[15]

Strikingly, *every one of these languages has full and obligatory agreement paradigms for both subject and object* (allowing for the possibility of some phonologically null third person forms). Not surprisingly, the languages also allow argument-drop and at least some degree of freedom in word order. This overall pattern is highly significant. There seems to be an implicational universal: all languages with full-fledged noun incorporation phenomena fall within the class of nonconfigurational head-marking languages.[16] Nothing in the theory of Jelinek (1984) or Baker (1988a), for example, predicts that this should be so. However, the Polysynthesis Parameter explains why the two properties are related. This set of languages I will henceforth refer to as the true polysynthetic languages, and I will draw on them for comparison purposes throughout this book.

(ii) The macrostructure of Mohawk. There is a curious functional complementarity between agreement morphemes and NI in Mohawk. As a general rule, NI is a property of inanimate nouns that fill the direct object role and meet certain morphological conditions. Interestingly, this is the only class of argument for which there is no trace of an overt agreement morpheme. Thus, the agreement morphology on a transitive verb with subject X and an inanimate object is always identical to the agreement morphology on an intransitive verb with subject X (Postal 1979, Mithun 1986b, Baker 1990b). An example of this is shown in (16).

(16)   a. Yu-[a]táwʌ-s.
          FsS-swim-HAB
          'She is swimming.'

       b. Ye-núhwe'-s   (ne áthere').
          FsS(NsO)-like-HAB NE basket
          'She likes it (the basket).'

On the other hand, NI of animate direct objects is limited and NI of subjects and indirect objects is completely impossible. There are, however, visible agreement morphemes for all of these categories in the Mohawk verbal paradigm.[17] Together, agreement and noun incorporation virtually partition the class of nominal arguments: for each type of argument there is one and only one mode of morphological expression available. This kind of complementarity makes sense if NI and agreement are part of the same system for expressing argument relationships; otherwise, it is a peculiar coincidence. Evans (1993) emphasizes the same kind of functional partitioning in the Gunwinjguan language Mayali.

(iii) The microstructure of Mohawk. An even more striking complementarity between agreement and noun incorporation is seen within that narrow range where there is a potential choice: the area of incorporable animate objects. There are some areas of Mohawk in which such examples can be found (see chapter 7). In this domain, one finds paradigms like the following:

(17) a. *Ra-núhwe'-s ne owirá'a.
        MsS-like-HAB NE baby
        'He likes babies.'

      b. Shako-núhwe'-s   (ne owirá'a).
         MsS/3pO-like-HAB NE baby
         'He likes them (babies).'

      c. Ra-wir-a-núhwe'-s.
         MsS-baby-Ø-like-HAB
         'He likes babies.'

      d. *?Shako-wir-a-núhwe'-s.
         MsS/3pO-baby-Ø-like-HAB
         'He likes babies.'

In these examples, either an object agreement morpheme or an incorporated noun root is permitted. However, it is ungrammatical to have neither, as shown by (17a). This form cannot be ruled out on purely morphological grounds: the verb is grammatical as 'he likes it', where 'it' refers to an inanimate object. One cannot even say that agreement is obligatory when the object of the verb refers to a baby, given the existence of (17c). The form is correctly ruled out by the MVC, however: the verb has an obligatory internal (object) θ-role, but there is no corresponding morpheme within the word to make visible an argument that receives that θ-role.

It must be conceded that the necessity of NI or agreement is not always apparent on the surface in Mohawk. I have already alluded to the fact that verbs with neuter objects and no incorporated noun root seem to have no morpheme on the verb that indicates the object. Thus, (17a) becomes perfectly grammatical when one replaces the animate NP *owirá'a* 'baby' with an inanimate one like *ká'sere'* 'car'. However, this problem disappears if we assume that Mohawk has a phonologically null third person neuter morpheme on the verb in these cases. Positing the existence of such zero morphemes is a common practice in both the descriptive and theoretical literature; for example, this device is used explicitly in Jelinek 1984, as well as in most descriptions or analyses of head-marking languages (e.g., Mithun 1986b for Mohawk).[18] The important point is that this Ø element is restricted to third person neuter; for other person–gender categories the form is not, in general, Ø and the need for either agreement or incorporation shows up clearly.

The Nahuatlan languages are particularly clear in this regard because they have overt object agreement even for neuter third person objects. Thus, the complementarity between object agreement and noun incorporation can be seen overtly in a much wider range of examples. Merlan (1976:187) gives the following minimal pair for the Huauhtla dialect:

(18) a. Neʔ Ø-ki-ca'ki   kallak-tli.
         he   3sS-3sO-closed door-NSF
         'He closed the door.'

      b. Neʔ Ø-kal-caʔ-ki.
         he   3sS-door-closed
         'He closed the door.'

The object agreement *ki* is absent in (18b), yet cannot be dropped in (18a). Again, either an agreement morpheme or an incorporated root is adequate to make the verb's internal argument visible, but one or the other is strictly required. Andrews (1975:ch. 23) and Launey (1981) present similar facts for Classical Nahautl. Comparable effects are found in Chukchee (Nedjalkov 1976:197) and one dialect of Ainu (Shibatani 1990:61).

So far I have contrasted the examples in (17b) and (17c) with (17a) to show that some morphological expression of the object argument is necessary. Interestingly, (17d) shows that one cannot have *both* agreement and an incorporated noun root in Mohawk.[19] Rather, when the noun root is incorporated, the object agreement morpheme on the verb must be lost. Significantly, this is true even when an overt NP is present that doubles the incorporated root, showing that the construction is still transitive in some sense:

(19)   a. Ra-wir-a-núhwe'-s   thíkʌ owirá'a.
          MsS-baby-Ø-like-HAB that   baby
          'He likes that baby.'

       b. *Shako-wir-a-núhwe'-s   thíkʌ owirá'a.
          MsS/FsO-baby-Ø-like-HAB that   baby
          'He likes that baby.'

The same complementarity is found in Nahuatl: the object agreement marker *ki* cannot be added to (18b). This is true even though the incorporated noun can be understood as definite, referring to something already present in the discourse, as Merlan shows with some care. Moreover, one cannot rule out the cooccurrence of NI and object agreement by saying that object agreement and INs compete for the same position in a morphological template. Object agreement and INs do appear on the same verb in both Mohawk (see (20)) and Nahuatl (see (21)) when the verb root is triadic, selecting two internal arguments.

(20)   T-a-shako-wír-u-'.
       CIS-FACT-MsS/FsO-baby-give-PUNC
       'He handed her the baby.'

(21)   ni-mic-tomi-maka   (Merlan 1976:184–185)
       1sS-2sO-money-give
       'I'll give you money'

This shows that it is not the cooccurrence of object agreement and noun root per se that is the problem in (17d), but rather the redundancy that results from having both the agreement morpheme and the noun root associated with the same argument.

Interestingly, the status of examples like (17d) is a point on which polysynthetic languages vary. Thus, agreement with the object is retained even when the head of the object is incorporated in the Northern Australian languages (as in (22) from Mayali) and the Tanoan languages (as in (23) from Southern Tiwa).

(22)   a. Nga-ban-yaw-na-ng.   (Evans, personal communication)
          1sS-3pO-baby-saw-PAST/PERF
          'I saw the babies.'

b. Bi-yau-ngune-nguneng   ginga.[20]   (Evans 1991:291)
3sS/3HO-child-eat-PAST/PERF crocodile.
'The crocodile ate the child.'

(23)   Bi-seuan-mū-ban.   (Allen et al. 1984:295)
1sS/3PO-man-see-PAST
'I saw the men.'

Example (22) would be ungrammatical on the given interpretation if the object agreement morpheme were omitted. Similarly, the agreement prefix in (23) is a portmanteau that indicates the gender class and number of the object; it is distinct from the prefix that would appear if there were a first person subject with an intransitive verb (the prefix would be *te*) or the one that would appear if the object were in a different gender/number class (*ti* or *te*). This difference between Iroquoian/Aztecan, on the one hand, and Australian/Tanoan, on the other, seems to be a rather superficial one that does not correlate with any other important properties of the languages. In particular, it does not correlate with the transitivity of the construction, as measured by the possibility of having an independent NP doubling the IN (contrary to the claim of Rosen 1989b): Mohawk and Mayali both allow full NP doubles, whereas Nahuatl and Southern Tiwa do not. Indeed, Shibatani (1990) shows that dialects of Ainu differ minimally in this regard.

This variation is significant because it confirms the decision to treat the Polysynthesis Parameter as a type of Visibility Condition rather than as a special way of applying the Theta Criterion. The Theta Criterion requires biuniqueness between arguments and positions in a θ-grid. This is what we find in (17) in Mohawk and (18) in Nahuatl, if agreement morphemes and incorporated noun roots count as arguments. In particular, (17d) would be ruled out because there are two argument-type morphemes associated with a single position in a θ-grid. However, this approach would also incorrectly rule out (22) and (23). We would be forced to conclude that Mayali and Southern Tiwa either are not polysynthetic after all or do not have syntactic noun incorporation—both undesirable conclusions. On the other hand, when the Polysynthesis Parameter is stated as a Visibility Condition, as in (15), it is sufficient to rule out (17a) in contrast to (17b,c), but is silent on the status of (17d). This formulation requires that the direct object NP be coindexed with a morpheme in the verb, but crucially does not require that that morpheme be unique. Thus, low-level variation within the class of polysynthetic languages is tolerated at exactly this point, corresponding to what we observe.

1.5 Other Implications and Prospectus

So far we have concentrated on the MVC's ability to explain interactions between agreement and incorporation. These interactions are crucial in motivating the basic idea of the parameter. However, it is easy to see that the MVC will influence languages in which it holds in many other ways as well. We are now in a position to map out some of the more straightforward of these influences, thereby providing a sense of the topics to be developed in the remainder of the book.

First, the MVC has a significant role to play within the analysis of nonconfigurationality proper. In particular, it determines the extent to which the Jelinek-style pronominal argument analysis applies to a given language. Part of Jelinek's idea is that inflections on the verb count as pronouns and satisfy the θ-positions of that verb. However, in order to properly account for the facts of Mohawk one must also stipulate that such inflections *must* appear on the verb. Translating this into my terms, the arguments of the verb must be made visible in this way, rather than in some other. Without this stipulation, an object agreement morpheme, for example, could simply be omitted. This, then, would allow an independent NP to be the syntactic argument of the verb, becoming visible by ordinary Case assignment as in English.[21] The ungrammaticality of (17a) shows that this is not an option in Mohawk. However, the possibility cannot be ruled out by Universal Grammar, since other languages do exactly this. Chichewa, as analyzed by Bresnan and Mchombo (1987), is one important example:

(24)   a. Njûchi zi-ná-lúm-a   alenje.
          bees   SM-PAST-bite-IND hunters
          'The bees bit the hunters.'
          OK: SVO and VOS orders, but *OVS, *VSO, *SOV, *OSV

       b. Njûchi zi-ná-wá-lum-a   (alenje).
          bees   SM-PAST-OM-bite-IND hunters
          'The bees bit the hunters.'
          OK: SVO, VOS, OVS, VSO, SOV, and OSV orders

When there is no object marker on a transitive verb, as in (24a), a full NP object must be right-adjacent to the verb. When there is an object marker on the verb, as in (24b), however, it acts as the true object of the verb. An additional NP can be adjoined to the clause, but it has no fixed syntactic position. Thus, Chichewa seems to have both an English-like configurational mode, and a Mohawk-like non-configurational mode. Similar facts hold in Northern Athapaskan languages, such as Slave (Rice 1989). Indeed, the pattern seems to be rather common cross-linguistically; perhaps even Spanish is to be analyzed in this way (Jelinek 1984:48–49). Mohawk, however, does not have a similar, partially configurational mode, as will be seen in detail in chapter 2. The MVC explains why this is so. Mohawk and Chichewa have comparable object agreement morphemes, but only Mohawk is required to use them. More generally, the MVC explains why polysynthetic languages must have obligatory agreement with all NP argument positions: subject, object, indirect object. It seems correct to say that such languages are of a distinctly different type than languages like Chichewa, Slave, and Spanish, where agreement is partial and/or optional. In a sense, the MVC puts teeth into Jelinek's proposals concerning nonconfigurationality.

   This reasoning has implications that go beyond the familiar configurationality cluster. Suppose, for example, that a given category had no agreement associated with it and could not be incorporated. The MVC then implies that such a category could never appear as an argument. In chapter 9 I will argue that this explains the systematic absence of adpositional phrase (PP) arguments in Mohawk. Interestingly, argument PPs also appear to be lacking in other polysynthetic languages, although they are certainly found in nonpolysynthetic languages like Slave (Rice

1989). The condition that all arguments must correspond to a morpheme on the head also has important implications for the internal structure of NPs in polysynthetic languages, as will be discussed in chapter 5.

The MVC also implies that a polysynthetic language will not be able to have anything comparable to the infinitives found in English and other Indo-European languages. The reason is simple: infinitival forms lack agreement inflection for the subject;[22] hence, any verb that selected a subject θ-role and appeared in an infinitival form would violate the MVC. Example (25) shows how typical infinitival constructions in English are translated into Mohawk.

(25) *K*-ate'nyʌ́t-ha' au-sa-*ke*-'sere-ht-a-hserúni-'.
      1sS-try-HAB   OPT-ITER-1sS-car-NOM-Ø-fix-PUNC
      'I am trying to fix the car.'

Here, the embedded verb form in the optative mood has exactly the same subject agreement as the matrix verb.

Most other languages tentatively identified as polysynthetic also lack infinitival verb forms: Nahuatl (Andrews 1975:14–15, 17), Kiowa (Watkins 1984:146–147), Nunggubuyu (Heath 1986:395), Mayali (Evans 1991:332–335), and Ainu (Shibatani 1990) all fit this generalization (see chapter 10). Indeed, this is a known typological feature of head-marking languages, noticed by a variety of researchers and confirmed by Nichols (1992).[23] In contrast, the Bantu languages do have infinitival forms; for example, in (26) from Swahili both the tense/aspect prefix and the otherwise obligatory subject agreement marker are replaced by invariant *ku* (Vitale 1981:sec. 4.1.3).

(26) Juma a-li-jaribu   ku-fungua mlango.
      Juma 3sS-PAST-try to-open   door
      'Juma tried to open the door.'

Such infinitival clauses have an obligatorily null subject, which can only be understood as coreferential with the matrix subject, as in English. This is permitted because the MVC does not hold in Swahili.[24] The MVC also predicts that polysynthetic languages will lack the special types of complementation inherently associated with infinitival constructions in English, such as obligatory control. Chapter 10 shows that this is true, with one principled class of exceptions.

Finally, the MVC can be interpreted as playing an important role in determining the kind of incorporation structures a language will have. We observed in connection with (3) that noun incorporation in Mohawk is impressive in terms of its frequency, productivity, and referential properties. In contrast, Mohawk is quite modest in its verb incorporation. There are at most five suffixes that can plausibly be analyzed as higher verbs. More importantly, those verb incorporation triggers that do exist are quite limited in their use by the standards of other languages. In particular, the causative morpheme attaches only to a subclass of the intransitive verbs; it is completely impossible on transitives verbs:[25]

(27) a. Wa'-t-ha-[a]'shar-á-'tsu-st-e'.
         FACT-DUP-MsS-knife-Ø-be.dirty-CAUS-PUNC
         'He made the knife dirty.'

    b. Uwári t-a-yú-[a]hsʌ-ht-e'   ne á'share'.
        Mary CIS-FACT-FsS-fall-CAUS-PUNC NE knife
        'Mary made the knife fall.'

(28) a. *(ÓnʌsteꞋ) wa-hi-yʌ́tho-ht-e'   Sak.
        corn   FACT-1sS/MsO-plant-CAUS-PUNC Sak
        'I made Sak plant it (corn).'

    b. *Ká'sere wa'-uk-hnínu-ht-e'.
        car   FACT-FsS/1sO-buy-CAUS-PUNC
        'She made me buy a car.'

Verbs differ from nouns in that they are canonically argument-*takers;* in general, they select for some kind of argument of their own. Consider, then, an abstract structure in which a transitive verb is incorporated, as in (29).

(29)

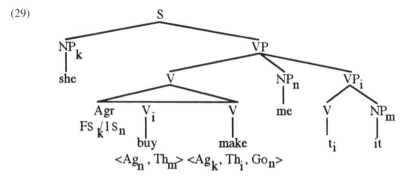

The derived word in structure (29) contains two lexical categories: the "incorpororee" and the host of the incorporation. So far, we have focused on how the MVC is satisfied with respect to the incorporation host. However, the principle presumably applies to the incorporee as well. For noun incorporation, the question did not arise, since nouns usually do not take arguments. The question does arise in (29), however, and proves problematic. The most flexible way to represent arguments is by agreement morphology. However, incorporated roots are always incorporated "bare," without the inflectional morphology they would have if they stood alone. This has been observed by many people across many languages, and there is presumably some deep theoretical reason for it (e.g., see Li 1990, Baker and Hale 1990, and later discussion in the present chapter). Neither will the agreement factors associated with the incorporation host be available to represent the arguments of the incorporee, since they will, in general, be needed to satisfy the host's θ-grid. Interpreted in this way, the MVC exerts pressure against the incorporation of verbs, particularly verbs with multiple arguments. From this perspective, it is no coincidence that Mohawk limits causatives to intransitive verbs only.

     Indeed, similar transitivity restrictions on morphological causatives are found in the other languages that are rich in noun incorporation, including the other Iroquoian languages (Chafe 1967, Williams 1976b), the Gunwinjguan languages (cf., e.g., Heath 1984:393–395 for Nunggubuyu), Chukchee (Nedjalkov 1976), and arguably Wichita (Rood 1976). Conversely, those languages that are known to allow causatives of transitive verbs typically do not allow productive noun incorporation: this includes Bantu languages in general, Chamorro, Malayalam, Turkish, and Japanese. This negative correlation between NI and verb incorporation (VI) could not be explained under the assumptions in Baker 1988a, where it was assumed that incorporation was triggered purely by morphological properties, such as whether a given morpheme was an affix or whether N–V compounding was allowed. The MVC, however, has the potential to explain this negative correlation by encouraging NI in languages where it holds, while discouraging most kinds of VI in those languages. However, many theoretical and empirical complexities arise in working out this intuitive idea, and it will by my task in chapters 7 and 8 to sort these out. This reasoning also has implications for the analysis of applicative constructions in polysynthetic languages (see chapter 9).

This preliminary survey suggests there is a property of polysynthetic languages that qualifies as a true parameter. Indeed, its implications are broad enough to be worthy of the term "macroparameter."

1.6 On Morphological Structure and Syntactic Structure

Before beginning the detailed exposition, it will helpful to clarify certain aspects of the hierarchical structure of polysynthetic languages. We have already seen that these languages have nonconfigurational syntax, where elements are rather freely ordered and give little evidence for phrasal grouping. In contrast, word-internal structure in these languages is very configurational indeed. Not surprisingly, the relative order of morphemes within words is almost always rigidly fixed, with few opportunities for alternative arrangements; this is a near-universal property of morphology. More remarkable is the fact that the order of basic morphemes is also quite consistent across the polysynthetic languages. Thus, readers will be better equipped to understand the examples if they have some awareness of this structure. Furthermore, I believe that this morpheme order provides a clue to the basic syntactic structure of these languages, something that is difficult (although not necessarily impossible) to establish by conventional syntactic means.

Consider first noun incorporation in the seven language families where it is syntactic: Iroquoian, Caddoan, Tanoan, Nahuatl, Gunwinjguan, Chukchee, and Ainu. In Mohawk, we have seen that an incorporated noun root comes just before the verb root (i.e., between the verb root and the preceding agreement prefixes). Strikingly, this is where the incorporated noun root appears in the other six languages as well:

(30) a. Wa-hake-*natar*-a-kwétar-ʌ-'.   MOHAWK
          FACT-MsS/1sO-*bread*-Ø-cut-BEN-PUNC
          'He cut the bread for me.'

      b. I-s-kí-ic-ʔ*asin*-nʔi.   WICHITA (Rood 1976:15)
          IMPER-2sS-1sO-ben-*shoe*-make/PL
          'Make me a pair of shoes.'

      c. Ka-'*u*'*u*-wia-ban.   SOUTHERN TIWA (Allen et al. 1984:303)
          1sS/2sO|AO-*baby*-give-PAST
          'I gave you the baby.'

   d. Ni-quin-*xōchi*-tēmo-lia. NAHUATL (Andrews 1975:164)
     1sS-3pO-*flower*-seek-BEN/PRES
     'I seek flowers for them.'

   e. Bandi-marne-*ganj*-ginje-ng. MAYALI (Evans 1991:210)
     3pS/3pO-ben-*meat*-cook-PAST/PERF
     'They cooked meat for them.'

   f. Mət-meč-*qora*-gərke-plətko-mək. CHUKCHEE (Spencer 1993:39)
     1pS-almost-*deer*-hunt-finish-1sS
     'We almost finished hunting reindeer.'

   g. A-Ø-ko-*tam*-enere. AINU (Shibatani 1990:69)
     1sS-3sO-APPL-*sword*-swing
     'I swung the sword at them.'

It is unlikely that this is coincidental. It is known that in lexical N–V compounds either the verb or the noun can appear first, depending perhaps on the basic word order parameters of the language (Lieber 1993). Suppose, then, for the sake of argument that an incorporated noun were equally likely to appear to the left or to the right of the verb root. Then the probability of it appearing to the left in all seven language families would be $(0.5)^7$, or 0.0078125. When one takes into account that the position as well as the direction of the IN is uniform, this becomes even more remarkable.

Verbal morphemes that trigger verb movement also show up in a very consistent place in the complex verb. We have seen two such morphemes in Mohawk: the causative and the purposive. Both are suffixes, appearing after the verb root but before any inflectional morphology, as seen in (3f) and (27) above. Exactly the same is true in the other polysynthetic languages. Thus, causative morphemes exist in Wichita, Kiowa, Southern Tiwa, Nahuatl, Ainu, and the various Gunwinjguan languages; in each case, it is a suffix that precedes tense/aspect morphology. The only complication is Chukchee, where the causative morpheme is a circumfix, consisting of the prefix *r* or *n* and the suffix *ew* or *aw* (Nedjalkov 1976:186, Bogoras 1922:819); even here the suffix part appears in the expected position. Similarly, purposive-like morphemes meaning 'go in order to' exist not only in Mohawk, but in Wichita (Rood 1976:169–170), Tanoan, Nahuatl, and (with a slightly different meaning) Mayali. Again, these all come after the verb root but before inflectional morphology. Desiderative elements meaning 'want' are found in at least Southern Tiwa, Nahuatl, and Chukchee, and probably in Ainu.[26] Again, they all come after the verb root except in Chukchee, where the desiderative is again a circumfix (*ra* plus *ng*) (Nedjalkov 1976:191, Bogoras 1922:821). Various other verb–verb combinations can be formed in these languages, and the same generalization holds throughout: the morpheme that one would treat semantically as the higher predicate consistently follows the morpheme that expresses the lower predicate. Examples of most of these types can be found in chapter 8. Again, this degree of uniformity in word structure cannot be a coincidence.

Significantly, a simple generalization covers both of these cases. This becomes obvious when we compare once again the simple NI structure in Mohawk with the VI structure of the purposive, as shown in (10); repeated here as (31).

(31)   a.

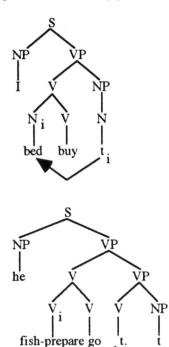

b.

The syntactic similarity between the two was pointed out earlier: in both constructions, the maximal projection of one morpheme is an argument of the other, and the lower morpheme moves to adjoin to the higher one. We now notice a morphological similarity, as well: in both cases, *the moved morpheme adjoins to the left of the target morpheme.* This is consistent with Kayne's (1995) hypothesis that there are no basic ordering parameters in natural language. In particular, it follows from Kayne's system that if an element X is adjoined to an element Y, then X must precede Y. One source of evidence that he gives for this is the claim that pronominal clitics in Romance always adjoin to the left of the functional category that hosts them, superficial appearances notwithstanding. In this work, I will not commit myself to Kayne's general claim,[27] but I adopt his view for the special case where X and Y are head-level categories. This is stated in (32).

(32)   If X and Y are X^0 categories and X is adjoined to Y in the syntax, then X precedes Y in linear order.

This explains why incorporated nouns always precede the verb root, and why the verb root always precedes an affix or root that expresses a higher verbal predicate.

The other point that is consistent across these languages is that incorporated noun roots follow inflectional prefixes such as agreement (see (30)), and verbal suffixes precede inflectional suffixes such as tense and aspect. This observation does not necessarily follow from (32). It does, however, fit naturally with the P&P claim that many inflectional morphemes count as phrase structure heads. If this is so, then it is possible for a verb to combine with these heads only after NI or VI has taken place. Indeed, there are morpheme order regularities that hold of "inflectional" morphemes as well. In particular, most of the polysynthetic languages have aspect morphology (e.g., perfective vs. imperfective) and some kind of tense and/or mood morphology (e.g., past vs. nonpast, factual vs. irrealis). Where these can be clearly distinguished from one another, their relative position is consistent: aspect is a suffix that follows the verb root and any "higher predicate" suffixes; tense/mood is a suffix that follows aspect. The following morpheme order in Mohawk is quite typical:

(33)   Ra-'wáhr-a-k-s-kwe.' (D&D:380)
        MsS-meat-Ø-eat-HAB-PAST
        'He used to eat meat.'

Aspect also follows the stem in Wichita, Kiowa, and Chukchee; it conditions the final vowel of the stem form in Nahuatl, and it is a suffix or a postverbal auxiliary in Ainu. Tense and/or mood morphology follows aspect in Kiowa, Nahuatl, and some examples in Mohawk. Finally, tense/mood and aspect combine to form a portmanteau in the Gunwinjguan languages; this portmanteau is a postverbal suffix.

    These generalizations are admittedly somewhat "noisier" than those involving incorporated noun roots: for example, tense/mood is a prefix in Wichita and sometimes in Mohawk, and it is expressed by a combination of prefix and suffix in Chukchee. There are also important details of the tense/aspect system in various languages that may be relevant. Since it is not my purpose to give a complete analysis of the tense/aspect system of any of the polysynthetic languages, I must put these concerns aside for the most part. Still, it seems clear that the order verb–aspect–tense/mood is found much more often than would occur by chance. Thus, I assume that the tense/mood morphemes generally head a functional category "Inflection Phrase" (IP), while aspect morphemes head a functional category "Aspect Phrase" (AspP). The universal order of embedding is, then, VP inside of AspP, which is inside of IP. This is the semantically natural order of embedding on most accounts, where tense and aspect are both operators over VP, with tense having scope over aspect (see, for example, Travis 1991, in preparation). Thus, a partial structure for (33) is (34). Incorporation then proceeds successive cyclically from the bottom of the tree to the top, adjoining the head of each phrase to the left of the next head, in accordance with (32). This derives [N–V–Asp–Infl] as the unmarked morpheme order, as observed.

    The last type of morphology to consider is agreement. This, too, is treated as the head of a functional category in much P&P work since Pollock 1989. However, there are some problems with this proposal for the polysynthetic languages. First, agreement morphemes, unlike tense and aspect, are semantically vacuous; thus, there is no way of locating them in a syntactic tree by investigating their scope with respect to other items. Second, and more important, this claim together with (32) predicts that agreement morphemes should show up as some kind of suffix. Exactly the opposite is true: in the vast majority of cases, agreement morphology is prefixal, appearing early in the verbal complex. This is consistently so in Mohawk, Wichita, Tanoan, Nahuatl, and Gunwinjguan (see (30a–e)). It is usually true in Ainu (see (30g)) (one first person subject agreement morpheme is a

(34)

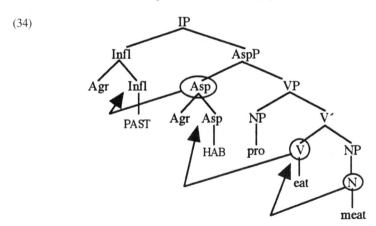

suffix in Ainu). The one problematic case is Chukchee, in which agreement is expressed by a combination of prefixes and suffixes (see (30f)); this may be yet another instance of Chukchee's unusual love of circumfixes. Moreover, in those cases where it can be determined, subject agreement markers appear outside of object agreement markers. This is clearly so in Wichita, Nahuatl, and Ainu; it is also true for those combinations in Mohawk that can be readily segmented, as in (35a). Other combinations of subject and object agreement form portmanteaux in which order cannot reliably be discerned, at least in a synchronic sense, as in (35b).

(35) a. Ye-sa-núhwe'-s. (D&D:385)
         FsS-2sO-like-HAB
         'She likes you.'

      b. Ya-núhwe'-s. (D&D:384)
         MsS/2sO-like-HAB
         'He likes you.'

Portmanteaux are also typical of Tanoan and Gunwinjguan. Thus, the position of agreement morphemes seems to be principled in this class of languages, but not in a way that is consistent with the claim that they are X-bar theoretical heads.

The principles developed so far converge on a simple proposal for what these agreement morphemes are. The fact that they are on the left side of the complex suggests that they are adjoined elements, placed by (32). The fact that they are relatively near the periphery of the morphological complex suggests that they are adjoined to heads that are relatively high in the structure. For these reasons, I assume that one agreement element (Agr) is adjoined to the Infl node; if there is a second, it is adjoined to Asp. This fits well with the familiar fact that there are dependencies between tense/aspect inflection and agreement in many languages. For example, subject agreement is missing on most infinitivals in Indo-European languages, a fact that motivated putting tense and subject agreement under the same node in Chomsky 1981. Similarly, the agreement paradigms are somewhat different in different tenses in Chukchee and Nunggubuyu. Finally, there is one context in which tense/aspect morphology is generally not found on a verb stem in the polysynthetic languages: that is when the verb is incorporated into another verb (see chapter 8). In exactly this case, there is no agreement morphology associated with the verb stem. For concreteness, I will assume that the agreement factors are adjoined to Infl and Asp in the base.[28] Thus, a fuller underlying structure for (33) is (36).

(36)

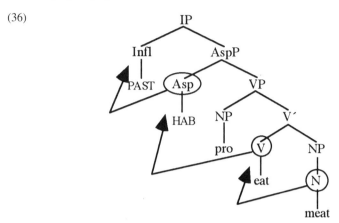

The head of the object noun phrase incorporates into the verb, and the derived verb then incorporates into Asp and Infl. In the latter two steps, I assume that the moved item adjoins not to the left of the target category as a whole, but rather to the head of the target category. This means that the verb and the incorporated noun root (if any) show up to the left of Asp and Infl, but inside of the associated agreement morphemes, as desired.[29]

I have stated (32) as a universal, but it is possible that it should be parameterized to say that moved heads adjoin to the left of the target category in some languages and to the right of it in others. This possibility is raised by interesting facts in Sora, a Munda language spoken in India, brought to my attention by David Stampe (personal communication). Sora is polysynthetic in the informal sense; it also has productive noun incorporation where the IN is understood as referential. The following two sentences are essentially equivalent:

(37)   a. Bɔŋtɛl-ən-ədɔŋ jom-t-ɛ-ji   pɔ?
           buffalo-NSF-ACC eat-NONPAST-3S-3PS Q
           'Will they eat the buffalo?' or 'Do they eat buffalo?'

       b. Jom-bɔŋ-t-ɛ-n-ji   pɔ?
           eat-buffalo-NONPAST-3S-INTR-3PS Q
           'Will they eat the buffalo?' or 'Do they eat buffalo?'

Thus, Sora is also polysynthetic in my technical sense. However, the IN follows the verb root, rather than preceding it as (32) predicts. This reversal is more general, as (38) shows (Donegan and Stampe 1983:341).

(38)   Ñɛn əd-məl-jom-jɛl-yɔ-aj-t-en-ay.
       I   NEG-want-eat-meat-fish-all-NONPAST-INTR-1sS
       'I don't want to eat all the fish.'

Not only does the IN follow the verb root, but the higher predicate morpheme 'want' precedes it; meanwhile, the agreement morphology is the final suffix, and the quantificational element 'all' is an intermediate suffix. In short, the order of morphemes in Sora is the mirror image of that found in the other polysynthetic languages. (The exception is the tense marker, which ought to be a prefix on this view; however, tense is the most common element to be out of position in the other polysynthetic languages as well.) These facts are elegantly explained if the direction of adjunction performed by head movement is simply reversed in Sora.[30]

We have now deduced most of the structure of the clause in these languages from their morphological structure. The most significant element that has not been placed by these means is the subject. What morphological structure tells us about the subject is mostly negative: it cannot be incorporated, the way the object can. In addition, subject agreement typically appears outside of object agreement, as previously noted. These facts, plus a bias in favor of assuming a relatively universal structure for the clause, lead me to claim that in polysynthetic languages, as in English, the subject is more loosely attached to the clause than the object, which it asymmetrically c-commands. Exactly what position the subject occupies is still open; for the time being, I will assume that the subject is generated as the specifier of VP, as in most current work. These assumptions will be confirmed and elaborated in the chapters that follow, particularly chapters 5 through 8. In contrast, the details of clause structure are not particularly important for most of the material in chapters 2 through 4; therefore, in those chapters I will often draw simplified structures from the era of S→NP VP and VP→V NP for convenience and clarity.

Some other representational conventions will be used as well. First, I will generally not show the base-generated internal structure of Asp and Infl, with Agrs adjoined to them; rather I will just write the Agr directly under the Asp or Infl head. Second, I will omit the specifiers of functional categories where they are not in use. Third, I will draw most of my phrase structures as if the polysynthetic languages were uniformly head-initial, SVO-type languages. There is no evidence that this is so: for the most part, clause kernels consist entirely of traces and null pronouns the order of which cannot be readily established. Indeed, some of the polysynthetic languages have head-final tendencies (Ainu and perhaps Kiowa). Nevertheless, the structures have to be drawn one way or another, and head-initial diagrams have two expository advantages: they are more familiar to some linguists, and they provide a clear non–string-vacuous representation of many head movements.

In closing, I would like to point out that if this account of verbal morphology in polysynthetic languages is more or less correct, it has some profound implications for the theory of morphology in general. Morphology has typically been considered the most idiosyncratic component of the grammar, with languages differing greatly in the expression and position of their morphological categories. This survey shows that much of the idiosyncrasy disappears when one carefully limits the analysis to a narrow class of languages that are similar in their syntactic structure. Significantly, this account of the gross morphological structure in polysynthetic languages makes no use of some of the stipulative devices or delicate distinctions that are important in the morphological literature. For example, there has been no use of morphological subcategorization frames of the type introduced by Lieber (1980) to determine whether a given morpheme is a suffix or a prefix, or what kind of host it attaches to. These are fully determined by a combination of syntactic selection, the locality of head movement, and the stipulation that adjunction is always to the left. Morphological subcategorization frames are not even needed to force incorporation in this class of languages, because for the most part this will be forced by the MVC (see, e.g., chapter 7). Similarly, there is no need for morpheme templates or ordered rule systems (see Anderson 1992) to determine the order of morphemes. We do not even need to distinguish between derivational and inflectional morphology: noun incorporation and causative formation have traditionally been considered derivational processes, while tense and aspect are inflectional; nevertheless, the same ordering generalizations apply to both types of morphology. The analysis also speaks against a wide range of lexicalist theories of morphology, including Chomsky's (1992) "checking theory." Chapter 7, in particular, presents new evidence that noun incorporation is a syntactic phenomenon. However, we have seen that noun incorporation is typically the first of the morphological combinations to take place. This, then, implies that all of the other morphological combinations are also performed in the syntax or later.

The view of morphology that emerges here is a very restrictive one, with some clear conceptual advantages. Principles like (32) begin to make sense out of how it could be possible for children learning a polysynthetic language to master both the word structures of their language (which are very complex) and the syntactic structures of their language (for which there is little other direct evidence). The principle given in (32) makes this problem almost trivial by guaranteeing that over a large range of cases, morphological order corresponds to morphological hierarchical structure, which, in turn, reflects syntactic hierarchical structure. Without such a principle, both the learning of such a language and the parsing of it would be very difficult.

It must be emphasized, however, that this is not a complete theory of morphology, even for the polysynthetic languages. First, the various polysynthetic languages have other morphemes that have no obvious role in the syntax, about which this theory says nothing. Some of these are only partially productive, derivational morphemes that appear close to the verb root (although these are not common in polysynthetic languages). Others are, broadly speaking, "modifying," "adverbial," or "quantificational" in nature. Most of the so-called prepronominal prefixes in Mohawk fall into this class (*s* iterative, meaning 'again' or 'back'; *y* translocative, 'away'; *t* cislocative, 'toward'; *te* duplicative, *th* contrastive, etc.). Wichita and the Gunwinjguan languages are particularly rich in these. For the most part, they are prefixes rather than suffixes in all three families; thus, both their position and interpretation suggest that they are base-generated adjoined modifiers of some kind. However, I cannot say more than this.

Even among the morphemes that this theory aspires to analyze, there are some minor variations in order and realization. I strongly suspect that there is no unified solution to this class of problems, but rather an individual solution for each case. In some cases, the difference in morpheme order probably is the result of a difference in underlying syntactic structure. For example, benefactive applicative morphemes appear in one of two places in polysynthetic languages: they can be suffixes between the verb root and aspect, as in Mohawk and Nahuatl, or they can be prefixes between object agreement and the incorporated noun, as in Gunwinjguan, Ainu, and Wichita. In section 9.3, I argue that the suffixes are actually incorporating verbs, whereas the prefixes are incorporated adpositions. A similar solution seems likely for the variable position of reflexive and reciprocal morphemes. Other variations in morpheme realization are obviously idiosyncratic, however, and call for a morphophonological analysis of some kind. The fact that first person intransitive subject agreement in Ainu is a suffix rather than a prefix clearly falls into this class; so, too, presumably does the fact that some tense/mood morphemes in Mohawk and all of them in Wichita are prefixes rather than suffixes.[31] However, these irregularities are not fatal to a syntactically oriented theory of morpheme order, as long as one adopts a framework that allows for "late lexical insertion" and a limited amount of readjustment in the postsyntactic component (see Halle and Marantz 1993 and related work). Which kind of solution is correct for any given case and what constraints should be placed on the whole system are very important topics that are the subject of some current work and probably deserve more attention. However, they are not the topic of this book. Having now oriented the reader to the basic morphological and syntactic structures of polysynthetic languages, it is time to start developing the main themes in earnest.

Notes

1. Sometimes such languages are called "nonconfigurational." However, this is a blurring of two notions that are better kept separate; see Speas 1990 for a discussion.

2. This work is presented in P&P terms, for a variety of reasons. Nevertheless, I have tried to make it accessible to people with various backgrounds and theoretical tastes by avoiding terminology of narrow usage and by giving brief characterizations of the principles of the theory as they become relevant. Thus, while some general familiarity with the P&P framework will undoubtedly make the reading easier, I have taken for granted as few specifics as possible.

P&P theory has undergone a change of emphasis in the last few years, due to the proposals in Chomsky 1992; how far-reaching that change will prove to be is not yet clear. Under the circumstances, I have taken a somewhat eclectic approach, using both some ideas of the Minimalist Program and some ideas from earlier work that may not be strictly compatible with that program. Since my primary interest here is to generalize the theorems of P&P theory to a broader class of linguistic phenomena, the exact axiomization of the theory is not directly relevant, as long as the mid-level theorems are more or less unchanged.

3. It is not clear how to count members of a parametric cluster. For example, does the fact that verbs appear before adverbs and floated quantifiers in French (Pollock 1989) count as one fact or two? Should the fact that the equivalents of both *who* and *what* remain in situ in Chinese (Huang 1982) be counted as one fact or two? Probably there is no principled way to answer such questions.

4. See also Webelhuth 1992 and recent writings of Richard Kayne, among many others.

5. See appendix B for information about how to pronounce the Mohawk examples and appendix A for an explanation of the abbreviations used in the literal glosses.

6. Indeed, this was considered to be another parameter in the sense of Chomsky 1981; these properties constituted the characteristic cluster associated with that parameter.

Moreover, the cluster has undergone the same fragmentation as others (see, for example, Austin and Bresnan 1994).

7. See also Deering and Delisle 1976. In the rather rare cases where agreement on the verb does not identify grammatical functions unambiguously, a sentence of the form NP–V–NP is usually interpreted as SVO rather than OVS (Mithun and Chafe 1979:11–12). It is not clear that this has any syntactic significance, however, and it is apparently not true for other, closely related Iroquoian languages (Mithun 1987).

8. Jelinek would not necessarily agree with all the details of the structure in (8). In particular, Jelinek (1984:50) does not distinguish VP from S and attaches NPs to the basic clause by sister-adjunction rather than Chomsky-adjunction. I believe that (8) is faithful to her basic idea, however. In addition, (8) is not exactly the structure used in Baker 1991a or the current work; in particular, I assume that the agreement markers license pro's in canonical argument positions, rather than literally being arguments themselves (see the discussion later in this chapter).

9. This may, in fact, be a lexicalized compound, specific to Akwesasne Mohawk. My Kahnawake consultant is not familiar with the word.

10. One important question left open here is whether there is a null subject (such as PRO) associated with the embedded VP in (10b) (see sections 8.3 and 10.2.2 for discussion).

11. Given this, it has been suggested to me that the word "polysynthesis" should be left as a general descriptive term and that I should coin a new term for the class of languages I am concerned with, which is a proper subset of the languages typically called polysynthetic. Nicholas Evans (personal communication) suggests the term "polysaturation" for the Mohawk class. However, I have not been able to tear myself away from the more familiar term.

12. For example, free word order in these languages seems to be due to syntactic movement (scrambling); see Saito 1985, 1990, Webelhuth 1992, and Mahajan 1990 for discussion. See also Chamorro 1992:ch. 3 for a comparison of free word order and its correlates in Mohawk and Japanese/Hindi.

13. Of these factors, (c) is the hardest to judge on the basis of standard grammars, and it may turn out that some of the languages listed actually fail this criterion.

14. This is a group of languages spoken in the western and central Arnhem Land area in the north of Australia. The name for the group comes from Evans 1991. A number of these languages have been quite well described, and there are some nontrivial differences in their morphosyntax. Those that I have looked at are: Nunggubuyu (Heath 1980, Heath 1984, Heath 1986), Mayali (Evans 1991, Evans 1993), Rembarrnga (McKay 1975), Ngandi (Heath 1978), and Ngalakan (Merlan 1983). For the most part, I will base my discussion on Nunggubuyu and Mayali, because the descriptions of these languages are more recent, more detailed, and in some cases more theoretically informed. Material from the other Gunwinjguan languages will only be cited when it fills out or corrects the picture formed by the first two in a significant way.

15. See also later discussion of Sora, a Munda language of India.

16. Sapir (1911:262ff.) claims that Paiute is an exception to this generalization. However, it is not clear from his examples and discussion whether NI in Paiute is referentially active, or whether it can be analyzed as lexical compounding. It is also the case that Paiute pronouns cliticize into an auxiliary element, and this might be considered sufficient to pass the MVC (see the discussion of Chukchee auxiliaries in section 10.2.2).

17. The zoic gender frequently shows up as a zero morpheme. Nevertheless, the zoic morpheme is not *systematically* null; thus, the agreement in (i) is distinct from that in (16):

(i) Kuwa-núhwe'-s   (ne takós).
FsS/ZsO-like-HAB NE cat
'She likes it (the cat).'

See Baker 1990b for further morphological distinctions between zoic and neuter consistent with this analysis.

18. More specifically, these authors assume that the languages in question have null agreement morphemes. In chapter 5 I will argue that the facts of Mohawk are better understood if the null morpheme has the status of an incorporated noun root; however, this issue is not essential to the point at hand.

19. Mohawk does have a few structures that look like (17d), but there is evidence that these are derived by ordinary compounding rather than by incorporation (see section 7.4).

20. The prefix *bi* is a special form of 3sS/3sO agreement that is used when the object is higher on an animacy hierarchy than the subject (see Evans 1991:205–209 for details). The important point is that this prefix is not identical to any used on purely intransitive verbs.

21. This possibility was not considered in Baker 1991a, where I took for granted the presence of agreement morphology.

22. Here I put aside the well-known case of inflected infinitives in Portuguese. Such constructions could perhaps exist in polysynthetic languages, but they would not necessarily be identified as infinitival forms in descriptive grammars. A possible case in point is the so-called participle form in Wichita: Rood (1976) sometimes refers to the participle form as nonfinite, but it still has full agreement with the subject.

23. Chukchee looks like a counterexample to this claim, but there is some evidence that what is commonly called the infinitive is, in fact, a kind of nominalization (see Bogoras 1922:784–788 and section 10.2.1).

24. However, a nonpolysynthetic language could lack an infinitival verb form simply because its lexicon does not have a [− finite] Infl. This would be a microparameter. Modern Greek is a language of this type (Terzi 1992).

25. The same affix can sometimes attach to transitive verbs with an instrumental meaning, however (see Lounsbury 1953).

26. Shibatani (1990:77–78) refers to *rusuy* 'want' as an auxiliary and leaves a space between it and the preceding verb root, as in (i).

(i) Icen   ku-kon   rusuy.
money 1sS-have want
'I want to have money.'

However, it is striking that whenever agreement is a prefix it attaches to the first verb, and whenever it is a suffix it attaches to the second verb:

(ii) Wakka-ku-rusuy-an.
water-drink-want-1sS
'I want to drink water.'

This strongly suggests that *rusuy* and the preceding verb root form a morphological constituent after all, which is perhaps obscured by the fact that Ainu has relatively little internal sandhi.

27. Adopting Kayne's proposal in full generality would require a major rethinking of the status of right dislocations and verb-initial orders in the polysynthetic languages. The problems this raises are no worse than the ones Kayne himself considers, but they are no better either. See chapter 3, particularly section 3.2.1, for some relevant discussion. See

also later discussion in the present chapter for possible evidence of parameterization in this respect.

28. Note that this is comparable to the position of clitics in Romance languages, but not to the position of true subject agreement or participle agreement in Romance languages, as pointed out to me by Dominique Sportiche (personal communication). Agreement morphemes in polysynthetic languages have other properties that are similar to those of clitics in Romance languages; for example, they absorb Case features (see section 2.2). These similarities merit further consideration. However, agreement morphemes in polysynthetic languages are clearly prefixes rather than clitics in the morphophonological sense.

The question of whether or not Agr is adjoined to functional categories in the base becomes meaningless if one implements Chomsky's (1992) proposal that the phrase marker is built up step by step by generalized transformations; then there is no "base" in the usual sense. One could also say that Agr factors are added to the edge of an appropriate functional category as soon as incorporation into that functional category has taken place in the course of building up the structure.

29. This assumption might also provide a way of analyzing the circumfixes in Chukchee. Suppose that these are two-part morphemes, where one part is considered the head, and the other part is adjoined to it, something like verb–particle combinations in Germanic languages. Then, when an element is incorporated into such a morpheme, it will show up between the two parts. Moreover, the suffix part of the circumfix (i.e., the head) will be in the same relative position in the final verb complex as conventional morphemes are in other languages. This seems to be a correct generalization for Chukchee.

30. This is compatible with Donegan and Stampe's (1983) view that very general principles of ordering pervade languages as a whole; they also point out a possible historical explanation based on the relationship of Munda languages to the head-initial Mon-Khmer languages. Unfortunately, it is difficult to find material on Sora, and I only learned of its relevance in the final stages of preparing this work; therefore, it was not possible to include it in the rest of the discussion.

31. For Mohawk, an autosegmental solution to this problem may be possible: the mood categories show up as the vocalism in a prefix template determined by the adverbial prepronominal prefixes. Hence, they may be floating segments underlyingly. (See Lounsbury 1953 for a description of the basic facts.) It may also be significant that mood morphemes show up as prefixes, whereas tense morphemes show up as suffixes in Mohawk; this generalization does not appear to carry over to other languages, however.

I

NONCONFIGURATIONALITY

2

The Position of NPs

In Chapter 1, I showed that Mohawk has the classical properties of a nonconfigurational language: any NP can be omitted; NPs are freely ordered with respect to each other and the verb; some discontinuous nominal expressions are allowed. I also briefly reviewed Jelinek's (1984) theory that in such languages the pronominal agreement morphemes are the real arguments of the verb and the NPs are independent adjuncts. This approach is attractive because it explains the nonconfigurational properties almost immediately. Thus, compare the following two paradigms:

(1) a. Wa'-ke-tshÁri-'.
         FACT-1sS-find-PUNC
         'I found it.'

     b. Wa'-ke-tshÁri-'   kíkʌ káhure'.
        FACT-1sS-find-PUNC this gun
        'I found this gun.'

     c. Kíkʌ káhure' wa'-ke-tshÁri-'.
        this gun   FACT-1sS-find-PUNC
        'I found this gun.'

     d. Ne kíkʌ wa'-ke-tshÁri-'   ne káhure'.
        NE this FACT-1sS-find-PUNC NE gun
        'I found this gun.'

(2) a. I will go to the store.

     b. I will go to the store tomorrow afternoon.

     c. Tomorrow afternoon I will go to the store.

     d. Tomorrow I will go to the store in the afternoon.

In (1), the nonconfigurational properties of Mohawk are illustrated; (2) shows the behavior of ordinary temporal adverbs in English. The parallelism is essentially perfect. An English clause can have zero, one, or more than one temporal adverbs. Moreover, if it has one such adverb, it can appear either at the beginning or at the

41

end of the clause. This freedom is possible because these adverbs are modifiers rather than arguments; thus, there are fewer syntactic restrictions on their presence or their position. On the other hand, the verb does have a unique and obligatory tense morpheme, with a fixed syntactic position; it must be in the Infl that governs the verb. This tense can be thought of as being in a thematic relation to the verb (Higginbotham 1985); temporal adjuncts are then licensed with respect to it (cf. Hornstein 1990). The Mohawk sentences in (1) have exactly the same properties with respect to the direct object: there can be zero, one, or two such NPs; when there is one NP it can occur on either side of the clause. Meanwhile, the verb has unique and obligatory object morphology, which can be considered the true argument of that verb. The NPs are somehow licensed as adjuncts with respect to this element. From this perspective, the nonconfigurational properties are nothing exotic or unfamiliar; rather they are familiar properties applied in a new domain.

However, it is one thing to say that this approach is attractive, and another to show that it is correct. Many important questions must be answered in some detail first. Some particularly interesting ones are the following:

(i) Must the NPs be in adjunct positions? The paradigm in (1) could be accounted for by saying that the postverbal NP in (1b) is a true direct object, while the preverbal NP in (1c) is in an adjoined position. Alternatively, the preverbal NP could be a direct object, while the postverbal one is adjoined. Either choice would presuppose that there is a true underlying word order in Mohawk that is largely masked by other factors. This is exactly what has been proposed for certain other languages with relatively free word order, such as Hindi, Japanese, Chichewa (Bresnan and Mchombo 1987), Slave (Rice 1989), and Papago (Hale 1992). Is this also true for Mohawk and other polysynthetic languages?

(ii) What is the nature of the relationship between the adjoined NP and the true argument? Our earlier discussion was vague on this point, and the same is true of much of the previous literature. In practice, Jelinek relies rather heavily on language-specific "linking rules" to associate NPs and agreement elements. Speas (1990) uses the mechanisms of modification, originally used for adjectives and adverbs, to account for this relationship. Ideally, however, one would want the properties of the construction to follow from the Polysynthesis Parameter plus the principles of Universal Grammar. It remains to be seen to what degree this is possible.

(iii) Why are discontinuous constituents so restricted? Although (1d) is acceptable, examples of this type are rather rare in texts and native speakers generally prefer (1b) or (1c). Moreover, the opposite split—with the demonstrative following the verb and the lexical noun root preceding it—is judged to be even worse. Examples like (1d) are also limited in some languages that are otherwise typologically similar to Mohawk. These restrictions are not found in Warlpiri, the prototypical nonconfigurational language, and they do not follow from the leading idea, as sketched above.

This chapter begins the process of developing a more articulated theory of configurationality in polysynthetic languages, so that these questions and others can be addressed. In particular, this chapter focuses on question (i) and shows that the MVC forces all overt NPs to be adjuncts. The distinctive structures created by this requirement account for a variety of important ways—involving anaphora, question formation, and quantification—in which the syntax of polysynthetic languages differs from that of other languages. Questions (ii) and (iii) will be the starting points for chapters 3 and 4, respectively.

One terminological note: in this chapter whenever I use a phrase like "all NPs are adjuncts," this is to be understood as referring to NPs with phonological content. Phonologically empty NPs, such as null pronominals (pro) and traces of movement, can and do appear in argument positions, as we shall see.

2.1 All NPs Are Adjuncts

I begin by presenting six syntactic differences between Mohawk and English that can be explained if overt NPs are base generated in a position adjoined to the clause.[1]

2.1.1 Disjoint Reference Effects

The first difference concerns cases where two NPs may be understood as referring to the same thing. Reinhart (1976, 1983a:43) argues for the following condition on the interpretation of NPs (I have changed her wording slightly):

(3) A given NP must be interpreted as non-coreferential with any distinct non-pronoun that it c-commands.

This assumes that a category X c-commands a category Y if and only if the smallest phrase properly containing X also contains Y. The principle in (3) is called *Condition C* in the Binding Theory of Chomsky 1981, and I will refer to it by that name. Lasnik (1989) discusses the status of this principle, as well as certain refinements, parameterizations, and residual problems; however, any structurally based version of the principle that covers the familiar English facts is adequate for our purposes. Among other things, Condition C accounts for the difference between subjects and objects found in sentences like (4) in English. A pronominal object position can readily be coreferential with an NP embedded in the subject (as in (4a)), because the object does not c-command the subject. In contrast, a pronominal subject cannot be coreferential with an NP embedded in the object, because the subject c-commands the object:

(4) a. *John's* knife helped *him* (to survive in the woods alone).

 b. *He broke *John's* knife (in a fit of rage).

There is good evidence that Condition C holds in Mohawk as well as in English. Consider the following sentences:

(5) a. Wa-hí-'nha'-ne'   ne tsi   Sak ra-yo'tʌ-hser-íyo.
         FACT-1sS/MsO-hire-PUNC because Sak MsS-work-NOM-be.good
         'I hired *him* because *Sak* is a good worker.' (coreference OK)

 b. Wá'-k-ko-'   ne tsi   yo-[a]hy-á-hri   ne sewahyówane.
         FACT-1sS-pick-PUNC because NsO-fruit-be.ripe NE apple
         'I picked *it* because the *apple* was ripe.' (coreference OK)

    c. S-a'-khé-kʌ-'   ohʌtu ne s-a'-[e]-íhey-e'
    ITER-FACT-1sS/FsO-see-PUNC before NE ITER-FACT-FsS-die-PUNC

    ne Uwári.
    NE Mary
    'I saw *her* before *Mary* died.' (coreference OK)

(6) a. Wa-hi-hróri-'   tsi Sak ruwa-núhwe'-s.
      FACT-1sS/MsO-tell-PUNC that Sak FsS/MsO-like-HAB
      'I told him that she likes Sak.' (disjoint only)

     b. ʌ-hi-rihw-a-nútu-'s-e'   úhka Sak wa-huwa-snyéna-'.
      FUT-1sS/MsO-matter-Ø-ask-BEN-PUNC who Sak FACT-FsS/MsO-help-PUNC
      'I will ask him who helped Sak.' (disjoint only)

     c. Wa'-t-hi-'nikuhr-a-kʌ́ni'   tsi Uwári ruwa-núhwe'-s
      FACT-DUP-1sS/MsO-mind-Ø-beat-PUNC that Mary FsS/MsO-like-HAB

     ne Sak.
     NE Sak
     'I convinced him that Mary likes Sak.' (disjoint only)

All of these sentences have a name inside an embedded clause and an agreement morpheme on the matrix verb that matches that name in gender and number features. These agreement morphemes license null pronouns (pro's) as the arguments of the matrix verbs, in accordance with the assumptions given in chapter 1. The question, then, is whether this pronominal can be interpreted as coreferential with the name. The answer is yes in (5), but no in (6). This correlates with the fact that the subordinate clauses are subcategorized complements of the verb in (6), but adjunct modifiers in (5). It is standardly assumed that these two types of clause appear in different structural positions: complement clauses are generated inside the VP, whereas adjunct clauses are outside it. More specifically, I assume that this type of adjunct is adjoined to S (= IP) in Mohawk, as in (7).

(7)

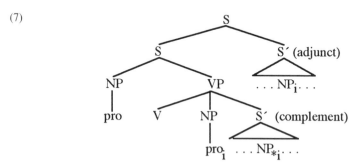

This structural difference is induced by the Projection Principle of Chomsky 1981, which requires that all and only the phrases subcategorized by a head be in the first projection of that head. In (7) both the subject and the object c-command an NP inside the complement clause, but neither c-commands an NP inside the adjunct. Coreference is thus possible in the latter case, but not in the former, in accordance with (3). This confirms that Condition C holds in Mohawk. Indeed, the judgments for (5) and (6) are essentially the same as the judgments for the

English glosses (Reinhart 1983a:34), as one would expect if the same principles are at work in both languages.

This contrast also supports the assumption that Mohawk has phonologically null pronouns, licensed by agreement (following Postal (1979:396ff.)). The alternative, proposed by Jelinek (1984), would be to say that the agreement morphemes *are* the pronouns, and there is no empty category. This proposal seems at first glance less abstract than the one assumed here. If, however, pro is omitted in (7), then the representation does not violate (3). We would no longer have a unified account that explains both the coreference patterns in (5) and (6) and their English equivalents.[2]

Consider now Mohawk sentences analogous to (4). Strikingly, this difference between subjects and objects found in English is not found in Mohawk. Verbal agreement indicates that the postverbal NP is the object in (8) and the subject in (9). Nevertheless, the possessor of the NP can be coreferential with the pronoun associated with the verb in both cases:

(8) a. Wa'-t-há-ya'k-e'　　　　　Sak raó-[a]'share'.
　　　　　FACT-DUP-1sS-break-PUNC Sak MsP-knife
　　　　　'*He* broke *Sak's* knife.' (coreference OK)

　　 b. Wa'-te-huwa-noru'kwányu-'　ne Uwári akó-skare'.
　　　　　FACT-DUP-FsS/MsS-kiss-PUNC NE　Mary　FsP-friend
　　　　　'*She* kissed *Mary's* boyfriend.' (coreference OK)

　　 c. Wa-huwá-hser-e'　　　　　eksá'a ako-[i]tshénʌ (érhar).
　　　　　FACT-FsS/MsO-chase-PUNC child　FsP-pet　　　dog
　　　　　'*She* chased the *girl's* dog.' (coreference OK)

(9) a. Ro-ya'takéhnha-s Sak raó-[a]'share'.
　　　　　MsO-help-HAB　　Sak MsP-knife
　　　　　'*Sak's* knife helps *him*.' (coreference OK)

　　 b. Wa'-te-shako-noru'kwányu-'　ne Uwári akó-skare'.
　　　　　FACT-DUP-MsS/FsO-kiss-PUNC NE Mary　FsP-friend
　　　　　'*Mary's* boyfriend kissed *her*.' (coreference possible)

　　 c. Wa-shakó-hser-e'　　　　　eksá'a ako-[i]tshénʌ (érhar).
　　　　　FACT-MsS/FsO-chase-PUNC child　FsP-pet　　　dog
　　　　　'The *child's* dog followed *her*.' (coreference possible)

There is nothing unexpected about the judgments in (9), but those in (8) are problematic.

The morphosyntactic properties of Mohawk make possible an alternative analysis of (8) that would eliminate the problem. Possessed nouns are inflected for the features of their possessor, making a null pronoun possessor possible. Furthermore, VSO word order is possible in Mohawk. Finally, Mohawk NPs are completely unmarked for Case. This means that *Sak* has no morphology to indicate that it is a dependent of the NP in (8a). Putting these factors together, it is not clear that the possessor NP and the possessed N form a constituent in (8a); (8a) could be analyzed as (10b)—where *Sak* is the postverbal subject and pro is the possessor—rather than as (10a), which was the intended structure.

(10)   a. pro he-it-broke [$_{NP}$ Sak his-knife]

       b. he-it-broke Sak [$_{NP}$ pro his-knife]

If so, then a proper gloss of (8a) could be 'Sak broke his knife,' and coreference would be expected. Now in point of fact, VSO is a rather rare word order in simple clauses in Mohawk; thus, the freedom with which the (8a) examples are accepted suggests that (10a) is the analysis that speakers have in mind when judging the sentences. Nevertheless, one would like to be sure.

In fact, there are ways to confirm that the possessor does form a constituent with the possessed noun, and when these are used the judgments given in (8) do not change. Thus, (11) is identical to (8) except that a demonstrative has been added. This demonstrative precedes the possessor and the head noun and is interpreted as specifying the head:

(11)   a. Wa'-t-há-ya'k-e'   ne thíkʌ Sak raó-[a]'share'.
          FACT-DUP-1sS-break-PUNC NE that Sak MsP-knife
          '*He* broke that knife of *Sak's*.' (coreference OK)

       b. Ro-ya'takéhnh-ʌ thíkʌ ne Sak raó-[a]'share'.
          MsO-help-STAT   that NE Sak MsP-knife
          'That knife of *Sak's* is helping *him*.' (coreference OK)

Mohawk demonstratives precede the noun that they modify in a single constituent. If the demonstrative and the head form a single constituent in (11), then *Sak* must be part of this constituent too. Thus, *Sak* is part of the object NP in (11a), and the subject is a null pronoun. Nevertheless, the two can still corefer. Other examples parallel to (11a) are:

(12)   a. Wa'-e-ratsú-ko-'   kíkʌ Uwári ako-[a]tyá'tawi.
          FACT-FsS-tear-REV-PUNC this Mary FsP-dress
          '*She* tore this dress of *Mary's*.' (coreference OK)

       b. Thíkʌ Sak raó-[a]'share' t-a-hák-u-'.
          that Sak MsP-knife   CIS-FACT-1sS/MsO-give-PUNC
          '*He* handed me that knife of *Sak's*.' (coreference OK)

Another test of constituenthood in Mohawk is provided by second position clitics. One such element is *kʌ,* a particle used to indicate yes/no questions. *Kʌ* typically appears after the first major constituent of the sentence; (13) is ungrammatical, because *kʌ* follows both the subject and the object.

(13)   ??Ánʌ akw-atyá'tawi kʌ wa'-e-nóhare-'?
         Anne 1sP-dress   Q FACT-FsS-wash-PUNC
         'Did Ann wash my dress?'

In (14), the position of *kʌ* shows that the name and the possessed noun are a single constituent.

(14)   a. Uwári akó-skare' kʌ wa'-t-huwa-noru'kwányu-'?
          Mary FsP-friend Q FACT-DUP-FsS/MsO-kiss-PUNC
          'Did *she* kiss *Mary's* boyfriend?' (coreference OK)

       b. Uwári akó-skare' kʌwa'-te-shako-noru'kwányu-'?
          Mary FsP-friend Q FACT-DUP-MsS/FsO-kiss-PUNC
          'Did *Mary's* boyfriend kiss *her*?' (coreference OK)

Again coreference is possible, regardless of whether the possessed NP is interpreted as the subject (as in (14b)), or as the object (as in (14a)).

Finally, the same pattern of judgments can be found when the name is embedded in a more complex NP; (15) gives examples with relative clauses.

(15) a. Wa'-t-huwa-noru'kwányu-'   ne rúkwe' ne Uwári ruwa-núhwe'-s.
       FACT-DUP-FsS/MsO-kiss-PUNC NE man   NE Mary FsS/MsO-like-HAB
       'She kissed the man that *Mary* likes.' (coreference OK)

    b. Wa'-te-shako-noru'kwányu-'   ne rúkwe'ne Uwári shako-núhwe'-s.
       FACT-DUP-MsS/FsO-kiss-PUNC NE man   NE Mary MsS/FsO-like-HAB
       'The man that likes *Mary* kissed her.' (coreference OK)

Here the word order precludes taking the name as the subject or object of the matrix verb. When the relative clause containing the name modifies the understood subject, the name can be coreferential with the pronominal object, as in English (see (15b)). However, coreference is also possible when the relative clause modifies the object and the subject is pronominal (as in (15a)), unlike in English. In (16), the same point is illustrated with conjoined NPs: the name is clearly embedded inside a conjoined object but can still corefer with the pronominal subject.

(16) a. Kanát-a-ku wa'-etsiseni-kʌ-'   ísi   tánu Sak raó-skare'.
       town-Ø-in FACT-MsS/2pO-see-PUNC you and Sak MsP-friend
       '*He* saw you and *Sak's* girlfriend in town.' (coreference OK)

    b. Ówise tánu Sak raó-[a]'share' t-a-hák-u-'.
       glass and Sak MsP-knife   CIS-FACT-MsS/1sO-give-PUNC
       '*He* handed me a glass and *Sak's* knife.' (coreference OK)

Thus, the subject–object asymmetry found in English is consistently absent in Mohawk.

Taking these Condition C facts at face value, the examples in this section show that the "object" NP can appear outside the c-command domain of the subject. If the basic clause structure of Mohawk is similar to that of English (as suggested by the behavior of subordinate clauses), the only position that meets this requirement is a position adjoined to the S (= IP) node. This is syntactic evidence that NPs may appear in adjoined positions in Mohawk, in accordance with our theory of nonconfigurationality. The Projection Principle then must be satisfied by a null object pronoun licensed by the agreement on the verb. The structure of (11a) would be (17), where the indicated indexing does not violate Condition C.

(17)

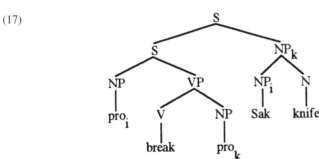

Although the NP is adjoined to the right side of S in (17), it can equally well be adjoined to the left side, without changing the basic hierarchical properties of the structure. In particular, the subject pronoun does not c-command into the understood object, whichever side that NP appears on. This explains the fact that the coreference possibilities in (14) are the same as those in (11).[3] These examples are not sufficient to show that overt NPs *must* be in adjoined positions in Mohawk, but they do show that overt NPs *may* be in adjoined positions.[4]

Before leaving this section, we must reconsider briefly the impossibility of coreference in examples like (6a) in the light of our analysis.

(6)   a. Wa-hi-hróri-'   tsi   Sak ruwa-núhwe'-s.
          FACT-1sS/MsO-tell-PUNC that Sak FsS/MsO-like-HAB
          'I told *him* that she likes *Sak*.' (disjoint only)

In particular, we must ask why (6a) cannot have a structure like (17), where the embedded clause is in an adjoined position and coindexed with a null pronoun object. If this were possible, then coreference between 'him' and 'Sak' should be allowed. The answer to this, I claim, is simply that in order for a dislocated phrase to be licensed in adjunct position, it must be nondistinct from a licensing argument position in all relevant features (see sections 3.3 and 9.2.2 for evidence and discussion). Since the argument position in (6a) is by hypothesis a pronoun, hence of category NP (or DP), it cannot license an adjoined phrase of category CP. It follows that the CP in (6a) must be in argument position, and hence in the c-command domain of the indirect object pronoun.[5]

This section has shown that patterns of coreference are different in English and Mohawk, because NPs in Mohawk can appear in positions adjoined to the clause. It would be interesting to know whether similar results hold in other nonconfigurational head-marking languages. Unfortunately, such information generally cannot be gleaned from standard grammars. However, apparent Condition C violations have been attested in some languages of this type. For example, the following sentence in Southern Tiwa allows coreference between the pronominal subject and the name inside the understood direct object (Donald Frantz, personal communication):

(18)   I-thã-ban [_NP   seuan-ide am-mukhin-we-'i].
         AS/BO-find-PAST man-SG   AO/BO-hat-be-SUB
         '*He* found the *man's* hat.' (coreference OK)

Williamson (1984:ch. 6) gives a lucid discussion of similar facts in Lakhota. Similarly, Speas (1990:222–229), building on work by Platero (1974), shows that in Navajo certain NPs inside an object relative clause can be coreferential with a subject pronoun. I take these to be encouraging signs that this analysis will generalize beyond Mohawk. However, it is not clear that these patterns hold true for all constructions in all nonconfigurational head-marking languages, and there are several other theoretical factors that ultimately need to be taken into account (see sections 3.1.3 and 6.2).[6]

2.1.2 The Absence of NP Anaphors

So far the focus has been on the interpretation of pronouns and referential expressions; we turn now to anaphors. The interesting fact about these in Mohawk is that they do not exist. Reflexive and reciprocal phrases like *herself, themselves,* and *each other* in English simply do not have Mohawk equivalents. Thus, there is no sentence like (19) with an interpretation in which the subject and the object refer to the same person.

(19)   #Sak ro-núhwe'-s   ra-úha.
        Sak MsS/MsO-like-HAB MsO-self
        'Sak likes himself.' (OK as: 'Sak$_i$ likes him$_k$.')

I use *raúha* as a potential anaphoric form for illustrative purposes because its internal morphological structure is comparable to that of *himself* in English and because like *himself* it can be used as a nonargumental emphatic element. However, neither this element nor any other can function as an anaphoric argument in Mohawk.

This fact can be derived from the hypothesis that all overt NPs are adjuncts. This hypothesis implies that the putative anaphor in (19) is an adjunct. Since *nuhwe'* 'like' is a transitive verb, it must have an empty category object, licensed by the masculine singular object agreement. This empty category presumably must be a pro, as it is when no anaphor is adjoined. Thus, the phrase structure of an example like (19) would be something like (20).

(20)

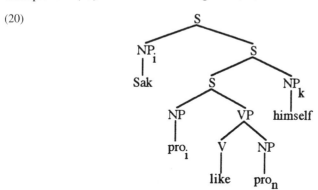

But there is no indexing for this structure that is consistent with the basic outline of Chomskian Binding Theory, given informally in (21).

(21)   A. An anaphor must have a c-commanding antecedent within its minimal clause.

       B. A pronominal must not have a c-commanding antecedent within its minimal clause.

Sak and the subject pro are straightforwardly coindexed in (20). Since 'himself' is an anaphor by hypothesis, it must be coindexed with an NP inside the same clause—in this case either *Sak* or the subject pro. Hence i must equal k in (20). At the same time, 'himself' must be coindexed with the object pro, since it is an adjunct that expresses this argument.[7] Hence n must equal k. But this implies that the object pro is coindexed with the subject pro. This violates its inherent properties as a pronominal, which must not have a c-commanding antecedent in the minimal sentence. Thus, there is no way to satisfy the properties of both the anaphor *raúha* and the null pronoun. Therefore, Mohawk could not have an overt reflexive NP, at least in a canonical context like (19).

To express the intended meaning of (19), Mohawk makes use of special reflexive verb forms. These differ from other verbs in that they contain the prefix *atat*. This morpheme has the effect of detransitivizing the verb, at least in the sense that it no longer takes an object agreement morpheme:

(22)   Sak ra-[a]tate-núhwe'-s.
        Sak MsS-REFL-like-HAB
        'Sak likes himself.'

Reciprocals are similar, except that the verb takes the duplicative prefix *te* in addition to *atat*. Thus, one finds pairs like the following:

(23)   a. Wa-hu-[a]tat-yénawa's-e'.   (D&D:375)
            FACT-MpS-REFL-help-PUNC
            'They helped themselves.'

        b. Wa'-t-hu-[a]tat-yénawa's-e'.   (D&D:375)
            FACT-DUP-MpS-REFL-help-PUNC
            'They helped each other.'

In this way, Mohawk sidesteps the contradiction outlined above. These examples still satisfy the MVC on either of two interpretations: *yenawa's* 'help' is a two-place verb, whose arguments are coindexed with the prefixes *hu* and *atat;* or *atat-yenawa's* 'self-help' is a one-place verb derived in the lexicon, whose single argument corresponds to the prefix *hu*. I return to these structures in section 5.2.3, arguing that the former interpretation is the correct one.

This analysis bears on the question of whether overt NPs must be in adjoined positions in polysynthetic languages. Suppose that this were an option, but not a necessity. Then we would predict that Mohawk could have lexical anaphors, but these would be limited to the true object position, wherever that might be. Thus, if Mohawk were underlyingly an SVO language, 'himself' could only appear immediately after the verb; if it were an SOV language, 'himself' could appear only before the verb. Anaphors would thus differ from other NPs in being restricted in their word order. However, Mohawk is not like this: anaphors are equally impossible in all positions and word orders. This fact alone could be accidental, but when combined with similar facts given in the next section it strongly suggests that argument positions must remain vacant.

This prediction can also be investigated comparatively: all polysynthetic languages will lack overt NP anaphors, at least as objects. Assuming that all languages have a way of expressing simple reflexive clauses for extralinguistic reasons, polysynthetic languages should have morphological reflexives that eliminate object agreement. This issue can be readily checked with conventional grammars, which provide substantial support for this view. Thus, most of the languages tentatively identified as polysynthetic have morphological reflexives of one kind or another:

(24) a. Ta-t-a-raː-rhe'e-s. WICHITA (Rood 1976:151)
         IND-1S-REFL-PL-make-IMPF
         'We created ourselves.'

      b. 'U-ide be-khoy-ban. SOUTHERN TIWA (Rosen 1990:691)
         baby-SG 3sS/REFL-bite-PAST[8]
         'The child bit himself.'

      c. Ti-mo-tlātia. NAHUATL (Launey 1981:61)
         2sS-REFL-hide
         'You hide yourself.'

      d. Gabarri-djobge-rre-n. MAYALI (Evans 1991:218)
         3PS-cut-REFL/RECIP-NONPAST
         'They are cutting themselves/each other.'

      e. Yay-rayke-an. AINU (Shibatani 1990:48)
         REFL-kill-1sS
         'I kill myself.'

On the other hand, nonpolysynthetic languages may (although they need not) have overt NP anaphors. For example, Hindi and Japanese are similar to Mohawk in that they allow rather free word order. However, these languages are not subject to the MVC. Moreover, both languages have anaphoric NPs. This counts as empirical evidence that the source of free word order is different in the two language types: in polysynthetic languages it crucially depends on null pronominals that are incompatible with anaphors; in other languages it may be a result of movement, which leaves traces that are compatible with anaphors (see Chamorro 1992 for examples and discussion). Similarly, most Bantu languages are like Mohawk in having morphological reflexives and reciprocals; nevertheless, this choice is not forced on them by the MVC, so it should be easier for a Bantu language to acquire an NP anaphor by language contact or historical change than it would be for an Iroquoian language to do so. This seems to be correct; the Chimwiini dialect of Swahili, for example, has apparently acquired a reflexive NP (Abasheikh 1979).

The polysynthetic language Chukchee provides an interesting case, which motivates a refinement of the analysis. It is unique among the polysynthetic languages surveyed in that it has an independent reflexive root *činit* 'self'. This element can appear in a semantic Case form as an adjunct to the clause; it is then understood as being coreferential with the local subject (Nedjalkov 1976:196, 201):

(25) Ǝtləg-e   čenet-etə qoraŋə tem-nen.
      father-ERG self-DAT reindeer slaughter-3sS/3sO
      'The father slaughtered a reindeer for himself.'

(Here *činit* becomes [čenet] by vowel harmony, a pervasive feature of Chukchee.) *Činit* can also be the possessor of the direct object, indicating that this function is coreferential with the subject of the governing verb (Kozinsky et al. 1988:682–683):

(26) . . . Iŋqun   nə-teyŋet-lʔu-ninet   činit-kin nenene-t.
            in-order-to 3sS-food-find-3sS/3PO self-POSS child-ABS/PL
         '. . . in order for him to find his children food.'

However, *činit* cannot appear in the absolutive Case, as the direct object of a transitive clause. Thus, a sentence like (27) is apparently not possible.

(27) *∃tləg-e   činit wiriŋe-rkə-nin.
       father-ERG self defend-PRES-3sS/3sO
       'The father defends himself.'
       (implied to be ungrammatical by Nedjalkov (1976))

Instead of (27), Chukchee speakers use the dummy noun root *uwik* 'body' as the head of the direct object, and *činit* is grammatically the possessor of this noun (Nedjalkov 1976:190, 201). The result is a syntactic structure identical to the one in (26):

(28) ∃tləg-e   činit-kin uwik wiriŋe-rkə-nin.
       father-ERG self-POSS body defend-PRES-3sS/3sO
       'The father defends himself (literally: his body).'

This is the only situation in which *činit* must cooccur with *uwik* to yield a reflexive interpretation. Moreover, there is reason to think that this construction is a marked one within the system of the language, in that if there is any other way to express a reflexive sense, that is prefered to the construction in (28). Thus, verbs that have an inherently reflexive interpretation when used intransitively (like *shave* or *wash* in English) typically do not appear in a structure like (28) (Nedjalkov 1976:201). Furthermore, verbs that normally allow a benefactive NP to be expressed in absolutive Case via something like dative shift do not allow such expression when the benefactive is reflexive; rather, the benefactive must remain in oblique Case, as in (25) (Nedjalkov 1976:201).

The theory of nonconfigurationality proposed here explains why (27) is ungrammatical; its structure would be the one illustrated in (20), which is ruled out by the principles of Binding Theory. In some ways, Chukchee is the most convincing example of all. It could simply be a coincidence that other polysynthetic languages do not have NP anaphors and do have reflexive verb morphemes. Indeed, if morphological reflexives turn out to be more common across languages in general than NP reflexives, this would not be too implausible. However, Chukchee clearly does have an NP reflexive; it simply cannot use that lexical item in the object position of a transitive clause, the most common position for such elements in a language like English. Something must actively rule out this particular use of the reflexive, and our theory of polysynthesis tells us what that something is.

We must still explain why a sentence like (28) is possible, with an ordinary reflexive interpretation. In ruling out structure (20), we assumed crucially that the anaphor was a syntactically unanalyzable unit associated with a single referential index. However, much recent work on anaphora has shown that this is not always the case: the behavior of some anaphors can be derived from the assumption that they are syntactically complex, consisting of a head noun 'self' and a possessor 'him' ('my', 'her', etc.). In such analyses, the possessor typically bears a distinct index from the NP as a whole. This idea has been proposed for both reciprocals such as *each other* (Heim et al. 1991) and reflexives like *myself* (Reinhart and Reuland 1991). It is natural to suppose that this also holds for *činit-kin uwik* 'self's body'. Then, for such an anaphor the representation in (29) should be legitimate.

(29)

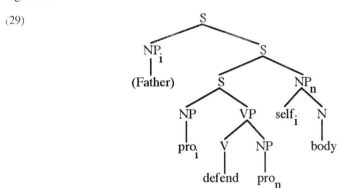

In particular, there is no violation of Binding Theory here, since the subject pro and the object pro are not coindexed in syntax. The fact that i and n refer to the same individual is derived in the semantics, presumably as a function of the meaning of the lexical item 'self', in ways that need not concern us here (see Reinhart and Reuland 1991 for discussion). Such a representation should then be possible, as Iatridou (1988) shows independently with Modern Greek examples. Thus, the theory actually claims that polysynthetic languages cannot have *morphologically simple* independent anaphors in argument position; morphologically complex anaphors are, however, possible (although apparently rather marked). This is a weaker claim than the one I stated at first, but it is still a substantive prediction, given that simple anaphors are quite common across languages.

2.1.3 The Absence of Nonreferential Quantified NPs

Another significant prediction of the view that all NPs are adjuncts in the polysynthetic languages is that such languages should not have nonreferential quantified NPs—that is, NPs comparable to *everyone, everything, nobody,* and *nothing* in English. Why this is so can be seen by observing that the basic clause structure of Mohawk is similar to that of dislocated constructions in English and the Romance languages.

Rizzi (1986b:395–397) observes that quantified NPs cannot be dislocated in Italian (see also Cinque 1990)[9]:

(30) a. *Nessuno, lo conosco in questa citta.
          'Nobody, I know him in this city.'

      b. *Tutto, lo diro' alla polizia.
          'Everything, I will say to the police.'

These examples contrast with ones in which *nessuno* or *tutto* is topicalized, which are acceptable. Rizzi accounts for the ungrammaticality of (30) in straightforward terms, which we may adopt for current purposes. He claims that the pronoun cannot be interpreted as a variable bound by the dislocated element at the level of

Logical Form (LF). This analysis has immediate plausibility, since the weak cross-over effect (reviewed briefly in section 2.1.6) independently shows that pronouns in the domain of a quantifier can only be interpreted as variables bound by that quantifier if certain specific conditions are met. In this light, Rizzi proposes the following:

(31)   A pronoun cannot be locally [A-bar] bound by a quantifier.

This condition presumably applies at LF, after quantifier raising has put quantified NPs in adjoined positions that represent their scope (although Rizzi is not fully explicit about this). Commenting on (31), Rizzi writes (1986b:395): "This statement essentially amounts to claiming that pronouns cannot function as primary variables, and can acquire variable status only parasitically, through binding [i.e., A-binding—MCB] from licit primary variables." The conclusion is that every quantifier must bind an actual trace (the prototypical variable) in argument position; pronouns only become variables "parasitically," by being c-commanded by a trace variable. Since (31) implies that the pronominal objects in (30) cannot count as variables bound by the dislocated quantifier, the sentences are ruled out as instances of vacuous quantification.

This account is readily applicable to Mohawk within our analysis. By hypothesis, all NPs in Mohawk are adjoined to the clause and coindexed with a null pronoun. Hence, they are like (30) in this respect. Therefore, no truly quantified NP will ever be associated with a legitimate variable. It follows that true quantifiers are impossible in Mohawk. In this way, we predict the absence of quantifiers like *every* and *nobody* in languages like Mohawk from more general properties of those languages. In this section, I will argue that this prediction is correct, although some further distinctions need to be made and each type of quantifier requires a separate discussion, as given in (i)–(iii).

(i) Universal quantification. When asked to translate English sentences using *everyone* or *everything*, Mohawk speakers invariably use the element *akwéku*, as in (32).

(32)   a. John akwéku wa-shakó-kʌ-'.
           John all   FACT-MsS/3O-see-PUNC
           'John saw everyone.'

        b. Akwéku wa-hó-[a]ti-'.
           all   FACT-MsO-lose-PUNC
           'He lost everything.'

However, there is good evidence that *akwéku* behaves more like English *all* than like English *every*. This evidence falls into two categories: (1) the behavior of *akwéku* with respect to number agreement, and (2) the fact that *akwéku* does not show scopal or weak crossover effects.

Vendler (1967) shows that when *all* has universal-like force in English, it acts like a plural in a variety of ways. *All* contrasts with *every* in these respects, *every* being grammatically singular. Thus, count nouns that head an NP including *all* must be plural, while the head of an NP including *every* is always singular. Furthermore, NPs with universal-like *all* trigger plural agreement on the verb, and a pronoun that is anaphorically related to the NP must be plural. In contrast, *every* triggers singular agreement on the verb, and a pronoun referring to an NP with *every* may be singular:

(33)   a. All men love their beer.   (*All man loves his beer.)

      b. Every man loves his beer. (*Every men love their beer.)

Akwéku in Mohawk behaves like *all* rather than *every* in these respects. Thus, count nouns in construction with *akwéku* are typically plural[10]:

(34)   a. Wa'-e-nóhare-'   akwéku ka'sere-shú'a.
         FACT-FsS-wash-PUNC all   car-PL
         'She washed all the cars.'

      b. Akwéku ne Uwári ako-[a]tya'tawi-shú'a yo-[a]te-ratsú-kw-ʌ.
         all   NE Mary FsP-dress-PL   NsO-SRFL-tear-REV-STAT
         'All of Mary's dresses are torn up.'

Verbal agreement with universal-like *akwéku* is also obligatorily plural. This is not apparent from the examples in (32) and (34), because Mohawk does not distinguish singular and plural agreement with neuter NPs or with some third person objects. However, (35) establishes this fact.

(35)   a. Akwéku wa-hoti-yéshu-'.   (*wa-ho-yéshu-')
         all   FACT-MpO-laugh-PUNC (*FACT-MsO-laugh-PUNC)
         'Everybody laughed.'

      b. Akwéku wa'-t-hu-[a]hsʌ́'tho-'.   (*wa'-t-ha-[a]hsʌ́'tho-')
         all   FACT-DUP-MpS-cry-PUNC (*FACT-DUP-MsS-cry-PUNC)
         'Everybody cried.'

Finally, universal-like *akwéku*, like *all*, can only be the antecedent of plural pronouns. Examples are given in (36).

(36)   a. Akwéku wa'-ti-shakoti-noru'kwányu-' ne raotí-skare'.
         all   FACT-DUP-MpS/3pO-kiss-PUNC NE MpP-friend
         'All of them kissed their girlfriends.'

      b. Akwéku ne ron-úkwe'   wa-hati-'sere-ht-óhare-'
         all   NE MsP-person FACT-MpS-car-NOM-wash-PUNC

         ne raoti-'sere-(shú'a).
         NE MpP-car-PL
         'All of the men washed their cars.'

If the object in (36a) were *raóskare'* 'his (sg.) girlfriend' rather than *raotískare'*, then the only interpretation would be that there is one specified girlfriend and all of the people kissed that one girl. In other words, a "bound" reading of the singular pronoun is impossible.

    The second type of evidence that *akwéku* is not quantificational comes from scopal phenomena. It is a well known that quantified NPs with *every* typically take scope only over the minimal clause that contains them. One consequence of this is that if a pronoun is not contained in that minimal clause, it cannot be interpreted as a variable bound by the quantified expression. Thus, the highlighted pronoun is not understood as a variable bound by the quantifier in examples like the following:

(37) a. *The guy who read *every book in the library* says that *it* is boring.

   b. **Every boy* came into the room. Then *he* sat down.

However, Reinhart (1983a) points out that NPs with *all* behave differently in this respect. Thus, the sentences in (38) are acceptable with the indicated referential dependencies.

(38) a. The guy who read *all the books in the library* says that *they* are boring.

   b. *All the boys* came into the room. Then *they* sat down.

Thus, the anaphoric possibilities of NPs with *all* are not like those of true quantifiers; indeed they are not significantly different from those of definite NPs.[11]

   Given this background, we can test whether NPs with *akwéku* in Mohawk act as though they are quantificational in this regard. In fact, they do not. In (39), *akwéku* is inside a relative clause, parallel to (37a). Nevertheless, this phrase can serve as an antecedent for the object pronoun in the matrix clause:

(39) Thíkv rúkwe akwéku kahure'-shú'a wa-ha-násko-',   karh-á-ku
     that   man   all   gun-PL   FACT-MsS-steal-PUNC forest-Ø-in

     y-a-ha-[a]shet-á-nyu-'.
     TRANS-FACT-MsS-hide-Ø-DIST-PUNC
     'The man who stole *all the guns* hid *them* in the woods.'

Another type of example is found in (40).

(40) R[a]-átu   akwéku rati-hnʌy-és-us   nónʌ
     MsS-say/HAB all   MpS-height-tall-PL when

     ʌ-shakó-kʌ-'.
     FUT-MsS/FsO-see-PUNC
     'He says *all (of them)* are tall whenever he sees *them*.'

Here *akwéku* is inside the complement of *rátu* 'he says'; hence, if it were a true quantifier, we would expect its scope to be limited to that embedded clause. Now the temporal adjunct clause in (40) cannot be within the embedded clause, because it modifies the matrix verb. This is clear because the predicate 'tall' in Mohawk (as in English) is perceived as a permanent property; therefore, it is rather bizarre with a temporal modifier. Nevertheless, *akwéku* in (40) can be interpreted as the antecedent of the pronoun in the adjunct clause, even though it should not be within its scope. In (41), another example of the same type is given.

(41) Wak-ateryʌ́tare-' tsi akwéku ʌ-t-hún-e-'   ne
     1sO-know-STAT that all   FUT-CIS-MpS-come-PUNC NE

     sh-a'-khe-hukarʌ-'.
     SIM-FACT-1sS/3pO-invite-PUNC
     'I knew that *all of them* would come when I invited *them*.'

The gross phrase structure of example (41) is given in (42).

(42)

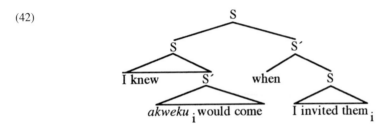

Finally, (43) shows that *akwéku* can be the discourse antecedent of pronouns that are not even in the same sentence.

(43) Akwéku t-a-hu-[a]táweya't-e'.   Sok wa-hú-[a]tyʌ-'.
      all   CIS-FACT-MpS-enter-PUNC then FACT-MpS-sit-PUNC
      '*Everyone* came in. Then *they* sat down.'

Thus, *akwéku* in Mohawk does not show the scope limitations of true quantified NPs in English. In all these respects, it is more like collective *all*, which has the properties of an ordinary definite noun phrase.

A further property of quantifiers of the *every* class in English is that they show the so-called weak crossover effect. Thus, (44) is impossible under the indicated interpretation, where one tries to interpret a pronoun inside the subject as a variable bound by the quantified object (contrast (44) with (33b)).

(44) *His* mother loves *every man*.
      ($\neq \forall$x, x a man, x's mother loves x)

Reinhart (1983a:122) captures this effect with the following statement (terminology slightly rephrased):[12]

(45) Quantified NPs (and *wh*-traces) can have anaphoric relations only with pronouns that they bind (i.e., c-command and are coindexed with) at S-structure.

For current purposes, it does not matter whether (45) is a primitive principle of the grammar, as Reinhart claims, or the consequence of a biuniqueness condition that holds of operator-variable structures at LF, as in Koopman and Sportiche 1981 and Safir 1984. What is crucial is that the condition does not apply to *all* phrases. Thus, anaphoric dependence is possible in (46) (Reinhart 1987:133).

(46) *Their* readers expect *all critics* to be boring.

Hence, *all* phrases must not count as quantified NPs. Sentences comparable to (46) are acceptable in Mohawk as well:

(47) a. Akwéku wa'-t-huwati-noru'kwányu-'   ne raotí-skare'.
          all   FACT-DUP-3pS/MpO-kiss-PUNC NE MpP-friend
          '*Their* girlfriends kissed *everyone*.' ($\forall$x, x's girlfriend kisses x)

      b. Raoti-[i]tshenʌ-shú'a wa-huwatí-hser-e'   akwéku
          MpP-pet-PL   FACT-3pS/MpO-follow-PUNC all

          rati-ksa'-okú'a.
          MpS-child-PL
          '*Their* pets followed *all of the boys*.' ($\forall$x, x's pet followed x)

Again, *akwéku* in Mohawk acts like referential *all* in English, not like truly quanti-ficational *every*.[13]

In the spirit of Reinhart (1983a, 1987), I interpret these differences between *all* and *every* as showing that *every* is a true quantifier but *all* is not. Thus, in *Every man loves his beer, every* functions as a universal quantifier whose range is re-stricted by the N′ *man*. Its LF representation is roughly:

(48)   ∀x, x a man, x loves x's beer

This explains why NPs that include *every* are treated as singular: each value that the variable assumes is itself singular. The predicate is applied distributively to the men considered one at a time. A sentence like *All (the) men love their beer,* on the other hand, is collective, and has essentially the same structure and interpre-tation as *The men love their beer.* Here, the plural subject refers to a certain set of men taken together as a group. This explains the use of plural agreement and plural pronouns with *all.* Thus, I will assume that *all* is not quantificational; it only emphasizes that the entire referent picked out by the NP is involved. With a plural NP, this gives an effect similar to universal quantification. This nonquanti-ficational account of the properties of English *all* is equally valid for Mohawk *akwéku.* (See section 4.2.1, however, for a refinement of this analysis.)

Of course, it is possible that there is a determiner that acts like a universal quantifier in Mohawk, but that *akwéku* happens not to be that determiner. How-ever, the only other plausible candidate that I have been able to find is *skátshu,* which is sometimes glossed as 'each'. *Skátshu* has a more distributive meaning than *akwéku;* nevertheless, it also appears with a plural head noun, triggers plural agreement on the verb, and binds plural pronouns:

(49)   Skátshu ne *ron*-úkwe' ne *raotí*-'sere' wa-*hati*-'sere-ht-óhare-'.
        each   NE MP-person NE MpP-car   FACT-MpS-car-NOM-wash-PUNC
        'Each of the men washed their car.'

Thus, a referential analysis is appropriate for *skátshu* as well. I conclude that there is no element in Mohawk that is parallel to *every* in English. This supports the broader generalization that purely quantificational NPs are not found in Mohawk.

(ii) Negative quantification. Next, let us consider the possibility of negative quantifiers. Deering and Delisle (1976:227) list *yahúhka* as a nominal meaning 'nobody'. Typical examples of its use include:

(50)   a. Shawátis yah-úhka   te-shakó-kʌ-Ø.
           John   not-someone NEG-MsS/FsO-see-STAT
           'John saw nobody.'

        b. Yah-úhka   thu-t-á-yʌ-[e]-'.   (D&D:227)
           not-someone CONTR-CIS-FACT-FsS-go-PUNC
           'Nobody is coming.'

However, closer inspection reveals that *yahúhka* is not even a constituent. As in English, the expression is bimorphemic: it can be divided into *yáh(tʌ)* 'no' (the sentential negation particle) and *úhka* 'someone'. Unlike English, however, *yah-úhka* is not a single word in the syntax. Thus, while it can appear before the verb, as in (50a), the supposed quantifier cannot appear after the verb:

(51) *Shawátis te-shakó-kʌ-Ø   yah-úhka.
      Shawatis NEG-MsS/FsO-see-STAT not-someone
      'John saw nobody.'

In this way, *yahúhka* differs from other NPs in Mohawk, including *akwéku*.
Rather, the near-equivalent of (50a) allowed by Mohawk's free word order is (52),
where the two parts of the supposed quantifier are split.

(52) Yah te-shakó-kʌ-Ø   úhka.
      not NEG-MsS/FsO-see-STAT someone
      'He saw nobody.'

This suggests that there is no quantifier equivalent to *nobody* in Mohawk after
all. Rather, (50a) is to be analyzed as the clausal negation of (53).[14]

(53) Uhkák   wa-shakó-kʌ-'.
      someone FACT-MsS/FsO-see-PUNC
      'He saw somebody.'

Indeed, the sentences in (50) have the surface characteristics of ordinary sentential
negation in Mohawk: (1) a particle *yáh(tʌ)* precedes the verb; (2) a special prefix
te (or *th*) is attached to the verb itself; (3) stative aspect forms replace factual-
punctual forms as the normal expression of past tense. In (54), these features are
shown in sentences with no potential quantifiers.

(54) a. Tyer yah te-ha-yéna-Ø   ne takós.
         Peter not NEG-MsS/ZsO-catch-STAT NE cat
         'Peter didn't catch the cat.'

      b. Sak yah kanúhsa' te-ho-hnínu-Ø.
         Sak not house   NEG-MsO-buy-STAT
         'Sak didn't buy a/the house.'

Thus, the most accurate gloss for (50a) or (52) is not 'He saw nobody', but 'He
did not see anybody'; these are not examples with a negatively quantified NP, but
examples with an indefinite NP under the scope of sentential negation.

      The Mohawk expressions for 'nothing' and 'nowhere' are treated in the same
way: both are made up of *yah* 'not' plus an independently existing indefinite word
(*thénʌ* 'thing'; *káneka* 'someplace'), where the two parts do not act like a single
lexical item (Deering and Delisle 1976:227–228). Some examples are given in
(55) and (56).

(55) a. Yah thénʌ   th-a-ye-hnínu-'.
         not something CONTR-OPT-FsS-buy-PUNC
         'She will buy nothing; She won't buy anything.'

      b. Thénʌ   ʌ-ye-hnínu-'.
         something FUT-FsS-buy-PUNC
         'She will buy something.'

(56) a. Yáhtʌ káneka   th-ye-haw-é-nu.
         not   anywhere CONTR-TRANS-MsO-go-STAT
         'He went nowhere; He didn't go anywhere.'

b. Káneka   kʌ wá-hs-e-'?
   anywhere Q FACT-2sS-go-PUNC
   'Are you going anywhere?'

Thus, Mohawk systematically lacks negatively quantified NPs as well as universally quantified NPs.

  (iii) Existential quantification. The negative sentences shown above raise a further issue, however. Although Mohawk does not have negatively quantified NPs,
it does have near-equivalents formed by having indefinite NPs under the scope of
sentential negation. If these indefinite NPs are a type of existential quantifier, as
often assumed, then Mohawk has at least one kind of quantified NP.

  This issue is not restricted to negative contexts. Even in affirmative sentences,
Mohawk seems to have existential quantifiers that correspond to 'someone',
'something', or 'some N'' in English. Simple examples are shown in (57).

(57) a. Uhkák   t-á'-yʌ-[e]-'.   (D&D:227)
         somebody CIS-FACT-FsS-go-PUNC
         'Somebody is coming.'

      b. Thénʌ   kʌ wa-hs-hnínu-'?   (D&D:227)
         something Q FACT-2sO-buy-PUNC
         'Did you buy anything?'

These structures do not have any known syntactic peculiarities that suggest that
they are not what they seem to be.

  Sentences like (57a) actually have two readings, one of which is not problematic. This is the reading in which *uhkák* is interpreted as specific indefinite, and
hence as referential. This reading is also found in English, and when it is present
there is no scope condition or weak crossover effect (see Heim 1982:220–225,
Reinhart 1983a:115–116 and references cited therein). Thus, (58) is grammatical
with the indicated coreference, as long as the speaker has a specific person in
mind when uttering the sentence (compare (37a)).

(58)   The guy who met *someone* in the library yesterday says that *she* was boring.

Sentences like this show that specific indefinites do not have the behavior of quantified NPs; hence, existence of *uhkák* in Mohawk is not problematic when it has
this reading.

  However, there are contexts in which this kind of referential interpretation is
inadequate. Examples (50), (52), (55a), and (56a) are of this type—that is, the
indefinite does not have a specific reading, but rather seems to have an existential
reading and takes narrow scope with respect to the negation. Similarly, (59) gives
examples in which *uhkák* receives a quantificational-like reading that has narrow
scope with respect to an adverb of quantification.

(59)   a. Tyótku uhkák   ʌ-yúk-kʌ-'   nónʌ kanát-a-ku
          always someone FUT-FsS/1sO-see-PUNC when town-Ø-LOC

          y-Á-k-e-'.
          TRANS-FUT-1sS-go-PUNC
          'Someone always sees me when I go to town.'

b. Niyesorek uhkák   yuk-yenawá's-e'.
   rarely   someone FsS/1sO-help-HAB
   'Rarely does someone help me.'

Here one cannot say that *uhkák* is referential, since it does not necessarily pick out a constant individual. Thus, (59a) means that every time I go to town I am seen, but it does not imply that there is some unnamed individual (say, John) such that that particular individual sees me every time. The same is true for (59b). Moreover, if we adopt the idea that there is a pronoun associated with the verbal agreement in Mohawk, then it is clear that the reference of that pronoun covaries with the reference of *uhkák*. In other words, we have some kind of bound pronoun reading in these cases.[15]

The key to understanding *uhkák* comes from Heim (1982), who treats indefinites like *someone* as free variables rather than as inherently quantificational elements. As such, *uhkák* has no quantificational force of its own; rather, it picks up quantificational force from other elements in the structure, such as the quantificational adverbs. Under this analysis, there is no need to abandon the claim that Mohawk has no truly quantificational NPs. Indeed, Reinhart (1987:159–160) shows that the presence of a quantificational adverb in English can allow an indefinite NP (but not an inherently quantificational NP) to bind a pronoun that it otherwise could not. Reinhart's examples are:

(60) a. *Lucie kisses *some guest* when *he* talks about Hegel.

    b. Often Lucie kisses *some guest* when *he* talks about Hegel.

Reinhart extends Heim's analysis of the so-called donkey-anaphora phenomenon to these cases as follows: *Some guest* is coindexed with the pronoun *he* but does not c-command it. Thus, the pronoun cannot be bound by *some guest* in (60a). In (60b), however, the index of 'some guest' is copied onto the c-commanding adverb of quantification by a rule of Quantifier Indexing.[16] Crucially, this adverb does c-command the pronoun in the adjunct clause. This, then, allows the pronoun to be translated as the same variable as *some guest* at LF.

This account can be carried over to the problematic case in Mohawk. The structure of the relevant part of (59a) is:

(61)   [$_S$ Always$_i$ [$_S$ someone$_i$ [$_S$ pro$_i$ sees me]]]

As in (60), the indefinite NP does not have to be taken as the direct binder of the pro. Rather, its index is copied onto the quantificational adverb, and the adverb binds the pronoun. Thus, *uhkák* and the pro are linked together by the mediation of the adverb rather than directly. This would be another way for a pronoun to become a variable "parasitically," to use Rizzi's term in describing the intuition behind condition (31). Thus, I maintain that Mohawk has no inherently quantificational NPs, but that it achieves a similar effect by using indefinite NPs in conjunction with quantificational adverbs.

Essentially the same analysis accounts for negative sentences like (62).

(62) Yah úhka   te-t-yakaw-é-nu.
     not someone NEG-CIS-FsO-come-STAT
     'Nobody came.' ($\neg$ ($\exists$x (x came)))

Again, there is an interaction between the indefinite NP *úhka* and the particle *yah* 'not'. *Úhka* is not referential here, inasmuch as the sentence does not mean that there is an unnamed person (say, John) and that person didn't come. Example (62) can be contrasted with (63), where the order of the first two words is reversed and the scope of the operators is also understood as reversed.

(63)   Uhkák   yah te-yako-yéshu-Ø.
       someone not NEG-FsO-laugh-STAT
       'Somebody didn't laugh.' ($\exists x$ ($\neg$ (x laugh)))

The difference between these sentences is readily understood if we assume that there is no rule of QR (Quantifier Raising) in Mohawk. This is reasonable: since all of the relevant NPs are already in S-adjoined positions at S-structure because of the syntax of the language, there is no need for a rule that adjoins them to S. Rather, *úhka* in (62) can be thought of as acquiring negative quantificational force by being bound by the negative adverbial particle *yah*; thus *úhka* in this context is an equivalent to *nobody*.[17] *Yah* also binds the null pronoun subject of the verb, creating the appropriate bound reading. Thus, the structure of (62) would be approximately (64).

(64)

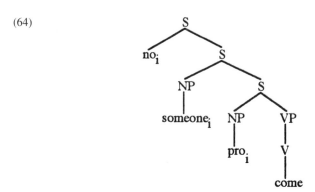

In (63), on the other hand, *uhkák* is attached outside the c-command domain of the adverb *yah,* rather than inside it. Hence, *yah* cannot bind *uhkák,* giving it a negative quantificational force. Thus, the referential (or default existential) reading of *uhkák* reemerges in this example.

   This account predicts that the functional equivalents of negative quantifiers in Mohawk should have neither the tightly restricted scope of quantified NPs, nor the unlimited scope of referential expressions, but something intermediate between the two. In particular, in order for a pronoun to be understood as bound by the apparent negative quantifier, it should not need to be c-commanded by the argument position associated with the NP *úhka;* it will need to be c-commanded by the negative particle *yah,* however. This is the general characteristic of donkey-type anaphora (Heim 1982). Although my data on this point are not particularly good, in part because of the difficulty of making up suitable examples, there is some support for the prediction. For example, in (65) *úhka* is in a subordinate clause, while its binder *yáhtʌ* is in the matrix clause—a degree of separation that is only possible with "negative raising" verbs.

(65) YáhtΛ tha-te-wak-atΛhutsoní-hne'   úhka   au-tá-yΛ-[e]-'
      Not   CONTR-DUP-1sO-want/STAT-PAST someone OPT-CIS-FsS-go-PUNC

      ohΛtu tsi niyóre Λ-khe-hukarΛ-'.
      before   FUT-1sS/FsO-invite-PUNC
      'I did not want *anyone* to come before I invited *them.*'
      (no x, x a person, I want x to come before I invite x)

Assuming that the temporal adjunct clause is attached no lower than the embedded
S/IP node (and perhaps higher), the pronoun object in this clause is c-commanded
by the negation, but not by the lower subject position. This configuration is sufficient to license a bound reading of that pronoun, as predicted. In contrast, both
the indefinite NP and the negative particle appear in the lower clause in (66). This
time, a pronoun inside an adjunct attached to the matrix clause cannot be understood as bound by the negative quantifier, again as predicted:

(66) NónΛ Λ-shakó-kΛ-'   rá-[a]tu   yáhtΛ úhka
      when FUT-MsS/3O-see-PUNC MsS-say/HAB not   someone

      te-ye-hnΛy-es.
      NEG-FsS-height-long
      'When he sees them, he says that no one is tall.'
      (when x sees y, x says that (no z, z is tall))
      NOT: (no z (when x see z, x says that z is tall)).

A truly quantified NP would not license a bound pronoun reading in either of
these sentences, whereas a truly referential NP would allow coreference in both
(compare (40) and (41) with *akwéku* 'all').

Putting these subcases together, we have seen that purely quantificational NPs
of the kind found in English are systematically not found in Mohawk. Moreover,
this fact is probably not learnable, given that Mohawk does have near equivalents
to these quantifiers. Mohawk children must have heard many sentences like (32),
with *akwéku* expressing some kind of universal statement in contexts where number agreement is neutralized. What, then, prevented them from overgeneralizing
and concluding that *akwéku* may, ambiguously, be a true quantifier of the *every*
type? Presumably, something that they already knew about the language held them
back from this generalization. The fact that all overt NPs are in adjoined positions
in Mohawk, together with a universal condition along the lines of (31), explains
this. Although certain important technical details remain to be clarified, this line
of reasoning seems promising. (See Baker, to appear b, for discussion of some
additional technicalities.)

This analysis is similar to the previous one in implying that overt NPs not only
may be in adjunct positions but *must* be. If this were not so, then we might expect
akwéku to act like *every/each* if and only if it were generated in an argument
position. However, this does not seem to be so. There is no designated position in
which *akwéku* may trigger singular agreement, just as there is no designated position where NP anaphors may appear. Similarly, there is no designated position
where *yahúhka* acts as an NP constituent. Indeed, this argument shows that NPs
understood as subjects must be in adjunct positions as well, because true quantifiers cannot be subjects either. In this respect, the argument from quantifiers is more

flexible than the earlier arguments, which only applied in a nontrivial way to direct objects.

Finally, these lines of reasoning should naturally carry over to other polysynthetic languages as well. All things being equal, we predict that true NP quantifiers are also not found in these languages. This is somewhat difficult to evaluate from most grammars, because even if they describe quantification, they may not provide facts that distinguish distributive (*every*-like) elements from collective (*all*-like) ones, nor indefinite NPs from those with inherent quantificational force. However, Launey (1981) gives important hints that the prediction is true for classical Nahuatl. Nahuatl has several universal-like quantifiers, some with a more collective sense and others with a more distributive sense. In spite of these semantic differences, all of them require plural morphology on both the head noun (if any) and the agreeing verb, as these examples from Launey 1981 show:

(67) a. Ø-tla-cua-'   in mochi-ntin pitzō-me'.   (p. 68)
          3S-3INDEF-eat-PL IN all-PL   pig-PL
          'All the pigs eat.'

      b. ō-Ø-micti-lō-que'   in īzquin-tin mā-mal-tin.   (p. 398)
          PAST-3S-kill-PASS-PERF/PL IN each-PL   RED-prisoner-PL
          'Each of the prisoners was killed (one by one, separately).'

      c. In īxquich-tin ye   ō-Ø-ya'-que'.   (p. 238)
          IN all-PL   already PAST-3s-go-PERF/PL
          'They have all left already (together, as a group).'

This is parallel to what we have seen in Mohawk and suggests that these are not true quantifiers of the *every* type. Furthermore, the so-called negative quantifiers are systematically combinations of a sentence-initial negative particle and an indefinite NP in a polarity form. Examples are from Launey (1981:47):

(68) a. Ay-āc   ni-qu-itta.
          not-someone 1sS-3sO-see
          'I see no one; I don't see anyone.'

      b. Ca a'-tle'   ni-c-chīhua.
          PRT not-something 1sS-3sO-make
          'I made nothing; I didn't make anything.'

Here *ay-āc* and *a'-tle'* are contractions of *a'mo āc* and *a'mo tle'*, respectively, where *a'mo* is the ordinary sentential negation particle. Launey mentions that the uncontracted forms can also be used with the same meaning. One sees the same noun roots used as indefinites without the negation marker in examples like (69) (from Launey 1981:249).

(69) a. A'zo ac-a'   ye   ōmpa Ø-ca'
          maybe someone-AFF already there 3sS-be
          'Maybe someone is already there.'

      b. Cuix i-tl-a'   ō-ti-qu-itta-c?
          Q   Ø-something-AFF PAST-2sS-3sO-see-PERF
          'Did you see anything?'

Again, this is extremely similar to Mohawk, suggesting that Nahuatl has no negative quantifiers and uses indefinite words under the scope of negative adverbs instead. This is confirmed by the fact that when two putative negative quantifiers appear in the same sentence, only one negative element *a'* appears. Thus, (70) can be compared to (68b).

(70)   Ay-āc   tle'   Ø-qui-chīhua.   (Launey 1981:47)
       not-someone something 3sS-3sO-make
       'Nobody made anything.' (for no x, y (x made y))

Here a single negative adverb unselectively binds two distinct indefinite NPs to give the desired reading, in keeping with the theory of Heim (1982). Thus, what has been said about Mohawk generalizes to Nahuatl.

Heath (1986:404–406) briefly surveys the types of quantification found in Nunggubuyu, concluding that this language does not have determiner-like quantifiers comparable to those in English. Thus, he states that there are no lexical stems meaning 'each', 'every', or even 'all'. The the elements that come closest to universal quantifiers in Nunggubuyu are certain verbal prefixes like *ngaraG* and *wara*; these indicate multiplicity of an argument, but not necessarily exhaustiveness. Mayali is also rich in this kind of element, as discussed in detail by Evans (to appear). One of Evans' examples is[18:]

(71)   Barri-djarrk-dulubom   gunj.
       3pS-all-shoot/PAST/PERF kangaroo
       'They all shot the kangaroo.'

Similarly, Heath states that Nunggubuyu has nothing comparable to English *nowhere, nobody*. Negative quantificational statements are formed by putting an ordinary NP under the scope of a clausal negation particle such as *wa:ri* or *yagi* 'not'. An example of this in Mayali is the following (Evans 1991:140):

(72)   Djama na-ngamed an-marne-yolyolme-ninj.
       not   Ms-who   3sS/1sO-BEN-mention-IRR
       'Nobody ever talked about him/her to me.'

Hence, the patterns in these languages also fit our theory of polysynthesis.

The last case I will discuss is Wichita. Rood's (1976:124) brief list of quantifiers mentions *assé:hah* 'all' as a universal, but there is nothing that he glosses as 'every'. This is what we expect. In the area of negative quantifiers there is an apparent problem, however. Rood (1976:11) presents a series of negative pronouns that are formed by adding the negative prefix *ká:* to an appropriate indefinite noun root to form words such as *ká:-kiriʔ* 'nothing' and *ká:-kiyaʔ* 'nobody' (compare *ka:-kiriʔ* 'something', *e:-kiriʔ* 'what', *e:-kiyaʔ* 'who', and so on). If these are true negative quantifiers, then they are problematic for my claim. However, the fact that they are bimorphemic and morphologically related to indefinites gives us cause to hope that they are similar to the Mohawk examples in structure. Indeed, negative sentences have other peculiarities in Wichita that are consistent with this. First, while NPs can in general precede or follow the main verb, these negative NPs seem only to precede the verb; at least all of Rood's examples have this property, and it seems to be implied by his word order rule W9 (1976:204). Typical examples are (1976:195):

(73) a. Ká:-kiya? ?i-is-hiss-sisha.
          NEG-one NEG/IND/3sS-NEG/PAST-arrive.there-go
          'Nobody got there.'

      b. Ká:-kiri? ?i-is-ak?a-s.
          NEG-thing NEG/IND/3sS-NEG/PAST-say-IMPF
          'He didn't say anything.'

The normal negation particle in Wichita is *kíri?*, which appears in clause-initial position (1976:157); however, Rood also mentions that *kíri?* can be replaced by *ká:* in some situations—perhaps in a less formal speech register. An example is the following (1976:159; see also p. 163):

(74) Ka:-?ac-i-is-?a:cke?e-s.
      NEG-NEG/IND/1S-Ø-NEG/PAST-learn-IMPF
      'I never did learn it right.'

This *ka:* is presumably the same as the one that is prefixed to the noun roots in (73). Moreover, Rood gives one example in which *kíri?* combines with *kiyá?* 'someone' to give the effect of 'no one', a meaning more often rendered by *ká:kiya?:*

(75) Kíri? kiyá?   ki?i-s-ic-í:se?e:-kic-icaras.
      not someone FUT/IMPER-2S-PREV-for.a.while-water-touch
      'Don't anybody (of you) touch that water for a while.'

Thus, we can interpret the facts as follows. Negation is generated as a clause-initial particle in Wichita, perhaps generated as the head of CP or of some kind of "assertion phrase." It can be realized as either *kíri?* or *ka:* under conditions that are not entirely clear but may have to do with register and probably involve emphasis as well: *kíri?* would be the strong form and *ka:* the weak one.[19] Subsequently, *ka:* procliticizes onto the adjacent word. This can be the main verb as in (74). However, there can also be an indefinite NP such as *kiyá?* or *kíri?* under the scope of negation. If so, it gives the same kind of negative reading as in Mohawk. *Ka:* then procliticizes onto this NP, looking like a prefix. Nevertheless, the fact that *ká:kiri?* can only appear in initial position is evidence that it is not an ordinary NP, but rather an NP combined with a sentence-initial functional category. The only real difference between Mohawk and Wichita, then, is that Wichita apparently does not allow the indefinite NP to appear after the verb, clearly separate from the negative particle. This may be related to the independent fact that postverbal NPs are, in general, somewhat restricted in Wichita (Rood 1976:197), but not in Mohawk.

I conclude that the absence of purely quantificational NPs is a property of polysynthetic languages as a class, a direct result of their head-marking nonconfigurational structure.[20]

2.1.4 Interrogative Constructions

Interrogative constructions are known to be similar to quantificational constructions in a variety of syntactic and semantic respects. For example, both are subject to the Weak Crossover Condition given in (45) (see Chomsky 1976). More directly to the point, dislocated NPs in the Romance languages cannot be question words, just as they cannot be quantifiers as shown in this example from Spanish[21]:

(76)   *A quién la viste?   (Jaeggli 1982:45)
       'Who did you see (her)?'

Such sentences can be ruled out in the same way as those in (30) in Italian: question phrases, like other quantifiers must bind a variable in order to be properly interpreted at LF. However, in (76) the object position is pronominal, hence not capable of functioning as a primary variable by Rizzi's condition, given in (31), or its equivalent. Similarly, Bresnan and Mchombo (1987) show that question words in situ are incompatible with object clitics in Chichewa.

Given these similarities between interrogative phrases and quantifiers, it seems that we can extend the reasoning of the preceding section and predict that either interrogative phrases are impossible in Mohawk or their properties are different in some fundamental way from those in English. Such a prediction would not be correct, however; Mohawk has ordinary-looking constituent questions, such as those in (77).

(77)   a. Úhka t-á'-yʌ-[e]-'?
           who   CIS-FACT-FsS-go-PUNC
           'Who is coming?'

       b. Nahótʌ wa-hs-hnínu-'?
           what   FACT-2sS-buy-PUNC
           'What did you buy?'

Moreover, we shall see over the course of the next three sections that the syntactic properties of these constructions are remarkably similar to those in English.

Fortunately, we are not committed to the prediction that interrogative phrases are ruled out for the same reason as quantifiers. Although it is true that they show syntactic and semantic similarities, there are also important differences. The most obvious difference is that in many languages interrogative phrases overtly move into the specifier (Comp) of CP in the syntax. Quantifiers, on the other hand, do not move in this way. Rather, they adjoin to IP, and they wait until the LF component to do so. The distinction is clear in English, where one has *Who did I see?* but not **Everyone did I see.* Intuitively, this difference should be related to an important difference between interrogatives and quantifiers with respect to speech act theory: sentences with an interrogative phrase constitute a special type of speech act (a question), whereas sentences with, say, a universally quantified phrase do not (as pointed out to me by Norbert Hornstein (personal communication)). Along the general lines of much current work (see, in particular, Rizzi 1991 and Cheng 1991), this intuition can be implemented as follows. The type of speech act exemplified by a given clause is indicated by a feature on the complementizer (C) that heads that clause. Questions, in particular, will have a +*wh* feature on C (the Q morpheme of earlier work). This feature will then draw a +*wh* phrase into the specifier of C in many languages, so that a legitimate agreement relationship is established between the two +*wh* elements. Perhaps this is required to happen at S-structure in English because the +*wh* features on C are not realized morphologically; hence, they are similar to an empty category and need to be locally identified by something that bears that feature (Cheng 1991).[22] However, there is no reason to think that C will ever have a special [+every] feature, since the illocutionary force of universal statements is not significantly different from that of other statements. Therefore, there will not be anything to draw universally quantified phrases to the specifier of CP. The economy principles of Chomsky 1992 imply that overt movement never happens unless it is triggered by the morphosyntactic features of some morpheme. Hence, it is impossible for most quantified phrases to move to the specifier of CP in the syntax.[23]

What are the implications of this difference for the theory of nonconfigurationality in polysynthetic languages? In fact, there are three distinct structures to consider: the NP could be in argument position, as in (78a); it could be adjoined to IP, as in (78b); or it could be in the specifier of CP (i.e., Comp), as in (78c).

(78)   a. $[_{IP}$ Q-NP$_i$ verb]

       b. $[_{IP}$ Q-NP$_i$ $[_{IP}$ pro$_i$ verb]]

       c. $[_{CP}$ Q-NP$_i$ C $[_{IP}$ t$_i$ verb]]

Example (78a) is ruled out by hypothesis, regardless of whether Q-NP is an interrogative or a true quantifier. This is a distinctive property of head-marking nonconfigurational languages, to be explicated in section 2.2. Example (78b) is ruled out by (31) and the considerations discussed in the previous section. Indeed, we may maintain that this construction is ruled out even if Q-NP is interrogative (cf. (76)), as long as there is another possible analysis of the grammatical sentences in (77). In fact, there is: (78c). This structure is possible if Q-NP is interrogative, but not if it is a universal quantifier, because a phrase in Comp is required to agree with the C in features and +*wh* is a feature of Comp allowed by Universal Grammar, but "+universal" is not. Thus, the theory predicts that question phrases can exist in a language like Mohawk after all, *as long as they appear in Comp by S-structure.*

There is abundant evidence that this is true. In simple sentences like (77) it is not clear whether the question phrase is in Comp or adjoined to the clause (or even in an A-position). However, almost all of the reasons for saying that question phrases move to Comp in English carry over to Mohawk as well. One important difference between Comp and adjoined positions is that the location of Comp is fixed by principles of X-bar Theory. Comp is the specifier of CP (Chomsky 1986a), and as such it is subject to the ordering principles that govern specifiers. In fact, Comp and other subjects are overwhelmingly phrase initial across languages. If this is true in Mohawk as well, and if C is the highest head in a clause, then question words should be strictly clause initial, as in English. Adjoined NPs, however, are not subject to the ordering principles of X-bar Theory (at least not in the same way); hence, they can attach to either side of the clause, as I have assumed throughout. These expectations are fulfilled: question words appear only in clause-initial position, in contrast with other NPs:

(79)   a. Oh nahótʌ Sak wa-ha-hnínu-'?
          what   Sak FACT-MsS-buy-PUNC
          'What did Sak buy?'

    b. Oh nahótʌ wa-ha-hnínu-'   ne Sak?
       what   FACT-MsS-buy-PUNC NE Sak
       'What did Sak buy?'

    c. *Sak wa-ha-hnínu-'   oh nahótʌ?
       Sak FACT-MsS-buy-PUNC what
       'What did Sak buy?'

The same pattern holds with *ka nikáyʌ ká'sere'* 'which car' in place of *oh nahótʌ* 'what'. This confirms that question words are actually in Comp and may not be adjoined to the clause like other NPs.

Further evidence that question phrases appear in Comp in Mohawk comes from complement-taking verbs. As in English, these can be divided into three classes: those that require an indirect question, those that forbid an indirect question, and those that permit but do not require an indirect question. For those verbs that require an indirect question, the appearance of a question phrase at the beginning of the clause is sufficient to satisfy this requirement (see (81a)); for those verbs that cannot have an indirect question, the appearance of a question phrase at the beginning of the embedded clause induces ungrammaticality (see (80a)). Hence, the patterns are directly comparable to English and other familiar languages.

(80)   a. *Í-k-ehr-e'   oh nahótʌ Sak wa-ha-tshʌ́ri-'.
        Ø-1sS-think-IMPF what   Sak FACT-MsS-find-PUNC
        'I think what Sak found.'

      b. Oh nahótʌ í-hs-ehr-e'   Sak wa-ha-tshʌ́ri-'?
        what   Ø-2sS-think-IMPF Sak FACT-MsS-find-PUNC
        'What do you think Sak found?'

(81)   a. Wa-hake-rihwanútu's-e'   oh nahótʌ Uwári wa'-e-tshʌ́ri-'.
        FACT-MsS/1sO-ask-PUNC what   Mary FACT-FsS-find-PUNC
        'He asked me what Mary found.'

      b. *Oh nahótʌ wa-hya-rihwanútu's-e'   Uwári wa'-e-tshʌ́ri-'?
        what   FACT-MsS/2sO-ask-PUNC Mary FACT-FsS-find-PUNC
        'What did he ask you that Mary found?'

(82)   a. Wa'-ke-rihwáruk-e' oh nahótʌ Uwári wa'-e-tshʌ́ri-'.
        FACT-1sS-hear-PUNC what   Mary FACT-FsS-find-PUNC
        'I heard what Mary found.'

      b. Oh nahótʌ wa-hse-rihwáruk-e'   Uwári wa'-e-tshʌ́ri-'?
        what   FACT-2sS-hear-PUNC Mary FACT-FsS-find-PUNC
        'What did you hear that Mary found?'

Notice that the question word in the ungrammatical (81b) is in a licit structural position; it just happens to be the wrong position for satisfying the selectional properties of *rihwanutu's* 'ask'. Typically, verbs only select for grammatical properties of the head of their complement—in this case the embedded C. Hence, the question word can only satisfy the properties of the matrix verb via an appropriate relationship with this C. Under standard assumptions, this requires that the question word be the specifier of the CP. Positions adjoined within the clause would not be expected to satisfy selectional requirements in this way.

Another similarity between questions in Mohawk and English is that they may undergo successive-cyclic movement. Thus, when a question phrase has scope over a higher clause than the one that it is an argument of, it may and must appear at the beginning of that higher clause. This is exemplified in (80b) and (82b); two more examples are given in (83).

(83) a. Úhkʌ te-yo-[a]tohutsóh-u   n-au-sa-ha-[a]htʌ́ti-'?
      who DUP-NsO-be.necessary-STAT NE-OPT-ITER-MsS-home-PUNC
      'Who must go home?'

      b. Oh niyʌtyérʌ tsi wa-ts-hróri-'   tsi
      Why   that FACT-2sS/MsO-tell-PUNC that

      yu-s-a-hs-yákʌ'-ne'?
      TRANS-ITER-FACT-2sS-exit-PUNC
      'Why did you tell him that you went out?'
      (*Answer:* Ne tsi sótsi yonuhsaríhʌ. 'Because it's too warm in the house.')

This suggests that in Mohawk as in English interrogative phrases not only move to Comp, but can move cyclically from one Comp to another.[24]

In contrast, interrogative phrases in Mohawk cannot be moved out of a clause that is interpreted as a relative clause modifying an NP argument:

(84) a. *Nahótʌ wa'-hse-ríyo-'   ne érhar ne wa'-ka-nʌ́sko-'?
      what   FACT-2sS/ZsO-kill-PUNC NE dog NE FACT-ZsS-steal-PUNC
      'What did you kill the dog that stole?'

      b. *Úhka s-a-hse-tshʌ́ri-'   ne yako-hwist-ʌ́ty-u?
      who ITER-FACT-2sS-find-PUNC NE FsO-money-lose-STAT
      'Who did you find the money that she lost?'

      c. *Ka nikáyʌ áthere' she-yʌtéri   ne yakó-hs-u?
      which   basket 2sS/FsO-know/STAT NE FsO-finish-STAT
      'Which basket do you know the woman who made?'

This shows that interrogative dependencies in Mohawk obey standard island conditions—in this case the Complex NP Constraint. Since these are typical of *wh-*movement constructions but not necessarily other syntactic dependencies (see Chomsky 1977), the contrast between (84) and (83) supports the idea that movement to Comp is involved in Mohawk questions.[25] Similarly, the next section shows that question movement in Mohawk obeys the adjunct island condition. (The Sentential Subject Condition and the N-complement case of the Complex NP Constraint do not arise because Mohawk has no clausal subjects or complements to N; see section 10.1.1 and chapter 6 for discussion.)

The last and perhaps most striking evidence that *wh-*phrases occupy Comp is the fact that they create islands for further extraction. Thus, sentences like (85a) and (85b) are significantly degraded, with judgments ranging from ?? to *.[26]

(85) a. ??Ka nikáyʌ ká-'sere' wa-hse-rihwáruk-e'   úhka wa-ha-hnínu-'?
      which   car   FACT-2sS-hear-PUNC who FACT-MsS-buy-PUNC
      'Which car did you hear who bought?'

      b. *Úhka wa-hse-rihw-a-tshʌ́ri-'   ka nikáyʌ yakúkwe'
      who FACT-2sS-matter-Ø-find-PUNC which   woman .

shako-núhwe'-s?
MsS/FsO-like-HAB
'Who did you find out which woman likes?'

The sentences in (85) can be compared with the superficially parallel (86). The only difference is that the NP at the beginning of the lower clause is a referential NP rather than an interrogative word. However (86) is perfectly acceptable.

(86) Úhka wa-hs-íru-'　　　　Sak wa-huwá-kʌ-'?
　　 who FACT-2sS-say-PUNC Sak FACT-FsS/MsO-see-PUNC
　　 'Who did you say saw Sak?'

Thus, question phrases interfere with other long-distance relationships in a way that other NPs do not. This suggests that they fill the unique specifier of CP position, making that position unavailable for successive-cyclic movement of the other question word (Chomsky 1977). Since other NPs are adjoined to the clause, they do not fill the Comp position and no island effects are found.

The examples in (85) also suggest that question phrases not only appear in Comp, but they get there by movement rather than by base generation. The fact that the expression-initial question word is influenced by the presence of an interrogative phrase in the lower Comp indicates that it needs to move successive-cyclically through that position. This is a standard argument for *wh*-movement (Chomsky 1977). Moreover, the sentences improve if the initial interrogative phrase is replaced by a referential NP. Thus, (87) is more acceptable than (85).

(87) Thíkʌ ká'sere' wa'-ke-rihw-a-tshʌ́ri-'　　　　úhka wa-ha-hnínu-'.
　　 that　 car　 FACT-1sS-matter-Ø-find-PUNC who FACT-MsS-buy-PUNC
　　 'That car, I found out who bought it.'

This suggests that question phrases actually move from argument position to Comp, whereas referential NPs are base generated in peripheral (adjoined) positions.

So far, I have been emphasizing the similarities between Mohawk and English that follow from the claim that interrogative phrases must move to Comp. However, it is not the case that all such phrases move at S-structure in English: in multiple interrogatives, one and only one interrogative phrase moves to Comp; the others remain in their argument positions. This should not be possible in Mohawk, if I am correct that no overt NP can be in an argument position. Neither can *wh*-phrases be base generated adjoined to a clause, because of their nonreferential, quantificational nature. Thus, the only possibility for multiple questions in Mohawk is for all the interrogative phrases to move to clause-initial position. Thus, the following examples are grammatical:

(88) a. Tak-hróri　　　 úhka nahótʌ wa'-e-hnínu-'.
　　　　 2sSIMPER/1sO-tell who what FACT-FsS-buy-PUNC
　　　　 'Tell me who bought what.'

　　　 b. Wa-hse-rihwáruk-e' kʌ ka nikáyʌ úhka wa-ha-'sere-ht-a-hnínu-'?
　　　　 FACT-2sS-hear-PUNC Q which　 who FACT-MsS-car-NOM-Ø-buy-PUNC
　　　　 'Did you hear who bought which car?'

If any of the question words appear after the verb, then the sentence is ungrammatical, at least on a multiple interrogation reading[27]:

(89)   #Úhka wa'-e-tshÁri-'   nahótʌ?
       who FACT-FsS-find-PUNC what
       'Who found what?'

The same generalization holds true in more complex sentences: all of the interrogative phrases that have scope over the whole sentence appear to the left of that sentence. This is so regardless of whether the argument positions that the interrogative phrases are associated with are in the matrix clause or the embedded clause:

(90)   a. Úhka oh nahótʌ í-hr-ehr-e'   wá-hse-k-e'?
          who what   Ø-MsS-think-IMPF FACT-2sS-eat-PUNC
          'Who thinks you ate what?'

       b. Úhka oh nahótʌ í-hs-ehr-e'   wá-hra-k-e'?
          who what   Ø-2sS-think-IMPF FACT-MsS-eat-PUNC
          'Who do you think ate what?'

       c. ?*Úhka í-hr-ehr-e'   oh nahótʌ wá-hse-k-e'?
          who Ø-MsS-think-IMPF what   FACT-2sS-eat-PUNC
          'Who thinks you ate what?'

In these respects, Mohawk is similar to the Eastern European languages discussed by Rudin (1988), among others.[28] Thus, multiple *wh*-movement is not a phenomenon limited to polysynthetic languages. Nevertheless, the polysynthesis parameter does constrain the range of choices for expressing multiple questions in a substantive way.

To summarize so far, we have seen that Mohawk interrogatives have largely the same syntax as those of English. Thus, there is no incompatibility between *wh*-movement and polysynthesis. On the contrary, the Polysynthesis Parameter plays a role in forcing *wh*-movement to take place, ruling out *wh*–in situ in both simple questions and multiple questions.

Once again, other polysynthetic languages are similar to Mohawk in not having *wh*–in situ constructions. Although the range of evidence concerning *wh*-movement surveyed for Mohawk is not available in other polysynthetic languages, there is at least evidence that interrogative phrases are constrained to appear in clause-initial position. Launey (1981:45, 47) and Andrews (1975:197) state this explicitly for Nahuatl; the word order in these examples is particularly striking given that referential NPs more commonly follow the verb than precede it in Nahuatl:

(91)   a. Aquin Ø-chōca?   (Launey 1981:45)
          who 3sS-cry
          'Who is crying?'

       b. Tlein ti-c-nequi?   (Launey 1981:47)
          what 2sS-3sO-want
          'What do you want?'

Similarly, Heath (1984:508) states that in Nunggubuyu, "*WH interrogatives regularly precede other words* in the same (logical) clause" (his emphasis); this is one of the very few reliable word order generalizations that his text-based approach discovers in the language. (See Evans 1991:138–139, 299 for the same generalization in Mayali.) Watkins (1984:213) shows that question words front to clause-initial position in Kiowa.[29] Rood (1976) is not as explicit about the order of question words in Wichita as one might like, but in his examples the questioned phrase is always initial in the clause in both matrix questions and embedded questions (1976:155–156), and this generalization is apparently expressed in his rule W9 (p. 204). The same is true for the literature on Chukchee. The following pair of examples is very suggestive of *wh*-movement (Kozinsky et al. 1988:662–663):

(92) a. Mikəne   winren-nin ətləg-en?
          who(ERG) help-3S/3O father-ABS
          'Who helped the father?'

      b. Meŋin   winren-nin ekke-te?
          who(ABS) help-3S/3O son-ERG
          'Who did the son help?'

The word order in (92b), in particular, is claimed to be unusual in Chukchee, apart from *wh*-movement. Thus, there is good preliminary evidence that *wh*-movement takes place in other polysynthetic languages as well.[30]

2.1.5 CED Effects

We can take advantage of the fact that Mohawk has *wh*-movement in the syntax to test in yet another way the claim that all NPs are in adjoined positions. It is well known that it is possible to extract material out of an object in English, but not out of a subject:

(93) a.   Who did you see pictures of?

      b. ?*Who did pictures of upset you?

Example (93) illustrates the Subject Condition, familiar from Ross 1967, Chomsky 1973, and other work. Huang (1982) argues that the crucial property distinguishing subjects from objects in this regard is that of being governed by the verb. In this way, he collapses the Subject Condition and the Adjunct Island Condition together into the *Condition on Extraction Domains* (CED), stated in (94) (Huang 1982:505).

(94) A phrase A may be extracted out of a domain B only if B is properly governed.

This assumes that B is properly governed by C only if C is a lexical category that governs B. A lexical category governs a phrase only if it c-commands that phrase. Since the verb c-commands the object but not the subject (or an adjunct), the difference between (93a) and (93b) follows. Chomsky (1986a) derives (94) from a version of the principle of Subjacency, noting that both are S-structure conditions; however, the details of the analysis are not important here, as long as (94) is descriptively correct.

The behavior of embedded clauses provides evidence that the CED holds in Mohawk. The evidence comes from comparing complement clauses with adjunct clauses. Example (95) gives grammatical instances of extraction from a complement; other examples were given in the previous section.

(95) a. Úhka í-hs-ehr-e'   Λ-ye-hnínu-'   ne raó-'sere'?
         Who Ø-2sS-think-IMPF FUT-FsS-buy-PUNC NE MsP-car
         'Who do you think will buy his car?'

     b. Úhka í-hs-ehr-e'   Uwári ruwa-núhwe'-s?
        who Ø-2sS-think-IMPF Mary FsS/MsO-like-HAB
        'Who do you think Mary likes?'

However, (96) shows that similar extraction from various kinds of adjuncts is deviant.

(96) a. *Úhka wa'-te-hs-ahsΛ'tho-'   ne tsi   wa'-[e]-íhey-e'?
          who FACT-DUP-2sS-cry-PUNC because FACT-FsS-die-PUNC
          'Who did you cry because (she) died?'

      b. *Úhka wa'-te-sa-hΛreht-e'   ne tsi   Uwári
         who   FACT-DUP-2sO-shout-PUNC because Mary

         wa-huwa-rasΛtho-'?
         FACT-FsS/MsO-kick-PUNC
         'Who did you shout because Mary kicked?'

      c. *Úhka wa-hs-hnekíra-'   ne cáwhe ohΛtu tsi niyóre
         who   FACT-2sS-drink-PUNC NE coffee before

         wá-hra-w-e'?
         FACT-MsS-arrive-PUNC
         'Who did you drink the coffee before (he) arrived?'

      d. *NahótΛ ne Λ-hs-atst-e'   kíkΛ á'share' Λ-hs-kwétar-e'?
         what   NE FUT-2sS-use-PUNC this knife   FUT-2sS-cut-PUNC
         'What will you use this knife in order to cut?'

This contrast follows immediately from (94), given that complements are sisters to the verb and adjuncts are outside the VP, adjoined to the clause as a whole—as already established in section 2.1.1. The complement is governed by the verb, but the adjunct is not; hence, only (96) violates the CED. This is what one would expect given that Mohawk has ordinary *wh*-movement.

With this established, one can compare subject and object NPs as domains of extraction. In fact, the possibilities to be checked are very limited. Mohawk nouns rarely if ever take complements (see chapter 6). Thus, the only type of NP that can potentially be extracted from within an NP is the possessor of the head noun. Such movement proves to be impossible, regardless of whether the possessed noun is interpreted as the subject of the clause or as the object. There is no contrast between the (a) and (b) sentences in (97) and (98).

(97) a. *?Úhka se-núhwe'-s ne ako-kára'?
          who   2sS-like-HAB NE FsP-story
          'Whose story do you like?'

      b. *?Úhka we-sa-tsitúni-'   ne ako-kára'?
          who   FACT-2sO-make.cry-PUNC NE FsP-story
          'Whose story made you cry?'

(98) a. *?Úhka wa'-hse-tshÁri-'   ako-hwísta'?
    who FACT-2sS-find-PUNC FsP-money
    'Whose money did you find?'

   b. *?Úhka Λ-ka-kwétare-'   akó-[a]'share'?
    who FUT-NsS-cut-PUNC FsP-knife
    'Whose knife will cut it (a hard loaf of bread)?'

All of these examples become grammatical if the possessed noun immediately follows the question word; in this case, there is no extraction from NP, but rather movement of the NP as a whole—a kind of "pied piping" in the terminology of Ross 1967. Here, it is the (a) examples that are potentially surprising; the fact that extraction is impossible from subjects (the (b) examples) follows from the CED. One further example of this type is:

(99) *Úhka wa'-te-she-noru'kwányu-'   ne raó-skare'?
   who FACT-DUP-2sS/FsO-kiss-PUNC NE MsP-friend
   'Whose girlfriend did you kiss?'

However, these judgments are exactly what one would expect, given our hypothesis that overt NPs in Mohawk are always in adjoined positions. The structure of (98a) would be (100), which is ruled out by the CED.

(100)

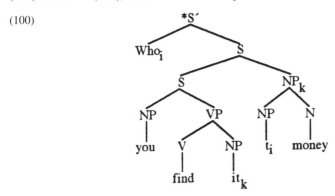

From this it follows that there is no subject–object asymmetry with respect to extraction in Mohawk; extraction from either violates the Adjunct Island subcase of the CED.

There is, however, an alternative interpretation of (97) and (98) that must be considered. These sentences involve the extraction of possessors, and it is clear that there is no subject–object asymmetry in their English translations either; (101a) and (101b) are equally bad.

(101) a. *Whose did you find [t money]?

   b. *Whose do you think [t knife] will cut it?

Thus, there may simply be a general ban against the extraction of possessors. In that case, (97) and (98) give no information about Mohawk clause structure.

It is not entirely clear what rules out (101) in English. There is certainly no universal restriction against the extraction of possessors; they can be extracted in the Romance languages, for example. One proposal is that inherent genitive Case cannot be realized on the question word once it is separated from the head (Giorgi and Longobardi 1991). Another proposal is that the trace left in the specifier position is not properly governed and therefore violates the Empty Category Principle (ECP) (Chomsky 1981, Kayne 1984). Neither of these English-specific approaches is likely to extend to Mohawk, however. Since Mohawk possessors are not marked overtly for genitive Case, there is no problem with Case realization. Moreover, possessed nouns in Mohawk agree with their possessors, and this agreement should be an adequate governor of the trace for purposes of the ECP, at least on some approaches.

Another reason for thinking that (97) and (98) are not comparable to (101) is that the ungrammaticality of possessor extraction in Mohawk can actually be rather mild, depending on the speaker and perhaps also the example. The asterisk is used for examples (97) and (98) because: (1) many speakers reject these sentences outright; (2) all speakers express a clear preference for sentences in which the possessed NP is pied-piped along with the possessor; (3) no speaker has spontaneously produced a sentence with this word order in my hearing; (4) I have found no examples of this type in texts. However, the fact remains that some speakers do permit some examples on some occasions. This type of variability is typical of sentences that violate the CED/Subjacency (Chomsky 1986a:34). In contrast, possessor extraction in English produces uniformly horrible results.

In fact, the extraction of the possessor in Mohawk becomes relatively acceptable when the question word does not appear in the Comp closest to the original extraction site, as in (102).

(102)   a.   ?Úhka í-hs-ehr-e'   wa-ha-tshÁri-'   ako-hwísta'?
             who Ø-2sS-think-IMPF FACT-MsS-find-PUNC FsP-money
             'Whose money do you think he found?'

        b.   ?Úhka í-hs-ehr-e'   ʌ-sa-ya'takéhnha-'   akó-[a]'share'?
             who Ø-2sS-think-IMPF FACT-NsS/2sO-help-PUNC FsP-knife
             'Whose knife do you think will help you?'

These sentences are still disfavored compared with their equivalents in which the whole possessed NP is pied-piped, but they are a significant improvement over the monoclausal versions. (The sentences are also acceptable if the possessed noun appears before the lower verb rather than after it, showing that linear order is not a significant factor in these constructions.) English possessor extractions do not improve in the same way: *Whose do you think you found money? is just as bad as (101a). This makes it very unlikely that the same principle is operative in Mohawk as in English. However, it has been noticed in the literature that CED violations sometimes improve in this way. Thus, Rizzi (1982:73–74, fn. 25) contrasts (103a), where the *wh*-phrase is in the nearest Comp, with (103b), where the *wh*-phrase is higher up. Both examples should violate the Subject Condition subcase of the CED, but (103b) sentence is judged to be much better than (103a).

(103)   a.   ??L'uomo di cui la sorella maggiore è innamorata di te è Gianni.
             'The man of whom the elder sister is in love with you is Gianni.'

        b.   L'uomo di cui ritengo che la sorella maggiore sia innamorata di te è Gianni.
             'The man of whom I believe that the elder sister is in love with you is Gianni.'

Some English speakers have similar intuitions, although the examples are somewhat degraded. Whatever the right technical analysis of this improvement is,[31] it seems to confirm that we are right to explain (97) in terms of the CED or whatever more basic principle of grammar it follows from. In short, extraction from any NP in Mohawk shows essentially the same pattern of behavior as extraction from ungoverned phrases does in English and Italian. From this we may conclude that these NPs must be in adjunct positions rather than argument positions.[32]

The system naturally predicts that all NPs should be islands to extraction in other polysynthetic languages as well. Unfortunately, the only language for which I have relevant data is Southern Tiwa, where, as in Mohawk, an interrogative word functioning as a possessor cannot be separated from the possessed noun, as shown in (104a) (Donald Frantz, personal communication).

(104)   a.   *?P'āyu a-thā-ban   betutu?
                who   2sS/AO-find-PAST 3s/sister
                'Whose sister did you find?'

        b.   P'āyu betutu   a-thā-ban?
                who   3s/sister 2sS/AO-find-PAST
                'Whose sister did you find?'

Example (104b) shows that if the NP as a whole is pied-piped to the beginning of the clause, the sentence is fine, as in Mohawk. These data, then, are consistent with the claim that all overt NPs are adjuncts in Southern Tiwa. For the other polysynthetic languages, I simply do not know the facts. Furthermore, in some of them the syntax of alienable possession is quite different from that of Mohawk in a way that affects the prediction (see chapter 6).

2.1.6 Weak Crossover Effects

The last topic to be discussed here concerns the weak crossover phenomenon. In section 2.1.3, I pointed out that there are few weak crossover effects in Mohawk because the language does not have true quantifiers. Mohawk does have interrogative quantifiers, however, as we have seen. Thus, consideration of weak crossover effects induced by *wh*-movement may shed further light on the clause structure of Mohawk.

The circumstances under which a pronoun can be interpreted as a bound variable are more restricted than those that allow ordinary coreference. Reinhart (1976, 1983a) argues that the condition in (45), repeated here as (105), applying at S-structure, defines when such an interpretation is possible.

(105)   Quantified NPs and *wh*-traces can have anaphoric relations only with pronouns that they c-command.

There are various controversies about the proper formulation of this principle and about how to characterize the set of elements it restricts; however, most of these issues are not crucial here. What is important is that (105) accounts for a difference between subjects and objects in English: a pronoun within the object can be interpreted with a questioned subject, but a pronoun inside the subject cannot be interpreted with a questioned object:

(106) a. *Who* t kissed *his* girlfriend?
           (= Wh x, x male, x kissed x's girlfriend)

       b. **Who* did *his* girlfriend kiss t?
           (NOT: Wh x, x male, x's girlfriend kissed x)

Consider in this light the possibility of question phrases binding overt pronouns in Mohawk. Sometimes this is allowed, as shown in (107).

(107) a. Úhka wa-ha-[a]t-hróri-'   tsi raúha wa-ha-nÁsko-'
           who FACT-MsS-SRFL-tell-PUNC that him   FACT-MsS-steal-PUNC

           ne ohwísta?
           NE money
           '*Who* told that *he* stole the money?'   (bound OK)

       b. Úhka í-hr-ehr-e'   Uwári raúha ruwa-núhwe'-s?
           who Ø-MsS-think-IMPF Mary him   FsS/MsO-like-HAB
           '*Who* thinks that Mary likes *him?*'   (bound OK)

In these sentences the overt pronoun is in the embedded clause, in a position where it is c-commanded by both the question word *úhka* and its trace in the subject position of the main clause. Hence, (105) allows an anaphoric relationship to hold between the two. The same result occurs when the pronoun is the possessor of an NP within an embedded clause:

(108) Úhka wa-ha-[a]t-hróri-'   tsi raúha raó-skare'
       who FACT-MsS-SRFL-tell-PUNC that him   MsP-friend

       yako-nuhwáktani?
       FsO-sick/STAT
       '*Who* told that *his* girlfriend was sick?'   (bound OK)

Suppose, however, that the relationships are reversed, such that the noun possessed by the pronoun is an argument of the matrix clause and the interrogative phrase originates in the embedded clause. Example (109) shows that a bound reading of the pronoun is not available under these circumstances.

(109) Úhka akaúha akó-skare' í-hr-ehr-e'   yako-ya't-á-hskats?
       who her   FsP-friend Ø-MsS-think-IMPF FsO-body-Ø-beautiful
       '*Who* does *her* boyfriend think is beautiful?' (not bound)

These judgments parallel those of the English glosses and are explained by (105). In (109), the trace of the interrogative phrase is inside the embedded clause, where it does not c-command anything in the matrix clause. Therefore, no anaphoric dependency between the pronoun and question word is possible in this example. Thus, the Weak Crossover Condition holds in Mohawk.

Now consider monoclausal examples parallel to (106) in English. Comparable pairs in Mohawk are:

(110) a. Úhka wa'-akó-[a]ti-'   ne akaúha ako-núhkwa?
           who FACT-FsO-lose-PUNC NE her   FsP-medicine
           '*Who* lost *her* medicine?'   (not bound)

    b. Úhka yako-ya'takéhnha-s ne akaúha ako-núhkwa?
       who NsS/FsO-help-HAB NE her   FsP-medicine
       '*Who* did *her* medicine help?' (not bound)

(111) a. Úhka raúha raó-skare' wa-shako-hranúhs-a-ya'k-e'?
       who him MsP-friend FACT-MsS/FsO-face-Ø-hit-PUNC
       '*Who* slapped *his* girlfriend?' (not bound)

    b. Úhka akaúha akó-skare' wa-shako-hranúhs-a-ya'k-e'?
       who her   FsP-friend FACT-MsS/FsO-face-Ø-hit-PUNC
       '*Who* did *her* boyfriend slap?' (not bound)

In the (a) sentences, *úhka* 'who' is understood as the subject of the verb and the possessed noun is the object; in the (b) sentences, *úhka* is understood as the object of the verb and the possessed noun is the subject. This distinction in grammatical function has no effect on the judgments, however: bound readings for these pronominal possessors are not available in either type of sentence. Thus, the subject–object asymmetry found in English does not show up in Mohawk.

This difference between Mohawk and English is immediately explained by our theory of nonconfigurationality. From an English point of view, the surprising sentences are the (a) ones, where a subject fails to bind into an object. In Mohawk, however, these putative object NPs are not in the argument position; rather they are adjoined to the clause as a whole,[33] as in (112).

(112)

In this configuration, the trace of the interrogative phrase in the subject position does not, in fact, c-command the pronoun inside the NP that expresses the object. (Note that the extraction site in this example must be the subject position, because the extraction of a possessor is blocked by the CED, as shown in the previous section.) Therefore, (105) rules out a bound interpretation of the pronoun. Once again, this NP must be required to adjoin to the clause for this result to occur; if overt NPs had the option of appearing in the true object position, then one would expect bound interpretations to be possible. Similarly (though less interestingly), the *wh*-traces in the (b) sentences are in the object position and do not c-command into the NP that is adjoined to the clause and linked to the subject position. Thus, bound pronouns are not available in these sentences either. Indeed, the parallelism between overt NPs and adjunct clauses seen throughout this chapter holds true in this case also: a *wh*-trace in the subject position cannot bind a pronoun inside an adjunct clause. Thus, (113) is parallel to (110a) and (111a).

(113)   Úhka wa'-t-ho-háreht-e'   ne tsi   Uwári raúha
         who   FACT-DUP-MsO-shout-PUNC because Mary   him

         wa-huwa-rasátho-'?
         FACT-FsS/MsO-kick-PUNC
         '*Who* shouted because Mary kicked *him?*' (not bound)

Example (113) contrasts with (107), where the pronoun in a complement clause can have a bound variable interpretation.

There is a sense in which this section presents data that are complementary to data presented in section 2.1.1. In section 2.1.1, I showed that in Mohawk the subject had to not c-command the possessor of the seeming object in order to explain why coreference was possible. In this section, the subject must not c-command the possessor of the seeming object in order to explain why an anaphoric dependency is not possible. Both point to the same conclusion: NPs interpreted as the object are outside the c-command domain of the subject and vice versa. This is only possible if those NPs are adjoined.

There is another sense in which this section is complementary to section 2.1.1: that section concentrated on pro as the core case of a pronoun in Mohawk, whereas here we have focused on the overt pronouns *raúha* 'him' and *akaúha* 'her'. In fact, when the overt pronouns in (110) and (111) are dropped, the judgments switch. Now bound readings are available for the (null) pronoun inside both the notional subject and the notional object[34]:

(114)   a. Úhka wa'-akó-[a]ti-'   ne ako-núhkwa?
            who   FACT-FsO-lose-PUNC   NE FsP-medicine
            '*Who* lost *her* medicine?'   (bound OK)

        b. Úhka yako-ya'takéhnha-s ne ako-núhkwa?
           who   NsS/FsO-help-HAB   NE FsP-medicine
           '*Who* did *her* medicine help?' (bound OK)

(115)   a. Úhka wa'-te-shako-noru'kwányu-'   raó-skare'?
            who   FACT-DUP-MsS/FsO-kiss-PUNC MsP-friend
            '*Who* kissed *his* girlfriend?'   (bound OK)

        b. Úhka wa'-te-shako-noru'kwányu-'   akó-skare'?
           who   FACT-DUP-MsS/FsO-kiss-PUNC FsP-friend
           '*Who* did *her* boyfriend kiss (her)?'   (bound OK)

It is significant that there is still no English-like subject–object asymmetry in these sentences. Nevertheless, this kind of difference between overt and null pronouns is not expected within the theory presented so far.

As in Baker 1991a, I claim that the key to this paradox is that the empty category possessor is actually not a pro in these sentences; rather, it is a parasitic gap. Parasitic gaps are known to be a way of avoiding certain weak crossover violations in English, as shown in (116).

(116) a. The linguist filed *the paper* without reading *it*.

   b. ?? *Which paper* did the linguist file *t* without reading *it* ?

   c. (?)*Which paper* did the linguist file *t* without reading *e* ?

In (116a) a pronoun is interpreted as coreferential with a definite NP. In (116b), this dependency becomes marginal when the antecedent is a *wh*-trace (at least for some speakers, including the author; see Safir 1984:606, fn. 3). This interpretation is ruled out by (105), assuming that the *without* phrase is outside the VP, and hence not c-commanded by the trace in direct object position. The sentence improves, however, if the offending pronoun is deleted, as in (116c) (Safir 1984). These parasitic gap constructions are familiar from Chomsky 1982, and 1986a and references cited therein; Chomsky 1986a analyzes them as instances of a *wh*-trace left by the movement of an empty operator (Op). Now, one cannot tell by simple inspection whether the possessor in (114) and (115) is a null pronoun or a null *wh*-trace bound by a null operator. Let us therefore consider the possibility that these sentences actually contain a *wh*-trace, avoiding the weak crossover problem.

Developing an account of (114) and (115) in terms of parasitic gaps is quite straightforward. The following properties are taken to be characteristic of the parasitic gap construction in the literature (Chomsky 1982):

(117) a. A parasitic gap must be associated with the trace of a legitimate *wh*-movement (the "real gap").

   b. The operator that binds the real gap must also c-command the parasitic gap.

   c. The real gap cannot c-command the parasitic gap, nor vice versa.

The structure of (115) is (118).

(118)

Properties (117a,b) are obviously obeyed in (118). Furthermore, the *wh*-trace does not c-command the possessor gap, in accordance with (117c); thus, the so-called anti-c-command condition is obeyed as well. The very lack of c-command that was problematic when we took the possessor to be a pronoun becomes an advantage when we analyze it as a parasitic gap.[35]

This analysis can be confirmed via a further property of parasitic gap constructions established by Chomsky (1986a). Chomsky shows that the relationship between the location of a parasitic gap and the top of the adjunct containing that gap is sensitive to island conditions. Consider, then, sentences similar in structure to (115) and (118), but where the position bound by the empty operator is not the possessor of the noun, but rather is embedded inside a relative clause that modifies the noun. The structure of such examples would be:

(119)

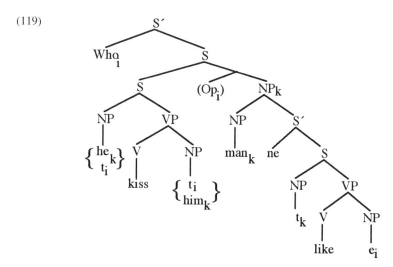

Here, e cannot be a parasitic gap, because it is not subjacent to a potential operator position with scope over NP_k. Neither can e be a bound pronoun, because it is not c-commanded by the trace of the *wh*-phrase. Hence, we predict that the position in question cannot be interpreted as the same as the questioned entity. This prediction proves true[36]:

(120)   a. Úhka wa'-ti-shako-noru'kwányu-'   ne rúkwe ne shako-núhwe'-s?
           who   FACT-DUP-MsS/FsO-kiss-PUNC NE man   NE MsS/FsO-like-HAB
           '*Who* did the man who likes *her* kiss?'   (not bound)

       b. Úhka wa'-t-huwa-noru'kwányu-'   ne rúkwe ne ruwa-núhwe'-s?
           who   FACT-DUP-FsS/MsO-kiss-PUNC NE man   NE FsS/MsO-like-HAB
           '*Who* kissed the man that *she* likes?'   (not bound)

The contrast between (120) and (115) suggests that parasitic gaps are crucially involved in the analysis of the latter. In (121) a second pair of examples is given with the same structure as those in (120).

(121)   a. Úhka wa-shako-[a]nisnuhsawí-tsher-u-'   ne shako-'nhá'-u?
           who   FACT-MsS/FsO-ring-NOM-give-PUNC NE MsS/FsO-hire-STAT
           '*Who* did the one who hired *her* give a ring?'   (not bound)

       b. Úhka s-a'-e-tshári-'   ne áthere' ne thetáre   yakó-[a]ty-u?
           who   ITER-FACT-FsS-find-PUNC NE basket NE yesterday FsO-lose-STAT
           '*Who* found the basket that *she* lost yesterday?' (not bound)

Notice that the bound readings are lost, regardless of whether the NP containing the gap in question is the subject or the object. This reinforces the conclusion drawn above that NPs associated with either grammatical function are in adjoined positions.[37]

As before, we would expect that similar patterns of bound pronouns should be found in other polysynthetic languages. In particular, no subject–object asymmetries are expected in this domain, since all overt NPs are structurally adjuncts. However, the empirical facts are quite subtle and simply are not available for any other language of my sample.

2.2 Why NPs Cannot Be in Argument Position

In this chapter we have seen that Mohawk and other polysynthetic languages differ syntactically from English in a variety of ways: they lack quantifiers and simple NP anaphors; they differ in the referential dependencies that can be found between pronouns and definite NPs; they differ in the dependencies that are allowed between pronouns and interrogative words; and they differ in the possibilities of extraction out of NP. Yet in spite of these extensive differences, we have not needed to posit a parameter in any of the major syntactic principles in question. On the contrary, Binding conditions A, B, and C, the Weak Crossover Condition, and the CED have all been shown to exist in Mohawk, where they account for patterns that are recognizably similar to those found in English and the Romance languages. Therefore, the differences in the Mohawk judgments have been attributed not to differences in the statement of the principles, but rather to differences in the structural configuration that those principles apply to. One simple and independently motivated difference underlies the differences seen in all these areas: the fact that in Mohawk overt NPs are adjoined to the clause rather than appearing in argument position.

This, however, raises a new question: Why can't NPs appear in argument positions in Mohawk? Should this property of the language be related to the Polysynthesis Parameter presented in chapter 1, and if so, how?

In Baker 1991a, I argued that the reason NPs could not appear in argument positions in Mohawk was because of the Case Filter. This accounted straightforwardly for the fact that certain other elements act as though they are in argument position in Mohawk. This is clearest for sentential complements. We have seen that these behave very similarly in Mohawk and in English: they can be extracted from (see section 2.1.5); pronouns in them can be bound by *wh*-phrases originating in the matrix clause (see section 2.1.6); and nonpronominal NPs in them cannot corefer with pronouns associated with the matrix clause (see section 2.1.1). In all these respects, complement clauses differ from object NPs in Mohawk. Thus, complement clauses do appear in argument positions, governed by the verb that selects them. Moreover, we have assumed throughout that null NPs appear in argument positions: in particular, we have seen evidence for pros and traces of *wh*-movement, both of which behave exactly like their counterparts in more familiar languages. Thus, there is a distinction between overt NPs on the one hand and null NPs and clauses on the other. This is exactly what one would expect if the Case Filter of Rouveret and Vergnaud 1980 and Chomsky 1980 were at work:

(122)   *The Case Filter*
        *NP without Case if NP has phonetic features and is in an argument position.

Suppose, then, that the following were true:

(123)   Heads cannot assign Case to argument positions in Mohawk (at S-structure/phonetic form (PF)).

This account explains why the class of elements that can appear in argument position in Mohawk is similar to the class of elements that can be objects of a passive verb in English: clauses and NP traces appear in this position, but not overt NPs:

(124)   a.   It is known [$_{CP}$ that elephants can't fly].

        b.   The solution is known [$_{NP}$ e].

        c.   *It/there is known [$_{NP}$ the solution].

In this way, an abstract similarity between English and Mohawk is captured, and yet another principle of UG is justified in Mohawk.

This analysis also plays an important role in explaining why polysynthetic languages have interrogative NPs but not quantified NPs. Thus, (122) is taken to apply at S-structure or somewhere between S-structure (the point where Spell-Out applies in Chomsky 1992) and PF. Now, *wh*-phrases are originally generated in argument position, then move to Comp prior to S-structure. At S-structure, a trace will be in the argument position, which is consistent with (122). However, if a quantifier phrase were generated in argument position, it would not be able to move out of that position until LF, since no morphosyntactic feature triggers its earlier movement (compare "Procrastinate" of Chomsky 1992). Hence, quantified phrases necessarily violate (122) at S-structure/PF. If NPs could not even be generated in argument positions, we would expect Mohawk to have neither quantified phrases nor interrogative phrases. If the ban held only at LF, one would expect both types of phrases to be possible. Only if the relevant condition holds at S-structure/PF is the contrast accounted for. This is another respect in which (122) and (123) have the desired effects.[38]

The Case-theoretic analysis has a third favorable consequence, also pointed out in Baker 1991a. Section 2.1.1 showed that embedded clauses had the same patterning with respect to Condition C in Mohawk and English. In fact, this is not entirely true. The examples in the earlier section all involved a pro object in the matrix clause; this object c-commands into complement clauses but not into adjunct clauses, as in English. Suppose, however, that one constructs similar examples where the pronoun is the subject of the matrix clause. Reinhart (1983a) shows that such pronouns must be disjoint in reference from a nonpronominal NP within an adjunct clause in English. Thus, one finds the subject–object asymmetry in (125):

(125)   a.   The chairman hit *him* on the head before *the lecturer* had a chance to speak.

        b.   **He* was hit on the head before *the lecturer* had a chance to speak.

This contrast is attributed to Condition C plus the assumption that adjunct clauses are generated outside the VP as daughters of S. Given this, the subject c-commands into the adjunct clause, but the object does not, and the coreference patterns follow. In Mohawk, however, a matrix clause subject pronoun can be coreferential with an NP in an adjunct clause. Some examples are:

(126) a. Wa-haké-'nha'-ne'   ne tsi   rake-núhwe'-s   ne Sak.
       FACT-MsS/1sO-hire-PUNC because MsS/1sO-like-HAB NE Sak
       '*He* hired me because *Sak* likes me.' (coreference OK)

       b. T-a'-uk-hyátu-'s-e'   ohÁtu ne Uwári
       TRANS-FACT-FsS/1sO-write-BEN-PUNC before NE Mary

       s-a'-[e]-íhey-e'.
       ITER-FACT-FsS-die-PUNC
       '*She* wrote to me before *Mary* died.' (coreference OK)

       c. Wa'-t-ho-hÁreht-e'   ne tsi   Uwári wa-huwa-rahsÁtho-'
       FACT-DUP-MsO-shout-PUNC because Mary FACT-FsS/MsO-kick-PUNC

       ne Sak.
       NE Sak
       '*He* shouted because Mary kicked *Sak*.' (coreference OK)

Of course, subject pronouns (like object pronouns) c-command into complement clauses in Mohawk; hence, the indicated coreferences are impossible in (127).

(127) a. Ro-[a]teryÁtar-e' tsi Sak ruwa-núhwe'-s
       MsO-know-STAT that Sak FsS/MsO-like-HAB
       '*He* knows that she loves *Sak*.' (disjoint only)

       b. Y-a'-t-ho-rihwayÁta's-e'   tsi Λ-ha-'sereht-a-hnínu-'   ne Sak.
       TRANS-FACT-DUP-MsO-decide-PUNC that FUT-MsS-car-Ø-buy-PUNC NE Sak
       '*He* decided that *Sak* would buy the car.' (disjoint only)

       c. Í-hr-ehr-e'   Uwári ruwa-núhwe'-s   ne Sak
       Ø-MsS-think-IMPF Mary FsS/MsO-like-HAB NE Sak
       '*He* thinks that Mary loves *Sak*.' (disjoint only)

Why should there be a difference between (125b) in English and (126) in Mohawk? Apparently, subjects c-command into sentential adjuncts in English but not in Mohawk. Conceivably one could achieve this result by saying that clausal and temporal modifiers attach higher in the tree in Mohawk than in English. This seems like a peculiar way for languages to differ, however, and it is unclear how this difference could be learned. A more promising analysis is to claim the opposite: that the position of the subject is lower in Mohawk than in English. Much recent research assumes that subject NPs are actually base generated inside the VP across languages (Koruda 1988, Kitagawa 1986, Fukui and Speas 1986, Koopman and Sportiche 1988). In English, the subject moves up to the "normal" subject position (specifier of IP) to receive nominative Case from Infl. Mohawk, however, is crucially different in this respect. Condition (123) states that there is no Case assignment to argument positions in Mohawk. Hence, there is no Case-theoretic motivation for the subject to raise to the specifier of IP in this language. In the economy framework of Chomsky 1992, unmotivated movements are barred;

hence, the subject must stay inside VP in Mohawk.[39] Holding constant the assumption that causal and temporal adjuncts are attached to IP, it follows that the subject c-commands such adjuncts at S-structure in English but not in Mohawk. The judgments in (126) are thus explained in terms of Condition C plus the assumption that there is no Case assignment to argument positions in Mohawk. This analysis is sketched in (128).

(128)

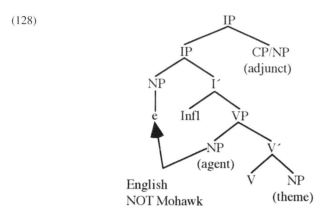

This gives additional support to (123) as a central property of Mohawk.

Notice that in order to obtain the correct results here, we must interpret the definition of c-command given in section 2.1.1 so that an NP in the specifier of IP c-commands phrases adjoined to that IP. In fact, the need for a notion of c-command with this property has been recognized from the introduction of the notion of c-command in Reinhart 1976. In the terminology of Chomsky 1986a, the desired result comes from recognizing that the lower IP in (128) does not count as a "complete" phrase in itself, but only a segment of a phrase, the higher IP being essentially the same category. Thus, the smallest *complete* phrase properly containing the specifier of IP is the largest IP, which also contains the adjoined CP or NP. On this interpretation, the subject in English c-commands IP adjuncts and everything contained in them, although the subject in Mohawk does not. Henceforth, I shall consistently use the term c-command in this way.

We have now found an analysis explaining why NPs cannot be in argument position that has the right properties and is embedded in an articulated theory of Universal Grammar. We can then go on to ask the next question: Why can't heads in Mohawk assign Case? In this respect, Mohawk categories seem radically different from English ones. The obvious next step is to relate this to the fact that all Mohawk heads are inflected with agreement morphemes, unlike their counterparts in English. Thus, (123) can be taken as a consequence of (129).

(129)   An agreement morpheme adjoined to a head X receives that head's Case at S-structure/PF.

This is a rather conservative proposal in several respects. First, it means that Mohawk does not differ in any fundamental way from English in the way that Case features are associated with lexical heads; we will find evidence that this is true in chapter 5. Second, (129) is a specific development of the traditional Amerindianist view that the nonconfigurational properties of polysynthetic languages are somehow a result of the presence of extensive agreement morphology on the heads. Third, (129) recalls the classical Government-Binding (GB) analyses of the early 1980s, in which clitics in the Romance and Semitic languages absorbed the Case features of the head they were attached to; this accounted for "Kayne's Generalization," for example (see especially Borer 1984). Independent motivation for (129) will be found when the syntax of agreement is considered in chapter 5.

One important question left open in the statement of (129) is whether it is a statement of Universal Grammar, a morpheme-specific property, or a parameter. If only certain agreement morphemes absorb Case, which ones are they? Unfortunately, the current literature does not allow us to evaluate this as well as one would like. Apparently, (129) holds of all agreement morphemes in all polysynthetic languages. Moreover, it extends beyond the polysynthetic languages to many languages in which agreement is optional, rather than obligatory. Thus, overt NPs in object position are incompatible with object agreement morphemes/object clitics in most Romance languages (Borer 1984), Bantu (Bresnan and Mchombo 1987), and the Northern Athapaskan languages, among others. Whether overt NPs in subject position are incompatible with subject agreement or subject clitics is much more controversial and much harder to assess empirically. In part, this is because there are not many syntactic differences between subjects and adjuncts in the first place: this chapter has presented six arguments that NPs understood as objects are actually in adjunct position, but only two of these (the absence of quantifiers and the necessity of *wh*-movement) apply in a nontrivial way to NPs understood as subjects. Bresnan and Mchombo (1987) argue on the basis of *wh*–in situ that overt NPs related to subject agreement can be true subjects in Chichewa, but Demuth and Johnson (1989) show that such NPs cannot be true subjects in Setswana; furthermore, the Setswana pattern is more widespread in the Bantu family (Katherine Demuth, personal communication). Similarly, the standard view is that overt NPs can appear in the specifier of IP in the context of rich agreement in Italian and Spanish; however, Barbosa (1993) argues that this may not be true, based on complex interactions between quantified subjects, clitic placement, and verb-second phenomena. Agreement is clearly incompatible with overt NPs in argument positions in many of the Celtic languages (Anderson 1982). Thus, (129) seems rather general. On the other hand, subject agreement does not absorb nominative Case in English or French, for example. Indeed, subject agreement in English and French has little or no syntactic effect of any kind: it also does not license null-subject phenomena, for instance. Hence, one could say that agreement morphemes in these languages do not appear in the syntactic derivation at all; rather, they are added to the representation in the morphological component of PF, as proposed by Halle and Marantz (1993). Thus, pending more conclusive data from a wider range of languages, I conjecture that (129) holds of all agreement elements that are present in the syntax in the first place. Crucially this includes all agreement elements that play a role in satisfying the MVC in polysynthetic languages; it also holds of those that license null pronouns and perhaps others.

Returning to the main theme, a closer look shows that (123) does not follow from (129) directly. Rather, a second assumption is necessary, made explicit in (130).

(130)   All (Case-assigning) heads in Mohawk must have agreement morphemes.

Without (130), there would be the option of not generating, say, object agreement morphology on the verb. Then nothing would absorb the verb's structural Case, and the verb could Case-mark an overt NP in the complement position. This is exactly what happens in the Romance languages, Bantu languages, and Northern Athapaskan languages, where object clitics/agreement morphemes are optional (see section 1.5). However, this option does not exist in Mohawk and other poly-synthetic languages. We may once again ask, "Why?"

In Baker 1991a, I did not address this question. The implicit assumption there was that (130) was a primitive fact about the morphology of Mohawk—an as-sumption discussed explicitly by Ikeda (1991). However, the relevant property proves both difficult to state and empirically problematic. Ikeda considers the pos-sibility that (130) is related to the fact that Mohawk verb roots can be smaller than the "minimal word" required by the phonology of the language. For example, Mohawk roots can be as small as a single vowel (*e* 'go', *u* 'give'), a single conso-nant (*k* 'eat', *t* 'stand', *w* 'arrive'), or a consonant cluster (*hkw* 'to pick up'). Thus, affixation of agreement morphemes may be required to get a proper morphophono-logical entity. However, this property would have to be highly grammaticized, since agreement morphology is neither necessary nor sufficient to create a phono-logically well-formed word in Mohawk. On the one hand, there are many verb stems in Mohawk that are disyllabic or longer, but agreement morphology is still required on these. On the other hand, the shortest verb stems are still not disyllabic even after the addition of agreement morphology; this lack is made up by the use of epenthetic and prothetic vowels (see, for example, Michelson 1989):

(131)   a. k-k-s   → íkeks 'I eat'

      b. t-hra-t-' → íthrate' 'he is standing there'

      c. k-ehr-' → íkehre' 'I want to, I think'

Moreover, even if it were true that Mohawk verb roots needed to be affixed for some purely morphological reason, it in no way follows that *agreement* morphol-ogy is obligatory. Spanish verb roots also never appear by themselves, but this does not make subject agreement morphology obligatory: Spanish also has infini-tival and participial suffixes that can satisfy whatever morphological requirement is at work. The idea under consideration offers no reason why this could not be true in Mohawk as well.

Also relevant to this issue is the paradigm in (132), discussed in section 1.4.

(132)   a. *[$_{VP}$ ra-núhwe'-s ne owirá'a].
             MsS-like-HAB NE baby
        'He likes babies.'

      b. [$_{VP}$ shako-núhwe'-s pro$_i$] (ne owirá'a$_i$).
             MsS/3O-like-HAB   NE baby
        'He likes them (babies).'

c. Ra-wir-a-núhwe'-s.
   MsS-baby-Ø-like-HAB
   'He likes babies.'

We are trying to explain the ungrammaticality of a sentence like (132a), where object agreement on the verb has been omitted. However, the verb is not entirely without agreement either: it is still inflected for subject agreement. Presumably, this subject agreement is sufficient to satisfy any simple-minded morphological or morphophonological requirement. *Ranúhwe's* is a well-formed Mohawk word, meaning 'he likes it (neuter)'. In fact, *ra* is the very agreement morpheme that shows up with this combination of verb and object when the object NP is incorporated into the verb, as shown in (132c). Thus, the simple-minded, purely morphological answer to the question "Why is agreement obligatory?" is seriously flawed; it is not clear how it could be revised within a generative theory that aspires to be restrictive and explanatory.[40]

Thus, we need a (morpho)syntactic parameter that has the effect of (130), thereby distinguishing languages like Mohawk, Nahuatl, Southern Tiwa, and Mayali, in which clitics/agreement are obligatory for all syntactic positions and categories, from Spanish, Chichewa, Slave, and Alamblak, in which they are available but optional. The Morphological Visibility Criterion proposed in chapter 1 has exactly this effect. It states that there must be an agreement morpheme (or incorporated noun root) on the head for each thematic role listed in the argument structure of that head. This explains the ungrammaticality of (132a). More generally, it implies that whenever a head takes an argument, it also has to have a corresponding agreement morpheme attached to it. Hence, the Case that the head might otherwise have assigned to its argument is necessarily taken up by the agreement morpheme instead, by (129). The Case Filter then applies, with the effect that the argument may be a clause or an empty category, but not an NP with phonological features. This induces the widespread syntactic ramifications presented in this chapter. Crucially, the obligatoriness of agreement is not an idiosyncratic property of individual verbs, or even of classes of verbs, or even of the class of verbs as a whole (nouns must also be inflected; see chapter 6). Rather, it is a property of all heads involved in θ-role assignment in a polysynthetic language. Thus, it is inappropriate to encode it as a lexical property; rather, it is a global property of the language as a whole. On the other hand, it is clearly not a property of other languages. Thus, the use of a parameter is justified exactly here.

Notes

1. Much of the material in this section was presented in Baker 1991a and Baker, to appear b. Although certain extensions, improvements, and clarifications have been made, the basic ideas are the same as in those works.

2. Jelinek's hypothesis that there is no pro could be maintained by making certain assumptions about c-command and word internal structure. Thus, if the category V dominating the object prefix does not count as a dominating node for purposes of c-command, then the object prefix binds the NP directly in this example. This could then be interpreted

as a violation of Condition C. However, this approach would not account for the subject–object asymmetry found in ellipsis interpretation (see section 3.1.3).

3. Some speakers find coreference less natural when the adjoined NP follows the verb than when it precedes the verb. In the former case, the *pro* linearly precedes the constituent including the name; hence, it is an instance of backward pronominalization. Backward pronominalization is known to be more awkward for some speakers in English as well.

4. The examples in the text all test Condition C with respect to *pro* rather than overt pronominals. Mohawk does have overt pronouns (e.g., *raúha* 'him' and *akaúha* 'her'), but these are most readily interpreted as disjoint from another NP in the same clause, regardless of grammatical functions and c-command relationships. The same is true of overt pronouns in languages like Navajo and Siouan (Kenneth Hale, personal communication). Presumably, this is a result of the emphatic, contrastive nature of these pronouns.

5. However, see section 10.1.2 for a refinement. For other, probably related, restrictions of the relationship between clauses and pros, see Iatridou and Embick 1993.

Note that *Sak* may be in a nonargument position, adjoined to the lower clause in (6). However, Condition C is not sensitive to whether the c-commanded NP is in an argument position or not. Indeed, pronouns cannot be coreferential with adjoined NPs that they c-command in English: *He$_i$ thinks that John$_i$, Mary really likes (him$_i$)* is bad with the indicated coreference.

6. The additional factors are reconstruction effects and the difference between relative clauses and other dependents of NP.

7. Here I assume for the sake of discussion that one can have A-anaphors in A-bar positions. This is allowed in Aoun's (1985) typology of anaphora.

8. Subject agreement and reflexive morphology tend to combine into a portmanteau in Kiowa, although generally the initial consonant of the prefix is characteristic of the subject person features and the vowel quality is characteristic of the reflexive (Watkins 1984:115).

9. Both Rizzi (1986b) and Cinque (1990) mention that there is improvement if the quantifier appears with a lexical N'. This effect does not seem to carry over to Mohawk.

10. It is possible for the head noun to be morphologically singular in these examples. This goes along with the fact that in Mohawk, as in many other native American languages, explicit plural morphology on the noun is not obligatory even when the reference of the noun is clearly plural. Nevertheless, plural nouns are often preferred with *akwéku*.

11. Reinhart also points out that (37a) becomes acceptable if *it* is replaced by *they* in the lower clause. Thus, when *every* is treated like *all* with respect to plurality, the scope condition ceases to hold.

12. In fact, in Reinhart's system this condition also rules out "scope condition" violations of the kind discussed earlier. Many other researchers distinguish the two classes of examples, however, treating the scope condition as more fundamental.

13. An alternative account of (47) would be that *akwéku* is a quantificational NP, but Mohawk has a "flat" structure in which the subject and the object are in a relationship of mutual c-command. However, this alternative ignores the other parallels between *akwéku* and *all*. Also, the properties of ellipsis interpretation (see section 3.1.3) show that Mohawk does not have a flat structure.

14. Note that *úhka* ends with a /k/ when it is not in a negative or interrogative context. This suggests that it may be a polarity item. The /k/ may be related to one which means 'only' in pairs like *áhsʌ* 'three' vs. *áhsʌk* 'only three'. This /k/ is, in turn, a reduction of the particle *khok* (e.g., *ahsʌ khok* 'only three'). See Deering and Delisle 1976:148.

Káneka 'somewhere', 'anywhere' used in locative negative sentences like (56a) is also a polarity item. In a positive assertion, one would use *ka tyok* or *kak*. Thus, an answer to (56b) would be *HΛ, kak wá'ke'* 'Yes, somewhere I go.'

15. Notice that when *someone* is dislocated in the English equivalents of (59), the quantificational reading is lost and only the referential reading of *someone* survives, as predicted by (31):

(i) a. Someone, he always sees me when I go to town.

  b. Someone, he rarely helps me.

Cinque (1990:75–76) discusses similar facts in Italian. Given what has been said so far, the structure and interpretation of (59) would be expected to be the same as (i)–contrary to fact. (See section 3.3.2 for an analysis.)

16. Here Heim's (1982:ch. 2) analysis differs slightly from Reinhart's (1987). Heim would claim that in this configuration the index of *some guest* would not be copied onto the quantificational adverb *often* itself, but rather onto an existential quantifier that is introduced under the scope of *often* by a rule of Existential Closure. Thus, Heim's mapping of S-structure to LF is somewhat more complex than Reinhart's, but her interpretation of indexing is more straightforward. Heim's rule of Existential Closure also accounts explicitly for the fact that when there are no other quantificational elements present, the default reading of indefinites is an existential one—a fact that carries over to Mohawk. These technical differences between Reinhart's and Heim's formulations are not crucial for our primary concerns, however.

17. Again, Heim's (1982:ch. 2) approach is slightly different: she would have the index on the indefinite copied not onto *yah* but onto an existential quantifier within the scope of *yah,* created by Existential Closure (see fn. 16). Thus, for Heim the LF of (64) would be (i) rather than (ii), as given by the text account. The two are logically equivalent, however.

(i) Not ($\exists$ x, x a person & x came)

(ii) No x, x a person, x came

18. Evans (to appear a) does imply that Mayali has determiner quantifiers, as well as those that are adverbial prefixes on the verb, but he says very little about them. The one relevant example that he cites (p. 2) involves *rouk,* which is glossed as 'all' and triggers plural agreement on the verb; this is not problematic.

19. The rarity of *ka:* in Rood's corpus could simply be a result of his elicitation procedures, which may have favored a formal speech level where unreduced forms are avoided.

20. However, it must be acknowledged that many, perhaps most, *non*polysynthetic languages also do not have equivalents to English *everyone* and *nobody*. This does not make the prediction vacuous, but it does makes it less striking than it would otherwise be.

Some of the languages for which this has been shown may qualify as head-marking nonconfigurational languages; if so, they would fall under the same theory as that given in the text. See Jelinek (to appear) for Straits Salish, and Bittner and Hale (to appear) for Warlpiri.

Partly the same and partly different is Navajo, as analyzed by Parsons and Speas (to appear). Navajo also does not have true quantified NPs, which can be attributed to the fact that NPs must be linked to inherently pronominal elements occupying the θ-positions. However, Parsons and Speas claim that overt NPs in Navajo are in specifier (A-) positions rather than in adjoined (A-bar) positions. Among other things, this correlates with the fact that Navajo, unlike Mohawk, is an SOV language with relatively strict word order.

Eloise Jelinek (personal communication) mentions that Chinese, Japanese, and Indonesian also do not have truly quantificational NPs. Since these are not head-marking languages, a different explanation is presumably needed for them.

21. Sentences like (76) could also be derived from a clitic doubling source in varieties of the Romance languages that permit this. In that context, the status of (76) has sparked great debate, but the issues are not directly relevant here.

22. This is a good example of a microparameter: whether syntactic movement is found or not is a function of the lexical properties of the interrogative C in the language.

23. Less clear is the issue of negative quantifiers. Thus ?*No one will I see* is marginally possible in English, motivating Rizzi (1991) to propose a Negative Criterion parallel to the *Wh*-Criterion. Perhaps a denial can be considered a distinct speech act from an affirmation in some cases. I put this issue aside.

24. In the speech of two of my older and more conservative consultants, there is some evidence for a "partial" *wh*-movement construction, in which the interrogative phrase moves only to the nearest Comp and a dummy interrogative phrase appears in the higher Comp to mark the scope of the question. An example is (i).

(i) NahótΛ wa'-ts-hróri-'   ne Uwári nahótΛ wa'-e-hnínu-'?
    What   FACT-2sS/MsO-tell-PUNC NE Mary what   FACT-FsS-buy-PUNC
    'What did you tell him that Mary bought?'

This construction is presumably like the German/Romani construction discussed by McDaniel (1989). However, even the speakers in question do not produce these forms consistently; nor do they have robust judgments about them. Also I have not found any examples of this type even in older texts (perhaps because questions of all kinds are fairly rare in narrative texts). Hence, all I can do is mention the possibility that (i) represents an older form of the language, less influenced by English.

25. Here there is a contrast with adjoined referential NPs, which can be acceptable appearing outside of complex NPs. Thus, compare (i) with (84c).

(i) ThíkΛ áthere' khe-yΛtéri-'   ne yakó-hs-u.
    that basket 1sS/FsO-know-STAT NE FsO-finish-STAT
    'That basket, I know the woman who made it.'

This suggests that referential NPs are base generated in clause-peripheral positions, whereas interrogative phrases move there (see also the contrast between (85b) and (87)).

26. I mention in passing that no ECP-type subject–object asymmetries arise here, so (i) is not worse than (85a). This is expected given that Mohawk is a pro-drop language (as defined in Chomsky 1981, Rizzi 1982):

(i) Úhka wa-hse-rihwáruk-e' oh nahótΛ wa-ha-hnínu-'
    who FACT-2sS-hear-PUNC what   FACT-MsS-buy-PUNC?
    'Who did you hear what bought?'

27. Some question words in Mohawk are partially homophonous with indefinite NPs. This means that sentences such as (89) can sometimes be accepted with an irrelevant reading like "Who found something?" Such questions are felicitously answered with a single NP (e.g., *Sak*), proving that they are not multiple questions.

28. Rudin (1988) actually argues that these languages divide into two types: those in which all *wh*-phrases move into Comp (Bulgarian and Romanian) and those in which only one *wh*-phrase moves into Comp and the others adjoin to IP (Serbo-Croatian, Polish, Czech). Mohawk does not fit neatly into either of these types. Mohawk allows more than one interrogative phrase to move successive-cyclically to a higher Comp, as in Bulgarian

and Romanian (see (90b)). On the other hand, Mohawk is like Serbian/Polish/Czech in that *wh*-islands are respected by most speakers (see (85)), and word order of the initial *wh*-phrases is free, with no superiority-like effect. Hence, (i) is a perfectly grammatical alternative to (88a).

(i) Tak-hróri   nahótʌ úhka wa'-e-hnínu'.
     2sSIMPER/1sO-tell what   who FACT-FsS-buy-PUNC
     'Tell me what who bought.'

Finally, clitics can interrupt the sequence of interrogative words in Mohawk, as in Bulgarian and Romanian:

(ii) Wa-hse-rihwáruk-e' kʌ úhka *tóka*   oh nahótʌ ʌ-ha-hnínu-'?
      FACT-2sS-hear-PUNC Q   who *maybe* what   FUT-MsS-buy-PUNC
      'Did you hear who might buy what?'

Thus, Mohawk seems to have properties of both of the types Rudin distinguishes.

From a theoretical perspective, either setting of Rudin's parameter would be consistent with the structure of Mohawk as developed here. Clearly, there is no problem with moving a second *wh*-phrase to Comp. In fact, there is no reason why a second *wh*-phrase cannot adjoin to IP either, *as long as it gets there by movement*. In this case, it will leave behind a trace, and the principles invoked to rule out quantificational NPs base generated in adjunct position will not apply. As a plausible first approximation, one might conjecture that additional *wh*-phrases may move either to Comp or to IP-adjoined position in Mohawk. These issues deserve further investigation, however.

29. The same is true for Southern Tiwa. However, Donald Frantz (personal communication) has collected some examples of multiple questions in Southern Tiwa in which the second question word does not have to be clause initial. If this is confirmed, it presents a potential problem for this analysis.

30. However, there are head-marking nonconfigurational languages that seem to have *wh*–in situ. One relatively well-studied example is Lakhota. In this language, there is good evidence that so-called question words are simply indefinite NPs in the scope of an interrogative particle. These, then, are derived not by *wh*-movement at LF, but by unselective binding, exactly like the negative constructions in Mohawk discussed in section 2.1.3 (see Bonneau 1992 for this analysis, based on data from Williamson 1984).

In fact, there is no good reason why a truly polysynthetic language could not have this type of construction either, as long as it had overt interrogative particles. This is a possible alternative analysis for constituent questions in Wichita. Question words consist morphologically of an interrogative morpheme *e:* and an indefinite noun root (Rood 1976:11). As such, they are superficially parallel to the negation constructions discussed above. Thus, it is possible that they are structurally parallel as well; if so, then *e:* would be a question particle in the head of CP that cliticizes to the next element—an indefinite word in its scope. The result is equivalent to a standard interrogative interpretation. As usual, the Polysynthesis Parameter puts constraints on interrogative constructions but does not actually determine their structure.

Perhaps also related to this is the problematic case of Ainu. Shibatani (1990:82–83) describes the situation as follows: "The interrogative pronouns . . . tend to occur sentence initially because the subject pronoun is often deleted; but there is no need to move WH-elements to sentence initial position." One example he gives is:

(i) Eani hemanta e-e?
     you what   2sS-eat
     'What do you eat?'

Shibatani does not discuss whether the question words in Ainu bear any systematic similarity to indefinites; if they do, then Bonneau's (1992) analysis of Lakhota could carry over to Ainu as well. Alternatively, the possibility of *wh*–in situ might be a result of Japanese influence, together with the loss in colloquial Ainu of some of the polysynthetic properties of the classical language.

31. I know of no recent analysis of this effect; indeed, it is not even clear how the CED itself is derived in the Minimalist framework of Chomsky 1992. It is rather straightforward to develop an account of the difference between (97)/(98)/(103a) and (102)/(103b) in the Barriers framework of Chomsky 1986a. In that theory, CED reduces to Subjacency: a principle that states that no link of a movement chain can cross more than one barrier. Now the second barrier that is crossed in the bad sentences is an IP that inherits barrierhood from the non–L-marked constituent that it immediately contains. We get the right results if we modify the definition of "barrier by inheritance" such that X is only a barrier by inheritance between Y and its antecedent Z if X is immediately dominated by the same maximal projection as Z. Thus, the lower IP in (102) and (103b) is not a barrier to movement as long as the interrogative phrase moves into the matrix Comp in one step.

32. Certain interrogative elements such as *ka nikáyʌ* 'which' and *to níku* 'how many' seem to be extractable from NPs in Mohawk. However, these are properly analyzed as a type of discontinuous nominal constituent; therefore, a discussion of the facts is deferred until section 4.3.

33. This structure is simplified in certain respects. One is that the overt pronoun actually does not occupy the specifier position of NP but is adjoined to the NP (see chapter 6). However, this detail does not affect the point made here.

34. One consultant does not allow bound readings in these examples either, although three others do. This makes sense if this speaker does not allow parasitic gaps for some reason (this is also true of some speakers of English). For that speaker, the null possessor is unambiguously a pro, and the bound readings are ruled out by weak crossover as before.

35. Kenneth Hale (personal communication) observes that parasitic gaps seem to be possible in possessor positions if and only if that position is agreed with. Thus, they are found in Mohawk and Nahuatl and with kinship terms in Warlpiri, but not with normal possession in Warlpiri. If Hale's conjecture proves correct, it is not clear why this should be so.

36. This judgment was consistently given by one consultant on a variety of occasions, with a variety of sentences. Another consultant has not been able to confirm the judgment, however; she claims to get bound readings even in (120). I cannot account for this difference.

37. These sentences also imply that NP–plus–relative clause cannot be "reconstructed" into the position of the coindexed pro at LF, since this also would make a bound pronoun reading possible. The issue is an interesting one, since reconstruction effects are found in Mohawk in other contexts (see chapters 3 and 6 for discussion).

38. Interesting theoretical questions arise concerning the exact formulation of the Case Filter in (122) and its relationship to the Visibility Condition. In Baker 1991a, I developed ideas of Shlonsky (1987) in which the Case Filter follows from a Visibility Condition that is relevant to both PF and LF (the two interpretative levels; indeed, the only true levels in the conception of Chomsky 1992). Informally, I claim that in order for a phrase to be interpreted at level α it must be in a local configuration with a head that has suitable licensing features at that level. Since the type of interpretation relevant to PF is pronunciation, the PF Case Filter applies only to phonetically overt NPs; since the type of interpretation relevant to LF includes θ-role assignment, all arguments are subject to the LF Case Filter. This has several empirical consequences in English, Hebrew, and Mohawk (see Shlonsky 1987, Baker 1991a, and the references cited therein). I assume a similar frame-

work here, with the difference that the LF Visibility Condition is parameterized, one of its values being the MVC. How exactly this network of principles and concepts can be stated most elegantly so as to cover the widest range of languages remains open to further research.

39. This conclusion only follows if there is no other reason for the subject NP to move to specifier of IP in Mohawk. In Chomsky's theory, the pro subject would have to move in order to be licensed by entering into a specifier–head relationship with a suitable agreement node. However, there is independent evidence that NPs can trigger agreement without being in a specifier–head configuration in Mohawk (see section 5.4). Hence, I propose a different structural condition on the agreement relation in section 5.4 (see also chapter 8).

40. Traditional structuralist accounts of polysynthetic languages did not hesitate to analyze agreement morphemes as filling a given slot in the morphological template of a verb, and then stipulating that that slot was obligatory. However, I assume that the information encoded in this type of template should be derived from more general principles whenever possible. (See section 1.6 for some empirical motivation that these templates can to a large extent be derived in the polysynthetic languages.) It is interesting that the agreement slots seem to be the most common obligatory slots in languages of this type; certainly, agreement morphology is the only completely obligatory affix on the verb in Iroquoian. Finally, even a template theory is unable to account for the pattern of facts in this paragraph without significant additional machinery, including zero morphemes and separate templates for transitive and intransitive verbs.

3

The Licensing of NPs

Now that we have an account of why overt NPs in polysynthetic languages do not appear in argument position, we can address the converse question: Why do they appear in adjoined positions? On an intuitive level, the answer is obvious: NPs appear in adjoined positions because those are the only positions left, given the tacit assumption that all languages must be able to somehow make use of overt NPs. Although this answer is not tautological, it is extremely plausible. The question is an important one in the current context, however, because our purpose is to discover the basic parameters that characterize polysynthetic languages. We have seen that a parameter is required to force NPs out of argument positions. The question, then, is whether another parameter is necessary to welcome them into nonargument positions. Such a parameter might be functionally related to the Polysynthesis Parameter, but it would not necessarily be formally related to it.

Previous work on nonconfigurationality within P&P frameworks has devoted comparatively little attention to this question.[1] Jelinek (1984), in particular, is somewhat vague on this point. She states that overt NPs in Warlpiri are "in apposition" to the clitic pronouns on the verbal auxiliary, drawing a comparison with English sentences such as (1).

(1) She, the doctor, helped them, the patients.

However, it is not clear what theory of apposition Jelinek has in mind. Nor does she push this analysis further to show how it accounts for the properties of the NPs in Warlpiri, beyond the fact that they are optional. Moreover, her account relies on language-particular "linking rules" to match up adjoined NPs with the proper clitic pronouns. In Warlpiri, these rules refer to the morphological case on the adjoined NPs; in other languages, they can refer to word order (Navajo), inverse voice morphology on the verb (Algonquian), switch reference morphology (Choctaw), and so on (Jelinek 1988). The cross-linguistic constraints on these linking rules and their relationship to principles of Universal Grammar (UG) are relatively unexplored. Finally, it seems clear that at least some aspects of these linking rules are language-specific. In Jelinek's system they are, in effect, auxiliary parameters, supplementing the primary parameter that creates head-marking non-configurational languages as a class.

Speas (1990) takes a different view of overt NPs in Warlpiri. She analyzes them as modifiers in the syntax. As such, the R ("reference") θ-role of the head noun of a noun phrase is identified (in the sense of Higginbotham (1985)) with one of the θ-roles of the main verb. This θ-role is subsequently assigned to a pronominal clitic, which is the true argument. There is no equivalent to this kind of structure in English. However, using Higginbotham's proposal that the mechanism of θ-role identification accounts for adjectival and adverbial modification in English, (2) gives a sense of Speas' proposal.[2]

(2) Doctor-like she helped patient-like them.

This proposal does use mechanisms of clear status within UG. However, like Jelinek, Speas does not push her analysis to show that it accounts for other properties of NPs in Warlpiri. Moreover, her analysis attributes a special status to the Case morphemes on nouns in Warlpiri. These are responsible for transforming the noun into a kind of predicate that can undergo θ-identification (similar, perhaps, to the derivational morpheme *like* in English). Since all grammatical Case morphemes in Warlpiri have this property, it should be considered a parameter specific to this type of nonconfigurationality. Finally, it is not clear how this proposal should be generalized to nonconfigurational languages like Mohawk, which do not have comparable Case morphology.

This chapter investigates the properties of adjoined NPs in Mohawk and the other polysynthetic languages in some depth. In particular, I will show that these NPs have the properties of left-dislocated NPs in more familiar languages to a rather fine degree of detail. Thus, the correct English pseudo-equivalent of a Mohawk sentence would be:

(3) The doctor, the patients, she really helped them.

More specifically, Mohawk sentences have the distinctive properties of *clitic left dislocation* (CLLD) in Italian, where these properties differ in certain important respects from those of ordinary left dislocation found in English (Cinque 1990:57–60). This analysis was more or less taken for granted in Baker 1991a, partly justified in Baker 1992b, and alluded to at some points in chapter 2 of the present volume. Now is the time to consider it properly. If it is correct, it means that there is nothing distinctive in this regard about polysynthetic languages. Rather, this type of construction is found throughout the Romance family (Cinque 1990, Dobrovie-Sorin 1990), in Greek (Iatridou 1991), and apparently in Bantu (Bresnan and Mchombo 1987) and Slave (Rice 1989). Indeed, as far as one can tell from the current state of the literature, CLLD constructions are found in every language that allows null pronominals licensed by agreement or clitics. If so, then the licensing principles involved are truly part of UG. The only way in which polysynthetic languages are special is the theoretically trivial fact that they are forced to use the CLLD configuration more often, as a result of the Morphological Visibility Condition (MVC) plus the Case absorption property of agreement. Moreover, the fact that NPs in most polysynthetic languages are not marked with features for number, Case, or definiteness explains why these languages allow a wider range of NPs to be dislocated than, say, the Romance languages do, even though there is no essential difference in the principles governing dislocation.

3.1 Similarities with Clitic Left Dislocation

Cinque (1990:ch. 2) gives an extended discussion of the properties of CLLD constructions in Italian. The essential descriptive properties that he uncovers are the following:

(4) (i)   The dislocated NP is in an adjoined position, typically adjoined to IP.

    (ii) The dislocated NP is coindexed with a null pronominal argument.

    (iii) The dislocated NP must have inherent referential properties.

    (iv) The dislocated NP forms an A-bar chain with the null pronoun.

    (v)   The NP–pronoun relationship does not have other properties of movement.

One important effect of property (iii) was already discussed in section 2.1.3: it implies that nonreferential quantified NPs cannot be in CLLD constructions in Italian. Similarly, such NPs cannot exist in polysynthetic languages at all. Hence, CLLD constructions in Italian and basic clause structures in, say, Mohawk are alike in this regard.[3] In the following sections, I go through the other properties in (4) and show that they hold in Mohawk as well. Data from other polysynthetic languages are also included where they are available.

3.1.1 The Necessity of a Null Pronoun

Consider first property (4ii). This implies that in any structure with an adjoined NP there must be an appropriate null pronoun that can license that NP. This is not a universal requirement: languages such as Japanese and Chinese allow an NP to appear at the beginning of the sentence as long as the sentence can be construed as being "about" the NP in some general, pragmatic way. In (5), examples of this from Japanese (Kuno 1973:67–69) are given.

(5) a. Nihon-wa dansei-ga tanmei   desu.
       Japan-TOP male-NOM short-lived are
       'As for Japan, men have a short life-span.'

    b. Yama-ga   ki-ga   kirei desu.
       mountain-NOM tree-NOM pretty are
       'As for the mountains, the trees are pretty.'

Chomsky (1977) argues that certain English constructions also have this property. Mohawk is clearly not like Japanese in this regard, however, as shown by (6).

(6) a. ?*KÁtsu ne auhá'a te-wak-éka'-s   rabábhot.
       fish   NE most   CIS-1sO-like-HAB bullhead
       'Of fish, I like bullhead the best.'

    b. *ThíkΛ onúta' yó-hskats   ne okwire-shú'a.
       That   hill   NsO-be.pretty NE tree-PL
       'As for that hill, the trees are pretty.'

   c. *Kon-úkwe' w-ʌtóre'   ne atúnhets.
      Fp-person NsS-difficult NE life
      'For women, life is difficult.'

Significantly, a sentence like (6c) becomes grammatical if 'life' is inflected for a third person plural possessor:

(7)   Ukwe-húwe w-ʌtóre' tsi níyot   tsi run-únhe'.
      person-real NsS-hard that it-stand that MpS-be.alive
      'As for Indians, their life is hard.'

An interesting example in this regard is (8), taken from a published text in Akwesasne Mohawk (Bonvillain and Francis 1980:77).

(8)   (?*)Wa-ha-nu'kéla-'   ki kohsátʌs.
      FACT-MsS-suckle-PUNC this horse
      'He (the fox) breast-fed (from) the horse.'

This sentence has a feminine NP adjoined to it. Given certain quirks of the Mohawk agreement paradigm, it is not clear whether the verb *nu'kera* 'breast-feed, suckle' in this example is transitive or not. In fact, for my Kahnawake consultants, it is clearly intransitive:

(9) a. *Owirá'a wa-shako-nu'kéra-'   ro-nistʌ́ha.
        baby   FACT-MsS/FsO-suckle-PUNC his-mother
        'The baby breast-fed (from) his mother.'

    b. Owirá'a wa-ha-nu'kéra-'.
        baby   FACT-MsS-suckle-PUNC
        'The baby breast-fed.'

Significantly, the same consultants consider (8) quite ungrammatical. This is what we predict, since the intransitive verb will not license an object pronoun, and hence there is no pronoun appropriate for licensing *kohsátʌs* 'horse'. If adjoined NPs could be licensed by purely pragmatic factors, one would expect (8) to be grammatical for all speakers. (Presumably, *nu'kela* 'suckle' is actually transitive in Akwesasne Mohawk.[4])

All this is not to say that polysynthetic languages cannot have Japanese-style free topics. Rather, the claim is simply that they need not and that even if they do this does not by itself account for the normal mode of attaching NPs in such languages. One gets the impression from reading texts in the Gunwinjguan languages that free topics are licensed in those languages, although uncertainties about where clause boundaries are make it difficult to know whether this is so. For example, (10) is attested in Mayali (Evans 1991:150), in contrast to the unacceptable (6a) in Mohawk.

(10) Maih na-wu, gunj   na-wu bonj andi-wo,   gunj   andud.
       animal I-DEM kangaroo I-DEM OK 2pS/1sO-give kangaroo then
       'Right, that animal, that kangaroo, give it to me then!'

In fact, I cannot guarantee that such constructions are not possible in Mohawk—only that they are rare at best in texts and were not picked up by my elicitation

techniques. The unmarked case in the polysynthetic languages is clearly for an NP
to be licensed by a pronominal in some argument position.[5]

3.1.2 The NP Is Adjoined

Next we turn to (4i), the claim that the NPs are adjoined to a category, typically
IP. This has several effects in Italian, and similar effects are found in Mohawk.

In order to see the force of this claim, it is helpful to visualize the alternative.
In chapter 2, I established that the NPs must be in nonargument positions, outside
the government domain of the verb and the c-command domain of the subject.
Other than adjoined positions, the only position that would qualify is Comp (specifier of CP), or perhaps the specifier position of some other functional category.[6]
Specifier positions differ from adjoined positions in being fixed and unique. Contemporary X-Bar Theory implies that a given category can have only one specifier
position (Chomsky 1986a, Larson 1988), but it can have many adjoined elements.
It is clear that a single Mohawk clause can have more than one NP attached to it;
indeed, there can be at least three, with no sign of degradation:

(11) a. Sak ye-hyatú-hkw-a'   wa-shakóy-u-'   ne Uwári.
         Sak FsS-write-INSTR-HAB FACT-MsS/FsO-give-PUNC NE Mary
         'Sak gave Mary a pencil.'

      b. Sak wa-shakó-[a]hy-a-nut-e'   sewahyówane ne Uwári.
         Sak FACT-MsS/FsO-fruit-Ø-feed-PUNC apple   NE Mary
         'Sak fed Mary an apple.'

Many examples throughout this work show instances of two NPs attached to a
single clause. More than one noun phrase can be adjoined to the clause in the
other polysynthetic languages as well. In this respect, the polysynthetic languages
are like Italian CLLD, in which more than one constituent can be dislocated in a
single clause (Cinque 1990:58):

(12) Di vestiti, a me, Gianni, in quel negozio, non mi   ce
      clothes   to me Gianni in that shop   not to-me there

      ne   ha mai comprati.
      of-them has ever bought
      'Gianni has never bought me any clothes in that shop.'

On the other hand, questions and true topicalization typically allow no more than
one constituent to be questioned or topicalized in the syntax. This can be attributed
to the fact that these constructions crucially make use of the Comp position, which
is unique for any given clause.[7] Since there is no similar uniqueness condition on
NPs in simple Mohawk sentences, they must not make crucial use of Comp or
similar positions. Rather, they have the freedom of attachment that one expects
from adjunction.

Another difference between CLLD and topicalization in Italian is that topicalization is limited to clauses of particular types. Thus, topicalization is possible in
matrix clauses and a restricted set of CP complements (in particular, "logophoric"
propositional attitude complements). However, it is not possible in other clause

types: complements of other verbs, adjunct clauses, relative clauses, and so on. There are different views about why these restrictions are present; however, it is plausible to assume that (for one reason or another) the unique Comp position is either not present in these contexts or is already used.[8] If this is so, then it follows that topicalization will be impossible. However, CLLD is possible in any clause whatsoever in Italian. In particular, it is possible even in those clause types that do not allow topicalization (Cinque 1990:58). This is what we expect if CLLD is not restricted to a particular base-generated position. NP adjunction in the polysynthetic languages is clearly like CLLD in this respect: overt NPs can appear in clauses of all types, including adjunct clauses, relative clauses, and complements of all kinds. Examples of these are found throughout this book.

The uniqueness of the Comp position also means that different processes making use of Comp will interfere with each other. This is the standard syntactic account of *wh*-island phenomena and "topic islands." At least some speakers of Mohawk respect *wh*-islands, as discussed in section 2.1.4. An example is repeated in (13).[9]

(13) #Oh nahótʌ wa-hse-rihwáruk-e' úhka wa-ha-hnínu-'?
      what   FACT-2sS-hear-PUNC who FACT-MsS-buy-PUNC
      'What did you hear who bought?'

However, if one replaces *úhka* 'who' in the lower clause with an ordinary NP, the sentence becomes acceptable for all speakers:

(14) Oh nahótʌ wa-hse-rihwáruk-e' Sak wa-ha-hnínu-'?
      what   FACT-2sS-hear-PUNC Sak FACT-MsS-buy-PUNC
      'What did you hear Sak bought?'

The deviance of (13) is explained by saying that *úhka* 'who' occupies the lower Comp at S-structure. This forces *oh nahótʌ* 'what' to move directly to the matrix clause, in violation of the Subjacency Condition. The acceptability of (14) shows that *Sak* does not fill the Comp position. Since it is not in argument position either, it must be adjoined to the clause.

The final piece of evidence that NPs are adjoined rather than in Comp (or Comp-like) positions in Mohawk is perhaps the most obvious. Specifiers are part of the X-bar schemata of a language; hence, their order with respect to the sister X′ is generally fixed. By far the most common pattern cross-linguistically is for specifiers to precede heads and complements, and this seems to be the case in Mohawk as well: *wh*-phrases in particular are always initial in the clause that they have scope over, as shown in section 2.1.4:

(15) a. *Wa'-e-hnínu-'   nahótv?
        FACT-FsS-buy-PUNC what
        'What did she buy?'

     b. Nahótv wa'-e-hnínu-'?
        what   FACT-FsS-buy-PUNC
        'What did she buy?'

However, other NPs are not subject to any such restriction in word order:

(16)   a. Wa'-e-hnínu-'   áthere'.
          FACT-FsS-buy-PUNC basket
          'She bought a basket.'

       b. Áthere' wa'-e-hnínu-'.
          basket FACT-FsS-buy-PUNC
          'She bought a basket.'

Again, this implies that these NPs are not in Comp, or any similar specifier position. Rather, they are placed by adjunction, which can, in general, attach a phrase
to either side of the host phrase. This argument also carries over to most of the
other polysynthetic languages (see section 2.1.4 for examples and references).
However, there is some cross-linguistic variation on this point, which I return to
in section 3.3.1.

3.1.3 The NP Is Part of a Chain

Next, I seek to establish property (4iv) by showing that Mohawk NPs, like their
CLLD counterparts in Italian, form an A-bar chain with the pronoun that licenses
them. Chains in P&P theory are sequences of positions that act as though they
constitute a single item for certain linguistic processes, such as θ-role assignment
(Chomsky 1981). The members of such a chain must obey at least three conditions: (1) each member of the sequence c-commands the next member; (2) no
island contains one member but not the previous one (Subjacency); (3) the first
member acts in certain respects as though it were in the position of the last (connectivity). Let us consider each of these properties in turn.

   (i) C-command. The first testable consequence of the claim that dislocated NPs
form a chain with the associated pronoun is that the adjoined NP must c-command
that pronoun. Cinque does not explicitly mention this as a property of CLLD
constructions in Italian, perhaps because he considered it obvious, but all of his
examples have this property.

   Example (17) shows that an NP adjoined to the matrix clause in Mohawk can
be licensed by a pronoun inside a sentential complement. This means that the
licensing relationship does not have to be local in the strictest sense:

(17)   a. Thíkʌ ká'sere' wá'-k-ehr-e'   ní'i se-núhwe'-s kʌ.
          that   car   FACT-1sS-think-IMPF me 2sS-like-HAB Q
          'That car, I thought that you liked it.'

       b. Thíkʌ á'share' wa'-ke-rihwáruk-e' tsi Sak wa-ha-[a]táte-ni-'.
          that knife   FACT-1sS-hear-PUNC that Sak FACT-MsS-REFL-lend-PUNC
          'That knife, I heard that Sak helped himself to it.'

       c. Uwári wa'-k-at-hróri-'   tsi wa'-t-ye-núnyahkw-e'.
          Mary FACT-1sS-SRFL-tell-PUNC that FACT-DUP-FsS-dance-PUNC
          'Mary, I told that she danced.'

Mohawk speakers sometimes find these sentences stylistically marked and therefore less acceptable in pragmatically neutral contexts. In this respect, the sentences
are similar to English topicalization or dislocation. Nevertheless, a wide variety of
examples are acceptable in the appropriate style.

The examples in (17) contrast sharply with those in (18), where the adjoined NP fails to c-command the pronoun that could potentially license it. These are hopelessly bad in any context:

(18) a. *Wa-hi-natahrÁ-'sera-'   ne tsi k-atukáryak-s-kwe'   ne Sak.
         FACT-1sS/MsO-visit-PURP-PUNC because 1sS-hungry-HAB-PAST NE Sak
         'I went to visit him because, Sak, I was hungry.'

     b. *Tsi nikaríhwes Uwári uk-íta'w-e',   wa'-e-kh[w]-úni-'.
         while   Mary FACT/1sO-sleep-PUNC FACT-FsS-food-make-PUNC
         'While, Mary, I slept, she cooked dinner.'

     c. *OhÁtu tsi niyóre ne Uwári s-a'-k-ahtÁti-'
         before   NE Mary ITER-FACT-1sS-leave-PUNC

         wa'-t-ye-núnyahkw-e'.
         FACT-DUP-FsS-dance-PUNC
         'Before, Mary, I went home, she danced.'

There is nothing inherently wrong with having coreference between an NP in an adjunct clause and a pronoun in the matrix clause. Example (19) is minimally different from (18c) and has exactly this interpretation.

(19) OhÁtu tsi niyóre ne Uwári s-a-yu-[a]htÁti-'
     before   NE Mary ITER-FACT-FsS-leave-PUNC

     wa'-t-ye-núnyahkw-e'.
     FACT-DUP-FsS-dance-PUNC
     'Before Mary went home, she danced.'

The difference between (19) and (18c) is that in (19) *Uwári* is licensed by a pronoun inside the adjunct clause that it is attached to, while in (18c) it is not. Thus, although a referential dependency is possible in (18c), that dependency is not sufficient to license the NP in the absence of c-command. The structural difference between the acceptable (17c) and the deviant (18c) is shown in (20).

(20) a.   b.

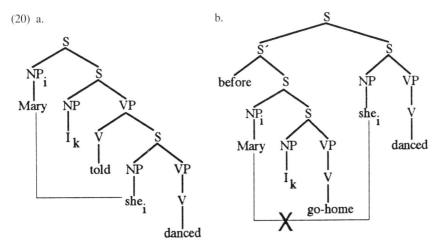

The fact that coreference is not sufficient and that c-command is also necessary suggests that the NP and the licensing pronoun form a chain.

(ii) Island effects. This impression is strengthened by the fact that the relationship between the adjoined NP and the licensing pronoun is sensitive to the presence of some of the standard islands. Cinque (1990:59–60) shows that this is true for CLLD in Italian (see also Iatridou 1991 for Modern Greek). The most striking illustration of this in Mohawk involves adjunct islands: an NP adjoined to a matrix clause is ungrammatical if the only pronoun appropriate for licensing it is inside an adjunct modifier clause. Thus, the sentences in (21) contrast minimally with the grammatical ones in (17), where the embedded clause was a complement of the verb.

(21)   a. *Sósan wa'-t-k-ahsʌ'tho-'   ne tsi   wa-ye-ya'tyénʌ'-ne'.
          Susan FACT-DUP-1sS-cry-PUNC because FACT-FsS-fall-PUNC
          'Susan, I cried because she fell down.'

       b. *John wa'-k-hnekíra-'   ne cáwhe ohʌtu tsi niyóre
          John FACT-1sS-drink-PUNC NE coffee before

          wá-hra-w-e'.
          FACT-MsS-arrive-PUNC
          'John, I drank the coffee before he arrived.'

       c. *Uwári wa'-k-ate-rórok-e'   tsi nikaríhwes
          Mary FACT-1sS-SRFL-watch-PUNC while

          wa'-t-ye-núnyahkw-e'.
          FACT-DUP-FsS-dance-PUNC
          'Mary, I watched while she danced.'

Similarly, NPs generally cannot be licensed by a pronoun inside a relative clause unless they themselves are in the relative clause. Thus, the following examples are bad:

(22)   a. ?*Kíkʌ áhta' wa-hse-ríyo-'   ne érhar ne wa'-ka-nʌsko-'.
          This shoe FACT-2sS/ZsO-kill-PUNC NE dog NE FACT-ZsS-steal-PUNC
          'This shoe, you killed the dog that stole it.'

       b. ?*Uwári s-a'-ke-tshʌri-'   ne yako-hwist-ʌty-u.
          Mary ITER-FACT-1sS-find-PUNC NE FsO-money-lose-STAT
          'Mary, I found the money that she lost.'

       c. ?*Ne thíkʌ áthere' khe-yʌtéri-Ø   ne yakó-hs-u.
          NE that   basket 1sS/FsO-know-STAT NE FsO-make-STAT
          'That basket, I know the one who made.'

These show that Mohawk dislocation respects at least one subcase of the Complex NP Constraint of Ross 1967. These are the only "strong" islands that can be tested in Mohawk, since the language does not have noun complement structures (see chapter 6) or sentential subjects (see section 10.1.1).[10] Nevertheless, the evidence that is available is sufficient to show that the NP–pro relationship is subject to some form of Subjacency.

Once again, ordinary coreference is not restricted in this way. It is perfectly possible for an NP adjoined to the matrix clause to be coreferential with a pronoun inside an adjunct clause:

(23) Sósan wa'-t-yu-[a]hsʌ'tho-'   ne tsi   wa-ye-ya'tyénʌ'-ne'.
       Susan FACT-DUP-FsS-cry-PUNC because FACT-FsS-fall-PUNC
       '*Susan, she* cried because *she* fell down.'

Thus, coreference in itself is not sufficient to license the NPs in (21); a chain relationship is apparently required. Since chains are not allowed to cross islands, the examples in (21) and (22) are ungrammatical.

Evans (1991:339) gives some evidence that suggests that Mayali is like Mohawk in this respect. In particular, he cites the following example:

(24) . . . wakkidj nungga ba-djare-ni   ba-m-wam
         fishing   he   3sS-want-PAST/IMPF 3sS-CIS-go/PAST/PERF

       ngadburrung.
       brother
       '. . . he wanted to come fishing, my brother.'

Here the NP *wakkidj* 'fishing' is a purpose adjunct associated with the embedded verb *wam* 'go'; nevertheless, it is adjoined to the matrix clause headed by *djare* 'want'. Moreover, Evans presents this example as evidence that some clauses in Mayali are true syntactic complements of the matrix verb. He clearly presupposes that a word order like that in (24) would not be possible if the embedded clause were an adjunct, although he does not present an actual ungrammatical sentence. If this is correct, then the licensing of adjoined NPs in Mayali is subject to the adjunct island effect, just as in Mohawk. Unfortunately, relevant data from other polysynthetic languages are not available.[11]

(iii) Connectivity. The last characteristic property of chains that Cinque 1990 demonstrates for CLLD constructions is the so-called connectivity effect: dislocated NPs in Italian act as though they occupied the position of the licensing pronoun for the purposes of binding and anaphora. Thus, Cinque (1990:59) points to the following contrast:

(25) a. A lei/*se stessa, Maria dice che non ci pensiamo mai
           'of her/herself, Maria says that (we) not-there-think ever'

      b. A ?*lei/se stessa, Maria non ci pensa
           'of her/herself Maria not-there-thinks'

The position of the dislocated element is the same in both (25a) and (25b), yet a pronominal is appropriate in one case and a reflexive in the other. Clearly, this is determined neither by the dislocated position, nor by its direct relationship to the antecedent *Maria,* but by the position associated with the licensing clitic *ci.* In (25a), *ci* is in a different clause from *Maria,* so a pronominal is needed; in (25b), *ci* is in the same clause as *Maria,* so a reflexive is called for. Thus, the anaphoric properties of the dislocated element are evaluated as if that element were "reconstructed" into the position governed by the clitic. Crucially, this effect is a property of chain relationships only; it is not found with control or with ordinary pronominal coreference (Barss 1986).

The contrast in (25) cannot be directly replicated in Mohawk, because there are no overt NP anaphors in the language (see section 2.1.2). Thus, the most familiar kind of connectivity effects are simply untestable. Nevertheless, Mohawk does permit a similar type of connectivity. In order to see this, we need to make some-thing of an excursus into the properties of ellipsis and "sloppy identity."

To begin with, consider the following English examples, inspired by Reinhart 1983b:

(26) a. John fed his dog and Peter did, too.

     b. His dog bit John, and Peter, too.

Even restricting attention to readings where the possessive pronoun refers to the subject in the first clause, (26a) is ambiguous: it can be understood as meaning that Peter fed John's dog, or that Peter fed his own dog. This second reading is called the *sloppy identity* reading, familiar from Ross 1967, Sag 1976, Williams 1977, and much recent work. Reinhart (1983a, 1983b) points out that sentences like (26b) do not have a similar ambiguity: (26b) has only the "strict" reading in which Peter was bitten by the same dog as John (i.e., by John's dog, if that is how the first clause is understood). Reinhart argues that this kind of difference can be explained by placing a c-command condition on bound variable interpreta-tions. Both sentences allow the position of *John* to be replaced by a variable, making ellipsis interpretation possible in the first place. In (26a), this primary variable c-commands the possessive pronoun, allowing that pronoun to be replaced by a second instance of the same variable. In (26b), however, the primary variable is in object position, and does not c-command the possessive pronoun inside the subject. Therefore, this pronoun cannot be replaced by a second instance of the variable, and only a strict reading is found. In this way, a parallelism is uncovered between the sloppy identity paradigm and other instances of bound variable anaph-ora, such as standard cases of weak crossover with quantified NPs.

In (27), potential cases of sloppy identity are given in Mohawk. In (27a), the subject and the possessor of the object are coreferential, and the elliptical conjunct can have the sloppy identity interpretation (reading (iii)), among others. In (27b), on the other hand, the object and the possessor of the subject are coreferential; in this situation the elliptical conjunct can only have one of the two strict interpreta-tions.[12]

(27) a. Sak rao-nekóta' wa-ha-kushráhrho-'   tánu Tyer óni.
       Jim MsP-ladder FACT-MsS/NsO-paint-PUNC and Peter too
       'Jim painted his (Jim's) ladder and. . . .'
         (i) '. . . Jim painted Peter's ladder, too.'
         (ii) '. . . Peter painted Jim's ladder, too.'
         (iii) '. . . Peter painted Peter's ladder, too.'

     b. Sak rao-nekóta' wa'-t-ho-ya'tórarak-e'   tánu' Tyer óni.
       Jim MsP-ladder FACT-DUP-NsS/MsO-hit-PUNC and   Peter too
       'His (Jim's) ladder fell on Jim and. . . .'
         (i) '. . . Jim's ladder fell on Peter, too.'
         (ii) '. . . Peter's ladder fell on Jim, too.'
         (iii) '. . . ?/*Peter's ladder fell on Peter, too.'

Thus, the subject–object asymmetry that Reinhart (1983a, 1983b) discusses for English is also found in Mohawk: the subject can bind a pronoun inside the object in both languages, but not vice versa. Example (28) gives a second pair illustrating the same contrast.

(28) a. Sak rao-[i]tshénʌ érhar wa-hó-nut-e'   tánu' Tyer óni.
          Jim MsP-pet   dog FACT-MsS/MsO-feed-PUNC and Peter too
          'Jim$_i$ fed his$_i$ pet dog and Peter$_k$ (fed his$_{i,k}$ dog), too.'

      b. Sak rao-[i]tshénʌ érhar wa-ho-kári-'   tánu' Tyer óni.
          Jim MsP-pet   dog FACT-MsS/MsO-bite-PUNC and Peter too
          'Jim's$_i$ pet dog bit him$_i$ and (his$_{i,*k}$ dog bit) Peter$_k$, too.'

That Mohawk is similar to English in this respect is somewhat strange when one takes into account the structural differences between the two languages. Given that NPs in Mohawk are not in their argument positions but rather are adjoined to the clause, (27a) and (27b) have exactly the same structure, apart from indexing, as shown in (29a) and (29b), respectively.

(29) a.

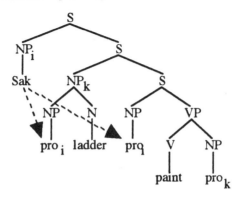

Sloppy Interpretation OK

      b.

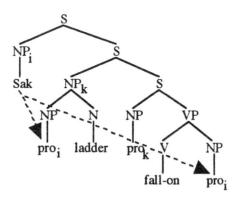

Sloppy Interpretation not OK

Surprisingly, *Sak* can bind a second variable in the possessor position of NP$_k$ in (29a) but not in (29b), even though it c-commands NP$_k$ in both structures. It is not immediately obvious why this should be so, given Reinhart's (1983a, 1983b) approach to sloppy identity.

In fact, there is nothing wrong with either pro in (29b) being a variable bound by *Sak*. Thus, the object pro becomes a variable in reading (i) of the ellipsis in (27b), while the possessive pro becomes a variable in reading (ii). Example (30) shows how the LFs could be derived from the S-structure in (29b) using relatively standard techniques of lambda insertion and copying.[13]

(30)   a. Jim_i [pro_i ladder]$_k$ [pro_k fall-on pro_i] and $Peter_n$ too.
                       ↓ lambda insertion
             Jim_i (λx ([pro_i ladder]$_k$ [pro_k fall-on pro_x])) and $Peter_n$ too.
                       ↓ copying
             Jim_i (λx ([pro_i ladder]$_k$ [pro_k fall-on pro_x]))
             and $Peter_n$ (λx ([pro_i ladder]$_k$ [pro_k fall-on pro_x])) too. $\Big\}$ LF

      b. Jim_i [pro_i ladder]$_k$ [pro_k fall-on pro_i] and $Peter_n$ too.
                       ↓ lambda insertion
             Jim_i (λx ([pro_x ladder]$_k$ [pro_k fall-on pro_i])) and $Peter_n$ too.
                       ↓ copying
             Jim_i (λx ([pro_x ladder]$_k$ [pro_k fall-on pro_i]))
             and $Peter_n$ (λx ([pro_x ladder]$_k$ [pro_k fall-on pro_i])) too. $\Big\}$ LF

The two interpretations follow from a choice of which instance of i is chosen to be the variable bound by the lambda operator when it is inserted. Thus, the problem with the unavailable third interpretation of (27b) must be that the lambda operator is not allowed to bind both pro's at once. This is presumably a special case of Koopman and Sportiche's (1981) Bijection Principle, which requires that operators and primary variables be in a one-to-one correspondence. This, then, blocks the sloppy identity interpretation, where there are two instances of the same bound variable.

Now we return to (29a) and ask why the third (sloppy) interpretation is possible here. Presumably, the lambda operator associated with *Sak* cannot directly bind both the subject of the verb and the possessor of the noun in this structure either. Therefore, there must be some kind of bound anaphora relationship between the pro's that allows one to become a variable identical to the other. However, neither pro c-commands the other, which is the necessary structural condition for a relationship of bound anaphora in Reinhart's system.

This internal contradiction can be resolved if we assume that adjoined NPs in Mohawk can indeed "reconstruct," so that they occupy (or act as though they occupy) the position of the pro's they are coindexed with. In (29a), the subject pro c-commands the possessor of the reconstructed object, as required. Similar techniques do not give a sloppy interpretation for (29b), however, since the object pro does not c-command the possessor, even if the NP containing the possessor is reconstructed into the subject position. These structural relationships are summarized in (31). I conclude that Mohawk sloppy identity works the same way as English sloppy identity, in spite of the structural differences between the two languages, because the relationship between the adjoined NP and the pro permits connectivity (reconstruction) effects. Thus, NP adjunction in Mohawk is similar to the CLLD construction in Italian in this respect as well.

For concreteness, I adopt a representational approach to connectivity along the lines of Barss (1986) and Roberts (1984), rather than a derivational approach in

(31) a.

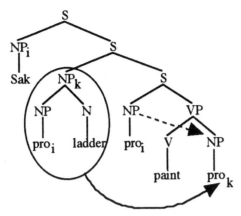

Sloppy Interpretation OK

b.

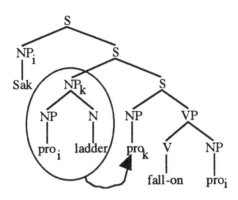

Sloppy Interpretation not OK

which the adjoined NP actually appears in the argument position at some level (see Baker, to appear b). The following condition, inspired by Barss (1986) and Roberts (1984), is sufficient for current purposes: [14]

(32)   Replace a pronoun or anaphor α with a variable associated with NP β only if there exists a series of nodes $(\gamma_1, \ldots, \gamma_n)$ such that:
   (i) $\alpha = \gamma_1$
   (ii) γ_n immediately dominates β
   (iii) for $1 < i < n$, either γ_{i+1} immediately dominates γ_i OR
         (γ_i, γ_{i+1}) is a link of a well-formed chain.

This is essentially a restatement of Reinhart's c-command condition, with the addition of the second disjunct in (iii), which allows a moved or dislocated phrase to count as being in the position it is associated with. This clause stipulates that only chain relationships are sufficient to extend binding domains (Barss 1986); hence, the connectivity effects in Mohawk show that a chain is formed between the adjoined NP and its licensing pronoun.

It is worth emphasizing that this analysis of sentences like (27) and (28) makes crucial use of the assumption that Mohawk is "configurational" in the sense that the subject argument position, c-commands the object argument position but not vice versa. I have assumed this to be true throughout, but there has been little evidence for the assumption because the primary focus has been overt NPs. Since these are never in the true argument position, their properties give little information about where the true argument positions are. When considering connectivity effects, however, the exact locations of the argument positions become very relevant. In exactly this situation, English-like subject–object asymmetries appear. This strongly suggests that a fundamental asymmetry between subjects and objects is part of innate Universal Grammar.

All this being said, there is another type of connectivity that one would expect to find in Mohawk but does not, namely reconstruction for purposes of Condition C. Recall from section 2.1.1 that a name contained in the apparent object (e.g., as its possessor) can be coreferential with a pronominal subject in Mohawk. One such example is repeated here:

(33)   Wa'-e-ratsú-ko-'   thíkʌ Uwári ako-[a]tyá'tawi.
       FACT-FsS-tear-REV-PUNC that   Mary FsP-dress
       '*She* tore that dress of *Mary's*.' (coreference OK)

A similar coreference is forbidden in English by Condition C. This was interpreted as evidence that NPs are dislocated in Mohawk to a position where they are not c-commanded by the (null) subject pronoun. This cannot be the whole answer, however, because when a possessed object is dislocated in the Romance languages, its possessor still cannot be understood as being coreferential with the subject pronoun. An example from Spanish is:

(34)   [$_{NP}$ El libro de Juan], lo perdió.
       'Juan's$_k$ book, he$_{i,*k}$ lost it.'

The same judgment is found in comparable Italian sentences (Luigi Rizzi, personal communication). Thus, (34) is another type of example that falls under Cinque's (1990) observation that CLLD shows connectivity effects, where the dislocated NP acts as though it occupies the argument position. However, this particular effect does not carry over to Mohawk for some reason. The solution to this problem will be deferred until section 6.2, where I will show that it is because the internal structure of possessed NPs in Mohawk is quite different from that in Spanish or Italian.

3.1.4 The NP Is Not Moved

The final property of CLLD constructions to be considered is (4v): The NP–pronoun relationship does not have the properties of movement, where those are distinct from those of a chain. Cinque (1990) argues for this at considerable length; indeed, it is crucial to his claim regarding the theoretical importance of CLLD constructions. Most of his arguments make use of properties that are highly specific to Italian and have no known correlates in Mohawk (Aux-to-Comp constructions, exceptional assignment of nominative Case, *ne*-cliticization, and so on). However, one of his arguments can be replicated in the context of the sloppy identity facts just presented. Thus, Cinque points out that CLLD chains differ from

other A-bar chains in Italian in that they do not license parasitic gaps (1990:60–
63). In section 2.1.6, I argued that parasitic gaps are found in Mohawk in interrogative constructions like (35).

(35) Úhka$_i$ [$_S$[$_{NPk}$ e$_i$ akó-skare'] [$_S$ pro$_k$ wa-shako-hranúhs-a-ya'k-e' t$_i$]]
     who   FsP-friend   FACT-MsS/FsO-face-Ø-hit-PUNC
     'Who did her boyfriend slap?'
     (which x, x a person, x's boyfriend slapped x)

Here, the interrogative phrase can be interpreted as binding both the object of the
verb and the possessor of the dislocated subject. If the possessor of the dislocated
subject NP is an overt pronoun, it cannot be interpreted as bound by *úhka*, an
instance of the weak crossover effect. If the empty possessor were a pro in (35),
a bound interpretation would be barred for the same reason. The conclusion was
that e$_i$ is not pro, but rather a parasitic gap. Now, compare this construction with
the minimally different (27b), repeated here as (36).

(36) Sak$_i$ [$_S$[$_{NPk}$ e$_i$ rao-nekóta'] [$_S$ pro$_k$ wa'-t-ho-ya'torárak-e' pro$_i$]]
     Jim   MsP-ladder   FACT-DUP-NsS/MsO-hit-PUNC
     'His (Jim's) ladder fell on Jim.'
     ≠ Jim (λ x (x's ladder fell-on x))

The two structures are nearly identical, except that the empty category in object
position in (36) is a pro, rather than a *wh*-trace. Now, suppose that e$_i$ in the
possessor position in (36) could be a parasitic gap, like the corresponding category
in (35). Then the Weak Crossover Condition is not relevant, and a bound reading
of the possessor would again be available. This would lead to a sloppy interpretation of an elliptical second clause conjoined with (36). However, we saw in the
previous section that such a sloppy interpretation is not found. Thus, we may
conclude that e$_i$ in (36) cannot be a parasitic gap. This, in turn, implies that the
referential NP–pro$_i$ relationship in (36) is not completely comparable to the *wh*-
phrase–t$_i$ relationship in (35). Both are A-bar chains, but only the latter is formed
by movement and can thereby license a parasitic gap.

    Recall also that *wh*-movement in Mohawk is sensitive to *wh*-islands, whereas
the dislocation of referential NPs is not (see fn. 10). This also supports the claim
that dislocated NPs are not moved from the argument position.

3.1.5 The Adjunct Licensing Condition

The preceding sections have shown that adjoined NPs in Mohawk have all the
essential characteristics of CLLD NPs in Romance languages, even down to the
subtle similarities and differences between these and *wh*-constructions. CLLD constructions seem to be available in any language that allows null pronouns, including languages that are clearly configurational. Mohawk allows null pronouns, and
therefore it is entirely expected that NPs adjoined to the clause would be found in
Mohawk, with the properties detailed earlier. We may tentatively conclude that no
addendum to the basic Polysynthesis Parameter is required in this domain.

    Before going on, it is useful to state in more formal terms the conditions under
which a phrase generated in an adjoined position is licensed. In formulating these

conditions I follow Cinque 1990 rather closely, partly for ease of exposition and partly to emphasize the similarity between NP licensing in Mohawk and dislocation in Italian. In fact, the theory is little more than a terse recapitulation of the properties that have already been enumerated.

The fundamental condition is stated very simply in (37).[15]

(37)   *The Adjunct Licensing Condition* (ALC; preliminary form)
       An argument-type phrase XP generated in adjoined position is licensed if and only
       if it forms a chain with a unique null pronominal in an argument position.

Among other things, this captures the facts in sections 3.1.1 and 3.1.2. Apparently, it is crucial that the licensing pronominal be an empty category, given Cinque's (1990) evidence that CLLD has chainlike properties but ordinary left dislocation does not. Why this difference should exist between null and overt pronouns warrants an explanation, but I do not have one to offer here. The ALC will be refined somewhat in chapters 4 and 7, but the essential idea will remain intact.

Of course, the ALC means little apart from a characterization of what chains are and how they are formed. As mentioned before, the basic intuition behind the notion of a chain is that it is an abstract, discontinuous representation of an argument. It is important to Cinque's system that chains can be formed not only by moving something from one position to another but by relating two base-generated positions. The conditions under which this is possible can be stated as in (38).

(38)   *The Chain Condition*
       X and Y may constitute a chain only if:
       (i)   X c-commands Y.
       (ii)   X and Y are coindexed.
       (iii) There is no barrier containing Y but not X.
       (iv)   X and Y are nondistinct in morphosyntactic features (i.e., category, person,
              number, gender, Case, etc.)

The c-command clause used in (i) is familiar and has already been defined; it accounts for the first set of facts in section 3.1.3. Condition (ii) indicates that the two elements must share the same referential index. At least in the case of base-generated structures, this presupposes that the adjoined NP must be inherently capable of bearing a referential index. In the theory presented in Rizzi 1990 and Cinque 1990, this means that pure quantifiers, most interrogative phrases, and perhaps idiom chunks cannot be licensed by (37), accounting for the facts in sections 2.1.3 and 2.1.4. Exactly what it means for two elements to be *co*indexed will be discussed in section 3.3.1. Condition (iv) is quite standard and seems innocuous enough, but its exact formulation has consequences. First of all, it states that the members of a chain must share major category features. The ALC says that a base-generated phrase must form a chain with a pronominal, and pronominals are inherently of category NP (or DP); hence, (37iv) implies that only NPs can be dislocated. This seems to be true, at least for Mohawk (see section 2.1.1 for clauses and 9.2.2 for PPs). The implications of (37iv) with respect to person, number, gender, and Case features are discussed in section 3.3.

Condition (37iii) is perhaps the least familiar part of the chain condition. Essentially, it says that the links of a chain are subject to Subjacency, a type of locality condition. In this respect, it is perfectly standard (Chomsky 1981, Chomsky 1986a). However, the format of the condition has been adjusted to fit with the assumption that some chains are base generated and thus unable to take advantage of the possibility of successive-cyclic movement. Cinque (1990:42) argues for the rather elegant definition of barrier given in (39).

(39)   Every maximal projection that fails to be selected in the canonical direction by a category nondistinct from [+ V] is a barrier for binding.

In Mohawk, the major type of islands that we need to be concerned with are adjunct phrases and relative clauses. According to (39), these are barriers because they are, almost by definition, maximal projections that are not selected by any category. Hence, the combination of (37), (38iii), and (39) explains the data given in example (21) through (24) in section 3.1.3. Beyond this, the notion of Subjacency is not crucial for anything that follows in this volume. (The interested reader is referred to Cinque 1990:ch. 1 for further details.)

   The last matter to be addressed in making these principles explicit is the question of where the ALC applies. In earlier versions of P&P theory, the obvious answer would have been S-structure; this is what I assumed in Baker 1992b and Baker, to appear b. The primary reason for this choice was that the bounding condition in (38) was thought to hold of S-structure dependencies but not LF dependencies, following Huang (1982) and Chomsky (1986a), among others. However, the issue is now less obvious, given Chomsky's (1992) conjecture that S-structure does not exist as a level where conditions can apply. In this newer framework, it is probably best to build (37) and (38) into the procedure that builds the phrase marker in the first place. Thus, Chomsky assumes a type of generalized transformation in which a syntactic structure is formed from the bottom up by combining well-formed phrases in accordance with some very simple rules. When, in the midst of this process, one has constructed, say, a well-formed IP, one has (in Mohawk and Italian) the option of combining that IP with a well-formed NP to create a new IP. This would be the modern equivalent of base-generated adjunction. The ALC could then be understood as a condition on the application of this type of generalized transformation. This is consistent with the partial theory of island phenomena sketched in Chomsky and Lasnik 1993:546–547 and Chomsky 1992, where the licitness of the movement is marked (by the mechanism of γ-marking) at the point where the movement is performed. Alternatively, the ALC could simply hold at LF, where it would be essentially a corollary of the Principle of Full Interpretation (a type of Economy of Representation in Chomsky 1992). Although I will tentatively assume the solution based on generalized transformations, the issue is independent of most of the material covered in this book.

3.2 Differences: I. Possible Adjunction Sites

Before we can accept with confidence the conclusion that NPs in polysynthetic languages are licensed by the same principles as dislocated NPs in Romance languages, there are some apparent differences between the two that must be sorted out. If these differences prove to be substantial, then further parameterization might be needed after all. For the most part, I believe that the differences are actually rather minor; however, there are a few topics that require further research. This general topic can be broken down into two parts: this section concentrates on issues of exactly where in a syntactic structure the dislocated NP can appear; the next section takes up issues concerning the morphosyntactic features of the dislocated NP.

3.2.1 *Left Adjunction vs. Right Adjunction*

The first and most obvious difference is that CLLD is, as its name suggests, *left* dislocation. The NP in CLLD constructions can only be adjoined to the left of the clause, whereas in Mohawk the NP can be adjoined to either side, as we have seen throughout. In fact, it is not clear whether this is a substantive difference or whether it is merely a terminological one. Clearly, if an NP were adjoined to the right of a clause in a Romance language, it would not be an instance of Clitic *Left* Dislocation. However, Romance languages do, in fact, allow right dislocation; (40) is a French example.

(40)   Il est parti, Jean.
        'He is gone, Jean.'

This construction has not attracted as much attention as CLLD in the literature because it is typically clause bound; hence it is not interesting from the point of view of island constraints and similar phenomena. It is not entirely clear, at least to me, whether the superficial differences between CLLD and right dislocation follow from independent principles, or whether they must be distinguished as two inherently different constructions, as is assumed in most work. In part, this is because of the rarity in the Romance languages of right-branching constructions, which are crucial to determining the locality conditions on dislocation.

   Indeed, similar problems arise in evaluating right adjunction in Mohawk. The earlier examples in (17) show that left adjunction is not clause bound in Mohawk. Suppose that we wanted to show that right adjunction was not clause bound as well. One can certainly find sentences like (41) in which an NP thematically associated with the lower clause is attached to the right periphery.

(41)   Sak í-hr-ehr-e'   ruwa-núhwe'-s   ne Uwári.
        Sak Ø-MsS-think-IMPF FsS/MsO-like-HAB NE Mary
        'Sak think that she likes him, Mary.'

The problem, of course, is that it is not easy to know whether the NP in question is attached to the right edge of the matrix clause or the right edge of the embedded clause. Nor can one put an unambiguously matrix clause element between the NP and the rest of its clause and thus clarify the position of the NP. The reason is that matrix clause elements such as adverbs never naturally follow a complement clause in Mohawk. An entirely similar effect is found in English. For example, it is difficult to interpret *yesterday* in (42) as modifying only the matrix clause.

(42) Mary said that Susan won an essay contest (??last week) yesterday.

This is probably a result of perceptual factors and/or the inherent "heaviness" of clauses.

Crucial data would be available if the complement clause preceded the verb; then we could see if an NP associated with that clause could appear to the right of the matrix verb. Such sentences would be exact mirror images of the sentences in (17):

(43) *Ruwa-núhwe'-s   í-hr-ehr-e'   ne Uwári.
      FsS/MsO-like-HAB Ø-MsS-think-IMPF NE Mary
      'He thinks she likes him, Mary.'

However, at this point, the free word order of Mohawk betrays us: complement clauses overwhelmingly follow the matrix verb:

(44) a. *(Tsi) Uwári ruwa-núhwe'-s   í-hr-ehr-e'.
          that Mary FsS/MsO-like-HAB Ø-MsS-think-IMPF
          'He thinks Mary likes him.'

     b. *Ro-nuhwáktani   wak-ateryÁtar-e'
          MsO-be.sick/STAT 1sO-know-STAT
          'I know that he is sick.'

     c. #Ra-[a]tukáryak-s   wa-hak-hróri-'.
          MsS-be.hungry-HAB FACT-MsS/1sO-tell-PUNC
          'He told me that he was hungry.'
          (OK as: 'The one who is hungry told me.')

This is the one strong instance of superficially fixed word order between a head and its argument in Mohawk.[16] Thus, test sentences such as (43) are not accepted for an independent reason.

Adjunct clauses, unlike complement clauses, do appear readily before the matrix verb. NPs associated with such a constituent cannot be adjoined to the right of the matrix verb:

(45) Tsi nikaríhwes yako-[a]terunót-e', wa'-k-hnekirÁ-ha-'
      while   FsO-sing-STAT   FACT-1sS-drink-PURP-PUNC

     (*ne Uwári).
     NE Mary
     'While *she* was singing, I went to get a drink, *Mary.*'

However, this tells us little, because we know that even left dislocation out of an adjunct is impossible, because of Subjacency (cf. (21)). Thus, circumstances conspire to make the bounding properties of right adjunction almost untestable.

One might also wonder whether there is any semantic or pragmatic difference between right adjunction and left adjunction in Mohawk. Mithun (1987) argues that there is such a difference in the related language Cayuga. NPs after the verb in Cayuga tend to be interpreted as definite or "less newsworthy" information. They typically repeat some referent that is already mentioned or implied in the discourse and are included to avoid unclearness or ambiguity. On the other hand, NPs before the verb tend to be interpreted as "more newsworthy" information.

This includes indefinites, which introduce a new participant into the speech situation, as well as changes of topic or contrastive information. My analysis of texts and elicited examples confirm that this pattern is typical of Mohawk as well. However, these observations are tendencies only; they fall short of being grammatical principles with predictive power. Thus, Chamorro (1992) shows that when one presents a Mohawk speaker with a sentence in isolation, both preverbal and postverbal NPs are ambiguous between a definite and indefinite interpretation. Significantly, this freedom of order is maintained even when the sentences are embedded in a context that makes it clear whether the NP in question is definite or not. Some illustrative examples are (Chamorro 1992:37, 53, 59–60):

(46) a. Sak wa-ha-tshΛri-'   ne á'share'.
         Sak FACT-MsS-find-PUNC NE knife
         'Sak found the/a knife.'

      b. Sak á'share' wa-ha-tshΛri-'.
         Sak knife   FACT-MsS-find-PUNC
         'Sak found the/a knife.'

(47) a. Tóka ne yenΛstahérha' t-Λ-há-yΛ-'   ne rúkwe'
         if   NE bingo   DUP-FUT-MsS-play-PUNC NE man

         tyótku te-ha-atΛtsha-s.
         always DUP-MsS-win-HAB
         'If the/a man plays bingo he always wins.'

      b. Tóka ne rúkwe' t-Λ-há-yΛ-'   ne yenΛstahérha'
         if   NE man   DUP-FUT-MsS-play-PUNC NE bingo

         tyótku te-ha-[a]tΛtsha-s.
         always DUP-MsS-win-HAB.
         'If the/a man plays bingo he always wins.'

Thus, while there are statistical tendencies, perhaps due to stylistics, there seems to be no firm grammatical difference between adjunction on the left and adjunction on the right in Mohawk in this respect either. Rather, we must admit that word order in Mohawk really is free to a significant degree. (See Chamorro 1992 for further evidence and discussion.)

It is also worth pointing out in this connection that Bresnan and Mchombo's (1987) study of Chichewa shows clearly that dislocated objects can attach to either side of the clause in that language. Their work pays explicit attention to discourse functions of various constructions, but they do not identify any difference of function between right and left adjunction. Rather, both are "topics" in their system (1987:745–746).

On balance then we have found no solid evidence to distinguish left adjunction from right adjunction in Mohawk, or to distinguish either from dislocation in Romance languages. Therefore, I tentatively assume that these are all instances of the same, basic UG phenomenon. This must remain subject to revision, however, if better evidence concerning right dislocation becomes available.

All this being said, it may be necessary to allow for some degree of parameterization in adjunction direction when the domain of inquiry is extended to other polysynthetic languages. Word order in the Gunwinjguan languages is as free as it is in Mohawk (Evans 1991:299–302, Heath 1984:509–513); it also seems to be quite free in Southern Tiwa (Donald Frantz, personal communication) and Chukchee, although the issue has not been studied in as much depth in those languages. Ainu, however, is described as an SOV language with OSV orders also being possible in some circumstances (Shibatani 1990:23):

(48) a. Kamuy aynu   rayke.   SOV
        bear   person kill
        'The bear killed the man.'

     b. Amam totto   esose   wa. . . .   OSV
        rice   mother borrow and
        'Mother borrowed rice and. . . .'

Other word orders are apparently not attested. If Ainu is otherwise syntactically similar to Mohawk, then this fact can be captured by stipulating that material can only be adjoined to the left side of the clause in this language. This would be a secondary parameter relevant to polysynthetic languages, albeit a rather superficial one. Moreover, this parameter should have consequences beyond the specific configurationality effects that we have been studying: for example, it predicts that adverbs, adjunct clauses, and other modifiers will appear only before the main verb in this type of language. This is correct (Shibatani 1990:80, 21):

(49) a. Tunas ipe wa tunas   mokor wa tunas   hopuni!
        quickly eat and quickly sleep and quickly get-up
        'Eat quickly, sleep quickly, and get up quickly!'

     b. E-eh   kusu   anekiroro-an.
        2sS-come because happy-1sS
        'Because you came, I am happy.'

In this way Ainu differs from Mohawk, where adjunct clauses can precede or follow the matrix clause.

Some polysynthetic languages may also have a bias concerning the direction of adjunction, even though it is not a strict condition. For example, Watkins (1984:204–208) states that the most neutral word order in Kiowa is (in my terms) SOV, and that "Kiowa is thus a verb-final language typologically but not strictly so." This might indicate that adjunction is on the left in Kiowa, as in Ainu. However, Watkins goes on to describe situations in which an NP may follow the verb that sound very much like Mithun's (1987) description of when NPs come late in the sentence in Cayuga. Thus, it is not clear whether there is a real grammatical difference between Iroquoian and Kiowa or not. Similarly, Rood (1976:197–199) alludes to a preference for verb-final orders in Wichita and states that verb-initial orders with two NPs after the verb are unattested in his data. Such orders are statistically rare in Mohawk, too, although they are possible.

Classical Nahuatl raises the same issues as Kiowa, only in reverse. Launey (1981:35–36) reports that in classical Nahuatl NPs typically follow the verb in neutral contexts. This might mean that NPs can be adjoined only on the right.[17] However, one NP and sometimes more can appear before the verb when the NP or NPs take on what Launey calls "thématisation." The result is that, again, a fairly wide range of word orders is found and it is not clear to what degree there is a grammatical difference at work. Indeed, Andrews (1975:204) emphasizes the freedom of word order in Nahuatl and suggests that there are no syntactic constraints on it. Clearly, more detailed comparative work is needed before we can draw firm conclusions about whether polysynthetic languages differ among themselves concerning which side of the clause NPs adjoin to.

3.2.2 The Category of the Adjoined-to Phrase

Next, let us consider in more detail exactly what categories the dislocated NP can adjoin to. I have assumed throughout that the most typical adjunction site is IP (= S) in both the Romance and the polysynthetic languages. However, further data suggest that adjunction to CP is also possible in Mohawk. The particle *tsi* seems to be a complementizer that appears before some sentential complements. NPs associated with the lower clause can show up either to the right or to the left of this particle. The examples in (50) show the less expected order where the NP comes first.

(50) a. Wa'-uk-hróri-'   ne Sak tsi wa-hrʌ́-[i]hey-e'.
         FACT-FsS/1sO-tell-PUNC NE Sak that FACT-MsS-die-PUNC
         'She told me that Sak died.'

      b. Í-k-ehr-e'   ne Sak tsi ʌ-ho-nuhwáktʌ-'.
         Ø-1sS-think-IMPF NE Sak that FUT-MsO-get.sick-PUNC
         'I think of Sak that he will get sick.'

Similarly, question phrases are known to move to the specifier of CP in Mohawk. Yet, NPs associated with the lower clause can appear on either side of this element as well:

(51) a. Wa'-ke-rihw-a-tshʌ́ri-'   úhka Uwári ruwa-núhwe'-s.
         FACT-1sS-matter-Ø-find-PUNC who Mary FsS/MsO-like-HAB
         'I found out who Mary likes.'

      b. Wa'-ke-rihw-a-tshʌ́ri-'   Uwári úhka ruwa-núhwe'-s.
         FACT-1sS-matter-Ø-find-PUNC Mary who FsS/MsO-like-HAB
         'I found out who Mary likes.'

The same freedom of word order is found in matrix questions as well as embedded ones:

(52) a. Oh nahótʌ Sak wa-ha-nʌ́sko-'?
         what   Sak FACT-MsS-steal-PUNC
         'What did Sak steal?'

      b. Sak oh nahótʌ wa-ha-nʌ́sko-'?
         Sak what   FACT-MsS-steal-PUNC
         'What did Sak steal?'

In the (a) sentences, the NP is presumably adjoined to IP; in the (b) sentences it must be adjoined to CP.

   Word order in Spanish is not as free. In particular, dislocated NPs are strongly deviant when they appear to the left of the complementizer[18]:

(53) a. Juan piensa que a María, la verá en la fiesta.
          'Juan thinks that Mary, he will see her at the party.'

      b. *Juan piensa a María, que la verá en la fiesta.
          'Juan thinks Mary, that he will see her at the party.'

The contrast between (53b) and (50b) suggests that adjunction to CP is allowed in Mohawk but not in Spanish.

Another possible adjunction site in Mohawk is NP. This arises in possessor constructions. Possessors are similar to clausal arguments in that they trigger Case-absorbing agreement on the head noun and can be pro-dropped. They also show a degree of free word order, appearing on either side of the possessed noun (although the order in (54a) is far more common) (see Launey 1981:91–92 for similar facts in Nahuatl).

(54) a. Sak rao-[i]tshénʌ wa-hák-hser-e'.
          Sak MsP-pet   FACT-MsS/1sO-chase-PUNC
          'Sak's pet chased me.'

      b. (?)Rao-[i]tshénʌ Sak wa-hák-hser-e'.
          MsP-pet   Sak FACT-MsS/1sO-chase-PUNC
          'Sak's pet chased me.'

Neither can a possessor be a true quantified NP of the 'everyone' or 'nobody' type (see section 6.2.1). These facts suggest that possessors also appear in adjoined positions. Nevertheless, they cannot be separated from their NP entirely in Mohawk, as shown by (55).

(55) a. *Rao-[i]tshénʌ wa-hák-hser-e'   ne Sak.
          MsP-pet   FACT-MsS/1sO-chase-PUNC NE Sak
          'Sak's pet chased me.'

      b. ?*Uwári ke-núhwe'-s ne ako-[a]tyá'tawi.[19]
          Mary 1sS-like-HAB NE FsP-dress
          'I like Mary's dress.'

The ungrammaticality of the examples in (55) is expected: they violate the Subjacency Condition on dislocation chains, since the only pronoun position that can license the understood possessor NP is inside an NP that is itself an adjunct. In effect, these examples are ruled out for the same reason as the adjunct island violations discussed in section 3.1.3. Indeed, comparable structures are ruled out in the Romance languages and Greek (Sabine Iatridou, personal communication).

(56)

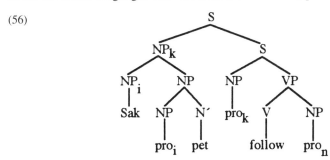

Given this, the possessor NP in (54) must be adjoined no higher than NP (or perhaps DP). The structure of these examples is given in (56). I conclude that NP is a possible adjunction site for dislocation in Mohawk. (See section 6.2 for some modifications and data from other languages.)

NP adjunction is probably not possible in the Romance languages. For example, although Spanish has clitic-like possessive pronouns, examples like (57) are nevertheless impossible.

(57)   *Juan leyó María, su libro.
        'Juan read Maria, her book.'

Again we find that Mohawk permits a wider range of adjunction sites than the Romance languages.[20]

Fortunately, P&P theory allows for some low-level parameterization of adjunction sites. Particularly interesting in this regard is Müller and Sternefeld's (1993) discussion of the differences in scrambling between Russian and German. They show that scrambling is considerably more restricted in German than in Russian in two respects. First, scrambling is clause bound in German, but not in Russian. Second, Russian allows a range of word orders that are not permitted in German, including those where constituents seem to be adjoined to CP. Müller and Sternefeld account for these facts by positing the following parameter (1993:470):

(58)   *Adjunction Site Parameter for Scrambling Positions*
        English: —
        German: VP, IP
        Russian: VP, IP, CP, (NP[21])

The adjunction sites they posit for scrambling in German are exactly the same as those we need for CLLD in the Romance languages. Moreover, the adjunction sites attributed to Russian are exactly those we need for Mohawk. This suggests that Müller and Sternefeld's parameter should be generalized beyond the domain of scrambling:

(59)   *Adjunction Site Parameter*
        English: —
        German, Spanish, . . . : VP, IP
        Russian, Mohawk, . . . : VP, IP, CP, NP

This parameter raises many interesting questions. First, it is not clear how this fits with current suggestions that all microparameters are morphological/lexical in nature. Second, one would like to know whether any arbitrary set of categories can be designated as adjunction sites in a given language, or whether the sets listed in (59) are the only possibilities, and if so why.[22] Third, one always wants to know whether parameter settings are predictable from other properties of the languages mentioned. Müller and Sternefeld have nothing to say about these questions, and neither do I. However, it seems clear that whatever status this parameter has in the theory, it describes a type of variation that is independent of the Polysynthesis Parameter. That is the crucial result for our purposes.

3.2.3 *Intonational Evidence*

A third difference between CLLD in Romance languages and adjoined NPs in polysynthetic languages that might bear on the issue of adjunction sites involves intonation. Kenneth Hale (personal communication) points out that dislocated NPs in Italian and other languages are typically set off from the rest of the clause intonationally. Cinque (1990) represents this by placing a comma between the dislocated NP and the material following it. In contrast, there need not be any such intonation break between, say, a preverbal NP and the verb in Mohawk:

(60) a. Gianni, lo conosciamo.
          'Gianni, we know him.'

      b. Sak ri-yΛtéri.
          Sak 1sS/MsO-know/STAT
          'I know Sak.'

What this contrast shows depends on details of the theory of phrasal phonology. If phonological phrasing is derived purely from syntactic structure, then the contrast in (60) suggests that NPs in Mohawk are in a different structural position than dislocated NPs in Italian. This would be problematic for my analysis. On the other hand, it is clear that CLLD constructions in Italian and simple clauses in Mohawk differ pragmatically, even if they are the same syntactically. CLLD constructions in Italian contrast with normal, unmarked clauses; hence, they are used for particular discourse purposes. In Mohawk, the same syntactic configuration is used for the full range of discourse contexts (with possible differences between left and right adjunction), because it is the only kind of structure that is available. Thus, if discourse-pragmatic notions can have a direct influence on the phrasal phonology, the contrast in (60) may not be problematic after all. Indeed, phrasal phonologies typically make use of a feature FOCUS as well as purely syntactic information; the semantics and pragmatics of this feature have not been worked out in detail (Sharon Inkelas, personal communication). Therefore, it is possible that all dislocated phrases bear FOCUS in Italian, but they need not in Mohawk. Moreover, the understanding of the phrasal phonology of polysynthetic languages is in its infancy, and the topic may produce some surprises.[23]

3.3 Differences: II. Features of the Adjoined NP

Having dealt with issues concerning the adjunction site of dislocated NPs in the polysynthetic languages, I turn now to issues concerning the morphosyntactic features of the adjoined NP. Here, too, there are some significant differences between the polysynthetic languages and the Romance languages that provide my analytic model. In general, the range of NPs that can be licensed via dislocation is broader in the polysynthetic languages. For example, nonsingular pronouns can license plural NPs in the polysynthetic languages, and vice versa. Similarly, definite pronouns can license indefinite NPs, and pronouns with structural Case can license NPs with inherent or semantic Case. None of these feature mismatches are possible with dislocation in the Romance languages. In this section, I present these differences and argue that they do not require any deep changes in the ALC; rather they are a result of the fact that NPs are formally unmarked for number, Case, and definiteness in the polysynthetic languages.

3.3.1 Number

Perhaps the most obvious of the feature mismatches are those that involve number. A striking fact about Mohawk is that a singular NP can be licensed by a plural pronoun. Simple examples are:

(61)   a. Sak t-ʌ-yaky-atskáhu-'.
          Sak DUP-FUT-1dS-eat-PUNC
          'I will eat with Sak.'
          (Literally: 'Sak, we two will eat.')

       b. Sak wa-shukení-kʌ-'   ne raó-skare' kanát-a-ku.
          Sak FACT-MsS/1dO-see-PUNC NE MsP-friend town-Ø-in
          'Sak saw me with his girlfriend in town.' (Literally: 'His girlfriend, Sak saw us two in town.')

       c. Uwári te-wak-atʌhutsóni   t-a-yakeni-núnyahkw-e'.
          Mary DUP-1sO-want/STAT DUP-OPT-1dS-dance-PUNC
          'Mary, I want to dance with her.' (Literally: 'Mary, I want that we two dance.')

Examples of this type are not at all rare in Mohawk; in fact, they are the standard way of expressing comitative relationships in the language, given that there is no preposition comparable to *with* (cf. Lounsbury 1953:99). Moreover, similar constructions are found in other polysynthetic languages, including Nahuatl (see (62a) from Launey 1981:246; see also Andrews 1975:201), Mayali (see (62b) from Evans 1991:205; see also Heath 1984:542, 544–545 for Nunggubuyu), and the Tanoan language Jemez (see (62c) from Kenneth Hale, personal communication).

(62)   a. Cuix ye   ō-an-tla-cua'-que'   in mo-nāmic?
          Q   already PAST-2pS-3INDEF-eat-PAST/PLUR IN 2sP-spouse
          'Have you and your spouse already eaten?'

       b. Al-gudji daluk   guni-djal-ni-n!
          II-one   woman 2dS-just-sit-NONPAST
          'You've got to stay with one woman!' (Literally: 'One woman, you two should stay together.')

       c. Nįį næ veela sǫ-the'ǫ-hų'.
          I   that man 1dS-speak-FUT
          'I will speak with that man.'

Such mismatches of number are clearly not possible in Romance language CLLD constructions, however. Thus, (63) in Spanish should be structurally parallel to (61b) in Mohawk, but it is ungrammatical.

(63)   #María, Juan nos vio en la fiesta.[24]
            'Maria, Juan saw us at the party.'

The opposite situation, in which a plural NP is licensed by a singular pronoun, is also found, at least in Mohawk. This situation arises, in particular, with certain nouns that express relations of friendship or kinship, where the members of the relationship have equal social status (friends, cousins, siblings-in-law). Such nouns are inherently plural, as shown by their prefix, and in neutral contexts they refer to all the people in the peer relationship. However, they also appear in construction with a singular pronominal argument position, as in (64).

(64) Ron-atÁro t-a-ha-[a]táweya't-e'.
      MP-friend CIS-FACT-MsS-enter-PUNC
      'His friend came in.' (Literally: 'The friends, he came in.')

Examples of this type are not found in the Romance languages.

In Baker 1992b, I discussed the syntax and semantics of these Mohawk constructions at some length as a way of learning about the linguistic representation of plural noun phrases. Among other things, that work establishes that these constructions have exactly the same chainlike properties as normal instances of CLLD. This fact can only be captured in the system if one broadens the notion "referential index" such that the indices of plural NPs can be sets of integers, along the lines proposed by Sportiche (1985) and Lasnik (1989:ch. 9). We then interpret the coindexing clause of the Chain Condition as in (65).

(65) X and Y are coindexed if and only if their referential indices are not disjoint.

In the special case where X and Y are both singular, (65) implies that their indices must be the same. When either X or Y is plural or both are plural, new possibilities are opened up, however. In particular, (61a) and (64) can have the rather natural representations in (66), now allowed by the ALC.

(66) a. $[_{NP\{i\}}$ Sak] $[_S$ pro$_{\{i, k\}}$ wa'-t-yaky-atskáhu-']
           Sak   (we)   FACT-DUP-1DS-eat-PUNC

      b. $[_{NP\{i, k\}}$ ron-atÁro] $[_S$ pro$_{\{i\}}$ t-a-ha-[a]táweya't-e']
           MP-friend   CIS-FACT-MsS-enter-PUNC

Although this interpretation of the coindexing relationship begins to explain why examples like (61), (62), and (64) are allowed by Universal Grammar, it does not provide an answer to the comparative question: Why are examples of this type allowed in the polysynthetic languages but not in, say, Spanish? In addressing this question, Baker (1992b) pointed out another way in which Mohawk and Romance languages differ: NPs are obligatorily marked for number (singular vs. plural) in Romance languages but not in Mohawk. Most common nouns in Mohawk are interpreted as either singular or plural, depending on the context. The language does have two plural suffixes (*shu'a* for nonhumans and *oku'a* for humans/animates), but these are optional and not particularly frequent in practice. For example, the distributive morphology on the verb in (67) indicates that the action is repeated, implying that more than one doll is involved. Nevertheless, the plural morpheme need not be used on the noun root (Deering and Delisle 1976:375):

(67) S-ahseht-á-nyu ne kaya'tuni'(-shú'a).
      2sS-hide-ø-DIST NE doll(-PL)
      'Hide the dolls here and there!'

Even, the morphologically simple independent pronouns *i'i* 'I/we', *ise* 'you sg/pl', and *ne* 'he, she, it, them' distinguish person but not number. The only overt nominals in Mohawk that are systematically marked for number distinctions are certain common nouns that refer to humans. These nouns have prefixes that are cognate with the subject prefixes on verbs and indicate the number and gender of the referent of the noun. For example (Deering and Delisle 1976:50):

(68) a. yak-úkwe
          FsS-person
          'woman'

      b. te-ken-úkwe
          DUP-FdS-person
          'two women'

      c. kun-úkwe
          FpS-person
          'women' (more than two)

(*Ronatáro* 'the friends' in (64) is another example of this type.) However, when these noun prefixes are analyzed in section 6.1, it will become clear that the features they register are not features of the NP as a whole, but rather those of an argument of the head noun. Thus, we can still maintain the generalization that NPs as a whole are formally unmarked for number features in Mohawk. Moreover, Nahuatl, Mayali, and Jemez are very much like Mohawk in this respect (Andrews 1975:143 and Evans 1991:96; see also section 6.1). All four languages contrast with Spanish and the Indo-European languages, where NPs are understood as referring to more than one entity of the class picked out by the head noun if and only if the head noun bears plural morphology.

This difference in morphosyntactic properties is relevant to dislocation constructions because of clause (iv) of the Chain Condition (see (38)), which states that X and Y may constitute a chain only if X and Y are *nondistinct* in morphosyntactic features. If both elements in question are fully specified for the same set of morphosyntactic features, this nondistinctness condition is equivalent to an identity condition. This is the situation in Spanish, where both overt NPs and clitic/agreement elements are consistently marked for number. Thus, in the Spanish example in (63), *María* cannot form a chain with the direct object position, because *María* is inherently singular and *nos* 'we' is plural. The result is that *María* is unlicensed. Mohawk nouns, on the other hand, are formally unmarked for number. This means that they are always morphosyntactically nondistinct in number from the pronoun, regardless of the cardinality of the referent of the NP. Similarly, we can assume that lexical nouns in Mohawk are formally unmarked for person features. This is reasonable, given that person is not distinctive for true nouns: there is no such thing as a first- or second-person noun. Thus, there are no morphosyntactic features associated with *Uwári* 'Mary' that prevent it from forming a chain with the first person dual pronominal object in an example like (61b) in Mohawk. More generally, the constructions in (61) and (64) are consistent with the Chain Condition as originally stated. This, then, accounts for the comparative problem, without resorting to significant additional parameterization. The constructions in (61) and (64) still present some difficult syntactic and semantic problems,[25] but close consideration of these would take us away from the main theme.

3.3.2 Definiteness

More subtle instances of apparent feature mismatch in the polysynthetic languages concern the matter of definiteness. In Italian and similar languages, nonspecific indefinite NPs cannot be dislocated. Thus, examples like (69) in Italian have only a specific reading, and not a true indefinite one (Cinque 1990:75–76).

(69) a. Qualcosa, la vedo anch'io.
'Something, I it-see as well.'

b. Qualcuno, l'ho trovato, non preoccuparti.
'Someone, I him-have found, don't worry.'

However, in Mohawk and the other polysynthetic languages, NPs adjoined to the clause can be indefinite; otherwise on my analysis there could be no indefinite NPs at all. Some examples of nonspecific indefinite NPs are (see also section 2.1.3):

(70) a. Tyótku úhkak   Λ-yúk-kΛ-'   nónΛ kanát-a-ku
always someone FUT-FsS/1sO-see-PUNC when town-Ø-in

y-Á-k-e-'.
TRANS-FUT-1sS-go-PUNC
'Someone always sees me when I go to town.'

b. Ne ónΛ érhar Λ-hó-kΛ-'   Λ-ho-tewékwΛ-'.
when   dog FUT-MsS/MsO-see-PUNC FUT-MsS/MsO-pet-PUNC
'Whenever he sees a dog he pets it.'

Here quantificational adverbs have been included to make it clear that the NPs *úhkak* 'someone' and *érhar* 'dog' are interpreted as true indefinites. Thus, (70b) does not mean simply that the male pets a certain dog whenever he sees it; it means that he pets all dogs that he sees. In other words, the NP is influenced by the universal quantifier in a way that is typical of indefinite NPs, but not definite NPs (Heim 1982). Similarly, (70a) does not necessarily mean that the same individual sees me on every occasion of my going to town. More generally, Chamorro (1992) shows that adjoined NPs in Mohawk may have all of the properties associated with indefinites in a language like English.

This topic is an important one because it has sometimes been used to argue against the Jelinek–Baker view of nonconfigurationality, in which NPs occur in nonargument positions related to pronominal elements. For example, Austin and Bresnan (1994) claim that Jelinek (1984) cannot account for the fact that NPs can have indefinite readings in Warlpiri. Similarly, Parsons and Speas (to appear) notice this difference between Italian and Mohawk and conclude that it can be used to argue against Baker's (1991a) analysis of Mohawk.

Parson and Speas, in particular, go on to propose an analysis of the definiteness effect in Italian and Navajo that is worth considering more closely. Following Heim (1982), they propose that indefinite NPs can only have quantificational-like readings when they are within the scope of appropriate operators, such as adverbs of quantification. If there is no overt operator in a given sentence, then a covert existential operator is added, in accordance with Heim's rule of Existential Closure. Up to this point, our assumptions are in agreement. They then stipulate that such operators always attach to the minimal S, while the position of the NP in a CLLD construction is higher up. This, then, accounts for the Italian facts in (69): *qualcosa* and *qualcuno* are simply too high in the tree to be bound by an existential operator. Hence, they must receive referential readings. Since the NPs in (70) are bound by operators, it follows that they must be inside the minimal S—perhaps even in A-positions.

There are, however, some problems with Parsons and Speas' approach to the lack of indefinite readings in (69). First, the analysis is based on a rather ad hoc stipulation. In section 3.1.2, I argued (following Cinque 1990) that dislocated NPs are adjoined to S; this is the only position that correctly accounts for the fact that they appear between the complementizer and the preverbal subject in Italian, and they are outside the binding domain of the subject in Mohawk. Now if adverbial operators also adjoin to S, it seems ad hoc to say that adverbial operators must adjoin first. Surely, the simplest assumption, consistent with the trend toward minimizing the extrinsic conditions on phrase structure (Speas 1990), is that elements can adjoin to a given category in any order. If so, then the restricted readings of (69) are not accounted for.

Second, the Parsons–Speas analysis makes the prediction that if there were some other kind of logical operator farther out than the landing site of dislocated NPs, this operator could bind the dislocated NP, giving a quantificational-like reading. This prediction seems to be false. The most plausible case in point concerns verbs which act like logical operators and select a CP complement. Heim (1982:257–263) notes that verbs such as *want* have essentially the same effect on indefinite NPs as negation and adverbs of quantification do. This is also true in Spanish; thus, (71) does not necessarily imply that there is a particular cake such that I want Maria to eat that cake.

(71)   Quiero que María coma una torta.
        'I-want that Maria eat a cake.'

In Heim's terms, this means that *querer* 'want' triggers the addition of an existential operator with scope over the clause that it selects. Heim is not very specific about the syntactic structure of sentential complements or the exact location of the existential operator in this kind of construction. However, standard principles of locality in syntax suggest that this operator should be at the level of the selected CP projection: either in the C itself, the specifier of the CP, or adjoined to the CP. If the operator were any lower, it would not be in a position where it could be selected by the matrix verb. Now, CLLD is possible in the complement of *querer*:

(72)   Quiero que esta torta, María la coma.
        'I-want that this cake, Maria eat it.'

Now consider (73), where an indefinite NP is dislocated in this context.

(73)   ??Quiero que una torta, María la coma.
        'I-want that a cake, Maria eat it.'

If the existential operator is introduced at the CP level, it should be in position to bind *una torta,* which is clearly lower than C. Thus, a normal existential-indefinite reading should be possible in this case. However, it is not; rather, the sentence is deviant. Indeed, even if CLLD places an NP out of the scope of lower-clause quantificational adverbs, this should simply put it into the domain of quantificational adverbs associated with the higher clause. A true indefinite reading should thus still be possible in (74b), parallel to that in (74a).

(74) a. Juan siempre cree que verá a alguien cuando va al parque.
'Juan always thinks he will see someone when he goes to the park.'

b. *Juan siempre cree que (a) alguien, lo verá cuando va al parque.
'Juan always thinks someone, he will see him when he goes to the park.'

Again, this is not the case. I conclude that the relative location of the dislocated NP and logical operators is not what is at issue. Rather, CLLD seems to be incompatible with indefinite NPs in Romance languages for some reason internal to the dislocation construction itself.

On an intuitive level, it is easy to see why this might be. Cinque (1990:74) points out that dislocated elements in Italian similar to those in (69) do have an indefinite meaning when the clitic pronoun on the verb is dropped:

(75) Qualcuno, troverò di sicuro per questo compito.
'Someone, I will-find surely for this task.'

Thus, it seems to be the presence of the clitic pronoun that forces the construction to be definite. This makes sense, because the clitic pronoun itself is definite, as are personal pronouns in general. Apparently, then, the pronoun and the NP that it forms a chain with must agree in definiteness in Romance languages. This result follows immediately from the nondistinctness clause of the Chain Condition, as long as we assume that $[\pm \text{definiteness}]$ counts as a morphosyntactic feature in Romance languages. This assumption is quite reasonable: common nouns in Romance languages are explicitly marked as definite or indefinite by the presence of a determiner (e.g., *una* vs. *la*, etc., in Spanish), and some such determiner is obligatory in most environments. Therefore, the indefinite dislocated NP in, for example, (73) clashes in definiteness features with the only pronoun that could license it, making the example ungrammatical. In contrast, both the dislocated NP and the object pronoun are [+definite] in (72); hence, the two can undergo chain formation, and the example is grammatical.

Now we are ready to return to the polysynthetic languages. Mohawk is different from Spanish and Italian in that it has no system of articles that mark definiteness. Rather, NPs are typically bare, and can ambiguously be interpreted as either definite or indefinite, depending on the context:

(76) a. Te-wak-atʌhutsóni ne érhar.
DUP-1sO-want/STAT NE dog
'I want a dog,' or 'I want the dog.'

b. Érhar te-wak-atʌhustóni.
dog DUP-1sO-want/STAT
'I want a dog,' or 'I want the dog.'

This ambiguity is independent of whether the NP precedes the verb or follows it. It is also independent of whether the particle *ne* appears or not. Although this particle is described as the Mohawk equivalent of *the* in some of the more descriptive literature, Chamorro (1992) shows in some detail that this is not so.[26] If NPs in Mohawk are not marked as [±definite] morphologically, they will always be nondistinct from the licensing pronoun in this respect, whatever their ultimate interpretation is. Hence, indefinites can be licensed by chain formation with a pronoun in Mohawk. Once again, we relate the fact that a wider class of NPs can be dislocated in Mohawk than in Spanish/Italian to an independent morphosyntactic difference between the languages.

Chichewa provides a useful point of comparison in this regard, because it is intermediate between Italian and Mohawk. Chichewa is like Italian in that its object clitics are optional; when they do not appear, the object NP has the opportunity to appear in argument position. On the other hand, Chichewa is like Mohawk in that there is no system of articles that mark the definite/indefinite distinction morphosyntactically:

(77)   Mw-a-bwerets-a   bûku?   (Bresnan and Mchombo 1987:761)
       2sS-PERF-bring-IND book
       'Have you brought a/the book?

The analysis I have sketched predicts that when the object is dislocated, it should still be ambiguous between a definite and indefinite interpretation, since the resulting chain does not clash in morphosyntactic features. Bresnan and Mchombo show that this is true:

(78)   Mw-a-lí-bwérets-a   bûku?
       2sS-PERF-OM-bring-IND book
       'Have you brought it, the book?' or 'Have you brought one, a book?'

This confirms that the effect of CLLD on definiteness found in the Romance languages is not an inherent property of dislocation constructions, even in languages where such dislocation is not forced by the Polysynthesis Parameter. Once again, there is no need to posit any fundamental difference between the UG principles that govern CLLD in Romance languages and nonconfigurational constructions in polysynthetic languages, even though the range of sentences generated is rather different.

From what has been said so far, one would expect to find the opposite dissociation as well: a language that is like Mohawk in that object clitics/agreement elements are obligatory, but like Italian in that definiteness is a morphosyntactic feature consistently marked on NPs. As far as I know, there is no such language; certainly none of the polysynthetic languages in my survey is of this type. Indeed, none of these polysynthetic languages has a true article system comparable to that in English or Italian.[27] The reason for this might be a broadly communicative one: on the one hand, my system predicts that such a language could not have indefinite NPs at all; on the other hand, it seems likely that humans simply cannot get by without using indefinite expressions in speech. Thus, this language type, although formally allowed by Universal Grammar, might never be attested in the actual languages of the world for extrinsic, practical reasons. Alternatively, the fact that polysynthetic languages do not have fixed article systems might follow as a formal consequence of the MVC as it applies to nouns. In fact, I will argue for this latter claim in section 6.1.2.

3.3.3 Case

Finally, there are also apparent mismatches between the dislocated NP and the licensing pronoun in the area of morphological Case. An important goal of Jelinek's original (1984) analysis of pronominal argument languages was to account for peculiarities in the patterns of morphological Case marking in nonconfigurational languages. In particular, she was concerned with the phenomenon of split ergativity in Warlpiri, where pronominal clitics on the auxiliary consistently show a nominative–accusative Case pattern, whereas the independent NPs that double those clitics show an ergative–absolutive Case pattern. Somewhat similar examples can be given for the Gunwinjguan language Ngandi (data from Heath 1978). We saw in chapter 2 that agreement morphemes absorb the Case of the head that they attach to in the polysynthetic languages (see also section 5.2). Thus, the subject agreement morpheme *rni* presumably absorbs nominative Case in both (79a) and (79b).

(79) a. Rni-rudhu-ni::: rni-wolo rni-yul-Ø-yung. (Heath 1978:221)
       MsS-go-PRES MsS-that MsS-man-ABS-NSF
       'That man goes along.'

   b. Rni-gu-ma-y   rni-yul-thu-yung   gu-jundu-Ø-yung. (Heath 1978:42)
       MsS-GU-get-PAST MsS-man-ERG-NSF GU-stone-ABS-NSF
       'The man got the stone.'

Nevertheless, the morphological Cases on the overt NPs related to this subject agreement are different in the two examples: in (79b) the NP is in ergative case, marked with the suffix *thu,* whereas in (79a) it is in the unmarked (nominative/absolutive) form. In (80), a different example of the same general type is given. Both (80a) and (80b) have a masculine singular object agreement factor that absorbs the accusative Case of the verb; however, the overt NP licensed by that pronominal is in unmarked nominative/absolutive Case in (80a) and in dative Case in (80b).

(80) a. Rnini-ja-ga-ng,   rni-wolo-Ø-yung. . . . (Heath 1978:267)
       MsS/MsO-now-carry-PAST/PUNC MsS-that-ABS-NSF
       'He took that man. . . .'

   b. Rno-wolo-thu Ø-ga-ba-ka-n-di   (Heath 1978: 267)
       FsS-that-ERG FsS/MsO-SUB-BEN-carry-AUG-PAST/CONT

       ma-ngic-ung rni-wolo-ku-yung rni-yul-ku-yung.
       MA-food-NSF MsS-that-DAT-NSF MsS-man-DAT-NSF
       'That woman was taking food to that man.'

Notice also that the Case form of the NP licensed by the accusative pronoun in (80a) is identical to the Case form of the NP licensed by the nominative pronoun in (79a). Thus, there seems to be a many-to-many correspondence between the

Cases on overt NPs and the Cases associated with the pronouns/agreement elements they are linked to. Similar issues arise in some of the other Gunwinjguan
languages and in Chukchee, which also has an ergative/absolutive/dative Case system (Bogoras 1922, Nedjalkov 1976). Jelinek (1984) used these facts to show that
NPs in languages like Warlpiri are adjuncts; hence, they are not governed by the
verb or by Infl and do not receive the usual structural Cases (nominative and
accusative). If, however, we maintain our idea that the adjoined NPs are licensed
by undergoing chain formation with the pronoun arguments, then those adjoined
NPs must be nondistinct from the pronouns in Case features. Thus, the split-
ergativity problem reappears in this version of the pronominal argument hypothesis.

Insight into this issue can be gained from looking at the polysynthetic languages more broadly. From this perspective, Ngandi and Chukchee are rather
atypical. The more common situation is the one found in Mohawk, where overt
NPs never show Case distinctions of any kind. Thus, an NP that binds a subject
pronoun looks exactly like an NP that binds an object pronoun or one that binds
an indirect object pronoun, as shown in (81).

(81)   a. Sak rake-núhwe'-s.
          Sak MsS/1sO-like-HAB
          'Sak likes me.'

       b. Sak ri-núhwe'-s.
          Sak 1sS/MsO-like-HAB
          'I like Sak.'

       c. Sak t-a-híy-u-'.
          Sak CIS-FACT-1sS/MsO-give-PUNC
          'I handed it to Sak.'

Sak in these examples is, of course, a proper noun, but the same is true for common nouns and even emphatic pronouns. This means that when there is more than
one pronominal in the clause that is compatible with an adjoined NP in gender
and person features, the sentence will be ambiguous in the absence of context.
This is correct, as shown in (82).

(82)   Sak wa-hó-[a]hseht-e'.
       Sak FACT-MsS/MsO-kill-PUNC
       'Sak killed him' or 'He killed Sak.'

In practice, such ambiguities are not overly common because of Mohawk's relatively rich gender system, which distinguishes masculine, feminine, zoic, and neuter; however, they do arise. In other polysynthetic languages such as Nahuatl,
where agreement makes fewer distinctions, this situation arises more frequently
(Launey 1981:38–39). Nevertheless, NPs are also completely unmarked for Case
in Wichita, Nahuatl, the Tanoan languages, Ainu, and Mayali.

Mayali is particularly instructive, inasmuch as it is rather closely related to
Ngandi, and genetically related to the other Australian languages (Dixon 1980,
Blake 1987). The vast majority of Australian languages have strong systems of
morphological Case marking. However, in precisely those Northern Australian
languages that have developed a polysynthetic system, the normal Australian Case

marking system has weakened. Thus, ergative Case is not strictly obligatory on the subjects of transitive verbs in Ngalakan and Rembarrnga, and it is lost entirely in Nunggubuyu and Mayali. Similarly, the use of dative or allative Case to mark NPs understood as indirect objects is not all that common in Rembarrnga and Ngalakan and apparently is lost altogether in Mayali. Thus, among Australian languages there seems to be an inverse relationship between the amount of Case marking used for the core arguments of the clause in a given language and the degree of polysynthesis in that language. This same negative correlation shows up in the large-scale typological study of Nichols (1992), who observes that languages that are predominantly head marking tend to be relatively low in overall "complexity"—that is, they do not use redundant dependent marking.[28]

Given, then, that the unmarked situation for a polysynthetic language is to not have structural Case on its NPs, this fits easily into the system developed here. Overt NPs in Mohawk and other languages are formally unmarked for Case features. Hence, their Case features are nondistinct from those of any potential licensing pronoun. An adjoined NP can therefore form a chain with a pronoun in any syntactic position with which it is otherwise compatible. This accounts for the Mohawk data in (81) and (82).

What can we say about Chukchee and Ngandi, which seem to have grammatical Case? Significantly, these two language families also differ from the other polysynthetic languages in their system of *semantic* Cases. Most of the polysynthetic languages have purely locational suffixes that attach to nouns; these are analyzed as adpositions in chapter 9. However, Chukchee and the Gunwinjguan languages also have Cases that are not purely locative. Some of these Cases have directional senses rather then pure locational ones: thus, Chukchee and Gunwinjguan differentiate allative (motion toward) and ablative (motion away from) from pure locative Case. Other Cases are more thoroughly nonspacial in meaning; for example, both Chukchee and Ngandi have an instrumental Case suffix, unlike Mohawk. The interesting point is that every putative grammatical Case suffix in these languages is systematically identical with some nonlocative semantic Case in the language. Thus, *thu* in Ngandi is used not only for transitive subjects, as in (79b), but also for instrumental phrases (Heath 1978:42):

(83) Rni-gung-Ø-yung njaru-ga-dho-ni   a-ja-mumbaʔ-dhu.
      NI-honey-ABS-NSF 1pS-SUB-chop-PRES A-now-axe-ERG
      'We chop down honey with axes now.'

The ergative Case is also identical to the instrumental in Chukchee (Bogoras 1922:697), Rembarrnga, and Ngalakan. Meanwhile, the dative Case *gu* in Ngandi is used not only for indirect objects, but for purposive adjuncts:

(84) Bari-bu-ydhi-ni   rna-dhingʔ-gu. (Heath 1978:44)
      3pS-hit-RECIP-PAST FsS-woman-DAT
      'They fought for (in order to get) a woman.'

Similarly, dative *gtə* in Chukchee is used for allative adjuncts that express the direction of a motion (Bogoras 1922:702). Finally, absolute Case is typically just the bare NP form. Thus, it seems that a given form must exist as a semantic Case in a polysynthetic language as a precondition to being used as a "grammati-

cal" Case. Note also that the meaning of the semantic Case is systematically related to its meaning as a putative grammatical Case: instruments are closely related to agents in θ-theory, as are goals and recipients (Jackendoff 1983, 1987).

The observed range of facts can be accounted for if we say that NPs do not
have grammatical Case in any polysynthetic language. Thus, there is never technically a problem with clause (iv) of the Chain Condition given in (38). The Case
endings one sees in a few of these languages are always semantic Cases. The
relationships of NPs in these Cases to null pronouns are determined not by the
sharing of morphosyntactic Case features, but rather by the inherent semantics of
the Case morpheme. This is very similar in spirit to Jelinek's (1984) discussion of
L(exical)-Cases in Warlpiri, which determine which NP adjunct is coindexed with
which argument position via a series of stipulated Case compatibility rules. However, the current proposal goes one step beyond Jelinek in suggesting that L-cases
must be a subset of the semantic cases. This means that the Case compatibility
rules can, for the most part, be deduced from the inherent meanings of the Cases
in question. Moreover, on this analysis it is not surprising that the use of ergative
and dative Cases is rather fluid, at least in the Gunwinjguan languages: the overt
Case forms are used when the grammatical function associated with the adjoined
NP is potentially ambiguous, but they are often omitted when no ambiguity would
arise.[29] For example, the transitive subject in (85) in Ngandi is in the bare NP
form, rather than in the ergative form that one might expect (Heath 1978:267).

(85)   . . . rni-ma-ga-nguni-ngu-ni   rni-wolo-yung rni-yul-yung.
       MsS-MA-SUB-RED-eat-PAST/CONT MsS-that-NSF MsS-man-NSF
       'That man was eating it (the food).'

See also Merlan 1983:40–46 for Ngalakan, Heath's (1978:46) description of the
"pseudo-accusative" in Ngandi, and Heath's (1984:204–205) discussion of when
ablative *wala* and allative *wuy* are used to mark subjects and objects in Nunggubuyu. This optionality of Case morphology would be surprising in a system of
true grammatical Case based on feature matching; however, it is not surprising if
the Case endings are playing a purely semantic/pragmatic role, as in this analysis.

3.4 Conclusion

This chapter has compared the syntax of overt NPs in Mohawk with that of CLLD
constructions in Romance languages in considerable detail. We have seen that
there are many striking similarities, suggesting that the same theory should apply
to both. This theory is expressed in terms of the Adjunct Licensing Condition,
together with the Chain Condition that it presupposes. Some of the differences
can be attributed to independent differences between Mohawk and the Romance
languages. For example, Mohawk NPs are morphologically unmarked for number,
definiteness, and Case; this means that Mohawk can have a wider range of dislocations than is possible in Romance languages without violating the feature-
matching constraint on chain formation. Thus, we do not have to introduce any
major new parameters or licensing conditions to govern the presence of NPs in
adjoined positions in polysynthetic languages.

Two problems remain: First, one would like to know why it is so common for NPs in the polysynthetic languages to be unmarked for morphosyntactic features; this question will be taken up in chapter 6. Second, individual languages seem to be able to specify to a certain extent which categories allow adjoined material, and perhaps which side of those categories such material can adjoin to. These specifications are relatively trivial from the point of view of syntactic theory, and they do not seem to be restricted to polysynthetic languages in any interesting way; the effects of the choices made will be more dramatic in the polysynthetic languages, however, since such a large percentage of the visible material is adjoined.

There is one more apparent difference between NPs in Mohawk and CLLD in Romance languages. However, this topic is important enough to deserve a separate chapter, and it will therefore be considered next, in chapter 4.

Notes

1. Similarly, work on these languages in other frameworks contains some information about the nature and properties of adjoined NPs, but few detailed discussions that I know of. Thus, it is difficult to establish good theoretical equivalents across frameworks in this domain.

2. To be still more accurate, the adjectives in (2) should be "floated" off the NPs into adverbial positions, similar to the way that quantifiers float in many languages.

3. Property (4iii) also has potential implications for the structure of idioms. Idiom chunks cannot, in general, be dislocated in English, Italian (Cinque 1990:89), or Chichewa (Bresnan and Mchombo 1987:763):

(i) a. Susan finally broke the ice [i.e. created a comfortable social setting].
     b. #The ice, Susan finally managed to break it at 11:30.

The reason for this is presumably that idiom chunks, like quantified NPs, do not refer and hence cannot be coindexed with a licensing pronoun in the relevant way (see also Rizzi 1990:78–80).

Transferring these observations directly to the polysynthetic languages, the prediction is that V–NP idioms, for example, should be impossible, because the idiomatic NP could not be licensed. As far as I can tell, this prediction is true for Mohawk. Mohawk has many idiomatic verb–object combinations when the object noun is incorporated; however, when the same noun is expressed as an independent NP, the result is either ungrammatical or it reverts to its literal meaning. The alternation in (ii) is typical in this respect.

(ii) a. Tu-s-a-yu-[a]t-háh-a-hkw-e'.   (based on Hewitt 1903)
          DUP-ITER-FACT-FsS-SRFL-road-Ø-pick.up-PUNC
          'She started her journey.' (Literally: 'She picked up the road.')

      b. #Tu-s-a-yú-([a]te)-hkw-e'   ne oháha'.
          DUP-ITER-FACT-FsS-SRFL-pick.up-PUNC NE road
          'She picked up the road.' (Only the literal reading is possible.)

Moreover, I have not found any clear instances of V–NP idioms in the Mohawk texts that I have studied. A native speaker was also directly asked if she could think of any idiomatic expressions and she failed to do so over the course of two weeks. However, evaluating this kind of prediction is difficult, and there have been few systematic studies of idioms in polysynthetic languages. (However, Evans (1991:311–313) claims that idioms are common in Mayali and gives some interesting examples.)

4. Alternatively, there may have been an error in the published text.

5. Ainu alone among the polysynthetic languages has a special particle for marking topics, comparable to *wa* in Japanese (Shibatani 1990:38–39). However, in all of Shibatani's examples the topic constituent corresponds to an empty position in the clause, as in Mohawk.

6. A great number of such categories have been proposed in the recent literature; however, most of them are held by, for example, Chomsky (1992) to have specifiers that are A-positions. Therefore, they can be ignored for current purposes.

7. Some Slavic languages apparently allow multiple *wh*-movement to Comp, but this is a parametric option and a somewhat unusual one. Moreover, most languages allow multiple *wh*-movement to Comp at LF. These facts emphasize the point at hand; clearly, there is no semantic/pragmatic constraint against multiple interrogatives. Rather, there is the syntactic constraint that only one of the interrogative phrases can occupy the syntactic position in question. This highlights the uniqueness of Comp as a syntactic position.

Many researchers have proposed that a CP can in some cases be the complement of another CP. However, in no case that I know of can the specifiers of both CPs be landing sites for A-bar movement; presumably any such structure would be ruled out as, at least, a *wh*-island/Relativized Minimality violation. (This would be true even if one of the heads was a functional category distinct from C with an A-bar specifier, such as the head of a "polarity phrase" or "focus phrase.")

8. This line is easy to develop for relative clauses, in which the Comp is necessarily occupied by the relative operator. The same might be true of at least some adjunct clauses, such as temporal adjuncts, if these have a null temporal operator in Comp as proposed by Richard Larson. Alternatively, these adjuncts might be adpositions selecting for an IP complement, rather than a CP; in that case, the crucial Comp position is not present at all.

Complements of nonlogophoric verbs probably need different techniques. One possibility that has been proposed is that embedded topicalization is possible only in instances of CP recursion. This would suggest that topics cannot appear in the Comp immediately under a selecting verb, perhaps because it makes it impossible for the matrix verb to select the complementizer.

Similar distributional restrictions hold for interrogative clauses, although the specific verbs that select for an interrogative are, of course, different from those that take an embedded topicalization.

Even if a pragmatic approach rather than a structural one is taken to the distribution of topicalization, the similarity between Mohawk clauses and CLLD is instructive.

9. This string was accepted as a type of multiple question, receiving paired answers, but crucially not as a simple question receiving an answer like "the car." See section 2.1.4 for discussion.

10. In fact, since NPs are in adjoined positions in Mohawk, the sentences in (22) could be considered to violate the adjunct condition instead of (or as well as) the Complex NP Constraint (CNPC). I have, however, collected one or two examples of this type that are accepted by native speakers.

Cinque (1990) distinguishes between strong islands and weak islands: weak islands block processes of adjunct extraction, but not CLLD relationships. If the distinction is valid for Mohawk, then we would expect NPs to be licensed out of *wh*-islands, for example. Example (i) shows that this is true.

(i) Thíkʌ ká'sere' wa'-ke-rihw-a-tshÁri-'   úhka wa-ha-hnínu-'.
    that   car   FACT-1sS-matter-Ø-find-PUNC who FACT-MsS-buy-PUNC
    'That car, I found out who bought.'

Recall that *wh*-movement out of an embedded question is not allowed. This contrast between questions and dislocation confirms the point made later that questions but not dislocations are formed by movement.

Other weak islands in Cinque's typology of islands are extraposed subjects and the complements of factive verbs. Apparently neither structure is found in Mohawk (see section 10.1).

11. Rood (1976:213) mentions a Wichita example in which an NP seems to be separated from the locative adverbial clause that it is related to semantically. However, he observes that these word orders are rare and suggests another possible analysis for the example in question, in which the NP is actually an adjunct of the matrix clause.

12. This judgment is clear and systematic for one consultant. For a second consultant, the sloppy interpretation of (27b) seems to be possible, but the nonsloppy interpretation is preferred, in contrast with (27a), where the sloppy interpretation is at least as felicitous as the nonsloppy one.

13. See Baker (to appear b) for a more precise formulation of some of these processes as they apply to ellipsis in Mohawk.

14. I have stated this as an interpretive rule that replaces pronoun indices with variables for ease of exposition and consistency with Roberts 1984, Williams 1977, and others. However, the same effect could presumably be achieved by interpreting the Bijection Principle as a filter that rules out multiple variables unless they are in the structural configuration defined in (32).

15. In stating this as a biconditional I assume that "free topics" of the Japanese type appear in a different structural position—perhaps one that is found only in root clauses.

16. A few examples like (44) have sporadically been accepted by my consultants. However, given the poverty of the complementizer system in Mohawk, it is possible that the examples in question are not really instances of preverbal complements at all, but rather a sequence of two independent clauses. I suspect that this accounts for the seeming variation.

The fixed V–CP order looks like evidence that Mohawk is underlyingly a head-initial language, in which verbs precede their complements in the rare circumstances when both are overt. The evidence is quite weak, however, given that there are many head-final languages in which clauses must extrapose to the right because of their "heaviness" and the desire to avoid center embedding. Indeed, (i) shows that some sort of clausal extraposition is needed in Mohawk in any case.

(i)   a. ???Í-hr-ehr-e'   wak-ya't-á-hskats   ne Sak.
         Ø-MsS-think-IMPF 1sO-body-Ø-be.beautiful NE Sak
         'Sak thinks I am beautiful.'

      b. Í-hr-ehr-e'   ne Sak wak-ya't-á-hskats.
          Ø-MsS-think-IMPF NE Sak 1sO-body-Ø-be.beautiful
          'Sak thinks I am beautiful.'

If clauses stayed in their complement position, then one would expect (ia) to be a natural order, with the matrix subject adjoined to the matrix clause and therefore appearing to the right of the clause inside the VP. In fact, (ib) is by far the preferred order. The NP must be adjoined to the matrix clause in this sentence, too; if it were adjoined to the embedded clause, it would not c-command the pronoun that licenses it. Thus, we are forced to the conclusion that the clause extraposes to the right periphery, and there is no clear evidence as to where it started. It might be that clausal extraposition takes place only at PF; this would explain the fact that clauses act as though they are in complement positions for the syntactic phenomena discussed in section 2.1.

17. Compare Jelinek (to appear), where she claims that NPs can only be adjoined to the right of the clause in Straits Salish, making the language strictly verb initial.

According to Launey, VOS order is found in Nahuatl only if the object is a determinerless indefinite. I will not speculate on the nature of this restriction.

18. The facts from embedded questions in Spanish seem contradictory. There, too, the order is fixed, but the dislocated NP appears outside the question word:

(i)   a.   *No sé quién este libro, lo revisará para mañana.
           'I don't know who, this book, will read it by tomorrow.'

      b.   No sé este libro, quién lo revisará para mañana.
           'I don't know this book, who will read it by tomorrow.'

This is surely related to the Spanish-peculiar fact that the verb usually must immediately follow the *wh*-phrase in Comp. One possible analysis of this is that *wh*-movement lands in the specifier of IP in Spanish. If this is correct, then the word order in (i) is perfectly consistent with the claim that dislocated NPs adjoin to IP only.

19. This word order is sometimes allowed in contexts where the sentence-initial possessor is heavily contrastive: for example, in the second clause of the Mohawk equivalent of *I don't like their dresses; I only like Mary's* dress. Such examples are also possible in Nahuatl, as is either order of possessor and possessed noun (Launey 1981:92). Perhaps in these examples the possessor is licensed as a kind of free topic, rather than by chain formation with the pronominal possessor of the NP (see section 3.1.1).

20. The Romance languages are also standardly held to allow adjunction to VP. This is the position of inverted subjects in Spanish and Italian in the classical Government-Binding works of the early 1980s, for example. In Mohawk, it is very hard to find a context in which VP adjunction can be distinguished from IP adjunction, however.

21. An earlier draft of Müller and Sternefeld's article (dated 1990) argued in favor of adjunction to NP (and AP) in Russian as well. The published (1993) version does not specify whether this claim proved empirically incorrect or was dropped because of space limitations; I tentatively assume the latter.

22. It is tempting to refer to Chomsky 1986a and say that all languages allow adjunction to nonargument categories (IP and VP), whereas only some allow adjunction to argument categories. On this formulation it would not be a coincidence that the same languages that allow adjunction to NPs also allow adjunction to CPs, these being the prototypical argument categories.

23. Interestingly, Heath (1986:378) comes close to saying that there are no phonological phrases in Nunggubuyu; he also makes very frequent use of commas in his Gunwinjguan texts. If this should be a property of polysynthetic languages more generally, this might be related in an important way to my syntactic analysis.

24. This sentence is acceptable if and only if *Maria* is interpreted as a vocative—if the sentence is addressed to Mary, and begins by calling her name. The same is true for French and for Italian (Luigi Rizzi, personal communication). The Mohawk sentences in (61) are not restricted in this way.

25. One problem considered in Baker 1992b is the fact that Spanish CLLD constructions require the dislocated NP to be identical in reference to the licensing pronoun, even when both are third person plural. Thus, Spanish requires identity of referential index as a condition for chain formation, whereas Mohawk requires only nondisjointness. This is apparently a secondary parameter, the setting of which in a given language is triggered indirectly by the presence or absence of number marking on NPs.

Another problem, not dealt with adequately in Baker 1992b, is raised by the possibility of sentences like (i).

(i) Úhka wa'-t-hni-núnyahkw-e'   ne Sak?
    who FACT-DUP-MDS-dance-PUNC NE Sak
    'Who danced with Sak?'

Here one and the same argument position (the subject of the intransitive verb) licenses both a moved *wh*-phrase and a dislocated referential NP. How these sentences can best be derived is unclear, although Chomsky's (1992) abandonment of the level of D-structure may be a step in the right direction.

26. What *ne* is remains somewhat mysterious; its core synchronic use seems to be simply to mark a postverbal NP constituent under certain conditions. However, there is a significant amount of variation in its use both within and across speakers.

27. In most cases, this claim is uncontroversial. The one polysynthetic language in which there is cause for doubt is Nahuatl; it has a particle *in* that is similar in many respects to *ne* in Mohawk but is more strongly associated with definite NPs. Nevertheless, *in* also has properties that are more like a demonstrative than a pure article (see section 6.1.2 for some data and discussion).

28. Bresnan and Mchombo (1987:sec. 3) present a related notion when they suggest that part of the reason why overt NPs do not bear morphological case in Bantu languages is because many of them do not bear true grammatical functions, but rather are anaphorically related to "incorporated pronouns."

29. Judging from the available literature, the Chukchee Case marking system is more rigid than the Gunwinjguan one, with ergative Case being used for all transitive subjects and allative Case being used for all indirect objects. Closer comparative work would be necessary to determine whether this is a substantive difference between the two language families.

4

Discontinuous Constituents

4.1 The Nature of the Problem

In chapters 2 and 3, a reasonably comprehensive theory of nonconfigurationality as it is found in polysynthetic languages was presented. In particular, I explained why overt NPs cannot appear in argument positions and why they can appear in adjunct positions in terms of familiar principles of Universal Grammar together with the Morphological Visibility Condition. This structural fact, in turn, explains why anaphora, quantification, and extraction work so differently in Mohawk and English, without having to posit any parameters specific to the principles that govern those domains. The theory also accounts for two characteristics of nonconfigurational languages discussed by Hale (1983). Both the fact that overt NPs are optional and the fact that they do not have fixed structural positions follow immediately from the claim that they have the status of adjuncts, as emphasized in Jelinek's (1984) original presentation.

However, we have not yet considered carefully the third of Hale's characteristics of nonconfigurationality: the existence of discontinuous expressions. These are quite common in Warlpiri. Some examples can be found in Mohawk and other polysynthetic languages as well:

(1) a. Akwéku wa'-e-tshÁri-'   ne onhúhsa'.
        all   FACT-FsS-find-PUNC NE egg
        'She found all the eggs.'

     b. Ka nikáyʌ wá-hse-nut-e'   ne kwéskwes?
        which   FACT-2sS/ZsO-feed-PUNC NE pig
        'Which pig did you feed?'

     c. KíkΛ wa-hi-yéna-'   ne kwéskwes.
        this FACT-1sS/MsO-catch-PUNC NE pig
        'I caught this pig.'

In each of these examples, a determiner-like element is split off from the NP it is associated with semantically: quantifier-like *akwéku* 'all' in (1a), a *wh*-word in

138

(1b), and a demonstrative in (1c). Such word orders are, of course, not found in English.

Jelinek (1984) makes a simple and elegant proposal to account for sentences like these, which I have implicitly adopted up to this point. She claims that sentences like these do not really have discontinuous NPs at all. Rather they have two simple NPs, both of which are independently linked to the same argument position. Again, this is made possible by the fact that overt NPs are adjuncts in these languages, so they are not relevant to the Theta-Criterion, which requires there to be only one argumental category for each θ-role specified by the verb. Thus, one can have zero NP adjuncts (the pro-drop case), one NP adjunct (the normal free word order case), or more than one NP adjunct (the discontinuous expressions case). Jelinek's analysis makes a nice further prediction: that both the preverbal and the postverbal material in (1) must qualify as complete, well-formed NPs in their own right in Mohawk This is correct: either the preverbal or the postverbal material can be dropped in these examples and the result is still grammatical. Jelinek's approach would rule out a discontinuous example equivalent to *John the bought book* for the same reason that something like *John bought the* is ruled out.

In spite of the elegance and initial success of this approach, there are several reasons to think that it should be abandoned. First, there is a theoretical problem that stems from the fact that many kinds of adjuncts are, in practice, unique within a single clause in a way that is not very different from the uniqueness associated with arguments (see, e.g., Grimshaw 1990:148–149). This is implicitly recognized by Chomsky's (1986b, 1992) recent replacement of the Theta-Criterion by the more general principles of Full Interpretation and Economy of Representation. According to these notions, every element in a structure must be associated with an interpretation, not just those occupying argument positions. The problem becomes sharper when one adopts the view (defended in chapter 3) that adjoined NPs in polysynthetic languages are licensed by the same mechanisms as clitic left dislocation constructions. It is clear that a given pronoun in these constructions can only license one NP at a time:

(2) a. *Este hombre,* lo ví en la fiesta.   (Spanish)
         'That man, I saw him at the party.'

     b. Lo ví en la fiesta, *este hombre.*
         'I saw him at the party, that man.'

     c. **Este,* lo ví en la fiesta, *(el) hombre.*
         'That, I saw him at the party, (the) man.'

     d. **Este,* creo que *(el) hombre,* lo ví en la fiesta.
         'That, I believe that (the) man I saw him at the party.'

Thus, there is a kind of uniqueness constraint on adjoined NPs in CLLD constructions such that only a single NP can be licensed by a given pronoun. All things being equal, one would expect the polysynthetic languages to be the same.

Empirical data from Mohawk also present problems for Jelinek's analysis of discontinuous expressions. Taken at face value, her analysis predicts that the possibilities for such expressions should be quite free. In fact, discontinuous expressions are both relatively rare and limited in Mohawk. Examples like (1c), in particular, are not often found in texts. Moreover, there are many other kinds of double or discontinuous NPs that are systematically impossible. For example, the NPs *rababhót* 'bullhead' and *kΛtsu* 'fish' can readily be used to refer to the same entity in Mohawk. Nevertheless, they cannot both be licensed by a single argument position. Hence, (3) is ungrammatical, although if either NP is omitted the structure becomes perfect.

(3) ?*KΛtsu ne auhá'a te-wak-éka'-s   rababhót.
      fish NE most CIS-1sO-like-HAB bullhead
      'I like bullhead fish the best.'

Similarly, (4a) has a composite NP made up of two roots in apposition, *itshenΛ* 'pet' and *érhar* 'dog'. Both of these can be well-formed NPs by themselves in Mohawk. Nevertheless, one cannot form a discontinuous expression, as shown in (4b).

(4) a. Ak-itshénΛ érhar wa-ha-níye-'.
        1sP-pet   dog FACT-MsS-bark-PUNC
        'My dog barked.'

     b. *Ak-itshénΛ wa-ha-níye-'   ne érhar.
        1sP-pet   FACT-MsS-bark-PUNC NE dog
        'My dog barked.'

Another example of the same type is given in (5).

(5) a. Éri   káhi wa'-é-ko-'.
        cherry fruit FACT-FsS-pick-PUNC
        'She picked the cherries.'

     b. *?Éri   wa'-é-ko-'   káhi.
        cherry FACT-FsS-pick-PUNC fruit
        'She picked the cherries.'

Jelinek's analysis offers no insight into why these sentences should be ruled out.

Even within the domain where discontinuous expressions are allowed, there are some curious restrictions. For example, the sentences in (1) all have the quantifier or demonstrative before the verb and the lexical noun after the verb. This is not a coincidence; the opposite order is ungrammatical in Mohawk[1]:

(6) a. *?Onhúhsa' wa'-e-tshΛri-'   akwéku.
        eggs   FACT-FsS-find-PUNC all
        'She found all the eggs.'

     b. ?*Kwéskwes wa-hi-yéna-'   kíkΛ.
        pig   FACT-1sS/MsO-catch-PUNC this
        'I caught this pig.'

Crucially, these sentences become grammatical if either the preverbal NP or the postverbal NP is omitted, thus showing that all of the elements in (6) can be licensed individually. Apparently, they cannot all be licensed at the same time, however.

Finally, there are unexpected locality restrictions on discontinuous NP constructions. Recall from section 3.1.3 that NPs need not adjoin to the smallest clause containing the licensing pronoun in Mohawk. Rather, they can be adjoined to a higher clause, as long as the NP c-commands the pronoun and no barrier intervenes. Additional examples of this are given in (7).

(7)   a. Akwéku kanataro-shú'a te-ho-[a]tʌhutsóni   á-hra-k-e'.
         all   bread-PL   DUP-MsO-want/STAT OPT-MsS-eat-PUNC
         'He wants to eat (taste) all the (kinds of) bread.'

      b. Akwéku athere'-shú'a ónʌ y-a'-t-ho-rihwayʌ́ta's-e'
         all   basket-PL   now TRANS-FACT-DUP-MsO-decide-PUNC

         a-ha-hnínu-'.
         OPT-MsS-buy-PUNC
         'He has now decided to buy all the baskets.'

Suppose, then, that we try to form a discontinuous expression as follows. First, we adjoin a lexical noun to the right of the lower verb and coindex it with the null pronoun object. Next, *akwéku* 'all' is adjoined to the matrix verb and is coindexed with the same embedded object position. On the assumption that the two NPs are licensed independently, such examples should always be grammatical, just as (7) is. In fact, (8a) is grammatical but (8b) is not.

(8)   a. Akwéku te-ho-[a]tʌhutsóni   á-hra-k-e'   ne kanátaro.
         all   DUP-MsO-want/STAT OPT-MsS-eat-PUNC NE bread
         'He wants to eat all the bread.'

      b. *Akwéku y-a'-t-ho-rihwayʌ́ta's-e'   a-ha-hnínu-'
         all   TRANS-FACT-DUP-MsO-decide-PUNC OPT-MsS-buy-PUNC

         ne áthere'.
         NE basket
         'He decided to buy all the baskets.'

This contrast suggests that elements like *akwéku* are not licensed by exactly the same principles as other NPs after all. If this is true, it may shed light on why *akwéku* participates in split NP constructions, but many other elements do not.

Summarizing these results, let us visualize the total range of discontinuous NP constructions that a language like Mohawk might have. We have seen that, in fact, only a rather small percentage of this range is actually attested; many kinds of examples turn out to be impossible. In this respect, Mohawk contrasts with nonconfigurational languages such as Warlpiri, in which examples parallel to (3) and (6) are grammatical (Kenneth Hale, personal communication).

These restrictions seem to carry over to the other polysynthetic languages as well. For some of them, discontinuous constituents are either outright impossible or are so rare and restricted that they go unobserved in standard grammars. This is true of Wichita (Rood 1976), Kiowa (Watkins 1984), Nahuatl (Andrews 1975, Launey 1981), and Ainu (Shibatani 1990). Only in grammars of the Gunwinjguan languages is the possibility of discontinuous NPs discussed explicitly—perhaps, in part, because the languages are distantly related to Warlpiri, where this phenomenon is so striking. However, even in these languages discontinuities seem to be rarer and more restricted than they are in Warlpiri. Thus, Evans (to appear a) writes: ". . . it is useful to recognize NP units in Mayali, and the words of exter-nal [i.e., nonincorporated—MCB] NPs are almost always contiguous. . . ." The only type of split NP explicitly discussed by Evans (1991:128) is one in which a modifying adjective is separated from the main noun, although there do seem to be a few examples of other types sprinkled throughout the grammar. His example is:

(9)   Na-marngorl ga-garrme   na-gimuk.
      I-barramundi 3sS-catch/NONPAST I-big
      'He's catching a big barramundi.'

Heath (1984:497–506) characterizes Nunggubuyu as having discontinuous nomi-nal expressions; however, other than N–A splits like that in (9), the only clear example he gives is the following:

(10) Nu:-'ba-gi-yung ni:-'maji-Ø, na-wulmur-injung.
      that(Ms)   he-stole   bachelor
      'That one committed theft, the bachelor.'

In (10), a demonstrative precedes the verb and an overt NP follows it—a possibil-ity that is within the range of discontinuous constituents allowed in Mohawk as well. This is also the only kind of discontinuous expression that Heath (1978:53) illustrates for Ngandi. We are thus left with the overall impression that discontinu-ous NPs are actually quite limited across the polysynthetic languages.[2]

This suggests that Jelinek's permissive approach to discontinuity is inappropri-ate for this class of languages. Inspired by the parallels with CLLD, let us begin by going to the opposite extreme and saying that a given pronoun can license no more than one adjoined NP. This can be achieved by explicitly building a unique-ness condition into the statement of the ALC, originally formulated in section 3.1.5:

(11) *The Adjunct Licensing Condition*   (revised)
      An argument-type phrase XP generated in adjoined position is licensed if and only if:
      (i) it forms a chain with a unique null pronominal Y in an argument position, and
      (ii) For each integer I contained in the index sets of both XP and Y, there is no phrase ZP distinct from XP that forms a chain with Y by virtue of sharing I.

The new clause (11ii) is clearly related to the idea, traditional in P&P theory, that two θ-chains cannot share the same θ-position. As such, it, too, can probably be understood as a corollary of the Principle of Full Interpretation; it helps to ensure that every well-formed sentence has a consistent interpretation at LF. With this clause added, (11) rules out all of the ungrammatical examples discussed in this section, because one or the other of the two nominal elements is not licensed.

Notice that the way (11) is phrased leaves open one situation in which a single pronoun can license two adjoined NPs after all: this is the situation where the pronoun is nonsingular. Nonsingular pronouns can have more than one integer in their referential index set, as reviewed in section 3.3.1 and the references cited there. Since the uniqueness condition in (11ii) is stated over integers in an index set and not over index sets as a whole, such a pronoun can, in principle, license two or more NPs. This is exactly what one finds in an example like (12a), which has the representation in (12b).

(12) a. Uwári wa'-t-hni-núnyahkw-e'   ne Sak.
          Mary FACT-DUP-MdS-dance-PUNC NE Sak
          'Mary danced with Sak.'

      b. [$_{NP\{i\}}$ Mary] [$_S$ pro$_{\{i,k\}}$ MdS-dance] [$_{NP\{k\}}$ Sak]

Indeed, it would not be too misleading to call (12) a "discontinuous conjunction" (see Baker 1992b for some semantic facts that go along with this). The crucial difference between this example and the ungrammatical ones given previously is that here the two NPs licensed by the pronoun are themselves disjoint in reference, whereas in the other cases they were coreferential. Thus, intuitively speaking, (12) does not present the same kind of danger of an inconsistent interpretation at LF. Having noted the existence of this case, I put it aside for the rest of this chapter; instead, I concentrate on examples where the licensing pronoun is singular and this possibility does not arise.

Another class of "discontinuous expressions" that I shall put aside in this chapter are those that consist of a relative clause separated from its head NP. These are rather common in the polysynthetic languages, particularly when the N precedes V and the relative clause follows V. An example of this type in Mohawk is the following:

(13) Áthere' ye-núhwe'-s ne wake-tsháry-u.
      basket FsS-like-HAB NE 1sO-find-STAT
      'She likes the basket that I found.'

Similar examples are found in the Gunwinjguan languages, Wichita, and probably many other languages as well. Noun–adjective splits such as that in (9) in Mayali may be instances of this type as well, given that bare "adjectives" can typically be the main predicate of a free-standing clause in the polysynthetic languages. Thus, a more literal gloss for (9) could be 'He's catching a barramundi, *which is big*.' My reason for putting this class of examples aside is that a relative clause can often be separated from its head even in fully configurational languages, such as English (e.g., *A man entered the room who was wearing a black hat*). Thus, it is not clear that examples like (13) have anything to do with polysynthesis or nonconfigurationality per se.

What does all of this imply for grammatical examples like (1) and (10), which are clearly not found in configurational languages? For these, the straightforward implication of (11) is that one member or the other of the "discontinuous NP" must be licensed by something other than the ALC. When and where such alternative licensing is possible, then, determines the range of discontinuous expressions that are found in the language. Not surprisingly, there turns out to be no single solution to all of the examples; rather quantifiers, *wh*-expressions, and demonstratives have separate licensing properties, resulting in subtly different syntactic behaviors. These will be discussed in turn. Along the way we will also have the opportunity to consider another very interesting kind of discontinuous dependency that is found in some polysynthetic languages but not in English: the internally headed relative clause.

4.2 Floated Quantifiers

4.2.1 All-type Quantifiers

I begin with discontinuous expressions in Mohawk involving *akwéku* 'all'. This is the most common type in Mohawk; indeed, it is the only type that is readily found in texts. For example:

(14)   a. Akwéku kʌ wá-hs-atst-e'   ne óhna'?   (D&D:388)
         all   Q FACT-2sS-use-PUNC NE leather
         'Did you use all of the leather?'

       b. Sak akwéku wa-híy-u-'   ye-hyatú-hkw-ha'.
         Sak all   FACT-1sS/MsO-give-PUNC FsS-write-INSTR-HAB
         'I gave Sak all the pencils.'

Such constructions are discussed explicitly for Onondaga by Woodbury (1975:71, 111). This is also the most common type from a cross-linguistic perspective. Very similar sentences are found in Nahuatl (Launey 1981:68), Chukchee (Nedjalkov 1979:248), and Southern Tiwa (Donald Frantz, personal communication)[3]:

(15)   a. Moch ni-c-cua   in nōchtli.   (NAHUATL)
         all   1sS-3sO-eat IN prickly.pear
         'I ate all the prickly pears.'

       b. ʔOrawetlʔa-ta əmelʔo na-twə-n ənə-kə ərg-in   (CHUKCHEE)
         man-ERG   all   3P-say-3s he-DAT they-POSS

         walom-yo-tte wetgaw-ət.
         hear-PART-PL word-ABS/PL
         'People told him all the words heard by them.'

       c. Shimba bi-mu-ban   seuan-nin.   (SOUTHERN TIWA)
         all   1sS/bO-see-PAST man-PL
         'I saw all the men.'

Why should elements meaning 'all' be exceptions to the rather general ban on discontinuous expressions? An obvious answer would appeal to the quantificational nature of such elements. Indeed, processes of quantifier floating are common even in configurational languages. In this light, I propose that *akwéku* in Mohawk is a particle[4] whose syntax is almost exactly like that of *tous* 'all' in French (see Kayne 1975:ch. 1 and Kayne 1984:ch. 4). Descriptively, both elements can appear either attached to an NP or in an adverbial position adjoined to VP. If attached to NP, they quantify over the parts of the referent of that NP, asserting that whatever is predicated of the NP is true of all of those parts. If adjoined to VP, then they are interpreted as quantifying over some empty category that is an argument of the V. This second alternative is the source of the sentences in (14).

Consider first the NP-adjoined construction. This has come up at various points in the discussion and particularly in section 2.1.3. Unambiguous instances are given in (16).

(16)   a. Sak wa-híy-u-'   akwéku ye-hyatú-hkw-ha'.
           Sak FACT-1sS/MsO-give-PUNC all   FsS-write-INSTR-HAB
           'I gave Sak all the pencils.'

       b. Shawátis wa-shakó-kʌ-'   akwéku.
           John   FACT-MsS/FsO-see-PUNC all
           'John saw everyone.'

In (16a), *akwéku* attaches to an overt noun 'pencil'; in (16b) it attaches to a null nominal head, perhaps pro.[5] As already mentioned, it adds the idea that every part of the referent of the NP it attaches to is involved in the action. This option is also found in Nahuatl (cf. (15a)):

(17)   Ni-c-cua   in mochi nōchtli.   (Launey 1981:68)
       1sS-3sO-eat IN all   prickly pear
       'I ate all the prickly pears.'

Notice that this need not imply that *akwéku* or *mochi* is a determiner syntactically. I have already mentioned that Mohawk does not have true determiners (section 6.1.2 derives this from the Polysynthesis Parameter). However, those elements that are most comparable to *akwéku*—*all* in English and *tous* in French—are not determiners either. On the contrary, they attach to phrases that already have definite determiners:

(18)   Elle lira tous *ces* livres.
       'She will read all *those* books.'

Thus, the absence of determiners in Mohawk has little bearing on this construction. *Akwéku* can be considered part of the nominal system, broadly construed, without having this status.

In section 2.1.3, I claimed that NPs with Mohawk *akwéku* and English *all* were not quantificational, contrasting them with NPs containing the determiner *every*. This view seems counterintuitive, however. Given that *akwéku* is not a determiner, there is a way to reconcile its intuitively quantificational nature with the theory given earlier. I tentatively suggest that Mohawk *akwéku* is to be analyzed along the same lines as the elements that Heim et al. (1991:75–79) call *distributors*. Distributors are elements that adjoin to a complete plural NP and "introduce a universal quantification over the individuals serving as the (plural) denotation of the NP" (Heim et al. 1991:75). One of their examples is postnominal *each* in a sentence like (19):

(19)   [[The men]$_{NPi}$ each]$_{NPk}$ left.

The crucial feature of this system for our purposes is that the basic NP and the larger NP formed by adding the distributor bear distinct referential indices, either of which can be the antecedent for anaphoric pronouns. This gives Heim et al. an explicit formalism for expressing at LF the various collective and distributive readings of plural NPs and the pronouns dependent on them. Suppose that this idea carries over to an example like (20) in Mohawk (here I suppress the possibility of set indices).

(20) [$_{NPk}$ akwéku [$_{NPi}$ ne ron-úkwe]] [$_S$ pro$_i$ wa-hoti-yéshu-']
        all   NE MP-person   FACT-MpO-laugh-PUNC
        'All the men laughed.'

It is natural to say that the smaller NP in this construction can have an index, given that it is thematically complete and capable of referring on its own. Now NP$_k$ cannot be directly licensed by the principles governing dislocation because coindexing it with the pro in argument position violates Cinque's (1990) referentiality condition on binding chains. However, NP$_i$ can be coindexed with pro, since NP$_i$ is an ordinary referential NP. This fits well with the fact that the pronoun/agreement in (20) must be plural, as one would expect if its true antecedent is NP$_i$ rather than NP$_k$. NP$_k$ can be deemed to be licensed indirectly by virtue of its close relationship to the properly licensed NP$_i$. In contrast, NPs comparable to *every man* are still be ruled out in Mohawk, because they do not contain an "inner" NP that is qualified to enter into coreference relationships; such nominals have the quantificational layer, but not the referential one. This maintains the crucial difference between *every* and *all/akwéku* that was the basis of the discussion in section 2.1.3, while still allowing the use of some quantificational techniques for the latter.

Next, consider the possibility of generating *akwéku* as an adverb in a VP-adjoined position.[6] This results in sentences such as (1a) and (14), in which *akwéku* is separated from the lexical NP it is interpreted with (if any). These examples are the Mohawk equivalents to the well-known "L-*tous*" phenomenon in French, in which a quantifier associated with the direct object appears in an adverbial position (Kayne 1975:ch. 1):

(21)   Elle les   a   tous lus.
        she them has all   read
        'She has read them all.'

An apparent dissimilarity between the French construction and the Mohawk one is that floated *tous* is not possible if the object is a full lexical NP, rather than an empty category associated with a clitic pronoun:

(22)   *Elle a   tous lu   ces   livres.
        she has all   read those books
        'She has read all those books.'

Kayne (1984) suggests that the reason for this is that *tous* must bind a variable in argument position in order not to violate the ban on vacuous quantification (now considered another instance of the Principle of Full Interpretation). Weak pronouns can serve as variables in this sense, but lexical NPs cannot. This is presumably a special case of a very general principle, related, for example, to the fact that many languages have resumptive pronouns in extraction constructions, but do not have resumptive lexical NPs. Examples (14) and (17) look as though they are directly comparable to (22), but they are grammatical. The dissimilarity is only apparent, however. On the neo-Jelinekian approach adopted here, lexical NPs are never in the direct object position in Mohawk either; rather, that position is filled by a null pronoun related to object agreement on the verb. This is, of course, true for (1a) and (14) as well. Hence, the phrase structure for (1a) is (23).

(23)

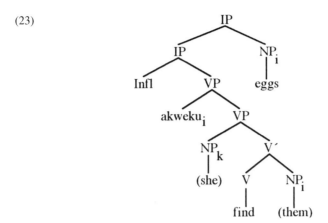

(In (23), I adopt the VP-internal subject hypothesis for Mohawk, argued for in section 2.2 but mostly suppressed until now.) The VP in (23) is directly parallel to that of (21) in French. In particular, there is a null pronoun inside the VP that *akwéku* can quantify over. This pronoun also serves to license the dislocated NP 'eggs', in accordance with (11). Even here, there is no principled difference between French and Mohawk, because the null pronoun associated with L-*tous* may license CLLD in French as well:

(24)   Ces livres, elle les a tous lus.
        'These books, she has read all of them.'

Of course, the dislocated NP in Mohawk can also be adjoined to the left side of IP, in which case it appears outside of the domain of *akwéku*, as in French.[7]

(25)   Onhúhsa' akwéku wa'-e-tshári-'.
        egg   all   FACT-FsS-find-PUNC
        'She found all the eggs.'

Thus, the only real difference between the two languages is the familiar one that Mohawk is forced to use dislocation to express a lexical NP, whereas it is a marked option in French.

Now we can consider more precisely why the representation in (23) does not violate the uniqueness clause of the ALC. The crucial factor is that floated *akwéku, mochi,* and *tous* are all adverbs syntactically. Kayne (1975) documents in considerable detail the evidence for saying that French *tous* appears in adverb positions. Since adverbs are not "argument-type phrases," the ALC is not directly relevant to them. Instead, *akwéku, mochi,* and *tous* are licensed according to the principles governing adverbs. For this, I follow the general outlines of Travis 1988, where it is argued that adverbs are heads adjoined to the projection of another head (here V). They are then integrated into the structure by entering into a relationship of θ-role identification with one of the arguments of the licensing head. If this view is approximately correct, then *akwéku* need not, and in fact must not, form a chain with the object pro in (23), because it is a head (an X^0), not a maximal projection. Hence, pro in (23) enters into only one chain (the one including 'eggs'), and the structure is well formed.

This theory explains part of the word order problem mentioned in section 4.1. Recall that split NPs are possible in Mohawk if *akwéku* is before the verb and the lexical NP after the verb, but not if the order is reversed. A minimal pair is repeated here:

(26) a. Akwéku wa'-e-tshÁri-'   ne onhúhsa'.
          all   FACT-FsS-find-PUNC NE egg
          'She found all the eggs.'

      b. *Onhúhsa' wa'-e-tshÁri-'   akwéku.
          eggs   FACT-FsS-find-PUNC all
          'She found all the eggs.'

Apparently the same word order asymmetry holds in Nahuatl (Launey 1981:68). Now, *akwéku* in (26b) cannot be licensed as an NP, because then the object *pro* would need to enter into two distinct dislocation chains. Thus, *akwéku* must be an adverb, as it is in (26a). However, this is not possible either, because X^0 adverbs modifying the VP typically only attach to the left side of VP in Mohawk. Example (27) gives independent evidence for this word order constraint using manner adverbs.

(27) a. Sak skʌnʌ-shú'a tsi   wa-ha-'wáhr-a-riht-e'.
          Sak slow-PL   that FACT-MsS-meat-Ø-cook-PUNC
          'Sak cooked the meat slowly.'

      b. ?*Sak wa-ha-'wáhr-a-riht-e'   skʌnʌ-shú'a.
          Sak FACT-MsS-meat-Ø-cook-PUNC slow-PL
          'Sak cooked the meat slowly.'

Indeed, it seems to be a general property of Mohawk that modifying particles are adjoined to the front of the modified category. Thus, demonstratives and *akwéku* within NP appear at the front of NP; the various particles indicating negation, evidential notions, and illocutionary force appear at or near the beginning of a clause, and so on. In this way, particles are different from full NPs, which can adjoin to either side of the target category. Leaving open exactly why this is so, I conclude that (26) confirms the hypothesis that floated *akwéku* functions as an adverb in Mohawk. In this way, it is parallel to the much more detailed evidence that Kayne presents for *tous* in French.

This being said, it must be conceded that adverbial *tous* and *akwéku* have some rather odd properties. In particular, they both lack what one might call a "pure" adverbial reading, in which they modify only the verb. Kayne (1975) illustrates this for French with the fact that sentences like (28) are ruled out in most varieties.

(28) *J'ai   tous lu   ce livre.
       I have all read this book
       'I have read this book completely.'

Similarly, (29) in Mohawk has no interpretation.

(29)   *Akwéku khe-núhwe'-s   ne Uwári.
       all   1sS/FsO-like-HAB NE Mary
       'I like all Mary; I like Mary completely.'

Nor does (30) seem to have the same kind of ambiguity that is attested in certain other Amerindian languages (see, e.g., Jelinek to appear).

(30)   Akwéku wa'-ka-na'ts-a-hútsi-'-ne'.
       all   FACT-NsS-pot-Ø-black-INCH-PUNC
       'All of the pot(s) turned black.'
       ??'The pot(s) turned completely black.'

This sentence could potentially have two representations: one in which *akwéku* is coindexed with the NP position associated with the incorporated noun *na'ts* 'pot', and one in which it simply modifies the verb 'turn black'. The first of these representations should correspond to a meaning in which every pot (or perhaps every part of a single pot) is discolored; the second could have the distinctive implication that the pot becomes fully black (as opposed to merely darkish gray). To the extent that speakers can distinguish these two readings, (30) seems to have only the first reading. Apparently, both *tous* and *akwéku,* in addition to being adverbs, must associate with a suitable NP position. Still following Kayne (1984:ch. 4), we may attribute this to their quantificational nature, which implies that they must bind an empty category or a pronoun in their domain to avoid the ban against vacuous quantification.

The theory sketched so far leaves open exactly which argument position these adverbial quantifiers bind. This is intentional, because, in fact, any position within their scope with suitable pronominal properties will do. Example (31) shows that *tous* in French can bind a subject position or an object position in the embedded clause equally well (Pollock 1978).

(31)   a. ?Il faut *tous* qu'*ils*   partent.
            it must all that they leave
            'They must all leave.'

       b. ?Il faut *tous* que Marie *les*   lise.
            it must all that Marie them read.
            'Marie must read them all.'

Similarly, *akwéku* can bind any null pronouns within the VP it adjoins to: direct object, indirect object, or subject. The examples so far have all involved direct objects, but that was simply for convenience. Split *akwéku* constructions are equally possible with subject arguments, as in (32), or indirect object arguments, as in (33).

(32)   a. Akwéku kʌ wa'-esá-kʌ-'   ne rati-ksa'-okú'a?
            all   Q FACT-3pS/2sO-see-PUNC NE MpS-child-PL
            'Did all the children see you?'

       b. Akwéku wa-hoti-yéshu-'   ne ukwe-húwe.
            all   FACT-MpO-laugh-PUNC NE person-real
            'All of the Indians laughed.'

(33)   Akwéku wa'-khe-tsikét-a-nut-e'   ne rati-ksa'-okú'a.
       all   FACT-1sS/FsO-candy-Ø-feed-PUNC NE MpS-child-PL
       'I gave candy to all the children.'

Similarly, *moch* 'all' in adverbial position can be associated with a subject argument as well as an object argument in Nahuatl. (Launey does not happen to give any examples with indirect objects.)

(34)   Moch-intin Ø-tla-cua-'   in pitzō-me'.   (Launey 1981:68)
       all-PL   3S-3INDEFO-eat-PL IN pig-PL
       'The pigs all ate.'

Thus, discontinuous expressions of this type are not restricted to any particular grammatical function.

    This analysis also sheds light on the contrast in (8), repeated here as (35).

(35)   a. Akwéku te-ho-[a]tΛhutsóni   á-hra-k-e'   ne kanátaro.
          all   DUP-MsO-want/STAT OPT-MsS-eat-PUNC NE bread
          'He wants to eat all the bread.'

       b. *Akwéku y-a'-t-ho-rihwayΛta's-e'   a-ha-hnínu-'
          all   TRANS-FACT-DUP-MsO-decide-PUNC OPT-MsS-buy-PUNC

          ne áthere'.
          NE basket
          'He decided to buy all the baskets.'

In these constructions, *akwéku* is adjoined to the matrix VP and is understood as quantifying over a variable contained within the complement of that VP. Whether or not this is possible apparently depends on the nature of the matrix verb in some way. Significantly, L-*tous* in French has similar properties (Kayne 1975, Pollock 1978). In particular, the following restrictions hold in French. First, the complement of the matrix verb must be in the infinitive or (marginally for some speakers) the subjunctive mood. This is illustrated by the following minimal pair (Pollock 1978:102–103):

(36)   a. ??Je dis tous qu'ils partent.
             'I say all that they ought to leave.'

       b. *Je dis tous qu'ils sont partis.
             'I say all that they have left.'

A similar condition is found in Mohawk; the complement of the matrix verb must be in the so-called optative mood in order for a long-distance interpretation of *akwéku* to be accepted. This mood is the closest Mohawk equivalent to a subjunctive or infinitive verb (see Lounsbury 1953:50). If the complement is in the factual (i.e., indicative) mood, long-distance *akwéku* interpretation is barred:

(37)   a. Akwéku í-hr-ehr-e'   a-ke-ks-oharé-nyu-'.
          all   Ø-MsS-think-IMPF OPT-1sS-dish-wash-DIST-PUNC
          'He wants me to wash all the dishes.'

       b. ??Akwéku í-hr-ehr-e'   wa'-ke-ks-oharé-nyu-'.
          all   Ø-MsS-think-IMPF FACT-1sS-dish-wash-DIST-PUNC
          'He thinks I washed all the dishes.'

(Notice that the Mohawk verb *ehr* translates into English as either 'want' or 'think', depending on the mood of its complement.) Second, even among the verbs that take infinitival or subjunctive complements, only a subset allow long-distance L-*tous*. Roughly, these seem to be verbs with modal-like meanings; in French the list includes *vouloir* 'want', *pouvoir* 'can,' *devoir* 'should', and *falloir* 'must' (see Pollock 1978 for discussion). Thus, one finds contrasts like the following, parallel to (35) in Mohawk (Bonneau and Zushi 1993):

(38) a. Jean a tous voulu les lire.
          'Jean has wanted to read them all.'

      b. *Jean a tous décidé de les lire.
          'Jean has decided to read them all.'

Again, Mohawk is strikingly similar: long-distance *akwéku* interpretation is allowed with the predicates *ehr* 'want', as in (37a), *atʌhutsoni* 'want', as in (35a), *onʌk tsi* 'must', and *atu* 'be possible'. Verbs that do not allow long-distance *akwéku* even though they take an optative complement include *rihwayʌta's* 'decide', as in (35b), *rako* 'choose', *askanek* 'wish', and *hrori* 'tell, order to'. Thus, the parallelism between L-*tous* in French and floated *akwéku* in Mohawk holds up in this empirical domain as well.

Unfortunately, the literature on French does not contain a fully satisfactory account of these facts that we can simply endorse. The analyses of Kayne 1975 and Pollock 1978 are dated and unstatable within current theoretical frameworks. Kayne 1984, which I have followed most closely, does not deal with this issue, although it is mentioned in a footnote. The list of verbs that allow long-distance L-*tous* looks, at first glance, very similar to the set of verbs that trigger restructuring phenomena in other Romance languages (Italian, Spanish, Catalan). This has led some to analyze examples like (38) as manifestations of restructuring in French (e.g., Bonneau and Zushi (1993)). However, there are a number of problems with this intuition. First, it is well known that Modern French allows none of the typical characteristics of restructuring found in the other Romance languages (see Kayne 1984). Second, long-distance L-*tous* is possible from subjunctive complements for some speakers of French, as shown in (36a) and other examples from Pollock 1978, but other properties of restructuring are not found with subjunctives in any of the standard Romance languages. Finally, a close look shows that the class of verbs that allow long-distance L-*tous* in French is not so similar to the class of restructuring verbs in cognate languages after all. Certainly, there is a nontrivial overlap in the form of *vouloir, pouvoir,* and *devoir.* However, aspectual verbs such as 'begin' and motion verbs such as 'go' and 'come' are restructuring triggers in Italian and Spanish, but do not allow long-distance L-*tous* in French (José Bonneau, personal communication; Nicole Domingue, personal communication). Conversely, *essayer* 'try' does allow long-distance L-*tous* in French, but its equivalent is not a restructuring verb in other Romance languages. Strikingly, Mohawk parallels French to a remarkable degree: the aspectual verb *atahsawʌ́* 'begin' and the motion verb *e* 'go' do not allow long-distance *akwéku* interpretation, whereas *ate'nyʌtʌ* 'try' does. For example:

(39) a. *Akwéku t-ho-[a]tahsáwe   a-há-ya'k-e'   ne ókwire'.
          all   CIS-MsO-start/STAT OPT-MsS-break-PUNC NE tree
          'He has started to cut all the trees.'

      b. Akwéku wa-ha-[a]te'nyʌ́tʌ-' a-ha-hnínu-'   óyʌte'.
          all   FACT-MsS-try-PUNC OPT-MsS-buy-PUNC wood
          'He tried to buy all the wood.'

This strongly suggests that the lexical factors that make long-distance quantifier interpretation possible are not idiosyncratic. Moreover, the lexical semantic property that permits restructuring in Spanish and Italian seems to be somewhat different from the one that potentiates long-distance quantifier interpretation in French and Mohawk. Thus, I conclude that restructuring is not crucially involved in long-distance quantifier interpretations.

Given this, I can only speculate as to the nature of the effect in question. The class of verbs that allow long-distance quantifier interpretation seems to consist distinctively of verbs that have modal interpretations. Verbs of this class are typically treated as quantificational elements by semanticists; they quantify over events of the type defined by the complement clause in a subset of the possible worlds—those that are desirable, those that are reachable from the real world, and so on. One may imagine that this type of quantification over the embedded complement somehow keeps that complement open to other types of quantification from the matrix clause. Thus, *tous* is able to find a variable inside the CP complement by virtue of the fact that its licensing verb (say, *vouloir*) quantifies over that complement. If the matrix verb is not quantificational, then its complement is sealed off as a fixed expression referring to a proposition; in that case, *tous* in the matrix fails to find a variable it can bind. This would account for the deviance of (35b) and (38b). Similarly, indicative/factual mood presumably has the function of fixing the event picked out by the verb, making the clause a referential expression. This makes it impossible for the matrix verb to quantify over the event position of the embedded verb, which, in turn, means that *tous* cannot piggyback on the matrix verb to quantify over an argument of the lower clause. This would account for the contrasts in (36) and (37). Obviously, to make these suggestions precise would involve venturing into the deep waters of the semantics of modality, mood, and tense, which is not my purpose here. However, to the extent that an account along these lines looks promising, we may safely attribute these effects to UG. Indeed, it seems all but certain that whatever accounts for facts about long-distance L-*tous* in French will also generalize to explain the contrasts seen in Mohawk. The fact that verbs like the one in (35b) allow long-distance dislocation but not long-distance *akwéku* is, then, not problematic. Like the other puzzles considered in this section, this one is solved by the fact that bare *akwéku* is not an NP licensed by dislocation, but a quantificational head licensed by bearing an adverbial relationship to the verb.

4.2.2 A Lot–type Quantifiers

Similar but not identical to the *akwéku* facts are those involving *éso* 'a lot' in Mohawk. *Éso* is like *akwéku* in that it can either form a constituent with a lexical NP or be separated from it by the verb:

(40) a. Éso onhúhsa' wa-ha-tshÁri-'.
a.lot egg   FACT-MsS-find-PUNC
'He found a lot of eggs.'

b. Éso wa-ha-tshÁri-'   ne onhúhsa'.
a.lot FACT-MsS-find-PUNC NE egg
'He found a lot of eggs.'

The same is true for *miyac* 'a lot' in Nahuatl (Launey 1981:68):

(41) a. Ø-Huītze-' miyaqu-intin tlāca'.
3S-come-PL a.lot-PL   person-PL
'A lot of people come.'

b. Miyaqu-intin Ø-huītze-' in tlāca'.
a.lot-PL   3S-come-PL IN person-PL
'A lot of people come.'

Presumably, the explanation for these facts is, broadly speaking, the same as the one offered for the facts involving *akwéku:* that is, *éso* and *miyac* can be licensed as an adverb with quantificational properties instead of as a full NP. Moreover, the parallelism with French continues to hold; (40b) and (41b) are comparable to (42) with adverbial *beaucoup.*

(42) Il a   beaucoup trouvé de pièces d'or.   (Obenauer 1984)
He has many   found of gold coins
'He found many gold coins.'

Nevertheless, although *éso, miyac,* and *beaucoup* are like *akwéku, mochi,* and *tous* in being adverbs with quantificational force, it is clear that they are quite a different kind of adverb. Some of the differences in French are documented by Obenauer (1984) and they carry over to Mohawk quite well. Thus, unlike *tous* and *akwéku, beaucoup* and *éso* can have pure adverbial meanings, in which they modify the verb alone. This means that there need not be any NP position in the sentence that they are understood as quantifying over:

(43) a. Éso tsi ke-núhwe'-s thíkʌ ká'sere'.
a.lot that 1sS-like-HAB that   car
'I like that car a lot (to a large degree).'

b. J'ai beaucoup lu ce livre.
'I have read that book a lot (many times).'

Indeed, sometimes the same example is ambiguous between these two different readings:

(44) Érhar éso wa-shako-[a]hterúhkwʌ-'   ne rati-ksa'-okú'a
dog   a.lot FACT-MsS/3pO-scare-PUNC NE MpS-child-PL
'The dog scared the children a lot (to a large degree of fear).'
OR: 'The dog scared a lot of children.'

Building on this observation, Obenauer argues that *beaucoup* in adverbial position always modifies the verb, even in examples like (42). The apparent dependency between *beaucoup* and the direct object is thus only an indirect one. Indeed, there is a semantic difference between adverbial *beaucoup* and nominal *beaucoup* that comes out more clearly in examples like (45).

(45) a. Dans cette marmite il a trouvé beaucoup de pièces d'or.
           'In this pot he found many pieces of gold.'

      b. #Dans cette marmite il a beaucoup trouvé de pièces d'or.
           'In this pot he many found pieces of gold.'

Adverbial *beaucoup* in (45b) carries with it the implication that not only were many coins found, but there were many distinct events of coin finding. This interpretation is pragmatically incompatible with the adverbial PP, so the sentence is anomalous. However, (45a) has no similar anomaly. This suggests that *beaucoup* is really modifying 'find' in (45b). The fact that many coins were found is a consequence of the fact that there were many findings. Similar differences in interpretation are sometimes found in Mohawk between split and nonsplit *éso*. Thus, consider (46).

(46) a. Éso ke-núhwe'-s ne ka'sere-shú'a.
           a.lot 1sS-like-HAB NE car-PL
           'I like many cars (there are many brands that I like).'

      b. Ke-núhwe'-s éso ka-sere-shú'a (nónʌ wakatʌyʌte').
           1sS-like-HAB a.lot car-PL   when wedding
           'I like a lot of cars (together when there is a wedding).'

Example (46a) is naturally interpreted as meaning that there are many different types of cars that I like; in other words, I enter into many different relationships of car-liking. Example (46b) is spontaneously understood in a somewhat different way. Here, I like a state of affairs in which there are many cars present, for example, for a particular purpose. Thus, while there are many cars, there is only one relationship of liking asserted. As in French, the adverbial *éso* quantifies over the verb itself in a way that the nominal position of the same element does not.[8]

   This analysis forms a plausible basis of an explanation of the fact that adverbial *éso* and *beaucoup* can only be interpreted with the direct object of the verb. For French, this is discussed by Kayne (1984:ch. 3) and Obenauer (1984), who analyze the effect in terms of Chomsky's (1981) Empty Category Principle. The same generalization holds in Mohawk. Thus, in the following examples the adverbial *éso* is not understood as asserting that many agents were involved in the action:

(47) a. Éso wa-hati-kar-atú-nyu-'   ne roti-kstʌ-'okú'a.
           a.lot FACT-MpS-story-tell-DIST-PUNC NE MpO-old.person-PL
           'The old men told a lot of stories/the old men told stories a lot.'
           NOT: 'A lot of old men told stories.'

      b. Éso wa-hoti-yéshu-'   ne ukwe-húwe.
           a.lot FACT-MpO-laugh-PUNC NE person-real
           'The Indians laughed a lot.' NOT: 'Many Indians laughed.'

Nor can adverbial *éso* be understood as quantifying over the indirect object in (48).

(48) Éso wa'-khe-tsikét-a-nut-e'   ne rati-ksa'-okú'a.
      a.lot FACT-1sS/3pO-candy-Ø-feed-PUNC NE MpS-child-PL
      'I gave a lot of candy to the children.' NOT: 'I gave candy to a lot of children.'

It is well known from the literature on aspect that the direct objects of many verbs have the property of "delimiting" or "measuring out" the event. Thus, there are important correspondences between the definiteness and number of the object and the aspectual character of the verb phrase as a whole; for example, *I ate an apple* counts as an accomplishment, whereas *I ate apples* is an ongoing activity (Dowty 1979, Tenny 1987). Given this, it is not surprising that quantification over the VP and quantification over the object turn out to be more or less equivalent in some cases. If an adverbial element implies that there were many events of a certain type, and if events are individuated and "measured out" by their direct object arguments, then it follows that there were many elements of the type referred to by the direct object as well. Agentive subjects and goals are not inherently related to the aspect of the verb in this way. Therefore, there is no general linguistic inference from a multiplicity of events to a multiplicity of subjects or indirect objects. This explains the contrast between (47)/(48) and (40). Example (47) also contrasts with (32), where adverbial *akwéku* does modify the subject. The difference is that *akwéku* enters into a direct binding relationship with an NP position, whereas *éso* does not. Hence, *akwéku* can bind any suitable variable within its domain, whereas *éso,* strictly speaking, modifies the verb, thereby influencing the interpretation of the NP that the verb is tied to aspectually.

In stating that *éso* can only be understood as modifying the direct object, I left vague whether I was referring to underlying direct objects or to surface/derived direct objects. The line of analysis just sketched leads one to expect that it is *underlying* grammatical functions that are relevant here. For example, Tenny (1987) proposes the Aspectual Interface Hypothesis, according to which the NP argument of the verb that "measures out the event" named by the verb is always projected as the internal argument of that verb. Similarly, Dowty (1991:570–574) identifies the "incremental theme" as one of the factors (although not the only one) that determines which argument of the verb will be its patient, where patients are always expressed as underlying direct objects in the theory assumed here.[9] Example (48) already gives some evidence that this is correct: the floated quantifier is understood as quantifying over the theme argument rather than the goal argument, even though the goal argument might reasonably be considered a derived direct object in some sense—it triggers object agreement on the verb, for example. More interestingly, intransitive verbs divide into two classes with respect to the interpretation of adverbial *éso.* With some, the "subject" of the intransitive is easily construed as being modified by *éso:*

(49) a. Éso t-úhsʌ'-ne'   ne ówise'-(shú'a).
          a.lot CIS-FACT/NsS/fall-PUNC NE glass-PL
          'Many glasses fell.'

      b. Éso wa'-t-ká-hri'-ne'   ne ówise'-(shú'a).
          a.lot FACT-DUP-NsS-break-PUNC NE glass(ice)-PL
          'Many glasses broke; much ice broke.'[10]

   c. Éso wa-hoti-ké'tot-e'   ne rati-[i]hn-a-rákʌ.
       a.lot FACT-MpO-arrive-PUNC NE MpS-skin-Ø-white
       'Many whitemen arrived.'

   d. Éso wa-hatí-ye-'   ne rati-ksa-'okú'a.
       a.lot FACT-MpS-awaken-PUNC NE MpS-child-PL
       'Many children woke up.'

   e. Éso yo-nánawʌ ne kahyatúhsera-(shú'a).
       a.lot NsO-be.wet NE paper-PL
       'Many papers are wet.' OR: 'The paper is very wet.'

   f. Éso wa-hun-íhey-e'   ne roti-kstʌ-'okú'a.
       a.lot FACT-MpS-die-PUNC NE MpO-old.person-PL
       'Many old people died.'

However, with other intransitive verbs this interpretation is not found; rather, *éso* is understood as a frequency or intensity adverb. One example of this was given in (47b); others are given in (50).

(50) a. Éso yoti-yó't[ʌ]-e' ne kon-úkwe.
       a.lot FpO-work-HAB NE FpS-person
       'Women work a lot, do a lot of work.'

    b. Éso te-hoti-nunyáhkw-ʌ   ne rati-ksa'-okú'a.
       a.lot DUP-MpO-dance-STAT NE MpS-child-PL
       'The children danced a lot.'

    c. Éso rati-yʌ́tho-s-kwe'   ne Kahnawake-hrónu.
       a.lot MpS-plant-HAB-PAST NE Kahnawake-RESID
       'Kahnawakeans used to farm a lot.'

    d. Éso ru-[a]tórat-s   ne Kahnawake-hrónu.
       a.lot MpS-hunt-HAB NE Kahnawake-RESID
       'Kahnawakeans hunt a lot.'

    e. Éso rotí-[i]ta'-s   ne rati-ksa'-okú'a.
       a.lot MpO-sleep-HAB NE MpS-child-PL
       'The children sleep a lot.'

A sentence like (50a) is, of course, consistent with the idea that many women work, but that is not what the sentence is asserting. If one wants to bring out that meaning, it is necessary to attach *éso* directly to the NP. In this respect, the intransitive verbs in (50) are different from those in (49). Now the fact that floated *éso* modifies the "subject" NP in (49) but not (50) implies that the subject NP delimits the verb in (49) but not (50). This, in turn, implies that the subject NP is underlyingly generated in the object position in (49) but not (50). In other words, we have found syntactico-semantic evidence that distinguishes between unaccusative verbs and unergative verbs in Mohawk: the verbs in (49) are unaccusative, while the verbs in (50) are unergative. Indeed, this partition fits well with the one we would expect, based on lexical semantics and what is known about the distinction between unaccusative and unergative verbs across languages. This distinction will prove to be very important when we turn to the morphosyntactic topics in Part II.

    Similar considerations explain one further difference between *éso* and *akwéku.*

Recall that in a few cases *akwéku* (like *tous*) can be attached to a higher verb rather than the most local verb, with little or no change in meaning. This is never possible with *éso*; rather, there is always an important meaning shift that goes along with a change in placement of the adverb:

(51) a. Te-wak-atΛhutsóni éso a-ke-nhúhs-a-k-e'.
          DUP-1sO-want/STAT a.lot OPT-1sS-egg-Ø-eat-PUNC
          'I want to eat many eggs.'

      b. Éso ?(tsi) te-wak-atΛhutsóni á-ke-k-e'   ne onhúhsa'.
          a.lot that DUP-1sO-want/STAT OPT-1sS-eat-PUNC NE egg
          'I really want to eat eggs.' NOT: 'I want to eat many eggs.'

This, too, follows from the fact that floated *éso* inherently quantifies over the verb, whereas *akwéku* quantifies directly over an NP position. Thus, whatever verb *éso* attaches to, that is the verb that *éso* modifies with an intensive or repetitive meaning. Since there is no aspectual relationship between the higher verb and the object of the lower one, putting *éso* on the higher verb will not be the semantic equivalent of quantifying over the lower object. Again, *beaucoup* works like *éso* in this regard:

(52) a. Je voulait beaucoup manger de pommes.
          'I wanted to eat many apples.'

      b. J'ai beaucoup voulu manger de pommes.
          'I have wanted very much to eat some apples.' NOT: 'I have wanted to eat many apples.'

This confirms that *éso* and *beaucoup* do not link directly to the argument position, but rather modify the VP.

The last few paragraphs have focused on the fact that *éso* and *akwéku* are different kinds of adverbs. However, the most important result is that the difference between the two is almost exactly the same as the difference between *beaucoup* and *tous* in French. This means that "discontinuous constituents" of these types are not dependent in any fundamental way on the theory of nonconfigurationality in general, or on the Polysynthesis Parameter in particular. The only essential property that Mohawk and French share to make these constructions possible is that both have null pronoun arguments that are suitable variables for an *all*-class adverb; this property is shared by languages of all typological classes (although not English). Moreover, there is no need to weaken the claim that only one dislocated phrase can be licensed by a given pronoun. On the contrary, *akwéku* and *éso* can appear separated from a noun only if they are licensed in a distinct way, as adverbial heads adjoined to the projection of the verb. The fact that the specific licensing conditions for the two elements are somewhat different explains the subtle syntax differences between "discontinuous expressions" of the two types.

4.3 Operator Constructions

4.3.1 Split Interrogatives

The next class of discontinuous expressions to be considered are those involving
an interrogative such as *ka nikáyʌ* 'which'. Such interrogatives also may precede
the verb, while the lexical noun that they are construed with follows it:

(53)   a. Ka nikáyʌ wa-há-kʌ-'   (ne) kwéskwes?
           which   FACT-MsS/ZsO-see-PUNC NE pig
           'Which pig did he see?'

       b. Ka nikáyʌ í-hs-ehr-e'   a-hs-hnínu-'   ne ká'sere?
           which   Ø-2sS-think-IMPF OPT-2sS-buy-PUNC NE car
           'Which car do you want to buy?'

Examples of this type are harder to find in texts than examples with floated *akwéku,* but all my consultants accepted them quite freely.[11] Moreover, the possibility of separating *ka nikáyʌ* from the head noun does not depend on the understood
grammatical function of that noun. The examples in (53) show split objects; (54)
shows an example of a split subject, and (55) an example of a split indirect object.

(54)   Ka nikáyʌ wa'-ka-nʌ́st-a-k-e'   ne kwéskwes?
       which   FACT-NsS-corn-Ø-eat-PUNC NE pig
       'Which pig ate the corn?'

(55)   Ka nikáyʌ wá-hse-nut-e'   ne kwéskwes?
       which   FACT-2sS-feed-PUNC NE pig
       'Which pig did you feed?'

In this respect, *ka nikáyʌ* is more like *akwéku* 'all' than like *éso* 'a lot'. Similar
examples are found in Southern Tiwa (Donald Frantz, personal communication):

(56)   Yoadeu a-mu-ban   seuan-ide?
       Which   2sS/3sO-see-PAST man-SG?
       'Which man did you see?'

I do not have relevant data for the other polysynthetic languages, in part because
the sections on question formation in most grammars are rather brief.

   The key to understanding *akwéku* and *éso* was recognizing that they could be
licensed as adverbs as well as NPs. This is unlikely to work for *ka nikáyʌ*. Rather,
the key factor in this case is presumably the interrogative nature of the element,
which causes it to undergo movement to Comp. More specifically, *ka nikáyʌ* is
presumably the interrogative version of a demonstrative, comparable to *thíkʌ* 'that'
or *kʌ'íkʌ* 'this'. Thus, one natural way of answering a question like *ka nikáyʌ
á'share'. . .* ? 'Which knife. . . ?' is with a phrase like *thíkʌ á'share'* (that knife)
or *kíkʌ á'share'* 'this knife'.

   In this connection, it is significant that the syntax of demonstratives in Mohawk
is somewhat different from that in English. In English, demonstratives are generally assumed to be members of the category Det(erminer). Thus, they appear invariably at the beginning of a nominal expression, as expected of a head that
selects an NP in a head-initial language. They are also in complementary distribu-

tion with other members of category Det, such as *the, a,* strong quantifiers like *every,* and perhaps possessive *'s:*

(57) a. *a that book, that a book

     b. *the that book, that the book

     c. *every that book, that every book

     d. *John's that book, that John's book

However, I have mentioned several times that Mohawk and other polysynthetic languages systematically lack these other elements: there are no definite or indefinite articles and no strong quantifiers. This suggests that Mohawk lacks the category Det altogether, a claim that will be discussed in chapter 6. If this is correct, then, clearly, demonstratives in polysynthetic languages cannot be Dets. Rather, I assume that they are adjoined to a thematically complete NP, perhaps in a kind of appositional structure. Confirmation of this is the fact that demonstratives can appear either before the noun or after the noun in free variation in many polysynthetic languages. This is true of the demonstratives *in* 'this' and *on* 'that' in Nahuatl, for example (Launey 1981:46):

(58) a. A'mo ni-c-nequi   in-on michin.
         not   1sS-3sO-want IN-that fish
         'I do not want that fish.'

     b. Ni-quin-nōtza in pī-pil-tin   on.
         1sS-3pO-call IN RED-child-PL that
         'I call those children.'

Similarly, although demonstratives most often precede the head noun in Kiowa (Watkins 1984), Mayali (Evans 1991:125), Nunggubuyu (Heath 1984:501–502), and Wichita (Rood 1976:23), the grammars state that they may follow the head noun as well. This freedom of word order is characteristic of adjuncts, but not of heads in the X-bar schema. Demonstratives cannot follow the noun in Mohawk; however, this is because particles, in general, must be adjoined to the left of the phrase they modify in Mohawk, as mentioned previously.

    Suppose, then, that *ka nikáyʌ* 'which' is like the demonstratives in this respect: it is generated as an adjunct to a complete NP. One possibility is that it is adjoined to a lexical NP generated in argument position. It then moves to Comp, pied piping the rest of the NP along with it. This produces sentences like (59), which are perhaps even more common than split variants such as (53b).

(59) Ka nikáyʌ ká'sere í-hs-ehr-e'   a-hs-hnínu-'?
     which   car   Ø-2sS-think-IMPF OPT-2sS-buy-PUNC
     'Which car do you want to buy?'

Alternatively, *ka nikáyʌ* could, in principle, move by itself, stranding the rest of the NP. This is a possibility in Mohawk but not in English, as a result of the category difference described above. *Which* is a Det and thus a head; hence, it cannot move by itself to the specifier of CP, a position that must be filled by a maximal projection. *Ka nikáyʌ,* on the other hand, is not a Det, but rather is in apposition to a maximal projection. This means that *ka nikáyʌ* itself must presumably be a maximal projection, if Chomsky's (1986a) restrictions on adjunction are correct. Therefore, *ka nikáyʌ* is eligible for movement to Comp. However, all this is academic in the case of (59) because if the lexical NP is left in the argument position, it will violate the Case Filter in PF, just like any other overt NP in Mohawk.

Suppose, then, that *ka nikáyʌ* is generated as an adjunct to a lexical NP in dislocated position. However, this structure is ruled out on general principles. If the entire NP is pied-piped to Comp, then the *wh*-operator binds no legitimate variable. Thus, the construction is ruled out as an instance of vacuous quantification, for the same reason that other dislocated NPs cannot be questioned (see section 2.1.4). Neither can *ka nikáyʌ* move by itself, stranding the rest of the NP; this would violate the ban on extracting from adjoined positions (see section 2.1.5). Thus, no grammatical structure can be derived from this source.

So far, we have not found a derivation for sentences like (53), which are our primary interest. Fortunately, there is one further possibility: *ka nikáyʌ* can be generated as an adjunct to a pro in argument position. Nothing rules this out: the resulting phrase would be interpreted in a way comparable to expressions such as *which one* or *which of them* in English. From this position, *ka nikáyʌ* can move to Comp in the syntax, stranding the pro. This results in an argument that is phonetically empty by S-structure, so the Case Filter is not violated. Finally, a dislocated NP can be licensed by forming a chain with the stranded pro. This yields (60) as a grammatical representation for (53a).

(60)

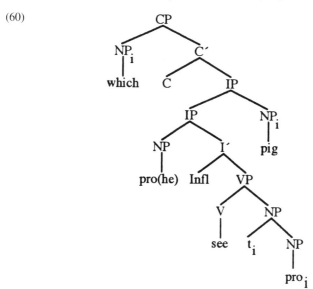

Thus, we explain the possibility of this type of discontinuous expression by combining *wh*-movement with a plausible assumption about the structure of demonstratives in a determinerless language.[12]

This appeal to *wh*-movement implies that the split *which* construction will be sensitive to the same locality conditions as other movement in Mohawk. By and large, this is true.[13] *Ka nikáyʌ* can move successive-cyclically out of complement clauses, rendering the following examples perfect:

(61) a. Ka nikáyʌ y-a'-te-sa-rihwayʌ́ta's-e'   a-hs-hnínu-'
      which   TRANS-FACT-DUP-2sO-decide-PUNC OPT-2sS-buy-PUNC

      ne áthere'?
      NE basket
      'Which basket did you decide to buy?'

    b. Ka nikáyʌ wa-hya-hróri-'   wa'-k-hnínu-'   áthere'?
      which   FACT-MsS/2sO-tell-PUNC FACT-1sS-buy-PUNC basket
      'Which basket did he tell you that I bought?'

Note that the matrix verbs in these examples are not members of the class that allow long-distance interpretation of *akwéku*. This confirms our assumption that different mechanisms are at work in the two cases: adverb interpretation in the one, and *wh*-movement in the other. However, *ka nikáyʌ* cannot be extracted out of an embedded question (see (62)), an adjunct clause (see (63)), or a relative clauses (see (64)).

(62) ??Ka nikáyʌ wa-hse-rihwanútu-' úhka ʌ-ha-hnínu-'   ne
      which   FACT-2sS-ask-PUNC who FUT-MsS-buy-PUNC NE

     ká'sere'?
     car
     'Which car did you ask who will buy?'

(63) *Ka nikáyʌ s-a-hs-ahtʌ́ti-'   ohʌ́tu tsi niyóre' kwéskwes
      which   ITER-FACT-2sS-leave-PUNC before   pig

     wá-hse-nut-e'?
     FACT-2sS/ZsO-feed-PUNC
     'Which pig did you go home before you fed?'

(64) *Ka nikáyʌ she-yʌtéri-Ø   ne yakó-hs-u   áthere?
      which   2sS/FsO-know-STAT NE FsO-finish-STAT basket
      'Which basket do you know the one (female) who made?'

Additional technical questions arise with respect to examples like (54), in which *ka nikáyʌ* is separated from an NP understood as the subject. Here *ka nikáyʌ* must extract a position adjoined to the subject pro, and we must ask why this extraction does not violate the Condition on Extraction Domains (stated in section 2.1.5). There are two possibilities. First, we know that the subject remains inside the VP at all levels in Mohawk, contrary to English (see section 2.2). Hence, the subject might count as lexically governed by the verb and therefore not an island, depending on details of how the principles are formulated. The second possibility is that since *ka nikáyʌ* is adjoined to the subject NP, it is not contained in all segments of that NP. Thus, the subject NP does not count as a barrier between the trace and its antecedent in Comp under the assumptions of Chomsky 1986a.[14] Either of these approaches (or their heirs in a Minimalist framework) should be sufficient.

Finally, it is worth pointing out that other interrogative expressions in Mohawk, such as *úhka* 'who' and *oh nahótʌ* 'what', cannot form discontinuous constituents in this way. Thus, the sentences in (65) contrast with those in (53).

(65) a. ??Úhka wa-shé-kʌ-'   ne eksá'a?
          who FACT-2sS/FsO-see-PUNC NE child
          'Which (who) child did you see?'

      b. ??Oh nahótʌ wa-hs-úni-'   ne atyá'tawi?
          what   FACT-2sS-make-PUNC NE dress
          'What dress did you make?'

These sentences become perfect if the initial *úhka* or *oh nahótʌ* are replaced with *ka nikáyʌ*. The explanation for this is quite straightforward. *Ka nikáyʌ* is a +*wh* demonstrative; as such, it can be adjoined to NPs just as other demonstratives can. *Úhka* and *oh nahótʌ*, on the other hand, are +*wh* NPs. As such, they cannot, in general, be adjoined to another NP. Therefore, examples like (66) are also bad.

(66) a. ??Úhka eksá'a wa-shé-kʌ-'?
          who child FACT-2sS/FsO-see-PUNC
          'Which children did you see?'

      b. ??Oh nahótʌ atyá'tawi wa-hs-úni-'?
          what   dress FACT-2sS-make-PUNC
          'What dress did you make?'

(These also become perfect if *úhka* and *oh nahótʌ* are replaced by *ka nikáyʌ*.) By the same token, *úhka* and *oh nahótʌ* cannot be generated adjoined to pro either. Thus, (60) is impossible with one of these elements replacing *ka nikáyʌ* . *Úhka* and *oh nahótʌ* are only licit if they bind a trace that occupies the entire argument position. Thus, the structure for (65b) would have to be either (67a) or (67b).

(67) a. what$_i$ [$_{IP}$ pro make t$_i$] [$_{NPi}$ dress]

      b. what$_i$ [$_{IP}$ pro make pro$_i$] [$_{NPi}$ dress]

Structure (67b) is ruled out because pro does not constitute an appropriate primary variable for *úhka;* (67a) is ruled out because there is no pro that can license the dislocated NP in accordance with the ALC, given in (11). In this way, we explain the ungrammaticality of (65). Thus, split interrogative constructions are only possible if the question word is an NP modifier, not if it is itself an NP.[15]

4.3.2 Relative Clauses: Internally Headed and Otherwise

Although relative clauses may not, at first glance, seem to be related to the topic of discontinuous expressions, we will see that they turn out to be very much related indeed. It is not surprising that relatives should be considered along with "which"-type questions, since the two share syntactic features in many languages, including English. In fact, the ideas of the last section extend naturally to relative clauses to explain the range of such constructions found in Mohawk, including certain typologically exotic "internally headed" relatives. Moreover, this topic turns out to be essential background for understanding the split demonstrative construction illustrated previously, in (1c).

It is no coincidence that the basic relative pronoun in English is *which,* the same form used in discourse-linked questions. Thus, it comes as no surprise that Mohawk has a relative pronoun *tsi nikáyʌ,* which is morphologically related to the interrogative *ka nikáyʌ.*[16] This expression occasionally appears in ordinary-looking headed relatives like (68).

(68) a. Atyá'tawi tsi nikáyʌ í-k-ehr-e'   a-k-hnínu-'
         dress   which   Ø-1sS-think-IMPF OPT-1sS-buy-PUNC
         ka-hutsí-nyu.
         NsS-black-DIST
         'The dress that I want to buy is black.'

      b. Sak ra-núhwe'-s   ne áthere tsi nikáyʌ i: k-úni-s.
         Sak MsS-like-HAB NE basket which   me 1sS-make-HAB
         'Sak likes the kind of baskets that I make.'

Somewhat more common are examples in which the head is dropped:

(69) a. Tsi nikáyʌ wa-hí-kʌ-'   wa'-te-shako-noru'kwányu-'
         which   FACT-1sS/MsO-see-PUNC FACT-DUP-MsS/FsO-kiss-PUNC

         tsi ni-yako-ya't-á-hskats.
         so PART-FsO-body-Ø-beautiful
         'The one that I saw him kiss is so beautiful.'

      b. Tsi nikáyʌ ne wa-hiy-ahta-hk[w]-úny-ʌ-'
         which   NE FACT-1sS/MsO-shoe-NOM-make-BEN-PUNC
         ro-[a]tshʌnúni.
         MsO-happy/STAT
         'The one who I made shoes for is happy.'

Presumably, these have approximately the same structure as the sentences in (68), but the head NP has been pro-dropped, something which is always possible in Mohawk.

More interestingly, examples like (70) are also possible.

(70) a. Sak ra-núhwe'-s   tsi nikáyʌ i: k-úni-s   ne áthere'.
         Sak MsS-like-HAB which   me 1sS-make-HAB NE basket
         'Sak likes the (kind of) baskets that I make.'

      b. (?)Sak wa-hó-[a]ti-'   tsi nikáyʌ wak-hnínu-Ø (ne) áthere'.
         Sak FACT-MsO-lose-PUNC which   1sO-buy-STAT NE   basket
         'Sak lost the basket that I bought.'

Here, the relative operator *tsi nikáyʌ* appears separated form the "head" noun, which appears inside the relative clause. This, then, is a type of *internally headed relative clause* (IHRC)—a construction found in various Amerindian languages as well as other languages.[17] This can also be considered a type of discontinuous expression, since the relative operator *tsi nikáyʌ* and the NP *áthere'* are noncontinguous but express the same argument (the object of the lower verb). Indeed, there is an obvious similarity between (70) and (71), a sentence of the type discussed in the previous section.

(71) Ka nikáyʌ wa-hs-hnínu-'   ne áthere'?
      which   FACT-2sS-buy-PUNC NE basket
      'Which basket did you buy?'

The analysis of (71) generalizes readily to (70). *Tsi nikáyʌ* is of the same
syntactic category as *ka nikáyʌ, thíkʌ* 'that', and *kíkʌ* 'this'; it is generated as an
adjunct to a complete NP. In (70a), for example, it is adjoined to the pro object
of 'make'. It then undergoes *wh*-movement to Comp to create an open sentence
of the kind typically required for a relative clause. The object pro is left stranded
by this movement; it then has the option of licensing a dislocated NP within the
relative clause. Thus, the structure of (70) is (72).

(72)

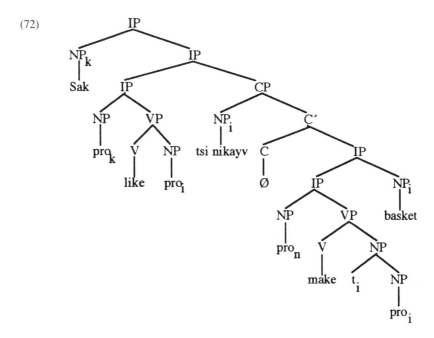

The existence of IHRCs in Mohawk follows with no additional machinery. Indeed,
it is predicted that such constructions should exist, given the other things we know
about the language.

However, none of the types of relative clauses considered so far is the most
typical one found in Mohawk.[18] Rather, the most common relative clauses look
exactly like any other kind of sentence: they are simply verbal forms that receive
a nominal interpretation. The use of verbal forms as NPs is a very salient feature
of Mohawk, remarked on by many observers of the language. (See Postal 1979
for Mohawk; see also Chafe 1970:86–87 and Woodbury 1974 for Onondaga, and
Williams 1976b:29–32 for Tuscarora.) Such forms have all the inflectional possibilities of other verbs and have no trace of nominalizing morphology. They may
or may not have an internal head or other material in addition to the basic verb.
They are often preceded by the particle *ne* or a demonstrative (*thíkʌ* or *kíkʌ*),
but this is not required. Some examples are in (73), with the verb-used-as-noun
italicized.

(73) a. Uwári ruwa-nákw-a-'s-e'   ne *ro-whahs-a-rátsu-Ø.*
         Mary FsS/MsO-mad-Ø-BEN-STAT NE MsO-skirt-Ø-tear-STAT
         'Mary is mad at the guy who tore her skirt.'

     b. *Ra-[a]tukárya'k-s*   wa-hak-hróri-'.
         MsS-be.hungry-HAB FACT-MsS/1sO-tell-PUNC
         'The hungry man told me.'

     c. Ke-'sere-ht-ísak-s   ne *tyótku te-w-atáhsawʌ-s.*
         1sS-car-NOM-seek-HAB NE always DUP-NsS-start-HAB
         'I'm looking for a car that always starts.'

     d. Wa-shakoti-yéna-'   ótya'ke ne *wa-shakoti-'shʌ́ni-'.* (KO: 127)
         FACT-MpS/3pO-hold-PUNC some   NE FACT-MpS/3pO-defeat-PUNC
         'They held some of the ones that they defeated (in battle).'

Forms like those in (73) are spontaneously generated in accordance with the needs of the situation, just like relative clauses in English. However, a large number of verbal forms have become conventionalized expressions with "nominal" meanings in Mohawk. In this way they make up for the fact that the language has relatively few basic noun roots and no productive nominalizing morphology. For example, most of the profession names are verbal forms in the habitual aspect. In isolation, these may be translated as either a nominal or a verb (Deering and Delisle 1976:77):

(74) a. ra-natar-úni-s
         MsS-bread-make-HAB
         'he makes bread, the baker'

     b. yu-[a]tétsʌ't-s
         FsS-heal-HAB
         'she heals, the doctor'

     c. shako-hah-áwi-s
         MsS/FsO-road-give-HAB
         'he gives one the road, the guide'

Similarly, many manmade artifacts are verb forms in either the habitual or stative aspect:

(75) a. ye-hyatú-hkw-ha'
         FsS-write-INSTR-HAB
         'one writes with it, a pencil'

     b. ye-natar-a-kwetar-á-ht-ha'
         FsS-bread-Ø-cut-Ø-INSTR-HAB
         'one uses it to cut bread, a bread-knife.'

     c. ka-'níkhu-s
         NsS-sew-HAB
         'it sews, a sewing machine'

     d. te-ka-htórarak-s
         DUP-NsS-press-HAB
         'it presses together, pliers'

Many more examples like these could be given.

Interestingly, over time some expressions that were originally in this class have been reanalyzed as true nouns. This happens when the aspect suffix is dropped (a particularly easy development for stative verbs ending in Ø) and the pronominal prefix takes on its nominal form, without word-initial glides (e.g., (76b)). Some examples of this that are common in my data are the following:

(76)   a. ka-ya'túni
           ka-ya't-úni-Ø
           NsS-body-make-STAT
           'doll' (Literally: 'its body was made')

       b. Ø-atya'tawi
           w-at-ya't-awi-Ø
           NsS-SRFL-body-wrap-STAT
           'shirt, dress, jacket' (Literally: 'it is wrapped around self's torso')

       c. ka-'sere'
           ka-'ser-e'
           NsS-drag-IMPF
           'car, vehicle' (Literally: 'it drags'; originally referred to sleds, then carriages)

One clear way of telling reanalyzed nouns from forms that are still verbal is that only the reanalyzed forms can take nominal possessive prefixes. Thus, one has *ako-ya'túni* 'her doll', *rao-[a]tya'táwi* 'his shirt', and *aké-'sere* 'my car', but not **rao-hyatúhkwha'* 'his pencil.' Similarly, only forms that have been reanalyzed as nouns can undergo noun incorporation. Such nouns that have evolved from verbs are also very common; virtually all articles of clothing can be analyzed this way, for example. Other nouns show signs of a similar history, even though the verb stems they originally came from have been lost. It is hard to overestimate the practical importance of the fact that verb forms can be used as nominals in discussions of Mohawk communication, lexicography, and language history.

Significantly, very much the same range of constructions is found in other polysynthetic languages as well. It is widespread in the Northern Iroquoian languages, and also shows up in Wichita (Rood 1976:9–10), Mayali (Evans 1991:119–123), Ainu (Shibatani 1990:32–34), and Southern Tiwa. Thus, the ability to use verbal clauses as functional nominals seems to be a typological feature of this class of languages as a whole. Indeed, Evans (1991:123) observes that within Australian languages this property is common in the head-marking languages but rare among the dependent-marking languages.

I claim that "pseudonominals" that still have verbal inflection are structurally identical to the *tsi nikáyʌ* relative clauses, except that the relative operator is phonologically null. There is nothing remarkable about this proposal: for example, English routinely allows null relative operators in free variation with overt ones (*John lost the book (which) I bought*). Indeed, null relative operators are preferred or even required in some constructions and in many languages. This is the most straightforward possible approach to these constructions, and hence the null hypothesis. Presumably, it holds not only for the examples in (73), but those in (74) and (75) as well. In the paragraphs that follow, I argue for this analysis by showing that pseudonominals have the properties of *wh*-movement in Mohawk. Thus, the range of things that can be expressed by pseudonominals in a polysynthetic language is much wider than what can be expressed by true nominalizations, but not as wide as one would expect if they were simply adjoined modifier clauses with no relationship to the matrix clause other than coreference.

One of the most striking properties of pseudonominals is that the understood reference of a verbal form can, in general, be any of the arguments of the verb. Thus (73a,b,c) are examples where the reference is to the subject argument of the verb; in (73d), reference is to the object of a transitive verb. It is also possible for a verbal form to be interpreted as referring to a goal or benefactive argument:

(77) Wa-hrʌ́-[i]hey-e'   ne t-hi-hwist-áwi.
      FACT-MsS-die-PUNC NE CIS-1sS/MsO-money-give/STAT
      'The guy I gave money to died.'

Similarly, in (75a) and (75b) the verb conventionally refers to a kind of instrumental argument introduced by the instrumental morpheme *ht, hkw*. Indeed, a transitive verb form can be ambiguous, interpreted as referring to either the verb's subject or its object, depending on features of the context, such as the selectional restrictions and agreement morphology on the matrix verb. An example is given in (78).

(78) a. *R[a]-ather-úni-'*   wa'-k-atkátho-'.
         MsS-basket-make-IMPF FACT-1sS-see-PUNC
         'I saw the basket that he is making.'

      b. *R[a]-ather-úni-'*   wa-hí-kʌ-'.
         MsS-basket-make-IMPF FACT-1sS/MsO-see-PUNC
         'I saw the man who is making a basket.'

Example (79) gives a similar case, in which the same verbal constituent can be interpreted as referring to the theme of the verb or the benefactive/goal, depending on the context.

(79) a. Sak ra-núhwe'-s   ne *khey-uny-ʌ́ni*   *anúwarore.*
         Sak MsS-like-HAB NE 1sS/FsO-make-BEN/STAT hat
         'Sak likes the hat that I made for her.'

      b. Sak shako-núhwe'-s   ne *khey-uny-ʌ́ni*   *anúwarore.*
         Sak MsS/FsO-like-HAB NE 1sS/FsO-make-BEN/STAT hat
         'Sak likes the woman that I made a hat for.'

This carries over to the other polysynthetic languages as well. Heath (1984:563, 1986:389) explicitly points out that the understood reference of a verbal-relativized expression in Nunggubuyu can be any grammatical function in the clause; the range of examples cited by Rood (1976:174) for Wichita and by Shibatani (1990:33) for Ainu shows that the same is true for these languages.

This indeterminacy of reference distinguishes the pseudonominal constructions in the polysynthetic languages from true nominalizations or participle constructions in other languages. True nominalizations are usually limited to referring to some designated θ-role or argument position of the base verb. For example, *er* nominals in English typically refer to the agent of the verb root only, whereas *ion* nominals refer to the process or result but not the agent. However, if we hold that pseudonominals are relative clauses formed by *wh*-movement, their range of interpretations is immediately explained, since *wh*-movement is possible from any argument position. Thus, the structure of (78a) is (80b), while the structure of (78b) is (80a), where "Op" stands for a null operator.

(80) a.

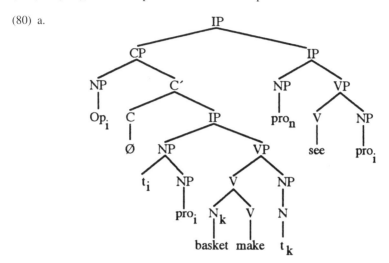

b

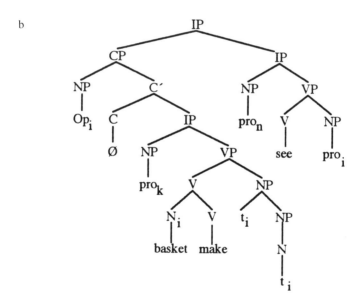

One point of detail that I leave open here is the question of whether or not the relative clause is embedded in an NP with a null head in these languages. Either assumption is reasonably natural. The null head of a full NP could plausibly be a pro, licensed by its link to a position governed by agreement. On the other hand, it is not clear that anything forces the CP to be embedded in an NP. The expression is in an adjoined position, which is not necessarily subject to the strictures of strict subcategorization: even if the verb 'see' selects an NP in (78), this categorial requirement is satisfied by the pro in argument position. Indeed, the structures in

(80) may not be significantly different from those of relative clauses extraposed from their heads in other languages. For concreteness, I will adopt this second alternative, since the structures are slightly simpler, but I know of nothing important that hinges on this choice.

Continuing to develop this theme, it is significant that the understood reference of a verbal construction need not be a direct argument of that verb at all. Rather, it can be an argument inside a sentential complement of the verb:

(81)　a.　Wa-hi-yá't-hew-e'　　　　　ne ye-hskeni-hnhá'-u　(Hopkins 1988:266)
　　　　　FACT-1sS/MsO-body-hold-PUNC NE TRANS-2DS/1sO-send-STAT

　　　　ne' a-hi-hnuksa-'.
　　　　NE OPT-1sS/MsO-fetch-PUNC
　　　　'I have got him here, the one you two sent me to fetch.'

　　　b.　Thíkʌ wa'-ke-rihwáruk-e'　ʌ-ha-'sere-ht-a-hnínu-'　　　　khere
　　　　that　FACT-1sS-hear-PUNC FUT-MsS-car-NOM-Ø-BUY-PUNC instead
　　　　wa-h[a]-ahtʌ́ti-'.
　　　　FACT-MsS-leave-PUNC
　　　　'The one that I heard would buy a car went away instead.'

Interpretations of this type are not found with ordinary nominalized or participial clauses, but they are routinely possible with true relative clauses. These examples

(82)

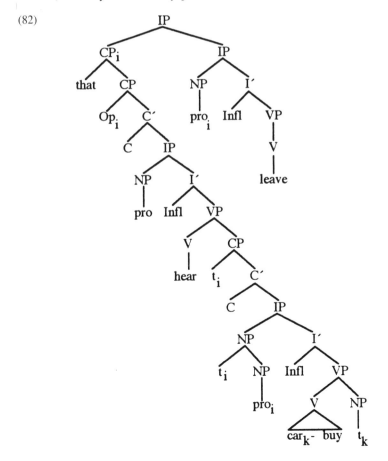

are thus readily derived by ordinary successive-cyclic movement of a relative operator. For example, in (81b) the relative operator starts out adjoined to the object of the embedded verb 'buy', then moves to the specifier of the CP dominating 'hear' via the specifier of the CP immediately dominating 'buy'. Its structure is given in (82).

It is not the case that any verbal expression imaginable can be a pseudonominal, however. Rather, this analysis predicts that these pseudonominal constructions should be limited by the same kinds of island phenomena that one finds elsewhere in Mohawk. The reason is that the movement of the relative operator is constrained by ordinary conditions on *wh*-movement, including Subjacency. The prediction is correct. In (83), examples are given that are no more complex than those in (81), but the intended relativized position is within an adjunct clause rather than a complement clause. The examples are deviant.[19]

(83) a. ??Uwári ye-núhwe'-s thíkʌ wa'-kuy-aterórok-e'
              Mary FsS-like-HAB that   FACT-1sS/2sO-watch-PUNC

          tsi nikaríhwes wa-hs-anitskwara-tsher-úni-'.
          while   FACT-2sS-chair-NOM-make-PUNC
          'Mary likes the chair that I watched you while you made.'

      b. ??Sak s-a-h[a]-anitskwara-tsher-a-kwatáko-' thíkʌ
          Sak ITER-FACT-MsS-chair-NOM-Ø-fix-PUNC that

          uke-nakúni-'   tsi Uwári wa'-t-yé-ya'k-e'.
          FACT/1sO-anger-PUNC that Mary FACT-DUP-FsS-break-PUNC
          'Sak fixed the chair that I got mad because Mary broke.'

This illustrates the adjunct island effect, which is the most important of the island conditions in Mohawk.

Similarly, one cannot have a relative operator originate embedded in an expression that is itself interpreted as a relative clause. Hence, (84) is ungrammatical, although it is no more complex than the examples in (81) in terms of superficial factors like number of words and their linear order.

(84) *Te-yu-[a]hsʌ'tho-s nene wa'-te-w-át-ya'k-e'   thíkʌ
       DUP-FsS-cry-HAB   NENE FACT-DUP-NsS-SRFL-break-PUNC that

       yako-ya'tuni-hser-íhs-u.
       FsO-doll-NOM-finish-STAT
       'The one who the doll that she made broke is crying.'

Example (84) can also be compared to the minimally different and perfectly acceptable (85).

(85) Te-yu-[a]hsʌ'tho-s ne tsi   wa'-te-w-át-ya'k-e'   thíkʌ
       DUP-FsS-cry-HAB   because FACT-DUP-NsS-SRFL-break-PUNC that
       yako-ya'tuni-hser-íhs-u.
       FsO-doll-NOM-finish-STAT
       'She is crying because the doll that she made broke.'

The only difference between these examples is that the complementizer-like particle in front of the complex adjunct CP has been changed from *nene* to *ne tsi* 'because'. This means that the clause is interpreted as a causal adjunct that modifies the matrix clause as a whole, rather than a relative clause that modifies the subject argument of the matrix verb. The acceptability of (85) shows that the relative construction within the adjoined clause is itself grammatical. Example (85) also shows that it is possible to have coreference between the matrix subject and the subject position of the relative verb inside the adjunct. These are the same two positions that are related in (84). Nevertheless, a truly relative interpretation is impossible under these conditions. This shows that operator movement is involved in these relative constructions and not simply coreference between the arguments of the two nearby clauses.

Finally, (86) shows that relative constructions in Mohawk are subject to the *wh*-island constraint.

(86) *Isi wa'-ka-tákh-e' thíkʌ wa'-ke-rihwáruk-e' úhka
    there FACT-NsS-go-IMPF that FACT-1sS-hear-PUNC who
    wa-ha-hnínu-'.
    FACT-MsS-buy-PUNC
    'There goes the one (a car) that I heard who bought.'

This example can be contrasted with the grammatical (81b), where the verbs in the relative clause are the same, but *rihwaruk* 'hear' takes a declarative complement rather than an interrogative one. Example (86) is another type that is ruled out by Subjacency under the assumption that null operator movement is involved in these constructions.[20]

Also relevant is an interesting word order effect in relative constructions where the understood head is a possessor. Normally, a possessed noun can either precede or follow the verb, in accordance with the general freedom of word order found in Mohawk. Possessor relatives, however, are possible if and only if the possessed noun precedes the verb. This is illustrated in (87).

(87) a. Uwári ruwa-núhwe'-s thíkʌ rao-[a]nitskwára s-a'-k-kwatáko-'.
      Mary FsS/MsO-like-HAB that MsP-chair ITER-FACT-1sS-fix-PUNC
      'Mary likes the man whose chair I fixed.'

   b. ??Uwári ruwa-núhwe'-s thíkʌ s-a'-k-kwatáko-' ne
      Mary FsS/MsO-like-HAB that ITER-FACT-1sS-fix-PUNC NE
      rao-[a]nitskwára.
      MsP-chair
      'Mary likes the man whose chair I fixed.'

This is predicted by the analysis. The relative operator is, by assumption, generated as an adjunct to the possessor argument of the noun. However, all overt NPs are adjuncts in Mohawk; hence, this operator cannot be extracted without violating Subjacency (see section 2.1.5). This explains the deviance of (87b). Possessed noun phrases can always be pied piped by *wh*-movement, however, as seen in (88).

(88) Úhka rao-[a]nitskwára s-a-hs-kwatáko-'?
    Who MsP-chair ITER-FACT-2sS-fix-PUNC
    'Whose chair did you fix?'

This then explains the grammaticality of (87a): the possessed noun has been pied piped to Comp along with the null operator. Since Comp is rigidly initial in the

Mohawk clause, the possessed noun ends up as the first visible element in the clause. Thus, although one cannot see empty operator movement per se, in this example one can detect the movement indirectly, via the displacement of material that forms a constituent with the null operator.[21] The structures of (87a,b) are given schematically in (89).

(89)   a. Mary$_i$ she$_i$-him$_k$-likes [$_{CP}$ [$_{NPn}$ Op$_k$ chair] [$_{IP}$ I-fixed t$_n$]]

       b. *Mary$_i$ she$_i$-him$_k$-likes [$_{CP}$ Op$_k$ [$_{IP}$ I-fixed-it$_n$ [$_{NPn}$ t$_k$ chair]]]

   Next, consider the interpretation of the pseudonominal in (90).

(90)   Wa'-t-hni-núnyahkw-e'   ne   shako-'nhá'-u.
       FACT-DUP-MdS-dance-PUNC NE MsS/FsO-hire-STAT
       'He danced with the one he hired.' NOT: 'The man and the woman such that the man hired the woman danced together.'

The main verb in (90) has a dual argument and the pseudonominal verb has two singular arguments. Moreover, the pragmatics of the example are such that it is perfectly possible that the two people involved in the hiring are exactly the same as the two people involved in the dancing. Thus, one might think that the verb form could be interpreted as a kind of "doubly headed" relative clause, which is used to identify both members of the dual subject of the matrix verb. Such doubly headed relative clauses are known to exist in Japanese:

(91)   Taroo-wa [neko-ga nezumi-o   oikakete-iru-no-o]   ni-hiki-tomo
       Taro-TOP cat-NOM mouse-ACC chase-PROG-REL-ACC both
       tukamaeta.
       caught
       'Taro caught both the cat and the mouse such that the cat was chasing the mouse.'

Similar structures are found with correlative constructions in Hindi (Srivastav 1991:650). However, this type of interpretation does not seem to be possible for the Mohawk example. Rather, it can only be interpreted as a single-headed relative clause specifying one member of the plural subject; the other member must be recoverable from the previous speech context. (It may, of course, be "accidentally" coreferential with the other pronoun in the relative clause.) If the arguments of the two verbs in (90) were simply related by some kind of pronoun coreference, then there would be no explanation of this restriction, since pronouns are allowed to have overlapping reference. If empty operator movement is involved, however, this restriction makes sense: the desired interpretation would require that two distinct operators move separately into the specifier of the relative CP. Thus, (90) is impossible in Mohawk under the indicated interpretation, for essentially the same reason that one cannot say something like *The two people which$_i$ which$_k$ t$_i$ hired t$_k$ danced in English.[22]

   We have now established that pseudonominals in Mohawk have a rather ordinary null relative operator. I have also assumed implicitly that this null operator is a member of the same syntactic category as the interrogative *ka nikáyʌ* and relative *tsi nikáyʌ*. Thus, we predict that this element can also be separated from an overt noun that it is associated with. More accurately, it can be adjoined to an argument and move to Comp by itself, leaving the rest of the argument inside the relative clause. This will give the effect of an IHRC. In fact, such IHRCs are found in Mohawk. The most striking IHRCs in the language are those in which the "internal head" is incorporated into a verb within the relative clause. Relative clauses of this type are rather common in texts and were an important focus of Postal 1979; they are also the topic of discussion in Woodbury 1974 and are mentioned in Chafe 1970. One example was seen in (78a); others are given in (92).

(92) a. Uwári wa-huwʌ́-[i]tʌhr-e'   ne *wa'-ke-ksá-ht-a-ya'k-e'*.
      Mary FACT-FsS/MsO-pity-PUNC NE FACT-1sS-child-NOM-Ø-hit-PUNC
      'Mary pitied the child I slapped.'

    b. Uwári ʌ-ye-'níkhu-'   ne *ute-whahs-a-rátsu-'*.
      Mary FUT-FsS-sew-PUNC NE FACT/NsS/SRFL-skirt-Ø-tear-PUNC
      'Mary will sew the skirt that just tore.'

    c. Uwári wa'-e-núhwe'-ne'   thíkʌ *wa'-ku-snyéna-'*
      Mary FACT-FsS-like-PUNC that FACT-1sS/2sO-help-PUNC

      wa-hs-anitskwara-tsher-úni-'.
      FACT-2sS-chair-NOM-make-PUNC
      'Mary liked the chair that I helped you to make.'

In these cases, the relative operator is generated adjoined to the (underlying) direct object of the verb. Two movements then take place. The operator moves to Comp to create a predicate as before. Meanwhile, the head of the NP left behind incorporates into the verb. The result is sentences of the type illustrated. In fact, the structure of such an example was illustrated previously in (80b). Similar constructions are found in at least some of the other polysynthetic languages, as in (93a) from Southern Tiwa and (93b) from Ngalakan.

(93) a. Bi-k'uru-tha-ba-'i   i-k'euwe-m.   (Allen et al. 1984:308)
      1sS/BO-dipper-find-PAST-SUB BS-old-PRES
      'The dipper I found is old.'

    b. Bonji mu-wolo   yimi-birtin-marninjʔ-minj-gin.   (Merlan 1983:146)
      now   MU-cooked 1DINS/MUO-damper-make-PAST/PUNC-SUB
      'Now the damper you and I made is cooked.'

The other type of IHRC arises when the operator is adjoined to a pro and moves to Comp. The stranded pro then has the option of licensing a dislocated NP adjoined somewhere within the relative clause. This type of "internal head" is somewhat harder to recognize because of Mohawk's highly polysynthetic nature. The problem is simply that so much information is expressed in the verb that Mohawk clauses often have little else. Thus, it is common for a relative construction to contain only a verb and an NP interpreted as the head (if that). In this case, it is not obvious whether the NP is inside or outside of the relative clause. However, clear examples can be constructed. Thus, in (94) the NP interpreted as the head precedes the embedded verb but follows a time adverbial that modifies that verb.

(94) a. ʌ-k-atkáhto-'   ne thetʌ́re' atyá'tawi wa'-e-hnínu-'.
      FUT-1sS-see-PUNC NE yesterday dress   FACT-FsS-buy-PUNC
      'I will see the dress that she bought yesterday.'

b. Yoti-nuhwáktani ne thetΛre' kítkit wa-shé-nut-e'.
ZpO-be.sick/STAT NE yesterday chicken FACT-2sS/3pO-feed-PUNC
'The chickens that you fed yesterday are sick.'

Given that the time adverbial is adjoined to the clause that it modifies, the NP must also be adjoined to that clause. Hence, these are cases of IHRCs. This is the typical way of arguing for head-internal structures in other Amerindian languages. Moreover, it is clear that "heads" in Mohawk can appear on either side of the relative verb in free variation. For example, the following variants are all perfectly natural (and found in texts):

(95) a. Sak wa-hó-[a]ti-'   ne wak-hnínu-Ø áthere'.
         Sak FACT-MsO-lose-PUNC NE 1sO-buy-STAT basket
         'Sak lost the basket I bought.'

      b. Sak wa-hó-[a]ti-'   áthere' ne wak-hnínu-Ø.
         Sak FACT-MsO-lose-PUNC basket NE 1sO-buy-STAT
         'Sak lost the basket I bought.'

      c. Sak wa-hó-[a]ti-'   ne áthere' wak-hnínu-Ø.
         Sak FACT-MsO-lose-PUNC NE basket 1sO-buy-STAT
         'Sak lost the basket I bought.'

Now languages do not usually allow a relative clause to precede or follow its head in free variation. To the extent that this is true, the examples in (95) cannot all be externally headed relatives. Whichever one is not externally headed is then internally headed, an example of the type we have predicted to occur. More concretely, I conjecture that examples in which the "head" follows the verb such as (95a) are unambiguously IHRCs in Mohawk. This guess is motivated by the well-known cross-linguistic tendency for relative clauses to follow their (external) heads, particularly in languages where overt movement takes place to an initial Comp. A textual example of this type is given in (96) (KO: 127).

(96) T-Λ-hshakoti-ya't-a-yestáhsi-'   néne kwáh
      DUP-FUT-MpS/3pO-body-Ø-look.over-PUNC NENE truly

      roti-ya't-a-hníru-s   tánu' kΛ'   ni-t-hoti-yΛha
      MpO-body-Ø-be.hard-HAB and small PART-CIS-MpO-have.age
      roti-skΛ'rakéhte'.
      MpO-male
      'They would look over the boys that were strong and young.'

It is also interesting that the particle *ne* can either precede or follow the head NP when that head is to the left of the relative verb (see (95b,c)). Whenever the head is not initial in a relative construction and *ne* is present, *ne* comes immediately before the relative clause, marking the beginning of that clause. If this is a true generalization, it suggests that the head is external in (95b) and internal to the relative clause in (95c). In that case, the internal head of an IHRC has the same freedom of placement as an arbitrary NP in a simple clause, as our theory predicts. Similarly, Evans (1991:336–337) shows that in Mayali the understood head of the relative clause (the demonstrative *nawu* or *ngalu*) can be in any position with respect to that clause: preceding the clause as a whole, as in (97a); coming between the verb and one of its arguments, as in (97b); or following the verb, as in (97c).

(97)   a. Na-mege bininj ga-m-re,   na-wu gogok bi-yame-ng.
          I-that   man   3sS-CIS-go I-REL   brother 3sS/3HO-spear-PAST/PERF
          'The man is coming, whom your brother speared.'

       b. Na-mege ga-m-re   gogok na-wu gun-marne-yame-ng.
          I-that   3sS-CIS-go brother I-REL   3sS/2sO-BEN-spear-PAST/PERF
          'Here comes the (man) who speared your brother (on you).'

       c. Al-ege daluk, gogok gun-marne-bom   ngal-u.
          II-that woman brother 3sS/2sO-BEN-hit/PAST/PUNC II-REL
          'This is the woman who your brother hit (on you).'

At least (97b), and probably also (97c), is an example of an IHRC.

The examples of IHRCs still have all of the properties of operator movement that we saw with headless relative clauses. For example, interpretations derived by cyclic movement are possible:

(98)   Uwári wa'-akó-[a]ti-'   thíkʌ wa-hsek-hróri-'
       Mary FACT-FsO-lose-PUNC this   FACT-2sS/1sO-tell-PUNC

       á-k-atst-e'   ne á'share'.
       OPT-1sS-use-PUNC NE knife
       'Mary lost the knife that you told me to use.'

However, island conditions are obeyed; (99) illustrates the adjunct island, and (100) the *wh*-island.

(99)   *R-ukwe-ht-áksʌ   ne wá'-k-ye-'   ne thíkʌ rúkwe'
        MsS-person-NOM-bad NE FACT-1sS-wake-PUNC NE this   man

        shu-t-a-ha-[a]táweya't-e'.
        SIM-CIS-FACT-MsS-enter-PUNC
        'This man that I woke up when (he) came in is a bad man.'

(100) *Ísi wa'-ka-tákh-e'   thíkʌ wa'-ke-rihwáruk-e' úhka
        there FACT-NsS-go-IMPF that   FACT-1sS-hear-PUNC who

        wa-ha-hnínu-'   ká'sere'.
        FACT-MsS-buy-PUNC car
        'There goes the car that I heard who bought.'

Compare also (92c) with (83a), where the internal heads are incorporated. This is exactly what we would expect, since IHRCs and headless relatives are minimally different on this analysis. Both involve operator movement from a position adjoined to an argument pro; therefore both have the same range of possibilities. The only difference between the two constructions is the rather trivial matter of whether the pro in question also licenses a dislocated NP within the relative clause.

This section has considered verbal constructions used as NPs in the polysynthetic languages. This topic has inherent interest not only because of its exotic nature, but also because of its central importance in expressing oneself in such languages. I have argued that the constructions are, in fact, rather ordinary relative clauses, that are somewhat masked by the use of null rather than overt relative pronouns. The most exotic-looking cases are those in which an NP interpreted as the head is found inside the relative clause. However, this possibility has been seen to follow from exactly the same mechanisms that allowed split interrogative phrases, discussed in section 4.3.1. Indeed, IHRCs in Mohawk can be thought of as another case of discontinuous expressions, where the head is separated from its relative operator. Ultimately, this is traceable to the fact that Mohawk lacks a true determiner system; therefore, *which*-like elements are maximal projections that may undergo operator movement by themselves.

4.3.3 Split Demonstratives

Finally, we come to examples in which demonstratives appear separated from a noun with which they are interpreted. Example (1c) was of this type; two others are the following:

(101) a. (?)Ne kíkʌ wake-tshÁry-u ne káhure'.
            NE this 1sO-find-STAT NE gun
            'I found this gun.'

       b. Ákwa kʌ'náhe kíkʌ wa'-ku-[a]táwʌ-'   ne' tsonathuwísʌ. . . . (M: 11)
            quite later   these FACT-FpS-swim-PUNC NE women
            'Quite some time later, these women went swimming. . . .'

Similar examples are found in the Gunwinjguan languages (see section 4.1 and later in this chapter), as well as Southern Tiwa (Donald Frantz, personal communication):

(102) Yede ti-mu-ban   seuan-ide.
          that 1sS/3sO-see-PAST man-SG
          'I saw that man.'

These examples look superficially like the quantifier splits analyzed in section 4.2. This makes it tempting to treat the two cases in the same way. However, quantifiers and demonstratives do not form a natural semantic class in any obvious way. Indeed, we have seen that quantifier splits in Mohawk are little different from *tous* float in French; however, there are no comparable examples of "demonstrative float" in French.

Example (101) is also the rarest type of discontinuous NP in Mohawk; (103b) is the only clear example that I have found in a text.[23] Native speakers always consider them marked alternatives that emphasize the discontinuous argument: often they spontaneously correct the order to one in which the demonstrative and the NP are adjacent; sometimes they even rate the sentences as questionable or worse. In contrast, *akwéku* is usually considered at least as natural when separated from its head as when adjacent to it.

One further peculiarity of the split demonstrative construction is that the particle *ne* must precede the demonstrative, at least for some speakers.

(103) *(Ne) thíkʌ ʌ-k-hnínu-'   ne ká'sere'.
           NE   that FUT-1sS-buy-PUNC NE car
           'I will buy that car.'

This constraint does not hold for clause-initial demonstratives apart from this construction.

These peculiarities begin to make sense if one compares (103) with (104).

(104) *Thíkʌ wa'-k-hnínu-'*   *ká'sere' ísi* *t-ká-yʌ.*
      that   FACT-1sS-buy-PUNC car   there CIS-NsS-lie
      'There is the car that I bought.'

Example (103) is a split demonstrative construction, whereas (104) is an IHRC of the type analyzed in the last section. Notice that they are virtually identical in form. Thus, I suggest split demonstrative constructions are actually a degenerate case of an IHRC, in which there is little or no matrix predicate. The structure of (103) is then (105).[24]

(105)

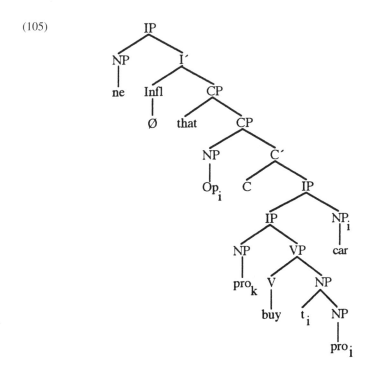

Essentially, this is a kind of cleft construction, comparable to *It is that car which I will buy* in English. More accurately, it is an "internally headed cleft construction," bearing the same relationship to ordinary clefts that IHRCs bear to standard relative clauses. This explains the marked pragmatic nature of the construction: the cleft is only appropriate when the "split" constituent is associated with focal emphasis. This analysis also suggests a reason why *ne* is required; *ne* serves as the pleonastic pronoun often found in clefts (or perhaps as the copula).

The cleft analysis also accounts for the fact mentioned in section 4.1 that the demonstrative must precede the verb and the head must follow it in a split construction, rather than vice versa. Thus, (101a) contrasts with (106).[25]

(106) *Káhure' wa'-ke-tshÁri-'   kíkʌ .
      gun   FACT-1sS-find-PUNC this
      'I found this gun.'

In (105), the demonstrative is actually adjoined to the predicate clause as a whole, just as it can be freely adjoined to ordinary NPs or to relative clauses. As pointed out in section 4.2.1, modifying particles in Mohawk quite generally adjoin to the left of a constituent rather than to the right. Given this, (106) cannot be analyzed as a cleft. The only other possibility would be to consider *kíkʌ* an NP in its own right. However, in that case, both it and the initial lexical NP would have to be licensed by the same argument pro, in violation of the uniqueness clause of the ALC. Thus, the sentence is ungrammatical. In this way, the generalization that *thíkʌ* and *akwéku* must both be the initial member of a split receives a unified explanation based on the fact that both are clausal modifiers, even though the actual syntactic structures they enter into are rather different.

Since the explanation of the deviance of (106) hinges on an idiosyncratic property of Mohawk, we might expect such examples to be possible in other languages. This seems to be true. Earlier I mentioned in passing that demonstratives in the Gunwinjguan languages can be adjoined to either the left side of NP or to the right side in more or less free variation. Thus, a Mayali expression meaning 'that creature of ours' can come out as either *namege maih ngarrgu* 'that creature ours' or *maih ngarrgu namege* 'creature ours that' (Evans 1993:125). All things being equal, one would expect that demonstratives could adjoin to either side of the relative-like clause in a cleft construction as well. This is true; Mayali has not only the split order in (107a), but also the split order in (107b).

(107) a. Wanjh, na-behne barri-m-golu-rr-inj   maih, ...   (Evans 1991:
        well   I-that   3PS-CIS-descend-REFL-PAST/PERF bird   155)
        'Well, those birds just came down here, ...'

     b. Gun-nud ba-rrolga-ng   an-ege. (Evans 1991:327)
        IV-pus   3sS-arise-PAST/PERF III-that
        'All that pus rushed out.'

The cleft analysis also predicts that demonstrative splits should have the same distributional properties as *wh*-movement. Demonstratives separated from their apparent head noun should be able to adjoin to a higher verb if and only if that higher verb is a "bridge" verb, taking a clausal complement. In this respect, they should contrast with split *akwéku*, which can only adjoin to a higher verb if that verb is one of a small set of quantificational verbs. This prediction is correct, as can be seen in the following Mohawk sentences:

(108) a. Ne *thíkʌ* te-wak-atʌhutsóni   a-ku-hnínu-'   ne *ká'sere'*.
        NE that   DUP-1sO-want/STAT OPT-1sS/2sO-buy-PUNC NE car
        'I want to buy that car from you.'

     b. Ne *thí* y-a'-te-wake-rihwayÁta's-e'   ʌ-k-hnínu-'
        NE that TRANS-FACT-DUP-1sO-decide-PUNC FUT-1sS-buy-PUNC

        ne *áthere'*.
        NE basket
        'I decided that I will buy that basket.'

c. Ne *kíkʌ* wa'-ku-hróri-'   tsi   wá-hr-atst-e'   ne
   NE this FACT-1sS/2sO-tell-PUNC that FACT-MsS-use-PUNC NE
   onyatará'a.
   cloth
   'This is the cloth that I told you that he used.'

The matrix verb in the first example allows long-distance interpretation of *akwéku,* but the matrix verb in the second example does not; nevertheless, the two examples with split demonstratives are equally grammatical. Similarly, in (108c) the split demonstrative construction crosses an indicative complement, something that is never possible with split quantifier constructions. Thus, although split demonstratives are pragmatically more restricted than split quantifiers, they are syntactically less restricted. This is what we predict; all of these examples are derived by successive-cyclic *wh*-movement of a relative-like null operator.

Of course, this analysis also predicts that split demonstrative constructions should be sensitive to the same island conditions as other instances of *wh*-movement in Mohawk. Examples (109)–(111) show that this is the case.

Adjunct Island:
(109) *Ne kíkʌ wa'-t-k-ahsʌ́'tho-'   ne tsi   Sak wa-ha-ráta'-ne'
       NE this FACT-DUP-1sS-cry-PUNC because Sak FACT-MsS-step.on-PUNC

       ne kaya'túni.
       NE doll
       'I cried because Sak stepped on this doll.'

Complex NP Constraint:
(110) *Thíkʌ khe-yʌtéri-'   ne yakó-hs-u   áthere.
       that   1sS/FsO-know-IMPF NE FsO-finish-STAT basket
       'That basket, I know the woman who made.'

Wh-*Island:*
(111) #Ne thí wa'-ke-rihw-a-tshʌ́ri-'   úhka wa-ha-hnínu-'
       NE that FACT-1sS-matter-Ø-find-PUNC who FACT-MsS-buy-PUNC

       ne ká'sere'.
       NE car
       'That car, I found out who bought.'

Example (111) contrasts minimally with the acceptable sentence in (112), where the demonstrative and the noun form a constituent at the beginning of the sentence. This contrast confirms that split demonstrative constructions are derived by *wh*-movement, and hence are sensitive to "weak" islands, even though simple dislocation constructions are not.

(112) Thíkʌ ká'sere' wa'-ke-rihw-a-tshʌ́ri-'   úhka wa-ha-hnínu-'.
       that   car   FACT-1sS-matter-Ø-find-PUNC who FACT-MsS-buy-PUNC
       'That car, I found out who bought.'

Finally, this analysis predicts that split demonstratives should also *form* islands. Since they have an operator-variable structure internal to them, no other operator should be able to move out of that domain. This is also confirmed. Example (113) shows that split demonstrative constructions can be embedded under another predicate.

(113) a. Í-hs-ehr-e'   kʌ ne thíkʌ a-ku-hnínu-'   ne
          Ø-2sS-think-IMPF Q NE that OPT-1sS/2sO-buy-PUNC NE

          ká'sere'?
          car
          'Do you want me to buy that car from you?'

       b. Í-hs-ehr-e'   kʌ ne kíkʌ ʌ-kúy-u-'   ne
          Ø-2sS-think-IMPF Q NE this FUT-1sS/2sO-give-PUNC NE

          áthere'?
          basket
          'Do you think I will give you this basket?'

If, however, one then attempts to question another argument of the lower clause in these examples, the result is substantially degraded:

(114) a. ??Úhka í-hs-ehr-e'   ne thíkʌ a-yesa-hnínu-'
          who Ø-2sS-think-IMPF NE that OPT-FsS/2sO-buy-PUNC

          ne ká'sere'?
          NE car
          'Who do you want to buy that car from you?'

       b. *?Úhka í-hs-ehr-e'   ne kíkʌ ʌ-khéy-u-'   ne
          who Ø-2sS-think-IMPF NE this FUT-1sS/FsO-give-PUNC NE

          áthere'?
          basket
          'Who do you think I will give this basket to?'

The structure of (114a) is given in (115). In contrast, split quantifiers of the type analyzed in section 4.2 do not involve *wh*-movement; they are simply adverbial heads. As such, they do not create islands for *wh*-movement. Thus, (116) is grammatical, unlike the superficially similar (114b).

(116) Úhka í-hs-ehr-e'   akwéku ʌ-híy-u-'
       who Ø-2sS-think-IMPF all   FUT-1sS/MsO-give-PUNC

       yehyatúhkwa?
       pencil
       'Who do you think I will give all the pencils to?'

This confirms that split quantifier constructions and split demonstrative constructions are not really parallel phenomena in Mohawk, but rather are subject to different principles.

4.4 Conclusion

This chapter has presented an analysis of the principal instances of discontinuous constituents in Mohawk and the other polysynthetic languages. This account is

(115)

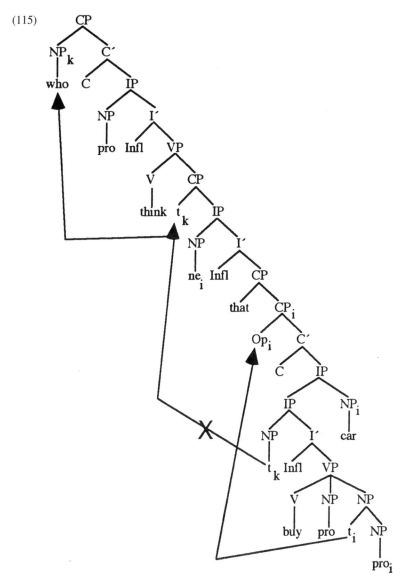

based on the fundamental idea that only one NP can be licensed by any given (singular) pro, as is the case for dislocation constructions in other languages. This rules out many easily imaginable but unattested discontinuous expressions immediately. Those split NPs that do exist are caused by either quantifiers that can be licensed as adverbs as well as NP modifiers, or NP modifiers that undergo *wh*-movement. Thus, discontinuous constituents factor into two rather different constructions. The elements licensed as adverbs must, in general, be in the same clause as the associated NP, but they do not create islands. In contrast, the elements placed by *wh*-movement can show up an unbounded distance away from the associated NP, but they do create islands.[26] This second class of structures is theoretically more interesting; it includes not only split interrogative constructions and split demonstrative constructions, but also the internally headed relative clauses found in Mohawk and at least some other polysynthetic languages. That specifier-like elements can undergo this kind of *wh*-movement has been attributed to the fact that polysynthetic languages typically lack a true determiner system; hence, demonstratives act like full NPs in these languages.

Since these two types of discontinuous constituents are licensed by somewhat different properties, they are not necessarily found together across languages. This is what we observe. Thus, Nahuatl allows split quantifier constructions, but Nunggubuyu does not. On the other hand, Nunggubuyu allows split demonstrative constructions, but Nahuatl does not—at least I have found no sign of them in the grammars. Mohawk and Southern Tiwa happen to have both types of constructions. I conclude that the range of discontinuous constituents in a polysynthetic language is determined more by lexical factors (microparameters) than by the MVC itself. This material also suggests that languages that allow a much wider range of discontinuous constituents—particularly some Pama-Nyungan languages of Australia—must license nominal fragments in some way other than dislocation.[27] This, then, completes our discussion of the nonconfigurational properties found in polysynthetic languages.

Notes

1. Example (6a) may be marginally possible in special discourse situations and with a heavy pause after the first NP. In this case, a more accurate gloss would be: 'As for the eggs, she found all of them.' The same is true for (3a), which can marginally be interpreted as 'As for fish, I like bullhead the best.' This kind of discourse topic is presumably licensed by principles different from the ALC (compare the discussion of "free topics" in Japanese in section 3.1.1).

2. Southern Tiwa also allows more or less the same range of discontinuous constituents as Mohawk does (Donald Frantz, personal communication). Some examples are given later in this chapter.

3. Examples of this type are probably not found in Nunggubuyu, simply because the language does not have a word comparable to *all* (Heath 1986:404).

4. This means that it is uninflected and does not fit neatly into either major lexical category (noun or verb) in Mohawk.

5. Alternatively, one could say that *akwéku* itself heads an NP in this example.

6. Alternatively, *akwéku* could be generated adjoined to a functional category that is part of the V-system; for simplicity I ignore such details here. See Bonneau and Zushi 1993 for detailed discussion of the French case.

7. A potentially interesting question is whether the lexical NP can adjoin inside of *akwéku*, as well as outside of it. If so, this might show that VP adjunction is possible in Mohawk, something left open in section 3.2.2. The word order *Akwéku onhúhsa' wa'etshʌ́ri'* is clearly also possible in Mohawk, but one cannot tell if *akwéku* is adjoined to VP or directly to the NP *onhúhsa'*. More complicated examples could probably resolve this question, but I have not looked into it.

8. French and Mohawk are not exactly the same on this point, however. Example (i) is an exact translation of (45b), but my consultant does not consider it semantically deviant.

(i) Kaná'ts-a-ku sh-y-a-ha-[a]tketóta-' éso wa-ha-tshÁri-'
pot-Ø-in SIM-TRANS-FACT-MsS-look-PUNC a.lot FACT-MsS-find-PUNC

ne onhúhsa'.
NE egg
'When he looked in the pot, he found many eggs.'

Similarly, Obenauer (1984:sec. 3.1) reports that some noneventive verbs in French do not allow *beaucoup*-type adverbs to indirectly modify their direct objects, presumably because the semantics of the verb is wrong. I have not found any transitive verbs that do not permit adverbial *éso* in Mohawk. Thus, the semantics of the two elements are similar, but apparently not identical.

9. Thus, I assume a version of the Uniformity of Theta Role Assignment Hypothesis (UTAH), in which thematic roles determine underlying structure (Baker 1988a). See chapters 5 and 7 for discussion of the particular version of the UTAH assumed here.

10. The noun root *wis* originally meant 'ice' and has become the normal word for 'drinking glass'. Many of my examples with this element are ambiguous between these two meanings.

11. The rarity of such examples in texts is probably because most of them are narratives, with a low density of questions of any kind.

12. The definition of a syntactic variable may have to be revised to include structures like (60); I put this aside as a technical issue.

It is well known that Russian and Polish allow extraction of 'which', stranding the rest of the NP. Interestingly, they also lack the determiner system found in Western Indo-European languages. (I wish to thank Steve Franks for helpful discussion of this point.) This gives further evidence that there is a true correlation between these factors and shows that the structures are not unique to polysynthetic languages.

13. In fact, one might expect islands to be even stronger for split *which* constructions. This depends on whether the trace adjoined to the argument counts as being lexically governed by the verb. If it does not, then the trace must be governed by its antecedent in order to pass the ECP. However, antecedent government is impossible into an island. Therefore, these examples violate not only Subjacency, but the much stronger ECP. The matter is difficult to assess, because my consultants have rather strong *wh*-island effects even when the extracted element is a full argument.

14. Perhaps this also implies that *ka nikáyʌ* could be extracted from an adjoined NP after all, by the same reasoning.

15. Paradigms similar to those with *ka nikáyʌ* 'which' are also found with *to níku* 'how many'. An example is (Deering and Delisle 1976):

(i) To ni-kúti wa-hse-nahskw-a-hnínu-' ne kwéskwes?
How-PART-ZpS FACT-2sS-animal-Ø-buy-PUNC NE pig
'How many pigs did you buy?'

However, it is not clear at this point whether *to níku* should be analyzed exactly like *ka nikáyʌ,* or whether it is more closely related to the split numeral construction mentioned in note 26.

16. Historically *ka* is 'where' and *tsi* is 'place where', while *nikáyʌ* is a form of the verb root *yʌ* 'to lie'. Thus, 'which basket did you buy?' in Mohawk comes from a collocation something like 'Where does the basket you bought lie?' I believe that this complex structure has been simplified in contemporary Mohawk, however.

17. See, among others, Platero 1974 for Navajo, Munro 1976 for Mojave, Cole 1987

for Quechua and other languages, Williamson 1987 for Lakhota, and Rice 1989 for Slave. Bonneau (1992) provides a recent survey and a discussion of the theoretical issues.

18. Indeed, for one consultant *tsi nikáyʌ* only appears in relative clauses with a distinctive interpretation, where *tsi nikáyʌ* + N means 'the kind of N', rather than 'the N'. Thus, examples like (70a) are perfect, while (70b) is only possible with the pragmatically odd reading 'Sak lost a basket of the kind that I bought.' The same pattern holds for comparable examples in which the head (*áthere*') is outside the relative clause. However, two other consultants do not seem to have this restriction on *tsi nikáyʌ* relatives and spontaneously gave the examples cited.

19. These sentences improve considerably when there is an NP "head" external to the relative clause. For example, (i) is better than (83a).

(i) Uwári ye-núhwe'-s thíkʌ anitskwára wa'-kuy-aterórok-e'
     Mary FsS-like-HAB that   chair   FACT-1sS/2sO-watch-PUNC

     tsi nikaríhwes wa-hs-úni-'.
     while   FACT-2sS-make-PUNC
     'Mary liked the chair that I watched you while you made.'

This suggests that Mohawk has a marginal resumptive pronoun strategy that makes operator movement unnecessary under these conditions.

20. Again, headed relatives are less sensitive to island effects, suggesting the use of a resumptive pronoun strategy:

(i) Isi   wa'-ka-tákh-e'   ne ká'sere' wa'-ke-rihwáruk-e' úhka
     there FACT-NsS-go-IMPF NE car   FACT-1sS-hear-PUNC who

     wa-ha-hnínu-'.
     FACT-MsS-buy-PUNC
     'There goes the car that I heard who bought.'

21. Mayali is different from Mohawk in this regard: the relative-pronoun-like demonstrative can be separated from the possessed noun in Mayali (Evans 1991:337). However, this is surely related to the fact that the syntax of possession in Mayali is different from that in Mohawk (see section 6.2).

22. At least in Mohawk. The grammaticality of (91) may imply that no operator movement is involved in IHRCs in Japanese, contrary to arguments given by Watanabe (1991) and Bonneau (1992). Alternatively, Japanese may allow some kind of "absorption" of two relative operators into a single complex relative operator, similar to the absorption that allows multiple questions in many languages. Perhaps this is only possible if the relative operators can be interpreted "quantificationally" (see Srivastav 1991).

23. Identifying such cases is complicated by the fact that *thíkʌ* 'that' and *kʌ'íkʌ* 'this' are often shortened to *thi* and *ki,* respectively. These elements often occur in particle clusters in Mohawk, and it is not easy to tell whether some of these might qualify as split demonstratives or not.

24. The exact structure of the matrix clause is not crucial here. Presumably it is similar to ordinary copular clauses in Mohawk, but this is not a topic of investigation in this work.

25. I have collected two examples of this word order that were accepted by one consultant (as well as several that were not). I assume that this variability is related to the factors pointed out in note 1.

26. In fact, there is one more kind of discontinuous expression found in Mohawk: numerals can be separated from the noun they modify, as in (i).

(i)   Wisk ni-a'-t-hatí-nerʌk-e'   ne kayʌ́kwire'.   (KO:96)
      five   PART-FACT-DUP-MpS-bind-PUNC NE arrow
      'They (leaders of the Iroquois) tied up five arrows.'

This is a relatively common structure in Mohawk; it is also attested in Nahuatl. Unfortunately, it does not fit neatly into either class of constructions discussed in the text. Floated numerals in a matrix clause can be interpreted with an NP in the embedded clause of virtually any bridge verb—like demonstratives and unlike *akwéku*. However, a floated numeral does not form an island for further extraction—like *akwéku* and unlike demonstratives. Numeral constructions also have some morphological quirks that are highly specific to the Iroquoian languages (see Postal 1979). I speculate that these constructions involve the movement of some kind of QP or "degree phrase" operator. This accounts for the possibility of long-distance dependencies. On the other hand, if the QP operator were categorially different from the NP/DetP operators involved in normal questions or relatives, perhaps it would not create islands for them, by some version of Rizzi's (1990) theory of Relativized Minimality.

27. See Austin and Bresnan 1994 for other arguments that the kind of nonconfigurationality found in Warlpiri and Jiwarli cannot be derived entirely from Jelinek's pronominal argument hypothesis. Discontinuous constituents in these languages are apparently licensed by properties of the Case system, rather than by head-marking phenomena.

II

WORD STRUCTURE AND PHRASE STRUCTURE

5

Agreement and Clause Structure

5.1. Introduction

Part I discussed nonconfigurationality in polysynthetic languages. In the course of the investigation, it became clear that there are normally three distinct elements involved in expressing the argument of, say, a verb: an empty category that is the true argument of the verb; a morpheme in the word containing that verb that makes the argument visible for θ-role assignment; and, optionally, an NP in adjunct position that expresses most of the semantic content associated with the argument. For the most part, part I concentrated on the relationship between the null argument and the adjoined NP. In part II we now turn to the more fundamental relationship: the one that holds between the null argument and the morpheme on the verb. This inquiry yields a better picture of basic clausal relations in the polysynthetic languages and clarifies some of the detailed operations of the Morphological Visibility Condition. It also develops the idea, introduced in chapter 1, that much of the phrase structure in polysynthetic languages shows up on the surface as word structure. Recall that there are two types of morphological entities that can satisfy the MVC: agreement elements and incorporated roots. There are also two major categories that one needs to be concerned with: nouns and verbs. Hence, part II naturally divides into four topics: agreement on verbs, agreement on nouns, incorporation of nouns, and incorporation of verbs. I begin with the most basic of these topics—the syntax of agreement relationships within verbal domains.

In chapters 1 and 2, the central importance of agreement morphology in polysynthetic languages in general and Mohawk in particular was shown. According to the Polysynthesis Parameter proposed in chapter 1, all of the θ-roles of the head must be expressed morphologically within the word. Agreement morphemes are the primary way of satisfying this requirement, because they (unlike incorporated noun roots) are available for all classes of syntactic positions. Moreover, in chapter 2 we saw that overt NPs always appear in nonargument positions. This analysis depends on the agreement morphemes in at least two ways. First, the agreement morphemes must be present to license null pronouns, which, in turn, satisfy the Theta Criterion. Second, the agreement morphemes absorb the Case-assigning properties of the head: this is what forces overt NPs to be in nonargument positions.

This chapter takes up the topic of agreement more directly, seeking to develop a theory that both fits these general requirements and explains the specific morphological forms that agreement takes in Mohawk. In particular, I will concentrate on the following three questions: (1) What determines the number of agreement elements found on a given verb? (2) How can the special properties of neuter gender be explained within the system? (3) What determines the form of the agreement morphemes found on a verb? The answer to question (1) provides independent evidence that agreement morphemes absorb Case in Mohawk, thereby supporting the analysis in chapter 2. Question (2) is particularly relevant to evaluating the MVC, since it involves a range of cases in which arguments of the verb do not seem to trigger agreement. Question (3) deals with the well-known descriptive fact that the Iroquoian languages have a so-called active agreement system, in which some intransitive verbs take "subject" agreement, whereas others take "object" agreement. This fact has been given widely different interpretations in the literature, many of which I claim to be on the wrong track. Also, in the course of the chapter I will present evidence that bears on recent controversies about the position of agreement in phrase structure and the nature of the agreement relationship, triggered by Pollock 1989, Chomsky 1991, and related work.

Up to this point, our focus has been primarily on phrases that are adjoined to the clause, and therefore specific assumptions about clause structure have been relatively unimportant. However, now clause structure becomes quite important. This is an area where there has been considerable activity in recent years. Rather than assuming the more recent developments from the outset, I will begin with fairly conservative, classical Government-Binding assumptions and add more recent developments as they are needed. In particular, I begin with ternary branching structures and with Infl as the only functional category; however, both of these positions will be revised as the discussion proceeds. I hope that this method of exposition will have two advantages. First, readers who are less familiar with these innovations will have an opportunity to get accustomed to them somewhat gradually. Second, this format will make clear exactly which aspects of the analysis crucially depend on and/or support some of the more controversial aspects of current theory.

Mohawk agreement paradigms are somewhat formidable. Mohawk distinguishes three non–third persons (first inclusive, first exclusive, and second) as well as four third person genders (masculine, feminine, zoic, and neuter).[1] Added to these categories are three number distinctions (singular, plural, and dual). Hence, there are on the order of 21 distinct person/number/gender combinations that are potentially possible. To make matters worse, subject and object agreement elements are not always kept distinct; rather, they often merge into portmanteau forms that are not always easily recognized from their parts. Thus, there could be as many as $21 \times 21 = 441$ separate prefixes. In fact, many of the distinctions are neutralized in certain environments, so that only 58 forms are used. There are interesting patterns to this neutralization that suggest that a system of rules or principles is at work in reducing the number of prefixes (see Postal 1979:ch. 3 for discussion). However, these neutralization patterns are not sufficiently simple to be of much mnemonic help to the non-Iroquoianist. Then, as the final insult, some of these prefixes undergo rather opaque allomorphy triggered by the adjacent sounds. To make the system more tractable, I will, for the most part, limit the examples to singular subjects and singular objects. Thus, most of the forms are drawn from the 6 × 6 matrix given in Table 5–1. This range of examples is adequate to illustrate the basic morphosyntactic properties of the system that are of interest here. The complete list of forms, together with their various allomorphs, can be found in many references, including Lounsbury 1953, Postal 1979, Bonvillain 1973, and Deering and Delisle 1976.

Verbs can have three types of arguments that are relevant to agreement processes: agentive subjects, patient/theme objects (which can also be subjects if the verb has no agent), and source/goal arguments comparable to those that appear in the dative case in other languages. In fact, there are rather few morphologically underived verb roots that take source/goal arguments; the list includes *u* 'give', *ni* 'lend', *hninu* 'buy from', *nʌsko* 'steal from', and perhaps a few others. However, goals can be added to many other verbs by means of the benefactive morpheme *'s/ʌ;* since the resulting verb acts in almost every respect like a simple verb with a goal argument, for purposes of this chapter I treat benefactive verbs as syntactically simple verbs selecting a goal. (See section 9.3 for an explicit analysis of the Mohawk benefactive morpheme.) For methodological convenience, I largely avoid verb classes where the identification of θ-roles is in serious question, such as psychological predicates, although these do not present any obvious difficulties in Mohawk.

Finally, a note on terminology. When a language shows agreement with both arguments of a transitive verb, it is common to speak in terms of subject and

Table 5-1. Singular Agreement Prefixes in Mohawk*

A-Class	O-Class	*1*	*2*	*M*	*F*	*Z*	*N*
	No A / *No O*	*wak*	*sa*	*hro*	*yako*	*yo*	*o*
1	k	—	ku	hri	khe	k	k
2	hs	sk	—	tsh	she	hs	hs
M	hra	hrak	hya	hro	shako	hra	hra
F	ye	yuk	yesa	hruwa	yutat	kuwa	ye
Z	ka	wak	sa	hro	yako	yo	ka
N	ka	wak	sa	hro	yako	yo	ka

*See text for explanation of "A-Class" and "O-Class."

Masculine forms beginning with *hr* show up as [r] word initially, as [hr] before [u, Ʌ́] or following the stressed syllable, and as [h] otherwise; feminine *ye* becomes [yu] before [a] and yak before [e, Ʌ́, o, u]; neuter/zoic *ka* becomes [w] before [a, e, Ʌ́] and [y] before [o, u].

object agreement. However, one of the crucial questions to be considered is whether such terminology is appropriate for Mohawk's active system. One important question to investigate is whether or not intransitive verbs that take "object agreement" actually take a direct object argument at some level. Pending the results of this inquiry, it is best to avoid such terminology, which is overtly based on grammatical functions. For the same reason, semantically based terminology such as "agent prefix" and "patient prefix" (Chafe 1970) should also be avoided until we know that agreement forms are semantically determined. Thus, I refer to the forms normally used to indicate the subject of a transitive verb simply as "A-class agreements": this is inspired by the vowel [a] in the masculine, zoic, and neuter forms (*hra, ka, ka*); it is also evocative of "agent." The forms normally used to indicate the object of a transitive verb will be called "O-class agreements": this is inspired by the vowel [o] found in the masculine, feminine, zoic, and neuter forms (*hro, yako, yo, yo*), and is evocative of "object." This terminology differs slightly from that used in the rest of this book, where I am not so shy about grammatical function-based terminology and abbreviations.

5.2. Case and the Number of Agreement Morphemes

As a starting point, recall from chapter 1 that the position of the agreement morphemes in polysynthetic languages suggests that they are adjoined items, rather than X-bar theoretic heads in their own right. Furthermore, chapter 2 showed that agreement morphemes absorb the structural Case features of X^0 heads in Mohawk. Suppose that, in fact, they must absorb Case in this way. If this is true, then we should expect to see a correlation between agreement and Case features, as stated in (1).

(1) Agreement morphology is adjoined to all and only those heads that have structural Case-assigning features.

The "all" part of (1) follows from the MVC, as discussed in section 2.2. The "only" part of (1) might also be derivable from a suitable generalization of the PF Case Filter given in section 2.2. Agreement morphemes in Mohawk are nominal elements, at least in the sense that they are categorized for features of person, number, and gender. They also have phonological features. Thus, it is reasonable to say that they are like NPs in needing to receive Case in order to be visible in the PF component.

Suppose, furthermore, that the basic principles determining the distribution of structural Case-assigning features are relatively invariant across languages. Then there should be similarities between the distribution of agreement morphology in Mohawk and the distribution of structural Case in other languages, such as English. Although the existence of such a relationship will not surprise those familiar with recent work in the P&P framework, it is worth establishing with some care for Mohawk. Let us therefore survey the different types of verbs in Mohawk from this perspective.

5.2.1 Basic Verb Types

The first type of verb to consider is a transitive verb with an agent subject and a theme/patient object. Not surprisingly, such verbs agree with both their agent and their theme. In terms of Table 5–1, the form chosen is the one where the features of the agent determine the row while the features of the theme determine the column; (2) gives some representative examples.

(2) a. T-a-ha-yéna-'.
       CIS-FACT-MsA/ZsO-catch-PUNC
       'He caught it (e.g., a bear).'

     b. T-a-ho-yéna-'.
       CIS-FACT-ZsA/MsO-catch-PUNC
       'It (e.g., a bear) caught him.'

     c. T-a-hi-yéna-'.
       CIS-FACT-1sA/MsO-catch-PUNC
       'I caught him.'

     d. T-a-hak-yéna-'.
       CIS-FACT-MsA/1sO-catch-PUNC
       'HE CAUGHT ME.'

Similarly, in other polysynthetic languages "subject" agreement goes with the agent and "object" agreement with the theme, more or less by definition.

More interesting are verbs with three arguments—an agent, a patient, and a goal (or source). Such verbs agree with the agent as the A factor and the goal as the O factor. These verbs show no agreement with the theme whatsoever. Hence, the agreement prefixes are exactly the same as those found with simple transitive verbs:

(3) a. Wa-híy-u-'.
       FACT-1sA/MsO-give-PUNC
       'I gave it to him.'

     b. Wa-hák-u-'.
       FACT-MsA/1sO-give-PUNC
       'He gave it to me.'

In this situation, the theme argument is generally required to be neuter, as shown by (4).[2]

(4) a. #Érhar Λ-kú-nut-e'.
       dog FUT-1sA/2sO-feed-PUNC
       'I will feed you to the dog.'(OK as: 'Dog, I will feed you (something).')

     b. *Λ-ku-(ya't)-óhare-'s-e'   ne owirá'a.
       FUT-1sA/2sO-wash-BEN-PUNC NE baby.
       'I will wash the baby for you.'

Example (4a) attempts to express a second person theme with a zoic goal; (4b) attempts a feminine or masculine theme with a second person goal. In each case, some rather elaborate circumlocution is needed to express the intended idea. Example (5) illustrates this effect with a near-minimal pair; an example with a neuter theme is perfect, while one with an animate theme is ungrammatical.

(5)   Ká'sere'/ *káskare' ʌ-hi-tshʌ́ry-a-'s-e'.
        car   friend   FUT-1sA/MsO-find-BEN-PUNC
        'I will find him a car/*a girlfriend.'

Intuitively, the reason the theme of a triadic verb must be neuter is that agreement with a neuter object is phonologically null. This can be seen in Table 5–1, where the first and last columns are identical. Hence, this type of argument does not overtax the agreement system in Mohawk, which can only represent two elements at a time. This cannot be the whole story, however, because agreement with a neuter subject is also phonologically null, as shown by the fact that the first and last rows in Table 5–1 are identical. Nevertheless, having a neuter subject does not make a triadic verb well formed unless the object is neuter as well; hence, (6) is ungrammatical.

(6)   *Tsi yo-kʌnór-u   wa'-uk-ya't-óhare-'s-e'   ne khe-yʌ́'a.
        that NsO-rain-STAT FACT-FsA/1sO-body-wash-BEN-PUNC NE my-daughter
        'The rain washed my daughter for me.'

This example becomes grammatical if the feminine theme 'my daughter' is replaced with a neuter NP such as *akwatyá'tawi* 'my shirt' and the agreement prefix is adjusted accordingly. Similarly, triadic verbs are ungrammatical if the agent and theme are animate and only the goal is neuter:[3]

(7)   *Wa-hi-ya't-óhare-'s-e'.
        FACT-1sA/MsO-body-wash-BEN-PUNC
        'I washed him for it (e.g., a special school event).'

Thus, we see that it is not enough for one of the arguments of a three-place verb to be neuter; rather, it must be the theme/object that is neuter.

Here, we see the first nontrivial parallel between agreement in Mohawk and the assignment of structural Case in, say, English. In English triadic constructions where the goal is not expressed as the object of a preposition, the goal necessarily usurps the immediate postverbal position normally reserved for the theme:

(8)   a.   John sent Mary a book.
        b. *John sent a book Mary (vs. John sent a book).

This is normally taken to show that the goal receives structural accusative Case from the verb under adjacency (Chomsky 1981, Baker 1988a). Thus, the agent and the goal receive structural Case in (8a), and the theme is then left to get Case by other means. In the same way, the agent and the goal displace the theme for purposes of agreement in Mohawk.

Other polysynthetic languages are broadly similar to Mohawk in this regard, but have a few complications. The Gunwinjguan languages also show agreement with the agent and the goal, but not with the theme, in constructions where all three are present (see Heath 1984:552–555, Evans 1991:220–221). All attested examples in Ainu fit this pattern as well (Shibatani 1990:34–35). Wichita, Nahuatl, and Southern Tiwa are similar, but with an added wrinkle: they show agreement with a full range of person/number features for the agent and the goal only, but they also show an impoverished amount of agreement with the theme. Thus, in Nahuatl and Wichita it is possible to indicate the difference between a third singular theme and a third person plural theme (Launey 1981:172–174, Rood 1976:188); in Southern Tiwa, verbs show agreement with the noun class of the theme, where noun class is a combination of number (singular vs. plural) and gender (animate vs. two kinds of inanimate) (Allen et al. 1990, Rosen 1990). However, in these languages as in Mohawk one cannot have a full range of themes: it is impossible to say something like 'I will give you to the dog' for example. I assume that the impoverished agreement with the theme falls outside the core agreement system. If we then disregard this and restrict ourselves to full person/number agreement, Wichita, Nahuatl, and Southern Tiwa fit the same generalization as Mohawk and Gunwinjguan. Finally, agreement in Chukchee seems to depend on a choice in how the goal is realized. If the goal is expressed as an NP in the allative case, then the verb agrees with the theme and not the goal, with the sole exception being the verb yǝl 'to give', which has the option of agreeing with the goal instead (Nedjalkov 1976:208, Mel'cuk and Savvina 1978:19–20). If, however, the theme is incorporated into the verb, the goal may be expressed as an NP in the absolutive case; in these circumstances, the verb agrees with it as it would with any normal theme object (Nedjalkov 1976:189–190). These facts are more or less the same as those in Mohawk, as long as one makes two stipulations involving the morphological Case system of Chukchee: (1) goals cannot be expressed with absolutive Case unless there is no other absolutive NP in the clause, and (2) allative Case NPs only count as true arguments of the verb in Chukchee with the exceptional verb yǝl (see section 9.2). Throughout the polysynthetic languages, then, we see a tendency for the goal to supplant the theme for purposes of true or full agreement.

The next class of verbs to consider consists of simple intransitive verbs. In Mohawk, these agree with their sole argument, regardless of whether that argument is semantically an agent or a theme:

(9) a. Wa-ha-[a]táwʌ-'.
         FACT-MsA-swim-PUNC
         'He swam.'

     b. T-a-ha-yá't-ʌ'-ne'.
         CIS-FACT-MsA-body-fall-PUNC
         'He fell down (e.g., from in a tree).'

     c. Wa-ho-yó'tʌ-'.
         FACT-MsO-work-PUNC
         'He worked.'

     d. Wa-ho-ké'tot-e'
         FACT-MsO-appear-PUNC
         'He appeared, emerged, came into sight.'

In some cases, the morpheme used is from the A paradigm (the first column of Table 5–1), and thus is comparable to subject agreement; in other cases, it is from the O paradigm (the first row of Table 5–1), and thus is comparable to object agreement. At first glance, the difference seems to have little or nothing to do with what thematic role the verb assigns: examples (9a) and (9c) take volitional agents; examples (9b) and (9d) take nonvolitional themes. Moreover, this variation in the form of agreement is peculiar to the Iroquoian languages and the distantly related Caddoan languages (Mithun 1991); the other polysynthetic languages show the same "subject" agreement paradigm with all intransitive verbs. I return to the topic of split subject marking in detail in section 5.4.[4]

The next class to consider is verbs that select an agent and a goal. Such verbs freely show A-type agreement with the agent and O-type agreement with the goal:

(10)   a.   Λ-hi-yó'tΛ-hs-e'.   (D&D:427)
            FUT-1sA/MsO-work-BEN-PUNC
            'I will work for him.'

       b.   Uwári wa-huwa-[a]tyΛ-ha's-e'   ne Sak.
            Mary   FACT-FsA/MsO-sit-BEN-PUNC NE Sak
            'Mary sat down on Sak (walked in and stayed).'

       c.   (?)Sak s-a-shako-[a]htΛty-a-'s-e'   ro-nistΛha.
            Sak ITER-FACT-MsA/FsO-move-Ø-BEN-PUNC his-mother
            'Sak went home for his mother.'

       d.   Sak t-a-hakw-ataweyá't-Λ-'.
            Sak CIS-FACT-MsA/1sO-enter-BEN-PUNC
            'Sak broke in on me.'

Notice that the agreement morphemes used here are identical to those used with agent–theme verbs or with agent–goal–theme verbs. This is a further indication that the theme argument has no effect on verb agreement in the presence of a goal. Similar equivalencies hold in the other the polysynthetic languages as well.

The last class of verbs to consider are those that select a theme and a goal. Interestingly, in this situation the verb shows full agreement with the goal argument only:

(11)   a.   Sak wa-hó-[a]hsΛ'-s-e'   ne ówise'.
            Sak FACT-MsO-fall-BEN-PUNC NE glass
            'Sak dropped the glass.' (Literally: 'The glass fell on Sak.')

       b.   Wa'-ako-wir-a-kΛ-[i]héy-a-'s-e'.
            FACT-FsO-baby-Ø-??-die-Ø-BEN-PUNC
            'Her baby died on her.'

       c.   ?Ukw-ate-nóhare-'s-e'   ne atyá'tawi.
            FACT/1sO-SRFL-wash-BEN-PUNC NE shirt
            'The shirt came clean on me.'

       d.   (?)Wa-ho-'sere-ht-a-ke'tót-Λ-'.
            FACT-MsO-car-NOM-Ø-appear-BEN-PUNC
            'The car suddenly appeared before him.'

With these verbs, the theme is required to be neuter, just as it is with ditransitive verbs. Thus, the examples in (12) contrast with the corresponding examples in (11).

(12) a. *Sak wa-huwa-yá't-ʌ'-s-e'   ne owirá'a.
          Sak FACT-FsA/MsO-body-fall-BEN-PUNC NE baby
          'Sak dropped the baby.' (Literally: 'The baby fell on Sak.')

      b. *T-hní-[i]teru   wa-shako-[i]héy-a-'s-e'.
          CIS-MDA-stay FACT-MsA/FsO-die-Ø-BEN-PUNC
          'Her husband died on her.'

      c. *Wa'-ukw-at-ya't-óharé-'s-e'   ne eksá'a.
          FACT-FsA/1sO-SRFL-body-wash-BEN-PUNC NE girl
          'The girl became clean for me.'

      d. *Tutayawʌ́stsi wa-huwa-ke'tót-ʌ-'   ne Sak.
          suddenly   FACT-FsA/MsO-appear-BEN-PUNC NE Sak
          'She (the Virgin Mary) suddenly appeared before Sak.'

Significantly, these verbs are not limited to neuter themes when they are used without a goal NP, as demonstrated in (13).

(13) a. Wa'-e-yá't-ʌ'-ne'   ne owirá'a.
          FACT-FsA-body-fall-PUNC NE baby
          'The baby fell.'

      b. T-hní-[i]teru   wa-hrʌ́-[i]hey-e'.
          CIS-MDA-stay FACT-MsA-die-PUNC
          'Her husband died.'

      c. Wa'-u-[a]t-ya't-óhare-'   ne eksá'a
          FACT-FsA-SRFL-body-wash-PUNC NE girl
          'The girl got washed.'

      d. Tutayawʌ́stsi wa'-ako-ké'tot-e'   tsi núwe Sak í-hr[a]-et-e'.
          suddenly   FACT-FsO-appear-PUNC where Sak Ø-MsA-stand-PUNC
          'She suddenly appeared where Sak was standing.'

Therefore, the effect illustrated by (11) vs. (12) is morphosyntactic in nature, and not simply a reflection of the verbs' selectional restrictions. Thus, we have uncovered an important contrast between the so-called *unergative* verbs, which take an agent but no theme, and the *unaccusative* verbs, which select a theme but no agent: the unergative verbs can take a full range of transitive prefixes, while the unaccusative verbs cannot.

   This distinction recalls a well-known difference between unergatives and unaccusatives in the Romance languages: the fact that unergative verbs can assign structural accusative Case and unaccusatives cannot (Burzio's Generalization; see Burzio 1986). The difference can be seen overtly in the fact that cognate objects and dummy resultative objects are allowed with unergative verbs but not with unaccusative verbs:

(14) a. John swam a good swim.

      b. John swam himself home.

(15) a. *John fell a bad fall.

      b. *John fell himself down.

This is the second nontrivial parallelism between Case assignment in English and agreement in Mohawk. Notice, incidentally, that the form of agreement used with the goal is always the O-type "object" form, regardless of what agreement the verb root alone selects. This turns out to be of great importance in the discussion in section 5.4.

Goal/benefactive/malefactive arguments can also be expressed with unaccusative verbs under certain conditions in Southern Tiwa, Mayali, Chukchee, Wichita, and Ainu. However, the exact conditions vary from language to language in ways that depend on properties of the applicative morpheme. Therefore, comparative data on this point are deferred until section 9.3, where applicative constructions are analyzed in detail.

5.2.2. The Location of Agreement

Summarizing our survey of verb classes, we find the following:

(16)   *Verb Type*   *Agreement Behavior*
         Transitive   Two agreement morphemes (agent and theme)
         Ditransitive   Two agreement morphemes (agent and goal)
         Unergative   Two agreement morphemes (agent and goal, if any)
         Unaccusative   One agreement morpheme (theme or goal, if any)

This is directly parallel to the distribution of structural Case assignment in English; hence, the same theory should apply to both. Specifically, I assume that both the verb and Infl may, in principle, assign one Case each, but not more. The verb is a Case assigner if and only if it assigns an agent θ-role (or, perhaps, some other external role). Infl, on the other hand, is always a Case assigner in Mohawk, since the language has no infinitival or participial verb forms (see section 10.2.1). Finally, the addition of a goal does not add any new Case-assigning properties, at least in Mohawk.[5] This leads to the statement given previously in (1), that agreement morphology is adjoined to all and only those heads that have structural Case-assigning features. In essence, this is equivalent to Borer's (1984) proposal that clitics are "spell-outs" of the Case features of the head; that is, I do not distinguish between clitics and agreement from the point of view of syntax. A (di)transitive structure will then look something like (17).

(17)

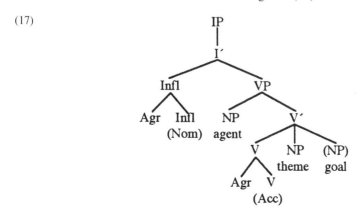

Infl agrees with the NP it governs—that is, the agent. The verb will agree with one of the NPs it governs; we shall return to how it chooses in situations where there are two candidates. These agreement morphemes can then license pros in the NP positions they govern. Since the agreement morphemes absorb the Case features associated with the heads, the argument positions must, in fact, be empty in the derived structure; if they do not contain a pro, then they contain the trace of either *wh*-movement or noun incorporation. Finally, V undergoes head movement, adjoining to Infl; this creates a single word that has agreement morphemes coindexed with two of the arguments of the verb, satisfying the MVC. (This structure will be revised later, when binary branching and the aspect morphemes mentioned in section 1.6 are taken into account.)

5.2.3 *Reflexive Verbs*

The hypothesis that agreement morphemes are dependent on Case features also predicts that agreement should show interesting interactions with Case-absorbing morphology. The best known example of such morphology is the English passive morpheme. Now, Mohawk does not have anything that corresponds directly to passives in English. This I take to be more or less accidental, given that passive/impersonal constructions are found in other polysynthetic languages, such as Nahuatl and Ainu. However, there is good evidence that reflexive verbs in Mohawk are to be analyzed in essentially the same way as passives. Passive-like analyses of morphological reflexives have been proposed by Marantz (1984) for Albanian and Icelandic and by Baker (1988d) for Chichewa, among others. Once such an analysis is justified for Mohawk, the interactions of reflexives with agreement morphology can be investigated.

Mohawk reflexive verbs were mentioned, but not analyzed, in section 2.1.2, where the concern was simply to show that there are no overt NP anaphors in Mohawk. A simple example of the construction is (18), where the presence of the morpheme *atat* is the key.

(18)   Sak r[a]-atate-núhwe'-s.
        Sak MsA-REFL-like-HAB
        'Sak likes himself.'

Clearly *atat* either expresses or suppresses one of the verb's two θ-roles; the question is, which role? The answer is far from obvious, given that semantically both argument slots of the verb are ultimately satisfied by the same entity, in this case the referent of *Sak*.

Suppose that *atat* were related to the object θ-role. This idea could be developed in at least three ways: (1) *atat* could be an anaphoric N united with the verb by the general process of noun incorporation; (2) *atat* could be a special object agreement form that licenses a null anaphor instead of a pro; (3) *atat* could be a derivational morpheme that suppresses the object θ-role, turning the two-place predicate 'like' into a one-place predicate 'self-like' (cf. Di Sciullo and Williams 1987). Indeed, one or the other of these proposals may be correct for other languages; however, there are three empirical arguments that suggest that they are all on the wrong track for Mohawk.

First, there are a few transitive verbs in Mohawk that have the special lexical property that their subject argument triggers O-class agreement morphemes, rather than the usual A-class agreement morphemes. In (19), examples of two such verbs are given.

(19) a. Y-a'-akó-[a]ti-'.
TRANS-FACT-FsO-throw-PUNC
'She threw it away.'

b. Y-a'-t-hon-úko-'.
TRANS-FACT-DUP-MpO-bump-PUNC
'They bumped it.'

However, when these verbs appear with the reflexive morpheme, this property is lost; the reflexive forms of the verbs take A-class agreement forms obligatorily:

(20) a. Y-a-*ha*-[a]tat-ya't-úti-'.
TRANS-FACT-MsA-REFL-body-throw-PUNC
'He threw himself in.'

b. Y-a'-t-*ha*-[a]tat-ya't-úko-'.
TRANS-FACT-DUP-MsA-REFL-body-bump-PUNC
'He bumped into himself.'

This switch in agreement is unexpected if *atat* simply expresses or suppresses the object. On the other hand, it is readily explained if *atat* expresses/suppresses the subject argument of the verb root. Since the subject θ-role is no longer expressed by verbal agreement, the fact that it would have triggered O-class agreement automatically becomes moot. Put another way, (20) shows that the argument of the reflexive verb is not subject to the same constraint on expression as the agent of the nonreflexive verb. From this we can conclude that it is not the agent argument that remains in a morphological reflexive.[6]

Noun incorporation facts point to the same conclusion. Suppose that we take an example in which an inanimate NP appears with a reflexive verb form. Such examples require some imagination to construct, but they are possible. For example:

(21) K-askánek-s   ne karístatsi autate-nóhare-'.
1sA-wish-HAB NE stove   OPT/NsA/REFL-wash-PUNC
I wish the stove would wash itself.'

Interestingly, such an NP can be incorporated into the verb, with little or no further degradation.

(22) K-askánek-s   autate-rist-óhare-'.
1sS-wish-HAB OPT/NsA/REFL-stove-wash-PUNC
'I wish the stove would wash itself.'

In (23), another example of the same type is given.

(23) W-atat-a'shar-othíyo-s.
NsA-REFL-knife-sharpen-HAB
'The knife sharpens itself.'

Now it is known that theme-objects generally can be incorporated in Mohawk, but agent-subjects cannot be. Thus, 'stove' in (22) must be the theme-object of *ohare* 'wash'. Therefore, it must be the agent-subject of the verb that is affected by *atat*.

Finally, *atat* is clearly a reduplicated version of *at*, which is called the "semire-flexive" morpheme by Iroquoianists. One of the relatively productive uses of this morpheme is that it is added to a transitive change-of-state verb to derive its unaccusative, anticausativized variant (Lounsbury 1953, Bonvillain 1973, Deering and Delisle 1976). Examples of *at* used in this way are[7]:

(24)   a. Auhá'a w-ate-rist-óhare-s.
      itself   NsA-SRFL-stove-wash-HAB
      'The stove comes clean by itself.'

    b. W-ate-nhot-ú-kw-as.   (D&D:374)
      NsA-SRFL-door-close-REV-HAB
      'The door opens.'

    c. Wa'-te-w-át-ya'k-e'.   (D&D:374)
      FACT-DUP-NsA-SRFL-break-PUNC
      'It broke in half.'

In these examples, *at* is clearly suppressing the agent θ-role of the transitive verb, leaving only the patient role to be expressed. Moreover, the similarity in form between this morpheme and the reflexive morpheme is clearly not coincidental. On the contrary, many languages use exactly the same morpheme to form reflex-ives and anticausatives; the reflexive clitic *se/si* in Romance languages is probably the best known example. If *at* suppresses the external θ-role of a verb, it is likely that its cousin *atat* affects the external θ-role as well.

These facts all point to a passive-like analysis of Mohawk reflexive verbs, in which *atat* takes away or receives the external argument of the verb to which it attaches. Presumably, it also absorbs the Case features associated with that verb. Meanwhile, the theme argument of the verb projects into the direct object position, as usual. If it is not incorporated, then it is identified by the agreement in Infl. Ultimately, the lexical properties of *atat* guarantee that the agent of the verb will be interpreted as the same as the referent of the syntactically expressed theme argument. Thus, the syntactic structure of an example like (18) is roughly (25).

(25)

There is some debate in the literature on passives about whether the passive morpheme deletes the agent θ-role of the verb in the lexicon, as in Chomsky 1981, or
is literally assigned the agent θ-role in the syntax (see Baker et al. 1989). Exactly
the same question arises with respect to *atat* in (25). I will leave this question
open for now, returning to it later. For our present purposes, the relevant fact
is that the reflexive morpheme reduces the structural Cases available in a given
structure.

We can now look at how *atat* interacts with agreement. The interesting examples are those where a goal NP is present. Consider first a ditransitive verb. Such
verbs have three arguments; hence, in principle there are three conceivable reflexive interpretations: agent = patient, agent = goal/benefactive, and patient =
goal/benefactive. In fact, only the agent = goal/benefactive possibility is allowed:

(26)   a. Wa-h[a]-atát-u-'.
           FACT-MsA-REFL-give-PUNC
           'He gave it to himself.' NOT: 'He gave himself to it/her.'

       b. Λ-k-atat-ahy-óhare-'s-e'.
           FUT-1sA-REFL-fruit-wash-BEN-PUNC
           'I will wash the fruit for myself.'

This is expected on the passive-style analysis; *atat* has the property of tying up
the external (agent) argument of the verb, and hence, the agent must be involved
in the reflexive interpretation. At the same time, *atat* absorbs the structural Case
of the verb. We saw in section 5.2.1 that the structural Case of a ditransitive verb
is generally assigned to the goal argument, not the theme. For example, the goal
must be the argument to move to the subject position in passives of ditransitives
in many dialects of English:

(27)   a.   The farmer was given a new car.

       b.   ??A new car was given the farmer.

Similarly, it is the goal argument that is forced to associate with the subject position in Mohawk reflexive verbs, thereby being interpreted as the same as the agent;
I return to the details of how this takes place later. In this way, the interpretation
of (26) is accounted for.

Consider now the theme argument in a ditransitive reflexive. We have seen that
this cannot be part of the reflexive interpretation. However, now that the goal
argument no longer determines object agreement on the verb, one could imagine
that object agreement would be free to express the theme argument. In fact, object
agreement with the theme is still not possible, as shown by (28).

(28)   a. *Wa'-khey-atat-ya't-óhare-'s-e'.
           FACT-1sA/FsO-REFL-body-wash-BEN-PUNC
           'I washed her for myself.' (Also bad as: 'I washed myself for her.')

       b. *Wa-hiy-atate-náhsk[w]-u-'.
           FACT-1sA/MsO-REFL-animal-give-PUNC
           'I gave him (e.g., a male dog) to myself.' (Also bad as: 'I gave myself to him.')

The ungrammaticality of these examples cannot be explained by saying that *atat*
and O-class agreement compete for the same slot in some kind of morphological

template, because the two can cooccur in other circumstances (see note 6 for an example). It is, however, explained by (1), together with our analysis of reflexive verbs. Verbs in Mohawk can assign at most one structural Case, and this Case is absorbed by the reflexive morpheme. Thus, only the Case associated with Infl is available in reflexive structures. Therefore, (1) implies that only one agreement morpheme can appear in the clause—the one that identifies the goal argument moved to subject position. The sentences in (28) are bad because they have a second (object) agreement. Thus, they show once again that the presence of agreement morphology is determined by Case in Mohawk.

Finally, consider the possibility of reflexives with intransitive verbs that take a goal argument. Here, we predict another contrast between unaccusatives and unergatives. Unergative verbs can assign structural Case, so they pattern with transitives. The verb's Case is absorbed by *atat,* and the goal moves to subject position, where it is identified by the agreement in Infl. Thus, examples of this type are perfectly grammatical:

(29)   I'i k-atat-yó'tʌ-'s-e'.
       me 1sA-REFL-work-BEN-PUNC
       'I work for myself.'

The situation is different with unaccusative verbs. These do not assign Case, by Burzio's Generalization. Hence, there is only one structural Case assigner present in the clause. However, there will be two elements that need to absorb structural Case: the reflexive morpheme and the agreement morpheme needed to identify the remaining argument. Thus, we correctly predict that reflexives of unaccusative verbs with a goal argument are ungrammatical:

(30)   *Sak wa-h[a]-atat-yá't-ʌ'-s-e'.
        Sak FACT-MsA-REFL-body-fall-BEN-PUNC
        'Sak fell on himself' (i.e., he fell through his own carelessness and was adversely affected).

Thus, agreement morphology interacts with passive-like morphemes in a way that confirms that it is crucially related to structural Case.[8]

5.3. Arguments Without Agreement

One result of the discussion in the previous section is that neuter seems to play a special role in the Mohawk agreement system. Whenever the verb complex does not have enough agreement morphemes for all of its arguments, the "left out" argument is required to be neuter. This happens in three distinct situations: active ditransitive verbs, unaccusative verbs that take a goal argument, and reflexive ditransitive verbs. This situation threatens to falsify the MVC, because there is a systematic class of arguments for which there seems to be no corresponding morpheme in the verbal complex.

The obvious solution to this problem would be to say that neuter arguments are identified by agreement morphemes that just happen to be spelled out as "Ø" in the morphophonology. At first this seems attractive, since the use of Ø forms for neuter agreement is independently motivated in Mohawk. As mentioned before, the "no object" column and the "neuter object" column in Table 5–1 are identical. A pair of examples illustrating this homophony is given in (31).

(31) a. Ye-núhwe'-s.
         FsA/(NsO)-like-HAB
         'She likes it.'

      b. Ye-atáwʌ-s.
         FsA-swim-HAB
         'She swims.' (Note: e + a → u)

Similarly, the agreement on a transitive verb with a neuter subject is identical to the agreement on an intransitive verb that selects O forms for its sole argument, as seen by comparing the "No A" ("no subject") row with the "Neuter A" ("neuter subject") row in Table 5–1.[9]

(32) a. Yako-ya'takéhnha-s.
         (NsA)/FsO-help-HAB
         'It helps her.'

      b. Yako-yó't[ʌ]-e'.
         FsO-work-HAB
         'She works.'

Moreover, it is clear that pro or something like it can still be licensed in these examples; (31a) and (32a) are complete and grammatical as they stand. This, then, could count as evidence that a neuter agreement morpheme is present in the syntax, but happens to be null at PF. The same null agreement that licenses pro is also sufficient to satisfy the MVC at LF.

Turning now to the crucial cases, we observe that a neuter pro seems to be possible as the object theme of a ditransitive verb or a benefactive unaccusative verb as well. Thus, the sentences in (33) are as grammatical and complete as (31a) and (32a).

(33) a. T-a-híy-u-'.
         CIS-FACT-1sA/MsO-give-PUNC
         'I gave it to him (e.g., a specific knife).'

      b. Sak t-a-hó-[a]hsʌ-'s-e'.
         Sak CIS-FACT-MsO-fall-BEN-PUNC
         'It fell on Sak; Sak dropped it (e.g., a drinking glass).'

It is tempting to say that these pros are also identified by a null agreement morpheme. However, this would require an undesirable weakening of the generalizations about agreement discovered in the previous section. Instead of saying that a verb can have no more than two agreement morphemes in Mohawk, we would have to say that it can have three, as long as one of them is spelled out as Ø. Instead of saying that an unaccusative verb can have only one agreement morpheme, we would have to say that it can have two, as long as one of them is spelled out as Ø. However, the syntax is generally blind to aspects of how individual morphemes are realized phonologically. This is an important aspect of modularity, constraining the power of the grammar. For example, one does not find systems with principles like "an agreement morpheme can license a null pronoun only if it contains the phoneme /k/," or "NPs can move to Comp only if their head noun contains a high vowel." Similarly, it should not be relevant to syntactic principles determining the distribution of agreement that a certain member of the paradigm is spelled out as Ø. Therefore, we cannot posit a Ø affix coindexed with the theme argument in (33). Most importantly, even if we did we would have no explanation for the fact demonstrated in section 5.2.1 that null affixes, in general, do not solve the agreement problems of triadic verbs—only null affixes associated with the theme argument do.

What is the alternative? In fact, only one other possibility is consistent with the MVC. There are two types of morphemes that can satisfy this condition in general: agreement morphemes and incorporated roots (see section 1.4). Therefore, since there can be no agreement morpheme associated with theme argument in (33), it follows that the theme must be an incorporated noun root. Since we see no incorporated material, a noun that is phonologically null must be incorporated. Thus, the structure of (33a) is approximately (34).

(34)

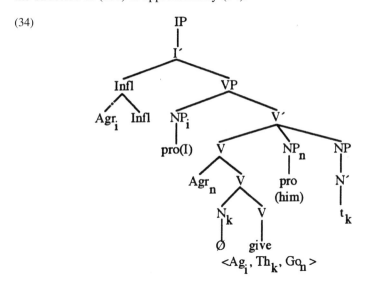

Here, two arguments of the verb (the agent and the goal) are made visible by the two agreement morphemes; the third argument (the theme) is made visible by an incorporated noun root. Thus, (33a) is exactly like the grammatical (35), except that the incorporated theme is a null morpheme in (33a).

(35) Wa-hiy-a'shár-u-'.
      FACT-1sA/MsO-knife-give-PUNC
      'I gave a/the knife to him.'

Positing a null noun root in examples like (33) may seem rather ad hoc at first sight. However, there is no a priori reason why a phonologically null noun root is any more problematic than a phonologically null agreement morpheme, and the latter is routinely posited in many grammars and other descriptive works. Furthermore, the incorporated noun root needed on this account is not always so invisible after all. It is an interesting lexical feature of Mohawk that a substantial number of verbs seem to lose phonological material when their theme argument is incorporated. For example, *(n)ohare* 'wash' loses its initial [n] when a noun is incorporated:

(36)   a.   Wa'-ke-n-óhare-'   (ne ó-wis-e').
            FACT-1sA-??-wash-PUNC   NE NsO-glass-NSF
            'I washed it (the glass).'

       b.   Wa'-ke-wis-óhare-'.
            FACT-1sA-glass-wash-PUNC
            'I washed the glass.'

'Fall' in (33b) is another member of this class; its initial [ahs] is lost under noun incorporation:

(37)   a.   Sak wa-hó-[a]hs-ʌ'-s-e'   (ne ó-wis-e').
            Sak FACT-MsO-??-fall-BEN-PUNC   NE NsO-glass-NSF
            'It (the glass) fell on Sak; Sak dropped it.'

       b.   Sak wa-ho-wís-ʌ'-s-e'.
            Sak FACT-MsO-glass-BEN-PUNC
            'The/A glass fell on Sak; Sak dropped the/a glass.'

Lounsbury (1953:75–76) analyzes such elements as dummy incorporated noun roots. His motivation for this seems to be distributional; it explains the fact that these elements are in complementary distribution with true INs. In this context, Lounsbury's suggestion takes on new meaning: the *n* in (36) and the *ahs* in (37) can be taken as the incorporated theme. Thus, for a significant class of verbs in Mohawk the claim that a neuter object must incorporate is not so abstract after all.

Consider in this light the observation that themes in triadic constructions or benefactive unaccusative constructions must, in general, be understood as neuter. This was illustrated by sentences like (5), repeated here as (38).

(38)   Ká'sere' / *káskare' ʌ-hi-tshÁry-a-'s-e'.
       car   friend   FUT-1sA/MsO-find-BEN-PUNC
       'I will find him a car/*a girlfriend.'

In the current context, this means that the null incorporated theme in (38) and similar examples must be inherently inanimate in meaning. In other words, Ø must mean 'thing', and not 'person' in Mohawk. Indeed, this is an observable property of most of the non-null dummy INs. Thus, the *n* associated with *ohare* 'wash' and the *ahs* of *ʌ'* 'fall' cannot be used when the theme argument of the verb is animate:

(39)   a.   *Wa'-ke-n-óhare-'   ne owíra'a.
            FACT-1sA-thing-wash-PUNC NE baby
            'I washed the baby.'

       b.   *T-a-w-áhs-ʌ'-ne'   ne owirá'a.
            CIS-FACT-NsA-thing-fall-PUNC NE baby
            'The baby fell.' (Note: a + w + a → u)

Rather, a distinct nominal element *ya't* 'body' must be incorporated in these cases; indeed, a great many verbs in Mohawk include this morpheme in the IN position when their theme is animate. Thus, the ungrammaticality of (38a) can be identified with that of (39); in both cases, the adjunct noun phrase is incompatible with the incorporated noun root (null or overt) that it supposedly doubles.[10] The real prediction of this system, then, is not that the theme in a ditransitive or benefactive unaccusative sentence must be neuter, but rather that it must be incorporated. This often works out to almost the same thing, because the dummy objects always seem to refer to things, and many animate nouns resist incorporation. However, these verbs can perfectly well take an animate theme as long as that theme is both incorporable and incorporated. Thus, the sentences in (40) are perfect.

(40) a. Λ-hi-skar-a-tshΛ́ry-a-'s-e'. (cf. (38a))
          FUT-1sA/MsO-friend-Ø-find-Ø-BEN-PUNC
          'I will find him a girlfriend.'

      b. Sak wa-ho-wír-Λ'-s-e'. (cf. (12a))
          Sak FACT-MsO-baby-fall-BEN-PUNC
          'The baby fell on Sak.'

This analysis also explains the important distributional fact that whenever there are fewer agreement factors than NP arguments in a given clause, it is always the theme that fails to trigger agreement; there is no way that agreement with the agent or a goal can be omitted instead. On the null noun analysis this follows immediately from the well-known cross-linguistic fact that only theme-objects can incorporate (Baker 1988a). Thus, (41) shows that agents are not incorporable in Mohawk; (42) shows that goals are not incorporable, even when other factors are controlled for.

(41) a. KíkΛ á'shar-e' ka-natar-a-kwétar-Λs.
          this knife-NSF NsA-bread-Ø-cut-HAB
          'This knife cuts bread.'

      b. #Ka-nátar-o w-a'shar-a-kwétar-Λs.
          NsS-bread-NSF NsA-knife-Ø-cut-HAB
          NOT: 'The knife cuts bread.' (OK as: 'The bread is cutting the knife.')

(42) a. T-a'-khey-athΛnó-tsher-u-'   ne owirá'a.
          CIS-FACT-1sA/FsO-ball-NOM-give-PUNC NE baby
          'I gave the ball to the baby.'

      b. #T-a'-ke-wír-u-'   ne athΛno'.
          CIS-FACT-1sA-baby-give-PUNC NE ball
          NOT: 'I gave the ball to the baby.' (OK as: 'I gave the baby to the ball.')

This generalization is discussed in detail in section 7.3. Thus, the theme argument is the only one that has a legitimate way of satisfying the MVC apart from agreement. This means that in contexts where there are not enough agreement factors to go around, the theme must be the one to do without. In this way, we draw an interesting and nontrivial connection between the incorporation patterns of Mohawk and its agreement patterns.

For the most part, this analysis carries over rather well to the other polysynthetic languages. It is true for all of them that if one argument of a three-place verb cannot be agreed with, that argument must be the theme (see section 5.2.1 for references and discussion). Moreover, the fact that this theme must be incorporated shows up overtly in some cases. For example, Evans (1993) points out that when the theme argument of an agent–theme–goal verb is animate in Mayali, it incorporates into the verb. This is true in spite of the fact that the incorporation of animates is otherwise quite rare. The example Evans cites is the following:

(43)   Nga-marne-beywurd-berrebbom
        1sS/3sO-BEN-child-promise/PAST/PERF
        I promised him/her my daughter/son.

Thus, Mayali, like Mohawk, must incorporate the theme of a ditransitive verb. In many cases, this is hidden by the fact that the incorporated noun may be a phonologically null "cognate object." However, such null nominals are grammatically inanimate. Thus, when the theme is animate it is forced to incorporate itself. This overriding of the general tendency for animate nouns to resist incorporation is motivated by the need for the theme argument to pass the MVC.

The claim that the theme must incorporate in ditransitive sentences or unaccusative sentences with a goal argument is also confirmed in the Tanoan languages. Allen et al. (1984) state explicitly that visible incorporation is obligatory under these conditions in Southern Tiwa, citing contrasts like the following:

(44) a. *'U'u-de ka-wia-ban. (p. 303)
          baby-SG 1sS/2sO\AO-give-PAST
          'I gave you the baby.'

      b. Ka-'u'u-wia-ban.
          1sS/2sO\AO-baby-give-PAST
          'I gave you the baby.'

(45) a. *Seuan-ide ka-wan-ban.   (p. 305)
          man-SG   2sO\AO-come-PAST
          'The man came to you.'

      b. Ka-seuan-wan-ban
          2sO\AO-man-come-PAST
          'The man came to you.'

This is clearly similar to (40) in Mohawk and (43) in Mayali. However, Southern Tiwa is slightly different in that this pattern of facts is found not only with animate themes, but with inanimates as well. Thus, it is tempting to say that Southern Tiwa does not have the null cognate nouns that are found in Mohawk and (presumably) Mayali. This cannot be quite correct, however, because there is no overt IN representing the theme in (46).

(46) Tow-wia-ban. (Rosen 1990:677)
      1sS/cO\AO-give-PAST
      'I gave them to him/her.'

Since there is no overt IN, this kind of example must have a null IN as well. However, Southern Tiwa differs crucially from Mohawk in that an incorporated noun stem cannot be doubled by a lexical noun root. Thus, examples like (47) are impossible in Southern Tiwa, although similar examples are fine in Mohawk and Mayali.

(47) *Yede diru-de   a-diru-k'ar-hi. (Baker 1988b:275)
     that chicken-SG 2sS/AO-chicken-eat-FUT
     'You will eat that chicken.'

Examples (44a) and (45a), therefore, are bad for the same reason that (47) is bad: the incorporated noun (null or overt) is improperly doubled by a full lexical NP. Thus, the underlying obligatoriness of noun incorporation is more obvious in Tanoan languages than it is in Iroquoian or Gunwinjguan languages, thanks to this independent factor.

Chukchee is very much like Southern Tiwa in these respects. Benefactive and malefactive NPs can appear as direct arguments and trigger agreement on a transitive verb or unaccusative verb; however, this is possible only if the theme of the verb has been visibly incorporated:

(48) a. Ǝtlǝg-e   akka-*(gtǝ) qoraNǝ   tǝm-nen.
          father-ERG son-DAT   reindeer(ABS) kill-3sS/3sO
          'The father slaughtered a reindeer for the son.'

     b. Ǝtlǝg-e   ekǝk qaa-nm-ǝ-nen. (Nedjalkov 1976:198–199, Kozinsky et al. 1988)
          father-ERG son   reindeer-kill-Ø-3sS/3sO
          'The father slaughtered the son a reindeer.'

(49) a. Ǝtlǝg-*(ǝk) ǝ'tw'et rǝr'et-g'i.
          father-LOC boat   fill.up-3sS
          'The boat filled up on the father.'

     b. Ǝtlǝg-ǝn ǝ'tw'-ǝ-yǝr'et-g'i. (Nedjalkov 1976:188–189, Polinskaja and
          father-ABS boat-Ø-fill.up-3sS   Nedjalkov 1987:258–260)
          'The boat filled up on the father; the father was boat-filled up.'

(I assume that the dative and locative NPs in the (a) examples are adjuncts, not arguments of the verb.) This correlates with the fact that Chukchee, like Southern Tiwa, does not, in general, allow an IN to be doubled by an external NP; thus, Mithun (1984a:861–862) classifies Chukchee as having Type III (discourse relevant) noun incorporation, but not the Type IV ("classificatory") noun incorporation found in Iroquoian, Gunwinjguan, and Caddoan languages. The one IN that does allow a kind of doubling in Chukchee is the so-called antipassive morpheme *ine*.[11] This morpheme is sufficient to express the theme argument of the verb, but it also allows an NP in an appropriate oblique Case to be present (Nedjalkov 1976:200–201):

(50) a. Ǝnan   qaa-t   qǝrir-ninet. (Kozinsky et al. 1988:652)
          he/ERG reindeer-ABS/PL seek-3sS/3pO
          'He looked for (the) deer.'

     b. Ine-lqǝrir-ǝ-rkǝn   (qora-ta). (Kozinsky et al. 1988:665)
          APASS-seek-Ø-PRES/3sS deer-INSTR
          'He is seeking (for deer).'

Thus, examples like (51) are possible, where the benefactive is agreed with and there is an independent NP that expresses the theme, thanks to the *ine* on the verb.

(51)   Ǝtləg-e   ekək ena-nmə-nen   qora-ta.   (Kozinsky et al. 1988:664)
       father-ERG son   APASS-kill-3sS/3sO deer-INSTR
       'The father slaughtered the son a reindeer.'

Ine can thus be thought of as an overt instance of the dummy incorporated noun, which is usually phonologically null in Mohawk, Mayali, and Southern Tiwa.

These Chukchee paradigms might help make sense of Nahautl, the polysynthetic language with perhaps the least evidence for these proposals. Nahautl is like Southern Tiwa and Chukchee in that it does not permit independent NPs to double incorporated noun roots; it, too, is a "Type III" language in Mithun's (1984a) typology. However, Nahautl is unlike Southern Tiwa and Chukchee in that an independent NP can express the theme of a three-place verb:

(52)   Ni-mitz-maca in xōchitl.   (Launey 1981:173)
       1sS-2sO-give IN flower
       'I give you the flower.'

Examples of this type are potentially problematic. The good news, however, is that Chukchee shows us that the INs may differ within a single language as to whether they can be doubled by an adjoined NP or not. Thus, it is at least possible that examples like (52) have a null incorporated noun root and that this noun root is like *ine* in Chukchee in that it licenses adjoined NPs in a language where this is otherwise not possible. In other words, Nahuatl has a null antipassive morpheme. Given this possibility, Nahuatl does not falsify the analysis developed here, even though it does not give much evidence in favor of that analysis.[12]

Finally, let us briefly reconsider theme arguments in contexts where there is no goal argument. If my analysis is correct, then these arguments have a rather special status in the theory, in that they have the possibility of satisfying the MVC in either of two ways. First, they could be coindexed with an agreement factor since one is available: the agreement licensed by accusative features on the verb if that verb is transitive, or the agreement licensed by nominative features on the Infl if the verb is unaccusative. Alternatively, they could be expressed by cognate objects

(53)   a.   b.

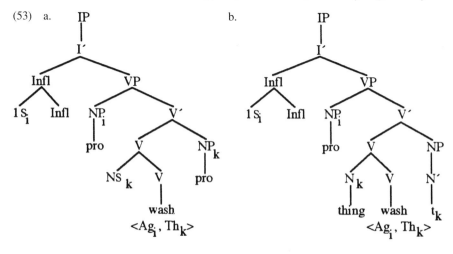

that incorporate into the verb, as in the structures with goals. The two possible structures for a transitive verb are compared in (53). In fact, there is evidence that only (53b) is found in Mohawk. Thus, for those verbs that take a visible cognate object, that element must appear on the verb when no other root has been incorporated. This means that such verbs never take a neuter pro object, even when there should be an agreement factor available to license that pro. Thus, one finds the following:

(54) a. Wa'-ke-*(n)-óhare-'.
       FACT-1sA/(NsO)-thing-wash-PUNC
       'I washed it.'

     b. T-a-w-*(áhs)-ʌ'-ne'.
        CIS-FACT-NsA-thing-fall-PUNC
        'It fell.' (Note: a + w + a → u)

The same conclusion holds in Southern Tiwa: Allen et al. (1984:293–298) point out that inanimate direct objects must obligatorily be incorporated, although animate direct objects may remain unincorporated under certain conditions (see also Rosen 1990). A partial account for this might be to say that these languages simply lack transitive prefixes with features that would identify a neuter object; this would be a kind of systematic gap in the paradigm. Then, the ungrammaticality of (53a) would be due to the fact that there is simply no morpheme "Ns." Such an account would only be partial, however, and would leave open the question of why the paradigm is deficient in just this way.[13] Nevertheless, it seems to be descriptively correct for these two languages.

5.4. The Form of Agreement

So far, we have accounted for the number of full agreement factors that can be present in a clause (determined by Case Theory) and the distribution of arguments not related to agreement (they must be in incorporable positions). The next topic to consider is the factors that determine the morphological form that agreement with a particular argument takes. Recall that there are two sets of agreement morphemes in Mohawk: the A-class "subject" agreements and the O-class "object" agreements. Which type of agreement is used to identify a given argument seems to depend on both lexical and syntactic factors. Thus, the direct object of a transitive verb is without exception associated with O-class agreement; apparently this is determined syntactically. However, the subject of an intransitive verb may be licensed with either "subject" or "object" agreement, depending on the verb involved. Here, we see the influence of lexical factors. This section discusses the interplay of these two factors in determining the form of agreement in Mohawk, the result of which is what is known as an *active* agreement system (see Merlan 1985 and Mithun 1991 for general surveys of active agreement systems). Parts of the account are quite specific to Mohawk; except for Wichita, the other polysynthetic languages are not active in precisely this way. It is a well-known property that overlaps with the class of polysynthetic languages, however, and thus it merits an account.

5.4.1. *Lexically Determined Form*

Let us begin by considering the lexical factors that influence the form of agreement. As mentioned above, some intransitive verbs show "object" agreement with their sole argument, whereas other intransitive verbs show "subject" agreement. At first sight, this brings to mind the unaccusative hypothesis, where it is assumed that some intransitive verbs select an object underlyingly, whereas others select a subject. Thus, we have a potential case of agreement with initial grammatical relations rather than surface grammatical relations. Indeed, this is how active systems have been analyzed in certain other Amerindian languages, including Lakhota (Williamson 1984), Choctaw (Davies 1986, Broadwell 1988), and others discussed in the Relational Grammar literature.

Closer examination shows that there is little or no direct correlation between selecting an underlying object and taking O-class "object" agreement, however. Thus, the following Mohawk verbs would all be classed as unaccusative verbs by the original characterization of the classes given in Perlmutter and Postal 1984; they take a theme or patient argument rather than an agent argument. Nevertheless, some of them take A-class agreement and others take O-class agreement:

(55)   a. *O-class unaccusative verbs*
      wa-*ho*-ké'tot-e'   'he appeared'
      ro-tʌ'kéwhʌ   'he is jealous'
      ro-ya't-ákste   'he is heavy'
      ro-na'khwʌ́'ʌ   'he is angry'
      ro-ta'kárite'   'he is healthy'
      yo-nánawʌ   'it is wet'
      yo-hníru   'it is hard'

     b. *A-class unaccusative verbs*
      ʌ-te-*w*-áhsʌ'-ne'   'it will fall'
      ká-nyu-s   'it is growing'
      wa'-t-*ká*-hri'-ne'   'it broke'
      wa-*ha*-[a]totahsi-'   'he appeared'
      ra-ya't-akérahs   'he stinks'
      ra-kowánʌ   'he is big'
      *r*ʌ-[i]tórha   'he is lazy'
      ka-hútsi   'it is black'

On the other hand, (56) lists verbs that one would expect to be unergative on lexical semantic grounds. Again, some of these take A-class agreement, and others take O-class agreement.

(56)   a. *O-class unergative verbs*
      ro-yó't[ʌ]-e'   'he works'
      wa'-t-*ho*-hʌ́reht-e'   'he yelled'
      wa-*hó*-[a]hta'-ne'   'he ate his fill'
      wa-*ho*-yéshu-'   'he laughed'

     b. *A-class unergative verbs*
      ra-yʌ́tho-s   'he plants'
      wa'-t-*ha*-[a]hshʌ́'tho-'   'he cried'

wa'-t-*ha*-[a]tskáhu'   'he ate'
t-ʌ-*ha*-ríhwahkw-e'   'he will sing'
wa-*há*-[a]tyʌ-'   'he sat down'

Several morphosyntactic tests are available to confirm that the verbs in (55) are unaccusative, whereas the verbs in (56) are unergative. For example, many of the verbs in (55) allow their argument to be incorporated. This is true regardless of the type of agreement prefix selected:

O-class verbs

(57) a. Ónʌ wa'-o-'sere-ht-a-ké'tot-e'.
          now FACT-NsS-car-NOM-Ø-appear-PUNC
          'The car appeared; the car stuck out (e.g., of a garage).'

   b. Yo-na'ts-ákste.
          NsS-pail-heavy
          'The pail is heavy.'

   c. Te-yo-[a]'shar-á-'tsu.
          DUP-NsO-knife-Ø-dirty
          'The knife is dirty.'

   d. Yo-[a]tya'tawi-tsher-a-ná(na)wʌ.
          NsO-dress-NOM-Ø-wet
          'The dress is wet.'

A-class verbs

(58) a. T-a'-ka-wís-ʌ'-ne'.
          CIS-FACT-NsA-glass-fall-PUNC
          'The glass fell.'

   b. Ka-na'ts-a-hútsi.
          NsS-pail-Ø-black
          'The pail is black.'

   c. Wa'-t-ka-ks-á-hri'-ne'.
          FACT-DUP-NsA-dish-Ø-break-PUNC
          'The dish broke.'

   d. Ka-ris-er-akérʌs.
          NsA-sock-NOM-stink
          'The socks stink.'

Assuming my (Baker 1988a) theory of noun incorporation (or, indeed, most other current theories), incorporation is only possible if the verb selects an internal (object) NP argument. In contrast, none of the verbs in (56) allows its argument to be incorporated. I illustrate this only for the O-class verbs, where the morphology makes it tempting to analyze them as unaccusative:

(59) a. ?*Wa'-t-yo-wir-a-hʌ́reht-e'.
          FACT-DUP-NsO-baby-Ø-yell-PUNC
          'The baby yelled.'

   b. *Wa'-ako-wir-áhta'-ne'.
          FACT-FsO-baby-eat.full-PUNC
          'The baby finished eating.'

    c. *Wa'-o-wir-a-yéshu-'.
       FACT-NsO-baby-Ø-laugh-PUNC
       'The baby laughed.'

The second piece of evidence that agreement does not correlate with unaccusativity comes from the fact that there are verbs from both lists that have benefactive forms with transitive agreements:

(60) a. Λ-hi-yó'tΛ-hs-e'   (D&D:427)
        FUT-1sA/MsO-work-BEN-PUNC
        'I will work for him.'

      b. Uwári wa-huwa-[a]tyÁ-ha's-e'   ne Sak.
        Mary FACT-FsA/MsO-sit-BEN-PUNC NE Sak
        'Mary sat down on Sak.'

As discussed in section 5.2, this is only possible if the verb root is a Case assigner that can license a second agreement morpheme. If it is a Case assigner, then it must also be an unergative verb, by Burzio's Generalization. Again, we see that taking an external argument underlyingly does not correlate with taking an A-class agreement morpheme, as one might have expected. Conversely, there are both A- and O-class verbs that cannot show transitive agreement in the benefactive construction. This confirms that there are also unaccusative verbs in both agreement classes (see (12) for examples, where *Λ'* 'fall' takes A-class prefixes and *ke'tot* 'appear' takes O-class prefixes).

The third piece of evidence comes from facts about the interpretation of the adverb *éso* 'a lot' discussed in the previous chapter. There it was shown that preverbal *éso* can have the effect of quantifying over a postverbal NP if and only if the verb involved is unaccusative. Once again, the verbs that are unaccusatives by this test may take either A- or O-class agreement with the argument; the same is true for verbs that are unergative by this test. In (61), an example of an A-class unaccusative is given, and (62) gives an example of an O-class unergative (see section 4.2.2 for further examples of each type).

(61) Éso wa-*hatí*-ye-'   ne rati-ksa-'okú'a.
      a.lot FACT-MpA-awaken-PUNC NE MpA-child-PL
      'Many children woke up.'

(62) Éso *yoti*-yó't-e'   ne kon-úkwe.
      a.lot FpO-work-HAB NE FpS-person
      'Women work a lot.' (NOT: 'Many women work.')

Thus, we have at least four ways of distinguishing unergative verbs from unaccusative verbs in Mohawk: lexical semantics, noun incorporation, the possibility of transitive benefactives, and adverbial *éso* interpretation. Two more morphosyntactic tests will be discussed in chapter 8: only unaccusative verbs can occur with causative morphology in Mohawk and only unergative verbs can have the purposive morpheme attached (see also Chafe 1970 for Onondaga). The results of these six tests all correlate with one another to a very substantial degree.[14] However, there seems to be little correlation between these criteria and the form of the agreement on the verb.

Finally, it is significant that the intransitive versions of verbs that appear in "anticausative" transitivity alternations almost always take A-class agreement morphemes rather than O-class agreement morphemes. This is so even though according to standard principles of argument projection, their argument must be generated in the object position underlyingly. (As mentioned in section 5.2.3, the intransitive verb is marked with the so-called semireflexive prefix *at*, in a way comparable to the "ergative" use of the reflexive clitic in the Romance languages (see Burzio 1986).)

(63) a. Wa-w-ate-nóhare-'   ne atyá'tawi.
          FACT-NsA-SRFL-wash-PUNC NE dress
          'The dress became clean.' (NOTE: wa + w + a → u)

      b. Wa-w-ate-nhotúko-'   ne o'neróhkwa.
          FACT-NsA-SRFL-open-PUNC NE box
          'The box opened.' (NOTE: wa + w + a → u)

This confirms once again that verbs that take O-class agreement are not the same as verbs that select object arguments. On the contrary, there are few or no examples like (63) where the intransitive verb shows object agreement. I return to this systematic gap below.

Of course, it is always possible that the difference between the O-class verbs and the A-class verbs is syntactically and/or semantically predictable, but the correct distinction has not been found yet. However, other lexical semantic classifications of known utility, such as Kratzer's (1989) stage-level/individual-level distinction, or the Vendler/Dowty aspectual classes (Dowty 1979), do not look any more promising for Mohawk, as a quick survey of the cited examples will show. For example, 'being wet' and 'being stinky' are both temporary (stage-level) properties when predicated of, say, a pair of socks; yet the first takes an O-class prefix and the second takes an A-class prefix. Similarly, 'to fall' and 'to appear' are both achievement-type verbs aspectually; the first takes an A-class prefix and the second an O-class prefix. Thus, my findings are compatible with those of Merlan (1985), who finds no simple semantic explanation for verb classes in Seneca. Similarly, Chafe (1970) states that agreement is determined by the agent–patient distinction in Onondaga, but he is forced to state a rule that changes agent to patient or vice versa to account for the agreement of certain verbs (1970:51–52). Mithun (1991) still seeks to explain which verbs take which prefixes in Mohawk in semantic terms. However, her account crucially makes use of a variety of semantic factors and involves knowing the etymology of the root involved. Thus, any one semantic generalization is only partially valid, and all of them have counterexamples, explicable only in diachronic terms. Similar remarks hold of the partial generalizations pointed out for Oneida by Michelson (1991c). Thus, these discussions are compatible with my claim that there is no independently motivated syntactic or semantic basis for agreement on intransitive verbs in *synchronic* Mohawk. If there was a rule-based system in an older stage of the language, it has now become opaque. Whether a given verb takes O- or A-class agreement must be listed as a separate property in its lexical entry. Whatever partial generalizations there may be because of historical factors can easily be captured with lexical redundancy rules.

Finally, although the vast majority of transitive verbs in Mohawk show A-class agreement with their subject, there are a few that take object agreement, as mentioned in section 5.2.3. Two relatively clear examples of this are:

(64)   a. Y-a'-te-wak-úko-'   ne anitskwára.
          TRANS-FACT-DUP-1sO-bump-PUNC NE chair
          'I bumped into the chair.'

       b. Ats-ákta   y-a'-akó-[a]ti-'.
          river-near TRANS-FACT-FsO-throw-PUNC
          'She threw it toward the river.'

There are other examples in which the subject is less agentive: *kate'* 'to have in abundance', *eka'w* 'to like the taste of', and so on. This property is only visible when the object of the verb is inanimate, for reasons that we will return to later. However, these examples confirm that verbal morphology is not determined by independently testable grammatical relations or thematic roles.

Given that the type of agreement that an argument shows does not follow from its grammatical function or lexical semantic properties of the selecting verb, there must be a (semi-)arbitrary lexical feature on verbs that determines it. Let us try to clarify how this lexical feature works.

Notice first of all that there is an aspect of the agreement relation that is not entirely local in the system assumed here. Unaccusative verbs, for example, take a single internal argument that is θ-marked by the verb. However, the verb has no structural Case-assigning features; hence, it cannot host an agreement morpheme. Rather, the agreement morpheme is adjoined to Infl. Nevertheless, it is the lexical properties of the verb that determine the form this agreement will take, not the lexical properties of the Infl. The following paradigm illustrates this more clearly:

(65)   *verbs* Λ', *'fall'*   *ké'tot, 'appear'*

         Habitual aspect   t-*ye*-yá't-Λ'-s   *yako*-ke'tót-ha'
         Future-punctual Λ-t-*ye*-yá't-Λ'-ne' Λ-*yako*-ké'tot-e'
         Factual-punctual   t-a-*ye*-yá't-Λ'-ne'   wa'-*ako*-ké'tot-e'

The form of the agreement clearly varies with the verb root, not the tense/aspect/ mood morphology.[15] Only the so-called stative/perfective aspect changes the agreement class of the verb in Mohawk, and there is some evidence that this is not a simple aspect associated with the Aspect or Infl node in Mohawk (see Ormston 1993). Thus, it is the θ-marking head rather than the head that hosts agreement that determines the form that agreement takes.

This behavior is reminiscent of "quirky" Case marking in Icelandic. It is well known that the Case morphology of certain NPs in Icelandic is determined by the verb that θ-marks them, rather than by the head that locally assigns them Case. Such quirky Case forms are preserved even when the NP raises into a higher clause. A typical example is:

(66)   a. Drengina   vantar mat.   (Andrews 1982:462)
          the-boys(ACC) lacks food(ACC)
          'The boys lack food.'

b. Hana   virðist vanta   peninga.   (Andrews 1982:464)
her(ACC) seems to-lack money
'She seems to lack money.'

Similar mechanisms apparently underlie the Mohawk paradigms. Specifically:

(67)   a. As an idiosyncratic lexical property, a verb may associate the feature [+O] with a position in its θ-grid.

    b. If morpheme X is coindexed with a [+O] NP, then X will show up as a form from the O-class paradigm. Otherwise, X will show up as a form from the A-class paradigm.

Here O-class "object" agreement is taken to be the marked choice. This corresponds to the fact that there seem to be fewer verbs that take O-class agreement than A-class agreement, particularly among the transitive verbs. Further justification of this decision will be given later. Thus, the forms in the third column of (65) will be determined as in (68).

(68)

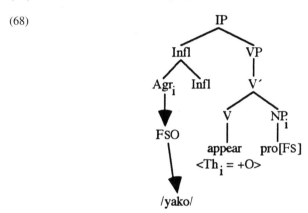

The statement of (67a) is such that the verb may assign quirky agreement features to its agent argument as well as to its theme argument. Thus, the subject of an unergative verb or even a transitive verb may be specified as taking quirky O-class agreement. This is apparently different from Icelandic, where it seems true agents are never marked with quirky Case (Marantz 1984). However, this possibility fits with the fact that the verb and not the Infl θ-marks the agent argument.

5.4.2. Configurationally Determined Form

Next, we turn our attention to configurational factors that determine the form of agreement. There are three cases to consider under this heading.

The first structural effect of agreement is a relatively minor one that involves subjects of transitive verbs. Even if a subject argument is marked [+O] by the verb, it still shows up with A-class agreement whenever the verb has an animate object. Thus the examples in (69) can be compared with those in (64).

(69)   a. Y-a'-t-khe-ya't-úko-'.
       TRANS-FACT-DUP-1sA/FsO-body-bump-PUNC
       'I bumped into her.'

   b. Ats-ákta   y-a-huwa-ya't-úti-'   ne raksá'a.
      river-near TRANS-FACT-FsA/MsO-body-throw-PUNC NE boy
      'She threw the boy toward the river.'

The motivation for this effect is fairly obvious: the subject cannot show O-class agreement because O-class agreement is required for the object in these cases. Now one might expect that such examples would simply have two object agreement prefixes. This is exactly what one finds in comparable cases in other active languages, such as Lakhota (Williamson 1984) and Choctaw (Davies 1986). However, this is impossible in Mohawk, for a rather superficial morphological reason: there is (in most cases) no readily segmentable object agreement morpheme. Rather, the two agreement morphemes combine into a single portmanteau form. Thus, one cannot combine O-class agreement forms at will, productively creating the desired combination. The only double-agreement forms available in Mohawk are the ordinary transitive prefixes. If the object has already claimed the O-class part of this form, than the subject is forced into the A-class part of the transitive prefix. This can be thought of as a low-level morphological fixup process that applies in the PF component of the grammar with no consequences for the syntax.[16]

   At the end of section 5.3 I observed in passing that Mohawk prefers incorporating (null) neuter objects to having (null) neuter object agreement. The contrast between (64) and (69) gives independent evidence for this. Suppose that object agreement with a neuter pro were possible in sentences like (64). Then this agreement, even though it is phonologically null, would prevent the subject argument from being realized with +O agreement, just as phonologically null zoic agreement does. Therefore, the subjects in (64) should trigger A-class agreement, at least optionally. This is not the case; rather O-class agreement is obligatory in these sentences. This confirms that sentences with neuter objects involve incorporation, not null object agreement.

   The second and more important configurational effect on agreement is that the direct objects of transitive verbs invariably take O-class agreement. Since there are no exceptions to this generalization, it seems inappropriate to stipulate lexically that each transitive verb assigns +O to its object. Indeed, there is evidence that such a stipulation would not only be redundant but incorrect. Thus, I have already mentioned that Mohawk has many transitive verb stems where the agent role can be omitted when the verb root is marked with the semireflexive morpheme. Moreover, we have seen that the versions of these verbs without the agent always show A-class agreement with the theme argument; see (24) and (63) for examples. Two additional examples of this are the following:

(70)   a. wa-w-ate-whahs-a-rátsu-'
          FACT-NsA-SRFL-skirt-Ø-tear-STAT
          'the skirt just tore' (Note: wa + w + a → u)

       b. Wa-ha-[a]t-kwatáko-'   Sak.
          FACT-MsA-SRFL-fix-PUNC Sak
          'Sak got better.'

Clearly, these verbs do not lexically assign +O to the theme in their intransitive variants; the minimal assumption is that they do not lexically assign +O in the transitive variant either. This allows us to hold the lexical properties of a root as constant as possible across the different uses of that root. Rather, the O-class agreement in transitive constructions must come from elsewhere. Essentially the same type of argument can be made from reflexive verbs: I have argued that these are intransitive forms whose agent argument has been suppressed; nevertheless, the surviving theme argument always triggers A-class agreement, not O-class agreement (see section 5.2.3 for examples).

It is tempting to think of this as the inverse of the situation illustrated in (69): transitive objects cannot show A-class agreement because this is taken by the subject. If one uses the same idea twice, however, one faces a tricky ordering problem: one must decide which argument associates with agreement first, and the second argument cannot affect this first association. This problem is particularly acute with verbs that mark their agent argument +O and their patient argument −O. In this case, it seems like the agreement factors should cross, with the syntactic subject showing O-type "object" agreement and the syntactic object showing A-type "subject" agreement. However, this does not happen. The verbs *ati* 'throw' and *uko* 'hit, bump into' are relevant cases. Example (64) has already shown that their subjects are +O. Their detransitivized and reflexive forms show that their object arguments are inherently −O:

(71) a. Y-a-ha-[a]t-ya't-úti-'. (PB:551)
        TRANS-FACT-MsA-SRFL-body-throw-PUNC
        'He threw himself down.'

      b. Y-a'-t-yu-[a]tat-ya't-úko-'.
        TRANS-FACT-DUP-FsA-REFL-body-bump-PUNC
        'She bumped into herself.'

However, when both arguments are present and animate, A-class agreement goes with the agent and O-class agreement goes with the theme, rather than vice versa, as shown by (69). Example (69b) means 'she threw him', *not* 'he threw her'. Thus, objects are associated with O-class agreement, even when the A-class agreement might reasonably be considered to be available. Apparently, the principle that associates transitive objects with "object" agreement is a relatively deep one.[17]

Before choosing a way of expressing the rule that associates direct objects with O-class agreement, it is useful to consider the treatment of goal arguments. In active sentences these, too, always appear with O-class agreement. When the verb also has an agent, this is rather unremarkable; it is easily subsumed under the previous generalization, given that both goals and themes are "internal" arguments, whereas agents are "external" arguments in the terminology of Williams (1980). However, there is one class of examples that raises important new issues: those where a goal appears together with the theme of an unaccusative verb. In connection with example (11), I mentioned that the goal argument consistently triggers O-class agreement under these conditions; additional examples illustrating this are the following:

(72) a. Wa'-t-ho-wis-á-hri'-s-e'.
          FACT-DUP-MsO-glass-Ø-break-BEN-PUNC
          'The glass broke on him.'

      b. wa-ho-nakt-íyo-hs-e'   (D&D:481)
          FACT-MsO-bed-good-BEN-PUNC
          'it was a nice place for him'

      c. Terés, we-sa-[a]te-na'tar-á-tsha-'s-e'   kʌ?   (D&D:461)
          Teresa FACT-2sO-SRFL-bread-Ø-burn-BEN-PUNC Q
          'Teresa, did your pies burn (on you)?'

This is quite independent of the inherent lexical properties of the verb; indeed, all of the verbs in (72) and most of those in (11) take A-class agreement when no goal is expressed.

The easiest account of this fact would be to say that verbs lexically assign the +O feature to their goal arguments. This does not lead to such a massive degree of redundancy in the lexicon, given that in most cases the goal is added to the verb stem by the benefactive morpheme *'s/ʌ*. If this single morpheme associated the +O feature with its argument, the majority of the examples would be accounted for. However, this would not account for the agreement in an example like (73).

(73)   ʌ-k-atat-yó'tʌ-'s-e'.
          FUT-1sS-REFL-work-BEN-PUNC
          'I will work for myself.'

Here, the reflexive morphology suppresses the external argument, allowing the internal goal argument to appear as the only argument of the verb relevant to agreement. Since the agreement is an A-class form, the goal argument introduced by the benefactive morpheme must be inherently [− O]. Assuming that this carries over to other examples, we are forced to conclude that the "object" agreement in (72) is configurationally determined, not lexically assigned. Let us consider how this could be.

It is useful to compare the examples in (72) with other languages that have productive benefactive/goal-adding morphology, such as the Bantu languages. Machobane (1989) shows that in Sesotho, goals can be added to unergative verbs as in (74), but not to unaccusative verbs, as in (75) (see Alsina and Mchombo 1988 for similar data in Chichewa).

(74)   Bashanyana ba-hobel-l-a   morena.   (p. 62)
          boys   SM-dance-APPL-IND chief
          'The boys are dancing for the chief.'

(75)   a. *Lintja li-hol-el-a   nkhono.   (p. 59)
             dogs SM-grow-APPL-IND grandmother
             'The dogs are growing for my grandmother.'

      b. *Baeti   ba-fihl-ets-e   morena.   (p. 60)
             visitors SM-arrive-APPL-IND chief
             'The visitors have arrived for the chief.'

Alsina, Mchombo, and Machobane treat this as a kind of thematic restriction on applicative formation, to the effect that it is impossible to have a goal/benefactive argument without having an agent. However, this seems like a dubious interpretation. First, the Mohawk examples show that there is nothing in the universal principles of θ-theory that rules out the presence of a goal in the absence of an agent. Second, (75) seems to provide sources for grammatical examples in Sesotho. Such sentences become grammatical if the goal is expressed as an object clitic, as in (76a), or if it becomes the subject via passivization, as in (76b).

(76) a. Letebele leo le-re-hol-el-e! (p. 65)
       Letelbele that SM-1PO-grow-APPL-SUBJ
       'May that Letebele (clan name) grow up for us!'

     b. Morena o-fihl-ets-o-e   ke-baeti. (p. 81)
        chief SM-arrive-APPL-PASS-IND by-visitors
        'The visitors have arrived for the chief.'

This shows that there is nothing semantically ill formed about having a theme and a goal without an agent, even in Sesotho. Rather, it seems preferable to account for the difference between (75) and (74) in terms of the independently motivated Case theoretic difference between unergative verbs and unaccusative verbs (Baker 1992a, 1992c). Unergative verbs are Case assigners; hence, they can assign structural Case directly to the goal argument, making (74) possible. Unaccusative verbs cannot assign structural Case, however. Furthermore, Infl's Case is assigned to the theme-subject, and goals are not eligible to receive inherent Case. Thus, there is no Case available for the goal in (74), and the sentence violates the Case Filter. Example (76a) is grammatical because the goal is a pronominal clitic that does not need to receive Case (see Baker 1992c).

There is another derivation that must be considered, however. The underlying structure of (75a) is presumably something like (77).

(77) [IP e Infl [VP grow-for dogs grandma]]

In this structure, we must ask what prevents the goal NP from moving to the subject position to receive nominative Case from Infl. This would leave the theme NP inside the VP, where it—unlike the goal—would qualify for inherent Case. There is no Case theoretic problem with such a derivation; in fact, passives of applicatives have essentially this derivation (see Baker 1992c and section 5.4.3 of the current work). Nevertheless, examples formed in this way are at least as bad as those in (75) ('Malillo Machobane, personal communication):

(78) *Nkhono o-hol-el-a   lintja.
       grandma SM-grow-APPL-IND dogs
       'The dogs are growing for my grandma.'

The problem with this type of example must be that it is impossible to move the goal to subject position in the first place. Apparently, NP movement of this type is somehow blocked by the presence of the theme NP. Example (76b) supports this interpretation. In this sentence, the theme is expressed as a by-phrase adjunct rather than as an argument; movement of the goal to subject position then becomes possible, deriving a grammatical sentence.

This blocking effect of the theme NP becomes understandable when we integrate certain innovations of Larson (1988) into the theory used here. He argues that Vs can take only a single complement (see also Kayne 1984). This implies there must be a structural asymmetry between themes and goals. In particular, Larson assumes that goals project as the complements of the verb, whereas themes are associated with a higher position, as specifier of the verb. Hence, the underlying structure of (75b) is actually (79).

(79)

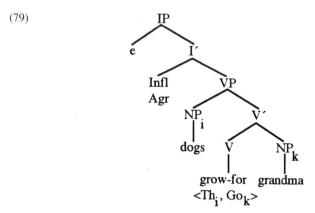

In (79), it is easy to see intuitively why the theme blocks NP movement of the goal: the theme creates a kind of Specified Subject Condition violation (Chomsky 1973). More technically, I adopt the Binding theoretic notions in (80), based on Chomsky's (1986b) version of Binding Theory.

(80) a. A *complete functional complex* (CFC) is a category in which all the grammatical functions compatible with the head are present, and all the head's θ-roles are assigned.

b. The *governing category* of an anaphor X is the smallest CFC containing X, a governor of X, and a c-commanding NP distinct from X.

c. Anaphors (including NP trace) must have an antecedent within their governing category.

The VP in (79) contains all of the arguments θ-marked by the head verb and qualifies as a Complete Functional Complex. The VP also contains the head verb, which governs the goal NP. Hence, the VP counts as the governing category for the goal in this structure. If the goal moved directly to the subject position, its trace would not have an antecedent in this governing category, in violation of principle A of Binding Theory. It follows that this movement is impossible. This completes the explanation of the ungrammaticality of (74) in Sesotho.[18]

Now we may return to examples like (72) in Mohawk. They also have the structure in (79), but they are grammatical as long as the goal determines O-class agreement. Movement of the goal to the subject position is presumably blocked in Mohawk, too. This correctly distinguishes (72) from examples like (73), where the goal determines A-class agreement. The goal pro does not need Case in PF, but it does need to be coindexed with agreement by the MVC. The only Case-assigning head in (79) is the Infl node; hence, the agreement factor that is coindexed with the goal must be there. The theme argument is then realized apart from agreement by incorporating into the verb, as discussed in section 5.3. In this way, the essentials of (72) are accounted for. The structure of (72a) is given in (81).

(81)

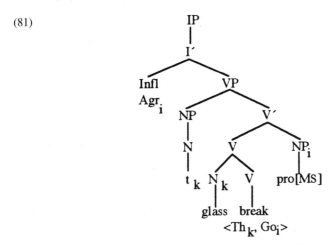

In other examples, the incorporated theme may be only a null cognate object.

Now we are in a position to ask why Infl's agreement with the goal must be from the O-class paradigm, even though the goal argument is not lexically marked +O. Many reasons that look plausible for simple transitive verbs do not generalize to this construction. First, the Case features that license the agreement are in Infl, not V; thus, we cannot say that +O is the accusative form of agreement. If anything, the agreement in (81) should be considered nominative. Second, there is no other agreement relationship in this sentence that could force an agreement shift; we cannot say that the goal takes the +O form as an accommodation to some other argument that requires an A-class form. Third, there is no reason to say that the goal is assigned +O by its θ-marker. The only thing that distinguishes the goal in this construction from other NPs that are known to trigger A-class agreement is that it is c-commanded by another NP, the theme. Of course, normal direct objects also have this property: the object of a transitive verb is c-commanded by the agentive subject. Hence, all of the configurationally determined examples are accounted for if we assume that the feature +O is assigned to NPs by the following rule:

(82) *The Structural Agreement Principle* (SAP)
      Assign +O to NP if it is c-commanded by another XP that is its co-argument.

In (82), X and Y are co-arguments if and only if they are both coindexed with positions in the θ-grid of the same lexical head. The SAP adds +O features in addition to those that are assigned lexically; it explains why transitive objects use the O-class agreement paradigm—and hence why that paradigm was called "objective" in Lounsbury 1953:58–59 and related work. The restriction that only NPs that are co-arguments trigger +O assignment is needed because of examples like (83), where the subject of a matrix verb has no effect on the agreement used to represent the theme argument in a complement clause.

(83)   Sak í-hr-ehr-e'   Uwári wa'-u(*ako)-[a]t-ya't-óhare-'.
       Sak Ø-MsS-think-IMPF Mary   FACT-FsA(*FsO)-SRFL-body-wash-PUNC
       'Sak thinks Mary washed.'

Here, the theme in the lower clause is not realized as a +O agreement form, even though it is c-commanded by another NP. This type of locality condition is a natural one, given the inherently local nature of agreement phenomena.[19]

As it is stated, the SAP seems to be quite specific to Mohawk. However, there is reason to think that many of the notions it is based on are much more general. Indeed, the account of agreement in Mohawk fits very well within the broader approach to morphological Case and agreement phenomena developed by Marantz (1991). Marantz's framework is built around two leading ideas. The first is that the principles that license the presence of an NP are distinct from the principles that spell out the morphological forms of that NP; thus, standard Case theory breaks up into two quite different subtheories. In the same way, we have seen that the principles that license agreement factors in Mohawk are distinct from the ones that determine the morphological form of those agreement factors. Second, Marantz distinguishes four types of morphological Case and agreement: lexically governed (i.e., "quirky"), dependent, unmarked, and default. Dependent Case and agreement forms are the ones that are usually called accusative or ergative; they are realized on a given NP precisely when that NP is the clausemate of a distinct NP not marked for lexical Case. Clearly, O-class agreement in Mohawk is a "dependent agreement" in Marantz's terms. Significantly, Marantz points out that the realization of a dependent Case or agreement form does not require that there be another NP in the unmarked Case or agreement form, only that there be another NP of some kind. This is what we see in (81), where the theme triggers a dependent form for the goal even though there is no agreement with the theme itself. Thus, the SAP is no more than a Mohawk-specific version of a much more general principle of dependent form realization. There are some technical inconsistencies between the details of my analysis and those of Marantz's paper that do not permit one analysis to be entirely subsumed by the other at this time, but these can presumably be resolved by further research.[20]

5.4.3. Some Refinements

Now that we have considered almost all of the relevant examples and have the basic ideas in place, it is worthwhile to go back over some simpler examples and be more specific about how they work. In doing this, I introduce some other aspects of the current theory of phrase structure that have not been necessary up to this point. I will also be more specific about the status of the SAP and about the structural configurations in which agreement takes place.

The structure in (81) is the most detailed so far, and there will be little reason to modify it.[21] The single agreement generated in Infl licenses the goal in the V' projection; the theme must then satisfy the MVC by undergoing NI in accordance with principles to be discussed in chapter 7.

A simple unaccusative construction has essentially the same structure, given in (84), except that there is no NP in V'. Thus, the agreement morpheme in Infl is free to be coindexed with the theme in this construction. The theme need not incorporate, and can be a pro of any person, number, and gender. Since there is no other NP in the clause to trigger the SAP, the agreement morpheme in Infl will be realized as an O-class form only if the verb that θ-marks the theme assigns it the $+O$ feature as a lexical property (yes for *ke'tot* 'appear'; no for *ʌ'* 'fall'). This is essentially the analysis in (68), except that we now take the theme to be generated in the specifier of VP rather than the complement position, to be consistent with (81). In this I adopt a rigid interpretation of the *Uniformity of Theta Assignment Hypothesis* (UTAH) of Baker 1988a, where thematic roles are assigned in the same structural configuration across comparable verbs (see Hale and Keyser 1992, Travis 1991, Noonan 1992, Baker 1992c).[22] Or, the head of the theme NP in (84) may incorporate into the verb.

(84)

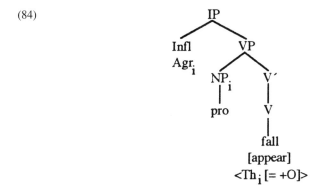

Next, consider structures with agents. Up to this point, I have assumed that these are generated in the specifier of VP; we now take that position to be the canonical position of the theme. Indeed, if both specifier and complement positions are unique in a given phrase, as Larson (1988) assumes, there is no position in the VP of a structure like (81) where an agent could go. Larson's solution is to assume that a higher VP "shell" is generated. This VP has a null head, and takes the basic VP as a complement. The agent role is then assigned

(85)

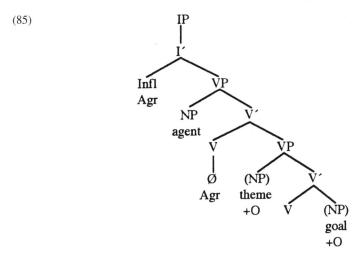

to NPs in the specifier position of this higher VP shell. Thus, agentive verbs have structures like the one in (85). In (85), the agent argument is "external" in the sense that it is assigned outside the smallest maximal projection of the verb. However, it is "internal" in the sense that it is assigned inside a VP projection. Thus, the complete statement of the UTAH that I assume is given in (86), from Baker 1992c.

(86)   *The Uniformity of Theta Assignment Hypothesis* (UTAH)
       Thematic roles are always assigned in the following configurations:
       (i)   Theme to the specifier of the minimal VP;
       (ii)   Goal (more generally, path) to the complement of minimal VP;
       (iii) Agent outside the minimal VP (typically, to the specifier of a VP shell).

Burzio's Generalization states that only verbs that assign agent arguments can assign accusative Case, and thus can host an agreement factor. In this framework, then, it is natural to say that the agreement features are generated along with the null higher verb whose projection is the locus of the assignment of the external argument. This will be revised later in this section.

Suppose that the verb takes an agent and a theme, but no goal. Then the agreement in Infl is coindexed with the agent and the agreement on the V is coindexed with the theme. Both agent and theme can be pros of any person/number/gender. Since the theme is c-commanded by the agent, it is assigned the feature $+O$ by the SAP, and this feature is copied onto the agreement adjoined to the null verb. The verb root then undergoes head movement, moving first to the null verb position, and finally to Infl. In this way, tense, both agreement features, and the verb root end up as one morphological complex. The agreement features are spelled out at PF as the appropriate portmanteau morpheme, perhaps by some kind of "lookup" procedure in which the mental equivalent of Table 5–1 is accessed. Thus, the features of the object end up determining the O-factor (i.e., which column to use in Table 5–1); the features of the subject, in turn, determine the A-factor (i.e., which row to use) by default. Even if the verb lexically marks the agent as $+O$, this feature has no effect because there are no "double object" agreement forms in the inflectional system of Mohawk. The agent's $+O$ feature will have an effect if and only if the object is incorporated, which is always the case if the object is neuter; in that situation, a transitive verb is identical to an unergative verb from the point of view of agreement (see later in this section). This explains the properties of ordinary transitive verbs in Mohawk.

Suppose now that the verb takes an agent and a goal, but no theme. Then the agreement in Infl is coindexed with the agent and the agreement on the V is coindexed with the goal. Everything else proceeds just as in the previous case, resulting in a verb that shows A-class agreement with the agent and O-class agreement with the goal. The only significant difference is that goals do not have the possibility of incorporating; hence, they can never be neuter, and O-class agreement will never be associated with the agent, regardless of the lexical properties of the verb root. This explains the properties of unergative verbs with the benefactive morpheme.

Minimally different is the case of ditransitive verbs, which take an agent, a theme, and a goal. Since there are only two agreement factors licensed by Case, one of the three arguments must satisfy the MVC by way of incorporation. According to the theory of incorporation, this can only be the theme. From this it follows that the theme of such verbs must be third person, and generally inanimate. The agreements in Infl and the null verb are then coindexed with the agent and the goal, respectively. Everything else proceeds as in the previous case, resulting in a verb that shows A-class agreement with the agent, O-class agreement with the goal, and no agreement with the theme.

Finally, in a framework that assumes the rigid UTAH, ordinary unergative verbs are those in which there is an agent phrase in the specifier of the VP shell, but no NPs in the lower VP. Once again, the agreement in Infl will be coindexed with this NP. Now, however, there is nothing for the agreement in the null V to be coindexed with. Hence, this agreement is not realized (or, equivalently, is never generated). In this situation, the lexical features of the verb do have an opportunity to influence the expression of the agent. If the verb associates $+O$ with its agent argument, that feature will be copied onto the agreement (e.g., the Mohawk verbs meaning 'work', 'sleep', 'eat one's fill', 'shout', 'laugh'). Then, when the agreement feature is spelled out at PF there will be a $+O$ factor but no $+A$ factor; therefore, a form from the first row of Table 5–1 is chosen. If the verb does not associate $+O$ with its agent argument (e.g., the Mohawk verbs meaning 'plant', 'cry', 'eat', 'sing'), then the PF spell-out process will have a $+A$ factor but no $+O$ factor. This results in a form from the first column of Table 5–1 being chosen. In this way, we explain the fact that either type of agreement can appear on an unergative verb, just as either type can appear on an unaccusative verb, and all of the basic verb classes in Mohawk are accounted for.[23]

Mohawk verbs show one further regularity that does not have a purely syntactic account. I have assumed that any argument of a head may, in principle, be marked as $+O$ by that head. To some extent this is true: in particular, both internal (theme) and external (agent) arguments can be specified as $+O$, as shown by unaccusative and unergative verbs, respectively. There is a gap in the pattern, however: no transitive verb associates $+O$ with its object. This is shown by (70), where the intransitivized versions of basically transitive verb roots never take O-class agreement. However, there seems to be no need for a special stipulation to rule out this possibility. In the large majority of cases, the SAP will cause the object of a transitive verb to be $+O$ regardless of the verb's lexical features. Thus, any difference between transitive verbs with $+O$ objects and verbs with $-O$ objects would be completely neutralized by this principle. Suppose, furthermore, that the anticausative examples in (70) do not count as part of the primary linguistic data that a child considers in learning a given verb—either because they are not sufficiently common, or (more likely) because their added morphological complexity (the *at* prefix) disqualifies them. This means that the child never finds any evidence as to whether the transitive verb associates $+O$ with its object or not; such a feature is simply unlearnable. Therefore, it is left unspecified. When the theme argument does appear by itself as a result of derivational morphology, it always takes the default value, which I have assumed is A-class agreement. This explains the observed gap. The same reasoning accounts for why no verb associates $+O$ with a goal argument.[24]

There remains one extremely interesting derived verb type to discuss, however.

Recall from section 5.2.3 that Mohawk has reflexive verbs derived by the prefix *atat*. These behave like unaccusative verbs in several important ways: (1) their sole argument may be incorporated; (2) any idiosyncratic +O feature associated with the agent of the verb root is suppressed; and (3) they can have only a single agreement factor, even when a goal is present. *Atat* is also related to *at,* the prefix that derives unaccusative verbs from transitive roots. For these reasons, I claimed that *atat* somehow takes away the agent argument of the verb root. Reflexives based on simple transitive stems then work exactly as expected: the theme θ-role is the only one expressed syntactically and this always shows A-class agreement by default, for the reasons discussed in the previous paragraph. Consider, however, reflexives based on ditransitive stems. Once the agent argument is taken away, a theme and a goal argument remain. Hence, the structure of such a verb should be essentially identical to (81). In one respect, this is true: a reflexive verb, like an unaccusative, must agree with its goal argument and incorporate its theme argument (see (26) and (28)). However, there is a clear difference in the form of the agreement: the agreement on the reflexive verb is always A-class, whereas the agreement on the unaccusative is O-class. A minimal pair illustrating this is given in (87).

(87)   a. Atyá'tawi *ukw*-ate-nóhare-'s-e'.
          shirt   FACT/*1sO*-SRFL-wash-BEN-PUNC
          'The shirt came clean for (on) me.'

       b. Atyá'tawi wa'-*k*-atate-nóhare-'s-e'.
          shirt   FACT-*1sA*-REFL-wash-BEN-PUNC
          'I washed the shirt for myself.' (Literally: 'I was self-washed the shirt.')

In both examples, the basic verb is *ohare* 'wash'. In (87a), the agent is suppressed by *at* to give the unaccusative 'come clean'. In (87b), the agent is suppressed by *atat* to give 'self-wash'. Other than that, the only difference is in the verb agreement. The other examples found in section 5.2.3 all point to the same difference.

   The theory as it stands predicts the agreement in (87a), but not (87b). This is as it should be, because (87a) is morphologically more basic. Something about the *atat* affix must change how things work out in (87b). Now, the O-class agreement in (87a) is a result of the SAP, since the goal is c-commanded by the theme. Therefore, if the goal NP were for some reason not c-commanded by the theme NP in (87b), the SAP would not apply, and the goal would trigger A-class agreement. Assuming that the principles for constructing underlying structures are invariant across constructions (as stated in the UTAH), this can only mean that the goal has moved to a position higher than the theme prior to the application of the agreement principles in the PF component. However, we have seen that NP movement of the goal past the theme is ungrammatical with simple unaccusatives in both Bantu and Mohawk. Thus, the difference in agreement in (87) boils down to a question of why the goal can move past the theme in reflexive clauses but not in simple unaccusative ones.

   This situation recalls the following paradigm in English, discussed in Baker 1992c:

(88) a. John passed a ring to Mary.

      b. John passed Mary a ring (t).

      c. A ring passed t to Mary.

      d. *Mary passed t a ring (t).

      e. A ring was passed t to Mary.

      f. Mary was passed t a ring (t).

The crucial contrast is (88d) vs. (88f): the goal phrase of a dative shift–type verb can move past the theme into the subject position in a passive clause but not an unaccusative one. Baker shows that the same pattern holds in Sesotho, Chichewa, and Japanese; see also Everaert 1990, where similar facts in English and Dutch are presented. Thus, the pattern in (87) will be accounted for if we can develop the idea, hinted at in section 5.2.3, that Mohawk reflexives are syntactically similar to English passives and combine this idea with Baker's (1992c) account of the paradigm in (88).

Example (87) shows that reflexive verbs are not syntactically identical to unaccusatives after all, even though the two share many properties.[25] Hence, one cannot say that the reflexive morpheme attaches to the verb root in the Lexicon to create an unaccusative verb stem with a reflexive interpretation. The alternative is to say that the reflexive morpheme is generated as a separate element in the syntax. Then the verb root must assign its agent role in the syntax after all, but not to a canonical NP position. The most natural way to meet these requirements is to say that the verb assigns its agent θ-role to *atat*. Thus, *atat* is presumably adjoined to the head of some functional category outside the minimal VP (since the agent θ-role must be assigned "externally" by the UTAH). In other words, *atat receives* the agent role in the syntax, rather than *suppressing* it in the Lexicon. This is directly parallel to the analysis of the passive in English and other languages by Baker et al. (1989). Thus, the structure of (87b) in Mohawk is approximately (89); this can be compared with the structure of (87a), given in (90) (identical to (81) except for lexical items). In (90), the goal cannot move out of VP (e.g., to the specifier of IP) because to do so constitutes a kind of Specified Subject Condition violation: the trace does not have an antecedent in the VP, a thematically complete domain containing a distinct structural subject (the theme NP). However, (89) is crucially different in that the VP is *not* thematically complete in the same sense. Rather, the verb θ-marks an agent argument, which is not discharged within this category. Hence, the VP does not qualify as a CFC or a governing category, according to the definitions in (80). Therefore, the goal NP may move out of the VP by NP movement, landing in the specifier of FP (functional phrase) without violating any structural condition. Moreover, we can say that this movement is actually forced for another reason: an NP must move to the specifier of FP in order to provide the anaphoric element *atat* with a proper antecedent. Thus, the representation in (89) is incomplete as it stands in one important respect: there is no indication that i = n, that the first person goal is the same as the agent of 'wash'. Once the goal NP moves to the specifier of the category for which *atat* is the head, this equation is established by the general convention of specifier–head

(89)

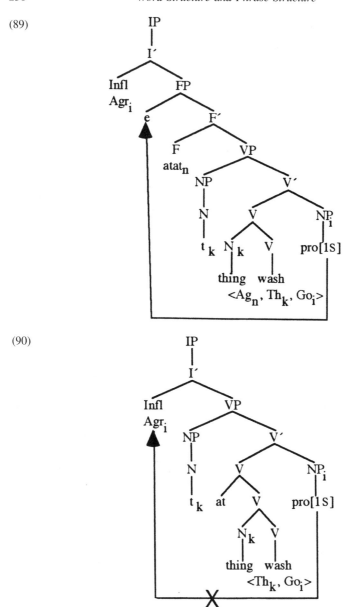

(90)

agreement, introduced in Chomsky 1986a. There is nothing unusual in this; indeed, it has been claimed that some such agreement relation underlies all antecedent–reflexive anaphor relationships at LF (see Pica 1987 and subsequent work). Therefore, the argumental nature of *atat* makes NP movement of the goal possible (just like passive morphology), and the anaphoric nature of *atat* makes NP movement necessary.[26] In this way, we complete the analysis of reflexives in Mohawk, begun in section 5.2.3. We also explain why there is A-type agreement in sentences like (87b): the first person pro in (89) is not c-commanded by any other NP in the derived structure and therefore it is not assigned +O either by lexical properties or by the SAP. Notice here that the SAP must apply in PF, after NP-movement, as in Marantz 1991; if it applied to the argument structure of the verb in the Lexicon, or as the structure is built in the base, then the difference between (87a) and (87b) could not be accounted for in these terms.

We may ask in passing what the mystery category called "FP" in (89) is. Since its specifier is a landing site for movement, it must be a functional category (Travis 1991). Since it is a landing site for A movement, it must be a category associated with the inherent morphological features of the verb (Chomsky 1992). It must be lower than Infl, given that *atat* systematically appears closer to the verb stem than tense/mood morphology or agreement in Mohawk. The most natural place for it, then, is in the head of an Aspect Phrase (AspP), since aspect is the only other (nearly) obligatory inflectional category in Mohawk, showing up as either ' 'punctual' (perfective) or *s* 'habitual' (imperfective). Indeed, section 1.6 showed that aspect morphemes in the polysynthetic languages consistently appear as suffixes placed between the verb root and the tense/mood inflection, a position that is explained if they head a phrase that is lower than the IP but higher than the lowest VP. In clauses with a true agent, the further question arises of whether this category is above or below the higher VP shell where the agent phrase is generated. Although the standard position is that all functional categories are above the VP projections (see, for example, Chomsky 1992), Travis (1991) and Noonan (1992) give interesting arguments that AspP (with the associated object agreement) should be between the two VPs of the Larsonian structure. Although the issue is not a crucial one for current purposes, this latter suggestion fits some-what better in the current system because it provides a legitimate landing site for movement of the goal that is still lower than the agent; this seems to be needed for sentences like (88b) in English[27]; Travis (1991) also gives some quasisemantic arguments for this structure, claiming that tense operators have scope over the subject, whereas aspect operators have scope over the verb and the object only. Thus, I take the final structure of a simple transitive clause in Mohawk to be (91).

(91)

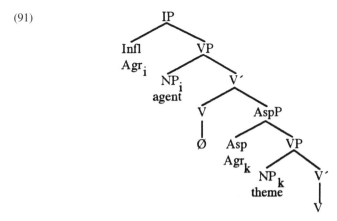

Of course, if the verb takes a goal argument, it will appear inside the lowest V'. Whether or not the agent NP or the theme NP is generated is also determined by the θ-grid of the lexical verb. If the agent NP is not generated, than neither will the higher VP shell be generated. Notice that I have also moved the "object"

agreement features down from the null verb to the head of AspP. This is not crucial to the analysis, but brings it more in line with other current work and makes possible the attractive generalization that agreement features are generated only on functional heads. In this system, Burzio's Generalization takes the following form (from Noonan 1992, which develops a suggestion of Dominique Sportiche):

(92)   The head of AspP is a Case assigner (and thus a legitimate host for agreement features) if and only if AspP is the sister of a V.

Aspect is selected by V only if a higher VP shell is generated, which, in turn, happens only if there is an agent θ-role to be assigned. Thus, (92) is equivalent to more familiar statements of Burzio's Generalization. Finally, the specifiers of Infl and Aspect will generally be empty in Mohawk, since NP movement is not triggered by Case; thus, I will frequently omit them in my phrase structure trees and will not distinguish between IP and I', AspP and Asp', as in (91). Thus, we end up with a theory of basic clause structure in Mohawk that is very similar to that adopted in much recent work in the P&P framework.[28]

There is one important way in which our analysis must differ from current practice, however. That has to do with the conditions under which one category can agree with another. Much current work assumes that a head A can agree with a phrase B only if B is in the specifier of the projection headed by A at some level (see, e.g., Chomsky 1992). However, the analysis of unaccusative verbs with goals is fundamentally incompatible with this restriction. To see this, consider once again a structure of the type in (90). This structure has only a single agreement factor, located in Infl (by Burzio's Generalization). This agreement manifestly reflects features of the goal phrase. However, the goal phrase is trapped in the VP, unable to move to the specifier of IP, the standard agreement configuration. The fact that the goal does not move by S-structure is crucial to the explanation of why the goal takes O-class agreement in this construction, but not in reflexive constructions; it also fits naturally with an explanation of why constructions consisting of an unaccusative verb with a bare NP goal are impossible in languages like English and Sesotho. The impossibility of this NP movement has been attributed to Binding Theory. Furthermore, the goal NP will not be better able to move out of the VP at LF. Such movement would be possible only if (1) the theme NP somehow deleted without a trace at LF; or (2) Principle A of Binding Theory did not hold at LF. Both possibilities would violate fundamental tenets of the theory, where LF is the linguistic interface with semantic and conceptual systems—tenets held in a particularly strong form in Chomsky 1992. Thus, we are virtually forced to the conclusion that Infl in a structure like this agrees with the goal, even though the goal is never in its specifier.

What, then, is the structural condition on agreement? The older position would be that a head A may agree with a phrase B only if A governs B. This works in (90), as long as the verb raises to the Infl position to combine with tense and agreement morphology in the syntax. It is now quite standard to assume that a category whose head has moved becomes transparent for purposes of government (the Government Transparency Corollary of Baker 1988a). However, by the same token, government turns out not to be a very restrictive locality condition. This is particularly so in a polysynthetic language like Mohawk, where almost every head seems to incorporate into the next higher head. When this happens, everything governs everything, and the government condition puts little substantive restriction on agreement relations. For this and other reasons, Chomsky (1992) suggests that the notion of government by a head should be eliminated from linguistic theory, in favor of more basic X-bar Theory notions.

Thus, the specifier–head condition is too strong in Mohawk, whereas the government condition is too weak. To replace them, I propose (93).[29]

(93)   *Condition on Agreement Relations* (CAR)
An agreement factor X can be coindexed with a phrase Y only if Y is coindexed with a position in the argument structure of a head Z and X is adjoined to Z .

The basic idea here is that head movement determines when agreement is possible, at least in the polysynthetic languages. In effect, an agreement can be related to any of the arguments of the head that incorporates into it. Structure (90) obeys the CAR in a straightforward way, as indicated in (94) (with AspP node omitted).

(94)

The verb incorporates into Infl; therefore, the agreement associated with Infl can be coindexed with either the theme of the verb or the goal of the verb. In this particular example, agreement must be coindexed with the goal for other reasons; however, if there were no goal in the structure, then the agreement could be coindexed with the theme of 'wash' as well. This is the result we need. It is easy to see that the CAR also works for the other, less problematic, structures discussed in this section. Notice that although there is no deep reason why ordinary agent-subjects and theme-objects could not move to the specifiers of IP or AspP to trigger agreement, the CAR makes it unnecessary for them to do so. The most economical assumption, then, is that they do not move, but rather remain in their base positions. This is also consistent with the evidence from Condition C that shows that subjects remain inside the VP (shell) in Mohawk, as discussed in section 2.2.[30] Moreover, chapter 8 shows that the CAR also plays an important role in determining what kinds of incorporation processes are possible in a polysynthetic language. This is not the formulation that the agreement condition generally takes in English, however; thus, I leave open the question of whether the CAR is a parameter that holds in polysynthetic languages or is a true principle of UG.

5.4.4. *Agreement in Other Languages*

So far, most of the principles in the analysis of agreement have been phrased with only Mohawk in mind. One window into the generality of these principles is to consider briefly how they apply to other polysynthetic languages.

In fact, for many of the other polysynthetic languages the account is rather trivial, because they do not have active agreement systems. In other words, there are no verbs in these languages that assign +O to their arguments. Thus, the quirky agreement principle in (67) applies vacuously in these languages. However, all of the other principles can be taken to apply to the other polysynthetic languages more or less as stated. In particular, there is some evidence that agreement is generated only on Case-bearing functional categories in the other languages, since none of them allow full three-way agreement in clauses with a ditransitive verb, as shown in sections 5.2 and 5.3. Moreover, extensive evidence that the CAR applies in all the polysynthetic languages will be seen in chapter 8. Finally, we may assume that some version of the SAP stated in (82) accounts for the fact that objects trigger object agreement in the context of a subject, following Marantz (1991). However, most of these languages do not have the same facts concerning theme–goal verbs as Mohawk, which provided the best evidence for this formulation; this is because of a difference in the nature of the applicative morpheme, which is discussed in section 9.3. Thus, the theory of agreement developed for Mohawk is perfectly adequate for the other polysynthetic languages as well, but it is somewhat underdetermined by the facts of those languages.

The only other language in my survey that has an active system is Wichita, as described by Rood (1976); the quirky agreement system in this language has both points of similarity and points of difference with the Mohawk system. In Wichita, as in Mohawk, some intransitive verbs take the same subject prefixes as those on transitive verbs, whereas others take the same object prefixes as those on transitive verbs. Thus, the examples of intransitive verbs in (95) can be compared with the corresponding examples of transitive verbs in (96).

(95) a. Ta-*t*-i:-ʔa-s   (Rood 1976:32)
         IND-1sS-PREV-come-IMPF
         'I am coming.'

      b. Ára-*ki*ʔ-iweʔeha.   (Rood 1976:31)
         PERF-1sO-fall.over
         'I fell over.'

(96) a. Ta-*t*-ʔi::s.   (Rood 1976:217)
         IND-1sS-see
         'I saw him.'

b. Ta-*ki?*-[?]i::s   (Rood 1976:217)
   ind-*1O*-see
   'He saw me.'

However, crucial examples are somewhat rarer than in Mohawk, because the distinction is neutralized in the third person, in part because this category is marked with Ø-prefixes (Rood 1976:16–19, 140).

As in Mohawk, the subject prefix/object prefix distinction does not seem to correspond very well to the unergative/unaccusative distinction. Thus, Rood recognizes a small class of verbs that select a patient argument (i.e., are unaccusatives) but idiosyncratically take subject agreement prefixes (his rule T17, pp. 141–142); this class includes verbs meaning 'be long', 'hang' (but not 'hang outside'), 'be asleep' (but not 'go to sleep'), and 'be lazy' (but not 'be greedy'). He notes that some of these verbs can actually take classifier morphology that is normally sensitive only to patients. Furthermore, there are verbs of both agreement classes that allow noun incorporation; (97) shows subject agreement verbs with INs; (98) shows object agreement verbs with INs.

(97) a. ti'i has-k-wá-kiya-ki-rikic-kic-his   (p. 82)
         this PERM-Ø-now-QUOT-AOR/3S-little-water-go
         'until there was just a little trickle of water'

      b. Kiya-ki-ic-íwa:c-é:hir?a-s-?irhawi.   (p. 262)
         QUOT-AOR/3S-PREV-big-buffalo-NOM-be.lying
         'There was the big buffalo lying there.'

(98) a. Ara-wíra?a-s-kskwe?eha.   (p. 31)
         PERF-bear-NOM-fall.over/PL
         'The bears fall over.'

      b. i-yé:c-hi-k-wac-iti-s.   (p. 31)
         DUR-fire-PL-inside-out-exit-IMPF
         'Sparks fly out.'

(See Rood 1976:32–33 for evidence that the verbs in (97) take subject agreement and example (95b) above for evidence that 'fall' takes object agreement.) Notice that the subject agreement verbs that allow noun incorporation in Wichita go beyond the small class of verbs that Rood recognizes as taking semantic patients; it includes verbs of directed motion, as in (97a) and posture, as in (97b). These are verbs in which the sole argument can be considered as either a theme or an agent semantically. I claim that in Wichita these classes of verbs are unaccusative verbs that take subject prefixes systematically. This helps explain a contradiction in Rood's grammar: at one point (p. 206) he states categorically that "agents of verbs cannot be incorporated," whereas a few pages before (p. 198), he states that "the agent may be incorporated in an intransitive verb." The cause of this confusion seems to be that Rood has two criteria for agent in mind: those arguments that are pure agents semantically and those arguments that trigger subject agreement on the verb. He assumes that these two categories are the same, whereas, in fact, they are not, leading to the inconsistency in his exposition. Hence, agreement class is in part lexically determined in Wichita, as well; principle (67) applies in a nontrivial fashion.

Nevertheless, +O marking is apparently less idiosyncratic in Wichita than in Mohawk. We have seen that unaccusative verbs may take +O or −O agreement in Wichita, but Rood gives no evidence that suggests that the agent argument of unergative verbs can be marked as +O. Similarly, Mohawk has a few transitive verbs that take object agreement with their subject, but there is no sign of this in Wichita either.[31] Thus, we may want to restrict the use of the +O feature in Wichita to say that verbs may only assign +O to their *internal* arguments.

Next, we turn to possible instances of structurally determined +O assignment. In Wichita, as in Mohawk, theme-objects always show object agreement in transitive constructions, as in (96b). Similarly, the benefactive argument in agent–benefactive constructions always triggers object agreement:

(99) Ara-ki-ic-tarʔa:ti.   (Rood 1976:39)
      PERF-1sO-BEN-turn
      'He doctored me.' (Literally: 'He turned something for me.')

The key difference between Wichita and Mohawk is in the area of theme–benefactive verbs. Here, Rood reports variation. In some cases, the added goal triggers subject agreement, whereas in others it triggers object agreement (pp. 146–147). An example of each type is:

(100) I-s-té::ʔi-h   keʔe-s-i:r-í:-riwa:c-s-kita-wa:-ha.   (p. 196)
       COND-2sS-be.lazy-SUB FUT-2sS-POSS-PREV-big-Ø-be.scattered-DIST

       na-ʔawítat[a]-e:ha-rih.
       PART-yard-be.place-LOC
       'If you are lazy, you will have a lot (of trash) scattered around in the yard (on you).'

(101) Néʔaʔ ta-ki-ir-í:-ta:ras-iʔakhirʔi:-s.   (p. 147)
       bad   IND-1sO-POSS-PREV-horse-feel-IMPF
       'My horse is not feeling well (on me).'

The generalization that Rood states is that verbs that take agent arguments are marked with subject agreement in this construction, whereas verbs that take patient arguments are marked with object agreement (his rule T20, p. 143; see also p. 146).[32] However, we have seen that Rood's use of "agent" and "patient" confounds thematic roles and surface morphological marking. Hence, we must ask which is the operative notion here. The answer is clearly that surface morphology is the operative concept. The verbs of the (100) type that he lists are ʔirʔi:ʔariki 'protrude' (a compound formed from 'stand'), iki 'be', ʔiriwachisha 'leave' (a compound formed from 'go'), and kitaha 'be scattered'. All have unaccusative meanings, and the first three are known to allow noun incorporation. Hence, it seems that whether the benefactive argument triggers subject or object agreement in these examples is determined by the lexical properties of the root. This is in marked contrast with Mohawk, where examples of this type invariably have O-class "object" agreement.

Two adjustments are needed, therefore, to the system of quirky case marking for it to apply properly to these examples in Wichita. First, we need to restrict the

SAP somewhat so that it will uniformly assign $+O$ in agent–theme constructions and in agent–benefactive constructions but not in theme–benefactive constructions. Second, we need to loosen up the process of lexical $+O$ assignment so that verbs can "transfer" their $+O$ feature from the theme argument to the benefactive argument when one is present. The second of these changes basically means that $+O$ is lexically associated with verbs in Wichita, but not with specific arguments of those verbs. Thus, we have the following principle of $+O$ assignment (compare (67) in Mohawk):

(102)   If a verb is lexically associated with the diacritic feature $+O$, assign this feature to the lowest argument of that verb.

Thus, if a benefactive is present, this is marked $+O$; otherwise the theme is marked $+O$. This also accounts for the fact, mentioned previously, that transitive verbs can have $+O$ external arguments in Mohawk but not in Wichita; thus, these two differences can be elegantly captured in a single principle. As for the SAP, the difference between Mohawk and Wichita is apparently that structural $+O$ marking applies only when there are two agreement factors active in the structure—which, in turn, happens only if the verb has an external argument, by Burzio's Generalization. Thus, we can say that the SAP applies to NPs in Mohawk, but directly to agreement nodes in Wichita (compare with (82)):

(103)   *SAP2*
        Assign $+O$ to Agr if it is c-commanded by another Agr in the same minimal domain.

This, then, explains the differences between the two systems, with only minor adjustments to the structure of the system.[33] Thus, the contrast between Mohawk and Wichita gives some feel for which elements of the theory of agreement are universal and which are language particular. As far as I can tell, the same system should work for other "active" languages like Lakhota and Choctaw, perhaps with a few more language-specific adjustments.[34]

5.5   Conclusion

This chapter has worked through the intricate facts surrounding agreement in Mohawk and has made some comparisons with other polysynthetic languages. The Mohawk facts, in particular, provide a rather detailed window into the structure of clauses in the polysynthetic languages—a welcome result given that the syntax of full NPs tells us little about this topic. In the course of the study, we have found evidence for several features of current P&P theory, including binary branching; Larsonian "layered" VPs; the presence of at least two functional categories in the clause; and a tight connection between functional categories, Case features, and agreement. The paradigms analyzed are also consistent with a strong version of the UTAH; in fact, they give insight into how this general hypothesis should be developed into the specific mapping conditions stated in (86). Also supported is the general framework of Marantz 1991, in which the licensing of an element is distinguished from the spelling out of that element morphologically, and dependent forms are assigned in particular structural configurations (the SAP). The one important area in which P&P ideas have proven inadequate is in characterizing the structural relationship between an NP and its agreement; therefore, I have proposed the CAR as a basic principle in this domain. In several instances, further research is needed to determine how these Case and agreement principles can be stated in the simplest and most general way. Nevertheless, they are sufficiently well developed to warrant a basic conclusion: agreement in Mohawk is determined by a combination of UG principles and language-specific morphological spell-outs, with most of the real work being done by the former. These developments in the theory of agreement can now form the background for the study of NP internal structure, which is the topic of the next chapter.

Notes

1. This is the traditional analysis of Lounsbury 1953 and much subsequent Iroquoia-nist work. In fact, the neuter and zoic forms are usually identical, and should perhaps be collapsed into one gender. The primary difference between the two is treated in section 5.3. What I call the feminine gender is also used for generic statements, and there are some hints that this was its original use in Iroquoian languages. Thus, it might be slightly misleading to call it a "gender," at least in earlier stages of the language.

2. There are some exceptions to this found in the 1903 Prayer Book (*Kaiatonsera Ionterennaientakwa*); for example (p. 404):

(i)   KΛ kayΛ wa'-t-kwa-[a]tΛnyet-a-'s-e'   ne roti-tokΛse,
      here it-lies FACT-DUP-1sS/2pO-send-Ø-BEN-PUNC NE MpO-prophet

      ne ru-[a]ttokhas,nok rati-hyatu-s. . . .
      NE MpS-be.wise and MpS-write-HAB
      'Therefore I am sending you prophets and wise men and teachers. . . .' (Matt. 23:34).

Perhaps the existence of such examples in this particular source is a result of the fact that the material was translated from Indo-European languages in which there is no constraint against having both an animate theme and an animate goal.

3. This example may be bad for another reason: Mohawk speakers dislike neuter goals in general. Thus, (i) is rather bad even though both the theme and the goal are neuter.

(i)   *Wa'-k-hnínu-'s-e'   ne anitskwára.
      FACT-1sS-buy-BEN-PUNC NE chair
      'I bought it (a new cushion) for the chair.'

See section 5.3 for a possible analysis.

4. One might ask whether there are any verbs in Mohawk that take only a goal argument. The only examples would be a few experiencer verbs such as *atΛhutsoni* 'want', and *nuhwaktΛ* 'get/be sick', which represent their experiencer argument with O-type agreement and seem to have benefactive morphology in the verb root. I tentatively assume that these verbs take a quasi-argumental theme (similar to that found in weather predicates), as well as the experiencer/goal. If so, then this class reduces to the theme–goal verb class.

5. This is a point on which languages differ (see section 9.3). See Baker 1990a for discussion of this issue within the context of the Bantu languages.

6. One might think that the agreement in (20) could be explained by saying that *atat* counts as an animate object prefix. However, if this were so, one would expect the A-class

agreement form to be maintained even when the reflexive verb is put into the stative aspect (see later discussion). This is not the case; rather the A-class agreement is replaced by an O-class agreement form, just as it is with verbs that lack an animate object:

(i) Ro-[a]tate-nuhwé'-u.
     MsO-REFL-like-STAT
     'He has liked himself.'

7. However, this is not the only use of *at* in Mohawk. It has a number of others, including some that are quite lexicalized and have no obvious relationship to the external θ-role.

8. Alternatively, (30) could be ruled out because the verb has no external θ-role to assign to the reflexive morpheme *atat* (see Baker et al. 1989 for a similar account of why unaccusative verbs cannot be passivized in many languages).

Reciprocals differ from reflexives in that the duplicative morpheme *te* is added to the verb in addition to *atat* (see section 2.1.2). Otherwise, reciprocals have exactly the same morphological and syntactic behavior as reflexives in Mohawk.

Notice that I do *not* claim that this passive-like analysis of morphological reflexives in Mohawk generalizes to the other polysynthetic languages. The passive-like analysis is one commonly found possibility, but it is probably not the only one allowed by Universal Grammar. For example, Nahuatl and Southern Tiwa seem to have passive-like reflexive morphology that behaves much like Mohawk, but they also have an anaphoric element that can be generated as the direct object and incorporated into the verb (*ne* in Nahuatl (Launey 1981:196); *be* in Southern Tiwa (Rosen 1990:690–695)). This gives these languages a way to express coreference between an agent and a theme in the presence of a goal argument, something that is impossible in Mohawk.

Reciprocal morphemes in Chukchee and the Gunwinjguan languages differ from those in the other languages in that they are suffixes rather than prefixes. Given the correlations between syntactic structure and morpheme order presented in section 1.6, this suggests that these morphemes have the status of a higher predicate in a complex predicate construction. Indeed, in Chukchee the reciprocal morpheme is cognate with a main verb meaning 'bump together' (Nedjalkov 1976:202). In the Gunwinjguan languages, this analysis may be supported by the fact that the reflexive/reciprocal morpheme also has a collective reading (see Evans 1991:215–219, and to appear a for Mayali and Heath 1984:391–393 for Nunggubuyu). The corresponding morpheme in Mohawk has no such collective reading.

9. The sole exception is found in verbs with both a neuter subject and a neuter object, which cannot fit both generalizations simultaneously and still have an agreement morpheme.

10. See chapter 7 for discussion of adjunct NPs licensed by the trace of noun incorporation.

This account raises the question of why most or all of the dummy INs mean 'thing' rather than 'thing or person'. (One exception is the *rh* of *rhorok* 'to cover'.) I conjecture that this is the result of the rather deep tendency of human language to divide the world into categories of animate and inanimate. There are few or no basic vocabulary items that are neutral between these categories. Thus, 'person' can refer to any human and 'thing' can refer to any concrete inanimate, but there is no word that naturally refers to both. (Quasi-philosophical discourse might use words like 'entity' or 'substance' in this sense, but this is hardly ordinary language.) Similarly, there is no question word that readily varies over both humans and nonhumans: one must use either 'who' or 'what', thereby presupposing the class of the answer. The "dummy" noun roots in Mohawk are also subject to this general force: they must be categorized as animate or inanimate. In practice, they are categorized as inanimate, with *ya't* 'body' serving as the animate version.

It is interesting to note that the dummy inanimate N varies from verb to verb, while the dummy animate N is relatively constant across verbs. This suggests that the dummy N stems are really a kind of "cognate object." If so, then the correct gloss of *n* is something like 'washable thing', *ahs* is 'thing that can fall', and so on; Ø is a multiply ambiguous noun, meaning 'edible thing', 'findable thing', 'givable thing', and so on. The use of *ya't* 'body' is clearly related to the incorporation of body parts (see section 8.1 for brief discussion).

11. Kozinsky et al. (1988) and Polinskaja and Nedjalkov (1987) show in detail that antipassive and noun incorporation share most syntactic and semantic properties, justifying a unified treatment of the two. See Baker 1988a for a general analysis of antipassive that takes it to be a type of noun incorporation universally.

12. The fact that theme arguments are the only ones that can fail to trigger true agreement in Nahuatl might still count as indirect evidence for this analysis. Ainu may also have the same incorporation patterns as Nahuatl, but the available data are very limited.

Kenneth Hale (personal communication) points out a context in which the incorporated noun root in Nahuatl may show up overtly. He points out that reflexive triadic verbs can have third person *qui* representing the theme argument, even though first or second person object agreement is impossible:

(ii)   a. ni-c-no-cuī-lia
          1sS-3sO-1REFL-get-BEN
          'I get it for myself'

       b. *ni-mitz-no-cuī-lia
          1sS-2sO-1REFL-get-BEN
          'I get you for myself.'

This peculiar fact begins to make sense if reflexive morphology in Nahuatl has a passive-like analysis, as in Mohawk. Then there is no Case to license a second agreement factor, ruling out (iib). Therefore, *qui* in (iia) must be a spell-out of the null incorporated noun root, rather than a true object agreement. In this respect, *qui* patterns with the indefinite prefixes *tē* and *tla* and true INs, all of which can express the theme argument of a triadic verb (cf. section 8.2.3).

An alternative analysis could build on the fact that Nahuatl does show an impoverished degree of agreement with its theme argument in a three-place verb. In particular, one can mark the theme as plural by including the morpheme *im:*

(i)   Ni-mitz-im-maca   in huē-hue'xōlo-'.   (Launey 1981:174)
      1sS-2sO-3pO-give IN RED-turkey-PL
      'I give you the turkeys.'

Thus, it is possible that Nahuatl uses triple agreement to satisfy the MVC with this class of verbs, rather than double agreement plus noun incorporation. One would then have to modify the Case-based theory of how agreement factors are licensed to allow for this possibility.

Although this alternative deserves more careful consideration, I am doubtful that it will prove to be correct for two reasons. First, by itself it may not account for the fact that the agreement with the theme is very impoverished, distinguishing only third singular from third plural (Launey 1981:172–174). Second, Southern Tiwa has a system of triple agreement that is even richer than Nahuatl's, but this does not eliminate the need for NI in the language (Allen et al. 1984). These facts suggest that the third agreement factor in these languages is part of a very different system and not relevant to the MVC.

13. In particular, the account does not generalize to the unaccusative examples (54b).

We know that there are agreement forms for neuter subjects in Mohawk (although perhaps not in Southern Tiwa), because such subjects are possible in transitive verbs. Nevertheless, such agreement cannot license a pro in order to make the cognate IN unnecessary. Thus, there must be some grammatical preference for NI over agreement where both are possible in Mohawk. This, then, underlies the paradigmatic gap pointed out in the text. It is tempting to think that this preference for NI over null agreement might be a result of economy in the sense of Chomsky 1992, but I do not see how any of the economy effects proposed in the literature would have this consequence. Moreover, the preference is probably not universal; Nahuatl has an overt agreement morpheme *k(i)* that is used with inanimate objects, for example.

14. The correlations may not be perfect, however, because of other factors. For example, some unaccusative verbs such as *ihey* 'die' do not readily allow NI because their argument is prototypically animate (but see section 5.2.1 for an example). Similarly, there may also be a few verbs that can ambiguously be unergative or unaccusative, and hence have properties of both classes. A few verbs of motion may allow both a purposive form and a causative form, for example.

15. In traditional Iroquoian work, the so-called stative (perfective) form is considered part of the aspect/mood system. This does seem to change the inflectional class of the predicate: intransitive verbs in the stative always take O-class agreement with their subjects. However, Ormston (1993) shows that the stative is not, in fact, an aspect at all. Rather, Mohawk has a rather simple two-way aspectual distinction between perfective (called punctual) and imperfective (called habitual). The stative is most comparable to the perfect in English, and like it consists of an auxiliary verb (*u*) as well as the main verb. The peculiar agreement properties of the stative can then be explained in terms of this complex syntactic structure (see Ormston 1993 for details and discussion).

16. One possible way of implementing this is by using a kind of autosegmental linking formalism, as sketched in Baker 1990b.

These same patterns are found with ordinary transitive verbs that are in the stative aspect (see note 15 and Ormston 1993 and the references cited therein).

The same fixup process also applies when a goal is added to an unergative verb that assigns +O to its agent argument, such as *yo'tʌ* 'work'. The goal argument then triggers +O agreement, and the agent argument shifts to +A agreement. An example of this is (10a).

17. This can also be seen cross-linguistically: Lakhota and Choctaw have verbs that take two object agreement morphemes but no verbs that take two subject agreement morphemes. Thus, the association of objects to object agreement is relatively invariant.

18. NP movement of the goal to subject position in (79) could also be blocked by a notion of Relativized Minimality (Rizzi 1990) or Economy (Chomsky 1992), since the goal passes over another position of the same type. However, these approaches as they stand are not sufficient to distinguish (89) from (90); thus, I adopt the older approach in the text. These examples may also be interpreted as showing that something like the CFC must be built into Rizzi's notion of "closer potential antecedent" or Chomsky's notion of "equidistant."

19. Compare the Condition on Agreement Relations, introduced later in this chapter; it, too, is defined in terms of argument structure. Ormston (1993) proposes a slightly different version of the SAP, based on her study of stative clauses, which are a type of complex predicate. However, the difference between the two versions is not important here.

20. For example, Marantz's system taken literally would give the wrong agreement pattern for transitive verbs with quirky subject agreement, such as (69).

Bittner (1994) and Bittner and Hale (1994) also develop a sophisticated version of

Case theory based on the notion of a competing NP. Bittner and Hale's work is less directly relevant, however, because it uses concepts that are specific to morphological Case; generalizing these to agreement would be a valuable but nontrivial exercise.

21. Based on what is said below, this should also have an AspP projection dominating the VP but contained within the IP. This category is inert with respect to Case and agreement; its only contribution to the structure is that the aspect morphemes ' 'punctual' (better 'perfective') and *s* 'habitual' (better 'imperfective') are generated in its head.

22. This differs from relativized versions of the UTAH adopted by Belletti and Rizzi (1988), Larson (1988), Speas (1990), and others. On the relativized version of the UTAH, the exact position in which a given θ-role is assigned is immaterial, as long as its position is structurally higher than all XPs bearing lower ranked θ-roles. Under this assumption, the theme of an unaccusative verb could be generated in V′ as long as no goal (a lower-ranked argument) is present. An immediate advantage of the rigid UTAH is that it induces a structural distinction between unergative verbs and unaccusative verbs, a distinction well supported by this study. With such verbs, it is clearly not the relative position of NPs that is crucial (since there is only one), but rather their absolute position. I also take the rigid UTAH to be preferable to the relative UTAH on conceptual grounds, all other things being equal.

Like (81), (84) also has an Aspect Phrase between VP and IP that is inert for purposes of Case and agreement.

23. The last logical possibility is a verb that takes only a goal. I assume that there are no such verbs in Mohawk (see note 4).

The terms "agent" and "theme" throughout this discussion (and indeed throughout this book) should be understood as "argument having the most proto-agent entailments" and "argument having the most proto-patient entailments," respectively, in the sense of Dowty 1991. Thus, a verb like *nuhwe'* 'like' acts just like normal agent–theme transitive verb for these purposes, even though its arguments are probably not true agents or themes in a rigorous semantic sense. However, the liker is necessarily animate and the liked one is not, so the liker argument is closer to a prototypical agent and projects into the specifier of the VP shell. The liked one projects into the specifier of the lower VP. The syntax and morphology are then quite oblivious to these subtleties of Theta Theory.

24. Similar effects are found with Case assignment in Icelandic: no transitive verb assigns quirky accusative Case to its object, although there are unaccusatives that do so.

Parallel reasoning gives a partial account for the fact that +O is relatively rare on the subjects of transitive verbs. This feature will only be visible if the verb takes an inanimate object, for reasons discussed in the text. Hence, the lexical property of such a verb will only be learnable if that verb appears frequently with inanimate objects. (There may also be historical reasons why this type of verb is rare; see Mithun 1991).

25. Another difference between the two involves their interaction with purposive morphology in Mohawk: the purposive suffix can combine with reflexive verbs but not with unaccusative verbs (see section 8.3).

26. There is, however, no need to assume that the goal in these sentences raises to specifier of IP in Mohawk. In fact, Chomsky's (1992) Economy Principles would forbid such movement, given that specifier of IP is not a Case position. This fits with the fact that even the goal-subject does not c-command into adjunct phrases; hence, it is relatively 'low'. (See section 2.1.1 for discussion.)

27. See Baker 1992c. With some adjustments to the notion of a governing category along the lines sketched by Chomsky (1992), the idea that goals move above the base position of the subject might be made compatible with Condition A. However, this would crucially require that the agent would raise out of VP to a position that is higher still,

presumably the specifier of IP. This would require a different account of the Condition C patterns discussed in section 2.2.

28. I do not follow the common practice of separating Infl into two distinct nodes: tense and (subject) agreement; neither do I divide aspect into aspect and (object) agreement. Readers who wish to do so may consider this merely a typographical convenience, to keep the tree structures smaller and thus more readable. However, the fact that agreement morphemes show up near the left periphery of the verbal complex in the polysynthetic languages strongly suggests that they are base generated as adjoined items, rather than as heads in the X-bar system (see section 1.6 for discussion).

29. An alternative formulation of (93) that I used in previous work is the following: "A head X can agree with a phrase Y only if Y is contained in the argument structure of the X-bar theoretic sister of X"—where it was assumed that argument structures percolate from the head of a phrase to the phrase as a whole. The two formulations are nearly equivalent since the category that incorporates into X is normally the same as the head of the sister of X, by the Head Movement Constraint. However, I now find (93) somewhat more intuitive. The two conditions also give crucially different results in the unusual situation where one head incorporates from the specifier of an agreement-bearing head and another incorporates from the complement of such a head (see section 9.3.2 for such a case).

30. See also Bittner 1994:9–16 for evidence that NPs do not raise into the specifier positions associated with agreement in some ergative languages.

31. However, there are verbs of this type in the related language Caddo, according to Mithun (1991).

32. Unfortunately, Rood's examples do not illustrate his generalization as well as one would like because many of them have third person benefactives and the difference between subject and object agreement is neutralized in the third person. However, he does present at least one good example of each type, so I will assume he is correct.

33. Chukchee is like (100) in Wichita in that the affected argument added to unaccusative verbs in Chukchee triggers ordinary intransitive subject agreement (Nedjalkov 1976:188–189):

(i)   Ǝtlǝg-ǝn   ǝ'tw'-ǝ-yǝr'et-g'i.
      father-ABS boat-ø-fill.up-3sS
      'The boat filled up on the father.'

This suggests that Chukchee also obeys SAP2, rather than the original version. Chukchee is not an active language, however, so it never has examples like (101).

34. Minimally, the particular verbs that assign +O will vary from language to language. Lakhota and Choctaw may also have a more robust lexical redundancy rule than Mohawk, which assigns +O to the argument of unaccusative verbs. This depends on how convinced one is by the claims in the literature that it is the unaccusative verbs in these languages that take object agreement forms (Williamson 1984 for Lakhota; Davies 1986 and Broadwell 1988 for Choctaw; see also Merlan 1985 and Mithun 1991 for relevant discussion). All of these languages have at least a few idiosyncratic forms, suggesting that one cannot avoid the use of a diacritic feature entirely.

6

Agreement and the Structure
of NP

In Chapter 5, we saw that details about agreement on the verb and its relationship to the arguments of that verb revealed aspects of the structure of clauses in polysynthetic languages. This chapter examines agreement on nouns to gain similar insight into the internal structure of NPs.

Nominals in the polysynthetic languages share several unusual properties that distinguish them from nominals in a language like English. Morphologically, nouns in these languages often have agreement prefixes that are cognate, in curious ways, to the agreement prefixes of verbs. Syntactically, the internal structure of nominals in these languages is often quite simple: NPs do not have determiners or complements, for example; even possessors are much more restricted than one might expect. Ideally, these peculiarities should follow from the Morphological Visibility Condition, plus the theory of agreement developed in chapter 5. In this chapter, I will show that this ideal can be met, once one considers the implications of the MVC for the "R" argument of nouns.

6.1. The R Argument

6.1.1 Noun Prefixes in Mohawk

Let us begin with simple, unpossessed nouns. Virtually all native nouns in Mohawk start with an "agreement" prefix. This prefix indicates the number and gender of the referent of that noun. The prefix is taken from the A-class or the O-class, depending on lexical properties of the noun. In general, which type of prefix a given noun will appear with is not predictable from any known lexical semantic distinctions. The data in (1) are from Deering and Delisle 1976.[1]

(1)   a. *Nouns taking A-class prefixes:*
      ká-tshe-'   'bottle' (N)
      ka-ná'ts-u   'pot, pail' (N)

ka-ríhtu'	'black oak' (N)
ka-nátar-o'	'bread' (N)
ká-'sere-'	'car' (N)
ka-núhs-a'	'house' (N)
e-ksá-'a	'girl' (Fs)
ra-ksá-'a	'boy' (Ms)
kuti-ksa'-okú'a	'girls' (Fp)
rati-ksa'-okú'a	'boys' (Mp)

b. *Nouns taking O-class prefixes:*

ó-wis-e'	'ice, drinking glass' (N)
o-'neróhkw-a'	'box' (N)
o-tokΛha	'white oak' (N)
ó-nΛst-e'	'corn' (N)
o-háhser-a'	'lamp' (N)
o-kár-a'	'story' (N)
ako-kstΛ-ha	'old woman' (Fs)
ro-kstΛ-ha	'old man' (Ms)
oti-kstΛh-okú'a	'old women' (Fp)
roti-kstΛh-okú'a	'old men' (Mp)

These prefixes are the same as the verbal prefixes, except that initial glides are lost the noun form: thus the FsA form is *e* rather than *ye*, the NsO form is *o* instead of *yo*, and so on. Some nouns, such as *ksa* 'child' and *kstΛ* 'old person', can take virtually any third person prefix. Most nouns, however, appear only with one or the other of the neuter prefixes, based on their lexical meaning; it does not make much sense to talk about a masculine or feminine pail, for example. In some cases, even when the referent of the noun is animate, the gender prefix is grammaticized to neuter: for example, *o-wirá'a*, 'baby'; *ká-skare'*, 'lover'; *o-hkwári*, 'bear'. It is also important to realize that the difference between the nouns in (1a) and those in (1b) is not a gender distinction in the normal sense, because the difference has no effect on verb agreement. *Raksá'a* 'boy' and *rokstΛha* 'old man' have different prefixes but trigger exactly the same (masculine singular) agreement on an associated verb:

(2) a. *Ra*-ksá'a wa-*ho*-yéshu-'.
        MsA-child FACT-MsO-laugh-PUNC
        'The boy laughed.'

    b. *Ro*-kstΛha   wa-*ho*-yéshu-'.
        MsO-old.person FACT-MsO-laugh-PUNC
        'The old man laughed.'

If instead of *yeshu* 'laugh' the verb root were *ahsΛ'tho* 'cry', then the form in both examples would have the A-class prefix *ha (wa'thahsΛ'tho')*.

Why should Mohawk use its agreement prefixes in this way? What could the nouns be agreeing with? In fact, there is a rather straightforward answer. Virtually any semantic analysis requires that nouns have an argument structure that contains at least one position. This argument structure is most obvious when the noun is used predicatively; thus, in an example like *I consider John a fool, fool* assigns a θ-role to *John*. The same θ-role also appears covertly as a free variable in referential uses of an NP; thus, *A fool walked in* is semantically something like 'x is a fool and x walked in' (see Heim 1982). Syntacticians often call this θ-role "R," following the usage of Williams 1981 (R is intended to suggest "referent"). Apparently, then, the noun is agreeing with this R role.

In fact, the existence of this agreement can be derived from the Polysynthesis Parameter if we strengthen it slightly. As presented in section 1.3, the Polysynthesis Parameter states that if a given θ-role is assigned by a head Y to a phrase X, then X must be coindexed with a suitable morpheme in the word containing Y. Assuming transitivity of coindexing, this means that the θ-role associated with Y is also coindexed with a morpheme in the word containing Y. We may say that this element *morphologically expresses* the θ-role in question. Strictly speaking, this says nothing about θ-roles that are not assigned to phrasal positions. Suppose, however, that we strengthen this condition so that it says that *every* θ-role associated with a head Y must be coindexed with a distinct morpheme in the word containing Y—either an incorporated root or an agreement morpheme. Since there is no stipulation to the contrary, this condition applies to nouns as well as to verbs. In particular, it applies to the R argument of the noun. Putting aside incorporation, which seems to be impossible in this case (see section 6.2.2 below), we explain the fact that a noun in Mohawk must agree with its R argument, as shown in (1).

Developing this simple idea leads to some rather radical consequences, however. I have assumed throughout that agreement morphemes cannot be coindexed with a position in a θ-grid directly; rather, the agreement relationship must always involve a syntactic NP (often pro) as well. This is built into the formulation of the Condition on Agreement Relations, stated in chapter 5. Thus, it is not enough for an agent argument associated with the verb to be matched with an agreement morpheme on the verb; there must also be an NP in the subject position that the θ-role is assigned to and that is coindexed with the agreement morpheme. This allows for a straightforward account of why anaphora possibilities are comparable in Mohawk and English, for example. When this is carried over into the domain of NP, we derive the following consequence from the strengthened MVC:

(3) The R role of the noun must be assigned to an NP position in the syntax in a polysynthetic language.

To be more specific, the R argument must be assigned to a subject position, given that it is the external argument of the N in Williams' (1981) terminology; indeed, it is clearly assigned to a subject position in predication constructions in English.

Given this, the theory of agreement can be applied to Mohawk nominals as follows. Agreement features are generated in a Case-assigning functional category. In English, the Case-assigning functional category is Det(erminer), which has genitive Case. Carrying this over to Mohawk, the structure of a typical N like *ó-wis-e'* 'ice, glass' will be as shown in (4). The R of the noun is assigned to the specifier of NP, just as the theme argument of the verb is assigned to the specifier of VP.[2] The N then incorporates into Det, allowing the agreement factor adjoined to Det to be coindexed with an argument of N by the CAR. If that agreement is, in fact, coindexed with the R argument, then the structure satisfies the MVC. Finally, nouns, like verbs, may or may not associate the "quirky" agreement feature $+O$ with their R-argument as an idiosyncratic lexical property. *Wis* and the other Ns in (1b) take advantage of this option; hence, the agreement in Det is spelled out

(4)

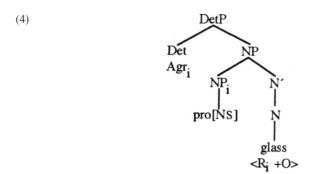

as an O-class prefix (*o*) at PF. The nouns in (1a) do not have this feature, so their structure is the same, but the agreement is realized as an A-class prefix, such as *ka*.[3]

The structure in (4) also posits a determiner head in Mohawk. I tentatively assume this position is filled with the meaningless noun suffixes *a'* and *(e)'* that appear on most morphologically independent nouns in Mohawk; this is the third morpheme in many of the words in (1), which I generally gloss simply as NSF (noun suffix). This suggestion fits nicely with the claim in section 1.6 that elements that show up as suffixes on a given root typically correspond to higher heads that that root incorporates into. It also more or less explains the fact that when the noun suffix is missing, so is the agreement morpheme on the noun. For example, non-native Mohawk words lack both the noun suffix and the agreement prefix; this includes not only borrowed words from French and English (including many proper names), but also onomatopoeic words like *kwéskwes* 'pig' and words of more obscure origin, such as *érhar* 'dog' and *takós* 'cat'. Similarly, when a noun is incorporated, both the noun suffix and the nominal agreement are absent (see chapter 7). Thus, the noun suffix and nominal agreement show the same kind of interdependence that agreement and functional categories do in the verbal system. In this way, the form of Mohawk nouns is accounted for; indeed, the structure in (4) is exactly like the structure of an unaccusative verb, apart from the different category labels.

The structure in (4) also sheds some light on a fact mentioned briefly as a potential problem in section 3.3.1. The basic observation was that the morphosyntactic features associated with the nominal prefix do not necessarily seem to count as features of the NP as a whole. In section 3.3.1, the focus was on number features, but the same is true of gender features as well. For example, a zoic/neuter prefix on a noun does not necessarily mean that the noun is treated as neuter for purposes of verbal agreement. Thus, sentences with mismatched genders, like (5), are rather common.

(5)   *O*-wirá'a   wa-*ho*-yéshu-'.
       N/ZsO-baby FACT-MsO-laugh-PUNC
       'The baby laughed.'

In fact, zoic agreement on the verb would be considered semantically inappropriate in this case. In this way, Mohawk differs from a language like French, in which agreement on, say, an adjective is strictly determined by the grammatical gender of the noun, not the sex of its intended referent. Structure (4) explains in part why this should be. Suppose that we put *wir* 'baby' in the place of *wis* 'glass'. Then the morphology tells us that the specifier of the NP is grammatically neuter, *but not that the NP as a whole is neuter.* Since there is no principle of grammar that percolates features from the specifier of a category to the category as a whole, the gender and number features of the larger NP in (4) are left open. This NP is therefore nondistinct from the pronominal argument of the verb in gender and number features and can be licensed by forming a chain with it. Thus, the gender matching that one finds between the prefix on the noun and the corresponding prefix on the verb is not a strict matching like that found in grammatical agreement, but rather a loose, semantically based matching induced by the fact that the specifier of the noun and the specifier of the verb refer to the same entity. On this view, the gender mismatch in (5) is similar to the possibility in English of referring to a baby as either 'he', 'she', or 'it', depending on the specific situation. Similarly, the *ra* in an NP such as *raksá'a* 'boy' shows that the specifier of the NP is singular, but not that the NP as a whole is singular; hence, it does not contradict the claim that NPs are unmarked for number in Mohawk. This was crucial to the account of comitative-like constructions in Mohawk given in section 3.3.1. Indeed, the existence of chains with elements that look as though they are unmatched in morphosyntactic features supports the view built around (3).

6.1.2 Noun Prefixes in Other Languages

Mohawk is somewhat unusual among the polysynthetic languages in showing such clear evidence of agreement with the R argument. Many of the other languages show fewer obvious signs of this. However, a careful look reveals evidence that the same sort of structure is found in most of them.

One factor that reduces the amount of overt evidence for this proposal in an entirely predictable way is the existence of null forms in the agreement paradigm. Many of the polysynthetic languages have null agreement forms for intransitive third person subjects of verbs. This is the situation in Nahautl, Wichita, and Ainu, for example. Since third person intransitive forms are exactly what we would predict for most nouns, it comes as no surprise that nouns seem to be morphologically unmarked in these languages. However, Andrews (1975:143–148) points out that nouns in Nahautl can be overtly inflected for first and second person.[4] Moreover, when they are, the forms used are identical to those that appear on intransitive verbs:

(6)   a. n-oquich-tli
         1sS-man-NSF/SG
         'I, the man; I am a man'

      b. am-oquich-tin
         2pS-man-NSF/PL
         'you men; you (pl.) are men'

      c. Ø-oquich-tli
         3S-man-NSF/SG
         the man; he is a man

These nouns can be used predicatively as nominal clauses, but they are also the forms that attach as adjuncts to a verbal clause (Andrews 1975:192–198, Launey 1981:246). From this it is a short step (which both grammars take explicitly) to say that nouns with third person reference have a subject agreement marker that is phonologically null in Nahuatl. Thus, what was said about Mohawk generalizes at least to Nahuatl and perhaps to Wichita and Ainu as well.

One can also find at least a little evidence for R agreement in Chukchee, although the sources do not discuss it in these terms. In the absolutive ("unmarked") Case, nouns show a singular/plural contrast. Plural is marked with a suffix *t*; singulars fall into several different patterns: some are unmarked, some have partial reduplication, some take an *n* suffix, and some undergo truncation (Bogoras 1922). Thus, one pattern for showing the contrast between a singular referent and a plural referent is an alternation between *n* and *t* (Nedjalkov 1976:185):

(7) a. ətləg-ə-*n*
         father-Ø-SG(ABS)
         'father'

     b. ətləg-ə-*t*
         father-Ø-PL(ABS)
         'fathers'

Interestingly, a parallel *n* vs. *t* alternation is found with intransitive verbs in the present/imperfective form, where it indicates singularity vs. plurality of the subject of the verb (Nedjalkov 1976:185):

(8) a. tergat-ə-rk-ə-*n*
         'cry-Ø-IMPF-Ø-SG
         'he/she cries'

     b. tergat-ə-rk-ə-*t*
         cry-Ø-IMPF-Ø-PL
         'they cry'

Here again, there is a parallelism between morphology that indicates the referent of a noun and morphology that indicates the subject of a verb, supporting the idea that the two are structurally parallel. Indeed, there are further parallels between verbal morphology and nominal morphology in the language; however, their significance is not entirely clear, and there are many endings unique to verbs as well. Nevertheless, the similarities—particularly in the use of *t* for third person plural in both—are suggestive.[5]

The Gunwinjguan languages vary a good deal in the area of nominal prefixes: some give clear evidence of R agreement, whereas others show instructive complications. The clearest support comes from Ngandi (Heath 1978), which has prefixes on nouns that indicate features of the referent of the noun. These distinguish five genders: masculine (*rni*), feminine (*rna*), and three distinct inanimate genders (*a, gu,* and *ma*). There is also a distinct prefix for animate plural nouns (*ba*) (Heath 1978:35). Exactly the same prefixes attach to intransitive verbs, where they indicate the gender, number, and noun class of the subject of the verb (Heath 1978:67, 71). Thus, examples like those in (9) are common in the language, where the same prefix appears twice, once on the subject and once on the predicate.

(9)   a. *A*-jenj-ung *a*-ja-wati-ni.   (Heath 1978:189)
        AS-fish-NSF AS-now-die-PAST/CONT
        'The fish died.'

      b. *Ma*-bergeʔ   *ma*-ja-rukba-n-di.   (Heath 1978:194)
        MAS-green.plum MAS-now-fall-AUG-PAST/CONT
        'Green plums fell (to the ground).'

Moreover, first and second person agreement markers from the verbal paradigm can also be attached to noun roots when circumstances warrant. For example, the 2PS prefix *rnar* can attach to *dhingʔ* 'woman' to give either *rnardhingʔ* 'you are women' (predicative) or *rnardhingʔyung* 'you women' (referential) (Heath 1978:37). The only slight complication in this picture mentioned by Heath is that the agreement prefixes on nouns are occasionally omitted in spontaneous discourse. Except for this, the R argument of Ns is treated exactly like the sole argument of an intransitive verb in Ngandi.

   Most of the other Gunwinjguan languages depart from this simple scenario in one way or another. For example, Nunggubuyu has more or less the same five classes as Ngandi, but the actual prefixes that appear on the noun are different from those that appear on the verb in this language. This is shown in the following comparison:

(10)   *N prefix*   *V prefix* (intransitive subject)
            Masc.   na-   ni-
            Fem.   ngara-   ngi-
            Pl/III   wara-   wuru-
            IV   ana-   wu-
            V   mana-   ma-

Thus, in a simple subject–predicate construction like (11) the same prefix is not repeated, as it is in Ngandi (Heath 1980:22).

(11)   *Wu*-yangga-yanggi:: na da-ga-waj   *ana:*-gugu.
        IVS-RED-go/PAST2   now IMM-Ø-PERGR IV-water
        'Now the water went up to there. . . .'

However, this superficial difference in form has little theoretical import. The important point is that a noun agrees with its R argument in a polysynthetic language, not that that agreement need be identical to the morphemes found on verbs. This is clearly the case in Nunggubuyu, just as much as in Ngandi. Languages in which N prefixes and V prefixes happen to be identical, or nearly so, are analytically useful because they help to show that the prefixes on Ns are actually *agreement* prefixes in some sense. However, it is no surprise if the actual inflections on Ns and Vs should differ in many languages, as a result of historical drift or other factors. Heath (1984) goes on to mention several other complications concerning noun class morphology in Nunggubuyu: (1) there is a second series of prefixes for both Ns (the punctual prefixes) and Vs (the B-set prefixes) that is used under certain syntactic/pragmatic conditions; (2) some nominals take V prefixes when used predicatively, whereas others continue to take N prefixes; (3) N prefixes are dropped (or replaced by Ø) in certain discourse situations, particularly if the NP is a focused indefinite. However, none of these details undermines the basic point.

Other Gunwinjguan languages show further deviations from the particularly transparent situation found in Ngandi. Thus, Mayali has four distinct prefixes showing noun classes on Ns (plus Ø forms), but the difference among them is neutralized in V prefixes, such that there is only one 3sS form (*ga*). Ngalakan also has four noun classes. Like Nunggubuyu, these can appear in any of three different forms on N: a "long" form, a "short" form, and a Ø form. Similar to Mayali, the noun class distinctions are largely—but not completely—lost in verbal agreement: two of the four genders always trigger Ø-agreement on the verb, whereas the other two optionally trigger either Ø-agreement or a distinctive agreement form identical to the "short" form of the noun class prefix. Finally, in Rembarrnga the whole noun class system has been lost, so R always triggers Ø-agreement on Ns and a single 3sS form on verbs (sometimes Ø). Rembarrnga thus has the same degenerate R agreement system as Wichita and Ainu. Therefore, in this single group of related languages one finds a whole range of agreement systems that goes all the way from the fully articulated and fully cognate system of Mohawk (the original motivation for the proposal) to the minimal system of Wichita and Ainu, which is merely consistent with that proposal.

The last and most problematic polysynthetic language to consider in this regard is Southern Tiwa. In this language, verbs show overt agreement with the gender class of their associated arguments, but there are no similar gender class prefixes on nouns. However, this problem is not as severe as it might seem, once certain other facts about Southern Tiwa are taken into account. Singular animate nouns fall into one gender class (called "A" in Allen et al. 1984 and related work) and plural animate nouns fall into another (class "B"). Moreover, animate nouns also have a suffix that marks whether that noun is singular or plural (Allen et al. 1984:294, fn. 6). Thus, examples like those in (12) differ in both the noun morphology and the verb morphology (Allen et al. 1990:321–322).

(12) a. 'U-ide   Ø-'aru-we.
          child-SG AS-cry-PRES
          'The child is crying.'

     b. 'U-mnin i-'aru-we.
          child-PL BS-cry-PRES
          'The child is crying.'

Inspired by a suggestion from Kenneth Hale (personal communication), I suggest that the suffix *ide* is actually an agreement marker that signals an R argument of noun class A (animate, singular), while *mnin* is an agreement marker that signals an R argument of noun class B (animate, plural). If this is correct, then Southern Tiwa is actually like Nunggubuyu; it has agreement morphology on nouns, but that morphology happens not to be cognate with the morphology found on verbs. Ideally, this suggestion should then extend to inanimate nouns in Southern Tiwa, which show up in all three genders. However, this case arguably does not arise for an independent reason: neuter nouns almost never appear as independent words in Southern Tiwa. Thus, if a neuter NP functions as the object of a transitive verb or the subject of an intransitive (unaccusative) verb, it must be incorporated into the verb (Allen et al. 1984:293–294, 299–300). Moreover, incorporated nouns lose all their inflectional morphology, including the R agreement, in Southern Tiwa and other languages. In the few cases where an inanimate noun appears as an unincorporated subject, it is treated as animate and takes the *ide* suffix, as well as triggering A agreement on the verb. Thus, either (13a) or (13b) can be used, but not an intermediate form in which the subject is unincorporated but triggers B agreement on the verb.

(13) a. I-mukhin-k'euwe-m.
         BS-hat-old-STAT/PRES
         'The hat is old.'

      b. Mukhin-ide Ø-k'euwe-m.
         hat-A   AS-old-STAT/PRES
         'The hat is old.'

The only other position that inanimate NPs can occur in is the object of a postposition or Case marker; however, these could also be instances of a kind of incorporation (see section 9.1).[6] Thus, animate nouns arguably do have R agreement affixes, whereas inanimate nouns do not because of independent constraints on where they can appear. Under this interpretation, Southern Tiwa might be compatible with the analysis after all.

6.1.3 The Absence of Determiners

So far we have seen that the MVC forces the R role of nouns to be assigned to an argument position so that it can be agreed with. This explains the fact that polysynthetic languages often have agreement morphology on nouns that is cognate to that found on intransitive verbs. However, this treatment of the R role has other implications for the structure of the language. If the R role is assigned to an NP position in polysynthetic languages, then it stands to reason that the R role cannot fulfill precisely the same grammatical functions that it does in other languages. This accounts for the important fact that polysynthetic languages do not have semantically meaningful determiners of the kind found in English.

Before justifying this claim, it is helpful to clarify what I mean by a "true determiner." Structurally, determiners are members of a closed class category that heads a phrase and may select an NP as a complement (Abney 1987). In English, some determiners obligatorily select an NP complement (the articles *the, a, every*), some optionally do so (the demonstratives *this, that*), and some never do so (the pronouns *him, her*). I take the existence of the first class to be essential to evaluating the claim that a language has determiners, since demonstratives and pronouns can be analyzed in other ways; they may be of category A or N, for example. A simple NP can have at most one determiner associated with it, so the above elements are in complementary distribution. Semantically, determiners help to specify the reference of the nominal they are associated with; for example, they often encode the definite vs. indefinite distinction. In many of the Western European languages, some determiner must appear with most or all NPs (depending on the analysis of certain mass nouns and bare plurals).

Although I claimed previously that there is a Det node in Mohawk that is usually associated with lexical material, it is nonetheless true that determiners in

Mohawk are degenerate when compared with those in English. In particular, Mohawk has no semantically significant determiners such as *the* and *a,* which mark an NP as definite or indefinite. Similarly, Mohawk lacks strong quantifiers such as *every* (see section 2.1.3). The only element that could be taken as a definite determiner is the mysterious particle *ne,* which appears more or less optionally before NPs that are not clause initial. Thus, Lounsbury (1953:99), in his early study, informally remarks that the cognate particle in Oneida "is often translatable as *the, the one who,* or . . . *if.*"[7] Although subsequent studies have not shown exactly what this element is, they agree that it is not reliably a definiteness marker, and my data confirm this. Thus, a postverbal NP preceded by *ne* can be understood as either definite or indefinite, as can a preverbal NP without *ne:*

(14) a. Te-wak-atΛhutsóni ne érhar.
       DUP-1sO-want/STAT NE dog
       'I want a dog,' OR 'I want the dog.'

     b. Érhar te-wak-atΛhutsóni.
       dog DUP-1sO-want/STAT
       'I want a dog,' OR 'I want the dog.'

See Chamorro 1992 for further examples and discussion. Thus, I follow Postal (1979:412–413) and Chafe (1970:70) in tentatively assuming that *ne* is a surface structure particle inserted before noninitial NPs. More generally, there is no minor class word that must be followed by an NP in Mohawk. The only truly determiner-like elements that are found in Mohawk are the demonstratives *thíkΛ* 'that' and *kΛ'íkΛ* 'this', and these have a rather different syntax (see chapter 4).

   This lack of semantically significant determiners seems to be a property of the polysynthetic languages as a class. For example, Spencer (1993:59) says of Chukchee that "There is no syntactically identifiable class of specifiers or determiners as opposed to other types of modifier. . . . Those elements which would be determiners in languages such as English, such as demonstrative adjectives, numerals and *wh*-word modifiers, can be incorporated just as easily as other modifiers." Allen et al. (1984) give Southern Tiwa examples in which independent NPs are determinerless and can be translated as either definite or indefinite:

(15) Seuan-ide ti-mū-ban. (AGF:295)
       man-SG 1sS/AO-see-PAST
       'I saw the/a man.'

Similarly, there is no article system in the Gunwinjguan languages; nominals typically appear as bare nouns, with no particle or inflection to indicate their role in the discourse. For example, Evans (1991:300–303) shows that discourse factors such as whether an NP indicates new or old information may influence word order in Mayali, but they do not influence how the NP itself is marked. Thus, in (16a) the eaten object is known from the previous discourse, whereas in (16b) it is not; nevertheless, both appear as bare nominals.

(16) a. Barri-h-ngu-ni   djilidjili, gorlobbarra barri-na-ng.
       3pS-IMM-eat-PAST/IMPF cane.grass kangaroo 3pS-see-PAST/PERF
       'As they were eating [the] cane-grass, they saw a kangaroo.'

b. Ba-ngarre-werrhm-i				gun-marlaworr, gun-boi
3sS-scrub-scratch-PAST/IMPF IV-leaf			IV-cooking.stone
ba-ngune-ng. . .
3sS-eat-PAST/PERF
'While she was scratching around in the leaves, she ate a cooking stone.'

Apparently this is also true of the other Gunwinjguan languages.[8] Shibatani (1990) also does not present any true articles in Ainu. Ainu does have certain modifiers that optionally precede the noun, including attributive adjectives, quantifier/numerals, and demonstratives (Shibatani 1990:23–24); however, there are no markers of definiteness per se. Furthermore, these elements do not follow the head noun, as one would expect if they were X-bar theoretic heads in a head-final language.

The polysynthetic language that comes the closest to having a true determiner system is Nahuatl. NPs in this language can appear as bare forms or preceded by *in* or *cē*. Launey (1981:24) says that *in* "has multiple uses, one of which corresponds roughly to the definite article in French [my translation]." Elsewhere he writes (Launey 1981:38): "The absence of *in* is most often the equivalent of either the partitive article or the indefinite plural." Unlike *ne* in Mohawk, *in* never appears in texts before a nominal that is clearly understood as indefinite (Kenneth Hale, personal communication). Finally, Launey (1981:66) points out that "The numeral *cē* 'one' can as in French serve as an indefinite article." Thus, Launey gives contrasts like the following:

(17)	a. Ni-qu-itta	cal-li.	(1981:38)
		1sS-3O-see house-NSF
		'I see (some) houses.'

	b. Ni-qu-itta	in cal-li.	(1981:37)
		1sS-3O-see IN house-NSF
		'I see the house(s).'

	c. Ni-qu-itta	cē	cuahui-tl.	(1981:66)
		1sS-3O-see one tree-NSF
		'I see a tree.'

If one looks only at these examples, this seems to be a conclusive case of a determiner system. However, both *in* and *cē* in (17) need to be understood in the context of their other uses in the language. As already mentioned, *cē* is the numeral 'one'; as such, it has the same syntax as other numerals in Nahuatl. Among other things, it can be used as the predicate of a clause, in which case it is inflected for the person and number of its argument:

(18)	ti-cē-meh	(Andrews 1975:184)
		1pS-one-PL
		'we are one in number; we are a unit.'

Cē can also be incorporated into a verb, in which case it means 'together' or 'completely':

(19)	ti-ce-ya-z-queh	(Andrews 1975:184)
		1pS-one-go-FUT-PL
		'we will go together' (Literally: 'we will go as one')

In these respects *cē* acts like an open class element (presumably a noun), rather than a true determiner. Meanwhile, *in* is homophonous with the demonstrative meaning 'this'; as such, it can appear with no head noun following it:

(20) Ca te-tl   in. (Launey 1981:45)
      PRED rock-NSF this
      'This is a rock.'

Moreover, demonstratives in Nahuatl act like adjuncts rather than like determiner heads, inasmuch as they can appear either before or after a noun they are associated with (see section 4.3.1). Thus, even though *cē* and *in* may be used rather systematically to indicate definiteness in Nahuatl, their syntax is not that of a determiner. In particular, Nahuatl has no elements that necessarily select an NP. I conclude that even Nahuatl supports the generalization that polysynthetic languages do not have semantically significant determiners.[9]

The absence of most determiners in the polysynthetic languages also has repercussions for other aspects of their structure, some of which have already been discussed in earlier chapters. Thus, the absence of definite and indefinite determiners, in particular, explains why dislocated NPs can be semantically indefinite in the polysynthetic languages, unlike the Romance languages (see section 3.3.1). Also, the fact that there is no class of determiners in these languages means that demonstrative-like elements cannot be determiners; rather, they are adjoined elements in apposition to the NP. This, then, explains why demonstrative-like elements that are +*wh* can be moved away from the noun, giving rise to certain kinds of discontinuous expressions (see section 4.3). These features of the polysynthetic languages bear further witness to the fact that they are different from more familiar languages in exactly this domain.

Now let us see how this fact about polysynthetic languages can be derived from the MVC, again focusing on the crucial case of articles. In order to do this, we must have in mind a clear idea of what articles do in English. In the framework of Heim 1982, which I adopted in section 2.1.3, articles in English have no direct representation at the level of Logical Form; rather they provide a kind of flag that indicates how the free variable associated with the R argument of their NP complement is to be interpreted. For example, NPs marked with *a* undergo the rule of Quantifier Indexing and are perceived as novel in the discourse, whereas NPs marked with *the* do not undergo Quantifier Indexing and are understood as familiar. Thus, articles are closely related to the R argument of their complement noun. However, this R argument is assigned as a conventional θ-role to an NP position in the polysynthetic languages, as a consequence of the MVC. Intuitively speaking, it makes sense that this kind of θ-role assignment is incompatible with the use of a determiner.

One way of implementing this intuition technically would be as follows. Suppose that the semantic relationship of the determiner to the R role of its NP complement falls under the general rubric of "modification," broadly construed. Then (21) is a plausible structural condition of modificational relationships.

(21) X modifies an argument position Y in the θ-grid of its sister Z only if Y is not saturated within Z.

Here, "saturation" is a general term that includes θ-role assignment, as well as perhaps thematic relationships of other types (Higginbotham 1985). In other words, only θ-positions that are still open are available for modification. Among other things, this principle guarantees that (apart from extrapositions derived by movement) the modifiers of a noun must be inside the nominal rather than outside it, attached, say, to the verb phrase. Evidence for this principle from the domain of determiners is given in (22).

(22)   a.   I consider [Mary [the smartest student in the class]].

     b.   I consider [John [a genius].

     c.   *I consider [the [Mary smartest student]].

     d.   *I consider [a [John genius]].

These sentences show that a determiner can be attached to a predicative NP if and only if that determiner, which modifies the R role, is generated lower in the structure than the subject of the predicate, which receives the R role. This is precisely what (21) stipulates should happen.

Now suppose that we apply principle (21) to a structure like (4) in Mohawk, keeping our other structural assumptions as before. This structure is repeated as (23).

(23)

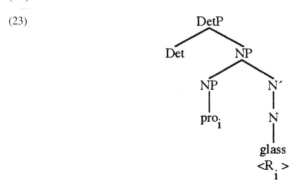

The determiner is by assumption the head of a functional category that selects an NP complement. Meanwhile, the R θ-role of the head N is necessarily assigned to the specifier of NP in order to satisfy the MVC, as already discussed. Thus, (21) states that the determiner cannot modify the R argument of the NP. This does not rule out the possibility of a determiner entirely; we can still analyze meaningless morphemes such as the noun suffixes in Mohawk as instances of the category Det if it is useful to do so from a morphosyntactic viewpoint. Indeed, similar elements are found in several other polysynthetic languages as well: examples include the so-called absolutive suffix *tl(i)* in Nahuatl, the absolutive suffix *yung* in Ngandi (Heath 1978:48–49), and the suffix *(k)ʔa* in Wichita (Rood 1976:7). These suffixes simply need to be attached to free-standing nouns as a formal requirement; in many cases, their existence as a distinct morpheme is recognizable only because they disappear when the noun root is incorporated into the verb or certain other items. Nevertheless, (21) does combine with the MVC to explain the fact that polysynthetic languages never have more than a degenerate determiner system.[10]

6.2. Other NP-Internal Arguments

So far the focus has been entirely on one argument of the head noun: the R argument. However, nouns can take other, more conventional arguments in English and related languages, as shown by Chomsky (1970) and others. This, then, is another area where one would expect the MVC to have implications. Indeed, NP-internal structure in the polysynthetic languages appears to be rather simple by English standards; for the most part, Ns cannot take arguments. The only exception of any generality is alienable possessors, and even these are not as widespread as one might expect. This section surveys the empirical facts in this domain and develops an account based on what is already known about the syntax of agreement and the nature of NPs in the polysynthetic languages. For the most part, the discussion concentrates on alienable possessors, but at the end there will be a few remarks about how the theory generalizes to noun complements.

6.2.1 The Markedness of Possessor Agreement
(Nichols' Problem)

Given the overall genius of the polysynthetic languages, one would expect a possessed noun to agree with its alienable possessor. Indeed, the MVC seems to require this, assuming that the possessor is a kind of optional argument of the noun.[11]

This expectation seems to be fulfilled in Mohawk. Alienable possessors are indicated by an agreement prefix on the noun, which is cognate to a verb agreement from the O-class paradigm. This prefix replaces the usual R agreement prefix found on the noun, thereby neutralizing the difference between A-class and O-class nouns:

(24) a. *A-class nouns:*
ake-núhs-a'	'my house'
sá-'sere-'	'your car'
raó-'sere-'	'his car'
ako-ná'ts-u'	'her pail'

 b. *O-class nouns:*
ak-kár-a'	'my story'
sa-sahét-a'	'your beans'
raó-wis-e'	'his glass'
akó-nʌst-e'	'her corn'

Again, there are a few phonological differences between the nominal forms and the verbal forms of these prefixes. As before, initial glides are lost in the nominal forms, giving [ak] instead of [wak] for 1sO, [ako] instead of [yako] for FsO, and so on. In addition, the sound [o] splits into [ao] in many of the forms: for example, [ro] MsO becomes [rao] in possessed nouns.

This analysis also predicts that the behavior of a possessor phrase inside NP should be very much like that of an NP associated with the agent or patient role inside a clause. Specifically, the agreement morpheme associated with the possessor licenses a pro possessor, but also absorbs any Case (e.g., genitive) associated with the noun. The Case Filter then implies that overt NPs appear only in nonargument positions, adjoined to NP and coindexed with a pro in the argument position. Thus, NPs in Mohawk should have a nonconfigurational syntax very much like that of the clause. To the extent that one can test it, this prediction is correct. Thus, in section 3.2.2 we observed that possessors can be pro-dropped in Mohawk and that the word order between an overt possessor and the possessed noun is relatively free:

(25)   a. Rao-[i]tshénʌ wa-hák-hser-e'.
          MsO-pet   FACT-MsS/1sO-chase-PUNC
          'His pet chased me.'

       b. Sak rao-[i]tshénʌ wa-hák-hser-e'.
          Sak MsO-pet   FACT-MsS/1sO-chase-PUNC
          'Sak's pet chased me.'

       c. (?)Rao-[i]tshénʌ Sak wa-hák-hser-e'.
            MsP-pet   Sak FACT-MsS/1sO-chase-PUNC
          'Sak's dog chased me.'

Furthermore, NPs understood as possessors cannot be nonreferential quantifiers in Mohawk any more than verbal arguments can be. Thus, universal quantification of the possessor is expressed by the referential element *akwéku* 'all', and not by an element comparable to English *everyone*. (26) shows that *akwéku* in this role triggers plural agreement on the possessed noun, and its scope is not restricted to NP as the scope of *everyone* is for some English speakers.

(26)   Akwéku raoti-[i]tshenʌ-'óku s-a-huwatí-hser-e'.
       all   MpO-pet-PL   ITER-FACT-3pS/MpO-follow-PUNC
       '*Everyone's* dog followed *them* home.'

Similarly, negative quantification over the possessor argument is expressed not by a true negative quantifier, but rather by an indefinite NP in the scope of sentential negation:

(27)   Yah úhka   rao-[i]tshénʌ te-hák-hser-u.
       not anyone MsP-pet   NEG-MsS/1sO-chase-STAT
       'Nobody's dog chased me.'

Notice that (27) has all the characteristics of clausal negation: the particle *yah(tʌ)*, the verbal prefix *te,* and the switch from factual–punctual aspect to stative form. The fact that nonreferential quantifiers are impossible inside NP suggests that the nominal understood as the possessor is dislocated from the true possessor position, which has inherently pronominal properties. Together, these facts confirm that the structure of possessed NPs in Mohawk is approximately (28); this is perfectly parallel to the structure that has been established for clauses.

However, a cross-linguistic perspective adds considerable complications to this rosy picture. The reader might already be somewhat surprised to see that possessors trigger object agreement in Mohawk; we are more familiar with possessors being treated like NP-internal subjects in English and certain other languages. One might think that this is an accommodation to the fact that the R role must be

(28)

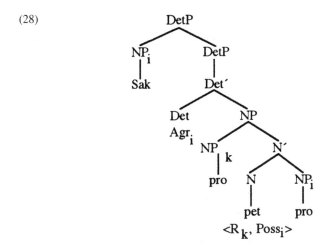

assigned to the NP-internal subject position in Mohawk. Even so, the poly-synthetic languages are not consistent on this point. Thus, nouns in Ainu and Nahuatl also agree with their possessors, but they do so in different ways. Ainu uses subject agreement prefixes for this purpose (Shibatani 1990). Nahuatl, on the other hand, has a special set of agreement prefixes for the possessor; these prefixes have some similarities to subject and object agreement markers (as well as to reflexive prefixes), but they are not systematically identical to either of them (Launey 1981, Andrews 1975). Thus, the assignment of grammatical functions inside noun phrases seems to be inconsistent—a challenge to the UTAH.

Even more threatening is the fact that the noun does not agree with its pos-sessor at all in some polysynthetic languages. Rather, the possessor is marked by a suffix in what looks like a dependent-marking construction. This is the case in Chukchee and the various Gunwinjguan languages. Thus, possessors seem to be an exception to the general head-marking character of these languages. Indeed, this fact is widespread enough to show up in large-grain typological studies: Nich-ols (1992:69–72) observes on the basis of her statistical survey that NPs tend to show less head marking and more dependent marking than clauses. This, then, is a challenge to the MVC.

Finally, some polysynthetic languages eschew a distinctive possessive construc-tion altogether. This is what one finds in Southern Tiwa and Wichita. In these languages, alienable possession can only be expressed by a relative clause in which the noun is incorporated into a possessive verb meaning 'be'(see discussion later in this chapter for examples).[12]

This preliminary survey suggests that the possessive NP construction is both fragile and variable in polysynthetic languages. This contrasts strikingly with what we found in verbal contexts, where the basic principles of agreement are quite universal and consistent. One would like to know why this should be so, and how it can be reconciled with the MVC. I refer to this as "Nichols' problem" in recog-nition of her typological observation cited above (although Nichols apparently did not view it as a problem).

6.2.2 Why Possessor Agreement Is Marked

Insight into the reason for these curious facts is gained when one tries to analyze the relatively expected pattern in Mohawk, beginning with the structure in (28). This structure is essentially parallel to that of unaccusative verbs, where Det corresponds to Infl, the R argument of N corresponds to the theme argument of V, and the possessor argument of N corresponds to a goal argument of V.[13] This parallelism between possessors and goals is plausible on several grounds. Many have pointed out a semantic connection between the two; for example, *I gave John a book* implies that it is now John's book (Kayne 1984, Tremblay 1990). There is also morphosyntactic evidence for this parallelism in some languages. For example, the same morphological Case is used to mark both possessors and goals in Ngalakan, Rembarrnga, and Ngandi, as well as in French (Tremblay 1990) and other Indo-European languages. In Mohawk, this assumption accounts for the fact that possessors consistently trigger O-class "object" agreement, just as goals do. Technically, then, we can say that the SAP marks the possessor as having the "dependent" agreement form, because it is c-commanded by another NP (the R argument) within the same thematic domain. So far then, the parallelism looks promising.

However, (28) has a serious problem with regard to the MVC: once the agreement factor adjoined to Det is coindexed with the possessor, there is no longer any morpheme in the complex word that expresses the R argument. More generally, the N has two arguments that need to be related to morphemes inside the word containing that N. However, it is well known that Ns do not, in general, license structural Case (see, for example, Chomsky 1981, 1986b). We may tentatively assume that this follows from a suitable version of Burzio's Generalization, given that nouns never take a true external argument and do not project a higher NP shell; in this I continue to develop the analogy between nouns and unaccusative verbs, which also do not assign structural Case. Therefore, there is at most one structural Case-assigning head in a nominal construction (Det, parallel to tensed Infl); hence, only one agreement factor is licensed. This, then, is inadequate to make both arguments of the N visible for θ-role assignment.

A similar scarcity of agreement is found in unaccusative verbs, where it is made up for by incorporating one of the arguments into the head (see section 5.3). However, this solution cannot be used in nominals, because noun incorporation into a noun is never possible, at least in this class of languages. Thus, both of the following expressions are completely ungrammatical in Mohawk:

(29) a. *ake-'nerohkw-a-núhs-a'   (NI of R argument)
          1sP-box-Ø-house-NSF
          'the box that is my (toy) house'

      b. *ka-wir-a-núhs-a'   (NI of possessor argument)
          NsS-baby-Ø-house-NSF
          'the baby's (toy) house'

Example (29a) should be compared with the grammatical (30), which shows that 'box' can receive the R θ-role from 'house' in the context of nominal predication.

(30) Néne ake-núhs-a'   thíkʌ o'neróhkwa.
     NE   1sP-house-NSF that   box
     'That box is my (toy) house' (spoken by a child).

Presumably, the impossibility of possessor incorporation can be explained in the same way as the impossibility of goal incorporation in verbal constructions (see sections 7.3.3 and 9.2.3 for discussion). The impossibility of incorporating the R argument is more mysterious theoretically. It is, however, very well supported empirically; none of the languages in my sample allows anything like (29), where the second root is a true noun. Since incorporation is impossible in (28) and only one agreement factor is available, the structure violates the MVC; therefore, it should be ruled out.

Although this analysis looks like it gives the wrong result for Mohawk, I take it to be the explanation for why simple head-marking possessive constructions are not found in roughly half of the polysynthetic languages. This is clearest in Southern Tiwa and Wichita, which use relative clauses with a copular verb in place of true possessor constructions. Typical examples of this are (31) in Southern Tiwa (Frantz 1993a) and (32) in Wichita (Rood 1976:146).

(31) Ti-thã-ban   kam-mukhin-we-'in.
     1sS/ʙO-find-PAST 2sO\ʙO-hat-be-SUB.
     'I found your hat.'

(32) I-s-aː-kí-c-ha-ra-ʔa   n-iy-aː-taːh-iːki-h.
     IMPER-2sS-PREV-1sO-BEN-PL-PORT-come PART-3INDEFS-POSS-knife-be-SUB
     'Bring me their knives.'

A more literal gloss of (31) would be 'I found the hat that is to you,' or (more idiomatically) 'I found the hat you own.' The structure of these expressions is, in fact, very much like (28), in that the head takes an NP specifier that expresses the ultimate referent of the construction and an oblique complement that expresses the possessor, as shown in (33).

(33)

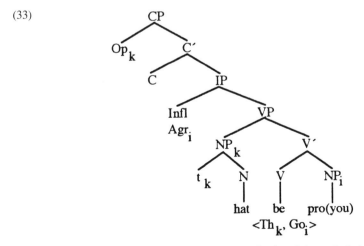

However, the crucial difference is that here the head is verbal; hence the theme noun can and does incorporate into it. The sole agreement factor then identifies the possessor/goal, and the structure is grammatical. A relative operator is adjoined to the theme noun phrase and then extracted in order to produce a relative clause structure and interpretation, as discussed in section 4.3.2. Similarly, structures like (28) are impossible in Chukchee and many of the Gunwinjguan languages; however, the dependent-marking constructions that these languages actually use to express possession require further discussion.

6.2.3 Dependent-Marked Possessors

The natural bridge between Southern Tiwa/Wichita and Chukchee/Gunwinjguan is provided by Nunggubuyu. In this language, the possessor noun is marked with the so-called relative affix; (34) gives an example (from Heath 1980:512).

(34)   . . . mari na-runggal-yung ngara-Katherine-*jinjung* na-rlandhur-jung,
       and   Ms-big-ABS   Fs-Katherine-REL   Ms-dog-ABS

       ardaba   ni-yara-ng.
       then   MsS-smell-PAST
       '. . . and then Katherine's big male dog smelled it (a buffalo).'

Interestingly, Heath (1984) shows that this same suffix also attaches to verbal constituents to form relative clauses. Hence, (34) can be compared with (35) (Heath 1980:544).

(35)   Aba ni-ngambi-nj   na-baba, na-lha:-'nguru
       then MsS-go.in.water-PAST Ms-father Ms-place.name

       wunu-ra-ni-*yinjung* . . .
       3pS/MsO-spear-PAST-REL
       'Then my father, whom they speared later at Anguru . . . , jumped in.'

Thus, Nunggubuyu is not very different from Southern Tiwa or Wichita in this respect. However, it is probably not quite right to say that *ngara-Katherine-jinjung* in (34) is a relative clause, because it contains no overt verb, and analyzing 'Katherine' as the predicate of a nonverbal clause would give the wrong interpretation. Rather, the connection between the relative usage of *yinjung* and the possessive usage is probably slightly more abstract. Heath (1984:546–547, 1986:393) suggests that when *yinjung* attaches to nouns it acts as a kind of derivational affix; in particular, it creates a new nominal meaning roughly 'thing belonging to Katherine'. In support of view, he cites the fact that when the possessed noun is in an oblique Case, the Case morpheme may show up on the "possessor" as well (Heath 1980:208):

(36)   . . . wu:-jarari-nj nga nigawi-*ruj* a:-'nga-*ruj*.
       3pS-move-PAST   then him-LOC ANA-camp-LOC
       '. . . then they arrived at his camp.'

(It should be noted that *yinjung* usually deletes before an overt Case suffix such as *ruj*.) Furthermore, the "possessor" can appear even when there is no overt possessum whose possessor argument could license it syntactically. The possessor can even be separated from the possessum in a kind of discontinuous dependency (Heath 1980:428):

(37) . . . marya yamba ya:-ni   nanggu-dharlarliga-nj
food   because it.is.here 3sS/1pO-attract-PAST

wara-munu-munanga-yinjung.
3pS-RED-white.person-REL
'. . . because we have come to like white man's food.'

Comparable configurations in Mohawk violate the CED, because the NP interpreted as a possessor binds a position inside an adjunct (see section 3.2.2). However, (37) in Mayali is grammatical because it has quite a different structure: *waramunumunangayinjung* can be glossed as 'thing belonging to the white man'; this modifies or is coreferential with 'food'. Hence, (37) is like an extraposed modifier, rather than a dislocated NP. Its structure is simply (38) (with details suppressed).[14]

(33)

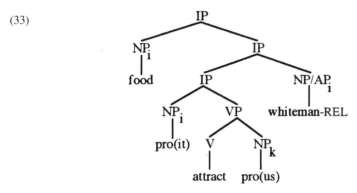

The construction in (38) is not as exotic as it might seem: English has something similar in the form of adjectives derived by the suffix *(i)an* and its synonyms. These can act as the functional equivalent of a true possessor, even though their syntax is clearly adjectival: thus, *the American proposal for ending the war* is comparable to *America's proposal for ending the war* (Kayne 1984, Zubizarreta 1985, Grimshaw 1990, Giorgi and Longobardi 1991). When this kind of derivational element exists in a language with nonconfigurational syntax, the result is what we see in Nunggubuyu. The productive use of this kind of derivation is thus a way of compensating for the fact that simple possessive constructions run afoul of the MVC.

Although the morpheme *yinjung* does not generalize from Nunggubuyu to the other Gunwinjguan languages, there is evidence that Heath's analysis of possession does. Possession in Mayali, Ngalakan, Rembarrnga, and Ngandi is indicated by the so-called dative/genitive Case suffix attached to the possessor (*gen/ʔgVn/ kan/ku*). A Ngalakan example is the following (Merlan 1983:44):

(39) '. . . balinjʔ rnu-gunʔbirri mirparra ju-rnangari-ʔgin yinimbala.
        like   Ms-that   child   Fs-Nangari-GEN just-the-same
        '[That child cried and cried,] just like that child of Nangari's.'

Since this suffix does not appear on relative clauses and is used to mark goal or purpose nominals in verbal constructions, it seems much more like a standard Case marker. Nevertheless, Evans (1991:132) observes that a possessive expression in Mayali need not be contiguous with its head, as in Nunggubuyu:

(40) Al-yau nga-bu-n   nguddanggi.
      II-child 1sS-hit-NONPAST your (GEN)
      'I will hit your daughter.'

In this example, the possessive is a pronoun, which has a suppletive genitive form; however, other examples show that the same is true of common nouns with the suffix *gen*. Evans tentatively concludes that possessive expressions are implicitly derived nominals in apposition to the NP that expresses the possessed noun, and that the proper gloss of (40) is 'I will hit the child, your one.' Furthermore, Evans shows that the genitive suffix creates a range of nominal modifying expressions that go beyond what one would normally expect to be marked by ordinary genitive Case (Evans 1991:78–80). Some of the examples do indeed have idiosyncratic, lexicalized meanings:

(41) a. ku-djorr-ken
         LOC-torso-GEN
         'shirt', lit. 'for on the torso'

      b. dalk-gen
         grass-GEN
         'dingo' (Literally: 'one of the grass')

The existence of such examples supports the idea that the so-called genitive is actually a derivational affix that derives nouns from nouns in this language, and not a true Case marker.[15] I assume that the same is true for its cognates in the other Gunwinjguan languages.

This analysis also extends to the apparent use of dependent marking for possessors in Chukchee. In an ordinary example of possession, such as (42), the possessed noun does not change its form, while the possessor appears with a suffix *in* (Polinskaja and Nedjalkov 1987:259).

(42) Эtləg-in   qaa-t   gəntek-w'e-t.
      father-POSS reindeer-PL run.away-3S-PL
      'The father's reindeer ran away.'

However, Bogoras (1922:686, 707–710) and Mel'cuk and Savvina (1978:25, fn. 5) deny that the *in* ending is a Case marker comparable to the other Cases in Chukchee. Rather, Mel'cuk and Savvina write "nor is there a genitive, its function being fulfilled by the relative adjective." Bogoras (1922:686, 707–710) also treats *in* as one of a set of related derivational suffixes (*kin, qin, lin*) that create adjectives of various kinds from nouns. Thus, *ətləg-in* in (42) is not 'father' in the genitive, but rather 'thing belonging to father'. Such forms can be pluralized, just like other nominals:

(43) ekk-in-et   (Bogoras 1922:709)
      son-POSS-PL
      'those of the son' NOT: 'that of the sons'

Furthermore, possessor expressions often appear separated from the possessed noun in Chukchee texts. In this, Chukchee is like Nunggubuyu and Mayali, but unlike Mohawk (Polinskaja and Nedjalkov 1987:254):

(44) Ɜmel'o məngə-t čəwi-nin-et kel'-in.
     all   arms-PL cut-3S/3O-PL devil-POSS
     'All the devil's arms he did cut!' (Literally: 'All the arms did he cut, those belonging
     to the devil.')

Finally, it makes sense on this view to take *in* forms to be nominals in absolute
Case form, since modifiers typically agree with the modified element in Case (Bogoras 1922:708). This view predicts that possessive forms can only modify absolutive Case NPs—transitive objects or intransitive subjects. Indeed, the majority of
the examples in the literature are of this type. Consider in this light the following
minimal pair (Kozinsky et al. 1988:682–683):

(45)   a. . . . iŋqun nə-teyŋet-l'u-nin-et činit-kin nenene-t.
          in.order.to ?-food-find-3S/3O-PL self-POSS children-PL
          '. . . in order for him to find food for his (self's) children.'

       b. . . . iŋqun teyŋet nə-l'u-nin čenet-nanana-gtə.
          in.order.to food ?-find-3S/3O self-children-DAT
          '. . . in order for him to find food for his (self's) children.'

In (45a) the benefactive phrase is in absolutive Case, and the (reflexive) possessor
is an independent form with the *in* suffix, as before. In (45b), however, the benefactive phrase is in an oblique Case (dative) and the separate possessor is no
longer found; rather the possessor is united with the possessed noun in a kind of
compound. I do not know if this is a general pattern in Chukchee, but if it is it
supports the analysis given.[16]

We can now summarize the solution to Nichols' Problem. The problem is, Why
do otherwise pure head-marking languages sometimes show dependent marking
inside NP? Part of the answer is that nouns in these languages must already agree
(overtly or covertly) with their R argument. Since nouns are not associated with
structural Case features, they cannot license enough agreement factors to agree
with a possessor as well. This explains why head-marking strategies of representing possession are not as common as one might think. How, then, can possession
be represented, consistent with the MVC? One way is to derive from the "possessor" noun X a new noun or adjective that means '(thing) belonging to X.' This
noun/adjective is not an argument of the possessed noun, so the MVC does not
require person/number agreement on the possessed noun; rather, the two nominals
are in apposition to one another. Thus, this construction is compatible with the
Polysynthesis Parameter. Since the derivational affix is attached to the possessor,
not the possessed noun, it is easily mistaken for a genitive Case affix. However, a
careful look at the syntax and distribution of forms bearing the suffix can reveal
the difference.

6.2.4 Head-Marked Possessors

We now return to polysynthetic languages where nouns do agree with their alienable possessors: Mohawk, Ainu, and Nahuatl. In explaining why other polysynthetic languages do not do this, we have rendered mysterious what at first looked
like the straightforward case. The fact that the structure in (28) is ruled out by the

MVC helps explain why Southern Tiwa, Wichita, Gunwinjguan, and Chukchee are the way they are, but (28) seems to be grammatical in Mohawk. This calls for an explanation.

In fact, I suggest that (28) is ungrammatical in Mohawk, too, and that examples like those in (24) are actually disguised relative clauses. Their structure is like that of (33), except that the copular possessive verb in Mohawk happens to be null. On this view, the nonconfigurational relationship between the possessor and the possessed noun in Mohawk that was documented in section 6.2.1 is reinterpreted: it does not show that NPs are nonconfigurational for the same reasons that clauses are, but rather that these NPs are, in fact, a special type of clause.

There are several pieces of evidence for this proposal, in addition to the fact that it saves the theory. The first is comparative evidence. Tuscarora is a Northern Iroquoian language related to Mohawk. According to Williams (1976b:218–220), its alienable possession construction is an interesting intermediate case between the obvious relative clauses of distantly related Wichita and the seeming nominals of Mohawk:

(46)   akò:-nʌ́hs-a-wʌ
       FsO-house-Ø-belong.to/PERF
       'her house'

Here the noun 'house' is incorporated into a stative verb *wʌ* 'belong to'; its understood possessor is a goal argument of that verb. Interestingly, however, the FsO agreement prefix shows up in the [y]-less form characteristic of nouns. From this, it is a relatively short and natural step to the Mohawk form in (47), where the possessive verb has eroded away to nothing.[17]

(47)   ako-núhs-(Ø)-a'
       FsP-house-(be)-NSF
       'her house'

Indeed, this is precisely the analysis that Chafe (1970:88–89) gives for similar forms in Onondaga, within a different theoretical framework.

The second advantage of this analysis is that it explains why possessed nouns in Mohawk do not agree with their R argument, as unpossessed nouns do. In standard examples like those in (24) or (47), this is not obvious, because the R argument of the noun is neuter, and this category is realized as Ø in the context of another agreement factor (see Table 5–1). The effect does show up, however, when one tries to construct nominals like 'her child', 'my girlfriend' or 'their people' in Mohawk. One might expect these to have transitive prefixes that agree with both the referent of the noun and the possessor of the noun. However, such forms are ungrammatical[18]:

(48)   a. *ruwa-ksá-'a
           FsA/MsO-child-NSF
           'his girl'

       b. *yúk-skar-e'
           FsA/1sO-person-NSF
           'my girlfriend'

c. *shakon-ukwe-'t-a'-shú'a
   MpS/3pO-person-NOM-NSF-PL
   'their people'

However, some of these nouns can be possessed, as long as agreement with the R argument is suppressed. Thus, one has the grammatical forms in (49).

(49) a. ák-skar-e'
          1sO-friend-NSF
          'my girlfriend'

      b. raon-ukwe-'t-a'-shú'a   (KO:97)
          MpO-person-NOM-NSF-PL
          'their people'

      c. rao-ruhy-a-'ke-hrónu   (PB:400)
          MsO-sky-Ø-LOC-RESID
          'his (God's) angel' (Literally: 'his sky-dweller')

If the purely nominal structure in (28) were somehow grammatical in Mohawk, this would be perplexing. However, it makes sense when one adopts the covert verbal structure in (33). On this view, the noun roots in (49) are incorporated into a null verb, and we have already seen that incorporated nouns are not agreed with in Mohawk (see sections 1.4 and, especially, 7.4.2). Thus, this account explains why the examples in (49) do not violate the MVC.

The last and most important evidence for the claim that possessive constructions are disguised relative clauses in Mohawk is that it resolves a paradox for the theory of connectivity that arose in chapter 3. Recall that dislocation constructions generally show connectivity effects, where the dislocated phrase acts as if it occupied the argument position that licenses it. Such connectivity effects exist with respect to ellipsis interpretation in Mohawk, but not with respect to disjoint reference (Condition C). Thus, the possessor in a dislocated object can be understood as coreferential with the pronominal subject in Mohawk, as in (50a), but not in Italian or Spanish, as in (50b).

(50) a. Kík Uwári ako-[a]tyá'tawi wa'-e-ratsú-ko-'
          this Mary FsP-dress   FACT-FsS-tear-REV-PUNC
          'She$_i$ tore this dress of Mary's$_i$'. (coreference OK)

      b. El libro de Juan, lo perdío.
          'Juan's$_{i,*k}$ book, he$_k$ lost it.' (disjoint only)

In the current context, this peculiar difference begins to make sense. It is a well-known fact about connectivity that material contained in a relative clause does not act as though it is reconstructed for purposes of Condition C (see Lebeaux 1989 and Chomsky 1992 and references cited therein). Thus, 'John' can be coreferential with 'he' when it is in a pied-piped relative clause, as in (51b), but not when it is an ordinary argument of the moved NP, as in (51a).

(51) a. *Which picture of John$_i$ did he$_i$ later buy?

      b.   Which claim that John$_i$ made did he$_i$ later deny?

Exactly the same contrast appears in CLLD constructions in the Romance languages. Thus, the indicated coreference is possible in the Spanish sentence (52), where *Juan* is in a relative clause.

(52)   El hecho que Juan descubrío, nunca me lo dijo.
        'The fact that Juan$_i$ discovered, he$_i$ never told me it.'

This contrasts with (50b), where *Juan* is a possessive phrase and coreference is impossible. Luigi Rizzi (personal communication) reports the same facts for Italian. A similar contrast is found in Navajo, a possible head-marking nonconfigurational language in which coreference possibilities have been fairly well studied: a referential NP inside a possessive NP cannot be coreferential with the matrix subject, but a referential NP inside a relative clause can be:

(53)   a. Adą́ą́dą́ą́' [ńléí John bi-łį́į́'] yi-zloh. (Kenneth Hale, personal communication)
           yesterday that John his-horse 3O/3S-rope
           *'Yesterday, he$_i$ roped that horse of John's$_{i.}$'   (disjoint only)

        b. [Adą́ą́dą́' ashkii at'ééd yi-yiiłtsą́(n)-ę́ę] yi-doots'ǫs.   (Platero 1974)
           yesterday boy   girl   3O/3S-saw-REL 3O/3S-will.kiss
           'He$_i$ will kiss the girl that the boy$_i$ saw yesterday.' (coreference OK)

Why relative clauses have this peculiar property is far from clear,[19] but it seems to be a rather robust fact across languages; hence, we can take it as a given for present purposes. Now, if attributions of alienable possession happen to be expressed by relative clauses in a given language, we expect no obligatory connectivity effect after all. Example (54) shows that this is correct for Southern Tiwa; the indicated coreference in this example is acceptable for the same reason that (51b), (52), and (53b) are (Donald Frantz, personal communication).

(54)   I-thã-ban [$_{XP}$ seuan-ide am-mukhin-we-'i]
        AS/BO-find-PAST man-SG   AO\BO-hat-be-SUB
        'He$_i$ found the man's$_i$ hat.' (coreference OK)

Now the claim is that the possessive construction of (50a) in Mohawk is a relative clause as well, even though its surface morphology looks nominal. This explains why there is no connectivity for Condition C examples of this type. Thus, we not only support the analysis of possession proposed here, but we explain a troubling residual difference between CLLD in the Romance languages and the syntax of adjoined NPs in Mohawk.[20]

   Nouns also agree with their possessors in Ainu, as shown in (55).

(55)   a-(Ø)-mac-i   (Shibatani 1990:30)
        1sS-(3sO)-wife-POSS
        'my wife'

Although my knowledge of Ainu is too slight to provide a full analysis of this construction, I tentatively assume that it is like Mohawk: seemingly possessed nouns are actually simple nouns incorporated into a covert possessive verb. Indeed, in the case of Ainu, the verb might not be so covert after all; the possessive suffix *i(hi)* (or *a(ha)*) seen in (55) could be taken as a defective verb (cf. Shibatani

1990:30–31). Indeed, the relative clause strategy for expressing possession is independently attested in Ainu; (56) is a rough equivalent to (55).

(56) ku-(Ø)-kor   mat   (Shibatani 1990:37)
      1sS-(3sO)-have wife
      'my wife' (Literally: 'the wife that I have')

Thus, it is not far-fetched to think of (55) as derived from a structure like (56) by noun incorporation, 'have' having a suppletive stem under incorporation. (The different agreement prefixes in these languages reflect a difference in dialect: *a* is the classical form, *ku* the colloquial.) This has the advantage of explaining the form of the possessor agreement in (55). As mentioned previously, possessors in Ainu trigger subject agreement on the noun, whereas possessors in Mohawk trigger object agreement, suggesting that possessors bear very different grammatical functions in the two languages—a problem for the UTAH. If, however, possessive constructions involve a possessive verb in both languages, this difference is explained. It so happens that the standard verb of possession in Mohawk, *yʌ*, treats the possessor as a (goal) object, whereas the basic verb of possession in Ainu treats the possessor as a subject, as shown in (56). This second difference is not very surprising; it is well known that possessive verbs can have these two distinct argument structures across languages (e.g., compare *John owns the hat* and *The hat belongs to John* in English).[21] The first difference reduces harmlessly to the second one on my analysis, as long as we make the natural assumption that the covert possessive verb has the same argument structure as overt possessive verbs in the language.

The last language to consider is Nahuatl. Nouns in this language agree with their possessors, using a set of prefixes that is not identical to any found in the verbal system for this purpose. Examples are given in (57) (Launey 1981:89–92).

(57) a. (Ø)-no-te-uh
          3sS-1sP-rock-POSS
          'my rock(s)'

      b. (Ø)-mo-chichi-uh
          (3sS)-2sP-dog-POSS
          'your dog'

      c. (Ø)-ī-mich-Ø
          (3sS)-3sP-fish-POSS
          'his/her fish'

This morphological difference makes it less likely that the possessive construction is a verbal relative clause in Nahuatl. Another important difference between Nahuatl and Mohawk is that in Nahuatl overt agreement with both the possessor and the referent of the noun is possible (Andrews 1975:149–153, Launey 1981:91). Thus, the grammatical Nahuatl expressions in (58) contrast with the ungrammatical ones in (48).

(58) a. ni-m-oquich-hui-Ø (Andrews 1975:152)
          1sS-2sP-man-POSS-SG
          'I am your husband' or 'I, your husband'

b. an-to-pil-huā-n   (Launey 1981:91)
2PO-1PP-child-POSS-PL
'You are our children' or 'you, our children'

This suggests the fully nominal possession structure in (28) is grammatical in Nahuatl after all. This forces us to be a bit more precise about why only one agreement factor can be present in Mohawk nouns. One possible reason is simply that there is only one functional category in the nominal system in Mohawk; hence, there is only one potential agreement host. This corresponds to the fact that Mohawk nouns typically have only one inflectional suffix: the degenerate determiner suffix. Verbs, in contrast, can have two agreement factors because they have both aspect and tense morphology. Interestingly, nouns in Nahuatl have two inflectional suffixes: one that indicates whether the noun is possessed (*tl* absolute state, vs. *hu(ā)*, possessive state) and one that indicates whether the noun is singular or plural (the possessive state forms are Ø, sg, and *n*, pl). These two affixes are seen most clearly in (58b). If they correspond to two distinct functional heads, as the fact that they are suffixes suggests (see section 1.6), then one has two potential hosts for agreement in Nahuatl NPs. In particular, Nahuatl is unique among the languages in my sample in having a distinct "possessive state" suffix; it is reasonable to think that this bears the extra Case feature that licenses a second agreement factor.[22] Thus, the structure of a Nahuatl possessive noun like (58a) is (59), where the exact labeling of the two functional categories is not crucial.[23]

(59)

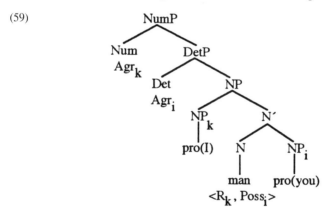

The structure in (59) provides further support for the claim made in chapter 5 that agreement is parasitic on the presence of other functional categories with semantic content. This also predicts that possessed NPs in Nahuatl should show obligatory connectivity for purposes of Condition C, because they do not have the structure of a relative clause. In other words, we predict that the subject of the verb must be disjoint from the possessor of the object in an example like (60):

(60)   Ō-Ø-qui-mictih   [inon Juan i-pitzo-h].
PAST-3sS-3sO-kill/PERF   that Juan 3sP-pig-POSS
'He killed that pig of Juan's.'

Kenneth Hale (personal communication) believes this to be true, but it has not yet been confirmed with a native speaker.[24]

We have now successfully come to grips with the syntax of alienable possession in polysynthetic languages. The bare-bones features of Universal Grammar
do not allow a straightforward solution to the problems raised by this construction.
In particular, the characteristic need of polysynthetic languages for nouns to agree
with their R argument combines with the limited availability of structural Case in
nominals to make the obvious constructions ungrammatical. This, then, is an area
where the features of specific lexical entries have much influence. Specifically, a
particular grammar could have an additional Case-bearing functional category in
its nominal system (as in Nahuatl), an N-to-N/A derivational affix with appropriate
meaning (as in Gunwinjguan and Chukchee), or copular verbs suitable for making
possessive IHRCs. Within this last category, there is further lexical variation as to
whether the copular verb has phonological content (as in Southern Tiwa and
Wichita) or not, and whether it has an argument structure like 'own' (as in Ainu)
or like 'belong to' (as in Mohawk). All these lexical matters influence the way
possessive expressions are realized in polysynthetic languages; yet all are elaborated in a way that is consistent with the Polysynthesis Parameter.

6.2.5 Noun Complements

Although the focus so far has been entirely on alienable possessors, the reasoning
also carries over to other NP arguments. In English, nouns of certain classes can
take agent and/or theme arguments; in particular, this is true of derived nominals
and "picture" nouns (Chomsky 1970). However, we predict that polysynthetic languages will not have nouns of exactly this type. Any argument of the noun must
either be coindexed with an agreement morpheme on the noun, or it must be
incorporated. However, incorporation into a noun is generally impossible (for un-
known reasons), and usually only a single agreement factor can be present, because of the limited number of Case features. Hence, nouns in polysynthetic languages should be limited to only one argument—the R argument. Therefore,
barring the influence of microparameters, there should be no argument-taking
nouns in the polysynthetic languages.

This prediction seems to be correct, at least for Mohawk. Clearly, there are no
derived nominals parallel to those that have been studied so intensively in English.
Mohawk does have a suffix *(t)sher* of rather low frequency that derives nouns
from verbs. Some examples of its use are the following:

(61) a. ka-yo'tÁ-hser-a'   (KO:221)
         NsS-work-NOM-NSF
         'job, beadwork'

      b. ka-'nhá'-tsher-a'
         NsS-hire-NOM-NSF
         'maid, hired hand'

      c. ka-yanerÁ-hser-a'   (PB:544)
         NsS-be.good-NOM-NSF
         'the law (of Moses)'

However, these are simple result nominals, not argument-taking process nominals.
In Mohawk, one never says something like 'I witnessed Rome's destruction of

Carthage,' but only a fully verbal construction, such as 'I saw Rome destroy Carthage.' Similarly, abstract nouns are occasionally derived from verbs in Mayali by adding a noun class prefix to a verb stem (Evans 1991:123–124), but Evans gives no indication that nouns formed in this way ever take arguments; on the contrary, they are used as simple nouns. For the most part, the topic of derived nominals is not discussed in the grammars of other polysynthetic languages. I take this to be some evidence that such nominalizations are not found in those languages.

The only polysynthetic language that is said to have a rich system of nouns derived from verbs is Nahuatl.[25] This language has a full array of agent nominalizations, action nominalizations, patient/result nominalizations, nominalizations of passives, and several other kinds. This, then, is the area where one is most likely to find nominals that take arguments. However, they are not found. For example, consider the following set of forms illustrating the agent nominalization.

(62)   a. tē-pix-qui   (Launey 1981:154–155)
          3INDEF-guard-NOM
          'guard'

       b. ti-tē-pix-qui   (constructed by MCB; see Launey 1981)
          2sS-3INDEF-guard-NOM
          'you are a guard(er) (of people)'

       c. teō-pix-qui   (Andrews 1975:214)
          god-guard-NOM
          'god-guarder, priest'

       d. *ti-nēch-pix-qui   (Launey 1981:154–155)
          2sS-1sO-guard-NOM
          'you are the guarder of me.'

       e. ti-no-tē-pix-cā-uh   (Launey 1981:154–155)
          2sS-1sP-3INDEF-guard-NOM-POSS
          'you are my guard'

Example (62a) shows a simple example of this kind of nominalization. Example (62b) shows that such nominals can be predicated of a subject, like any other nominal in Nahuatl. As one would expect from the semantics of an agent nominalization, the R argument of the derived noun is interpreted as an agent of the act of guarding. Interestingly, the theme argument of the verb root crucially does not become the theme argument of the derived nominal. Rather, it must be discharged by some morphological element within the verb prior to nominalization: either one of the indefinite prefixes *tē* (animate) or *tla* (inanimate) (see (62a,b,e)), or a nonreferential noun root as in (62c). The theme argument cannot be assigned to a referential element by the derived noun as a whole, as shown by (62d). Example (62e) is semantically the near equivalent of (62d), where the person being guarded is expressed as the possessor rather than as an object. However, in this example the *tē* prefix is maintained, showing that the possessor is not receiving the theme role of the verb root in the syntactic sense. Rather, the possessor is understood as the person being guarded by a kind of pragmatic inference, as in English. The same is true for the other types of nominalization in Nahuatl; in each case, the theme argument of a transitive verb is expressed by an indefinite prefix or incorporated noun and is not assignable to an NP argument in the syntax.

The other class of nouns that take arguments in English are the "picture" nouns. 'Picture' itself is not a noun in Mohawk, but rather a verbal expression of the kind discussed in section 4.3.2. There is noun *okára* meaning 'story'; however, this noun does not seem to take an internal argument. Thus, *Sak's story about Mary* is translated into Mohawk with a circumlocution such as 'Sak's story on Mary's matter', where the locative PP is clearly an adjunct modifier (cf. chapter 9):

(63)   Sak rao-kára' Uwári ako-rihw-á'-ke
       Sak MsP-story Mary FsP-matter-NSF-LOC
       'Sak's story concerning Mary.'

It is probably true that in an expression such as *Sak raokára'*, *Sak* can be understood as either the owner of the story or as the teller of the story, the latter being a kind of agent. Similarly, *akonúhkwa'* 'her medicine' can be understood as either 'the medicine she made', with 'her' a kind of agent, or as 'the medicine she uses'. However, I take these examples as merely showing that a range of relationships can fall under the rubric of possession in Mohawk as in English (Higginbotham 1983), not as evidence that nouns in Mohawk can assign an agent θ-role. Moreover, Mohawk speakers generally have difficulty understanding *Sak raokára'* as 'the story about Sak', with a theme-like interpretation for the possessor.[26] I conclude that nouns never actually assign θ-roles such as agent or theme in Mohawk—a fact that is explained by the MVC.

6.3 Conclusion

This chapter has explored the internal syntax of free-standing NPs in the polysynthetic languages. We have seen that a strengthened version of the MVC has a cluster of related implications in this domain. First and foremost is that the R role of the head noun must be assigned to an argument position so that that position can trigger agreement, thereby satisfying the MVC. This accounts for the fact that nouns in most polysynthetic languages have an agreement morpheme that indicates the morphosyntactic features of the referent of the noun. The other special properties of NPs are consequences of this one. Thus, polysynthetic languages cannot have semantically significant determiners because the θ-role that a determiner would modify has already been assigned to another position. This, in turn, broadens the possibilities for dislocation and discontinuous constituents, contributing to the nonconfigurationality of these languages, as discussed in previous chapters. Finally, nouns in polysynthetic languages cannot, in general, have arguments other than R, because expressing the R argument morphologically already exhausts the resources available for satisfying the MVC within an NP. Some argument-taking nouns the polysynthetic languages do very well without, such as derived nominals. Possessor arguments are too important to communication to do without entirely, however, so microparameters typically make available a way of expressing possession within the boundary conditions set by the MVC.

Notes

1. Michelson (1991c) points out certain subregularities: manmade objects have a tendency to have A-class prefixes, whereas naturally occurring objects tend to be O-class. Body parts are almost exclusively O-class. Even if this were fully systematic (which I believe it is not), it would not motivate a difference in syntactic structure, however. Chafe (1970:67) emphasizes the idiosyncratic aspect of prefix choice in the related language Onondaga.

2. In (4), the specifier position is filled with pro, a phonologically null pronoun. This assumption may have to be modified somewhat to account for the fact that NPs in Mohawk can be understood as semantically indefinite as well as definite; however, pro is usually only definite. Apparently, then, the specifier position can also contain a null indefinite element similar to *one*.

A potential problem for this account is that the null argument that receives the R θ-role cannot license an adjoined NP double. Thus, sentences like (i) are not possible in Mohawk.

(i)   *[$_{NPk}$[$_{NPi}$ o'nerohkwa'] pro$_i$ ka-núhs-a'] [$_{IP}$ pro ke-núhwe'-s pro$_k$].
            box   NsS-house-NSF   1sS-like-hab
      'I like the box-house, I like the house that is (made of) a box.'

In this respect, the R argument differs from most others in Mohawk. More precisely, the structure marked NP$_k$ is allowed as a nominal clause meaning 'The box is a house' (see (30)), but not as the argument of some other predicate. Intuitively, this is because the R element has the special role of defining the reference of the argument as a whole; thus i = k in sentences like (i), creating a kind of referential circularity similar to that ruled out by the i-within-i condition of Chomsky 1981. However, it is not clear to me exactly how this intuition can be insightfully built into the analysis.

3. There is some evidence, however, that the default value of this feature in nouns is +O, whereas it is −O in verbs. Thus, body parts virtually all take *o*, not *ka* (Michelson 1991c). Since these are very rarely used without their possessor, any marked feature would be difficult to learn and we expect to see only the default value. I will not speculate as to why the default value of this feature should differ in nouns and verbs.

4. This option is only attested with a few nouns in Mohawk: thus one finds *ke-ksá-'a'* 'I am a child' but not **wak-ahkwári* 'I am a bear'. I do not know why Mohawk should be more restrictive than Nahuatl in this respect.

5. When used predicatively, nouns take a series of suffixes that agree with their subject. These same suffixes are used on verbs in the so-called past II and present II forms (Bogoras 1922). For example:

(i)   ilila-*muri*.   (Bogoras 1922:759)
      island.dweller-1pS
      'we are islanders'

(ii) ge-wiri-*muri*   (Comrie 1979:231)
      PASTII-descend-1pS
      'we have descended'

(iii) nə-wiri-*muri*.   (Comrie 1979:231)
      PRESII-descend-1pS
      'We are descending.'

This may constitute further evidence for my claim. However, Bogoras claims that the prefixes in (ii) and (iii) truly nominalize the verbs; thus, he glosses examples like (ii) as something like 'we are the descended ones' and (iii) as something like 'we are the descending ones'. If he is correct, then the parallelism is less significant. Also, I do not know if forms like (i) can be used referentially in Chukchee to give something like 'we, the islanders, must leave early', as they can in Nahuatl and Ngandi.

Notice that the agreement morphemes on Ns are suffixes in Chukchee, whereas they are prefixes in most of the other polysynthetic languages. See section 1.6 for discussion of some of the complications of affix order in Chukchee.

6. However, animate nouns retain their number/agreement suffixes when they appear as the object of a postposition, and one might expect inanimate nouns to do the same. I leave this difference between the two unexplained.

7. Deering and Delisle (1976) and Woodbury (1975) also call *ne* a "definitizer," but acknowledge that it often has no equivalent in English.

8. However, the noun class prefixes in some Gunwinjguan languages (Ngalakan, Ngandi, and Nunggubuyu) alternate; there is a long form, a short form, and a null form. What governs these alternations is not particularly clear. By far the most extensive discussion of this phenomenon is by Heath (1984:163–173). He identifies several factors that influence the form of the prefix in Nunggubuyu, one of which is definiteness/givenness vs. focus/foregrounding. However, this is presented only as a correlation, not a rule of the grammar. Moreover, many other factors also influence prefix choice, including whether the NP is in oblique or unmarked Case, whether it is in the context of a negative, and what the aspect of the clause is. Thus, these noun class prefixes do not act like determiners in any straightforward sense. However, until one has a better understanding of their syntax and semantics, the possibility that they are a kind of determiner cannot be ruled out with full confidence.

9. For completeness, I mention that Wichita has a rather strange morpheme *re:R* that Rood (1976:6, 120–122) glosses as 'the'. What is odd about this morpheme is that it generally appears not on the noun itself but rather inside the V complex or inside a relative clause with the dummy verb 'be' in construction with the noun. I do not understand what this element is, but clearly it is not a standard determiner in the syntax.

10. Principle (21) is not needed to achieve this result if one adopts Higginbotham's (1985) view that determiners discharge the R role of the noun they are associated with by entering into a relationship of θ-role binding. Specifically, it follows from Higginbotham's extension of the Theta Criterion so that the same R role cannot be discharged by both θ-role assignment and θ-role binding. This, then, is a legitimate alternative to the view taken in the text. However, Higginbotham's analysis fits into the Russellian tradition in which determiners are a type of quantifier; this tradition is questioned by Heim (1982), who I have followed here. Higginbotham's assumptions also do not provide a good explanation of how the Theta Criterion is satisfied in noun incorporation structures, where there is no determiner (see section 7.1).

This section can usefully be compared with Bittner and Hale to appear, where the fact that there is no class of determiners in Warlpiri is discussed, along with some of its semantic consequences.

11. The claim that alienable possessors are arguments of the head noun is controversial, in part because virtually any noun can be possessed and in part because the notion "possessor" includes a wide range of semantic roles (Higginbotham 1983). However, it is well known that possessors usually count as A-position subjects for purposes of Binding Theory (see, e.g., Chomsky 1981 and Giorgi and Longobardi 1991:esp. 210, fn. 31). This suggests that possessors are, in fact, treated as (optional) arguments by natural language.

Inalienable possession (e.g., body part possession) is often treated rather differently from alienable possession in the polysynthetic languages. For example, the noun representing the body part and the noun representing the whole may be in apposition to each other, as in the Australian languages. See also section 8.1 for an example of a very common construction involving incorporation of the body part. I cannot go into this complex topic here.

12. If the possessed noun is the theme of the clause, both Wichita and Southern Tiwa prefer to express its understood possessor with a benefactive applicative construction (Rood 1976, Frantz 1993a). This is a favored option in other languages as well (see, e.g., Evans 1991:132 on Mayali). This construction is discussed in sections 8.1 and 9.3.

13. Compare the Relational Grammar analysis of Southern Tiwa in Rosen 1990, where the R argument of an N is its initial 2 (direct object) and the possessor argument is its initial 3 (indirect object).

14. The discontinuous constituent here is not one of the types analyzed in detail in chapter 4. However, it was mentioned there that most languages allow a postverbal adjective or relative clause to be construed with a preverbal NP in a way that is reminiscent of relative clause extraposition in English. I assume that (38) is an example of this type.

15. See also Heath 1984:214–216 for a similar range of examples with *yinjung* in Nunggubuyu.

16. A very similar pair involving the expression 'self's antlers' can be found in Comrie 1981:274. Compare also Spencer's (1993:57–61) discussion of nominal modifiers in general: the oblique forms have a type of incorporation, while absolutive Case nominals have an independent modifier with one of the *in* family of suffixes. The fact that possessors can "incorporate" into the noun may itself be evidence that they are modifiers rather than true NP possessors: possessors cannot generally incorporate into a noun as mentioned above, while N and A can be combined together, as shown in section 8.4.

The claim in the text is probably slightly too strong, because *in* forms can apparently modify ergative Case nominals; constructed examples are found in Kozinsky et al. 1988:682 and Polinskaja and Nedjalkov 1987:254. Perhaps *in* forms are not absolutive, but rather a neutralized structural Case form. This would imply that they can be associated with absolutive or ergative nominals, but not with nominals in an oblique Case. In fact, this fits rather well with the view that ergative Case is not a structural Case in Chukchee, as argued in section 3.3.3.

17. This account is, however, incompatible with my tentative claim that the meaningless noun suffixes such as *a'* in (47) are a kind of determiner; if so, then they should not show up after the noun is incorporated. Perhaps the correct analysis of these suffixes is one in which they are added in the PF derivation to any word that terminates in a noun root. This alternative is compatible with the fact that the suffixes have no interpretation at LF.

18. A closed class of kinship terms do take transitive prefixes. Typical examples are:

(i)   a.   rake-'ní-ha
        MsS/1sO-father-??
        'my father'

      b.   ri-yʌ́'-a
        1sS/MsO-child-??
        'my son'

There is ample reason to think that these must be treated somewhat differently from other possessors in Mohawk, however. They are not consistent with the otherwise valid correlation between agreement and grammatical role. In (ia), the possessor is realized as O-class agreement and the R argument is realized as A-class agreement, while the reverse is found in (ib). The grammatical functions are the same in the two examples, but the agreement prefixes are not. Agreement on kinship terms follows a simple rule of a different type: the older member of the relationship triggers A-agreement and the younger triggers O-agreement, regardless of which is the referent (Bonvillain 1973:151–162, Deering and Delisle 1976:40).

The kinship terms have another peculiar property: all of them end in *ha* or *'a*. There is evidence from locative morphology that this is actually a distinct morpheme (Deering and Delisle 1976:94, 104). The presence of transitive prefixes on (i) can then be explained if we analyze *ha* as a three-place quasiverb that means something like 'X is dominantly related to Y as a Z'. The noun root receives the Z role of the quasi-verb, thereby specifying the exact relationship involved. This noun incorporates into the quasi-verb, which then agrees with its other two arguments in the normal way. Thus, the correct literal gloss of (ia) would actually be 'he is related to me as father'. The difference between the two possession constructions, then, is simply that they involve quasiverbs (*ha* and Ø 'belong to') with somewhat different lexical properties.

19. Interesting proposals have been made by Lebeaux (1989) and Chomsky (1992). However, both rely heavily on the idea that movement is involved in the relevant constructions. For Lebeaux, Condition C applies before the *wh*-phrase is moved out of the c-command domain of the subject; for Chomsky, movement leaves behind a "layered trace" containing a copy of the name within the c-command domain of the subject. If Cinque (1990) and the present work are correct in claiming that dislocation constructions are not formed by movement, then a more abstract approach to these asymmetries is necessary, perhaps one involving chain binding in Barss' (1986) sense.

20. It is important to realize that this analysis does not undercut the argument that nominals in Mohawk are in adjoined positions. The reason is that relative clauses adjoined to NPs in argument position do show Condition C effects. Thus, (i) contrasts with (51b) (see references cited above):

(i) *He$_i$ later denied the claim that John$_i$ made.

Therefore, possessive expressions would not escape Condition C effects in Mohawk and Southern Tiwa unless they were adjoined to the matrix clause in addition to having a relative clause–like internal structure.

21. Of course, this more familiar fact also needs to be reconciled with the UTAH. One possible approach would be to use a prototype theory of thematic roles like that outlined by Dowty (1991). On this view, the participants in an event or situation are categorized as agents, patients, or (extending Dowty's idea slightly) paths depending on the kinds of semantic entailments they have. A possessor has both agent-like entailments and path-like entailments: it is like an agent in that it is typically sentient and has some control over the state; it is like a path in that it defines in some abstract sense where the theme may be found. If its similarity to agents and paths is roughly equal, then either way of categorizing it will be legitimate in Dowty's system. If it is categorized as an agent, it is projected as the specifier of a higher V; if it is categorized as a path, it is projected as an oblique complement of the base V, in accordance with my version of the UTAH. Perhaps this idea can also be extended to the NP domain to explain why possessors are treated like subjects in some languages (such as English), but as dative-like complements in others.

22. By "extra" Case, I mean a second Case that is not attributable to Burzio's Generalization. This idea was inspired by a remark made by Kenneth Hale (personal communication).

23. See Ritter 1991 and related work on functional categories in the nominal systems for relevant discussion. Ritter argues that Num(ber) is a functional head distinct from Det; however, one would normally expect Num to be below Det in the phrase structure. I leave these issues open here.

24. The Gunwinjguan languages Ngalakan, Rembarrnga, and Ngandi also have a special set of affixes that attaches to nouns to indicate the possessor. An example from Ngalakan is given in (i) (Merlan 1983:168).

(i) Ju-goʔje jugu-bolo-ʔgon gajaʔ-*ngoji* jeki Ø-yininj.
     Fs-that Fs-woman-DAT dog-FsP   first 3sS-do/PAST/PERF
     'The old woman's dog did like that at first.'

However, these affixes differ from possessive agreement in Nahuatl in that they are optional. They are also suffixes, whereas the vast majority of true agreement morphemes in the polysynthetic languages are prefixes (section 1.6). Thus, I am inclined to analyze them as independent appositional constituents in the syntax that are encliticized to the host noun at PF. They might, however, be the first step in a diachronic movement toward creating a favored head-marking pattern for possession within this language family (see Evans 1991 for remarks about Mayali possession along these lines).

25. In chapter 10, I argue that the nonfinite verb forms in Chukchee are actually nominalizations as well; part of the evidence for this claim is the very fact that the forms in question do not (typically) take arguments.

26. The theme-like interpretation can exist when the possessor is inanimate, perhaps because there is no competition from an agent-like reading. Thus, the first line of KO:124 has an example of *ao-kára'* 'its story', where 'it' refers to a famous church bell; this is clearly the story *about* that bell. However, this is presumably no more than a further illustration of the vagueness of the possession relationship, not an illustration of the ability of *okára* to assign a theme role.

7

Noun Incorporation

Chapters 5 and 6 focused on agreement phenomena as a way of satisfying the Polysynthesis Parameter and as a window on clause-internal structure. In this chapter and the next, I turn to the second major way of satisfying the Polysynthesis Parameter: incorporation. In particular, this chapter concentrates on the basic properties of the incorporation relation in the simplest case, that of ordinary noun incorporation. Chapter 8 then extends the results to more complicated cases in which the incorporated element has a nontrivial argument structure of its own.

Noun incorporation (NI) is a very salient property of the Northern Iroquoian languages, noticed by all observers. From a cross-linguistic perspective, NI is unusually frequent and productive in these languages, as noted by Boas (1911) and Sapir (1911). Thus, alternations like (1) are quite common in Mohawk.

(1)   a. Wa'-k-hnínu-'   ne ka-nákt-a'.
            FACT-1sS-buy-PUNC NE NsS-bed-NSF
            'I bought the/a bed.'

      b. Wa'-ke-nakt-a-hnínu-'.
            FACT-1sS-bed-Ø-buy-PUNC
            'I bought the/a bed.'

Many other examples are found throughout this book. Similar alternations occur in the other polysynthetic languages; indeed, this was the criterial feature that was used to identify languages as polysynthetic in the first place.

Noun incorporation has been a relatively well-studied topic, starting with the exchange between Kroeber (1909) and Sapir (1911). Part of the interest in the topic no doubt stems from the desire to come to grips with its "exotic" nature. In the Iroquoian literature alone, NI is a special focus of Postal 1979, Woodbury 1975, Mithun 1984a, and Hopkins 1988, in addition to the larger or smaller discussions found in every grammar of these languages. The literature on other language families is similar: see Allen et al. 1984 for Tanoan, Merlan 1976 for Nahuatl, McKay 1975 for Rembarrnga, Heath 1984:463–478 for Nunggubuyu, Evans to appear b for Mayali, and Spencer 1993 for Chukchee. Recently, there has also been a theoretically oriented discussion of whether NI is fundamentally a syntactic phenomenon or a morphological one, which recalls in some respects the original Kroeber/Sapir interchange. Thus, Sadock (1980, 1985, 1986) and Baker (1988a, 1988b) have defended the idea that NI has an integral syntactic component, while Mithun (1984a, 1986a), Di Sciullo and Williams (1987), and Rosen (1989b) have argued that it is simply a slightly different kind of lexical compounding. At stake in this controversy is the Lexicalist Hypothesis, and with it the whole issue of how morphology and syntax should be related in a general theory of grammar.

In the context of this book, it is natural to ask how the Polysynthesis Parameter might contribute to an understanding of NI. In fact, it makes three contributions. First, it sheds some light on the question of why NI exists in some languages and not in others. This question has not been discussed much in the previous literature. Second, since the Polysynthesis Parameter treats incorporated roots on a par with agreement morphemes, it should help to explain certain issues concerning the interaction of NI and agreement, briefly touched on in chapter 1. Third, and most importantly, the insight that it gives into the syntax of Mohawk makes it possible to formulate some sophisticated and convincing arguments that distinguish the syntactic approach to NI from the purely lexical one. In investigating these questions, my point of departure will be the theory of NI as syntactic head movement presented in Baker 1988a and briefly reviewed in chapter 1 of the present volume. However, some significant problems arise when one tries to use my analysis together with the current assumptions about phrase structure, defended in chapter 5, and these problems will need to be resolved. These, then, are the themes to be explored in this chapter.

7.1. The Cross-linguistic Distribution of NI

7.1.1 Why Some Languages Cannot Have NI

Let us begin with the most general issue: Why do some languages allow NI, whereas others do not? Within a P&P framework, this is a nontrivial matter, since the theory does not allow for language-specific rules or constructions. In Baker 1988a, I argued that the structure of a sentence like (1b) is approximately (2), where the head of the object noun phrase moves in the syntax to adjoin to the verb that governs it. (Notice that I return to old-fashioned clause structures here for consistency with the earlier work; newer phrase structures are reintroduced in section 7.3.) The question that arises is, Why can't exactly the same movement take place in English, deriving a sentence like **I bed-bought yesterday*? Such sentences are perfectly understandable, but clearly deviant. Why should this be?

We cannot attribute this to a difference in the basic phrase structure of Mohawk and English. On the contrary, scattered throughout this book are various scraps of evidence that the two are very much alike, inasmuch as the object forms a constituent with the verb and is asymmetrically c-commanded by the subject.[1] Thus, the difference must be attributed to the movement process itself. However, (2) is taken to be simply an instance of Move α, the general transformation schema that says little more than "move anything anywhere." Obviously, Move α exists in English. Nor can we maintain that Move α applies only to XP level categories in English;

(2)

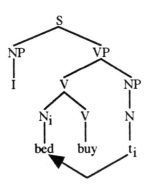

auxiliary verbs, for example, are analyzed as moving into Infl positions. From there, such verbs can move on to C in matrix interrogatives (Pollock 1989, Chomsky 1991). We cannot even stipulate that Move α does not apply to N^0, because there is evidence that Ns raise into higher functional category projections such Det and Num(ber) to derive Noun–Subject–Object orders in, for example, Hebrew and the Scandinavian languages. However, these languages do not have NI, even though they have N movement. Thus, it seems that we must explicitly stipulate both the target and the landing site of the missing movement, stating in the grammar of English, Swedish, and Hebrew that N cannot move so as to adjoin to a V. This is the equivalent of saying that these languages do not allow noun incorporation, and nothing more. It clearly violates the theoretical goal of eliminating construction-specific rules from the grammar. Thus, Baker 1988a had no good way of ruling out NI in English, a significant theoretical embarrassment.[2]

Certain changes of perspective in recent theory allow us to make progress on this question. Chomsky 1992 and related writings reverse the way the question is formulated. Rather than viewing Move α as fundamentally optional, Chomsky considers it to be a "last-resort" mechanism that applies only to save a sentence from violating conditions of a certain kind. The paradigm example is the passive construction, in which the direct object must move in order to be licensed by Case features on an appropriate head; without this pressure, NP movement is impossible. From this perspective, the question of why the movement in (2) does not happen in English is trivial: the movement does not happen because it does not need to, the structure being well formed without it. Conceptually, this is attractive: many languages of a wide variety of types are like English in not having productive noun incorporation, suggesting that this is, indeed, the unmarked situation.

The question now becomes, What is wrong with a base structure like (2) in Mohawk, such that movement is required to fix it? This is immediately answered by the Polysynthesis Parameter. Without movement, (2) violates the Morphological Visibility Conditin, because the object receives a θ-role from the verb but is not coindexed with any morpheme on the verb. This problem cannot be fixed by generating object agreement features somewhere in the verbal complex, because those features would absorb the verb's Case-assigning features. The object NP, then, passes the MVC but violates the Case Filter. Thus, the structure in (2) can only lead to a well-formed structure if N^0-movement happens, thereby placing a morpheme in the verb that is coindexed with the direct object. Movement is indeed triggered as a "last resort." The parallelism with NP movement in English passives is almost perfect: NP in English moves to a position where it can get Case in order to become visible for θ-role assignment at LF (the standard Visibility Condition); in the same way, N° in Mohawk moves to a position where it is in the verb complex in order to make the NP it heads visible for θ-role assignment at LF (the Morphological Visibility Condition). Since English is not subject to the MVC, NI is not forced; therefore, it is impossible.

This explanation of why NI is allowed in some languages but not others depends crucially on the assumption that NI is obligatory in a structure like (2) in Mohawk. At first glance, this seems to be incorrect: (1) shows that NI in Mohawk is in some sense optional. However, chapter 2 presented excellent evidence that *kanákta'* 'bed' in (1a) is *not* generated in the direct object position; rather, it is adjoined to IP. The true syntactic object of the verb in this case is an empty category: either pro (if the object is animate) or a null "cognate object" noun root. If it is a pro, then it may be coindexed with agreement without violating Case theory; if it is a null N root, then incorporation takes place after all. In either case, the basic structure of (1a) is quite different from that of (1b), as shown in (3).

(3)

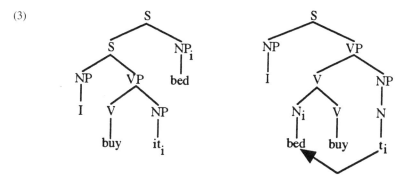

Thus, it is compatible with what we know about Mohawk to claim that incorporation is required whenever a lexical N is generated in argument position. Similar facts hold in other polysynthetic languages, where NI looks optional but is, in fact, obligatory when a certain type of structure is generated.

This analysis makes the clear prediction that productive noun incorporation will not be found in languages of all types. Rather, it will be found only if it is forced by some other property of the language in question, such as the MVC. But, as pointed out in chapter 1, languages in which the MVC holds can never get by with only noun incorporation; rather they must have rich subject and object agreement paradigms as well. The reason is that NI is not sufficiently flexible to allow a full range of arguments to be morphologically expressed: it only applies to third person (typically inanimate) themes, for reasons I will return to. Thus, languages with productive NI must be of the head-marking type. Moreover, if it is a general fact that agreement in such languages always absorbs Case, languages with productive NI will also be nonconfigurational, in the sense that their NPs are adjoined to the clause and hence freely ordered with respect to one another. In chapter 1, I claimed that this prediction is correct: at least Iroquoian, Tanoan, Nahuatl, Wichita, Gunwinjguan, Chukchee, and Ainu all have these properties.[3] The typological homogeneity of incorporating languages stands in sharp contrast to the diversity of languages that do not allow productive NI. These latter languages can be head initial or head final in word order, head marking or dependent marking in morphological type, and may have strict word order or free word order. This is a positive empirical result for our theory: absence of NI is the unmarked case, and the presence of productive NI has to be triggered by a specific parametric property.[4]

7.1.2 How NI Satisfies the MVC

Before I can boast about the advantages of this approach, however, I must clarify the claim that NI satisfies the MVC. In particular, one must consider not only how this principle is satisfied with respect to the theme argument of the verb—which is rather straightforward—but also how it applies to the R argument of the incorporated noun. This is less straightforward.

In section 6.1, I showed that the R argument of a noun is subject to the MVC in essentially the same way that the arguments of verbs are. This implied that the R role must be assigned to an NP position so that agreement can be triggered. However, the discussion in chapter 6 was implicitly concerned only with NPs in adjunct positions, since that is where independent, overt NPs occur in a polysynthetic language (chapter 2). Suppose that the same kind of structure were generated in the object position of a suitable verb as a prelude to incorporation. Then, the structure of the VP of, say, (4b) would be something like (5), where a pro in the specifier of NP has been left behind by N movement.

(4)   a. Shako-núhwe'-s   ne owirá'a.
          MsS/3pO-like-HAB NE baby
          'He likes them (babies).'

      b. Ra-wir-a-núhwe'-s.
          MsS-baby-Ø-like-HAB
          'He likes babies.'

(5)

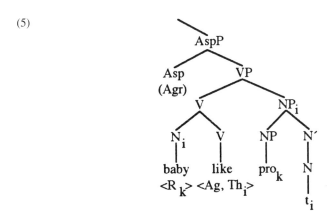

The substructure in (5) is thematically complete in the sense that every θ-role is assigned to an appropriate NP. Moreover, the theme NP is visible for θ-role assignment by virtue of its head being incorporated. However, the pro in the specifier of NP is not visible for θ-role assignment in this structure. Normally, pro would be licensed by agreement features on some functional head, but both empirical evidence and theoretical considerations suggest that this is not possible in a configuration like (5). The empirical evidence is simply that there is no agreement with this pro in (4b). This pro would be third person animate plural, as is the object pro in (4a). However, adding the appropriate agreement to the verb is not only unnecessary, but impossible in Mohawk[5]:

(6) *Shako-wir-a-núhwe'-s.
     MsS/3pO-baby-Ø-like-HAB
     'He likes babies.'

Apparently, then, the object agreement factor adjoined to Asp in (5) cannot be coindexed with the pro specifier of NP. Indeed, this follows from the Condition on Agreement Relations, introduced in chapter 5. According to this condition, an agreement factor can only be coindexed with a given argument if that argument is contained in the θ-grid of the head that the agreement factor is adjoined to. This is not the case in (5); pro is not coindexed directly with any position in the θ-grid of 'like', the (head of the) head that incorporates into Asp.

One might think that the structure in (5) would fare better if a DetP structure were generated above the theme NP. The head of this DetP could then host an agreement node coindexed with the pro; indeed, this is how R arguments were morphologically expressed in chapter 6. However, this cure proves to be worse than the disease: if a DetP is generated, then it no longer is possible to incorporate the noun into the verb at all. There are two possibilities to consider. Suppose first that the N head skipped over the Det head and adjoined directly to V. This movement path violates a very deep constraint on head movement, often called the Head Movement Constraint, following Travis (1984).[6]

(7) *The Head Movement Constraint* (HMC)
     An X^0 category Y can only adjoin to the head of the phrase that immediately dominates the maximal projection of Y.

In Baker 1988a, I derived this constraint from the Empty Category Principle of Chomsky 1981; in more recent works, it is derived from a Relativized Minimality Condition (Rizzi 1990) or a still more general Economy Condition (Chomsky 1992); I return to these issues below. The other possibility is for the N to adjoin first to Det, followed by movement of the N–Det combination to V. This movement path is consistent with the HMC; however, it violates another very general condition on head movement, which for convenience can be stated as follows:

(8) *The Proper Head Movement Generalization* (PHMG)
     A lexical category cannot move into a functional category and then back into a lexical category.

This statement is inspired by Li's (1990) study of verb incorporation (see also Baker and Hale 1990). Although the PHMG is presumably not a primitive principle of grammar, its nature remains rather unclear. Li relates it to the ban on improper NP movement, which states that one cannot move an NP from an A-position to an A-bar-position and back to an A-position again. However, this is achieved by stipulating that Binding Theory applies to verbal traces—a notion that

I find conceptually problematic. The Baker and Hale approach rested on an empirical assumption that I now believe to be mistaken (see note 6). A simpler approach with some empirical advantages is to simply stipulate that inflectional morphology cannot be inside derivational morphology, as a kind of filter at PF. This subsumes (8) as long as the morphology picked up from functional nodes counts as inflectional and that picked up from lexical nodes counts as derivational. Although I feel uneasy about giving this generalization the status of a basic principle of grammar, I must admit that it has much independent support, and it is hard to find anything else that works as well. Whatever its nature, the truth of (8) is easy to observe. If movement from N to Det to V were possible in Mohawk, then one would expect nouns to be incorporated along with their inflectional noun suffix *a'* or *e'*; however, this is quite impossible:

(9)   *Wa'-k-[nakt-a']-úni-'.
         FACT-1sS-bed-NSF-make-PUNC
         'I made the/a bed.'

(See chapter 8 for other examples of the PHMG, as well as one exception.) I conclude that NI is only possible if no DetP is generated above the NP. This, in turn, means that there is no host for agreement in a position where the agreement would have access to the R role of the head noun. Recall also from chapter 6 that a noun bearing the R argument cannot incorporate into the θ-marking noun. Therefore, there is no way for the R argument to satisfy the MVC, and structures like (5) are ruled out.

To see how these difficulties can be avoided, it is necessary to consider how the R role of a noun is discharged in a simple English example like (10).

(10)   I petted the dog.

This issue is discussed in Williams 1989. Williams claims that the relationship of θ-role assignment between a verb and an NP is precisely a matter of coindexing the R argument of that NP with the theme argument of the verb. From this it follows that θ-role assignment between V and NP is possible only if the NP has exactly one undischarged argument. Thus, the VP of (10) has roughly the structure in (11).

(11)

In other words, the θ-role assignment relation discharges one argument of the verb and one argument of the noun. Semantically, the coindexing means that the two argument slots are filled with instances of the same variable, giving an interpretation something like ((I pet x) and (dog x)). As in Heim 1982, the definite determiner *the* is not part of the thematic structure of the clause, but rather gives information about how the free variable associated with its NP complement is interpreted semantically.[7]

Suppose, then, that we apply this theory of θ-role assignment to NI structures in Mohawk. This means that the internal structure of NPs in argument position must be rather different from that of the adjoined NPs analyzed in chapter 6. In particular, when an NP is generated in an argument position, its head noun must not assign the R role to the specifier of NP. Rather, that argument is discharged by being coindexed with the theme position in the θ-grid of the verb. This leads to the partial representation in (12).

(12)

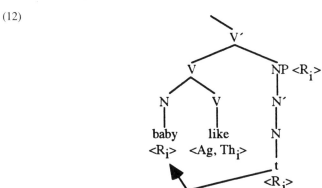

Now the question of how the specifier of NP is licensed does not arise. Is the MVC satisfied? In section 6.1.1, I proposed a strengthened version of this principle, which checks θ-role-to-morpheme relationships rather than argument phrase-to-morpheme relationships as originally proposed. This was stated as follows:

(13)   *Morphological Visibility Condition* (revised)
         Every θ-role associated with a head Y must be coindexed with a distinct morpheme in the word containing Y.

This formulation differs from the original only in its treatment of θ-roles that are not assigned to an argument position, such as R. Now it is easy to see that (13) is satisfied in the structure in (12). In particular, the noun 'baby' has a θ-role R; this is coindexed with the distinct morpheme 'like' via θ-role assignment. Conversely, the verb 'like' has a theme θ-role; this is coindexed with the distinct morpheme 'baby', again through θ-role assignment. Each morpheme satisfies the needs of the other in a kind of symbiotic relationship. Once the verb assigns its external argument to a pro subject and combines with the corresponding agreement in Infl (not shown here), the structure is fully grammatical. This, then, is the account of how NI satisfies the MVC with respect to both the noun and the verb.

7.2 The Semantics of NI

One result of the previous section was that NI in the polysynthetic languages is incompatible with the presence of any kind of determiner in the structure. This raises the question of how NI constructions are interpreted semantically. There has been a reasonable amount of discussion of this topic, much of it trying to discover differences in the interpretation of INs vs. independent NPs (e.g., Woodbury 1975, Mithun 1984a). Indeed, Bittner (1994) shows quite convincingly that there are such differences in Greenlandic Eskimo.

In contrast, the current theory predicts no such differences in interpretation in polysynthetic languages. In particular, the semantics of an NI structure in Mohawk should be essentially identical to those of an ordinary [$_{VP}$ V NP] construction in Williams' (1989) framework. He makes it clear (1989:426) that these structures are to be interpreted as having the same free variable fill both the R position of the N's θ-grid and the theme position of the V's θ-grid. Thus, a simple NI construction like (1b) (repeated here as (14a)) should have the partial semantic interpretation in (14b).

(14) a. Wa'-ke-nakt-a-hnínu-'.
          FACT-1sS-bed-Ø-buy-PUNC
          'I bought the/a bed.'

      b. bed (x) and buy (I, x)

Furthermore, since there is no possibility of a determiner in such a construction, one cannot mark the IN as being definite or indefinite. The simplest assumption, then, is that INs are ambiguous between indefinite and definite interpretations, just as determinerless NPs are in other languages (Heim 1982).

In fact, this describes the interpretation of incorporated noun roots in Mohawk quite accurately. Simple incorporations out of context are judged to have either a definite or an indefinite interpretation; thus, either determiner in the gloss of (1b) is considered an appropriate translation. This ambiguity becomes clearer when clauses with incorporated nouns are put in the kinds of environments that distinguish definite from indefinite NPs in English. For example, indefinite NPs are used to introduce new referents into the discourse, whereas definite NPs are used to refer to things already present in the speech situation (Heim 1982). Now, (15) is a natural Mohawk interchange, where two people have been working in the kitchen preparing for a large family gathering and one returns after a trip to the living room.

(15) A: Ónʌ akwéku kʌ́tho rún-e-s,   tánu Uwári
          now all   here MpS-come-HAB and Mary

          t-a-ye-na'ts-ʌ́haw-e'.
          CIS-FACT-FsS-pot-bring-PUNC
          'Everyone is here now, and Mary brought a pot.'

      B: Yo-yáner-e',   ne Á-k-atst-e'   ʌ-k-sahét-a-riht-e'.
          NsS-good-STAT NE FUT-1sS-use-PUNC FUT-1sS-bean-Ø-cook-PUNC
          'Good, I'll use it to cook the beans.'

The IN in A's utterance is indefinite, and has the effect of introducing a new referent into the discourse; B's utterance then refers to this element with an ordinary pronominal. (The IN in B's utterance is presumably definite, referring to a set of beans previously discussed or visibly present, but this was not the focus of investigation in this sentence.) A similar minitext is given in (16).

(16)   ThetÁre' wa'-ke-nakt-a-hnínu-'.   Í-k-ehr-e'   Uwári
        yesterday FACT-1sS-bed-Ø-buy-PUNC Ø-1sS-think-IMPF Mary

        Λ-ye-núhwe'-ne'.
        FUT-FsS-like-PUNC
        'I bought a bed yesterday. I think Mary will like it (the bed).'

On the other hand, (17) is a natural interchange in the context of someone walking into a craft shop and addressing the clerk.

(17)   A: K-ather-ísak-s.
           1sS-basket-seek-HAB
           'I am looking for a basket.'

        B: ThetÁre   Áska w-ather-a-yΛ-tah-kwe'   nek tsi Wíshe
           yesterday one NsS-basket-Ø-lie-HAB-PAST but   Michael

           í-k-ehr-e'   wa-ha-[a]ther-a-hnínu-'.
           1sS-think-IMPF FACT-MsS-basketØ-buy-PUNC
           'There was a basket (here) yesterday, but I think Michael (basket-)bought it.'

Each of the three verbs in this exchange contains the incorporated N root *ather* 'basket'. In A's original statement (in this context), this is clearly interpreted as indefinite and nonspecific. The IN in the first clause of B's response is also indefinite; however, the IN in the second clause of B's response is clearly definite—it refers to the same basket introduced in the previous clause. Indeed, B could even respond to A's inquiry as follows:

(18)   Yá'yak níku wak-ather-íhs-u,   tánu Wíshe   akwéku
        six   part 1sO-basket-finish-STAT and Michael all

        wa-ha-[a]ther-a-hnínu-'.
        FACT-MsS-basket-Ø-buy-PUNC
        'I made six baskets, but Michael bought them all.'

Again the IN in the first clause is indefinite and is modified by a weak numerical quantifier; the IN in the second clause, on the other hand, is definite and modified by a strong quantifier with a partitive interpretation. Properties of the context are crucial here. Example (17a) could also be uttered as a husband's response to a wife's inquiry as to why he is rummaging around in the cupboard, when both know that they own only one basket, which they use to serve bread in; in these circumstances, the IN is understood as definite. On the other hand, if the second clause of (18) were uttered at the beginning of a conversation after something like 'guess what!', the IN would probably be understood as indefinite. Thus, INs can be interpreted as either definite or indefinite, new or old information, depending on the context.[8]

Another difference between definite and indefinite NPs is brought out by quantificational adverbs and other sentential operators. Such elements act like they quantify over indefinites, but not over definites (Heim 1982). Again, INs in Mohawk are ambiguous between definite and indefinite readings in the context of these operators. One set of examples illustrating this is (19).

(19) a. NónΛ Λ-ke-'sere-ht-a-hnínu-'   Sak tyótku
          when FUT-1sS-car-NOM-Ø-buy-PUNC Sak always
          te-ha-hrí-ht-ha'.
          DUP-MsS-break-CAUS-HAB
          'Whenever I buy a car, Sak always wrecks it.'

      b. NónΛ Λ-ke-'sere-ht-óhare-'   Sak tyótku
          when FUT-1sS-car-NOM-wash-PUNC Sak always

          te-s-ha-'tsú-st-ha'.
          DUP-ITER-MsS-dirty-CAUS-HAB
          'Whenever I wash the car, Sak gets it dirty again.'

These examples are structurally parallel; both have an IN in the adjunct clause that restricts an adverb of quantification. However, based on real world knowledge, the IN in (19a) is understood as indefinite; it thus picks up universal quantificational force from the adverb *tyótku* 'always'. The resulting interpretation is essentially the same as "donkey-anaphora" sentences in English: For all x such that (car (x) & I buy (x)) (Sak wrecks (x)). In contrast, real world knowledge (the fact that one generally buys a given car only once but one washes it many times) guides the structurally parallel (19b) toward an interpretation in which the IN 'car' is definite. This makes it immune to the influence of the adverb of quantification, and it is understood that the same car is involved in each instance of washing and getting dirty. Another illustrative pair is given in (20).

(20) a. Te-wak-atΛhutsóni a-ke-'sere-ht-a-hnínu-'.   #S-atkátho-s
          DUP-1sO-want/STAT OPT-1sS-car-NOM-Ø-buy-PUNC 2sS-see-HAB

          kΛ nónΛ kΛtho t-Á-s-ta'-ne'?
          Q when here DUP-FUT-2sS-stand-PUNC
          'I want to buy a car. Can you see it from here?'

      b. Te-wak-atΛhutsóni a-k-ate-'sere-ht-a-hnínu-'.
          DUP-1sO-want/STAT OPT-1sS-SRFL-car-NOM-Ø-buy-PUNC

          A-hs-atútat-e'   kΛ a-hse-nóhare-'?
          OPT-2sS-be.willing-PUNC Q OPT-2sS-wash-PUNC
          'I want to sell the car. Would you be willing to wash it?'

Again, the sentences are structurally similar, but real world knowledge suggests an indefinite interpretation for the IN 'car' in (20a) and a definite one in (20b). This difference is brought out by discourse anaphora. The variable corresponding to the IN is bound by the operator associated with the modal verb *atΛhutsoni* 'want' in (20a); hence, it cannot provide a natural discourse antecedent for a pronoun in a later clause. However, the variable corresponding to the IN in (20b) remains free and can be the antecedent for a pronoun in a later clause. Both sets of sentences thus show that an IN may or may not be subject to Heim's semantic rule of Quantifier Indexing. This confirms that INs are free variables in Mohawk and may, in general, be definite or indefinite.

A somewhat different effect of determiners in English is the contribution that they make to the aspect of the clause (Dowty 1979, Tenny 1987). Here the difference is not between definite and indefinite determiners, but between determined NPs and bare plurals. Transitive verbs with determined objects count as *accomplishments.* On the other hand, transitive verbs with bare plural objects count as *activities.* These aspectual classes then determine what kinds of temporal modifiers can appear felicitously in the clause. Thus we have the following pattern:

(21)   a.   I ate the/an apple in five minutes.

       b.   ??I ate the/an apple for five minutes.

       c.   I ate apples for five minutes.

       d.   ??I ate apples in five minutes.

Now when an IN combines with a transitive verb in Mohawk, the result can be understood as either an activity or an accomplishment. Thus, (22) can have either of the two translations indicated.

(22)   Áska mínut ni-ka-ríhw-es   tsi wa'-ke-'wáhr-a-k-e'
       one   minute PART-NsS-matter-long that FACT-1sS-meat-Ø-eat-PUNC
       (i) 'I ate meat for (only) a minute.'
       (ii) 'I ate the meat in (only) one minute.'

In the reading in (i), it is understood that the speaker began to eat an unspecified amount of meat but was forced to stop after a specified (insufficient) amount of time. Here meat-eating is viewed as a continuous activity that could have gone on indefinitely. The reading in (ii) surfaces in the context of a speed-eating contest, where each contestant tries to eat a specified piece of meat the fastest. Example (22) under the reading in (ii) is thus an appropriate way to brag about one's winning time. Here meat-eating is clearly an accomplishment with an intrinsic temporal endpoint. The important point is that either the accomplishment reading or the activity reading can be expressed by an IN in Mohawk (as well as by an independent NP). Once again, incorporated nouns in Mohawk can have the full range of interpretations that phrasal NPs have in English.

   Why have researchers not believed that INs have the same interpretations as full NPs? To some extent, it is because they have confounded true noun incorporation in my sense with other constructions; thus, in languages like Hindi or Greenlandic where NI is triggered by factors other than the MVC, those factors might well have semantic consequences. However, this does not account for references like Mithun 1984a, which explicitly discusses NI in Mohawk. Now the one thing that INs clearly cannot do in Mohawk is bear focal or contrastive stress. This is true for a rather superficial phonological reason: the N loses perceptual prominence by being integrated into the verbal complex, which constitutes a single prosodic domain. Thus, if a speaker wants to *emphasize* or call attention to the introduction of a new referent to the discourse, that speaker will probably not use an NI form to do so. This could be the reason behind Mithun's statistical generalization that INs are not used as frequently to introduce new referents. This is, however, a subtle matter of style and pragmatics, not a clearcut matter of syntax or semantics. Example (20a) is an instructive example in this respect because the

focus of the sentence is on who arrived; what they brought is comparatively inci-
dental to the first speaker's message. Hence, there is no pragmatic reason to avoid
the incorporation of *na'ts* 'pot'. Nevertheless, the pot is a new referent, which can
be picked up in the subsequent discourse, as in (20b). Thus, although focus and
definiteness are often correlated, they can be distinguished. When they are, we see
more clearly that NI is not sensitive to definiteness per se.

I conclude from this discussion that INs in Mohawk can have the full range of
interpretations of any other nominal, except for those associated with focal stress.
Moreover, the same seems to be more or less true of the other polysynthetic languages, inasmuch as one can tell from the available sources. For example, Allen
et al. (1984:297–298) show clearly that INs may be definite, indefinite, or generic
in Southern Tiwa. Evans (1991:272–274) states that sentences with and without
incorporation are "essentially synonymous" in Mayali. INs in Mayali are often
used to express inanimate NPs already present in the text or the context (a definite
usage); however, they also appear in verbs of stance, appearance, and with verbs
such as 'have' and 'want' (an indefinite usage). Launey (1981:165–166) strongly
suggests that INs in Classical Nahuatl are only indefinite (see also Sapir 1911),
but Merlan (1976) gives examples that correspond to both definites and indefinites
in a modern dialect. Similarly INs are usually generic or nonreferential in
Chukchee, but this is not always the case; there are examples in which the IN
refers back to a previous NP, examples in which the IN provides the antecedent
for a subsequent pronoun, and examples where an IN is treated like an indefinite
in the scope of negation (Polinskaja and Nedjalkov 1987, Spencer 1993:19–21). (I
have no relevant information for Ainu.) Thus, NI in the polysynthetic languages
is a semantically vacuous operation, driven by the formal needs of the MVC and
not by some feature of a semantic representation.

7.3. The Language-Internal Distribution of NI

7.3.1 The Basic Generalization

I turn now to the question of which nouns in a given language may incorporate
into the verb, assuming that the language allows NI at all.

Throughout this book, I have assumed the descriptive generalization of Baker
1988a that noun incorporation is possible for underlying direct objects only. This
generalization is quite well known (see Baker 1988a for earlier references) and
has held up well under further inquiry. It is clearly correct for Mohawk, where
most morphologically simple inanimate noun roots can incorporate when they are
direct objects.[9] On the other hand, similar nouns cannot be incorporated when they
are associated with the subject function. For example, chapter 5 showed that in
the Mohawk equivalent of 'This knife cuts bread,' the word for 'bread' can incorporate into 'cut', but the word for 'knife' cannot. In fact, when a consultant was
exposed to the version with 'knife-cut', she laughed and said "You can't cut a
knife with bread." The fact that this sentence is associated with this silly meaning
indicates that the verb form is not ruled out for purely morphological reasons. It
also shows that the association of INs with the object role is not simply a prag-

matic inference based on the tendency for INs to be inanimate plus the tendency for agents of transitive sentences to be animate; even in situations where an inanimate subject is allowed, some kind of structural condition is strong enough to override the obvious pragmatic relationships between knives, bread, and cutting. Another example illustrating the difference between subject incorporation and object incorporation is given in (23).

(23)   a. O-nΛy-a'   wa'-t-ká-hri-ht-e'   ne o-tsíser-a'.
           NsO-stone-NSF FACT-DUP-NsS-shatter-CAUS-PUNC NE NsO-pane-NSF
           'The stone broke the window-pane.'

       b. O-nΛy-a'   wa'-t-ka-tsiser-á-hri-ht-e'.
           NsO-stone-NSF FACT-DUP-NsS-pane-Ø-shatter-CAUS-PUNC
           'The stone broke the window-pane.'

       c. *O-tsíser-a'   wa'-t-ka-nΛy-á-hri-ht-e'.
           NsO-pane-NSF FACT-DUP-NsS-stone-Ø-shatter-CAUS-PUNC
           'The stone broke the window.'

Nor can inanimate subjects incorporate in the examples in (24) and (25).

(24)   a. A'Λn-a'   wa'-ka-rátsu-'   ne yo-[a]'ar-Λ'tu.
           arrow-NSF FACT-NsS-tear-PUNC NE NsO-lace-hang
           'The arrow tore the curtains.'

       b. *Yo-[a]'ar-Λ'tu wa-w-a'Λn-a-rátsu-'.
           NsO-lace-hang FACT-NsS-arrow-Ø-tear-PUNC
           'The arrow tore the curtains.' (Note: wa + w + a → u)

(25)   a. KíkΛ o-núhkw-a'   wa'-ako-ya'takéhnha-'   ne Uwári.
           this NsO-medicine-NSF FACT-(NsS)/FsO-help-PUNC NE Mary
           'This medicine helped Mary.'

       b. *Uwári wa'-ako-nuhkw-a-(ya't)akénha-'.
           Mary FACT-(NsS)/FsO-medicine-Ø-help-PUNC
           'The medicine helped Mary; Mary was helped by the medicine.'

This generalization seems to hold in all languages, or at least all of those in our sample. Example (26) illustrates this for Southern Tiwa (Allen et al. 1984:299) and (27) for Mayali (Evans, to appear b).

(26)   Ø-hliawra-k'ar-hi   yede.
       AS/AO-lady-eat-FUT that
       'She ate that lady.' (*'The lady ate that.')

(27)   Bi-yaw-na-ng   daluk.
       3sS/3hO-baby-see-PAST/PERF woman.
       'The woman saw the baby.' (*'The baby saw the woman.')

The same is surely true in Nahuatl, where the grammars speak of "object incorporation," although they do not actually give ungrammatical examples of subject incorporation. (See also Heath 1984:472–473 for Nunggubuyu, Rood 1976:206 for Wichita, Nedjalkov 1976 and Spencer 1993 for Chukchee, and Shibatani 1990:61– 63 for Ainu.[10])

The second major contrast captured by the generalization is the fact that in ditransitive constructions, the theme/direct object may incorporate, but the goal/indirect object may not. Here, one cannot avoid the confounding factor of animacy, but my examples use roots like *wir* 'baby' and *nahskw* 'domestic animal'. These are the easiest of the animate noun roots to incorporate, appearing in a wide range of spontaneously produced verbs. Chapter 5 gave an example showing that in the Mohawk equivalent of 'I gave the ball to the baby', the noun meaning 'ball' could incorporate into the verb but the noun meaning 'baby' could not. This is true in spite of the fact that *wir* 'baby' can perfectly well incorporate into *u* 'give' as long as it is interpreted as the theme, as in a sentence 'I gave the baby to him.' Other examples illustrating the same contrast are:

(28) a. O-'wáhr-u   í-hse-nut   ne érhar.
         NsO-meat-NSF Ø-2sS-feed NE dog
         'Feed the dog some meat!'

      b. Se-'wáhr-a-nut   ne érhar.
         2sS-meat-Ø-feed NE dog
         'Feed the dog some meat!'

      c. *O-'wáhr-u   se-náhskw-a-nut.
         NsO-meat-NSF 2sS-pet-Ø-feed
         'Feed the pet some meat!'

(29) a. Áhsir-e'   Λ-khey-úny-Λ-'   ne o-wir-á'a.
         blanket-NSF FUT-1sS/FsO-make-BEN-PUNC NE baby
         'I will make a blanket for the baby.'

      b. Λ-khey-ahsir-úny-Λ-'   ne o-wir-á'a
         FUT-1sS/FsO-blanket-make-BEN-PUNC NE baby
         'I will make a blanket for the baby.'

      c. *Áhsir-e'   Λ-ke-wir-úny-Λ-'.
         blanket-NSF FUT-1sS-baby-make-BEN-PUNC
         'I will make a blanket for the baby.'

Here, the stipulation that only the *underlying* direct object may undergo NI becomes important. Goal phrases come to act like direct objects on the surface in many languages, via the process of dative shift. The fact that object agreement in Mohawk cross-references the goal rather than the theme when both are present is a potential example of this.[11] Nevertheless, such dative shift alternations never feed NI; even when there is good evidence that the goal has in some sense "become an object" it cannot be incorporated. Again, this carries over fairly straightforwardly to the other polysynthetic languages; see for example Allen et al. 1984 for Southern Tiwa and Evans 1991:287, McKay 1975, and Heath 1984:474–475 for various Gunwinjguan languages.[12]

The distinction between underlying and surface grammatical relations is also important for understanding the pattern of noun incorporation with intransitive verbs. Descriptively, some verbs allow incorporation of their sole argument and others do not (see section 5.4.1 for a wider range of examples):

(30) a. Wa'-ka-wír-Λ'-ne'.
         FACT-NsS-baby-fall-PUNC
         'The baby fell.'

    b. Ónʌ wa'-o-'sere-ht-a-ké'tot-e'.
       now FACT-NsS-car-NOM-Ø-appear-PUNC
       'The car stuck out (e.g., of the garage).'

(31) a. *Wa'-t-ka-wir-ahsʌ́'tho-'.
       FACT-DUP-NsS-baby-cry-PUNC
       'The baby cried.'

    b. ??Wa'-ka-'sere-ht-a-ráthʌ-'.
       FACT-NsS-car-NOM-Ø-climb-PUNC
       'The car climbed (on it, e.g., a hill).'

In Baker 1988a, I claimed that the intransitive verbs that allow incorporation are those that take a direct object argument underlyingly—the unaccusative verbs. Unergative verbs, on the other hand, never allow incorporation. This is one of the more controversial aspects of that generalization, due in part to the well-known difficulty of establishing which verbs are unaccusative and which are unergative on semantic grounds alone.[13] However, the current work supports the original claim by providing independent tests for the unergative or unaccusative status of a given verb in Mohawk. Thus, the verbs in (30) also fail to take transitive agreement prefixes in benefactive constructions, a fact that was derived from their unaccusativity via Burzio's Generalization in chapter 5. They also allow adverbial *éso* 'a lot' to modify their NP argument, as shown in chapter 4. Two further diagnostics of unaccusativity will be discovered in chapter 8. In each case, there is a substantial correlation between the verbs that allow NI and those that act like unaccusatives in other respects.

So far, we have seen the three primary contrasts that motivated my generalization (Baker 1988a) that only underlying direct objects can be incorporated. In more semantically oriented presentations, one often finds the generalization that only nominals associated with a patient (theme) role can be incorporated (see, e.g., Chafe 1970). In fact, the two generalizations are nearly equivalent, given that my framework includes a strong version of the UTAH, which states that NPs with theme/patient θ-roles are systematically mapped onto underlying direct object positions in the syntax. The two views can only be distinguished empirically if one can find verbs that assign a theme role to a position other than direct object, or verbs that assign a θ-role other than theme to a direct object position. The first case cannot arise on the version of the UTAH assumed here. The second case may or may not be possible, depending on how one interprets Theta Theory. There are certainly verbs with direct objects that are not patients in the ordinary semantic sense, such as *nuhwe'* 'like' and *yahya'k* 'cross' in Mohawk or *mū* 'see' in Southern Tiwa. Moreover, the objects of such verbs easily incorporate, in apparent support of the structure-based theory. However, using Dowty's (1991) prototype approach to thematic roles, one could well respond that the objects of such verbs are, in fact, categorized as themes; they just happen to be further from the prototype (see, for example, Di Sciullo and Williams 1987). In that case, the difference between the two approaches to NI ceases to be a directly empirical one. Rather, it hinges on the broad question of what aspects of the grammar should have direct access to thematic information and what aspects should have access only to structural information. For various views on this deep issue, see Bresnan and Kanerva

1989, Grimshaw 1990, Rappaport and Levin 1988, Belletti and Rizzi 1988, Van Valin 1987, and Baker 1992c, among others. Since the issue is not readily decidable, I continue to adopt the syntactically oriented version of the generalization that fits best with my overall framework, without arguing for that choice directly.

Finally, languages are sometimes said to allow the incorporation of nominals other than patients, such as instruments, locatives (Mithun 1984a), predicative modifiers (Launey 1981:167–169), or other kinds of adjuncts (Shibatani 1990, Spencer 1993). None of these kinds of incorporation is possible with any degree of generality in Mohawk, however. I tentatively assume those types that do exist in other languages are not true instances of movement in the syntax, but rather are cases of N–V compounding formed in the Lexicon. This claim could, in principle, be tested by means of the phenomena presented in section 7.4, but I do not have access to the crucial data. In any case, it seems clear that such examples are a second-order effect at best, and hence will be put aside in this work.[14]

7.3.2 Problems With the Previous Analysis

Although the empirical generalization of Baker 1988a has held up well, my theoretical explanation of that generalization needs to be reexamined. The account hinged crucially on the fact that in traditional phrase structure configurations there is a special relationship between the direct object and the verb: the direct object is the only NP that is governed by the verb. The structure of a ditransitive construction is given in (32).

(32)

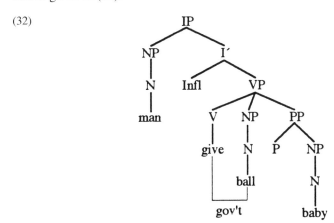

Roughly, a head X *governs* an element Y if and only if Y is within X's maximal projection and there is no other maximal projection Z that contains Y but not X. The fact that only the direct object is governed by the verb becomes relevant once noun incorporation is analyzed as movement leaving a trace. Like all traces, the trace of NI must be governed by its antecedent, according to the Empty Category Principle (Chomsky 1981, Rizzi 1990). In the case of NI, the antecedent is, by definition, in the verb. Thus, it follows that the trace of the moved N can only be in the direct object (at least if movement occurred in a single step), and hence only direct objects can incorporate.

This analysis claimed to capture a subtle but important similarity between

incorporation and more standard movement processes. *Wh*-movement, in particular, is also known to favor direct objects, because the fact that they are governed
by the verb makes them the easiest constituents to move. Structural subjects can
be *wh*-moved, but only if certain special conditions are met such that the complementizer becomes a proper governor of the subject position. Similarly, the objects
of prepositions can be *wh*-moved in English due to some special verb-like properties of the category P, but they cannot be moved in many other languages. Thus,
both NI and *wh*-constructions are object-oriented. This similarity was captured by
analyzing both as movement processes where the traces needed to be governed in
an appropriate way.

The first change is that agentive subjects (and other "external" arguments) are
Unfortunately, the ground has eroded under this analysis. In particular, the
phrase structure in (32) is no longer considered adequate by most P&P-style theories. Two significant innovations to the theory of phrase structure are relevant,
both of which were motivated for Mohawk in chapter 5.

The first change is that agentive subjects (and other "external" arguments) are
base generated as a specifier of VP. From this position, they may or may not move
to the specifier of IP, depending on morphosyntactic properties of the language in
question. Some version of this basic idea has been widely accepted and profitably
applied to a wide range of languages, including English, French, Irish, Yiddish,
Tagalog, Malagasy, and others. It also accounts for the fact that subject pronouns in Mohawk do not c-command into adjunct clauses (see section 2.2). Thus,
it is attractive to adopt the VP-internal subject hypothesis in Mohawk. However, this may be interpreted as meaning that agentive subjects *are* in fact governed by the verb. If so, the account of why agents may not incorporate must be
revised.

The second change involves the realization that there is an asymmetrical
c-command relationship between the direct and indirect objects. According to Larson (1988), this shows that there must be more internal structure to the VP than
is shown in (32). In particular, phrase structure must be binary branching, with the
goal as the complement in V′ and the theme as the specifier of an inner VP.
Chapter 5 presented evidence from agreement for the same c-command asymmetry
in Mohawk: in particular, the presence of a theme argument consistently causes a
goal argument to take O-class "object" agreement, just as the presence of an agent
argument consistently causes the theme argument it c-commands to take O-class
agreement.

This second innovation makes it even harder to see how the distribution of NI
can be explained in syntactic terms. The revised structure of a ditransitive clause
is (33), where the verb moves stepwise through the higher head positions, thereby
combining with its associated inflectional features. Notice that themes and agents
are structurally parallel in (33), in that both are generated in specifier positions.
Thus, if government is defined so as to allow incorporation from a specifier position, then incorporation of the agent will be allowed as well as incorporation of
the theme. On the other hand, if specifiers are islands to incorporation, then NI of
both agents and themes should be banned. Indeed, the only NP that the verb c-
commands by the strictest possible definition is the goal; thus one might expect
goals to be the easiest argument to incorporate—contrary to the facts. In short,
there is probably no natural definition of government such that only the theme

(33)

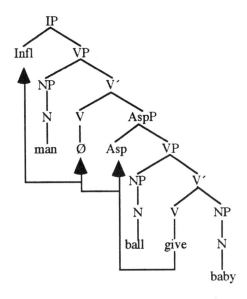

ball is governed by the verb in a structure like (33). Thus, if one wants to maintain a syntactic account of NI, a new analysis is necessary.

Since recent innovations have caused these problems for the analysis of NI, it is only fair that recent innovations should solve them as well. In particular, Chomsky (1992) makes some suggestions about how familiar generalizations must be adapted in the light of contemporary phrase structures. Let us consider, then, how some of the ideas sketched in that paper might be used to reconstruct a syntactic analysis of noun incorporation.

7.3.3 Goal Incorporation

Let us consider first the question of why goals cannot be incorporated. In Baker 1988a, this was blocked by the presence of an often silent goal/benefactive preposition. This idea can be carried over into the current framework with no decrease (or increase) in naturalness. None of the phrase structure innovations argues against the existence of such a preposition. On the contrary, the Case-theoretic considerations that motivated such a P in Kayne 1984, Czepluch 1982, and Baker 1988a carry over into the new framework. This P can also be motivated on rather general thematic grounds. Goal, source, benefactive, and malefactive roles can all be thought of as special cases of the more general θ-role "path," in Jackendoff's (1983) system; they all say something about the trajectory (perhaps in an extended sense) of the theme argument. It is clear that the canonical structural realization of a path argument is a PP. Thus, goals, sources, and benefactives should be PPs as well. What is special about goals and some sources is that they are part of the "possessional" semantic field, in which standard locative relationships are understood as possessional relationships (Jackendoff 1983). Now, the possessional field is degenerate, in that we do not have nearly as rich a vocabulary for possessional relationships as we do for other types of location. Although *The book is at John* may be comparable to *The book is John's,* there is no possessional equivalent to

The book is near John, or *The book is under John.* Thus, of all the path functions that natural language provides, the only ones that are appropriate in the possessional field are "to" and "from." Moreover, the inherent direction of a transfer of possession is often determined by the verb. Thus, in English one can say *I gave the book to John* and *I took the book from John,* but not **I gave the book from John.* Similarly, we have:

(34)   a.   I sold the book to John.

      b.   I bought the book from John.

      c.   *I sold the book from John.

      d.   *I bought the book to John.

Therefore, when a possessional verb with inherent directionality selects a goal or source argument, the canonical projection rules call for a PP argument, but there is no distinctive information for that P to express. In exactly this situation, a null preposition is generated. Thus, the structure of a ditransitive sentence is actually (35).

(35)

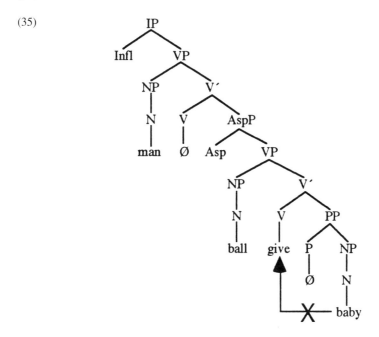

The empty preposition in (35) blocks NI of the goal by the HMC, as in Baker 1988a. In more current terms, we can say that an N root adjoined to the verb cannot antecedent govern its trace over the intervening preposition, because of Rizzi's (1990) Relativized Minimality Condition (or whatever deeper principles of Economy this follows from). Thus, direct incorporation of the goal is ruled out, essentially as before. The alternative derivation, in which the N incorporates first into P and then the combination incorporates into V, is also impossible, perhaps as a result of the PHMG.[15]

    This theory predicts that if there are verbs that take true NPs in the complement of V' position, then the heads of those NPs could incorporate even though they are not themes. There seem to be a handful of such verbs in Mohawk, including *yahya'k* 'cross' and *ra'* 'reach'. These verbs have two arguments, and their internal arguments usually incorporate:

(36) a. Te-wake-nyatar-iyá'k-u   thíkʌ.
       DUP-1sO-river-cross-STAT that
       'I have crossed that river.'

      b. Tsi ónʌ y-a'-k-háh-a-ra'-ne'   thíkʌ. . . .
         that when TRANS-FACT-1sS-road-Ø-reach-PUNC that
         'And when I reached that road. . . .'

In these examples, the demonstrative *thíkʌ* is understood as modifying the IN; this ensures that the forms are generated by syntactic NI rather than by lexical compounding (see section 7.4.1). The question, then, is what are the thematic roles involved here. It is plausible to say that 'I' is the theme argument, since it refers to the participant that changes location. Indeed, these sentences are close paraphrases of sentences with an unaccusative verb and a locative PP, such as 'I went through the river' or 'I arrived at the road'. Moreover, verbs like 'cross' and 'reach' often have syntactic properties in common with unaccusative verbs. For example, these verbs enter into the same serialization patterns as unaccusative verbs in West African languages (Baker 1989). In Mohawk, this explains why a benefactive argument cannot be added to *ra'*:

(37) *Y-a-hi-háh-a-ra'-s-e'.
      TRANS-FACT-1sS/MsO-road-Ø-reach-BEN-PUNC
      'I reached the right road for him.'

This structure requires two agreement factors: one to express the subject and one to express the benefactee. If, however, the subject of *ra'* is an internal theme argument rather than an external agent argument, there is only one Case available, by Burzio's Generalization. This means that there can be only one agreement factor, too, and (37) is ruled out. Its ungrammaticality is parallel to that of the unaccusative-plus-benefactive sentences discussed in section 5.2.[16] Further confirmation that *yahya'k* and *ra'* are like unaccusatives will be presented in section 8.2.2, where it will be shown that these are the only two-argument verbs in Mohawk that have a morphological causative.

Now if 'I' is the theme in (36), what is the thematic role of the INs? Clearly, they are not agents. They are not exactly paths either, because the path function is included in the lexical semantics of the verb: 'cross' means 'cross over' or 'cross through'; 'reach' means 'reach up to'. Thus, it makes sense to say that these verbs take the same kind of complement as prepositions normally do: an NP bearing what Jackendoff (1983) calls the "reference object" role.[17] Therefore, the structure of (36b) is (38). This confirms that NI can take place from the complement position as well as from the specifier position in the unusual case where there is no adposition in the way.

In fact, either argument of this type of verb should, in principle, be incorporable if other conditions are met. As far as I can tell, one never has a choice of which argument to incorporate in Mohawk. However, alternations are found in Mayali

(38)

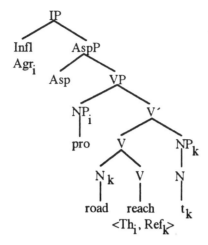

with exactly this kind of verb, according to Evans (1991:290). Thus, both examples in (39) have the N *rud* 'road' incorporated into the verb *djowkke* 'cross', but their interpretations are quite different.

(39)   a. A-rud-djoukge-ng.
          1sS/3sS-road-cross-PAST/PERF
          'I crossed the road.'

       b. Barri-bolk-ngeibu-ni   Gamirn, Gamirn gorrogo
          3PS/3O-place-name-PAST/IMPF Gamirn Gamirn before

          ba-rud-djoukbe-yi.
          3sS/3sO-road-cross-PAST/IMPF
          'They used to call that place Gamirn, in the olden days before the road crossed it (the river) at Gamirn.'

In (39a), the road is the object that is being crossed—it is the reference object—whereas in (39b), the road crosses something else and is thus the theme. Evans gives a similar example with the verb *bidbom* 'to climb'. Apparently, examples like (39b) are only possible when the verb has a noneventive reading, referring to spatial extent rather than actual movement. Although I have no explanation for this, I find it striking confirmation of the analysis that these two incorporation possibilities exist at all.[18]

7.3.4 Theme Incorporation

Next, let us turn our attention to NPs bearing the theme role. The challenge is to explain why they *may* incorporate. In fact, there are two plausible avenues by which incorporation could take place, given the structure in (35). On the one hand, the noun 'ball' could incorporate into the lower (base) position of the verb. The theoretical consequence of this proposal would be that m-command (to be defined later in this section) must be sufficient for antecedent government between heads, rather than strict c-command. In general, m-command is used for government purposes, whereas c-command is used for binding purposes (Chomsky 1986a); this means that antecedent government is more a special type of government than a special type of local binding. This is a reasonable choice, but not an obvious one.

The second possibility is that the head N of the theme incorporates into one of the higher positions that the verb moves through. Recall that the verb root 'give' in (35) moves successively into Asp, the Ø verb, and Infl, thereby combining with the inflectional morphemes generated in these positions. At the stage where the verb is in Asp, the N from the specifier of the lower VP could potentially incorporate upward into it. Such a derivation would satisfy a strict c-command condition on antecedent government. It would also satisfy the locality condition on antecedent government, as long as we assume that a head governs not only the head of its complement, but also the head of the specifier of its complement. The definitions of Chomsky 1986a have this effect; indeed, "Exceptional Case Marking" constructions and small clauses suggest that at least some specifiers are accessible to government from the outside. Thus, this is also a reasonable theoretical choice, although not an obvious one.

How shall we choose between these alternatives? In fact, there are empirical considerations that suggest that the N incorporates into the base position of the verb, rather than into a derived position. Suppose that the N crucially incorporates into the verb when the verb is in Asp. This predicts that in structures where the Asp node is not generated, NI would be impossible. If, however, the N incorporates into the base position of the verb, then NI should be unaffected by the lack of an Asp node. Now aspect suffixes are obligatory on most verbs in Mohawk. However, there is a class of stative/adjectival verbs that do not take aspect suffixes. Furthermore, these verbs select only a single theme argument, so there is no need for a higher verb position to assign the agent role. Neither do these verbs need to have any overt tense/mood morpheme. Thus, it is plausible to assume that at least the Asp position is missing with these verbs, and perhaps the higher head positions as well. Nevertheless, NI is perfectly possible (indeed more common than not) with these verbs (compare Postal 1979:288):

(40) a. Ka-na'ts-a-hútsi.
        NsS-pot-Ø-black
        'The pot is black.'

      b. Ka-nuhs-a-rákʌ.
        NsS-house-Ø-white
        'The house is white.'

These examples suggest that it would be a mistake to tie the possibility of NI too closely to the presence of higher functional categories.[19]

Facts about morpheme order also imply that NI targets the base position of the verb and not a derived position. In Baker 1988a:ch. 7 and section 1.6 of the present volume, I argue that the order of morphemes on a complex word generally reflects the history of incorporations that have taken place. If this is so, then the two incorporation routes should yield different morpheme orders. If the N incorporates into the verb before the verb moves to Asp, then the noun root will be inside of the morphemes associated with the Asp node. If, on the other hand, the N incorporates into the verb after the verb moves to the Asp node, then the noun root should appear outside the morphemes associated with aspect. Now the elements generated under Asp in our theory are the aspect morpheme itself and the object agreement features. Since the aspect is always a suffix and INs attach to the beginning of the verb in Mohawk, the order of attachment of these is not obvious. However, it is perfectly clear that the IN appears inside of object agreement:

(41)   a. Λ-t-ye-[sa-[athér-u]-']
           FUT-CIS-FsS-2sO-basket-give-PUNC
           'she will hand the basket to you'

       b. *Λ-t-ye-[ather-[sa-u-']]
           FUT-CIS-FsS-basket-FsO-give-PUNC
           'she will hand the basket to you'

Another morpheme generated in Asp on my account is the reflexive morpheme *atat* (see section 5.4.3). The IN necessarily attaches to the verb root before this element as well:

(42)   a. wa'-k-[atate-[nuhs-úny-Λ]-']
           FACT-1sS-REFL-house-make-BEN-PUNC
           'I made myself a house.'

       b. *wa'-ke-[nuhs-[atat-úny-Λ-']]
           FACT-1sS-house-REFL-make-BEN-PUNC
           'I made myself a house'

More generally, it is a striking fact about noun incorporation in all the polysynthetic languages that the N attaches inside of all standard inflectional morphemes, as shown in section 1.6. This shows that the N attaches to the verb in its base position, before the verb moves upward.

From this I conclude that the structure of a sentence with an IN is (43), prior to raising of the verb.

(43)

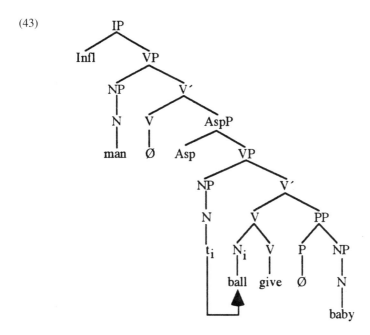

This is permitted as long as we take (44) as the definition of antecedent government, based on Rizzi (1990:6).

(44)   X antecedent governs Y if and only if:
    (i)   X and Y are members of the same chain,
    (ii) X m-commands Y,
    (iii) there is no barrier between X and Y, and
    (iv) Relativized Minimality is respected.

The crucial clause here is (ii); X *m-commands* Y if and only if the first *maximal projection* containing X also contains Y. Once this version of the command relation is adopted, the incorporated N antecedent governs its trace, satisfying the ECP.

    In order to explain the morpheme orders in (41) and (42), it is not quite enough that we allow the structure in (43); we must also rule out the alternative in which the N incorporates into the verb after the verb has moved to Asp. If this is not done, we predict that both morpheme orders should be possible, contrary to fact. This result could be achieved by tinkering with the definition of either barrierhood or Relativized Minimality presupposed in (44). However, perhaps the most natural approach in the framework of Chomsky 1992 is to say that the mere possibility of the derivation in (43) makes any other derivation from the same basic structure impossible. In other words, the derivation in (43) is "more economical" than the alternative. Here the relevant sense of Economy is presumably that any given movement must be as short as possible. Chomsky (1992) uses this principle to derive the superiority condition of Chomsky 1973 and sketches other uses that it might have (see also Collins 1994 and Nakamura 1993). For concreteness, we may assume that the Economy Principle is stated crudely as follows:

(45)   (i)   Minimize the length of chain links (Chomsky and Lasnik 1993, Nakamura 1993).

      (ii) The length of a chain link is the number of maximal projections that contain the trace but not the antecedent.

Now we can compare the two derivations in (46). The length of the movement of the verb to Asp is the same (one) in both derivations. In the first derivation, the length of the noun movement is also one; the N moves out of NP only. However, in the second derivation, the length of the noun movement is two: it moves out of NP and out of VP. Therefore, the total length of the chains is more in the second derivation, and this derivation is ruled out by (45a).

7.3.5 *Agent Incorporation*

The final case to consider is the possibility of incorporating agentive subjects. This we must rule out on principled grounds. Again, there are two plausible incorporation paths to be considered that are potentially compatible with locality requirements: (1) the N could incorporate "upward" into Infl after the verb has raised into that position, or (2) it could incorporate "downward" into the empty V position of a Larsonian VP shell. These derivations are exactly parallel to those we considered for the direct object, except that they are higher up in the tree. We can rule out possibility (1) immediately: it is less economical than possibility (2). If the N

(46)

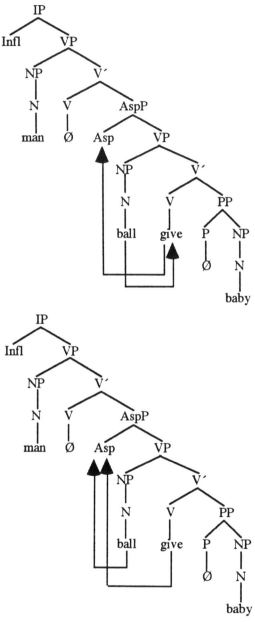

moves downward, it comes out of only its own NP, whereas if it moves upward directly it comes out of NP and VP. Crucially, using Chomsky's assumptions, the possibility of derivation (2) rules out derivation (1) even if derivation (2) proves ill formed for other reasons. This is a central property of the Minimalist Program, for otherwise it would be difficult to explain why some structures are ill formed under any possible derivation.

Therefore, the crucial derivation to be considered with respect to subject incorporation is the one shown in (47).

(47)

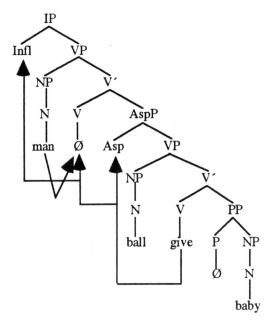

Here the chain links are all of minimal length (one), and antecedent government is obeyed. There is, however, an important structural difference between this and the grammatical cases of theme incorporation: the theme incorporates into the *base* position of a *lexical* verb, whereas the agent does not. The position into which the subject could potentially incorporate is a null, dummy position in the base and a derived position of the lower verb. This proves to be crucial. When could incorporation of the agent take place, relative to the successive raising of the verb? Presumably, the N cannot move into the V position before the lower verb raises, because there is really no verb to incorporate into. Since Ø is a truly empty position,[20] N cannot adjoin to it; nor can N substitute into it without violating X-bar Theory—the upper VP would then have an N head. Neither can the N move into the V position after the lower V has reached Infl: not only would this involve adjoining an N to a trace, it would fail to combine the N root and the V root into a single word. Thus, the N must incorporate into the higher V after the lower verb raises into that position but before it moves on to Infl. In other words, the derivation must be:

(48) (i) The V root moves to Asp.
   (ii) [V–Asp] moves into the higher V position.
   (iii) The N root adjoins to the higher V position.
   (iv) The V complex [N–V–Asp] moves to Infl.

However, this sequence violates another aspect of Chomsky's (1992) notion of "Economy of Derivation." In particular, it crucially requires that the movement of the verb from Asp through the higher V position and into Infl be broken into two discrete stages. However, Chomsky assumes that successive-cyclic movements through semantically irrelevant positions are one movement consisting of several steps, rather than a sequence of movements. In other words, they are a single instance of Form Chain that leaves several traces, not multiple instances of Move-α, each of which leaves one trace. A consequence of this view is that a successive-cyclic derivation cannot be interrupted in the middle to allow some other operation, as pointed out by Collins (1994). Assuming that the higher verb position is truly empty and not merely phonologically silent, moving through that position does not count as forming a separate chain, any more than moving a *wh*-phrase through an intermediate Comp does. On this conception, the only possible derivations are those in (49).

(49)   a.   (i) The V root moves to Asp.
            (ii) [V–Asp] moves to Infl via the higher V position.
            (iii) The N root moves to the higher V position.

       b.   (i) The V root moves to Asp.
            (ii) The N root moves to the higher V position.
            (iii) [V–Asp] moves to Infl via higher V position.

These three-step derivations block the four-step derivation in (48). Thus, there is simply no point in the derivation when the verb root is in the higher V position, and the agent never has an opportunity to incorporate into it. These derivations are ruled out by the quasimorphological considerations already discussed: (49b) violates X-bar Theory by substituting an N into a V position; (49a) fails to combine the verb root and the noun root. Thus, there is no way to incorporate an N from the higher specifier that is both economical and morphologically sound.[21]

In conclusion, we have seen that the basic distribution of NI can still be derived from the simple idea in Baker 1988a that NI is a result of an N^0 category moving in the syntax, subject to normal principles that govern movement. Although the basic structure of the clause is now somewhat different than it was in Baker 1988a, so are the principles that govern movement. The two types of theoretical innovations roughly cancel each other out, leaving the original account more or less intact. The head of the indirect object is still trapped inside a null-headed P; the head of the subject still fails to be in construction with a verbal position into which it could plausibly incorporate. The head of the direct object is thus left as the only X^0 position that is in the right structural configuration with a lexical verb to undergo NI. The phrase structures are more complex, and thus there are more possibilities to consider, but the fundamental idea is essentially unchanged.

7.4 The Syntactic Nature of NI

So far I have taken for granted that NI constructions in polysynthetic languages should be analyzed as movement in the syntax. However, this position is controversial. Various studies have argued that NI is a morphological process of compounding, including Mithun 1984a, Di Sciullo and Williams 1987, and Rosen 1989b (cf. also Sapir 1911). This position has also been accepted by more descriptively oriented studies, such as Spencer 1993 and Evans 1993. This alternative view has some immediate conceptual and empirical advantages over the range of data that has been published so far. Moreover, a morphological approach to NI is compatible with the Strict Lexicalist Hypothesis, which seems to be a more restrictive view of the organization of the grammar.[22] In the light of the complications created for the head-movement approach by current phrase structure assumptions, it might seem attractive to adopt a purely morpholexical solution. However, in this volume we have for the first time something like a comprehensive analysis of the syntax of polysynthetic languages. Hence, it should now be possible to build more conclusive arguments to determine the status of noun incorporation. In this section, I indicate how this can be done. The results show that whereas some N–V combinations are, indeed, formed by morphological compounding, most are clearly formed in the syntax.

7.4.1 A Preliminary Comparison

Let us begin by reviewing the debate so far and providing better examples than have previously been available. The starting point for morphological theories of NI is the observation that synthetic compounds in English and other languages are also "object-oriented": Ns associated with the theme role can be compounded with a verbal form, but Ns associated with the agent or goal role in general cannot be. Thus, the natural interpretation of *fish-eating* is that fish are being eaten; not that they are doing the eating or that they benefit from the eating (Roeper and Siegel 1978, Selkirk 1982, Di Scuillo and Williams 1987, and others). In this respect, there is an obvious similarity between compounding in English and NI in Mohawk. Thus, one might look to the principles that govern English compounding to account for the distributional facts described in the last section, rather than to the principles of movement. Di Scuillo and Williams (1987) give perhaps the best-known recent presentation of such principles from a lexicalist viewpoint.

There are, however, two salient differences between NI in a language like Mohawk and compounding in English that motivated the syntactic approach in the first place. The first, discussed in section 7.2, is that INs in some languages can readily introduce discourse referents and can receive definite, referential interpretations. This is not, in general, a property of compounded noun roots in English. For example, the two sentences in (50) seem nearly synonymous on first glance.

(50) a. John is a truck driver.

   b. John drives a truck for a living.

Nevertheless, a sentence like *It is parked over there behind the gas station,* with *it* referring to the truck John drives, is much more natural following (50b) than following (50a). The sequence in (51), however, is perfectly natural in Mohawk.

(51) Thetáre' wa'-ke-nakt-a-hnínu-'.   Í-k-ehr-e'   Uwári
      yesterday FACT-1sS-bed-Ø-buy-PUNC Ø-1sS-think-IMPF Mary

      ʌ-ye-núhwe'-ne'.
      FUT-FsS-like-PUNC
      'I bought a bed yesterday. I think Mary will like it (the bed).'

The syntactic approach interprets these facts as showing that incorporated noun roots function more like true objects than like compounded N roots. To account for this, the morphological approach must broaden its view of compounding somewhat.

The second way in which noun incorporation in some languages differs from compounding in English is that INs can be modified by elements that appear outside the verb. This is very common in Mohawk. Example (52) gives an illustrative range of examples: the incorporated root can be interpreted together with a demonstrative, as in (52a), an adjectival modifier, as in (52b), a quantifier or numeral, as in (52c), or a relative clause, as in (52d).

(52) a. Thíkʌ ʌ-ye-nakt-a-núhwe'-ne'.
         this   FUT-FsS-bed-Ø-like-PUNC
         'She will like this bed.'

     b. Aséhtsi ʌ-ye-nakt-a-núhwe'-ne'.
         new   FUT-FsS-bed-Ø-like-PUNC
         'She will like the new bed.'

     c. Akwéku ʌ-ye-nakt-a-núhwe'-ne'.
         all   FUT-FsS-bed-Ø-like-PUNC
         'She will like all the beds.'

     d. ʌ-ye-nakt-a-núhwe'-ne' ne thetʌ́re' wa'-k-hnínu-'.
         FUT-FsS-bed-Ø-like-PUNC NE yesterday FACT-1sS-buy-PUNC
         'She will like the bed that I bought yesterday.'

Indeed, virtually any element that can modify an external noun in Mohawk can modify an incorporated noun as well.[23] Such sentences are exactly what one would expect on the analysis of Baker 1988a; they are formed when the head of the object moves out, leaving behind the rest of the NP. On the other hand, expressions like *I met the truck driver of that* are distinctly weird in English. Again, the lexicalist approach must expand its view of compounding in order to account for these facts.[24]

Di Sucillo and Williams (1987) and Rosen (1989b) have an elegant way of approaching these apparent difficulties. In English, when a noun that forms a compound with a (de-) verbal form is associated with the object θ-role of the verb, the noun discharges that position in the θ-grid of the verb. This means that the θ-role cannot subsequently be assigned in syntax. Thus, examples like (53c) are ungrammatical.

(53) a. The eating of shark (is hazardous to one's health).

     b. Fish-eating (is hazardous to one's health).

     c. *Fish-eating of shark (is hazardous to one's health).

The leading idea of the lexicalists is that compounding in Mohawk does *not* discharge the object θ-role. Rather, it is interpreted as modifying or specifying that θ-role. On this analysis, a form like *nakt-a-hninu* 'bed-buy' is an ordinary transitive verb from the point of view of the syntax. The structures it enters into are identical in all relevant respects to those that *hninu* 'buy' does, except that *nakt-a-hninu* places more selectional restrictions on the object—it must refer to a type of bed.

This gives a new perspective on the examples in (52). The prediction of the lexicalist account is very simply that complex verbs with incorporated nouns take exactly the same range of objects as ordinary transitive verbs. Indeed, the "stranded modifiers" in (52) can all constitute complete NPs in Mohawk, as shown in (54).

(54) a. ThíkΛ Λ-ye-núhwe'-ne'.
         this   FUT-FsS-like-PUNC
         'She will like this.'

      b. Aséhtsi Λ-ye-núhwe'-ne'.
         new   FUT-FsS-like-PUNC
         'She will like the new one.'

      c. Akwéku Λ-ye-núhwe'-ne'.
         all   FUT-FsS-like-PUNC
         'She will like all of them.'

      d. Λ-ye-núhwe'-ne'   ne thetÁre' wa'-k-hnínu-'.
         FUT-FsS-like-PUNC NE yesterday FACT-1sS-buy-PUNC
         'She will like the one that I bought yesterday.'

Hence, there is no compulsion to say that there is a trace in the noun phrases in (52). Plausibly, the interpretation of the examples in (52) also follows from this view. For example, the lexical meaning of the object NP in (52a) would be 'that one', and from the selectional restrictions of the complex verb one can infer that a bed must be intended. Therefore, the meaning is equivalent to 'that bed'.

This also leads to an account of (51). One possible expression of the object of a transitive verb in Mohawk is a null pronoun. This is taken to be the object when no other object is present, as in simple noun incorporation structures. Such null pronouns can, of course, be the antecedents of other pronouns in the discourse. Thus, the discourse in (51) is parallel to the one in (55) on the compounding analysis.

(55) ThetÁre' wa'-k-hnínu-'.   Í-k-ehr-e'   Uwári L-ye-núhwe'-ne'.
      yesterday FACT-1sS-buy-PUNC Ø-1sS-think-IMPF Mary FUT-FsS-like-PUNC
      'I bought it yesterday. I think Mary will like it.'

Again, in (51) the invisible 'it' (or 'one', a null indefinite?) is interpreted as a bed because of the compound verb's very specific selectional restrictions. In this way, the lexicalist approach matches the initial successes of the syntactic approach.

The predictions of the lexicalist approach are not identical to those of the syntactic approach, however. On the contrary, lexicalist authors point to two advantages of their system. The first involves obligatorily transitive determiners. Thus, English has determiners such as *the* and *a* that (unlike *this* and *that*) must appear with a nominal head; one cannot say *Mary bought the*. Now consider the interaction of such a determiner with NI. Without further refinements, the syntactic approach predicts that sentences of the form in (56) should be possible, since the incorporated noun satisfies the selectional properties of the determiner before it moves.

(56)   Mary fish-bought [the (t)].

In contrast, the lexicalist analysis clearly predicts that such sentences will be impossible, since complex verbs take the same range of objects as simple transitive verbs (Rosen 1989b). In fact, such sentences have not been attested. This seems to support the lexicalist approach.

The second advantage of the lexicalist approach is that it captures immediately a fact about Mohawk NI emphasized by Postal (1979) and Mithun (1984a) but not analyzed in the discussion so far: complex verbs can take objects with full NP heads. In some cases, the head is identical to the incorporated noun root:

(57)   Uwári Λ-ye-nakt-a-núhwe'-ne'   ne Sak rao-nákt-a'.
       Mary FUT-FsS-bed-Ø-like-PUNC NE Sak MsP-bed-NSF
       'Mary likes Sak's bed.'

In other cases, the incorporated noun is distinct from the external noun and refers to a more general category that includes the reference of the external noun as a proper subset:

(58)   Sha'téku ni-kuti   rabahbót wa-hΛ-[i]tsy-a-hnínu-'   ki
       eight   PART-ZpS bullhead FACT-MsS-fish-Ø-buy-PUNC this

       rake-'níha.   (KO:198)
       my-father
       'My father bought eight bullheads.'

This type of example is sometimes referred to as "classifier incorporation." Its existence is exactly what one would expect if the lexicalist approach is correct: the complex verb can take any kind of object that an ordinary transitive verb can, including objects with an overt noun head. On the other hand, the existence of examples like (57) and (58) is somewhat awkward for the syntactic analysis of Baker 1988a. In particular, it is not clear what position the incorporated noun has at D-structure. If it can be base generated inside the verb, then the analysis is essentially identical to the lexicalist analysis. On the other hand, it cannot be generated as the head of the visible NP because that head position is otherwise occupied. This seems to be strong, perhaps decisive, evidence in favor of the lexicalist approach.[25]

However, once one considers these arguments for a lexicalist approach in the light of what we now know about polysynthetic languages, their force largely collapses. Consider first the stranded determiner argument based on structures like (56). It is understood as a defect of the syntactic approach that no grammatical instances of such structures are attested. In fact, no *ungrammatical* instances of this structure have been attested either. Thus the prediction of the lexicalist account has not been fully vindicated. This test for distinguishing the lexicalist approach from the syntactic approach crucially depends on the assumption that determiners of the relevant type exist in languages with noun incorporation. However, this is not the case: such determiners are systematically absent in Mohawk and the polysynthetic languages. Indeed, I have claimed that this is a predictable consequence of the theory: the same Polysynthesis Parameter that triggers NI in languages where it is set positively also explains why true determiner systems are not found in those languages (see sections 6.1.3 and 7.1.2). If this result holds up, then there could never be a structure like (56), simply because there could never be an underlying structure like 'Mary bought the fish.' This way of distinguishing the lexicalist approach from the syntactic approach becomes untestable in principle.

Consider next the noun doubling argument based on examples like (57) and (58). To account for cases of this type, in Baker 1988a I assumed that the visible NP is not actually the object of the verb, but rather an adjunct attached outside the verb phrase; the true object of the verb is the trace left by NI. On these assumptions, the structure of (57) would be (59).

(59)   Uwári [[$_{VP}$ Λ-ye-nakt$_i$-a-núhwe'-ne' t$_i$] [$_{NPi}$ ne Sak rao-nákt-a']].
         Mary   FUT-FsS-bed-Ø-like-PUNC   NE Sak MsP-bed-NSF
         'Mary likes Sak's bed.'

I compared the relationship between the visible NP and the trace NI to the phenomenon of clitic doubling found in some dialects of Spanish and Romanian. No real argument against this claim has been advanced in the subsequent literature. However, the system of Baker 1988a did make the counterintuitive prediction that the position of the overt NP in an NI construction is very different from the position of the overt NP in an otherwise similar sentence with no IN. Thus, the phrase *Sak raonákta'* in (57) was predicted to behave like an adjunct, whereas the corresponding phrase in the minimally different (60) was predicted to behave like a complement.

(60)   Uwári [$_{VP}$ Λ-ye-núhwe'-ne' [$_{NP}$ ne Sak rao-nákt-a']].
         Mary   FUT-FsS-like-PUNC   NE Sak MsP-bed-NSF
         'Mary likes Sak's bed.'

Baker 1988a gave no evidence in support of this distinction. The lexicalist approach, on the other hand, posits no structural difference between (57) and (60); the NP should act like an ordinary direct object in both cases. This might reasonably be considered the null hypothesis in the absence of clear evidence to the contrary.

This issue also appears in quite a different light once what we know about polysynthetic languages is taken into account. We established in chapter 2 that (60) is never a proper structure; rather, all NPs in Mohawk are in adjoined positions, "doubling" an empty category in the true argument position. Thus, the structure of (60) should, in fact, be (61).

(61)   Uwári [$_{VP}$ Λ-ye-núhwe'-ne' pro$_i$] [$_{NPi}$ ne Sak rao-nákt-a'].
         Mary   FUT-FsS-like-PUNC   NE Sak MsP-bed-NSF
         'Mary likes Sak's bed.'

Again, this is not an accident of Mohawk; rather the same parameter that triggers NI in a language also causes that language to be nonconfigurational (see section 7.1.1). Now, (61) is nearly identical to (59). Hence, the syntactic approach does not predict any clear-cut difference between noun-doubling constructions and ordinary transitive verbs after all; both should act like dislocated adjuncts. If the neo-Jelinekian theory of nonconfigurationality I have argued for here is combined with a lexicalist account of noun incorporation, then the lexicalist account makes the same prediction. Once again, what looked like a clear-cut empirical issue distinguishing the lexicalist and syntactic approaches collapses in the light of further knowledge of the languages in question.

The syntactic account does still posit one structural difference between (59) and (61): in the former case, the empty category that licenses the adjoined NP is headed by a trace, whereas in the latter it is headed by a pro. Thus, we must expand the ALC of chapters 3 and 4 slightly to include the bracketed phrase in (62).

(62)   *The Adjunct Licensing Condition* (revised)

An argument-type phrase XP generated in adjoined position is licensed only if it forms a chain with a unique null pronominal (or trace of head movement) in an argument position.

(For clarity, (62) does not include the uniqueness clause motivated in section 4.1, since that is not relevant here.) The lexicalist approach has the conceptual advantage of avoiding the disjunction in the statement of this principle. However, I take this advantage to be a very mild one, given that there is no theoretical reason why traces of this type should not license dislocated phrases. Here, a comparison with the Romance literature is instructive. There is a long-standing debate over whether the empty category associated with a clitic pronoun is a trace left behind by movement of the clitic, or a *pro* licensed by government with the clitic base generated on the verb, as in the following example from French:

(63)   Jean l_i'a lu $[e_i]$.
        Jean it-has read.

Crucial to this debate have been issues such as the proper account of clitic doubling, extraction, participle agreement, clitic climbing, and so on. However, the well-known fact that Romance languages allow Clitic Left Dislocation constructions like the example in (64) has never to my knowledge been considered an important factor in this debate.

(64)   Ce livre$_i$, Jean l_i'a lu $[e_i]$.
        'This book, Jean has read it.'

I take this as tacit evidence that there is no strong theoretical reason why a trace of head movement cannot act as the licenser for a dislocated NP.

Indeed, the bracketed material in (62) seems to be a low-level parameter within the polysynthetic languages. Thus, some polysynthetic languages permit a dislocated NP to double an IN, whereas others do not. Those that allow doubling include the Iroquoian languages, the Gunwinjguan languages (Heath 1984:464, Evans 1993:3–4), and the Caddoan languages (Mithun 1984a); those that do not include Nahuatl (Andrews 1975, Launey 1981), the Tanoan languages, Chukchee (Spencer 1993), and apparently Ainu (Shibatani (1990) does not mention the possibility). Crucially, these languages are typologically similar in most other respects. In particular, they all have nonconfigurational properties, showing that dislocated NPs can be licensed by pro. They also have INs that are referentially active in the discourse, suggesting that incorporation is of the syntactic type. Indeed, whether doubling of an IN is possible or not is precisely the difference between Class III noun incorporation and Class IV noun incorporation in Mithun's (1984a) typology.

A particularly interesting case is Southern Tiwa. This language clearly allows INs to have definite, referential interpretations (Allen et al. 1987:297). It also allows demonstratives, numerals, and relative clauses outside the verb to modify an incorporated N root:

(65) a. Yede a-diru-k'ar-hi. (AGF:296)
          that 2sS/AO-chicken-eat-FUT
          'You will eat that chicken.'

      b. Wim'a a-seuan-mū-ban. (AGF:295)
          one 2sS/AO-man-see-PAST
          'You saw one man.'

      c. A-shut-mū-ban   ti-pe-ba-'i. (AGF:297)
          2sS/AO-shirt-see-PAST 1sS/AO-make-past-SUB
          'Did you see the shirt I made?'

However, they do *not* allow a doubling NP with an overt nominal head (see Baker 1988b:275; data originally from Donald Frantz, personal communication):

(66) a. *Yede diru-de   a-diru-k'ar-hi.
          that chicken-SG 2sS/AO-chicken-eat-FUT
          'You will eat that chicken.'

      b. *Wim'a seuan-ide a-seuan-mū-ban.
          one   man-SG   2sS/AO-man-see-PAST
          'You saw one man.'

A lexicalist approach to NI has no natural way of accounting for this pattern. The ungrammaticality of (66) shows that complex verbs in Southern Tiwa do not have the same argument-taking properties as ordinary transitive verbs. On the other hand, the grammaticality of (65) shows that complex verbs do not have the same argument-taking properties as intransitive verbs either. Hence, there is no way of analyzing this case within the narrow typology permitted by a strictly lexicalist analysis. The syntactic analysis, however, has a natural way of approaching this pattern. The ungrammaticality of (66) is explained by saying that Southern Tiwa does not allow the more permissive setting of the licensing condition in (62). The sentences in (65), on the other hand, do not require that an NP be adjoined to the clause; rather the determiner-like elements or relative clauses can simply be adjoined to the NP headed by the trace of noun incorporation. Thus, the structure of (65a) is (67) (assuming Tanoan languages are underlyingly head final). This can be compared with the structures for operators split from their heads in Mohawk, discussed in chapter 4. Here, then, is an unambiguous case of "determiner-stranding" under noun incorporation similar to the one we were looking for in the discussion of (56).[26]

Taking stock of the situation as it stands so far, we find that the lexicalist analysis of NI and the syntactic analysis of NI are in a virtual deadlock. Both can derive the basic distribution of NI from more general considerations. Both can account for the fact that INs may be referentially active, and for the fact that they

(67)

may be modified or doubled by NP material outside of the verbal complex. Two places where we might have expected to find genuine empirical differences prove to be untestable once we take into account the nonconfigurational nature of the languages in question. The lexicalist theory has the small conceptual advantage that it permits a more unified view of when NP adjuncts may be licensed, but this is offset by the fact that the additional complexity of the syntactic theory allows it to analyze the Tanoan languages in a plausible way.

There is no reason to give up the inquiry in this unsatisfactory state, however. The two approaches are clearly not notational variants; on the contrary, they analyze the central constructions in quite a different way. Table 7-1 summarizes the two proposals, where each has been updated to include the neo-Jelinekian theory of nonconfigurationality. The previous literature has focused mostly on rows two and three, the exotic phenomena of modifier stranding and noun doubling. However, in the current context, the most striking difference actually involves row one—plain noun incorporation. Here, the syntactic approach and the lexicalist approach both posit an empty category, but the nature of that empty category is quite different: it is an ordinary pronominal in one theory and the trace of a referential item in the other. This clear-cut difference should be syntactically testable. The remainder of this section will show that it is.

7.4.2 *Agreement and the Null Argument*

The clearest and most straightforward difference between the two types of empty objects involves the licensing conditions that they must satisfy. Thus, suppose that the empty category in a plain NI construction is a pro, as the lexicalist theory claims. This pro must then be governed by agreement, which can identify its

Table 7-1. Theories of Noun Incorporation

Construction	Baker 1988a	Lexicalist Analysis
'I bed-like' (plain NI)	[N$_i$–V t$_i$]	[N–V pro]
'I bed-like that' (modifier stranding)	[N$_i$–V [that t$_i$]], or [N$_i$–V t$_i$] [$_{NPi}$ that]	[N–V [that pro]], or [N–V pro$_i$] [$_{NPi}$ that]
'I bed-like his-bed' (noun-doubling and classifier NI)	[N$_i$–V t$_i$] NP$_i$	[N–V pro$_i$] NP$_i$

person/number/gender features, according to standard assumptions presupposed in chapter 5. This effect is clearly seen in simple verbs, which must have an appropriate object agreement morpheme in order to have a null pronoun in Mohawk. Since the lexicalist analysis holds that verbs with an incorporated noun root are syntactically identical to simple transitive verbs, the same constraint should apply to them. Thus, this view predicts that an object agreement morpheme on the complex verb will be required to license the empty category.

On the other hand, suppose that the empty category in a plain NI construction is a trace, as in the syntactic analysis. As such, it is subject to well-formedness conditions on movement chains. These are satisfied if and only if the noun originates in the direct object position and adjoins to the local verb, as discussed in section 7.3. However, this is the only licensing requirement that traces must, in general, meet. Thus, nothing more than an IN in the nearby verb is required to license this empty category; in particular, no agreement morphology is needed. The two theories make clearly different predictions, therefore, with regard to whether agreement will be found in cases of NI.

Before this prediction can be checked, there is a complication that must be addressed. Recall that Mohawk has no overt agreement morpheme for neuter objects (see section 5.3). Thus, one cannot tell in any obvious way whether in an example like (68) the verb has phonologically null object agreement (as predicted by the lexicalist analysis) or no object agreement at all (consistent with the syntactic analysis).

(68) a. Wa'-k-(Ø)-hnínu-'   ne ka-nákt-a'.
          FACT-1sS-(NsO)-buy-PUNC NE NsS-bed-NSF
          'I bought the/a bed.'

      b. Wa'-ke-(Ø)-nakt-a-hnínu-'.
          FACT-1sS-(NsO)-bed-Ø-buy-PUNC
          'I bought the/a bed.'

Hence, the incorporation of neuter nouns does not give decisive evidence in this domain. However, most natural and spontaneous instances of NI in Mohawk generally involve neuter nouns. This has led to some confusion in the literature about whether INs are agreed with or not. For example, Woodbury (1975) claims that the Onondaga verb does still have transitive agreement, but none of her examples show this unambiguously.

Crucial evidence comes only from the incorporation of animate nouns; however, these often resist incorporation, for reasons that remain unclear. Descriptively, the facts are as roughly as follows. Textual examples of animate NI are few and far between, but do exist. Native speaker consultants find a few examples of this type perfectly acceptable, particularly those involving the noun *wir* 'baby' or *nahskw* 'domestic animal', or those involving verbs of evaluation (e.g., *nuhwe'* 'like') or possession (e.g., *yʌ,* 'to lie, to have'). A larger class of examples are marginally acceptable. These are judged to be well formed, but involve treating the person as a thing, without desires or self-control. As such, they are often considered disrespectful or pejorative.[27] Finally, many examples are rejected outright. As far as I know, this includes every verb that selects for a theme that must be animate, with the sole exception of benefactive forms of *ihey* 'die' (see also Woodbury 1975). Thus, there is a bias against the incorporation of animates in Mohawk, but no outright prohibition against it. I have no syntactic analysis of this effect, which seems to be found to varying degrees in other polysynthetic languages as well (see Allen et al. 1984 for Southern Tiwa, Evans 1993 for Mayali). However, it means that one can test the prediction as long as one is willing to explore the limits of the system and to be rather disrespectful to the elderly from time to time.

With this in mind, we find some good evidence for the syntactic approach. A particularly clear case is seen in the paradigm in examples (69) and (70), which I have discussed several times in this book.

(69) a. Shako-núhwe'-s   (ne owirá'a).
          MsS/3pO-like-HAB NE baby
          'He likes them (babies).'

      b. *Ra-núhwe'-s   (ne owirá'a).
          MsS-like-HAB NE baby
          'He likes them (babies).'

(70) a. *?Shako-wir-a-núhwe'-s.
          MsS/3pO-baby-Ø-like-HAB
          'He likes babies.'

      b. Ra-wir-a-nuhwe'-s.
          MsS-baby-Ø-like-HAB
          'He likes babies.'

Example (69a) shows that with an ordinary transitive verb, feminine or masculine agreement is required when the direct object is understood to be a baby; null/neuter agreement is considered inappropriate. However, when the noun incorporates, as in (70), the judgments reverse: now absence of object agreement is normal, and its presence is rare or impossible.[28] This is exactly what one expects on the syntactic approach. In contrast, the lexicalist approach predicts that the same pattern of judgments should be seen in (69) and (70), which is clearly not the case.[29] This pattern is typical of the wide range of examples in which *wir* may be incorporated.

Another minimal pair demonstrating the same point comes from a comparison of the two expressions for 'bus' in current use at Kahnawake:

(71) a. yako-ya't-a-karény-es
      NsS/FsO-body-Ø-transport-HAB
      'bus' (Literally: 'it transports one')

    b. w-at-ukwe-ht-a-karény-es
       NsS-SRFL-person-NOM-Ø-transport-HAB
       'bus' (Literally: 'it transports people.')

The verbal form in (71b) differs from the one in (71a) in that it incorporates the noun root *ukwe* 'person'.[30] Correlated with this is the fact that the transitive verb root in (71b) no longer shows third person object agreement: one finds the intransitive prefix *w* instead of the transitive animate prefix *yako* in (71a). Again we see the complementarity between NI and object agreement that the syntactic theory predicts, not the duplication that the lexicalist theory predicts.

A third instructive example comes from Bonvillain and Francis 1980. This text is a folktale concerning how a bear is tricked by a fox. As is typical of Mohawk tales of this genre, the bear is referred to with masculine singular agreement forms throughout the text. The only exception is in the following form, which is taken from almost the very end of the story (p. 85). This form is unique in the text in that the noun root *ahkwari* 'bear, furry animal' is incorporated into the verb. The form is also unique in that masculine agreement is absent:

(72) Tu-t-a-ha-[a]nijúhkwahkw-e'. O-huj-a-'ke
      DUP-CIS-FACT-MsS-jump-PUNC NsO-ground-Ø-LOC

      yu-s-a-*w-ahkwali*-'t-akwÁhta-la'-ne'.
      TRANS-ITER-FACT-*NsS-bear*-NOM-fall.spread.out-reach-PUNC
      'He jumped back down; onto the ground came the falling-down-bear.'

Again agreement is in complementary distribution with NI.

Example (72) is slightly different from the previous examples in that the verb is unaccusative rather than transitive. This means that once the N has incorporated, there is no argument left for the verb to agree with. Under these circumstances, the verb shows a default neuter agreement prefix. This I take to be an expletive, required for the formal reason that each Mohawk verb must have some agreement prefix (a fact that is probably related to the Extended Projection Principle of Chomsky 1981). Crucially, however, we do not find the agreement form for the bear that would be expected in the context of this story. The existence of a dummy agreement prefix on unaccusative verbs with NI is quite general; (73) gives an example with *wir* 'baby' that is directly comparable to (69) and (70) apart from this factor.

(73) a. T-a'-e (*ka)-yá't-Λ'-ne'   ne o-wir-á'a.
         CIS-FACT-FsS(*NsS)-body-fall-PUNC NE NsO-baby-NSF
         'The baby fell.'

    b. T-a'-ka (*e)-wír-Λ'-ne'.
       CIS-FACT-NsS (*FsS)-baby-fall-PUNC
       'The baby fell.'

The presence of the *ka* morpheme in (73b) has no doubt contributed to the impression in the literature that verbs in Mohawk do agree with incorporated nouns.[31]

However, it is wrong to call this agreement, when it is a form that cannot otherwise represent 'baby'. Rather, my claim is that this *ka* is not agreement at all, but rather the same expletive morpheme that appears with, say, meteorological predicates in Mohawk.

Other textual examples of animate NI are given in (74). None of them shows object agreement with the incorporated noun root.

(74) a. Yako-ksá-ht-a-yʌ. (OK:28)
          FsO-child-NOM-Ø-have
          'She has children.'

      b. Tu-t-a-yako-kétoht-e'   ts-e-wir-ʌháwi. (OK:28)
          DUP-CIS-FACT-FsO-appear-PUNC ITER-FsS-baby-carry/STAT
          'She appeared carrying a baby.'

      c. Wa-ha-'nha'-tsher-ísak-e'. (H:315)
          FACT-MsS-hire-NOM-seek-PUNC
          'He is looking for servants.'

      d. t-a-yo-nʌhl-a-kétoht-e' (B&F:91)
          CIS-FACT-NsO-crowd-Ø-appear-PUNC
          'The gang (three males) is coming into view.'

The grammaticality of these examples has also been confirmed by native speakers.

One might try to save the lexicalist approach by saying that the compound in, say, (70b) is simply intransitive syntactically. In other words, N and V combine to form a verb that happens to be an intransitive verb in this particular case. This would explain the absence of object agreement. However, it would not explain the fact that forms like (75) are possible, where there is an external modifier or doubling NP related to the IN.

(75) Ra-wir-a-núhwe'-s   thíkʌ (owirá'a).
      MsS-baby-Ø-like-HAB   that   baby
      'He likes that baby.'

This is perhaps the single most important example in this book for the theory of morphology and syntax, because it shows that verbs with incorporated nouns have a unique syntax, unlike that of any simple verb in the language. If the verb in (75) were truly intransitive, then there would be no argument position available to license the external NP in this sentence (see chapter 3). On the other hand, if the verb were a simple transitive, then it would have to agree with its object. However, there is a sharp contrast between (75) and (69), where there is no NI and object agreement is necessary.[32] Other examples illustrating animate NI without agreement but with external modification are[33]:

(76) a. ʌ-yo-wir-a-yʌ́ta'-ne'   roskʌrakéhte' nok Yésos (PB:401)
          FUT-ZsO-baby-Ø-acquire-PUNC male   and Jesus

          ʌ-tshe-nátu-hkw-e'.
          FUT-2sS/MsO-name-INSTR-PUNC
          'She will have a boy, and you will name him Jesus.' (Matt. 1:21)

      b. ʌ-ke-kstʌ-ser-áhset-e'   ne ro-nuhwáktʌni.
          FUT-1sS-old.person-NOM-hide-PUNC NE MsO-sick/STAT
          'I will hide the old man that is sick.'

Crucial examples like (75) and (76) can be formed in the Iroquoian languages, but not in the other polysynthetic languages, for independent reasons. In the Tanoan and Gunwinjguan languages, verbs still agree with their incorporated nouns, as mentioned in chapter 1. This is compatible with a syntactic analysis, since the MVC states only that the direct object must be coindexed with a morpheme in the word that contains its θ-marker; it does not say that that morpheme must be unique. Thus, while Mohawk prefers the economy of omitting the object agreement when incorporation makes it unnecessary, Southern Tiwa and Mayali prefer the uniformity of always agreeing with their syntactic object. This means, however, that lexicalists can more easily consider N–V combinations to be ordinary transitive verbs in these languages. (Whether this is the correct analysis or not remains to be seen; see later discussion.) On the other hand, in Nahuatl, Chukchee, and Ainu, INs cannot be doubled or modified regardless of the agreement; hence, lexicalists can analyze N–V combinations in these languages as being ordinary intransitive verbs. However, the fact that Mohawk does not fit well into either category deserves very careful consideration. Indeed, the situation in Mohawk is the reverse of that in Southern Tiwa, as described in the previous section: N–V combinations in Southern Tiwa cannot take a full range of external "objects" even though they take normal object agreement; N–V combinations in Mohawk can take a full range of external "objects" even though they do not take object agreement. Both deviations from the norm show that the syntax of N–V combinations is not identical to the syntax of any simple verb—a distinctive prediction of the head-movement account.

This is not quite the whole story, however. Although most or all of the textual examples of animate NI lack agreement, native speakers sometimes allow variation on this point. Thus, either an agreeing form or a nonagreeing form is accepted in the following examples:

(77)   a. Uwári ye (ruwa)-kstʌ-hser-Áhaw-e'   ne rake-'níha.
          Mary FsS(/MsO)-old.person-NOM-carry-IMPF NE my-father
          'Mary is holding my father.'

       b. Ke (ri)-ksa-ht-a-núhwe'-s   ne tshe-'ná'-u.
          1sS(/MsO)-child-NOM-Ø-like-HAB NE 2sS/MsO-hire-STAT
          'I like the child that you hired.'

       c. Wa'-ke (hi)-kstʌ-hser-áhset-e'.
          FACT-1sS(/MsO)-old.person-NOM-hide-PUNC
          'I hid the old person (the old man).'

       d. Wa'-o (ho)-ksa-ht-a-ké'tot-e'   ne ra-hútsi.
          FACT-N(M)sO-child-NOM-Ø-appear-PUNC NE MsS-black
          'A dark child has appeared, was born.'

How is this to be understood? I would like to suggest that the material in (77) shows that *both* the lexical compounding analysis and the syntactic incorporation analysis are valid after all. The two structures often exist side by side in Mohawk: if (77a) has the intransitive agreement *ye* (FsS), then the empty category in object position is a trace; if it has the transitive agreement *ruwa* (FsS/MsO), then the empty category in object position is a pro. This variability makes sense if learners of Mohawk are in essentially the same position as the linguist analyzing Mohawk when it comes to noun incorporation. Universal Grammar allows two plausible ways of analyzing the structure, both of which are compatible with the primary linguistic data. Hence, the native speaker acquires both analyses and uses them in parallel fashion. Since speakers have little practical experience with these forms for other reasons, their judgments are rather insecure and variable in exactly this domain, and individual differences in what is accepted or preferred are found. The claim that the agreeing and nonagreeing forms in (77) have quite different syntactic structures will be confirmed in the next two sections.

Nevertheless, I think it is fair to say that the syntactic incorporation analysis is the more fundamental one. The fact that nonagreeing forms are more common in texts than agreeing forms is one piece of evidence. Another is the fact that there are some instances of animate NI where speakers do not seem to permit agreement, such as (69), whereas I know of no comparable cases where speakers require agreement with the IN. Moreover, this is what one would expect on general grounds: as a syntactic process, noun incorporation should be relatively general and free from lexical exceptions, whereas lexical compounding can depend on idiosyncratic factors including the lexical semantics of the particular roots involved and differences in people's linguistic input. Thus, the syntactic pattern should always be possible (subject to other conditions), whereas there is considerable variability (and uncertainty) regarding the lexical pattern. This seems to correctly describe my consultants' behavior. Further evidence pointing in this direction is found in section 7.4.5.

7.4.3 Disjoint Reference Effects

A second way to distinguish between the lexicalist approach and the syntactic approach is via Binding Theory. The lexicalist analysis claims that the syntactic object of a simple NI clause is a null pronoun. If this is so, then the empty category is subject to Principle B of Chomsky 1981, which allows it to have a c-commanding antecedent as long as that antecedent is outside of the smallest clause containing the pronoun. In contrast, the syntactic analysis claims that the empty category in a simple NI construction is the trace of a lexical noun. Since this trace is locally bound by a lexical N, it presumably acts like a lexical N itself—either because the two share all relevant syntactic features or by virtue of some kind of reconstruction. In this case, the empty category should be subject to Condition C, meaning that it should resist being coreferential with any c-commanding NP, local or not. Thus, we want to look for Mohawk paradigms of the form in (78).

(78)   a. NP_i. . . [$_S$. . . V. . . pro_i. . .] coreference allowed

       b. NP_i. . . [$_S$. . . V. . . $NP*_i$. .] disjoint reference

       c. NP_i. . . [$_S$. . . N-V. . . ec_i. .] ???

The contrast between (78a) and (78b) would establish that Condition C is found in Mohawk in a way that is comparable to English (something we already know from section 2.1.1). The crucial sentence would then be (78c), where the lexicalist theory predicts judgments comparable to (78a), while the syntactic theory predicts judgments comparable to (78b).

Example (79) shows an instance of such a paradigm. Each sentence has *rabah-bót* 'bullhead' as the subject of the matrix clause and a potentially coreferential nominal in the embedded clause. When that nominal is a null pronoun, coreference is possible, as expected (see (79a)). When the nominal is an independent NP (*kÁtsu'*) 'fish', coreference is resisted. This confirms that Condition C is operative in Mohawk. (The context for these sentences was anthropomorphizing the feelings of a fish on sale at a pet store.)

(79) a. Rabahbót yah tha'-te-yo-[a]tΛhutsóni   ne úhka
          bullhead not CONTR-DUP-ZsO-want/STAT NE someone

          a-ye-hnínu-'.
          OPT-FsS/NsO-buy-PUNC
          '*The bullhead* doesn't want anyone to buy *it*.' (coreference OK)

      b. Rabahbót yah tha'-te-yo-[a]tΛhutsóni   ne úhka   a-ye-hnínu-'
          bullhead not CONTR-DUP-ZsS-want/STAT NE someone OPT-FsS-buy-PUNC

          ne kÁ-[i]ts-u'.
          NE NsS-fish-NSF
          '*The bullhead* doesn't want anyone to buy *fish*.' (disjoint only)

      c. Rabahbót yah tha'-te-yo-[a]tΛhutsóni   ne úhka
          bullhead not CONTR-DUP-ZsS-want/STAT NE someone

          a-ye-[i]ts-a-hnínu-'.
          OPT-FsS-fish-Ø-buy-PUNC
          '*The bullhead* doesn't want anyone to buy *the fish*.' (disjoint only)

The example of interest is (79c), where the noun root *its* 'fish' is incorporated. In fact, the three speakers consulted all interpret this as disjoint in reference from the subject of the higher clause, similar to (79b). Thus, the prediction of the syntactic theory is confirmed, rather than the prediction of the lexicalist theory.

Once again, the lexicalist theory cannot be saved by simply assuming that *its-a-hninu* 'fish-buy' is an intransitive N–V compound. If such an analysis were tenable, then there would simply be no NP position in (79c) that could corefer with 'bullhead', accounting for the observed judgment. However, (58) showed that it *is* possible to have an overt NP licensed by the object position with this verb. Furthermore, an incorporated noun can be coreferential with another NP in the sentence as long as that NP does not c-command the (trace of the) IN[34]:

(80) Rabahbót wa'-k-atkátho-'   tsi yutΛhninútha' sok wa'-k-its-a-hnínu-'.
      bullhead FACT-1sS-see-PUNC at-store   so FACT-1sS-fish-Ø-buy-PUNC
      'I saw a *bullhead* at the store and so I bought *the fish*.' (coreference OK)

(81) Rabahbót aon-atÁro yah té-w-ehr-e'   úhka
      bullhead its-friend not NEG-ZsS-want-IMPF someone

      a-ye-[i]ts-a-hnínu-'.
      OPT-FsS-fish-Ø-buy-PUNC
      '*The bullhead's* friend doesn't want anyone to buy the *fish*.' (coreference marginally OK)

Thus, one cannot simply say that coreference is bad in (79c) because INs are inherently nonreferential in Mohawk. Rather, the pattern of judgments is exactly what one expects if Condition C is at work.

This behavior of the IN seems to be quite consistent to the extent that it can be checked. Once again, the fact that animate INs are relatively rare means that one can only construct a limited range of examples. The problem stems from the fact that those verbs that take sentential complements—verbs of cognition, communication, and desire—typically take only animate arguments. Thus, it is virtually impossible to find cases where an inanimate NP c-commands another potentially coreferential NP. However, when examples with an animate IN are constructed, coreference is resisted as long as the IN does not trigger agreement. I have constructed many examples, of which those in (82) are representative.

(82)   a. (Sak) ra-tsháni-s   tóka   ʌ-ke-ksá-ht-a-ya'k-e'.
          Sak   MsS-fear-HAB maybe FUT-1sS-child-NOM-Ø-hit-PUNC
          '*He* (Sak*)* is afraid that maybe I will slap *the child.*' (coreference ??)

       b. Sak í-hr-ehr-e'   ka-kstʌ-hser-akéras.
          Sak Ø-MsS-think-IMPF NsS-old.person-NOM-stink
          '*Sak* thinks *the old person* smells bad.'   (coreference ??)

       c. Sak í-hr-ehr-e'   a-ke-kstʌ-hser-áhset-e'.
          Sak Ø-MsS-think-IMPF OPT-1sS-old.person-NOM-hide-PUNC
          '*Sak* wants me to hide *the old person.*'   (coreference ??)

This is strong evidence for the syntactic approach to NI. It shows rather clearly that an incorporated N root is equivalent to an independent NP for purposes of anaphora. This fits well with the results of section 6.2, where we saw that INs are equivalent to independent NPs for most semantic and pragmatic purposes.[35]

Finally, suppose that we construct the same test examples with verbs that agree with the IN. This gives the results in (83), which can be compared with (82a).

(83)   Sak ra-tsháni-s   tóka   ʌ-*hi*-ksá-ht-a-ya'k-e'.
       Sak MsS-fear-HAB maybe FUT-1sS/MsO-child-NOM-Ø-hit-PUNC
       '*Sak* is afraid that maybe I will slap *the child.*' (coreference OK)

In this example, coreference between the relevant argument of the matrix verb and the argument associated with the IN is very natural. This suggests that the empty category in (83) is pronominal, unlike those in (82). Exactly the same effect is seen in (82b,c): if the prefixes *ka* (NsS) and *ke* (1sS) in the final verbs are replaced by *ra* (MsS) and *hi* (1sS/MsO), respectively, then the indicated coreferences become perfectly natural. Apparently, the difference between agreeing NI and non-agreeing NI is not just a matter of superficial morphology. Rather, we have confirmed the conjecture that the two kinds of sentences have different syntactic structures. Once again, either syntactic noun incorporation or lexical compounding is possible in principle.

7.4.4 NI and Questions

The third way of distinguishing the lexicalist analysis from the syntactic analysis involves the interaction between NI and question formation. Section 2.1.4 showed that some question phrases must be generated in argument positions; they cannot be licensed by the ALC because of their nonreferential nature. Given this, the issue arises of whether one can both question and incorporate the same argument.

According to the lexicalist analysis, this should be possible, given the leading idea that complex verbs with an incorporated noun root are identical to ordinary transitive verbs. Since one can question the theme argument of a simple verb, one should also be able to question the theme argument of a N–V compound. The syntactic approach, however, anticipates a problem in this situation. The difficulty stems from the fact that the incorporated noun must have originated in the head of the direct object position, but the *wh*-phrase in Comp must also have originated in the direct object position. There is no way that these two requirements can be satisfied simultaneously. Hence, the syntactic analysis predicts that NI should be incompatible with ordinary questions, while the lexicalist analysis predicts that NI should be compatible with simple questions.

(84) a. Wh–NP$_i$ . . . [$_{VP}$ N–V t$_i$]   lexicalist approach

     b. *Wh–NP$_i$ . . . [$_{VP}$ N$_k$–V t$_k$/t$_i$] syntactic approach

In (85), a paradigm is given that is relevant to checking these predictions. Example (85a) shows that this particular N + V combination is "transitive" in the sense that its theme argument can be doubled by a referential NP. Nevertheless, the theme argument cannot be questioned using an interrogative word equivalent to English *who* (see (85b)); native speakers typically correct such sentences to ones that have the equivalent of English *which* (see (85c)).

(85) a. T-ʌ-ke-wír-a-hkw-e'   ne ka-wir-íyo.
        DUP-FUT-1sS-baby-Ø-pick.up-PUNC NE NsS-baby-nice
        'I will pick up the nice baby.'

     b. ?*Úhka t-ʌ-hse-wír-a-hkw-e'?
        who DUP-FUT-2sS-baby-Ø-pick.up-PUNC
        'Who are you going to pick up (a baby)?'

     c. Ka nikáyʌ t-ʌ-hse-wír-a-hkw-e'?
        which DUP-FUT-2sS-baby-Ø-pick.up-PUNC
        'Which baby are you going to pick up?'

The ungrammaticality of (85b) confirms the syntactic approach to NI.

Of course, to complete the analysis, we must also explain why (85c) is grammatical. The contrast between (85b) and (85c) recalls the contrast in (86), discussed in section 4.3.1.

(86) a. ??Úhka wa-shé-kʌ-'   ne eksá'a?
        who FACT-2sS/FsO-see-PUNC NE child
        'Who did you see, a child?'

     b. Ka nikáyʌ wa-shé-kʌ-'   ne eksá'a?
        which FACT-2sS/FsO-see-PUNC NE child
        'Which child did you see?'

These examples are similar to those in (85) in that *ka nikáyʌ* 'which' can be separated from its head N, whereas *úhka* 'who' cannot be. Example (86), in turn, is related to the more basic contrast in (87).

(87) a. ??Úhka eksá'a wa-shé-kʌ-'?
        who child FACT-2sS/FsO-see-PUNC
        'Who (a child) did you see?'

b. Ka nikáyʌ eksá'a wa-shé-kʌ-'?
    which   child FACT-2sS/FsO-see-PUNC
    'Which child did you see?'

Example (87) shows that *ka nikáyʌ* can adjoin to a complete NP projection, whereas *úhka* cannot. Thus, (86b) was generated by adjoining *ka nikáyʌ* to the pro in object position and then moving it to Comp; the pro left behind can then license an adjoined NP. Similarly, (85c) can be generated by adjoining *ka nikáyʌ* to the NP in object position headed by *wir* 'baby'. Then, *wir* incorporates into the verb, and *ka nikáyʌ* moves to Comp. Thus, the structure of (85c) is (88).

(88)

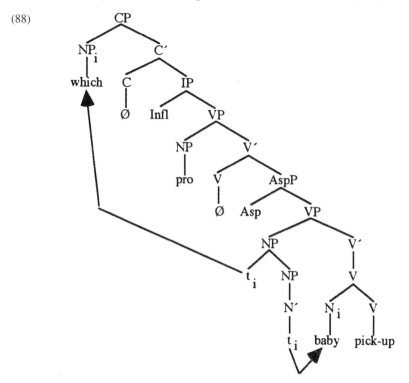

No such structure is possible when the question word is *úhka* 'who', since *úhka* cannot be adjoined to an argument position. Rather, *úhka* must fill an argument position itself. However, if it does, then there is no legitimate source for the incorporated noun root under the syntactic analysis.[36] This, then, completes the account of the paradigm in (85).

Other examples illustrating the incompatibility of *who*-type questions with NI are:

(89) a. *Úhka wa'-ke-ksá-ht-a-ya'k-e'?
          who FACT-1sS-child-NOM-Ø-hit-PUNC
          'Who (a child) did I slap?'

      b. ??Úhka ka-kstʌ-hser-akéras?
          Who NsS-old.person-NOM-stink
          'Who (an old person) smells?'

c. ??Úhka ye-'nha'-tsher-a-núhwe'-s ne Uwári?
  who FsS-hire-NOM-Ø-like-HAB NE Mary
  'Who of the hired help does Mary like?'

These sentences all become perfect if *úhka* 'who' is replaced by *ka nikáyʌ* 'which', as we expect. Interestingly, they also become perfect if the verb shows agreement with the IN, as is sometimes possible. Thus, (90) contrasts sharply with (89a).

(90) Úhka wa'-*khe*-ksá-ht-a-ya'k-e'?
  who FACT-1sS/FsO-child-NOM-hit-PUNC
  'Who (a child) did I slap?'

Similarly, (89b,c) become grammatical if the agreement prefixes *ka* (NsS) and *ye* (FsS) are replaced by *ra* (MsS) and *ruwa* (FsS/MsO), respectively. Thus, for sentences like (90) the natural prediction of the lexicalist analysis is borne out, whereas sentences like (89) validate the syntactic analysis. This confirms once again the conclusion that N + V combinations in Mohawk may be derived by either noun incorporation in the syntax or by lexical compounding (cf. Hopkins 1988, where a similar conclusion is reached).[37]

Unlike the other tests for distinguishing between lexical compounds and syntactic incorporations, question formation paradigms can be readily constructed using inanimate themes as well as animate ones. Thus, in this domain one can create a virtually unlimited range of examples. The general result is that questions using (*oh*) *nahótʌ* 'what' are ungrammatical:

(91) a. *Nahótʌ wa'-yu-[a]tya'tawi-tsher-a-hnínu-'?
      what FACT-FsS-dress-NOM-Ø-buy-PUNC
      'What did she garment-buy (a dress, shirt, or coat)?'

   b. *Nahótʌ wa'-t-ha-yʌ́t-ya'k-e'?
      what FACT-DUP-MsS-wood-cut-PUNC
      'What (kind of wood) did he wood-cut?'

   c. *Nahótʌ wa-hs-atsherunya-tsher-íhsa-'?
      what FACT-2sS-garment-NOM-finish-PUNC
      'What did you garment-make?'

   d. *Nahótʌ wa-hse-ks-óhare-'?
      what FACT-2sS-dish-wash-PUNC
      'What did you dish-wash?'

   e. *Nahótʌ wa-ha-'wáhr-a-k-e'?
      what FACT-MsS-meat-Ø-eat-PUNC
      'What did he meat-eat?'

As usual, these contrast with parallel questions using *ka nikáyʌ* 'which', are uniformly grammatical. There are a few examples that look like they have a similar structure to those in (91), but which are grammatical; these I take to be lexicalized compounds. Thus (92) is possible because (as in many languages) *hnek-íra* 'water-drink' is simply the normal transitive verb meaning 'drink'.

(92)   NahótΛ Λ-s-hnek-íra-'?
       what   FUT-2sS-liquid-drink-PUNC
       'What will you drink?'

I have found a few other examples like (92), but not many.[38]

    This pattern of facts reveals something important about the place of noun incor-poration in Universal Grammar. Although NI may be either syntactic or lexical in Mohawk, (91) indicates that it is *primarily* syntactic. Children learning Mohawk have essentially no data available concerning whether these N–V combinations (some of which are very common) are formed lexically or syntactically. Since the agreement paradigm is ambiguous, the only visible difference between the two constructions when the N is inanimate is these question formation patterns. How-ever, these facts are surely not available to children in the process of language acquisition. Children will hear examples like (92), which help them decide that these N–V combinations are formed lexically; however, they cannot conclude any-thing from the fact that they do not hear the examples in (91). Thus, the only explicit input they could receive would only mislead them as to the actual state of affairs. Hence, we have an interesting case of Chomsky's famous "poverty of stimulus" argument, where children get no evidence that helps them to decide between two competing analyses. Their choice then reveals something about Uni-versal Grammar. Now, the results indicate that they choose to analyze the majority of examples as syntactic incorporation. This means that syntactic NI must be in some sense the unmarked analysis. This is very counterintuitive, however, given that many languages have productive compounding, while relatively few have true noun incorporation. Much more likely is that children's innate linguistic compe-tence is set up in such a way that they consider syntactic NI the unmarked option *given what they already know about Mohawk.* What could they have previously learned about Mohawk that would guide them in analyzing these forms? The obvi-ous answer is the Polysynthesis Parameter. Once they have learned from the rich agreement morphology and the nonconfigurational properties of Mohawk that this parameter is set positively, they expect the N–V combinations that they see to be formed syntactically. Examples (91) and (92) thus constitute a subtle learnability argument in favor of the view that true NI must be triggered by a parametric feature. This supplements the conceptual and typological arguments given in sec-tion 7.1.1.

7.4.5 NI and Agreement in Other Languages

In section 7.4.2, I mentioned in passing that the Tanoan languages and the Gun-winjguan languages differ from Mohawk in that their verbs consistently show full agreement with the theme even when it is incorporated. Thus, the agreement mor-phology on the verb is the same with or without NI in these languages. This is quite obvious in Southern Tiwa, as (93) illustrates.

(93)   a. Wisi seuan-in bi-mū-ban.   (AGF:295)
          two   man-PL 1sS/bO-see-PAST
          'I saw two men.'

   b. Wisi bi-seuan-mū-ban.
      two 1sS/вO-man-see-PAST
      'I saw two men.'

If the verb in (93b) were grammatically intransitive with a first person singular subject, its agreement prefix would be *te* instead. Moreover, (94) shows that the agreement on the verb changes, depending on the number and noun class of the IN.

(94) a. Ti-seuan-mū-ban. (AGF:294)
         1sS/aO-man-see-PAST
         'I saw the/a man.'

      b. Te-shut-pe-ban. (AGF:293)
         1sS/cO-shirt-make-PAST
         'I made the/a shirt.'

Thus, the interaction of agreement and NI in Southern Tiwa is clearly different from that in Mohawk.

The facts are somewhat more subtle in the Gunwinjguan languages. Mayali is like Mohawk in that plural number is only marked for animate nouns. It is also like Mohawk in that the third person singular/unmarked object agreement is morphologically null. Thus, in an example like (95) one cannot tell by inspection whether the verb agrees with its theme or not.

(95) Nga-yaw-na-ng. (Nicholas Evans, personal communication)
      1sS/(3sO)-baby-see-PAST/PERF
      'I saw the baby.'

Hence, as in Mohawk, one must explore the peripheries of the system to get crucial evidence. One way of doing this is by incorporating an animate N understood as being plural; this changes the agreement prefix, as shown in (96).

(96) Ngaban-yaw-na-ng. (Nicholas Evans, personal communication)
      1sS/3pO-baby-see-PAST/PERF
      'I saw the babies.'

Mayali also has a special agreement prefix *bi* that indicates that the third person object of the verb is higher on an animacy hierarchy than the third person subject. This prefix is found on verbs even when the theme is incorporated:

(97) Bi-yau-ngune-nguneng   ginga. (Evans 1991:291)
      3sS/3hO-baby-eat-PAST/PERF crocodile
      'The crocodile ate the child.'

This gives further evidence that Mayali and Mohawk differ, even though this difference is not apparent in the most common examples of NI.[39]

Given these facts, it makes sense to ask whether NI in Southern Tiwa and Mayali is formed by syntactic head movement or by lexical compounding. A priori, one might expect their NI constructions to behave like lexical compounds, because that is how forms with agreeing INs behave in Mohawk. On the other hand, one might expect their NI constructions to behave like instances of syntactic head movement in light of their productivity and their referential properties.

Not surprisingly, the literature does not give the kinds of facts that are crucial to deciding between these two analyses. However, the information that I have been able to glean from those who work on the languages in question points consistently to the conclusion that NI is formed by syntactic movement. Thus, there is a contrast between the following sentences in Southern Tiwa (Donald Frantz, personal communication):

(98)   a. Seuan-ide a-na-kacha-m   (hi'a) ti-mū-mi-'i.
          man-SG   AS-q-know-PRES that 1sS/AO-see-PRES-SUB
          'The man knows (that) I see him.'   (coreference OK)

     b. A-na-kacha-m   hi'a ti-seuan-mū-mi-'i.
          AS-q-know-PRES that 1sS/AO-man-see-PRES-SUB
          'He knows that I see the man.'   (disjoint only)

Example (98a) shows that a null pronoun in an embedded clause can readily be understood as coreferential with the matrix subject, as expected. The native speaker responded quite differently to (98b), however, where the embedded object is represented by an IN (as well as verb agreement); here, coreference between the lower object and the matrix subject is impossible. This I take as showing that the empty category in object position is, indeed, the trace of the incorporated noun, and not the pronominal object of an ordinary transitive verb. Similarly, Nicholas Evans (personal communication) believes that an IN in an embedded complement clause cannot be coreferential with a matrix clause argument in Mayali—although this impression has not been confirmed with native speakers.

Data concerning the interaction between question formation and NI point in the same direction. Southern Tiwa shows the same clear contrast between 'who'-type questions and 'which'-type questions as is found in Mohawk (Donald Frantz, personal communication).

(99)   a. Yoade-u a-seuan-mu-we?
          which   2sS/AO-man-see-PRES
          'Which man do you see?'

     b. *B'āyu a-seuan-mu-we?
          who   2sS/AO-man-see-PRES
          'Who (a man) do you man?'

Again, this suggests that the direct object position in (99b) is filled by the trace of the IN, leaving no place for the trace of *b'āyu* 'who'. Example (99b) is then ruled out because it has a quantifier that binds no variable. Again, Nicolas Evans (personal communication) believes that the Mayali equivalent of (99b) is also ungrammatical.

Together, these similarities among Mohawk, Southern Tiwa, and Mayali suggest that whether or not the verbs of a language agree with an IN is a matter of low-level variation, having little impact on the syntax of NI. Certain facts of Ainu confirm this; according to Shibatani (1990:63–64), some dialects of Ainu show agreement with the IN and some do not. Thus, the incorporated version of (100a) is either (100b) or (100c), depending on the dialect.

(100) a. Wakka a-Ø-ta-re.
water 1sS-3sO-draw-CAUS
'I make (someone) draw water.'

b. Wakka-ta-re-an.
water-draw-CAUS-1sS
'I make (someone) draw water.'

c. A-Ø-wakka-ta-re.
1sS-3sO-water-draw-CAUS
'I make (someone) draw water.'

Here, the third person object agreement is null, but its presence or absence can be inferred from the form of the first person subject agreement, which is different in transitive and intransitive sentences. There is no evidence that this dialectal variation has any other effect on the syntax of the language.

If these results hold up under further investigation, they confirm the reasoning presented at the end of the last section. Once again, native speakers of polysynthetic languages seem to prefer a syntactic movement analysis of NI over a lexical compounding analysis, even when there are no obvious data to distinguish the two. If lexical compounding between N and V existed as a productive option to derive transitive verbs in Southern Tiwa or Mayali, then the contrasts in (98) and (99) should not appear. I conclude that syntactic NI is the unmarked option in languages where the Polysynthesis Parameter holds. Lexical compounding may exist as well, but speakers only analyze a given structure as a compound if they are forced to do so—say by an idiosyncrasy in the meaning of the form, by the fact that the IN does not bear a thematic relationship with respect to the verb, or (in Mohawk) by the presence of a visible object agreement morpheme. This implies that the Lexicalist Hypothesis cannot be maintained, at least in its strongest form. Thus, the essential theoretical point of Baker 1988a is supported over the reanalyses of Di Sciullo and Williams 1987, Anderson 1992, and other relatively pure lexicalist analyses.

7.5 Conclusion

One theme of this chapter has been that noun incorporation constructions in polysynthetic languages are virtually identical to ordinary verb–object constructions in other languages. Thus, NI constructions have the same range of interpretations as verb–object constructions with respect to definiteness and aspect (section 7.2), they are subject to the same disjoint reference conditions (section 7.4.3), and they form the same kinds of questions (section 7.4.4). In my analysis, this is explained by deriving the NI construction from an ordinary verb–object source by a semantically vacuous process of N movement. This type of N movement is subject to the normal principles that govern movements of all types, which explains why only themes and a few reference objects may incorporate (section 7.3).

The other theme of this chapter has been the role of the MVC in triggering the N movement that results in noun incorporation structures. This parameter plays a crucial part in explaining the fact that NI is essentially obligatory in a typologically homogenous class of languages (the polysynthetic languages), but is forbidden in all others (section 7.1). It also explains why speakers of Mohawk, Southern Tiwa, and Mayali typically analyze N–V combinations as noun incorporations even under conditions where there seems to be no good reason not to analyze them as compounds instead. Thus, noun incorporation is not really a primitive typological feature of languages; rather it is a reflection of a deeper property of language—namely the Polysynthesis Parameter.

Notes

1. The best evidence for this comes from: (1) the behavior of complement clauses with respect to binding and extraction (chapter 2), (2) the pattern of sloppy identity effects in ellipsis interpretation (chapter 3), and (3) the effect that the subject has on the agreement form of the object (chapter 5). The fact that floated *éso* 'many, a lot' can be interpreted with the object but not the subject (chapter 4) may also constitute evidence for this point.

2. Another, somewhat more attractive, approach is to have a morphological filter *[$_V$ N–V] in PF in English (see Baker 1988c). This filter is independently motivated by the fact that English lacks simple compounding of this type. However, the approach is ad hoc and unprincipled. It may also have empirical problems. Thus, English has acquired a number of N–V compounds through backformation from synthetic compounds; hence, there are verbs like *babysit, bartend, hand-wash, grocery-shop, air-condition,* and so on. Nevertheless, the addition of these forms to the language shows no sign of leading to the development of full-blown NI. Moreover, there seem to be languages where N–V compounding is permitted that still do not have syntactic noun incorporation in the Mohawk sense. The Oceanic languages may be of this type (Rosen 1989b; see also Mithun's (1984a) type I incorporation).

3. Chukchee has one part of the verb paradigm, consisting of the so-called present II forms, which does not show agreement with the transitive object (Comrie 1979). This is presumably a marked part of the grammar; Comrie points out that this tense is not found in closely related Koryak and seems to be an innovation. The forms are similar to those of predicative nouns and adjectives.

Ainu is constrained to be verb final, and thus looks rather like a configurational SOV language (see section 3.2.1).

4. This discussion assumes that the MVC is the only trigger for NI allowed by Universal Grammar. One might consider weakening this assumption somewhat. There are various claims that NI also takes place in some nonpolysynthetic languages, notably Turkish (Knecht 1985), Hindi (Mohanan 1991), and the Oceanic languages. In these languages, NI is possible only if the N has a generic, nonreferential interpretation. This is quite different from Mohawk, where INs can be generic, specific, definite, indefinite, or what you will (see later discussion). The question is how to understand this type of noun incorporation.

One possibility is to follow Rosen (1989b) and say that these forms like are simply N–V compounds. The generic interpretation of the Ns follows immediately from this, since other synthetic compounds have the same property (cf. Di Sciullo and Williams 1987). The MVC would then be the only trigger for incorporation in the syntax. Whether synthetic compounds are derived by a type of incorporation that applies in the Lexicon is a separate question (cf. Hale and Keyser 1992).

There is another possibility that may be worth considering. One might say that generic determiners in some languages are absent or somehow defective. This, then, might force N movement in the syntax to arrive at an interpretable structure. This would be an alternative way of accounting for the observed correlation of NI and genericity in these languages. Mohanan (1991) gives two arguments that NI structures in Hindi do not act just like morphologically complex verbs; this might point to an analysis of this type. This approach is being explored by Murvet Enç (unpublished data) for Turkish.

Apparently NI can also be triggered by morphological properties. In particular, it will happen if the noun is an affix that must attach to a verb, or if the verb is an affix that must attach to a noun. The first is Baker's (1988a) analysis of antipassive morphemes across languages; the second describes the well-known case of NI in the Eskimoan languages (cf. Baker 1988a, 1988c). If, however, the program of eliminating morphological subcategorization frames proposed in section 1.6 can be sustained, these examples will have to be rethought.

5. Examples of this type are possible in other polysynthetic languages, such as Southern Tiwa and Mayali (see section 7.4.5 for some discussion).

6. Baker and Hale 1990 claimed that NI could skip over an intervening Det; however, the crucial examples involved demonstratives, which I now believe are not determiners, for the reasons discussed in sections 4.3 and 6.1.3.

7. Note that Williams' system is rather different from Higginbotham's (1985) more traditional and well-known system. For Higginbotham, determiners play the role of discharging the R role of their NP complement, and the argument structure of a nominal must be fully discharged before it can serve as an argument of some other category. Higginbotham's analysis does not fit well with NI structures in Mohawk, in which NP can be the argument of a verb even though there can be no determiner present.

8. On this point, I am in partial agreement with Woodbury (1975). She states that INs in Onondaga may presuppose the existence of their referent, like definite NPs in English (Heim 1982), or they may not, like indefinite NPs in English. However, she eventually concludes that INs are basically indefinite, in contrast to NPs preceded by *ne'*. I suspect that this impression was a result of not putting the sentences in a suitable context to bring out the definite meaning. I have not tested Woodbury's claim that NI crucially involves an element of meaning glossable as 'kind of'.

9. The resistance of animate Ns to incorporation is discussed somewhat in section 7.4. Other than this, it seems that the restrictions on what nouns can be incorporated are mostly morphological in nature, as Woodbury (1975:17–20) suggests for Onondaga. Thus, expressions with the functional force of nouns but the morphological structure of verbs cannot be incorporated. This follows from the theory of such elements given in chapter 4, where they are treated as headless relative clauses. Also, uninflected nouns (including loan words from French and English) may sometimes be incorporated by adding a nominalizer suffix, but often are not. Proper nouns never incorporate; not only are they animate, but those of native origin have the morphological structure of verbs, and those taken from French or English are uninflected.

Given that Mohawk has what is known as "classifier incorporation," it has been suggested that only nouns that are intermediate in a hierarchy of classification may incorporate. For example, the basic root for fish (*its*) may be incorporated, but the words for specific species of fish may not. However, I am not convinced that this is an independent property of noun incorporation. To a large extent, it follows from the previous observations, given that the names for, say, specific fish species are either complex verbal forms (e.g., *tsi-kúhs-es kÁtsu* 'sturgeon', literally: 'fish with a long face') or borrowed terms (e.g., *rababhót* 'bullhead', from French). Typically, it is only the nouns of intermediate specificity that are simple noun roots in Mohawk; hence, they are the only ones that incorporate for morphological reasons. Moreover, there are cases where either a relatively specific N or a much more general, "classificatory" one can incorporate (see note 25 for examples).

10. The only major challenge to this generalization that I am aware of is in the Northern Athapaskan languages, which are not polysynthetic in my technical sense; see Rice (1989:ch. 24.10) for relevant data and arguments that "noun incorporation" is a lexical rather than a syntactic phenomenon in Slave.

11. Technically, my account of object agreement does not require that the goal move out of its base position in most sentences (see section 5.4).

12. I know of two classes of potential counterexamples, each involving a single morpheme in a single language.

Evans (1991:291–292) observes that the Mayali root *yau* 'baby' is a systematic exception to the generalization stated in the text; as an IN, it can express the goal argument of either simple ditransitive verbs such as 'give' or ditransitives formed by a benefactive applicative:

(i)   a. Gorrk   abanmani-yau-wo-ng.
          clothes 1sS/3DO-baby-give-PAST/PERF
          'I gave the clothes to the two babies.'

      b. Bi-marne-yau-wolngwo-ng.
          3sS/3HO-BEN-baby-warm.milk-PAST/PERF
          'He warmed the milk for the baby.'

It seems unlikely that this can be derived purely from the fact that *yau* is the most common animate IN and has borderline animacy status; these facts are equally true of *wir* 'baby' in Mohawk, but it never incorporates as a goal. Interestingly, *yau* violates other generalizations about incorporation as well. Thus, Evans claims (1991:286) that Mayali allows the agent argument of unergative verbs to incorporate, contrary to my generalization stated later in this section. Significantly, his most convincing examples use *yau:*

(ii) Ga-yau-wage-n.
      3sS-baby-crawl-NONPAST
      'The baby is crawling.'

Perhaps, then, we should simply say that *yau* is not always an incorporated noun root in Mayali, despite appearances. Rather, I conjecture that *yau* optionally counts as some kind of adverbial element in Mayali. Indeed, the language is rich in elements of this general type (Evans, to appear a).

The other apparent counterexample comes from Wichita. Rood (1976:207) notes that the indirect object of *wa:ri* 'tell' can be incorporated into the verb if and only if the direct object is a (quotative) clause:

(iii) A:?-á-ki-[i]c-iye:s-?ak-wa:ri. . . .
       QUOT-REFL-AOR-POSS-child-PL-tell
       'He told his children. . . .'

Elsewhere (1976:40), Rood mentions that this is the only verb in Wichita that inherently demands an agent, a patient, and a beneficiary, and he notes that the patient is always a clause. Hence, it is likely that examples like (iii) are found with this verb only. A reasonable way of approaching (iii) would be to say that 'his children' is actually the theme/direct object of the verb. This means that its argument structure is more like that of *inform* in English than like that of *tell.*

(iv) a. I told John my plans.

      b. I told John that I would leave early.

      c. I told my plans to John.

(v) a. I informed John of my plans.

   b. I informed John that I would leave early.

   c. *I informed my plans to John.

With CP arguments, the two verbs look quite similar, but when the communicated information is an NP it becomes clear that the animate argument is a goal with *tell* but a theme
with *inform*. If a more accurate gloss for *wa:ri* is 'inform', then (iii) is an unproblematic
instance of object incorporation after all.

   13. See note 12 for an apparent counterexample to this generalization from Mayali
and a possible interpretation.

   14. Perhaps also relevant to the issue of adjunct incorporation is the fact that the
argument–adjunct distinction is significantly blurred in the framework of Larson (1988).

   15. See chapter 9 for some discussion. Section 9.2.3 also discusses the status of the
null-headed PP with respect to the MVC.

   16. The equivalent of (37) is acceptable with *yahya'k* 'cross'. I take this to mean that
the higher argument of this verb can be categorized as either a theme or an agent in Mohawk. It is well known that motion verbs that can be volitional often have these two options
in other languages. The evidence from morphological causatives referred to is thus crucial
for showing that *yahya'k* may be unaccusative.

   17. The claim that 'cross'-type verbs take an NP complement whereas dative verbs
take a PP with a (possibly) null P is abstract but well motivated. It can perhaps be seen in
English nominals by the fact that *of*-insertion is possible with the former but not the latter:

(i)   The crossing of the river (took all day). (cf. I crossed the river today.)

(ii) *The writing of John (took all day). (cf. I wrote John today.)

The null P in (ii) blocks the assignment of inherent genitive Case in English (cf. Chomsky
1986b).

   18. The fact that reference objects incorporate as well as themes is prima facie support
for a structurally based analysis of NI rather than a thematic analysis. However, proponents
of the thematic analysis could respond that themes and reference objects form a natural
class in the typology of thematic roles.

   19. This argument does not completely rule out the possibility that NI is always upward, however. Stative verbs in Mohawk may take the suffix *hne'*, a kind of past morpheme. If this is generated in Infl, then at least one functional category may be present.
This Infl position would also be where agreement is generated on my account. Thus, it is
possible that the V in (40) raises directly to Infl, and then the N incorporates upward into
Infl as well.

   20. Here I am crucially following Larson's (1988) original conception of this higher
V position, where it is generated on purely formal X-bar theoretic grounds. It has no more
meaning than, say, the specifier position of a $-wh$ CP. Others have interpreted the higher
V as causative verb that is usually null phonologically. On this view, it is not clear how
the impossibility of agent NI can be derived. See also Zushi to appear.

   Another explanation for the impossibility of subject incorporation might be Koopman
and Sportiche's (1988) version of the VP-internal subject hypothesis. They argue that there
is no higher V position; the subject is base generated in a position adjoined to the VP that
contains the theme and goal. Thus, there is literally no verb position where one would have
to be for the agent to be able to incorporate.

   21. Technically, one could say that derivation (49b) "converges" into a legitimate LF
representation, but it has a deviant interpretation because the noun cannot be interpreted as

a verb. This is important because under minimalist assumptions only convergent derivations can block other derivations.

22. See for discussion Di Sciullo and Williams 1987 and Anderson 1992 among others. In fact, which theory is the most restrictive overall is not so clear. Lexicalist theories have restrictive morphologies and syntaxes, but there are problems characterizing the nature of the interface between the two (Baker 1985). The syntactic theory offers a potentially very restrictive solution to an important class of these problems (Baker 1988a:ch. 7 and section 1.6 of the present volume). Thus, which approach should be considered the most restrictive *overall* is far from obvious.

23. The exception is possessors; see section 8.1 for discussion.

24. It should be emphasized that not all instances of noun incorporation discussed in the literature have these distinctive properties. For example, "incorporated" nouns in the Oceanic languages discussed by Rosen (1989b) are not referential and cannot appear with external modifiers. These may well be formed lexically in the same manner as English deverbal compounds, as Rosen proposes. Baker 1988a is ambivalent on this point, and I will not discuss the matter here (see also note 4).

25. Actually, my data suggest that classifier incorporation in Mohawk is more restrictive than one might think. For example, (i) shows that a noun of rather general meaning such as *atahkwʌni* 'clothing' can incorporate into a verb, but it cannot license an external NP referring to a specific type of clothing.

(i) Uwári wa'-u-[a]tahkwʌny-a-hnínu-'   (*thíkʌ athásterʌ).
     Mary FACT-FsS-clothing-Ø-buy-PUNC   that   pants
     'Mary bought clothing (those pants).'

Apparently, (i) is blocked by the fact that *athasterʌ* can itself incorporate into the verb, as shown in (ii).

(ii) Wári wa'-u-[a]thasterʌ-tsher-a-hnínu-'.
      Mary FACT-FsS-pants-NOM-Ø-buy-PUNC
      'Mary bought pants.'

Similarly, one cannot say 'I food-bought the meat' nor 'I dish-washed the spoons' because one can say 'I meat-bought' and 'I spoon-washed'. Thus, classifier incorporation seems to be restricted to situations where the pragmatics call for NI, but the theme argument is not incorporable for morphological reasons (see note 9). These restrictions on classifier incorporation do not follow from the lexicalist analysis.

26. This analysis predicts that the word order of stranded demonstratives and numerals in Southern Tiwa should be relatively fixed, since they are related to the true object position. Ideally, then, they should be adjacent to the verb and either follow it or (more likely) precede it, depending on whether Southern Tiwa is underlyingly head initial or head final. In fact, the stranded demonstratives and numerals in Allen et al. 1984 are always given as adjacent to the verb and in all but one (unusual) case they precede it. This is encouraging, but since Allen et al. state no generalizations about word order in these sentences the regularity may be accidental. If the order of stranded demonstratives and numerals turns out to be relatively free, this might be analyzed by saying that they are base generated in the position indicated in (67), but can be moved by a process of scrambling.

As far as I know, the structure in (67) is not possible in Nahuatl or Chukchee. Spencer (1993:21) suggests that the reason that NI cannot strand elements such as demonstratives, quantifiers, and modifying adjectives in Chukchee is because these elements have the status of adjectival heads, rather than the status of maximal projections adjoined to NP, as in Mohawk. This difference in structure may prevent stranding, while permitting another possibility: one in which the N and its modifier together incorporate into the governing head.

Why (67) is not possible in Nahuatl is not clear.

27. Perhaps this helps to explain the relatively free incorporation of Mohawk *wir* 'baby' (and *yau* 'baby' in Mayali); it is not insulting to fail to take into account the desires of a small infant, or to deny its control over itself.

28. Here my data disagree with the pattern reported by Postal (1979:285). There are, however, cases where my consultants also allow examples similar to (70a); see later discussion in this section.

29. In the light of the previous paragraph, one might say that 'baby' can only incorporate if it is being viewed as inanimate; in that case, the pattern in (70) would be consistent with a lexicalist account. However, there is then no explanation for the complete ungrammaticality of (69b); if Mohawks can freely view babies as inanimate entities, then one would expect that they could trigger inanimate agreement even when not incorporated, contrary to fact.

30. Example (70b) also contains the semireflexive morpheme *at,* unlike (71a). I have no explanation for this difference, but it should have no effect on the agreement.

In fact, (71a) does have an incorporated noun *ya't* 'body'. This particular noun (and perhaps it alone) really does function as a classifier in Mohawk; many verbs simply require it to be present when their object is animate, and it has no known effect on the syntax of the sentence (see Woodbury 1975 for extensive discussion of its cognate in Onondaga). Its behavior is clearly related to the general phenomenon of body part incorporation, at least historically. Note that Rosen's (1989b:302) one crucial example of transitive agreement with NI in Iroquoian also has *ya't* as the IN. Thus, her lack of awareness of the special properties of this morpheme plus the precedent of Postal 1979 caused her to make the wrong empirical generalization regarding agreement and NI in these languages.

31. This impression is strengthened because the pleonastic agreement prefix is still sensitive to whether the sole argument of the unaccusative verb is lexically marked $+O$ or $-O$. Thus, the pleonastic agreement in (77d) is *yo,* a quirky "object" agreement form, not the subject agreement form *ka* found in (73b). This is clearly related to the fact that *ke'tot* 'appear' shows $+O$ agreement with its argument when there is no NI, whereas Λ' 'fall' shows $-O$ agreement (see chapter 5). The prefix on the unaccusative verb does, therefore, agree with the NI in this very limited sense. Indeed, when the theme argument of an unaccusative is neuter, the prefixes on the incorporated version and the unincorporated version look identical.

This feature of Mohawk can be built into our system as follows. Suppose that in Mohawk the default value for person is third, the default value for gender is neuter, and the default value for number is singular. These are probably universal default values; they are the same ones that English has, inasmuch the only pronoun that can be expletive is third person neuter singular *it.* However, the default value of $\pm O$ feature will clearly not follow from a universal theory of morphosyntactic features, since the feature is highly particular to Mohawk. Suppose, then, that there simply is no default value for the $\pm O$ feature. Nevertheless, the Mohawk agreement system is such that a value for this feature must be specified before a given agreement can be spelled out morphophonologically. Pleonastic agreements cannot get a value for this feature from their θ-marker as other nominals do, because they have no θ-marker. It follows that a pleonastic agreement morpheme must copy a value for the $\pm O$ feature from something in its immediate environment—namely, the theme argument of the verb. Since the situation only arises with unaccusative clauses, there is no indeterminacy in how this copying takes place.

32. Nor can the lexicalist approach say that the pro is licensed by the incorporated noun root. This would only be possible if some features from the noun root were passed on to the complex verb, by some kind of feature percolation. However, it is not clear what these features could be; positing features like [$\pm$infant] involves an absurd proliferation of pseudosyntactic features that are not otherwise motivated in the syntax.

33. Nevertheless, when the doubling material makes explicit the gender of the argument in question, the NI plus agreement construction is preferred where possible. I assume this is a stylistic effect resulting from the fact that gender cannot be marked in true instances of NI but often must be marked on unincorporated nouns. Thus, one often finds the Gricean effect that when the gender of the argument is known, true NI is avoided so it can be expressed, whereas when the gender is not known or not relevant NI is often a convenient way of avoiding having to specify it.

34. Judgments on (81) are less certain than those on (80): one speaker accepted a coreferential interpretation in (81), while another resisted it. In fact, I find coreference in the English gloss of (80) much more natural than that of (81) as well. Thus, I take this to be a matter to be clarified by a better understanding of Condition C and related discourse phenomena, and not a weakness in the syntactic analysis of NI.

35. It should be pointed out, however, that the impression of disjoint reference is not always as strong with NI constructions as it is with parallel examples where the theme nominal is not incorporated. Thus, for one consultant a coreferential interpretation of (i) is even worse than a coreferential interpretation of (82a).

(i) Sak wa-ha-[a]t-hróri-'   tsi wa-hi-kúrek-e'   ne ra-ksá-'a.
     Sak FACT-MsS-SRFL-tell-PUNC that FACT-1sS/MsO-hit-PUNC NE MsS-child-NSF
     '*Sak* told that I hit *the child.*' (disjoint only)

My consultant's first reaction to sentences like (82) was always to interpret them with disjoint reference; however, when I specifically drew her attention to the possibility of coreference in (82), she often accepted the possibility. In contrast, coreference in sentences like (i) was firmly rejected even under reconsideration. I have no account for this second-order contrast. Perhaps this is not a grammatical phenomenon at all, but a side effect of the uncertainty surrounding the difference between agreeing and nonagreeing NI—(82) is sometimes confused with the superficially similar (83). Other speakers seem to reject coreference in (82) more firmly than this one, but I have fewer data from them.

36. This account of the difference between *who* and *which* is somewhat different from one I proposed earlier in unpublished work. The earlier work was based on Cinque's (1990) intuition that *which* is more "referential" than *who* because it is D-linked in the sense of Pesetsky 1987. This referentiality then allows it to be licensed by forming a binding chain (the ALC) rather than by moving. However, this approach failed in two ways. First, it predicted that *which* questions should be sensitive only to strong islands, and not to weak islands. This does not seem to be the case: *ka nikáyʌ* 'which' cannot be extracted out of a *wh*-island any more than *úhka* 'who' can, although dislocation out of a *wh*-island is sometimes possible (see sections 2.1.4 and chapter 3 for examples). Second, this approach did not capture the obvious similarity between (85) and (86). *Wh*-traces cannot license adjoined NPs, as shown by the ungrammaticality of (86a). Hence the empty category in (86b) must be a pro. However, a (singular) pro cannot license two distinct NPs in A-bar positions, as shown in chapter 4. Hence, the theory of *which* reviewed here is independently necessary, making Cinque's assumption about *which* superfluous for Mohawk.

37. Examples like (90) also show elegantly that the examples in (89) are not ruled out because the selectional restrictions that the complex verb puts on the object are so narrow that 'who' questions are no longer appropriate pragmatically. The selectional restrictions on the object in (90) are just as narrow; nevertheless, 'who' questions are fine.

38. The one systematic class of cases is the "cognate object" INs of section 5.3; these are always compatible with *wh*-movement. For example, (i) has the dummy morpheme *n* as well as a question word linked to the direct object position. An explanation for these forms would require a deeper understanding of the dummy noun roots.

(i) Oh nahótʌᵢ se-nᵢ-óhare-s [eᵢ]?
     what   2sS-??-wash-HAB
     'What are you washing?"

39. These particular examples should be taken with a grain of salt, since there is some reason to believe that *yau* 'baby' does not always have the status of an incorporated N in Mayali (see note 12). However, the point is true more generally. Thus, in Rembarrnga, Nunggubuyu, and Ngandi transitive prefixes are (slightly) different from intransitive ones and verbs with incorporated objects take the transitive form of the prefix (McKay 1975, Heath 1978:117–118).

8

Complex Predicates

A striking fact about Mohawk polysynthesis observed in chapter 1 is that although it puts great emphasis on agreement and noun incorporation, certain other kinds of morphological structures are relatively restricted. Mohawk does not have the diversity of "complex predicate" constructions that some languages have, and, more importantly, some of those that it does have are restricted in their use. Moreover, similar restrictions appear to a greater or lesser degree in other polysynthetic languages as well. This observation goes against the conventional wisdom about polysynthetic languages, which is that they can express virtually any standard linguistic relationship by morphological means. In fact, the theoretical maximum of morphological complexity seems not to be reached. Rather, those languages that are rich in noun incorporation are poor(er) in other complex predicates, and those that are rich(er) in complex predicates are poor in noun incorporation.

In this chapter, I will refine and substantiate this claim empirically and show how it can be explained by the Polysynthesis Parameter. The special characteristic of nouns, I claim, is that they are the canonical way of representing arguments. Hence, NI is favored in polysynthetic languages as one way of satisfying the Morphological Visibility Condition, as seen in chapter 7. In contrast, verbs are canonically predicates; they are argument-*taking* elements, not argument-expressing elements. Thus, although incorporating a verb might properly express one argument of the higher verb, it runs the risk of making it impossible for the incorporated verb to express its own arguments morphologically. Therefore, the same principle that favors the incorporation of nouns limits the incorporation of verbs.

The term "complex predicate" has no precise technical meaning in current theory; it can refer to any predicate to which a given researcher attributes a representation with internal structure at some level. For purposes of this work, I define complex predicate as any inflectional domain that contains two distinct morphemes, each of which selects at least one phrasal argument in its θ-grid. Here "inflectional domain" means a domain in which there is one and only one set of tense/aspect/mood morphemes and associated agreement factors. Often in the polysynthetic languages, these two morphemes form a single morphological unit, but this is not part of the definition of the topic. There is also some indirect evidence that the two argument-taking morphemes compose with their arguments separately and thus create two different syntactic domains before they are combined by movement. In other words, complex predicates are syntactically complex as well as morphologically complex. In this, I will find some new support for the general approach of Baker 1988a.

To discuss fully all the complex predicate constructions found in each polysynthetic language would require a book of its own. The domain of inquiry must therefore be limited, perhaps in a somewhat arbitrary way. Thus, I concentrate on those types of complex predicates that are productive in Mohawk, that are central to the system of the language, and that are found in some recognizable version in many of the other polysynthetic languages. Satisfying these criteria are the incorporation of possessed nouns, morphological causatives, and control-like predicates such as desideratives and purposives. It seems like a good bet that these will illustrate the core properties of the system. Benefactive applicative constructions are also relevant; however, since they often involve adposition elements whose basic syntax has not yet been covered, discussion of these constructions is deferred until the next chapter.

8.1 Limitations on Possessor Raising

Although verbs may be the canonical argument-taking category, nouns sometimes take arguments as well. In particular, it is reasonable to say that nouns in Mohawk optionally take a possessor argument, just as some verbs optionally take a goal argument. In section 6.2, I argued that such nouns cannot be the heads of freestanding nominals in most polysynthetic languages because nominal projections do not have enough agreement factors to express the additional argument. Nevertheless, it is possible that such an argument-taking noun could be generated in an argument position and then incorporated into the verb; if so, the result would count as a complex predicate by the definition above. Indeed, this is essentially Rosen's (1990) analysis of "possessor raising" in Southern Tiwa (see also Baker 1988a). This potential case of complex predicate formation contrasts minimally with the incorporation of nouns that do not take possessors; hence, it is a natural starting place for our inquiry, since the basic facts about the distribution and morphology of NI are already familiar. The question, then, is, What happens to the possessor argument of a noun once that noun is incorporated?

There has been some confusion in the literature concerning the basic facts. Postal (1979) reports that when the N incorporates into a verb, its possessor can be left behind, in which case it triggers O-class agreement on the verb. In Baker 1988a, I assumed that this was correct, in part because the phenomenon seemed to be attested in other languages (especially Southern Tiwa) and in part because it fit naturally into my theory. Inasmuch as the possessor of the N ends up being treated like the object of the verb for agreement purposes, this can be called a *possessor raising* effect (Allen et al. 1984, Allen et al. 1990). However, this construction is notably absent from other Iroquoian grammars, such as Chafe 1970 and Williams 1976b. Moreover, Woodbury (1975:35–39), Mithun (1984a:868), and especially Michelson (1991b) argue that this kind of possessor raising is not found in the Northern Iroquoian languages. On the contrary, they claim that the verb cannot agree with the possessor of the incorporated N at all, once certain confounding lexical factors are controlled for, and that there is no way that an alienably possessed noun can be incorporated.

At the root of this confusion seems to be the need to distinguish between lexical verb classes. Consider first standard transitive verbs. Postal gave the following examples of the possessor raising effect:

(1) a. I'i ri-nuhs-óhare-s   ne Shawátis.   (1979:325)
        me 1sS/MsO-house-wash-HAB NE John
        'I wash John's house.'[1]

     b. I'i ri-nuhs-a-núhwe'-s   ne Shawátis.   (1979:320)
        me 1sS/MsO-house-Ø-like-HAB NE John
        'I like John's house.'

However, Mithun and Michelson argue strongly that this is not a true property of Mohawk/Oneida. Mithun gives (2) as ungrammatical, which is nearly identical to (1a) (see also Woodbury 1975:35).

(2)   *Wa-hi-'sere-ht-óhare-'.
       FACT-1sS/MsO-car-NOM-wash-PUNC
       'I washed his car.'[2]

Michelson (1991b:757) shows that in other apparent cases of possessor raising, such as (3a), the putative possessor of the IN is actually an indirect object of the verb thematically. One form of evidence for this is that such arguments trigger object agreement on the verb even if there is no overt noun and therefore nothing to θ-mark the putative possessor, as in (3b).

(3)   a. Wa-hi-'sleht-a-hni:nu: (ONEIDA)
         FACT-1sS/MsO-car-Ø-buy-PUNC
         'I bought his car, I bought a car from him.'

      b. Wa-hi-hni:nu:
         FACT-1sS/MsO-buy-PUNC
         'I bought it from him.'

Michelson's article also has a more subtle semantic argument pointing to the same conclusion. My own fieldwork confirms the Woodbury/Mithun/Michelson generalization. Additional examples are the following:

(4)   a. *Λ-hake-natar-a-kwétar-e'.
         FUT-MsS/1sO-bread-Ø-cut-PUNC
         'He will cut my bread.'

      b. *Wa-shako-[a]tya'tawi-tsher-a-rátsu-'.
         FACT-MsS/FsO-dress-NOM-Ø-tear-PUNC
         'He tore her dress.'

Simple NI is also permitted with unaccusative-type intransitive verbs. Example (5) shows that possessor raising with these verbs is also deviant in many cases.

(5) a. *T-a-ho-húr-ʌ'-ne'   ne Sak.
     CIS-FACT-MsO-gun-fall-PUNC NE Sak
     'Sak's gun fell.'

   b. *Sak wa'-t-ho-wis-á-hri'-ne'.
     Sak FACT-DUP-MsO-glass-Ø-break-PUNC
     'Sak's glass broke.'

   c. ?*Wa-ho-[a]te-'nerohkw-a-hnhot-ú-ko-'.
     FACT-MsO-SRFL-box-Ø-door-close-REV-PUNC
     'His box opened.'

There is, however, a subclass of the unaccusative verbs that works differently—namely "stative" verbs, whose meanings generally correspond to those of adjectives in English. These can be distinguished from the verbs given above on both formal and semantic grounds: semantically, they refer to states, rather than events; formally, they do not take the aspect suffixes that appear on eventive unaccusative verbs. These verbs clearly do allow possessor raising. Postal (1979:319) gives the following example:

(6) Ro-nuhs-a-rákʌ   ne Shawátis.
    MsO-house-Ø-white NE John
    'John's house is white.'

Mithun (1984a) does not discuss examples of this type, but they are mentioned by Michelson (1991b:fn. 5) and by Deering and Delisle (1976:305). Additional examples are:

(7) a. Ro-[a]ther-owánʌ   kíkʌ
     MsO-basket-be.big this
     'This guy's basket is large.'

   b. Ro-[a]nitskwara-tsher-a-hníru.
     MsO-chair-NOM-Ø-be.hard
     'His chair is hard.'

   c. Ro-ris-er-akérahs.
     MsO-sock-NOM-stink
     'His socks smell.'

One may guess that it was the existence of these examples that led Postal to overgeneralize the possessor-raising effect to examples like (1). It is clear that the putative possessor in (7) is not simply a kind of goal argument of the root, because with these verbs the understood possessor cannot be expressed when there is no IN. Thus, (8) contrasts with (7b) and (3).

(8) *Ro-hniru   ne anitskwara.
    MsO-hard NE chair.
    'His chair is hard; The chair is hard for/on him.'

The second situation where one finds what looks like a possessor-raising effect is when the IN refers to an inalienably possessed body part. This is a very productive phenomenon, observed by all researchers, including Mithun (1984a) and Michelson (1991b:759). Thus, (9) contrasts minimally with the ungrammatical (2).

(9)   Wa-hi-kuhs-óhare-'.
      FACT-1sS/MsO-face-wash-PUNC
      'I washed his face.'

In these examples, the verb agrees with the possessor of the incorporated body part in exactly the same way as it would if that possessor were itself the argument of the verb. This type of construction is very common in polysynthetic languages: it is also found in Nahuatl (Launey 1981:198–199), Mayali (Evans 1991:275–285), and Chukchee (Nedjalkov 1976:198); see also Rood (1976:149–150) for related facts in Wichita.

I mention the stative verb construction and the inalienable possession construction at this point for the purpose of putting them aside. For inalienable possession constructions like (9), one can plausibly deny that the masculine singular element is syntactically the argument of the noun; rather, it could simply be the theme argument of the verb. The IN would then be a kind of incorporated predicate modifying the theme. If so, the correct literal gloss for (9) would be something like 'I washed him facewise' or, more idiomatically, 'I washed him in the face'. This is the view of Evans (to appear b) for Mayali, Launey (1981:168, 199) for Nahuatl, and (implicitly) Michelson (1991b) for Iroquoian. It straightforwardly accounts for the basic morphosyntactic properties of the construction and is compatible with the general framework adopted here. The claim that these examples have a very different structure from other types of NI also fits with the well-known fact that body parts are the only nouns that can "incorporate" in many languages. If this suggestion is correct, then (9) is not a possessor raising construction at all; in fact, it may not even qualify as a complex predicate construction.[3]

The stative verb construction, on the other hand, is a clear case of a complex predicate, and a very interesting one. Nevertheless, I put it aside for now because we will be better equipped to understand it by the end of this chapter.

The correct empirical generalization, then, is that most noun–verb combinations in Mohawk do not allow a possessor-raising effect. Thus, the task at hand is to explain the ungrammaticality of examples like (4) and (5). This ungrammaticality implies that it is impossible to incorporate a possessed noun. If one wants to express a possessor for an incorporable noun, one must either refrain from incorporation or incorporate but repeat the noun root in a dislocated NP. Either way, agreement with the possessor appears on the independent noun root but never on the verb:

(10) Wa'-t-ka (*ho)-(hur-á)-hri'-ne'   ne Sak raó-hur-e'.
      FACT-DUP-NsS(*MsO)-(gun-Ø)-break-PUNC NE Sak MsP-gun-NSF
      'Sak's gun broke.'

Why is it impossible for a verbal complex to agree with the possessor of most incorporated nouns in Mohawk? The theory of Baker 1988a predicted that such agreement should be possible. We cannot say that the agreement potential of the verbal complex is already exhausted, because it is perfectly possible for a transitive or unaccusative verb to agree with another NP once its object has been incorporated. Such agreement is found in benefactive constructions, for example. Indeed, these benefactive constructions often have an interpretation that is very similar to what the possessor-raising construction would have if it were possible. Semantically, this is due to the fact, often noted in the literature, that if an event E causes a change of state or location to a thing X and X belongs to Y, then it is generally true that E affected Y, so Y is a benefactive (or malefactive). Thus, sentences like (11) and (12) are often offered spontaneously as corrections of the sentences in (4) and (5).

(11) Wa-hi-'sere-ht-óhare-'s-e'. (Mithun 1984a:868)
      FACT-1sS/MsO-car-NOM-wash-BEN-PUNC
      'I washed his car; I washed the car for him.'

(12) Wa'-t-ho-hur-á-hri'-*s*-e'.
      FACT-DUP-MsO-gun-Ø-break-BEN-PUNC
      'His gun broke; the gun broke on him'

(See also Woodbury 1975:36–37.) This contrast must presumably be accounted for in terms of the structural difference between possessor arguments and benefactive arguments.

Intuitively, it is clear what the relevant structural difference must be. The possessor is more deeply embedded than the benefactive—it is inside the object NP whereas the benefactive is outside of it as shown in (13).[4]

(13)   a. *Possessor-Raising Structure*

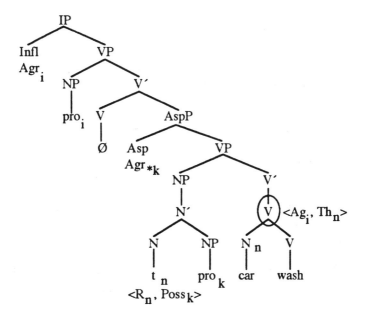

b. *Benefactive Structure*

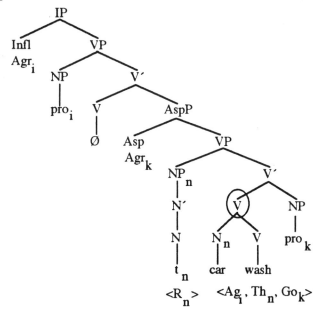

Thus, it is tempting to say that the node NP is a barrier to government, in which case the agreement in Asp in (13) would not be able to license the pro possessor. Unfortunately, it is unlikely that this NP would still block government once its head N has incorporated; it is generally accepted that once the head of a projection is incorporated, that projection becomes transparent to government from the outside (the Government Transparency Corollary of Baker 1988a).

There is another way to account for these facts. In section 5.4, I claimed that agreement is restricted by the Condition on Agreement Relations, at least in polysynthetic languages and perhaps more widely[5:]

(14)   *Condition on Agreement Relations* (CAR)
         An agreement factor X can be coindexed with a phrase Y only if Y is coindexed with a position in the argument structure of a head Z and X is adjoined to Z .

Thus, agreement possibilities are determined by a combination of argument structure and head movement. This accounts for the difference in grammaticality between (13a) and (13b) as follows. In (13b), the masculine singular element is a goal, which is an argument of the verb (added by the benefactive morphology) and is represented as such in the verb's θ-grid. Thus, when the verb incorporates into Asp, the agreement there can be coindexed with the goal. The pro is therefore licensed and visible for θ-role assignment at LF. On the other hand, in (13a), the masculine singular element is thematically a possessor argument of the noun. The incorporated noun is not the head of the derived verb; hence, it does not influence the argument structure of that verb. Rather, the argument structure of the circled verb is still simply <Ag, Th>. Therefore, when this verb incorporates into Asp, the agreement there cannot be associated with the possessor. For technical reasons, one might still want to say that after NI and V raising to Asp, the agreement in

Asp governs the possessor position, if such a relation has any meaning in current linguistic theory. This is irrelevant, however, because the agreement does not share features with the possessor.[6] Hence, the pro is not expressed morphologically, and the structure is ungrammatical.

It is important to realize that this account works crucially because incorporation does *not* compose the argument structures of the two heads involved into a complex argument structure. In particular, <Ag, Th> of the verb and <R, Poss> of the noun cannot combine to become <Ag, Th = R, Poss>. If this were possible, then the distinction between (13a) and (13b) would disappear. Rather, each head, complex or otherwise, must have a unique argument structure, and there is no mechanism for combining argument structures. In fact, this is the simplest and most desirable assumption within a syntactic movement framework; it is consistent with the claim in chapter 7 that N movement and incorporation in general are semantically vacuous. This, together with the CAR, limits the possibility of agreement.

The MVC also plays an important implicit role in this explanation of the impossibility of possessor raising in Mohawk. In particular, this is what guarantees that the possessor must be identified by agreement in the first place. If the MVC did not hold, then one could generate a lexical NP in the embedded possessor position. After NI, this possessor could be assigned accusative Case under government from the V or Asp position (assuming the Government Transparency Corollary). No universal condition would then be violated. The MVC is violated, however, because the noun root 'car' has an argument (the possessor) that does not correspond to any morpheme in the complex word. Thus, we predict that possessor raising might be found in a language with productive syntactic noun incorporation but not the MVC. This prediction is probably untestable because the MVC is what triggers syntactic noun incorporation in the first place (see section 7.1). However, the difference between complex predicates in languages with and without the MVC will be amply illustrated in the discussion of causatives in the next section.[7]

This reasoning has not made reference to any properties specific to Mohawk. Thus, the theory predicts that the incorporation of inalienably possessed nouns into eventive verbs should be impossible in other polysynthetic languages as well. This seems to be true. There is nothing like it in Nahuatl, judging from the grammars. Thus, one finds attestations of the inalienable possession construction in (15a), and the benefactive construction in (15b), but no true possessor-raising construction (Kenneth Hale, personal communication), which would look like (15c).

(15) a. Ni-mitz-cuā-pāca. (Launey 1981:198)
         1sS-2sO-head-wash
         'I wash your head.'

      b. Ni-quin-xōchi-tēmo-lia. (Andrews 1975:164)
         1sS-3pO-flower-seek-BEN
         'I seek flowers for them.'

      c. *Ni-mitz-xōchi-pāca.
         1sS-2sO-flower-wash
         'I wash your flower.'

The same is true for Mayali, according to Evans (1991:277)[8]:

(16)   a. Ngan-gorn-melme-ng.
          3sS/1sO-crotch-touch.with.foot-PAST/PERF
          'He felt my crotch with his foot.'

       b. Ngan-marne-yau-melme-ng.
          3sS/1sO-BEN-child-touch.with.foot-PAST/PERF
          'He kicked my child, he kicked the child on me.'

       c. *Ngan-yau-melme-ng.
          3sS/1sO-child-touch.with.foot-PAST/PERF
          'He kicked my child.'

Similarly, Rood (1976:146–149) discusses Wichita constructions in which the verb
is inflected to agree with a noun that is interpreted as the possessor of an argument
of the verb (whether it is incorporated or not). Not surprisingly, this is possible
only if the verb also bears one of two morphemes, which Rood transcribes as *uR*
and *uc;* these are the benefactive (or malefactive) applicative morphemes in the
language (Rood 1976:41). These paradigms are exactly like the one found in Mohawk. Moreover, Shibatani (1990:71) states clearly that there is no incorporation
of possessed nouns in Ainu.

   This brings us to Southern Tiwa, in which possessor raising in the context of
NI has been claimed to be fully productive by Allen et al. (1984) and (in most
detail) Allen et al. (1990). In (17), examples of this with both a transitive and an
unaccusative verb are given.[9]

(17)   a. Ka-khwian-mu-ban.   (Allen et al. 1990:325)
          1sS/2sO\AO-dog-see-PAST
          'I saw your dog.'

       b. Ka-khwian-chiapaw-m   (Allen et al. 1990:338)
          2sO\AO-dog-asleep-PRES
          'Your dog is asleep.'

Now, one certainly does not expect basic verbs meaning 'see' or 'sleep' to take a
goal argument. However, Southern Tiwa also differs from Mohawk, Nahuatl, and
Mayali in that it has no benefactive applicative morpheme comparable to *'s* or *lia*
or *marne*. Nevertheless, virtually any verb can optionally take a dative/benefactive
argument (Donald Frantz, personal communication). Suppose, then, that we say
that Southern Tiwa really does have benefactive applicatives, but the benefactive
applicative morpheme happens to be phonologically null, or perhaps disguised by
complex morphophonological processes, as in the related language Jemez (Kenneth Hale, personal communication). This means that one will not be able to tell
by the surface morphology whether any given Southern Tiwa example has a structure like (13a)—which is ungrammatical in other polysynthetic languages—or a
structure like (13b)—which is fine in the other languages. In fact, Rosen
(1990:702–703) observes that there is no evidence in the literature against the
claim that "raised possessors" in Southern Tiwa are simply base generated as indirect objects (technically, as "3s" in her Relational Grammar framework). On the
contrary, the multistratal agreement rules and constraints in Allen et al. 1990 are
for the most part designed precisely to capture the many similarities between
clauses with so-called raised possessors and clauses with ordinary goal arguments.

Thus, it is reasonable to say that structures like (13a) are ruled out in Southern Tiwa just as in other languages, and that the examples in (17) have the analysis in (13b). This saves the theory from an apparent counterexample and makes at least two further predictions. First, it predicts that a Southern Tiwa verb should be able to agree with an understood possessor of its theme argument even if the theme is not incorporated. This is so because the so-called possessor is actually an "affected object" θ-marked by the applicative verb; hence, it is not dependent on the existence of a noun root for its θ-role. Therefore, (18) should be just as good as (17b).

(18) Ka-chiapaw-m
      2sO\AO-asleep-PRES
      'Yours is asleep.' ('It is asleep on you.')

Rosen (1990:709, fn. 29) reports the impression of Barbara Allen that such sentences are, in fact, grammatical. This is parallel to the Oneida/Mohawk pattern in (3), pointed out by Michelson. Second, Kenneth Hale (personal communication) notes that there is diachronic evidence for the existence of an applicative morpheme in examples like (17); however, the morpheme is rather abstract phonologically and is merged into the agreement portmanteaux in the analysis of Allen et al. 1984. If this is correct, then the Southern Tiwa facts are no different from the Mohawk ones.

The prediction that emerges out of this discussion is that one should only find apparent cases of possessor-raising in a polysynthetic language X if X has no overt benefactive applicative morphology. If a language does have such morphology, then that morphology should appear in "possessor-raising" constructions with all but a few verbs that take goal arguments to begin with. Mohawk, Nahuatl, and Mayali illustrate one side of this prediction, while Chukchee illustrates the other side. Chukchee is typically described as having possessor raising under incorporation (Nedjalkov 1976:188–189, 198, Spencer 1993:21–22), as in (19b) (from Kozinsky et al. 1988:683).

(19) a. Ǝnan   remkel'-in poyg-ən   məčə-tku-nin.
          he(ERG) guest-POSS spear-ABS break-ITER-3sS/3sO
          'He broke the guest's spear (into many pieces).'

      b. Ǝnan   poygə-mča-tko-nen   remkel'-ən.
          he(ERG) spear-break-ITER-3sS/3sO guest-ABS
          'He broke the guest's spear (into many pieces).'

However, Chukchee also lacks overt applicative morphology; a benefactive or malefactive NP in absolutive case can be attached to a suitable clause with no change in verb morphology beyond that required for the verb to agree with its new object (Nedjalkov 1976:198–199):

(20) a. Ǝtləg-ən qaa-nm-at-g'e.
          father-ABS reindeer-kill-SRFL-3sS
          'The father slaughtered a reindeer.'

      b. Ǝtləg-e   ekək   qaa-nm-ə-nen.
          father-ERG son(ABS)   reindeer-kill-3sS/3sO
          'The father slaughtered the son a reindeer.'

Thus, it is perfectly reasonable to analyze 'guest' in (19b) as an affected object added by some kind of applicative process, like 'son' in (20b), rather than as a stranded possessor of the incorporated noun. Indeed, the discussion of Kozinsky et al. concerning the pragmatics of (19) supports this interpretation. They write (Kozinsky et al. 1988:684):

> The text is about the fight between the protagonist and the guest. The observed regularity implies that [a] should contain an assertion about the spear being broken, while nothing is definitely stated or denied concerning the guest's state. Accordingly, [a] may be used to represent the situation 'the guest is out for a time, and the spear is broken in his absence'. Meanwhile, [b] denotes obligatorily that the guest's state has changed too, i.e. he has been disarmed. Therefore, [b], strictly speaking, necessarily implies [a], but not vice versa; so the two sequences are not denotationally identical, though comparable.

Clearly, then 'the guest' is not merely a possessor in (19b), but rather a malefactive applied object, as predicted. Similar remarks hold for other instances of so-called possessor raising in Chukchee.

8.2 Morphological Causatives

8.2.1 *Limitations on the Mohawk Causative*

Next we turn to the paradigm case of complex predicates: combinations of two verbal morphemes. In fact, the same reasoning that rules out possessor raising in polysynthetic languages should carry over to this domain as well, limiting the kinds of structures that are possible.

The most important testing ground for this prediction is morphological causatives, which are quite common cross-linguistically. At a descriptive level, they are often considered to be valence-increasing operations. Thus, causativization adds a new causer argument, thereby changing intransitive verbs into transitive verbs, and monotransitive verbs into ditransitive verbs. There is also a relatively universal way of deploying these arguments: the new causer argument is treated as the subject of the causative construction, while the inherent subject of the verb root is treated as a kind of object.[10] Languages with causatives that fit this general description include Chamorro, Turkish, Japanese, and many Bantu languages. Rather typical examples are the following from Chichewa (Alsina 1992:518):

(21) a. Chatsalǐra a-ku-nám-íts-á   mwána.
          Chatsalira 3sS-PRES-lie-CAUS-IND child
          'Chatsalira is making the child tell lies.'

     b. Nŭngu   i-na-phík-íts-a   kadzidzi maûngu.
          porcupine SM-PAST-cook-CAUS-IND owl   pumpkins
          'The porcupine made the owl cook the pumpkins.'

Following a long generative tradition, in Baker 1988a I analyzed causatives in a way that was parallel to noun incorporation. The causative morpheme was treated as a separate verbal head in the syntax, which selected an external agent argument (the causer) and an internal event argument. The verb root then headed the phrase that expressed the event argument of the causative verb. In Baker 1988a, I took this complement to be a full CP, but following Li (1990) and others I will now assume that it is a bare VP. This change is made possible largely due to the adoption of the VP-internal subject hypothesis, so that there is a valid position for the agent even in such a reduced clause. The advantage of the change is that it helps to explain why there is typically little or no tense/aspect/agreement morphology associated with the lower verb in these constructions.[11] Thus, the underlying structure of an example like (21b) is something like (22).

(22)

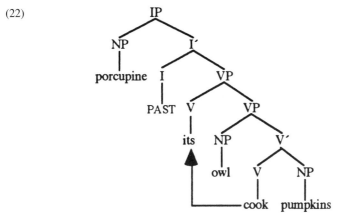

(In (22) I temporarily suppress the phrase structure innovations adopted in chapter 5 for clarity and ease of comparison with Baker 1988a). Move α takes the lower V and adjoins it to the higher V, thereby satisfying the latter's need to affix to a verb root. This is consistent with the conditions on movement (formerly the Empty Category Principle, now subsumed to Economy of movement) by the same reasoning used in chapter 7 in the context of NI. Finally, the complex higher verb governs the NP(s) inside the VP complement by the Government Transparency Corollary. Therefore, it can assign them structural Case, explaining the fact that they look like objects. If the lower V takes only one argument, the analysis ends there. If the lower V takes both an agent and a theme, then how they are both Case marked depends on the particular Case-theoretic properties of the language in question, in ways that we need not review here.

If the theoretical developments of the previous section are correct, then polysynthetic languages should not have morphological causatives of this type. The reason is simple. Although languages without the MVC can Case mark NPs stranded by the lower verb, languages with the MVC will not be able to express them morphologically. By hypothesis, there are no functional category projections within the complement of the causative verb (Li 1990). Indeed, if there were such functional categories, verb incorporation would be blocked by the combination of the HMC and the PHMG (see chapter 7). The lowest agreement, then, is adjoined to the Asp associated with the main verb. Thus, adopting the phrase structure innovations we have motivated in Mohawk, the structure of the Mohawk equivalent of (21b) would be (23), with head movements indicated by arrows.

(23)

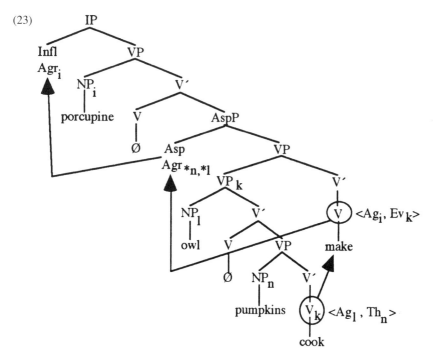

What this agreement can be coindexed with is determined by what incorporates into the Asp node, by the CAR. In this structure, what raises to Asp is a complex verb formed by adjoining the lower verb to the causative morpheme. Once again, incorporation does not lead to any kind of argument structure composition. Thus, the argument structure of the complex verb is the same as that of its head, the causative morpheme, and only the arguments of this morpheme can be agreed with. Apart from the possibility of noun incorporation, therefore, the arguments of the lower verb are left without morphological expression, in violation of the MVC. We can conclude that morphological causatives like (21) should not occur in Mohawk.

Of course, it is conceivable that NI could rescue this structure. However, this option does not help (23). The theme argument of 'cook' might incorporate into 'cook', but the agent argument will not be able to do so, for reasons discussed in section 7.3.5. In brief, it cannot incorporate downward into the base position of 'cook', because it would not c-command its trace. It cannot incorporate upward, directly into the causative verb, because the chain link would be longer than if it incorporated into the head of its own maximal projection. However, it cannot incorporate into that position either, because the position is lexically empty and hence unable to host incorporation. Therefore, the embedded agent cannot be agreed with and cannot be incorporated, so the structure is ruled out by the MVC. Similarly, goals are never able to incorporate (section 7.3.3), and they cannot trigger agreement when embedded under a causative verb. Therefore, it will be impossible to form a morphological causative of any verb taking either an agent or a goal argument in a language like Mohawk.

This prediction is true to a remarkable degree. Mohawk has a morphological causative, indicated by the morpheme *st/ht/'t*. However, unlike Turkish, Bantu, or Japanese, this causative attaches productively only to unaccusative verbs, whether eventive, as in (24), or stative, as in (25).

(24) a. Wa-ha-wis-a-náwʌ-ht-e'.
FACT-MsS-ice-Ø-melt-CAUS-PUNC
'He melted the ice.'

    b. Uwari t-a-yú-[a]hsʌ-ht-e'   ne á'share'.
Mary CIS-FACT-FsS-fall-CAUS-PUNC NE knife
'Mary made the knife fall; Mary dropped the knife.'

(25) a. . . . tanu te-hati-'tsú-st-a'   ne atsa'k-útye tsi núwe (OK:8)
and   DUP-MpS-be.dirty-CAUS-HAB NE river-along that where

yakwa-[a]táwʌ-s-kwe'.
1pS-swim-HAB-PAST
'. . . and they would dirty the river front where we used to swim.'

    b. Uwári wa'-e-rákʌ-st-e'   ako-[a]tyá'tawi tsi níyot
Mary FACT-FsS-white-CAUS-PUNC FsP-dress   that it-stands

ne ónyehte'.
NE snow
'Mary made her dress white as snow.'

Other verbs of the eventive unaccusative type that can be causativized include *hri'* 'shatter', *ye* 'wake up', *ateko* 'flee', and *ta'* 'stop, stand'; other verbs of the stative type include *iyo* 'be good', *hniru* 'be hard', *hutsi* 'be black', and *aksʌ* 'be bad'. However, these are the only classes of verbs that have morphological causatives. Thus, the causative is generally impossible with transitive verbs (cf. Lounsbury 1953:80):

(26) a. *ÓnʌSte' wa-hi-yʌtho-ht-e'   ne Sak.
corn   FACT-1sS/MsO-plant-CAUS-PUNC NE Sak
'I made Sak plant corn.'

    b. *Ká'sere' wa'-uk-hnínu-ht-e'.
car   FACT-FsS/1sO-buy-CAUS-PUNC
'She made me buy a car.'

    c. *Wa'-khe-ks-óhare-ht-e'.
FACT-1sS/FsO-dish-wash-CAUS-PUNC
'I made her wash the dishes.'

In order to express the sense of the examples in (26) in Mohawk, one must use a periphrastic construction involving a higher predicate *uni* 'make' and a distinct complement clause with full mood/aspect/agreement morphology:

(27) Wa-hiy-úny-ʌ-'   a-ha-ks-oharé-nyu-'   ne Sak.
FACT-1sS/MsO-make-BEN-PUNC OPT-MsS-dish-wash-DIST-PUNC NE Sak
'I made Sak wash the dishes.'

This is not a complex predicate construction, because there are two distinct inflectional domains.

Interestingly, one also cannot make morphological causatives from intransitive verbs of the unergative class, where the only argument is an agent:

(28) a. *Okwir-á-'ke wa-hake-ráthʌ-ht-e'.
          tree-Ø-LOC FACT-MsS/1sO-climb-CAUS-PUNC
          'He made me climb on the tree.'

      b. *Wa'-te-shako-[a]hsʌ'tho-ht-e'.
          FACT-DUP-MsS/FsO-cry-CAUS-PUNC
          'He made her cry.'

      c. *Wa'-te-shako-[a]tskáhu-ht-e'.
          FACT-DUP-MsS/FsO-eat-CAUS-PUNC
          'He made her eat.'

The causative morpheme cannot even be added to dyadic verbs that take a goal argument and a theme argument. The clearest example of a morphologically simple verb with this argument structure is *yʌ* 'lie, have':[12]

(29) a. Á'share' ró-yʌ
          knife   MsO-lie/have
          'He has a knife.' (Literally: 'A knife lies to him.')

      b. #Á'share' wa-hí-yʌ-ht-e'
          knife   FACT-1sS/MsO-have-CAUS-PUNC
          'I caused him to have a knife.'[13]

Thus, the range of verb roots that can be causativized morphologically is strictly limited in Mohawk.

What do these limitations mean? Certainly Mohawk is not the only language in which morphological causatives can be formed only from unaccusative verbs. Nevertheless, one can ask whether it is a coincidence that Mohawk has a causative that is limited in this way. One reason for thinking it might not be a coincidence is the fact that this type of causative has been very stable diachronically. Thus, none of the Northern Iroquoian languages has developed a full-blown unrestricted causative construction. This is true in spite of fact that the grammatical examples in (24) and (25) could be interpreted by children learning the language as evidence that there is a causative construction in the language, thereby tempting them to overgeneralize to constructions like (28). Since they resist this temptation, it seems likely that something else they know about the language is inhibiting them. Moreover, this restricted pattern of causativization is common in genetically unrelated polysynthetic languages: essentially the same facts are found in the Northern Australian languages, Kiowa, and arguably in Wichita and Chukchee (see later discussion). Thus, there seems to be a one-way implication to the effect that if a language is polysynthetic, its morphological causatives will be severely limited. In other words, all of the ungrammatical sentences in Mohawk cited above are ruled out, in part, by the Polysynthesis Parameter plus the CAR.

8.2.2 The "Light" Causative Construction

We need to further analyze why the examples in (24) and (25) are grammatical, however. On closer consideration, the analysis sketched in (23) turns out to be slightly too strong. As stated, it rules out any structure in which the embedded verb takes an argument, unless that argument undergoes noun incorporation. This correctly predicts that the root verb must be an unaccusative. However, it incorrectly predicts that the theme argument of the unaccusative verb root can never trigger agreement and must be incorporated. Example (30) shows that this is not the case; the theme argument of the verb may be incorporated, but it may also be an unincorporated animate triggering normal O-class agreement (cf. Lounsbury 1953:80).

(30)   Sak wa-shakó-ye-ht-e'   ne Uwári.
        Sak FACT-MsS/FsO-wake-CAUS-PUNC NE Mary
        'Sak woke Mary up.'

The analysis must be revised to account for sentences of this type.

Fortunately, there is a gap in the reasoning that seemed to prove that no argument of the lower verb can be agreed with. In fact, the CAR implies that an argument of the lower verb can trigger agreement morphology *if and only if the phrase in question is also an argument of the causative verb*. Up to this point, I have implicitly assumed that causative verbs all have the same argument structure: they are dyadic verbs that select an external agent argument (the causer) and an internal argument (the caused event), where the latter is perhaps a special kind of theme. This is probably correct for the verb *make* in English, which is also dyadic in its other, noncausative uses. However, there may well be other possibilities in other languages. For example, Alsina (1992) argues that the causative morpheme in Chichewa is actually triadic, selecting an agent, an event, and an affected object, where the affected object of the causative morpheme is also an argument of the embedded verb. If something like this were true for Mohawk, it would affect the agreement possibilities in a significant way.

With this intuition in mind, the specific suggestion that I would like to make is that the causative morpheme in Mohawk is a "light verb" in more or less the sense of Grimshaw and Mester 1988. The term light verb construction (LVC) is used for constructions like (31a) and (32a) in English (based on Jackendoff 1974).

(31)   a. John put the blame on Bill for the accident.

        b. John blamed Bill for the accident.

(32)   a. John gave Bill permission to buy a car.

        b. John permitted Bill to buy a car.

Examples (31a) and (32a) are fairly close paraphrases of the ordinary verbal constructions in (31b) and (32b), but they are structurally more complex. Intuitively speaking, the predicate is a simple verb in the (b) examples, whereas it is made up of a semantically rather neutral verb and a deverbal noun in construction with it in the (a) examples. I will refer to the former as the *light verb* and the latter as the *predicate noun*. Simplifying somewhat, these constructions seem to have the following properties: (1) The light verb and the predicate noun act as a unit for θ-marking purposes. (2) The total argument-taking properties of the construction are jointly determined by the light verb and the predicate noun. In general, lexical properties of the light verb determine the basic syntactic structure of the clause, while the predicate noun determines the semantic flavor of those arguments (Jackendoff 1974). (3) Some arguments—particularly themes—show up as either a phrase-structure dependent of the noun or a phrase-structure dependent of the verb, depending on the construction (Grimshaw and Mester 1988). For example, the infinitive *to buy a car* in (32a) forms a constituent with the noun *permission,* while the PP *on Bill* in (31a) does not form a constituent with the noun *blame.* This is demonstrated by the contrast between (33b) and (33c).

(33)   a.   The blame was put on Bill for the accident.

     b.   *The blame on Bill was put for the accident.

     c.   Permission to buy a car was given John.

The difference is more salient in languages like Japanese and Urdu, which mark NP dependents and VP dependents with different Cases. The following examples are from Urdu (Barker 1967:145):

(34)   a.   Mǝ̄y [ys   k-a   yntyzam]   kǝrūga.
         I   this GEN-MASC arrangement(MASC) make/FUT/1sS
         'I will arrange this.' (Literally: 'I will make its arrangement.').

     b.   Mǝ̄y [ys   pǝtthǝr ko] [khǝRa] kǝrūga.
         I   this stone   ACC   stand   make/FUT/1sS
         'I'll stand this stone up.'

In (34a), the theme of the construction as a whole is in the genitive Case and agrees with the masculine noun *yntyzam* 'arrangement'; in (34b), the theme of the construction as a whole is in the accusative/dative Case and has no agreement relation with *khǝRa* 'standing, upright'.[14] (4) Finally, if the predicate noun is Case marked by the light verb, it appears in the theme slot of the light verb. Thus, *blame* is structurally the direct object of *put* in (31a); *permission* is the second object of *give* in (32a); and 'arrangement' is the morphological object of 'make' in (34a).

    Unfortunately, the literature contains no standard account of LVCs that fully explains all these properties. The most influential analysis has been that of Grimshaw and Mester (1988), but although their article has much to say about property (3), it has little to say about properties (2) and (4).[15] On the other hand, Jackendoff (1974) has much to say about property (2), but he merely stipulates property (4). I cannot give a full-fledged analysis here of these constructions, which have many lexical intricacies. I will, however, sketch the outlines of an account that seems to be promising.

    Let us begin with property (4), the fact that the predicate noun must be the structural object of the light verb. This is a salient constraint on LVCs across a variety of languages (at least English, Japanese, and Urdu) that has often been observed but has drawn surprisingly little attention in the literature. Why should the theme position be special in this way? In fact, this constraint is strongly reminiscent of a constraint on noun incorporation discussed in chapter 7: the theme/ direct object is the only position from which noun incorporation can take place. Perhaps, then, an LVC interpretation is possible if and only if the predicate noun incorporates into the verb at some level of representation. This proposal elegantly reunites two distinct senses of the notion "word" that seem to diverge in LVCs: the sense of word as "basic predicate," and the sense of word as "X^0 constituent." On the surface, the light verb plus the predicate noun constitute a word in the first sense, but not the second; if this proposal is correct, then the two do, in fact, form an X^0 derived by incorporation by LF, if not before. The principle that allows LVCs to exist can then be stated roughly as in (35).

(35)   If the argument structure of X is nondistinct from the argument structure of Y, then the head chain $\{X_k + Y, t_k\}$ may assign θ-roles as a unit.

Such a formulation would have been impossible in the framework of Chomsky 1981 because of the Projection Principle, which stipulated that argument relationships had to be consistent at all levels. Thus, movement processes were never allowed to affect θ-role assignment. However, Chomsky (1992) abandons this claim and explicitly states that the θ-role relationships are properly defined at LF only. Principle (35), like the *tough*-movement constructions Chomsky discusses, crucially exploits this possibility. I will leave vague exactly what it means for the members of a head chain to "assign θ-roles as a unit." Minimally, it means that a given argument must meet the selectional restrictions of both heads (see Jackendoff 1974 for early discussion of some specific cases).

This approach analyzes an example like (32a) in the following way. The noun *permission* selects (at least) an infinitival phrase as a theme. This can be seen in non–light verb contexts such as (36).

(36)   [$_{NP}$ John's permission to buy a car] allowed his son to get a loan.

Give also selects a theme argument, as well as an agent and a goal. Thus, the argument structure of *permission* is a subset of the argument structure of *give*. Suppose, then, that an NP headed by *permission* is generated as the direct object of *give:*

(37)   John   gave   [$_{NP}$ Bill] [$_{NP}$ permission [$_{CPi}$ PRO to buy a car]]
            <Ag, Th, Go>   <Th$_i$>

Permission can then incorporate into *give* at LF. The conditions in (35) are satisfied, and *to buy a car* can be jointly θ-marked by *give* and *permission*. In this sense, it comes to be the theme argument of *give* as well as that of *permission* at LF.

(38)   John$_n$ permission$_m$-gave   [$_{NPk}$ Bill] [$_{NP}$ t$_m$[$_{CPi}$ PRO to buy a car]]
            <Th$_i$> <Ag$_n$, Th$_i$, Go$_k$>

Indeed, the infinitive behaves rather like a complement of the light verb in certain respects; for example, it is not an island for purposes of *wh*-extraction, as complex NPs usually are. Thus, (39b) is more like (39a) in its acceptability than like (39c).

(39)   a.   What did you permit John [to buy t]?

        b.   What did you give John [permission [to buy t]]?

        c.   ??What did you witness [a decision [to buy t]]?

Finally, the alternation between examples like (34a) and (34b) in Urdu can be thought of as a difference between whether the predicate noun incorporates into the light verb in the syntax, or only at LF.[16] In the first case, the theme argument already counts as the object of the light verb with respect to PF processes of Case marking and agreement; in the latter case, the theme will still be (only) the argument of the noun at this point. With respect to θ-role assignment at LF, however, the two are equivalent. This, then, is the beginning of an account of the major properties of LVCs.

The relevance of this for causative formation begins to appear when one considers pairs like (40) and (41) in Urdu.

(40) a. Mə̄y khəRa hū.
        I   stand   be
        'I am standing.'

      b. Mə̄y [ys pətthər ko] [khəRa] kərūga.
        I   this stone   ACC stand   make/FUT/1sS
        'I'll stand this stone up.'

(41) a. Nəmaz   šwru   hwi.
        prayer(FEM) beginning be(FEM)
        'The prayer began.'

      b. Mə̄y ne nəmaz   šwru   ki.
        I   ERG prayer(FEM) beginning make(FEM)
        'I began the prayer.'

These are LVCs in which the predicate noun combines either with the light verb *hona* 'be' or *kərna* 'do, make'. When it combines with *hona*, the effect is like that of a simple unaccusative verb. When it combines with the transitive *kərna*, however, the combination takes an agent argument as well as the shared theme argument. Semantically, the (b) examples can be considered a kind of causative version of the (a) examples. Indeed, the relationship of (40b) and (41b) to (40a) and (41a) is very similar to the relationship of a sentence with a causative verb in Mohawk to a sentence with the corresponding verb root. Notice also that although the theme *nəmaz* 'prayer' clearly is dependent on *šwru* 'beginning' for its thematic interpretation, it is treated morphosyntactically as the object of *kərna* as well, as indicated by the fact that they agree in gender. These examples with *kərna* are thus a suitable model for an analysis of the causative in Mohawk.

Suppose that the causative morpheme in Mohawk has the argument structure of a simple transitive verb and enters into light verb constructions with another predicate. Its lexical entry would be roughly as in (42).[17]

(42)   *st / ht / 't* 'do, make' <Agent, Theme>

The structure of a typical Mohawk causative like that given in (30) is (43). This structure is exactly like the one in (38) or (40b), except for one insignificant difference: instead of a predicate noun or adjective, we have a predicate verb. In particular, the argument structure of *ye* 'wake up' is nondistinct from that of *ht,* so after verb incorporation the theme of 'wake up' can count as the theme of *ht* as well, by (35). This makes all the difference with respect to the MVC. Since *ht* is the head of the derived V, its arguments will be accessible to the agreement factors once the complex incorporates into Asp and Infl. Since 'her' now qualifies

(43)

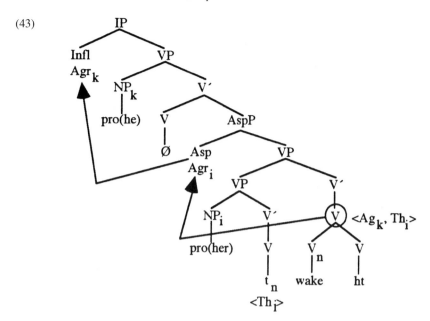

as such an argument, it can be agreed with, in accordance with the CAR. So, too, can the agent of the causative morpheme. Thus, the MVC is satisfied. In effect, 'wake up' satisfies the MVC even though it is not the morphological head of the complex predicate, because its sole argument is shared with an argument of the head. In this way, we explain the grammatical causatives in (24) and (25) in Mohawk. The conclusion is that although the CAR plus the MVC rules out English-style causatives in a polysynthetic language, it does not rule out an Urdu-style light verb causative.[18]

Not surprisingly, the jointly marked theme of a causative verb can be morphologically expressed by an incorporated noun root rather than by an agreement morpheme; (24a) was an example of this; another example is (44a).

(44)   Uwári t-a-yu-[a]'shár-ʌ-ht-e'.
       Mary CIS-FACT-FsS-knife-fall-CAUS-PUNC
       'Mary made the knife fall.'

Example (44) has exactly the same structure as (43), except that a lexical noun is generated in the specifier of the lower VP. This then adjoins to the left of the lower verb before the verb combines with the causative morpheme, deriving the structure [[knife-fall]-caus]. This complex then raises to Asp and Infl, thereby combining with agreement. The resulting structure again satisfies the MVC.

Support for this analysis comes from a detail regarding the behavior of quirky agreement in Mohawk causatives. Recall from chapter 5 that some unaccusative verbs in Mohawk associate with their theme arguments the feature +O, meaning that they trigger "object" agreement forms; other unaccusatives mark their themes as −O, so that they show "subject" agreement forms. Predictably this distinction vanishes when the verb is causativized, because then the theme is the lower of two arguments in a complete functional complex and is always marked +O by general rule (the SAP). Thus, the causer always triggers A-class agreement and the original theme triggers O-class agreement, as in (30), regardless of the properties of the verb root. So far, this is unremarkable. The interesting part is what happens when the agent argument added by the causative is suppressed—for example, by the addition of reflexive morphology (section 5.2.3). One might expect that since only the theme of the verb root is relevant to agreement, the original $+O/-O$ distinction would reappear. In fact, it does not; rather, the theme argument of a causative-reflexive verb always triggers A-class agreement, regardless of the properties of the original verb stem. The crucial type of example is (45), where *'tsu* 'dirty' by itself takes an O-class theme.

(45)   a. Te-*wak*-ya't-á-'tsu.
           DUP-1sO-body-Ø-be.dirty
           'I am dirty.'

       b. Wa'-t-*k*-atat-ya't-á-'tsu-st-e'.
           FACT-DUP-1sS-REFL-body-Ø-be.dirty-CAUS-PUNC
           'I made myself dirty.' (Literally: 'I was self-dirty-made.')

Assuming as before that reflexive morphology does not directly affect $\pm O$ values, (45b) shows that the causative morpheme somehow overrides the verb root, causing the theme to be marked $-O$ rather than $+O$. Now the theory of quirky agreement in section 5.4 is built around the assumption that a head X can determine the $\pm O$ feature for an NP Y only if X θ-marks Y. Thus, we conclude that the causative morpheme must itself θ-mark the theme NP at some level; otherwise, it would have no right to influence the agreement properties of that NP. This confirms the basic premise on which the LVC analysis of Mohawk causatives is based. Indeed, since the causative morpheme is the head of the derived word and thus the source of the argument structure that is visible to the Agr in Asp, it makes sense that the features of the causative morpheme predominate for purposes of agreement. Thus, the same principles that ensure that agreement with the theme argument is possible also account naturally for the form of that agreement.

We have now accounted for why causatives of unaccusative verbs are possible in Mohawk. The next step is to make sure that given our new understanding of the morpheme *ht* we still correctly rule out morphological causatives based on verbs of other types. Take, first, the fact that unergative verbs cannot be causativized. One example of this is repeated in (46).

(46)   *Wa'-te-shako-[a]tskáhu-ht-e'.
         FACT-DUP-MsS/FsO-eat-CAUS-PUNC
         'He made her eat.'

The basic hypothesis is that Mohawk causatives are like LVCs in other languages, except that the two heads are visibly joined by incorporation. Now Grimshaw and Mester (1988) show that an agent argument can never be a dependent of the predicate noun in an LVC, in contrast to the theme. A hypothetical example might look something like (47).

(47)   *John did [$_{NP}$ consumption by Mary].

Such examples are not attested in the literature on LVCs. Indeed, we can interpret (35) in such a way as to rule this out. Once we try to draw the structure of (46) we can see why this might be so. It would have to be something like the structure given in (48).

(48)

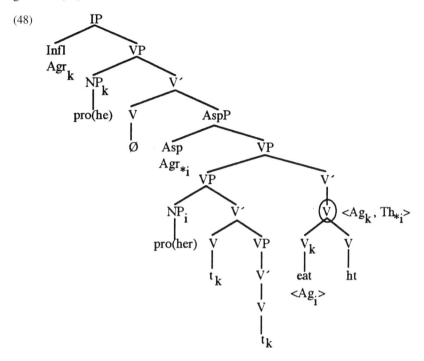

For (48) to be treated as an LVC construction, 'her' would have to receive the agent θ-role of 'eat' and the theme θ-role of the causative morpheme. Inasmuch as these are two very different θ-roles, we can say that the argument structures of 'eat' and 'cause' are not nondistinct in the sense required by (35). Thus, joint θ-marking fails in this case.[19] Now, if joint θ-marking is impossible, then 'her' is not coindexed with anything in the argument structure of *ht,* the head of the complex verb. Therefore, when the complex verb incorporates into Asp, this element does not become accessible to agreement. Neither can the embedded agent incorporate into the lower or higher verb, as discussed previously. Thus, 'her' never becomes visible for θ-role assignment, and the structure is ruled out.

These considerations also explain why it is impossible to causativize a transitive verb in Mohawk, as shown again in (49).

(49)   *Ká'sere' wa'-uk-hnínu-ht-e'.
        car   FACT-FsS/1sO-buy-CAUS-PUNC
        'She made me buy a car.'

This would have to be derived from an LVC source like (50), which again is unattested.

(50)   *She did [NP purchase of a car by me].

Such examples would have the same structure as (48), except that there would be a theme NP ('car') generated as the specifier of the lowest VP. Clearly, this will not solve any of the problems involved in finding a legitimate morphological expression for the causee 'me'. Therefore, Mohawk cannot use *ht* to causativize ordinary agent–theme verbs either.

The last class of verbs to consider consists of those with a theme–goal argument structure, such as *yʌ* 'to lie, to have'. These also fail to causativize:

(51)   #Á'share' wa-hí-yʌ-ht-e'.
       knife   FACT-1sS/MsO-have-CAUS-PUNC
       'I caused him to have a knife.' (Literally: 'I caused the knife to lie to him.')

Here the explanation is only slightly different. The predicate verb by hypothesis has the argument structure $<Th, Go>$, whereas the light verb has the argument structure $<Ag, Th>$. Its schematic structure would be something like:

(52)   I   do   [$_{VP}$ lie   knife to him].
          $<Ag_k, Th_i>$ $<Th_i, Go_n>$

The theme argument of this type of verb is compatible with the argument structure of the causative morpheme, but the goal argument clearly is not. Thus, even if the theme argument could be jointly θ-marked by the lower verb and the causative morpheme, the goal could not be. At best, this could be the argument of the lower verb alone. However, since only the argument structure of the higher verb is visible to the agreement factors in Asp and Infl, agreement with the goal will be impossible. Nor can goal arguments incorporate into the verb (section 7.3.3). Since neither agreement nor incorporation is possible for this argument, (51) is ruled out by the MVC.

In section 7.3.3, it was shown that Mohawk has a small class of verbs that are minimally different from standard theme–goal verbs in that the Jackendovian path function is already included in the meaning of the verb. Such verbs select an NP theme and an NP reference object, rather than an NP theme and a PP goal, and the head of this reference object can incorporate into the verb. Thus, our theory predicts that these verbs should be unique among the dyadic verbs of Mohawk in having causative forms. Strikingly, this is correct. The two clear examples of this class are *yahya'k* 'cross' and *ra'* 'reach, arrive at'. For most purposes, these verbs look like ordinary transitive verbs; nevertheless, the causative morpheme can attach to them:

(53)   a. Thíkʌ rúkwe y-a'-t-hi-nyatar-íya'k-t-e'
          that man   TRANS-FACT-DUP-1sS/MsO-river-cross-CAUS-PUNC
          'I took that man across the river.'

       b. Y-a-hi-háh-a-ra'-t-e'.
          TRANS-FACT-1sS/MsO-road-Ø-reach-CAUS-PUNC
          'I led him to the right road.'

The syntactic structure of (53a) is (54). After the verb combines with the relevant functional categories, the complex word in (55) is derived, which passes the MVC without any problems.

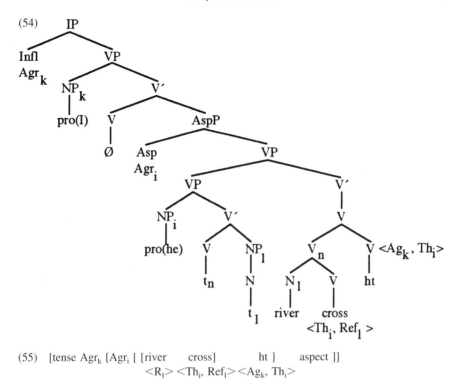

(54)

(55) [tense Agr$_k$ [Agr$_i$ [[river cross] ht] aspect]]
   $<$R$_1>$ $<$Th$_i$, Ref$_1>$$<Ag_k$, Th$_i>$

To summarize the results of this section, we have seen that the CAR, the MVC, and a theory of light verb constructions combine to explain quite precisely the range of verbs that can be found in morphological causative constructions in Mohawk. The MVC explains why the only kind of causative the language could have is one that makes use of some kind of argument sharing. Principles of light verb construction then explain why argument sharing is possible with unaccusative verbs but not with verbs that take an agent. Finally, the CAR explains why even theme-path verbs cannot be causativized, unless the path is of the very special kind that is eligible for noun incorporation.

8.2.3 Causatives in Other Languages

Of course, one might accept that Mohawk causatives are derived from an LVC-like source but deny that this fact has any inherent link to its polysynthetic character. It could simply be a historical accident that the causative construction happened to develop in this way in this particular language. The obvious way to show that this is not an accident is to demonstrate that the causatives of unrelated polysynthetic languages have similar properties. This section explores the prediction.

I have already mentioned that none of the languages that have guided the literature on the intricacies of morphological causatives is polysynthetic. Thus, the best-known and most important instances of morphological causatives are in languages such as Turkish (Aissen 1979), Japanese (Kuno 1973), Chamorro (Gibson 1980), Malayalam (Mohanan 1983), and the various Bantu languages (Alsina 1992). None of these languages is even remotely polysynthetic: only the Bantu languages have overt object agreement, and this is typically optional and discourse controlled (Bresnan and Mchombo 1987); only Turkish is said to have noun incorporation, and this is of the indefinite/generic type only.The Eskimoan languages are a more interesting case in that they are polysynthetic in the traditional sense and most of them have causatives of transitive as well as intransitive verbs (Woodbury and Sadock 1986). Nevertheless, these languages appear not to be polysynthetic in the technical sense of being subject to the MVC; rather, they differ from languages like Mohawk in a cluster of ways (see chapter 11 for a summary).

Working from the other direction, consider first Wichita (Rood 1976), a Caddoan language distantly related to Mohawk. Rood describes causatives in Wichita as being formed from verbs of any argument structure, but his examples do not bear this out. The majority of the causative forms he cites are excellent candidates for unaccusative status. A typical one is given in (56).

(56)   Hi-ta-kí-ic-ʔiriwara:r-ik-s.   (Rood 1976:62)
       3pS-IND-1sO-PREV-roll-CAUS-IMPF
       'They are rolling me.'

When discussing the fact that causatives can attach to agentive verbs (Rood 1976:152–153), the examples that he gives are instructive. He notes that the posture/location verbs 'stand', 'sit', and 'lie' are particularly common instances of agentive verbs that are causativized; an example is given in (57) (with reflexive).

(57)   I-t-a-ac-íseʔí:r-ʔirhaw[i]-iki.   (Rood 1976:153)
       IMPER-1sS-REFL-PREV-a.while-lie-CAUS
       'Let me lay myself down for a while.'

However, there is independent evidence that these verbs are really unaccusative in Wichita. For example, they allow incorporation of their sole argument:

(58)   Kiya-ki-ic-íwa:c-é:hirʔa-s-ʔirhawi.   (Rood 1976:262)
       QUOT/3S-AOR-PREV-big-buffalo-NOM-lie
       'There was the big buffalo lying here.'

Thus, I believe the main reason that Rood thinks morphological causatives are possible with agentive verbs is that the causative can attach to intransitive verbs that take subject agreement. In this, he underestimated the quirkiness of agreement in Wichita (see section 5.4.4). The glosses of his other examples are 'burst open', 'rain', 'be cooked', 'die in water', 'be on top', 'be dry', 'hang outside' (Rood 1976:62–63), 'be upright', 'sit/dwell', and 'dance' (Rood 1976:56, 178). Of these, only the root for 'dance' is potentially problematic. Finally, the one example that he gives of a causative attached to a transitive verb is the following (Rood 1976:56).

(59)   Kiyari:cé:hire:weʔekih ka:hí:kʔa té:s a:ki-ic-ʔí:s-ka-ʔahi-iki.
       God   woman   corn QUOT/AOR-BEN-hand-in-hold-CAUS
       'God gave corn to the woman.' (Literally: 'God made the woman hold corn in her hand.')

Rood elsewhere observes that *ʌahi-iki* is the normal lexeme meaning 'give' in the language, and hence presumably counts as a listed lexical item (Rood 1976:40). Given this, it seems reasonable to conjecture that (59) is not a productively formed causative, but some kind of frozen form. Perhaps there are a few other forms with similar structure. Nevertheless, Rood's grammar overall is consistent with the claim that the causative morpheme in Wichita only attaches productively to unaccusative verbs, as predicted.

Particularly clear support for the theory comes from the Gunwinjguan languages. These are spoken on the other side of the earth from Mohawk, yet their causatives are strikingly similar. Heath (1984:393–394) discusses in some detail the causative morpheme *jga* in Nunggubuyu. A typical example of its use is the following (Heath 1980:36):

(60) bama:-'ra:-'rndarrmi-jga-ng
2sS/MANAO-all-shake-CAUS-NONPAST
'Shake it (a rope)!'

Heath observes that the verbs to which *jga* is added are normally intransitive; the very few examples in which it seems to attach to a transitive verb (Heath cites two) are idiomatic. This is what we predict. Indeed, we predict a bit more than this—that the verbs that can be causativized are only the unaccusative ones. Heath does not distinguish between unaccusatives and unergatives in his grammar, but the list of verbs that have an attested causative form is very suggestive. This list includes verbs meaning 'to stand', 'to shift position', 'to go down', 'to be hot', 'to breathe', 'to flee', 'to sink', 'to die', 'to be straight', 'to shine', 'to enter', 'to shake', 'to be open', 'to jump', 'to fall', and 'to go to sleep' (Heath 1984:394, 402, 404). It is likely that these all belong to the unaccusative class; in some cases, there is direct confirmation of this in that the verb stem allows noun incorporation (e.g., *lha* 'to stand'). Moreover, these observations seem to be entirely typical of the Gunwinjguan languages as a whole. Thus, Merlan (1983:133–134) lists the following verbs as having causatives in Ngalakan: 'be sick', 'grow', 'stop', 'go in', 'bathe', 'come out', 'be ashamed', 'sit down', 'drown', 'break', 'go into water', 'die', and 'fall'. All of these verbs look like unaccusatives. Merlan makes the significant observation that the causative morpheme *ga* is also used as an independent verb meaning 'take'; 'take' is one of the most common elements to be used as a light verb across languages (cf. English *He took a bath*). McKay (1975:156–159) gives comparable facts for the cognate morpheme *ka* in Rembarrnga. Finally, Nicholas Evans (personal communication) confirms that the morphological causative is also very limited in Mayali; his impression is that it may not be productive even among the unaccusative verbs. (The examples listed in Evans 1991 mostly involve verbs of directed motion.)

The next polysynthetic language to consider is Chukchee. Like Mohawk, Chukchee has both a morphological causative and a periphrastic one; for current purposes the construction of interest is the morphological one.[20] Nedjalkov (1976) describes the morphological causative as being possible only with intransitive verbs. One of his examples is the following (Nedjalkov 1976:191):

(61) Gənan gəm ine-n-t'əl-ew-ə-rkən.
      you   me 2sS/1sO-CAUS-hurt-CAUS-Ø-PRES
      'You cause me pain, you hurt me.'

Another example has the gloss 'fall'; psychological verbs such as 'be frightened' also can be causativized in this way (Nedjalkov 1976:195). Certainly, these are good unaccusative verbs. This is confirmed by Bogoras (1922:819), who gives examples of morphological causatives where the meaning of the root is 'be un-well', 'sit down', 'awake', 'go out', 'appear', 'jump', 'be anointed', 'get married', 'be created'.[21] Although Nedjalkov describes this morpheme as attaching to transitive verbs as well, he notes (1976:202) that it is only possible with "10–15 transitive verbs of specific meaning"; thus, *l'u* 'see' with the causative becomes *re-l'u-ŋen* 'show'; *pəl* 'drink' becomes *rə-lp-əŋan* 'drench'. To this list, Bogoras adds *rə-keto-ŋat* 'remind', from *keto* 'remember'. These look like typical examples of lexical causatives; they are presumably idiosyncratic and listed. In general, unergative verbs and transitive verbs must use the periphrastic construction, whereas 'fall' and 'feel pain' are only grammatical with the morphological construction. An interesting minimal pair bringing out this difference is the following (Nedjalkov 1976:191):

(62) a. Ǝtləg-e   ekək   r-ikwici-w-ə-rkə-nin.
          father-ERG son(NOM) CAUS-drink-CAUS-Ø-PRES-3sS/3sO
          'The father drenches the son (with water).'

      b. Ǝtləg-e   ekək   ikwici-ygut rən-nin.
          father-ERG son(NOM) drink-CAUS have-3sS/3sO
          'The father lets the son drink (water).'

Apparently the verb *ikwici* 'drink' in Chukchee is ambiguous between the normal sense one would expect from English and a sense that means something like 'be drenched with water'. Semantically, one would expect this second sense to be unaccusative, whereas the standard sense is unergative. Interestingly, when the morphological causative is attached to the verb it has only its unaccusative meaning, as in (62a), whereas when the same verb appears in the periphrastic construction it has only its unergative meaning, as in (62b). This pair strongly suggests that morphological causatives are only possible with unaccusative verbs in Chukchee.

Consider next the Tanoan languages. Watkins (1984:153) says that causatives in Kiowa can be formed by compounding a root with the transitive verb *ɔ̀m* 'do, make', as in (63).

(63) Hóldà gyàt-kyɔ́y-ɔ̀:mɔ̀.
      dress 1sS/3pO-long-make/IMPF
      'I'm going to lengthen the dress.'

'Be long' is presumably an unaccusative, as are the other verbs Watkins uses in her examples ('be ripe/cooked', 'dry', 'start off', 'be sick', 'be hot'). Kenneth Hale (personal communication) believes that only unaccusatives can be causativized in Jemez as well.

There is another, much more interesting pattern with in Tanoan, however. Kiowa has a phenomenon that Watkins calls "raising incorporation." She writes (1984:228):

An extremely common type of incorporation is that of a subordinate verb or verb plus its object noun. Identity of participants in a pair of main and subordinate clauses results in the raising of the lower verb into the verb of the upper clause. . . . If the lower clause has an overt noun object, it too is raised. . . . Note that the pronominal prefix signals only the participants of the upper clause."

An example of this phenomenon is given in (64).

(64) Gyà-kí:-kɔ̀:tɔ̀-tòt.
      1sS/3sO-meat-buy-send/PERF
      'I sent him to buy meat.'

This sentence is not so different in meaning from a causative, such as 'I had him buy meat.'

Indeed, the normal causative in Southern Tiwa has exactly the same properties as the "raising incorporation" construction in Kiowa, according to Allen et al. 1984. The causative morpheme *'am* can attach to a transitive verb, as in (65).

(65) I-'u'u-kur-'am-ban.
      1sS/2sO-baby-hold-CAUS-PAST
      'I made you hold the baby.'

This example seems to be problematic for my theory. However, the Southern Tiwa construction has the same peculiarities as the one in Kiowa. Thus, the theme of the incorporated verb root must itself be incorporated into the verbal complex[22:]

(66) *'U'u-de i-kur-'am-ban.
       baby-SG 1sS/2sO-hold-CAUS-PAST
      'I made you hold the baby.'

Moreover, the verb as a whole does not agree with this lower theme. This can be seen by comparing the agreement prefix in (65) with the one in (67), where the same three participants are the arguments of a simple ditransitive verb and all three affect the agreement (see Allen et al. 1984, Allen et al. 1990, and Rosen 1990 for discussion).

(67) *Ka*-'u'u-wia-ban.
      1sS/2sO\AO-baby-give-PAST
      'I gave you the baby.'

Data from the appendices of Frantz 1993a confirm that this is a widespread pattern in Southern Tiwa, as it is in Kiowa. Thus, many complement-taking verbs can either take a full clausal complement or a construction with an incorporated verb. If the incorporated verb is transitive, its object must also be incorporated but does not trigger agreement on the verb complex. In contrast, the subject of the lower verb is not (necessarily) incorporated and does trigger agreement on the verb complex. Example (68) illustrates these characteristics for the verb *t'am* 'help'.

(68) a. Ow-t'am-ban   hliawra-de u-napir-hi-'i.
         2sS/AO\cO-help-PAST lady-SG   3sS/cO-sew-FUT-SUB
         'You helped the lady sew.'

b. Ow-napir-t'am-ban   hliawra-de.
   2sS/AO\cO-sew-help-PAST lady-SG
   'You helped the lady sew.'

c. Tow-musa-miki-t'am-ban.
   1sS/AO\cO-cat-feed-help-PAST
   'I helped him feed the cat.'

Other verbs that Frantz gives that fit this general pattern (with some differences in the argument structure of the matrix clause) are ones meaning 'allow', 'learn', 'try', 'start', 'decide' and 'forget'.

How much of the theory of polysynthesis must be revised to account for these facts? Clearly, I must retreat somewhat from my original claim that there are few complex predicate structures in polysynthetic languages; Southern Tiwa has as wide a range of verb incorporation constructions as one could hope for. However, these constructions are still limited as to their syntactic form in ways that provide elegant support for the essentials of my analysis. Watkins (1984) assumes that the verb 'send' in Kiowa takes an agent argument, a patient argument, and a clausal complement. She also assumes that the patient argument of 'send' controls the agent argument of the lower clause (although she does not use this terminology). Suppose that these assumptions are true not only for Kiowa 'send' but for *'am* in Southern Tiwa as well.[23] Then the structure of (65) is the one given in (69).

(69)

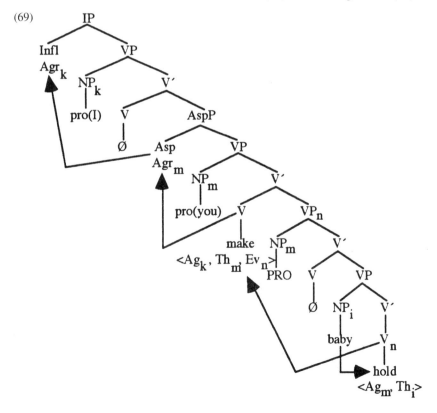

This is not an LVC, but rather an ordinary case of VP complementation. As before, there are no agreement-bearing functional heads inside the VP complement. Thus, the only agreement factors are those associated with the matrix verb, and only the argument structure of the matrix verb is visible to them after the relevant head movements. This explains immediately Watkins' (1984) and Rosen's (1990) observation that these sentences show agreement with the matrix subject and the matrix object but not with the embedded object. Indeed, these facts strongly support the idea that agreement is sensitive to argument structure, as expressed in the CAR. Since the matrix verb also assigns a θ-role to the projection of the lower verb, the lower verb must incorporate so that this argument will be morphologically expressed. Therefore, the two verbs must combine into a kind of verbal compound even if neither one of them is specified as an affix. (Sentences like (68a), in which there is no verb incorporation, have a slightly different structure; see section 10.1.)

Now consider the arguments of the lower verb. Since the subject of the lower verb is controlled by the object of the matrix verb, the agent position in the lower verb's θ-grid bears the same index as the theme position of the matrix verb.[24] Thus, when the two verbs combine, the agreement morpheme that expresses the matrix theme role can also count as expressing the embedded agent role. This leaves only the embedded theme role to be concerned with. This is too deeply embedded to be agreed with directly, and it cannot be agreed with indirectly because it is not associated with any argument of the matrix verb. Thus, this role cannot be made visible by agreement. However, it is possible for the lower theme to incorporate into the lower verb. Therefore, this incorporation is forced as the only way to satisfy the MVC. This explains the ungrammaticality of (66) in contrast to (65). The correct surface form is derived by having the lowest N incorporate into the lower V; then the lower V incorporates into the higher V, moving through the lower $\emptyset$ position. Finally, the resulting verbal complex combines with Asp and Infl, to give the following well-formed morphological structure:

(70)   [Agr_k [Agr_m [[baby $hold_n$]   make]   Asp] Tense]
                $<R_i><Ag_m, Th_i><Ag_k, Th_m, Ev_n>$

In this way, the special properties of sentences like (64) and (65) are elegantly accounted for by the theory of polysynthesis—in particular, the CAR and the MVC. Moreover, we see that causative-like constructions based on transitive verbs are possible in polysynthetic languages after all, but only under very specific conditions.[25]

The last polysynthetic language to discuss in depth is Classical Nahuatl. This language appears to be even more problematic in that morphological causatives are possible with base verbs of any argument structure, including unergatives and transitives as well as unaccusatives. Some examples are given in (71).

(71)   a. Ø-mitz-huetzī-tia.   (Launey 1981:190)
           3sS-2sO-fall-CAUS
           'He makes you fall.'

        b. Ti-nēch-tza'tzī-tia.   (Launey 1981:181)
           2sS-1sO-shout-CAUS
           'You make me shout.'

    c. Ni-mitz-cua-l-tia   in nacatl.   (Launey 1981:181)
       1sS-2sO-eat-x-CAUS the meat
       'I made you eat the meat.'

    d. Ni-quin-ne-tlazo'tla-l-tia.   (Launey 1981:186)
       1sS-3pO-REFL-like-x-CAUS
       'I reconcile them.' (Literally: 'I make them like each other.')

However, there is an important and revealing quirk to the forms in (71c) and (71d): the causative morpheme does not attach directly to the verb root, but rather to the root plus the formative *l*. This suggests that there may be more to this construction than meets the eye.

    Stems are commonly augmented by *l* in at least two other situations in Nahuatl. First, *l* appears when the passive/impersonal affix *hualo* is added to certain verb roots, as shown in (72) (Launey 1981:138–141).

(72)   a. Tla-cua-l-o.
       3INDEF-eat-x-PASS
       'Something is eaten; one eats things.'

     b. Ni-tlazo'tla-l-ō-z.
       1sS-like-x-PASS-FUT
       'I will be liked.'

This *l* appears on a particular conjugation class of verbs, most but not all of which are transitive; a few intransitive verbs also take *l* in the passive/impersonal, and a few transitive verbs fail to take *l*. The same verbs that take *l* in the impersonal also take *l* in the causative, apart from a small amount paradigm leveling.

    Another place where *l* appears productively is in the formation of nominalizations that refer to the object of the root verb (Launey 1981:283–286, Andrews 1975:232–239):[26]

(73)   a. tla-cua-l-li   (Launey 1981:283)
       3INDEF-eat-x-NSF
       'thing that one eats, food'

     b. tla-tlazo'tla-l-li   (Launey 1981:283)
       3INDEF-like-x-NSF
       'object or person that is liked'

Now these nominalizations and the passive/impersonal forms have something important in common: both have a suppressed external argument. In other words, the agent of the verb in both (72) and (73) is incapable of being expressed grammatically and is interpreted as indefinite or generic. This, then, seems to be the characteristic property of the *nonactive stem* form in *l*. For concreteness, we may assume that these stems are formed by a lexical rule such as the following:

(74) $[_{\text{verb}} \ X]$ $\rightarrow$ $[Xl]$ if X is of class A (mostly transitives)
                    $\rightarrow$ $[X]$ if X is of class B (mostly intransitives)
     $<\text{Arg}, \ . \ . \ .>$ $<\text{Arg}_{\text{arb}}, \ . \ . \ .>$

This rule has two effects. First, it assigns to the highest position in the stem's argument structure the special index "arb" (arbitrary); this means that this θ-role will not be available in the syntax (compare Rizzi 1986a). Second, it adds the formative *l* if the verb is of the right conjugation class. Notice that (74) does not specify whether the category of the resulting stem is N or V; thus, it leaves open the question of whether the nominalizations are derived from the verbal passives by truncation of *o/hua* (as Andrews claims), whether the passives are derived from the nominalizations by addition of *o/hua,* or whether both are derived from an abstract source neutral between the two.

The next question is, Why are causatives formed from the nonactive stem as well? In the context of this chapter, this fact makes sense. The general problem with morphological causatives in polysynthetic languages is that it is hard for the embedded verb to have its arguments expressed morphologically. By forming its causatives from the nonactive stem, Nahuatl decreases the magnitude of this problem: there is one less argument that needs to be expressed. If the stem to be causativized started out as monadic, its nonactive form will take no syntactic arguments. This means, of course, that the understood "causees" in (71) must be arguments of the matrix verb *tia.* Thus, *tia* must be a three-place predicate, which takes the causer as its agent argument, the caused action as its theme, and the causee as its goal.[27] The syntactic structure of (71a) and (71b) is then (75).

(75)

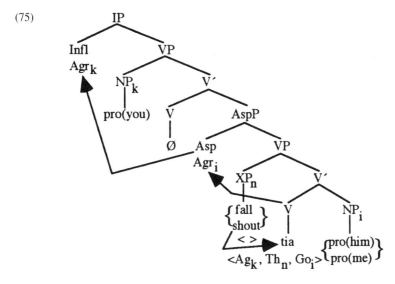

Semantically, the literal gloss for these sentences would be roughly, 'You gave falling to him' or 'You gave shouting to me'—which is a reasonable reconstruction of their meaning. The nonactive stem necessarily incorporates into *tia,* thereby expressing morphologically *tia*'s theme role. The two agreement factors then express the causer/agent and the causee/goal in a straightforward manner. The nonactive stem itself has no active arguments. Thus, the MVC is fully satisfied. Notice that the rule of nonactive stem formation effectively neutralizes the distinction between unaccusative verbs and unergative verbs, correctly accounting for the fact that both causitivize in essentially the same way in Nahuatl. This is in vivid contrast to the other polysynthetic languages, where the difference between the two types of intransitives is crucial—in part because they do not have impersonal verbs and nominalizations of the kind found in Nahuatl.

The situation with transitive verb roots is more complicated. Even after they have undergone nonactive stem formation, they still have an argument (typically a theme) that must be expressed. One straightforward possibility is for the theme argument of the stem to incorporate into the stem before the stem incorporates into the causative verb. This is certainly possible, resulting in forms like (76).

(76)   Ø-nēch-cac-chīhua-l-tia.   (Launey 1981:183)
       3sS-1sO-shoe-make-NONACT-CAUS
       'He makes me make shoes.'

Also possible are forms in which the lower object is expressed by the indefinite inanimate prefix *tla,* as in (77) or the indefinite animate prefix *tē* (see (80)). I tentatively assume that these are to be analyzed as incorporated noun roots as well.[28]

(77)   Ni-mitz-tla-cua-l-tia   (Launey 1981:181)
       1sS-2sO-3INDEF-eat-NONACT-CAUS
       'I make you eat (something), I give (something-)eating to you.'

The natural structure for (76) is given in (78).

(78)

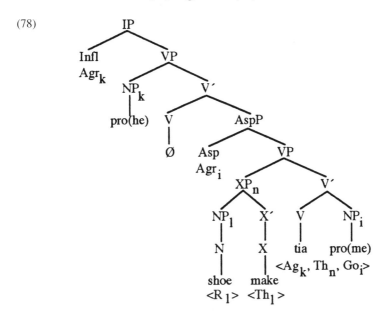

Structure (78) means roughly, 'He gave me making of shoes.' 'Shoe' then incorporates into the next highest head 'make', and the combination then incorporates into *tia* 'cause'. Finally, the complex verb headed by *tia* combines with the functional categories to derive the word structure in (79), which passes the MVC.

(79)   [Agr$_k$ [Agr$_i$ [[shoe$_l$ make]$_n$ *tia*   ] Asp] tense]
               <R$_l$><Th$_l$> <Ag$_k$, Th$_n$, Go$_i$>

The structure for (77) is analogous, with *tla* 'something' generated in the position occupied by 'shoe' in (78).

The one remaining question is whether under appropriate circumstances a true agreement morpheme can also express the theme of the verb root. On this point, the grammars give incomplete and partially contradictory information. Crucial evidence is only possible if the lower object is third person animate plural or the causee/goal is expressed by the animate indefinite prefix *tē*; in all other circumstances, the causee/goal's need for object agreement will make agreement with the lower object impossible (or invisible), in accordance with the normal principles governing agreement in triadic structures in Nahuatl. Launey (1981) does not give any forms with an animate third person plural lower object and does not discuss what happens in this case, but Kenneth Hale (personal communication) says that third person plural agreement with the lower object (*im*) is not attested. Launey (1981:189) does give the following example with *tē* and remarks that it is fixed in its interpretation:

(80) Ni-mitz-tē-nōtza-l-tia
      1sS-2sO-3INDEF-call-NONACT-CAUS
   (i) 'I made you call people.'
   (ii) *'I made people call you.'

The ungrammaticality of the second meaning again suggests that the lower object cannot trigger agreement. Thus, Launey's discussion makes it look like Nahuatl causatives are similar in this respect to Southern Tiwa causatives: agreement is impossible with arguments of the lower verb; hence, noun incorporation (possibly of a null "cognate" noun) is obligatory. If so, nothing needs to be added to the analysis in (78).

Andrews (1975:95–97), on the other hand, claims explicitly that causatives of transitive verbs show exactly the same agreement possibilities as simple ditransitive verbs in Nahuatl. As evidence, he presents the following two crucial forms of a kind not found in Launey's grammar:[29]

(81) a. Ti-nēch-in-nōtza-l-tia.
         2sS-1sO-3pO-call-NONACT-CAUS
         'You have me call them.'

      b. Ti-c-tē-chīhua-l-tia.
         2sS-3sO-3INDEF-make-NONACT-CAUS
         'You persuade someone to make it.'

In these forms, the lower object does trigger plural agreement (see (81a)) or definite object agreement (see (81b)) on the verb as a whole. It is not clear how much weight should be given to these forms, since Andrews clearly made them up to fit into his uniform paradigm and could not have checked them with native speakers. Thus, it is possible that his conception of the generative rules involved caused him to infer forms that are not actually attested. However, if these forms are correct, they can be accounted for by assuming that the incorporation of the lower verb into the causative predicate produces an LVC in Nahuatl. The structure of (81b) would then be (82). In (82), the nonactive form of 'make' takes only a theme argument, and the causative morpheme also selects a theme argument. Thus, once 'make' incorporates, the two heads can θ-mark 'it' as a unit. Now the goal argument of the complex is expressed by the indefinite morpheme *tē* (whatever that

(82)

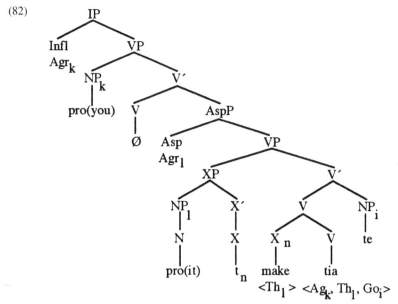

is); hence, it does not require agreement. Thus, the agreement factor in Asp is available to be coindexed with 'it'. Moreover, 'it' is coindexed with a position in the argument structure of the complex head, and the coindexing therefore satisfies the CAR. The result then passes the MVC. In essence, this structure is the same as that of causatives in Mohawk, except that the causative morpheme is triadic in Nahuatl and Nahuatl has a way of making new unaccusative stems from transitive verbs via (74). Thus, whether the forms in (81) are grammatical or not depends on whether the projection of the embedded verb is a true complement of the causative predicate, as in Southern Tiwa, or an LVC, as in Mohawk. Either is theoretically possible, and more conclusive data from Classical Nahuatl texts or modern dialects are needed to determine which is actually correct.

Finally, Ainu appears to be a true counterexample to my theory. Shibatani (1990:48–50) states that the Ainu causative suffixes *re, te,* and *yar* attach to both transitive and intransitive verbs, and illustrates the claim with appropriate examples. If there are any restrictions on their use with transitive verbs, Shibatani does not mention them. I can only speculate that this is a marked feature of the language, perhaps one caused by the influence of Japanese with its fully productive morphological causative. Furthermore, Ainu is the least robust of the polysynthetic languages, particularly in the colloquial variants. Thus, I will not abandon a relatively successful theory because of this one case, at least until more is known about it.

8.2.4 Conclusions

This rather detailed survey of causative patterns has shown that morphological causatives are indeed limited in the polysynthetic languages. This limitation can be manifested in one of two ways. First, the type of verb that is causativized may be limited to the unaccusative class; I have taken this to be a sign that the causatives are derived from the same underlying source as LVCs. This is the most common pattern, found in Iroquoian, Gunwinjguan, and probably Caddoan and Chukchee. Alternatively, the type of verb that is causativized may be relatively free, but the expression of its arguments extremely limited: the subject argument must be controlled and the object argument must be incorporated. This is a rarer pattern, found in the Tanoan languages. The Nahuatl causative combines features of both, taking advantage of the special resources it has in the nonactive stem form. What we have not found in true polysynthetic languages (except perhaps Ainu) is a morphological causative that can apply to verb roots of any argument structure, where the result has its arguments deployed with no more morphosyntactic restrictions than a simple transitive or ditransitive verb would have. Causatives meeting this description are fairly common in a wide variety of nonpolysynthetic languages, but they are not found in polysynthetic languages. This surprising gap gives striking support to the Polysynthesis Parameter, which (together with the CAR) provides an explanation for it.

If this form of reasoning is confirmed, it may have another, very deep theoretical implication. If what I have said about polysynthetic languages (and, by extension, head-marking nonconfigurational languages and certain "near polysynthetic" languages) is true, it suggests that there is no such thing as argument structure composition in the grammar. By "argument structure composition" I mean any process that takes as its input two lexical items, each with their own argument structure, and derives from them a new linguistic object with a new argument structure calculated as a combination of the two. Some such composition is a feature of virtually all lexicalist accounts of morphological causatives. For example, Di Sciullo and Williams (1987:34–40) make crucial use of this kind of function composition. One of their examples is the Japanese causative:

(83)   *tabe* (eat) + *sase* (make) →   *tabesase*
       <Ag, Th>   <Ag>   <<Ag, Th> Ag>

Indeed, it is hard to see how a lexical analysis of causatives could do without some process of this type. It expresses the traditional idea that causative is a systematic type of valence-increasing operation.

Now, suppose that (83) were a possible process in Universal Grammar. We would then be in danger of losing the explanation for the fact that polysynthetic languages do not have unrestricted morphological causatives. The reasoning presented in this section might explain why the causative of a transitive verb cannot be derived by verb incorporation (unless other conditions are met), but the language could still create causative verbs based on transitive verbs by argument structure composition in the Lexicon, as in (83). This would derive a verb with a rather ordinary looking three-place argument structure,[30] and there is no fundamental problem with having such a verb in a polysynthetic language. Indeed, all of the polysynthetic languages have simple three-place verbs like 'give'. Thus, we must assume that there is no possibility of argument structure composition in polysynthetic languages. Yet, it is not clear why polysynthetic languages should be restricted in this way; there is no obvious connection between this and any other known property of the languages. The easiest way to explain why polysynthetic languages have no argument structure composition is to say that Universal

Grammar rules out argument structure composition in general. This, then, suggests that two argument-taking items cannot combine before each combines with its own arguments. In other words, the only truly compositional system allowed by natural language is syntax. Whenever there is a productive and semantically transparent morphological device, it must be derived in the syntax.[31]

8.3 Control Constructions

8.3.1 The Mohawk Purposive

We will now consider another class of complex predicates found in the polysynthetic languages. These are morphemes that correspond to subject-control verbs and raising-to-subject verbs in other languages. The clearest member of this class in Mohawk is the purposive morpheme, which has the allomorphs *hn(a)*, *h(a)*, *r(a)*, and *hser(a)* and means roughly 'go to'. The purposive is of interest primarily because of the way it contrasts with causative constructions discussed in section 8.2. Although morphological causatives in the polysynthetic languages can only be formed from one-place verbs, the purposive in Mohawk can attach to verbs with any number of arguments:

(84)   a. Wa'-t-k-atskahú-hn-e'.
           FACT-DUP-1sS-eat-PURP-IMPF
           'I am going to eat.'

       b. Λ-ha-[a]torát-ha-'.
           FUT-MsS-hunt-PURP-PUNC
           'He will go hunting.'

       c. Ká'sere' ro-hninú-r-u.
           car   MsO-buy-PURP-STAT
           'He has already gone to buy a car.'

       d. Sák-hne riy-ahseht-á-hn-e'.
           Sak-LOC 1sS/MsO-kill-PURP-HAB
           'I'm going to Sak's place to kill him.'

       e. Λ-hi-'sere-ht-awí-ra-'.[32]
           FUT-1sS/MsO-car-NOM-give-PURP-PUNC
           'I will go to give him a car.'

Thus, we must account for why the restrictions on agreement in polysynthetic languages do not limit this type of construction in the same way that they limit the morphological causative.

The easiest way of dealing with this phenomenon is simply to deny that purposive forms are complex predicates in the syntactic sense at all. Rather, the purposive morpheme could simply be a derivational morpheme that attaches to a verb root in the lexicon without changing the verb's argument structure. If so, then the examples in (84) follow trivially. However, this simple approach does not fit well with the rest of our analysis. One reason is that the purposive morpheme may appear outside of the causative morpheme, as in (85). Since the causative morpheme combines with the verb root in the syntax, it is likely that the purposive does so as well. Certainly the alternative of saying that syntactic processes productively feed lexical ones is unpalatable.[33]

(85) T-ʌ-ha-hri'-t-á-hna-'.
      DUP-FUT-MsS-shatter-CAUS-Ø-PURP-PUNC
      'He will go to shatter it.'

There are also possible syntactico-semantic reasons for analyzing the purposive constructions as complex predicates in the syntax. Certainly, they interact in a complex manner with certain clause-level semantic operators, such as negation and tense/mood morphology—although this is often true of single-morpheme words (such as *kill*) as well. Stronger evidence might come from interesting contrasts like the following:

(86) a. Éso ʌ-ye-hnínu-'   ne áhsire'.
          a.lot FUT-FsS-buy-PUNC NE blanket.
          'She will buy many blankets.'

      b. ??Éso ʌ-ye-hninú-ra-'   ne ahsire(-shú'a)
          a.lot FUT-FsS-buy-PURP-PUNC NE blanket-PL
          'She will go to buy many blankets.'

Example (86a) has a discontinuous expression of the kind analyzed in section 4.2.2: the quantifier *éso* 'a lot' is separated from the noun that it is understood as modifying. In chapter 4, I drew a parallel between this construction and "quantification at a distance" constructions involving *beaucoup* in French (see Obenauer 1984). This means that *éso* is licensed as an adverbial modifying the verb 'buy'; its apparent interpretation with 'blanket' is established indirectly because 'blanket' is the argument that delimits the verb in the sense of Tenny 1987. As far as I know, this floated quantifier construction is allowed with any simple transitive verb in Mohawk. However, the floated quantifier construction is sometimes degraded when a purposive morpheme is attached to the verb, as in (86b). This makes sense if the purposive morpheme is really a higher predicate with the verb root functioning as its complement. Then the adverb *éso* modifies 'go' rather than 'buy'; since 'blanket' is not the delimiter of 'go', this is not the near-equivalent of having *éso* quantify over 'blanket'. Thus, under the complex predicate hypothesis, the deviance of (86b) is explained in the same way as the deviance of (87), repeated here from chapter 4.

(87) #Éso te-wak-atʌhutsóni á-ke-k-e'   ne onhúhsa'.
       many DUP-1sO-want/STAT OPT-1sS-eat-PUNC NE egg
       NOT: 'I want to eat many eggs.' (OK as: 'I really want to eat eggs.')

Unfortunately, my consultant's judgments on sentences like (86b) are not always sharp or consistent, so this argument must be classified as tentative.

The last reason for treating purposive constructions as complex predicates is a theoretically driven one. The purposive morpheme has identifiable thematic properties distinct from those of the verb root. In particular, it typically assigns an agentive 'goer' role to the subject position. This is brought out by contrasts like the one in (88). 'Knife' is an appropriate agent argument for the verb root 'cut', as shown by (88a). However, 'knife' is not an acceptable subject when the purposive morpheme is attached to the verb, as in (88b). The reason is intuitively obvious: knives are not capable of self-initiated motion, so they are not appropriate arguments of a verb meaning 'go'.

(88) a. KíkΛ á'share'Λ-ka-natar-a-kwétar-e'.
          This knife   FUT-NsS-bread-Ø-cut-PUNC
          'This knife will cut the bread.'

      b. #KíkΛ á'share' Λ-ka-natar-a-kwetarú-ha-'.
          this   knife   FUT-NsS-bread-Ø-cut(STAT)-PURP-PUNC
          'This knife will go to cut the bread.'

If *kíkΛ á'share'* 'this knife' were changed to *kíkΛ rúkwe'* 'this man' in (88b), the sentence would be fine.[34] This confirms that the purposive morpheme has a non-trivial argument structure associated with it. Now, our study of morphological causatives in the polysynthetic languages strongly suggests that there is no such thing as predicate composition in natural language—or at least in languages of this type. If this is so, then the fact that 'cut' and the purposive morpheme have distinct argument structures implies that they are distinct elements in the syntax, combined by head movement.

Having decided to treat purposive constructions as syntactically complex, we must now face in earnest the question of why the class of verbs they can combine with is so much freer than the class of verbs that can combine with a causative. Ideally, this should be derived from the fundamental difference between the two: the fact that the purposive is the polysynthetic equivalent of a control predicate and the causative is not. Thus, although both the causative morpheme and the purposive morpheme have an agent role in their argument structure, the agent of the purposive is always equated with the agent of the verb root, whereas the agent of the causative remains distinct from all arguments of the verb root. The first step, then, is to understand the nature of this equation.

In fact, two approaches are allowed under my assumptions, and I will develop both in parallel. The first possibility is that the purposive appears in structures that involve control in the standard P&P sense of the term. This means that the purposive selects a full VP complement that has a distinct syntactic subject, but the subject of that VP is the null anaphoric element PRO, which is necessarily bound by the matrix subject. The structure in (89) sketches what this would look like for the typical example (84d).[35] Since the lower verb is the head of a complement of the higher one, it can perfectly well incorporate into the higher verb without violating the conditions on movement.

The alternative is to say that both the purposive and the basic verb root θ-mark the same subject position. This could be achieved by giving an LVC-like analysis of the construction. Indeed, Rosen (1989a) argues that similar verbal predicates in Italian, such as *volere* 'want' and *andare* 'go to' are a kind of light verb. Rosen adopts Grimshaw and Mester's (1988) theory of light verbs in which the argument structure of the lower predicate entirely erases that of the higher predicate; however, her intuition can easily be transposed into the more Jackendovian view of

(89)

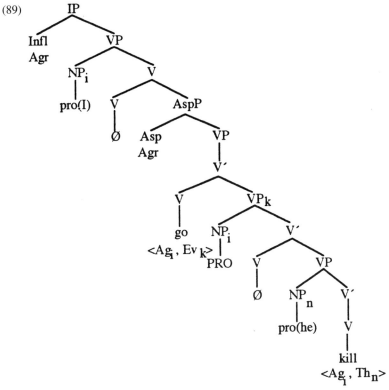

LVCs adopted here, in which the argument structures of the two predicates are overlaid. This would create a structure like (90).

(90)

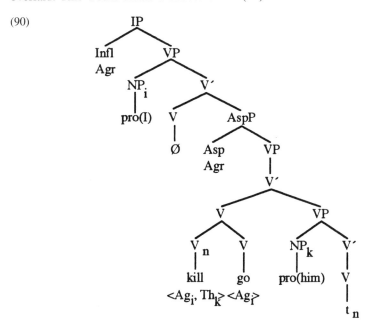

Here 'kill' heads a VP that is not interpreted as an argument of 'go'; nevertheless, it undergoes head movement, left adjoining to 'go'. The argument structures of the two verbs are nondistinct; in particular, the argument structure of 'go' is a subset of the argument structure of 'kill'. Thus, the conditions are fulfilled for an LVC interpretation, in which the two verbs assign θ-roles as a unit. In the previous examples, the jointly θ-marked argument was the object; this time it is the subject. The subject NP therefore counts as the agent of both verbs and must meet both sets of selectional restrictions. If Rosen (1989a) is correct, such structures are independently attested in Italian and other Romance languages.

The crucial question for a polysynthetic language is whether the MVC is satisfied in these constructions, and if so under what conditions. The answer is that the MVC is satisfied *if and only if the argument structure of the lower verb becomes the argument structure of the verbal complex.* Up to this point, I have assumed that the argument structure of a complex verb derived by incorporation is the same as the argument structure of the incorporation host, because the incorporation host counts as the head in the derived structure; the incorporated element has no effect on the argument structure. If that were the only possibility, then the argument structure of 'kill-go' would be <Ag> or <Ag, Ev>, the same as the argument structure of 'go'. Then, the theme argument of 'kill' could not be agreed with and would be in danger of violating the MVC. Nevertheless, (84d) and (84e) show that arguments of the lower verb can be agreed with.

In fact, we already have some reason to believe that the principles that determine the argument structure of a complex verb are somewhat freer than this. Thus, in every example the verb incorporates into Asp, and then into Infl. Strictly speaking, then, the argument structure of the [V–Asp] combination should be the same as that of Asp—which is presumably the null set. Then the agreement factor in Infl should not be able to be coindexed with anything; in particular, it cannot be coindexed with the external argument of the verb. This would mean that subject agreement is never possible, which is obviously the wrong result. Rather, we must conclude what I have implicitly assumed throughout: that the argument structure of [V–Asp] is the same as that of V, the nonhead.

Suppose that the inheritance of argument structures is actually rather free, as stated in (91).

(91)   An X^0 node can inherit its argument structure from any node that it immediately dominates (subject to other conditions).

Thus, either θ-grid associated with a part of a complex predicate can be passed on to the predicate as a whole, but not both. This gives the correct result for the [V–Asp] case; since Asp has no argument structure of its own, it is always advantageous to pick the argument structure of the V as the argument structure of the whole. Principle (91) also gives us a choice in the case of complexes involving the purposive morpheme. Suppose, then, that the argument structure of 'kill' is chosen to be the argument structure of 'kill-go', rather than the argument structure of 'go'. After verb raising to Asp, the agreement factor in Asp can be coindexed with the theme of 'kill', and at the next step the agreement in Infl can be coindexed with the agent argument of 'kill'. In both candidate structures, the agent argument of 'go' is coindexed with the agent argument of 'kill'; this is true by virtue of control in (89) and by virtue of joint θ-marking in (90). Thus, the agreement that morphologically expresses the agent role of 'kill' also adequately expresses the agent role of 'go'. For (90), this is all there is to say; in (89), 'go' also takes an event argument, but this is morphologically expressed by the incorporation of the head of that argument ('kill') into 'go'. Thus, both (90) and (89) satisfy the MVC under these assumptions, with the morphological structure given in (92).

(92)　[Agr$_i$ [Agr$_n$ [　　kill$_k$　　　　go　　　] Asp] tense]
　　　　　　　　　　 $<$Ag$_i$, Th$_n$$>$ $<$Ag$_i$, (Ev$_k$)$>$

More generally, we account for the fact that any array of arguments that is possible for simple verbs in Mohawk is also possible for a purposive construction. The reason is simply that including 'go' in the structure does not inhibit in any way the ability of the lower verb root to express its arguments by agreement, given that the argument structure of the lower verb can be inherited by the verbal complex. Nor does the purposive prevent the lower verb from expressing an argument by incorporation, given that such incorporation takes place entirely within the lower VP. The only major issue left open is how the PRO subject of the embedded VP is licensed in (89); I will return to this briefly in section 10.2.3.

At first sight, (91) looks dangerously unconstrained. In fact, the freedom that it allows does no harm to our earlier analyses. It raises the possibility that in causative constructions and possessor-raising constructions the argument structure of the incorporated root can take precedence over the argument structure of the host. However, this option is of no help in most cases. Suppose, for example, that from an underlying structure like 'I made [$_{VP}$ him buy it]' one chose the argument structure of 'buy' rather than the argument structure of 'make' to be the argument structure of the complex verb. Then the agreement factors would be able to express the agent and the theme of 'buy', unlike the analysis sketched in section 8.2.1. However, the agreement factors would no longer be able to express the agent of 'make'. Since agents are not incorporable, this choice always leads to a violation of the MVC. The essential problem with causative constructions, then, is that each predicate has at least one argument that is not incorporable and is not shared with the other. This makes it impossible to morphologically express all of the arguments. On the other hand, in the purposive construction, one of the predicates does, in effect, θ-mark all the arguments in the construction. The MVC can then be satisfied as long as it is the argument structure of this predicate that is inherited.

The claim that the argument structure of the embedded verb is inherited by the complex verb in purposive constructions also fits well with the data in (93) (from Deering and Delisle 1976).

(93)　a. Wa'-t-*ha*-[a]tskahú-hn-e'.　(D&D:90)
　　　　　FACT-DUP-MsS-eat-PURP-IMPF
　　　　　'He is going to eat.'

　　　b. Wa-*ho*-yo'tá-hser-e'.　(D&D:339)
　　　　　FACT-MsO-work-PURP-IMPF
　　　　　'He's going to work.'

The form of the agreement is different in these two examples: in (93a), the agent is indicated by an A-class agreement, while in (93b) it is indicated by an O-class agreement. This difference is inherited from a lexical difference between the verb roots: *yo'tʌ* 'work' assigns the quirky agreement feature +O to its agent argument, whereas *atskahu* 'eat' does not (see section 5.4). In other words, *yo'tʌ* has the argument structure <Ag = +O>. Since it is this argument structure that is inherited by the complex verb, this argument structure determines the form of the agreement as well.[36] In this way, we explain the fact that the purposive morpheme has no influence on quirky agreement. In this respect, the purposive contrasts with the causative, which does influence the form of agreement on the derived verb complex (see (45)).

8.3.2 Other Languages

Purposive constructions and other control-like complex predicates are found in other polysynthetic languages as well, and the same theory extends readily to them. In particular, one generally finds that the restrictions placed on morphological causatives do not hold for these other constructions. The following are simple examples of purposives in Wichita (see (94a)) and Nahuatl (see (94b)), as well as a desiderative in Chukchee (see (94c)).

(94)   a. É:ʔ-iy-a:-kí-ʔi::s-ʔa.   (Rood 1976:170)
         QUOT-3INDEFS-PREV-AOR-see-come
         'She came to see him.'

       b. Ō-Ø-tēch-māquixti-co   in To-tēucyo.   (Launey 1981:396)
         PAST-3sS-1pO-save-come/PERF IN 1pP-lord
         'Our Lord has come to save us.'

       c. Ne-re-luᵉ-ŋə-rkən-i-git.   (Bogoras 1922:821)
         3pS-want-see-want-PRES-Ø-2sO
         'They want to see you.'

In Wichita, causatives can, in general, only be formed from unaccusatives, but purposive V–V compounds are not restricted in this way. In Nahuatl, causatives can be formed from verb roots with any argument structure, but they have to be formed from the nonactive stem, which characteristically ends in *l* for transitive verbs. Example (94b) shows that purposive predicates are formed from the active stem instead. In Chukchee, the causative circumfix can go productively only on unaccusative verbs; (94c) shows that the desiderative circumfix can go on transitive verbs as well. (See also Evans (1991:296–298) for a set of partially similar constructions in Mayali.) In all these languages, purposive and desiderative complexes have the same agreement and incorporation behavior as simple verbs. This is expected on our analysis, in which these complexes acquire the argument structure of the first root.[37]

Nahuatl is particularly interesting because it is especially rich in complex predicates of this type, called auxiliaries by Launey (1981) and compound verbs by Andrews (1975). Moreover, many of the morphemes involved in these constructions can be used as independent verb roots, unlike the purposive in Mohawk, allowing one to see the system at work in a more spectacular way. For example, *nequi* 'want' can appear as either a free verb root or in a complex predicate construction. As a free verb root, it is not restricted to a control interpretation; the subject of its complement may be the same as or different from its subject (Launey 1981:295):

(95) a. Cuix ti-c-nequi   ni-c-chīhua-z?
       Q   2sS-3sO-want 1sS-3sO-make-FUT
       'Do you want me to make it?'

   b. Ni-c-nequi   ni-c-chīhua-z.
      1sS-3sO-want 1sS-3sO-make-FUT
      'I want to make it.' (Literally: 'I want that I make it.')

However, the lower verb can incorporate into *nequi* only if there is a control relationship between the two subjects. Thus, there is a complex predicate version of (95b) but not of (95a).

(96) Ni-c-chīhua-z-nequi.
     1sS-3sO-make-FUT-want
     'I want to make it.'

This is exactly what our theory predicts. The structure of (96) is the one in (89), except that the meaning of the matrix verb is different. However, if one were to try to form a complex predicate with the meaning of (95a) by incorporation, an irresolvable agreement problem would arise. Here the external argument of 'want' and the external argument of 'make' are distinct. Since neither is incorporable, both need to be coindexed with an agreement morpheme in order to pass the MVC. However, this is impossible: only one argument structure can be chosen to be the argument structure of the verbal complex; hence, only one will be visible to agreement. A complex predicate of this type is ruled out for essentially the same reason that causatives of ordinary transitive verbs are in these languages. This illustrates clearly the role that control plays in making this class of complex predicates possible. Exactly parallel paradigms are found with verbs like *khiwi* 'try' in Southern Tiwa (Donald Frantz, personal communication).

   Another set of examples in Nahautl that makes the same point involves epistemic verbs like *mati* 'know, consider' and *toca* 'believe, consider'. These can occur in complex predicates of several types (Launey 1981:269–271). First, they can be compounded with a noun or an intransitive (unaccusative) verb:

(97) Ni-c-teō-mati   in To-tēucyo.
     1sS-3sO-god-know IN 1pP-lord
     'I know our Lord to be God.'

(98) ō-ni-c-mic-cā-toca-ca.
     PAST-1sS-3sO-die-PART-consider-PAST/PERF
     'I had believed him dead.'

They can also be compounded with a transitive verb, but here restrictions begin to appear. First, the embedded verb must appear in the nonactive form, with *l*.

Moreover, if the matrix verb is transitive, the embedded verb must be understood as a passive:

(99)   Ni-c-telchīhua-l-mati   in Pedro.
       1sS-3sO-despise-NONACT-know IN Pedro
       'I believe that Pedro is despised; I consider Pedro despised.'

Alternatively, the matrix verb can be a detransitivized reflexive form; in this case the embedded verb can be understood as an active:

(100)   A'mo ni-c-no-chīhua-l-toca.
        not   1sS-3sO-1REFL-make-NONACT-consider
        'I don't pretend to have made it.'

It is apparently impossible for both the matrix verb and the embedded verb to be active and transitive. Thus, there is no way to say something like 'I believe Pedro to have made it' with this kind of complex predicate construction.

   I assume these verbs have basically three arguments: the external "believer" argument, the internal "object of belief" argument, and a propositional argument that expresses the content of the belief. In (97) and (98) the root that heads the propositional argument has only one argument and it is controlled by or predicated of the object of belief. Thus, it can incorporate into the matrix verb. The argument structure of the matrix verb will be inherited, and the MVC can be satisfied. The same holds true for (99), except here one argument of the transitive verb must be suppressed so that it has only one argument—the one that is coindexed with the object of belief. This explains the need for the nonactive morphology in (99), as well as the passive-like interpretation. If the lower verb were fully transitive, then each verb would have at least one argument that is not shared by the other, and agreement would be impossible, as in causatives. The clincher is (100). Here, a lexical process similar to the semireflexive in Mohawk identifies the believer and the object of belief. (The claim that this is a lexical process seems justified by the slightly idiosyncratic meaning of *toca,* together with the fact that *mati* 'know' does not have a similar alternation.) Now the matrix verb has only one argument apart from the content of belief one. Moreover, this argument is coindexed with an argument of the embedded verb. Thus, we have essentially the same configuration as in purposive clauses: the argument structure of a transitive embedded verb can now percolate and the MVC is satisfied.[38] The final morphological structures of (99) and (100) are (101a) and (101b), respectively, where the argument structure that is inherited by the whole word and is thus visible to agreement is in italics.

(101)   a. Agr_k- Agr_i- [[despise-nonact]$_n$ know   ]
                        $<\text{Th}_i>$ $<Exp_k, Obj_i, Prop_n>$

        b. Agr_i- Agr_k- [refl [make (-l)   ]$_n$ consider]
                        $<Ag_i, Th_k>$ $<\text{Exp} = \text{Obj}_i, Prop_n>$

Again, we see clearly that all the unincorporated arguments of a complex predicate must either be arguments of the higher verb, as in (101a), or arguments of the lower verb, as in (101b).

8.3.3 *Distinguishing Control From LVCs*

So far, I have not chosen between the LVC analysis of purposive constructions and the control analysis. However, there is reason to think that the LVC analysis is the correct one for Mohawk. Thus, it is not quite true that the purposive can combine with verbs of any argument structure in Mohawk; in fact, it cannot combine with unaccusative verbs:

(102) a. *Sak ʌ-t-ha-ya't-Á'-hsera-'.
           Sak FUT-CIS-MsS-body-fall-PURP-PUNC
           'Sak will go to fall.'

       b. *T-ʌ-ka-wis-a-hrí'-hsera-'.
           DUP-FUT-NsS-glass-Ø-break-PURP-PUNC
           'That glass will go there to break.'

       c. *Uwari ʌ-yako-ketoht-á-hna-'
           Mary FUT-FsS-appear-Ø-PURP-PUNC
           'Mary will go to show up.'

In contrast, the purposive combines productively with unergative verbs, as shown previously (see also Chafe 1970:19 for Onondaga). This follows if the purposive construction is a light verb, with an argument structure of <Ag>. For an LVC interpretation to be possible, the lower verb must have an agent role in its argument structure as well; otherwise, the two argument structures would be nondistinct, and joint θ-role assignment would be impossible.[39] The verbs in (102) do not take agent arguments; hence, the examples are ruled out. Thus, the set of verb roots that can appear with the causative morpheme and the set of verb roots that appear with the purposive morpheme are nearly disjoint.[40]

Interestingly, Nahuatl seems to be minimally different from Mohawk in this respect. It is not entirely clear whether the Nahuatl purposive morphemes can appear with simple unaccusative verbs or not. The element *co* 'come' can attach to verbs such as *ahci* 'arrive', *quiza* 'exit', *calaqui* 'enter', *miqui* 'die', and *tlami* 'end' (Kenneth Hale, personal communication); these verbs are often unaccusative across languages, but I do not have decisive evidence as to their argument structure in Nahuatl. However, Andrews (1975:128) does show that passive verbs can appear in the purposive construction:

(103) ō-ni-pōhua-l-ō-t-o.
       PAST-1sS-count-NONACT-PASS-Ø-go/PERF
       'I went in order to be counted.'

In this example, the null pronoun 'I' is clearly the agent of 'go' but the theme of *pōhua* 'to count', a pattern that is never attested in Mohawk. The control structure allows for this degree of flexibility. PRO can be generated as the theme of the lower verb and still be controlled by the matrix verb, as shown in (104).

(104)

As long as there is no agent argument in the lower clause, this configuration is allowed.[41] Similarly, passive verbs can be found in desiderative complexes in Nahuatl:

(105)   Ti-tlazohtla-l-ō-z-nequi-ah.   (Andrews 1975:139)
         1pS-love-NONACT-PASS-FUT-want-PL
         'We wanted to be loved.'

Thus, Nahuatl has control constructions where Mohawk has LVCs.

This contrast raises the intriguing question of whether there is some underlying reason why control structures are impossible in principle in Mohawk. In addition to explaining the ungrammaticality of the examples in (102), this might explain why there are fewer control-like complex predicates in Mohawk than in other polysynthetic languages. For example, Mohawk has no desiderative suffix meaning 'want', even though desiderative complexes are found in Nahuatl, Ngalakan, Chukchee, and probably Ainu. It is a reasonable conjecture that desideratives can only have a true control structure, and not the LVC structure, because their semantics (unlike that of 'go' verbs) requires that they select a VP complement. If this is so, and if control is impossible in Mohawk, then the fact that Mohawk has no desiderative has a principled explanation. Unfortunately, I have no proposal about why Mohawk should not have the control structure; it may be that the only account for this is a historical one.

8.4 Adjectival Predicates and Possessor Raising

Finally, we are ready to return to an unsolved issue concerning the incorporation of possessed nouns. In section 8.1, I showed that such incorporation is possible if and only if the host is an unaccusative verb of the stative class. The complex verb then shows O-class agreement with the possessor of the noun. Additional examples illustrating the generality of the effect are:

(106) a. Ro-[a]nitskwara-tsher-a-hníru.
MsO-chair-NOM-Ø-be.hard
'His chair is hard.'

b. Sa-na'ts-a-hútsi.
2sO-pot-Ø-black
'Your pot is black.'

c. Te-ho-hur-á-'tsu ne Sak.
DUP-MsO-gun-Ø-dirty NE Sak
'Sak's gun is dirty.'

In section 8.1, the reason that "possessor raising" is impossible with other verbs was explained, but not why it is possible with this particular class. In fact, given what we learned from the study of control verbs in the previous section, we can now fill in this gap in the account in a rather straightforward way.

The first step is to understand what is special about this class of stative verbs. Their meanings are more or less like those of adjectives in English, and they are similar to unaccusatives in that they take a single nominal argument, which may be incorporated. However, these verbs differ from other verbs in Mohawk in that they and they alone do not need to take one of the three aspectual morphemes: *s*, habitual; *'* punctual; *u* stative.[42] I take this to be the key hint to their nature. Suppose that the reason aspect suffixes are necessary on most verbs in Mohawk is that they serve to bind the special event argument (indicated by "e") in the θ-grid of the verb, as motivated by Donald Davidson and introduced into P&P theory by Higginbotham (1985). In fact, Higginbotham assumes that the e-role is bound by tense in English. In Mohawk, however, aspect morphology is obligatory with most verbs but tense morphology is not, so it is natural to transfer the role of binding the e-argument to Asp in this language.[43] Since aspect morphology is not needed on stative verbs, we say that these verbs lack an e-position in their argument structure. This fits well with the intuition that these verbs do not refer to events and cannot take the same range of adverbial modifiers as other verbs. The θ-grids of a typical eventive verb and a typical stative are compared in (107).

(107) a. *(ahs)Λ'* 'fall' <Th, e>

b. *hniru* 'be hard' <Th>

Since *hniru* 'be hard' does not include an e-role in its lexical entry, there is no need for an aspect morpheme to appear in clauses containing it; the verb's argument structure is fully satisfied with only a theme NP.

These θ-grids are confirmed by some peculiarities in the interpretation of the habitual/imperfective morpheme *s*. On ordinary eventive verbs, this morpheme typically has the effect of a kind of quantification over events of the type referred to by the verb root. Thus, (108) implies that there have been and will be various events in which the subject falls.

(108)   T-ye-yá't-ʌ'-s.
        CIS-FsS-body-fall-HAB
        'She falls (all the time, e.g., whenever she climbs a tree).'

However, the interpretation of *s* is somewhat different when it is added to a stative verb. In this case, it becomes a kind of plural morpheme (Deering and Delisle 1976:439). Thus, (109) is interpreted as meaning that there are various entities such that those entities are chairs that are hard.

(109)   Yo-hníru-s   ne anitskwára.
        NsO-hard-HAB NE chair
        'The chairs are hard.'

This makes sense, given the argument structure for *hniru* shown in (107b). Since the verb has no event argument, it is clear that *s* cannot be understood as quantifying over events. The only argument position that *hniru* and other verbs of this class have is the theme argument; therefore, *s* can only be understood as quantifying over the theme. It implies that there are multiple referents that satisfy that position and serves as a kind of plural marker.

   With this as background, we can now explain the fact of primary interest. The special property of stative verbs is that they have only one position in their θ-grid, and this is a theme role that can be assigned to an NP in direct object position. Thus, stative verbs are the only NP-selecting verbs whose arguments can be completely expressed by incorporation. In particular, (106c) can have the structure in (110).

(110)

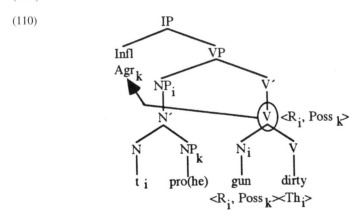

In (110), NI has taken place, so the bigger NP is visible for θ-role assignment from the verb 'be dirty'. Thus, the MVC does not force the argument structure of the main verb to be inherited by the complex V. Suppose, then, that the argument structure of the N is inherited by the complex V instead, taking advantage of the flexibility provided by (91). The agreement factor in Infl can then be coindexed with this possessor role subsequent to verb raising, and the structure passes the MVC. In this way, we explain why possessor raising is possible with these verbs alone.

   This structure also makes possible an account of the form of agreement in these sentences. Notice that the agreement features are coindexed with the possessor of the NP, and this possessor is the innermost argument of that NP. In particular, it is discharged lower in the structure than its co-argument, the R role: Poss is assigned within N', whereas the R role is discharged at the level of the NP as a whole. Thus, the possessor is assigned the feature +O by a slight generalization of the Structural Agreement Principle of section 5.4. This explains the fact that the verbs in (106) always show O-class agreement with the possessor of the incorporated noun, regardless of the inherent lexical properties of the verb root and the noun root. The "raised" possessors trigger O-class agreement on the verb for essentially the same reason that goals do, in keeping with the thematic parallels between possessors and goals in this approach.[44]

Contrasting minimally with the examples in (106) are those in which possessor raising takes place with an eventive unaccusative verb. Such structures are impossible, as was shown in section 8.1:

(111)   *T-a-ho-húr-ʌ'-ne'   ne Sak.
        DUP-FACT-MsO-gun-fall-PUNC NE Sak
        'Sak's gun fell.'

The verb ʌ' 'fall' differs from 'tsu 'be dirty' in that it has an event position in its argument structure that must be discharged. I have said that the event position is bound by an aspect morpheme, but I have not said how this is accomplished mechanically. Clearly, a kind of locality condition is at work; the e-position of a verb can only be bound by the aspect in the same clause as that verb. This kind of locality is very similar to the locality between agreement morphemes and the arguments they represent. The two can be subsumed under the same condition if one generalizes the CAR as follows:

(112)   *Condition on Agreement Relations* (revised)
        A functional element X can be coindexed with Y only if Y is (coindexed with) a position in the argument structure of a head Z and X is adjoined to Z or Z is adjoined to X.

Now the structure of (111) is (113).

(113)

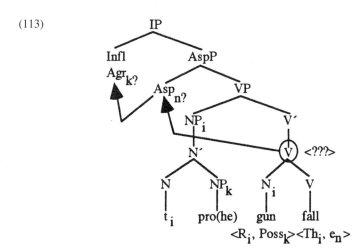

In (113), there are two relationships between functional categories and argument positions that must be established. The agreement features in Infl must be coindexed with the possessor of the noun to make it visible for θ-role assignment. On the other hand, the aspect morpheme must be coindexed with the event argument of the verb in order to discharge it. Unfortunately, these two arguments are not contained in the same argument structure. Either the argument structure of the N or the argument structure of the V can be inherited by the complex verb, but they cannot both be; neither can they be combined by some kind of argument structure composition. Whichever θ-grid is chosen, an argument in the other will be inaccessible to the functional categories. The result is a structure that violates the MVC, and hence the Theta Criterion. Since all verbs except the stative/adjectival verbs have an e-position, possessor raising is impossible with them. This, then, completes the analysis of the complex predicates formed by noun incorporation in Mohawk.

It is unclear to what extent complex predicates of this type are possible in the other polysynthetic languages. On the positive side, many references mention that nouns form special kinds of combinations with adjective-like elements; however, the data given are often somewhat fragmentary, and there seem to be important differences as well. For example, Wichita (Rood 1976:8–9) and the Gunwinjguan languages Ngandi (Heath 1978:120) and Nunggubuyu (Heath 1984:471–472) allow N–A combinations, more or less as in Mohawk. In Ngandi in particular, the agreement prefix of the combination is the same as the one that the noun would have taken in isolation, suggesting that the noun's argument structure is inherited by the whole complex in these cases. I do not know if there can be any possessor-raising effect, however; the issue may not even arise, given that there is no evidence that nouns θ-mark a possessor argument in these languages (see section 6.2). The one case in which a noun–adjective complex is known to show agreement with the possessor of the noun is in Ainu (Shibatani 1990:43–44, 72–75):

(114)   ku-pon-tresi
         1sS-little-younger.sister
         'my little younger sister'

This is much like Mohawk, except for an important difference in morpheme order: the noun root follows the modifying adjective in Ainu, while the noun root precedes the adjectival morpheme in Mohawk, Wichita, and Gunwinjguan. Given the correlations between morpheme order and structure discovered in section 1.6, this suggests that the Ainu combinations have a rather different phrase structure, in which the N is the head of the construction and the A incorporates into it. This A–N order is also found with modifier incorporation in Chukchee, as discussed by Spencer (1993:57–62) (see also Bogoras 1922:829). Unfortunately, I do not know enough about the Chukchee and Ainu constructions to make an informed proposal about their underlying structure. Thus, while complex predicates formed from a noun and an adjective or stative verb seem to be a separate class in the polysynthetic languages, the task of sorting out the various language-particular details is best left to future research.

8.5 Conclusion

In this chapter, we have seen that the MVC accounts for the range of complex predicates that are possible in a polysynthetic language. The basic generalization that follows from the theory is that the θ-grid of one of the morphemes in the complex predicate must in most cases be a subset of the θ-grid of the other. Thus, stative verbs or adjectives can combine with nouns of any argument structure (possessed or unpossessed) because their only θ-role (theme) is coindexed with the R role of the noun. All other verbs have arguments (e, agent, and/or goal) that cannot be identified with any argument of the noun; hence, these verbs' argument structures are never a subset of that of the noun. The noun's argument structure must then be a subset of the verb's: it can have nothing but the R argument that is coindexed with the theme argument of the verb. Similarly, control and raising verbs can combine with verbs of any argument structure (monadic, dyadic, or triadic) because their only θ-roles (agent/experiencer and event) are coindexed with arguments of the verb that heads their VP complement.[45] In contrast, causative morphemes have at least one argument (the "causer" agent) that is not identified with anything in the θ-grid of their argument. The embedded verb must then have a θ-grid that is a subset of the θ-grid of the causative morpheme (except perhaps for an incorporated argument). Typically, this means that the embedded verb can only have a theme argument and perhaps an event argument; in other words, the verb must be unaccusative. A few other alignments also show up, thanks to the possibility of incorporating an argument; this is seen particularly in Tanoan languages. However, most other combinations are systematically ruled out in polysynthetic languages, although they may exist in languages where the MVC does not hold.

Several auxiliary assumptions have been added to the MVC in order to derive these results. First and foremost among these is the CAR. Stated in its final form (see (112)), this is a locality condition on coindexing relationships between argument structure positions and functional categories, including agreement relationships. Although this principle is an innovation of this work, it is reasonably natural and well supported by a variety of facts in the polysynthetic languages. The question, of course, is whether it is universal; I return to this in a moment.

Also playing an important role in the analysis are the assumptions about when the θ-grid associated with a lexical category can be inherited by a larger phrase. These θ-grids then determine when agreement is possible via the CAR, which, in turn, determines whether the MVC is satisfied or not. My basic assumption is that any given X^0 node must have a unique argument structure, but that argument structure may, in principle, be inherited from any daughter of the node, not simply the head. This was stated in (91), as: An X^0 node can inherit its argument structure from any node that it immediately dominates (subject to other conditions). Condition (91) implies that the argument structures are not inherited by the same principles as true morphosyntactic features. In principle, this could lead to strange mixtures in which a word has the argument structure of, say, a noun but the morphosyntactic features of, say, a verb. This is exactly what we find in the possessor-raising constructions discussed in the last section. The complex word in

(110) has the argument structure of a noun; hence, it agrees with a possessor and even has the O-class agreement characteristic of possessors. Nevertheless, these complex forms are clearly Vs morphologically, not Ns. This is illustrated in (115). Example (115a) shows that the allomorph of the O-class agreement prefix that is used is the one that is characteristic of verbs, not nouns, since the initial glide is present. Example (115a) also shows that the complex predicate can take inflectional affixes that attach to verbs, such as the past tense morpheme *hne'*; however, it cannot take postnominal suffixes like *kʌha* 'former, deceased', as shown in (115b).

(115)   a. Wake-nuhs-a-rakʎ-hne'.
             1sO-house-Ø-white-PAST
             'My house was white.'

        b. *Wake-nuhs-a-rakʌ-kʎha.
             1sO-house-Ø-white-DEC
             'My former house was white.'

Nouns have the opposite possibilities: one can say *kanuhsa'kʎha* 'the former house', but not **kanuhsáhne'* 'it was a house.' Thus, the hybrid properties of these noun-plus-stative-verb forms provide rather dramatic support for (91).

With this in mind, we can return to the question of whether the CAR is universal or not. At first glance, it seems that it could not possibly be, because of raising constructions like (116) in English.[46]

(116)   John$_i$ seems [$_{IPk}$ t$_i$ to have laughed].
             <Th$_k$>   <Ag$_i$>

Here the matrix Infl agrees with *John,* even though *John* is not an argument of the verb *seem,* which ultimately raises to Infl at LF (Chomsky 1992). However, whether this is a real problem depends very much on the exact LF representation of (116). Thus, suppose that the head of the complement of *seem* incorporates into *seem* at LF to form a complex predicate. Then, one has a choice about which argument structure is chosen to be that of the newly formed complex. If the argument structure of the lower verb is chosen, then the agreement in (116) would be licit. Thus, examples like (116) do not show that the CAR cannot be universal, but rather that the CAR cannot be universal unless (91) is also universal and we make certain assumptions about the LF representation of raising predicates. I conclude that there are no obvious barriers to the claim that the CAR is universal. Of course, proving that it is universal is another matter, and one that goes far beyond the scope of the current work.

Finally, it was pointed out in section 8.2.4 that the entire system depends on the assumption that there is no such thing as argument structure composition. If there were, then whenever two heads had θ-grids such that neither one was a subset of the other, the two θ-grids could combine into a single θ-grid by argument structure composition. This composed θ-grid could then be inherited by higher nodes, and all the arguments contained in it would be accessible to agreement. This would allow complex predicates of the forbidden kind to be generated in polysynthetic languages after all. Since such complex predicates are not found, argument structure composition must not be possible. This has potentially important implications for the construction of linguistic theory: it points away from lexicalist analyses and toward syntactic head-movement analyses for a wide range of constructions where either kind of analysis would otherwise be possible. This, then, is potentially one of the deepest lessons we learn from the study of polysynthetic languages.

Notes

1. I have corrected an obvious mistake in Postal's translation, which has 'car' for 'house'.

2. Again, I have corrected a mistake in Mithun's gloss and translation; she translates the form as 'He car-washed me.' The same mistake is present in example (11). Something about this particular example must lead to errors!

3. I am not entirely convinced that this standard approach is correct, however. My doubts come from two sources. One involves some subtle semantic nuances of the construction that suggest that the body part is referential, not predicative in (9). The other is that the distributional parallels between body part incorporation and true noun incorporation are in danger of being lost on this account. In short, incorporated body parts can only refer to the theme/underlying object of the verb, just like other argument-type INs, at least in Mohawk and Mayali. This parallelism does not follow if the body part is a modifier. The construction deserves closer attention, but I must put it aside to pursue my main topic.

4. In these diagrams, I suppress the null preposition that governs the goal NP discussed in section 7.3.3. This is a constant factor, since the same null preposition presumably governs the possessor NP as well, given their thematic parallels. The implications of this element for agreement are discussed in section 9.2.3.

5. The details of this principle were undermotivated in the context of chapter 5 and were formulated with the needs of this chapter in mind. Raising constructions in languages like English appear to show immediately that the CAR cannot be universal, but this is not necessarily the case; see the conclusion to this chapter for a brief discussion.

6. Of course, one cannot allow "accidental licensing" to arise as a result of free generation of the right features or index in Agr. I assume crucially that an Agr can only bear features by virtue of the CAR.

7. To complete the explanation of why possessed nouns cannot be incorporated in the polysynthetic languages, one must also rule out the possibility that the possessor is expressed by incorporating into the noun or the verb. However, possessor incorporation is already known to be impossible (see section 6.2), perhaps due to a null preposition like the one discussed in section 7.3.3.

8. McKay (1975) claims that possessor raising (although this is not his term) occurs with NI in the related language Rembarrnga. One of his most convincing examples is the following (1975:304):

(i) Nga-thenj-rtungʔ-minj.
     1sS-fish-fall-PAST
     'My fish fell.'

This construction is said to exist in addition to the expected one, where there is a benefactive morpheme *pak* between the IN and the agreement prefix. However, examples like (i) are not attested in the grammars of any of the other Gunwinjguan languages nor in

McKay's texts; Nicholas Evans (personal communication) confirms that such sentences are ungrammatical in Mayali. Thus, it seems clear that (16) is the normal pattern in Gunwinjguan languages and perhaps the only one.

9. Allen et al. (1990) show that Southern Tiwa also allows NI and possessor raising with the sole argument of an unergative verb. I have no good explanation for this phenomenon, which seems to be unique to that language. Perhaps unergatives in Southern Tiwa are "coerced" into an unaccusative structure because of Southern Tiwa's inability to express possession in any other simple way.

10. More specifically, when the verb root is intransitive, its thematic subject always shows up as a direct object; when it is transitive, languages vary as to whether the thematic subject shows up as a direct object or an indirect object. For discussion of this point, see Marantz 1984, Baker 1988a, Alsina 1992, and references cited therein.

11. What is lost in this change is my (Baker 1988a) account of the two patterns found with causatives of transitive verbs. I assumed a distinction between VP movement and V movement, which only makes sense if the embedded clause is a full CP. Li gives an alternative account based purely on Case theory, but it is flawed. The correct answer probably comes from an interaction between the lexical properties of the causative affix (the fundamental insight of Alsina (1992)) and the general Case theory resources of the language (preserving this element from Baker 1988a). My topic does not allow me to explore these ideas here, however.

12. This verb has exactly the same morphosyntactic properties as the unaccusative-plus-benefactive verbs discussed in chapter 5: the verb can host only one agreement factor; the theme argument ('knife') may incorporate into the verb and must do so if it is animate; the goal argument (the possessor, 'him') triggers O-class agreement on the verb. If there is no goal/possessor argument, then the verb is one of posture/position, meaning 'lie'.

13. This form has an irrelevant instrumental reading ('I hit him with a knife'), due to the homophony between causative suffixes and instrumental suffixes in Iroquoian (Lounsbury 1953:80).

14. Barker lists *khəRa* as a predicate adjective, rather than a noun. However, the exact category of the predicate is not a systematic feature distinguishing the two types of LVC.

15. Property (2) is not a very salient issue in Japanese, the language Grimshaw and Mester (1988) were directly concerned with, because *suru* seems to have almost no lexical properties of its own. This is not typical of LVCs in other languages, however, as Grimshaw and Mester acknowledge at the end of their article.

16. However, the predicate noun and the light verb do not necessarily form a single word in the morphological sense, even in this case. This could be explained by saying that the verb "excorporates" out of the N–V compound formed by incorporation and by itself raises into the higher functional categories. Guasti (1992) argues that this is the case for causatives in Italian. (See also section 10.2.2.)

17. I leave open exactly what property of a given item allows it to be used as a light verb, and whether it is idiosyncratic or predictable by other means. The common intuition is that only "bland" verbs without much semantic meaning of their own qualify as light verbs. See Jackendoff 1974 for an early discussion of this issue.

18. In Baker (to appear a) and earlier versions of this work, I claimed that a different kind of argument sharing was involved in Mohawk causatives. In addition to the kind of argument sharing found in LVCs, there is another kind found in serial verb constructions (SVCs) such as (i) in Yoruba (Baker 1989):

(i) Olú ti   ọmọ náà ṣubú.
     Olu push child the fall
     'Olu pushed the child down; Olu caused the child to fall by pushing him.'

Here *o̜mo̜* 'child' is understood as the theme of both the transitive verb 'push' and the unaccusative verb 'fall'; the total effect is somewhat like a causative. Thus, the Mohawk causative could be derived by incorporation from an SVC source like (i) rather than a light verb source like (43). This derivation would also satisfy the MVC.

My principal reason for adopting the LVC analysis is that it provides a better account of morpheme orders. In particular, the unaccusative verb must adjoin to the left of the causative morpheme in the LVC structure, so the causative morpheme shows up as a suffix. In contrast, the verbs in a verbal complex derived from an SVC typically appear in the same order as they would in an SVC with no incorporation (Durie, to appear). Thus, if Mohawk causatives were derived from SVCs, one would expect the causative morpheme to precede the unaccusative verb root, contrary to the facts. Causatives probably are derived from SVCs in other languages, however, such as Yimas (Foley 1991). Thus (ii) can be contrasted with (43).

(ii) Na-ŋa-tar-kwalca-t
      3sS-1sO-CAUS-rise-PERF
      'She woke me up.'

Note that *tar* 'cause' is a prefix rather than a suffix in this example. Furthermore, this morpheme is a version of *tal* 'hold', which is used both as an independent verb and in other, more obvious serializations in Yimas. Apart from this difference in morpheme order, however, SVC causatives and LVC causatives look very much alike. Apparently no language that is polysynthetic in my narrow sense has SVC constructions with or without morphological union of the verbs; I do not know if this is a coincidence or not.

19. Perhaps this effect can ultimately be deduced from a proper formulation of the UTAH. For an NP to receive an agent role from one head, it must be in a certain kind of structural configuration; for it to receive a theme role from another head, it must be in a different kind of structural position. Since these contradictory requirements cannot be met by the same structure, argument sharing is only possible when both heads assign the same kind of θ-role.

20. However, in contrast to Mohawk, the embedded verb bears no agreement morphemes in Chukchee. This is a potential problem for the MVC of a different sort, related to the apparent existence of nonfinite complementation in Chukchee (see section 10.2.2).

21. Bogoras also gives an example with a verb meaning 'eat'; however, 'eat-caus' is a lexicalized form for 'feed' in many languages.

22. More recent data reported in Frantz 1993b suggest that this must be weakened somewhat. Apparently, the object of the lower verb need not incorporate if it is animate and definite—either a first or second person pronominal, or an animate with a demonstrative. Thus, (i) is acceptable.

(i) Yede 'u'u-de bey-khoa-'am-ban.
     that baby-SG 2sS/1sO-carry-CAUS-PAST
     'You made me carry that baby.'

Donald Frantz (personal communication) has conjectured that (i) may be grammatical only if the unincorporated NP is a topic of some kind. Taking this as a hint, I tentatively assume that this NP is not the grammatical object of the verb, but rather a "free topic" of the kind found in Japanese. The true object of the verb is then a null cognate object incorporated into the verbal complex, as is generally possible in Southern Tiwa.

23. The argument structure of *t'am* 'help' and some of the other examples in Frantz 1993a are probably minimally different from this in that the VP argument is the theme of the verb and thus in the specifier of the lower VP, while the "causee" argument is the goal, and hence the complement of the lower VP. The result is basically the same, however,

because the head of the VP can incorporate from either the specifier position or the complement position (compare NI with 'cross'-type verbs, section 7.3.3). Related to this is the fact that *t'am* has a kind of agreement with its VP/CP argument (the C class factor in (68)); this will be touched on in chapter 10.

24. Here the graphic device of coindexing is not subtle enough. The relationship between PRO and its controller and the relationship between a pronoun and its binder are both standardly indicated by coindexing. However, they are different types of linguistic relationships, subject to different principles. In particular, I assume that the coindexing involved with obligatory control is an argument structure relation that counts for purposes of the MVC, but the "accidental coindexing" between a pure pronoun and its antecedent is not. In a more careful exposition, these relationships would be expressed in different ways, thereby avoiding potential confusion on this point.

25. Apparently something about this structure is quite marked; otherwise one would expect to find it in more polysynthetic languages than we do. Perhaps the argument structure <Ag, Th, Ev> is a marked one, compared with <Ag, Th> (for LVC causatives) and <Ag, Ev> (for English-type causatives). If so, language learners would only assign this argument structure to a morpheme if they had independent evidence for it; in Tanoan languages this evidence would come from the use of the morphemes in question as simple verbs.

Allen et al. (1984) also show that the "causee" argument can be incorporated in Southern Tiwa, an unusual fact cross-linguistically. This follows from the analysis, since the causee is the direct object of the matrix verb. If it were only the subject argument of the embedded verb, it could not be incorporated, for the reasons discussed previously.

26. Thanks to Kenneth Hale (personal communication) for pointing out to me the existence and relevance of these examples.

27. This fits well with the fact that the verb meaning 'give' is often used as a causative predicate across languages. Examples include Urdu (Butt, to appear), Tzotzil and Alamblak (Bruce 1984), and others.

The fact that the causee in Nahuatl is projected as the goal of a give-type verb predicts that the causee will not be able to incorporate in this language, in contrast with Southern Tiwa. This seems to be true; Andrews and Launey give examples of the lower object in Nahuatl incorporating into the causative verb, but none of the causee incorporating.

28. *Tla* is usually described as being a special kind of object agreement morpheme. However, this does not explain the fact that *tla* occurs in a different position within the verb complex than true object agreements do (closer to the verb root), nor the fact that verbs with *tla* can be the input to derivational morphology (e.g., nominalization, as in (73)). Both of these facts are consistent with the view that *tla* is actually a noun root.

Animate *tē* patterns like *tla* in many respects. However, a pure NI analysis cannot be the whole story for this element, because *tē* can express the goal argument of a ditransitive verb, something that normal INs never do. More research is needed on this interesting element.

29. Launey does give one form comparable to (81b), namely *ni-c-tē-mach-tia,* literally, 'I made people know it'. However, he shows that this form is both morphologically and syntactically peculiar; it has probably been lexicalized as a simple triadic verb meaning 'teach'. It may also be important that (81b) has third singular agreement *c,* whereas (80) has 2sO agreement *mitz*; Kenneth Hale has suggested that *c* may be the spell-out of an incorporated noun root rather than a true agreement in some cases (see section 5.3).

30. This is probably the weakest point of the reasoning. One might say that argument structure composition does happen in the Lexicon, but it does not derive an argument structure that is comparable to any simple argument structure in the language. For example, the layers of the argument structure could be preserved through the lexical derivation. Then

there could be a morphosyntactic principle that says that agreement can only be sensitive to the outermost layer of an argument structure, as suggested by Joan Bresnan (personal communication). This would correspond rather closely to my assumptions that complex syntactic structure is preserved under incorporation and agreement is sensitive to this syntactic structure via the CAR. Although this could probably be made to work, it means that the Lexicalist Hypothesis would no longer derive the "structure preservation effect," arguably its strongest, most distinctive, and most attractive result (see Grimshaw 1982, Bresnan 1982, Grimshaw and Mester 1985).

31. This reasoning tells equally against the existence of some kind of predicate composition in the syntax, such as the kind worked out by Alsina (to appear) for Catalan causatives.

32. In this example and several others presented later, the purposive morpheme attaches to the stative form of the verb root. This does not seem to be a systematic property of the purposive, however.

33. Less unpalatable would be saying that the purposive morpheme attaches to the causative morpheme in the Lexicon, creating a kind of complex affix. Whether this is possible or not depends on one's theory of morphology.

34. Example (88b) also becomes grammatical when it is put into the imperfective aspect with the suffix *e'*. Such sentences are acceptable with a special "immediate future interpretation," just as in the acceptable English sentence *This knife is going to cut the bread.* (See also note 40.)

35. For current purposes, it does not matter whether the VP complement of 'go' appears in the specifier position of the lower VP (like a theme) or in the complement position of the lower VP (like a goal or path). For concreteness, I assume the latter, because the purpose-clause-like interpretation of the VP seems thematically analogous to a goal phrase.

36. Since both predicates θ-mark only an agent in these examples, one might expect that either could be inherited. Perhaps the purposive morpheme simply has no specification for the $\pm$O feature, because it is never used as an independent root.

37. Control-like verbs in Southern Tiwa and Kiowa use the pattern described in section 8.2.3, where the matrix verb does not agree with the object of the embedded verb and the embedded object is required to incorporate. A purposive-like example is given in (i) (Frantz 1993b).

(i) Yedi(n) seuan-nin i-hliara-pû-mi-ban.
    those   man-PL   BS-lady-see-go-PAST
    'Those men went to see the lady/ladies.'

This is shown for verbs like 'learn', 'try', 'start', 'decide', and 'forget' in Frantz 1993a. Apparently, a complex verb cannot inherit the argument structure of its nonhead in this language, for reasons that are unclear to me.

38. Note, however, that the nonactive stem form is used, even though the external argument of the lower verb is not unspecified or generic. My theory does not explain this.

39. Again, this condition on joint θ-role assignment can perhaps be derived from the UTAH. Since 'go' requires an agent, the NP must be in the specifier of a higher VP shell; since 'fall', 'break', and 'appear' require themes, the NP must be in the immediate specifier of the lower VP. These contradictory requirements cannot be met by a single NP.

40. I leave open the possibility that Mohawk may have a few verb roots that can ambiguously be treated as unergative or unaccusative.

Of course, it is possible for both the causative morpheme and the purposive morpheme to attach to the same unaccusative root, as long as the causative morpheme starts lower than the purposive morpheme; the purposive can share the agent argument selected by the causative morpheme. An example of this type was given in (85).

The examples in (102) become grammatical if they are put into the imperfective aspect (with suffix *e'*). They then have the same immediate future interpretation mentioned in note 34 (e.g., 'The glass is going to break'). Apparently, the agent argument otherwise associated with the purposive morpheme is suspended in this context, for some reason. Then, since the purposive has no remaining arguments, its θ-grid is always nondistinct from that of the embedded verb, and complex predicate formation is completely free. Alternatively, the purposive-plus-imperfective combination may have ceased to be a true complex predicate and become part of the tense/aspect/mood paradigm of the verb.

41. Perhaps PRO must first move to the specifier of some higher functional category within the complement of 'go' to avoid being governed. See section 10.2.3 for some discussion about what this position might be.

42. Most Iroquoianists claim that these verbs are in the stative aspect, both because of their meaning and because the stative is independently known to have a Ø allomorph. Even if this is correct, these verbs are special in that they appear *only* in the stative. However, there are important syntactic differences between these inherently stative verbs and eventive verbs in the stative aspect that motivate a different analysis.

43. More generally, which functional category binds the e-position could then be the core difference between so-called tense-oriented languages and aspect-oriented languages.

44. If an unpossessed O-class noun incorporates into an A-class stative verb, or vice versa, one might expect that the complex verb could take either class of agreement prefix. This is not usually so; rather, the agreement form is determined by the properties of the verb root. Thus, one says *ka-nʌst-a-rákʌ* 'the corn is white' rather than **yo-nʌst-a-rákʌ*, and *yo-na'ts-a-náwʌ* 'the pot is wet' rather than **ka-na'ts-a-náwʌ*. Apparently, the argument structure of the morphosyntactic head of the construction takes precedence over that of the nonhead if: (1) the head is specified for ±O features (unlike the purposive morpheme, adpositions, and a few exceptional verbs such as *ot* 'stand' (Michelson 1991c)), and (2) the MVC is not violated by doing so.

45. The treatment of event roles was not discussed in sections 8.2 and 8.3 because they were not introduced yet; however, the theory is easily extended to include them. In VP complementation constructions, I assume that the e-role of the embedded verb is coindexed with the theme (or goal) argument of the matrix verb as a part of the θ-role assignment process. This is directly parallel to the way that the R role of a nominal argument is coindexed with a position in the θ-grid of the verb as a part of θ-role assignment in the theory of Williams 1989 (see section 7.1.2). On the other hand, in LVCs the e-role of the light verb and the e-role of the predicate verb can be jointly discharged by the same aspect; this is essentially another type of argument sharing, formally parallel to the shared-theme and the shared-agent constructions that we have seen.

46. Thanks to Jan Voskuil (personal communication) for forcing me to come to grips with such examples.

III

NONNOMINAL CATEGORIES

9

Adpositional Phrases

Parts I and II focused primarily on nouns and noun phrases as the prototypical arguments and verbs as the prototypical predicates. Only in chapter 8 was this perspective opened up somewhat as we considered certain VPs that functioned as arguments and certain nouns that assigned θ-roles. This emphasis has been natural and appropriate for exploring the basic properties of polysynthetic syntax. However, NP is not the only category that can function as the argument of a predicate; for example, English also allows at least adpositional phrases (PPs) and clausal complements. Part III explores the implications of the Polysynthesis Parameter for these category types. This chapter focuses on the morphosyntax of adpositional phrases, and chapter 10 will cover embedded clauses.

At the level of superficial impressions, the most striking aspect of PPs in Mohawk is their rarity. Indeed, Mohawk has no clear and uncontroversial instances of the category P. It has no dative or benefactive adposition, no instrumental or comitative adposition, nothing corresponding to *about* or *of* in English. Instead, dative and benefactive notions are expressed primarily through the benefactive applicative constructions mentioned in chapter 5; instruments are normally expressed with periphrastic verbal constructions with literal translations like "I used a knife as I cut the bread."

There are, however, certain locative morphemes that might plausibly be analyzed as Ps; these are the four locative suffixes: *'ke/hne* 'at, on, general location', *ku* 'in', *oku* 'under', and *akta* 'near'. Typical examples of these morphemes in use are given in (1).

(1) a. Wa'-khé-kʌ-'   Uwári ka-hvt-á-'*ke*.
        FACT-1sS/FsO-see-PUNC Mary NsS-field-Ø-LOC
        'I saw Mary in the field.'

     b. Ka-ruto-tsher-á-*ku*   wa-hi-ya't-áhset-e'   ne Sak.
        NsS-chest-NOM-Ø-in FACT-1sS/MsO-body-hide-PUNC NE Sak
        'I hid Sak in the chest.'

     c. Ka-nakt-*óku*   wa-hi-ya't-áhset-e'   ne Sak.
        NsS-bed-under FACT-1sS/MsO-hide-PUNC NE Sak
        'I hid Sak under the bed.'

    d. Ka-'sere-ht-*ákta*   wa'-khe-ya't-a-tshári-'   ne Uwári.
       NsS-car-NOM-near FACT-1sS/FsO-body-Ø-find-PUNC NE Mary
       'I found Mary near the car.'

Some Iroquoianists have treated these morphemes as stative verb roots; others have considered them noun suffixes (see Michelson 1991a for an overview of the issues). Similar controversies over category membership arise in other polysynthetic languages; for example, Andrews (1975) claims that Nahuatl has no prepositions, but only a class of "relational nouns." In fact, these locative expressions typically display mixed behavior, acting in certain superficial ways like nouns or verbs, but showing subtle differences from both.[1] This unique behavior suggests that there is a category P in these languages, after all, albeit one whose use is circumscribed by the Polysynthesis Parameter. Thus, I assume that these are Ps without argument at this point; the properties that distinguish Ps from other categories will become clear as the chapter unfolds.

    We will look at PPs from three perspectives. First, I consider the Polysynthesis Parameter's implications for the relationship between the P itself and its arguments—the internal structure of PP. Next, I consider its implications for the relationship between the PP as a whole and other sentential elements—the external distribution of PPs. Finally, I consider the possibility of incorporating a P into some higher category. In all three domains, the Morphological Visibility Condition (MVC) will be seen to have important consequences, explaining why all of the adpositional elements are suffixes, why PPs appear only as adverbial modifiers, and why applicative morphemes are positioned where they are.

9.1 The Internal Structure of PPs

The basic idea of the Polysynthesis Parameter is that every argument of a head must be associated with a morpheme in the word containing that head. To see the implications of this idea for PPs, one must first determine what the argument structure of a typical locative adposition is. Indeed, this is a nontrivial matter, because there is an important controversy concerning this point. Once this controversy is resolved, however, the morphosyntactic expressions of the P's arguments turn out to be more or less what one would expect, given what we have seen for other categories.

9.1.1 The Argument Structure of the P

What, then, is the argument structure of simple locative adpositions? All agree that they may take a complement, usually of category NP. There is no widely accepted terminology for the θ-role that the P assigns to its complement, however, and it is best to avoid terms such as "location" that can ambiguously be used to refer to the PP as a whole or the NP that it contains. Thus, I follow Jackendoff (1983) in calling this NP the *reference object* argument (Ref) of the adposition.

    The controversial question is whether or not locative Ps are two-place predicates, which also assign a theme θ-role to an external argument. Probably the majority of researchers in P&P-style theories assume that they are, particularly those researchers who rely heavily on small clauses. On this view, the NP *the book* receives a theme θ-role from the PP *on the table* in both of the following sentences:

(2) a. The book is on the table.

   b. John put the book on the table.

Example (2a) is typically given a raising analysis, in which the copula takes a PP-headed small clause: [$_{IP}$ *e* is [$_{SC}$ the book [on the table]]]. The subject of the small clause then raises to become the subject of the clause as a whole. This captures the intuition that the copula is nearly meaningless in (2a). Some research-ers claim that *the book* and *on the table* also constitute a small clause constituent in (2b); others deny this, saying rather that the PP assigns its theme role to the object of *put* via a kind of predication.

In contrast to this widely accepted view, Jackendoff (1983) analyzes adposi-tions as one-place functions that take only the reference object as an argument. On Jackendoff's view, adpositions are essentially referential items referring to places, and they have no predicative power of their own. Thus, for Jackendoff, *put* in (2b) does not take a predicative small clause complement; rather, it takes two distinct internal arguments, an NP referring to an object, and a PP referring to a location. The relationship between the object and the location is a function of the meaning of *put* itself, and would not exist without it. Similarly, within Jacken-doff's assumptions one would have to analyze *be* in (2a) as a semantically mean-ingful verb with a true argument structure; it would be a dyadic predicate, select-ing a theme NP and a location PP.

There is no obvious incoherence in either of these views, so it is an empirical question which one is correct. In fact, polysynthetic languages present rather good evidence in favor of the view that adpositions are monadic. This evidence comes from two sources: agreement patterns and verbless clauses.

Consider first agreement. One pervasive fact about Mohawk is that heads al-ways agree with their arguments. Thus, verbs agree with their subjects, objects, and indirect objects, while nouns agree with their R argument and their possessor (if any). What, then, about Ps? If we look at the morphology of the examples in (1), we see that the putative PPs do have a neuter singular prefix; this could plausibly be understood as an agreement morpheme representing features of the P's reference object. Strikingly, however, there is no agreement on the P that indicates the features of the P's putative theme argument. Such agreement would show up clearly in (1), because the theme NPs are animate. Indeed, when one tries to add the relevant masculine or feminine agreement morphemes to the PPs, the examples become completely ungrammatical:

(3) a. *Wa'-khé-kʌ-'   Uwári ye-hʌt-á-'ke.
       FACT-1sS/FsO-see-PUNC Mary FsS-field-Ø-LOC
       'I saw Mary in the field.'

   b. *Ra-ruto-tsher-á-ku   wa-hi-ya't-áhset-e'   ne Sak.
       MsS-chest-NOM-Ø-in FACT-1sS/MsO-body-hide-PUNC NE Sak
       'I hid Sak in the chest.'

    c. *Ra-nakt-óku   wa-hi-ya't-áhset-e'   ne Sak.
        MsS-bed-under FACT-1sS/MsO-body-hide-PUNC NE Sak
        'I hid Sak under the bed.'

    d. *Ye-'sere-ht-ákta   wa'-khe-ya't-a-tshÁri-'   ne Uwári.
        FsS-car-NOM-near FACT-1sS/FsO-body-Ø-find-PUNC NE Mary
        'I found Mary near the car.'

Thus, not only is agreement with the putative theme of the PP unnecessary in these examples; such agreement is not possible. Nor is this just a quirk of Mohawk. As far as I know, no language inflects adpositions for the person, number, and gender features of the NP of which they are supposedly predicated.[2] For example, locative expressions in Nahuatl do not agree with the theme as a subject (Launey 1981:384):

(4)   Petla-pan, icpal-pan ni-ca'.
       mat-on   chair-on 1sS-be
       'I am on a mat, on a chair (i.e., I govern).'
       NOT: *Ni-petla-pan, n-icpal-pan ni-ca'.

In this respect, PPs differ from NP, VP, and AP predicates, which often do agree with their subjects. Nor is this restricted only to polysynthetic languages. Many languages have Ps that take agreement morphology, including the Celtic languages and the Athapaskan languages. Nevertheless, this agreement is always with the reference object, not the theme. If the theme were in some sense the subject/ outermost argument of the adposition, then both current theory and standard descriptive generalizations would lead one to expect the opposite: a category is more likely to agree with its subject than with its complement. These agreement patterns seen across languages only make sense if the theme NP does not in fact count as an argument of the adposition.

    The properties of predication in Mohawk also support this conclusion. Mohawk is like many other languages in that it allows verbless clauses, in which a nominal is directly predicated of an NP without the need for a copular verb. Some examples are:

(5)   a. Á'share' kʌ ne thi? Yah, atókʌ ne thi.   (D&D:129)
       knife   Q NE that No axe   NE that
       'Is that a knife?'   'No, that's an axe.'

      b. Uwári akó-skare' ne Sak.
        Mary FsP-friend NE Sak
        'Sak is Mary's boyfriend.'

It is not clear whether stative-adjectival roots in Mohawk are categorially distinct from true verbs or not (section 8.4). If they are, then they, too, can form verbless main clause predications:

(6)   Ka-rákʌ   ne kanúhsa'.   (Postal 1979:319)
       NsS-white NE house
       'The house is white.'

It is not entirely clear why English requires a copular verb in sentences such as these, while other languages do not. Part of the answer presumably has to do with the fact that tense and agreement morphology cannot be attached to nonverbs in English for morphological reasons; hence, a copular verb is needed to support these features originating in Infl. However, this is not the whole story, because the clauses in (5) and (6) are at least superficially tenseless. Whatever the exact nature of this difference is, verbless clauses like these are quite common across languages.

This property of Mohawk is relevant because it brings to light an important property of the locative expressions: these are the only major lexical class that cannot be used as matrix clause predicates in Mohawk. This is shown in (7) (see also Michelson 1991a).

(7) a. Sak ka-'seré-ht-a-ku   *(t-ha-yá't-i)
         Sak NsS-car-NOM-Ø-in   CIS-MsS-body-be.in
         'Sak is over there in the car.'

     b. Uwári ka-wehnó-'ke   *(í-t-yʌ-[e]-s).
         Mary NsS-island-LOC   Ø-CIS-FsS-go-HAB
         'Mary is on the island.'

     c. Sak ka-nakt-óku   *(t-ha-ya't-óru).
         Sak NsS-bed-under   CIS-MsS-body-be.covered
         'Sak is under the bed.'

     d. Sak ats-ákta   *(yé-hr[a]-e-s).
         Sak river-near   TRANS-MsS-go-hab
         'Sak is near the river.'

In each of these cases, a locative morpheme plus noun root is not enough to predicate location of the subject; rather a fully inflected verb of posture or location is needed as well. This is true even if the subject of predication is a neuter NP such as *o'nerohkwa* 'box', instead of an animate NP like *Sak*. Example (8) emphasizes the difference by contrasting simple noun and adjective predicates with locative expressions.

(8) a. O-'neróhkw-a'   thíkʌ.   (noun)
         NsO-box-NSF   that
         'That is a box.'

     b. Te-yó-'tsu   thíkʌ.   (adjective/verb)
         DUP-NsO-dirty   that
         'That is dirty.'

     c. Ka-'nerohk-owánʌ thíkʌ.   (adjective/verb with NI)
         NsS-box-big   that
         'That is a big box.'

     d. *O-'neróhkw-a-ku thíkʌ.[3] (locative with NI)
         NsO-box-Ø-in   that
         'That is in the box.'

The ungrammaticality of the examples in (7) and (8d) cannot be explained by the absence of tense or any other such feature; this would not distinguish the locative expressions from ordinary nominal clauses. Rather, I claim that the explanation is to be found in terms of Theta Theory: if there is no verbal element and if the preposition does not have a theme role in its argument structure, then the subject in the verbless clauses receives no θ-role. Such clauses are then ruled out immediately by the Theta Criterion. Thus, the lexical entry of a typical locative adpositions is simply:

(9)   *ku,* 'in', P, <Ref>

The argument structure of Ps is different from that of other categories in that their single argument is maximally "internal." By this, I mean that Ps select a single NP, and that NP is generated as a complement under the P′ projection. In this way, they are different from nouns, adjectives, and unaccusative verbs, whose single internal argument (R for Ns; theme for Vs and As) is generated in the specifier position. Suppose, then, that we make the rather natural assumption that X′ level categories are, in general, predicates.[4] Then it follows that V, N, and A can be predicates, but P cannot; the P′ simply does not have a θ-role to assign to a subject position.

Moreover, the other polysynthetic languages seem to be similar to Mohawk in this respect. For example, Nahuatl also allows verbless clauses headed by a nominal predicate. In this case, the noun is inflected to agree with the subject of which it is predicated:

(10)   Ni-mexi'-ca-tl.   (Launey 1981:26)
       1sS-Mexican-PART-NSF
       'I am a Mexican.'

However, locative expressions cannot be used as main clause predicates in this way; rather the copular verb *ca'* 'be' is needed in predications of location (Launey 1981:51):

(11)   a. *Ni-mexi'-co.
          1sS-Mexican-LOC
          'I am in Mexico.'

       b. Mexi'-co   ti-cat-e'.
          Mexican-LOC 1pS-be-PL
          'We are in Mexico.'

Thus, adpositions in Nahuatl appear to have the same type of one-place argument structure as those in Mohawk. Similarly, Evans (1991:304–309) gives a fairly thorough discussion of nonverbal predication in Mayali. He shows that simple Ns and adjectival Ns can be predicates in that language, but there is no indication that Ns in locative or directional Cases can be. Neither does his discussion of the various cases, prepositions, and postpositions in Mayali include any examples where the PP itself is the predicate (Evans 1991:73–87). This is also consistent with the description of locative expressions in the other Gunwinjguan languages. Rood (1976:41–42) also implies that locatives in Wichita cannot be predicated directly of an NP, but must be in construction with some verb that has semantic content of its own. Thus, it seems that the argument structure proposed for Ps in Mohawk in (9) generalizes to similar elements in the other polysynthetic languages and beyond.[5]

9.1.2 The P-Complement Relation

Now that we know what the argument structure of an adposition looks like, we can investigate how the MVC is satisfied with respect to the adposition. The predictions of the theory are perfectly straightforward: since the reference object is the only argument of the P, it (and it alone) must be expressed morphologically. In principle, there are two ways that this could happen: the reference object could trigger agreement on the P, or its head could be incorporated into the P. In fact, both possibilities are attested in the polysynthetic languages, although which appears in a given situation depends on the details of the language in question.

It will not have escaped the reader's attention that all of the elements analyzed as Ps in Mohawk undergo a kind of morphological union with their nominal complement. Such morphological union is absolutely obligatory[6]:

(12) a. *Óku ne ka-nákt-a'   y-a-há-yʌ-'.
          under NE NsS-bed-NSF TRANS-FACT-MsS-put.down-PUNC
          'He put it down under the bed.'

      b. *?Áktane atekhwára wa-há-yʌ-'.
          near NE table   FACT-MsS-put.down-PUNC
          'He put it down near the table.'

Indeed, with *'ke* 'at' and *ku* 'in' it is not even clear what kind of examples to form, because these violate the phonological conditions on wordhood in Mohawk.

Moreover, the union between the noun and the locative element has many of the distinctive morphological characteristics associated with noun incorporation into verbs. This can be seen by studying the paradigm of locative forms given in Table 9-1. First, the meaningless noun suffix *a'* that attaches to bare noun roots like *nakt* 'bed' and *'nerohkw* 'box' is lost when the noun combines with a locative element[7]; this is particularly clear in the 'under' forms, which have no [a] (*ka-nakta'óku*). This loss of nominal inflection is also seen with noun incorporation into verbs (see section 7.1.2 for discussion). Moreover, with one or two exceptions, nouns that take an idiosyncratic "nominalizer" suffix when they incorporate into a verb also take that same suffix when they appear with locative morphology; in other words, the nouns appear in their distinctive "incorporating" form.[8] This is seen in the forms for *atekhwara* 'table' and *'sere* 'car' in Table 9-1, which take the augments *tsher* and *ht,* respectively. These forms can be compared with those in (13), where these same roots are incorporated into a verb.

(13) a. Λ-k-atekhwara-*tsher*-úni-'.
          FUT-1sS-table-NOM-make-PUNC
          'I will make a table.'

      b. Wa'-ke-'sere-*ht*-óhare-'.
          FACT-1sS-car-NOM-wash-PUNC
          'I washed the car.'

Third, the noun root and the locative suffix *ku* are separated by the epenthetic "joiner" vowel [a]. It is clear that this vowel is the joiner and not the noun suffix *a'* or part of the locative suffix, because it is invisible to stress placement (cf.

Table 9-1. Locative Forms of Mohawk Nouns

Adposition	'Bed'	'Box'	'Table'	'Car'
Ø	ka-nákt-a'	o-'neróhkw-a'	atekhwára	ká-'sere-'
'at'	ka-nakt-á-'ke	o-'nerohkw-á-'ke	atekhwará-hne[10]	ka-'sere-ht-á-'ke
'in'	ka-nákt-a-ku	o-'neróhkw-a-ku	atekhwara-tsher-á-ku	ka-'seré-ht-a-ku
'under'	ka-nakt-óku	o-'nerohk-óku	atekhwara-tsher-óku	ka-'sere-ht-óku
'near'	ka-nakt-ákta	o-'nerohkw-ákta	atekhwara-tsher-ákta	ka-'sere-ht-ákta

Michelson 1989); thus, stress is on the antepenult in forms like *ka-'seré-ht-(a)-ku* 'in the car', in contrast to forms like *ka-'sere-ht-óku* 'under the car', where stress is always on the penult. This same vowel also appears when a root incorporates into a verb if the verb begins in a consonant and the noun ends in one[9]:

(14)   Yukwa-'seré-ht-(a)-yʌ.   (D&D:292)
       1PO-car-NOM-Ø-have
       'We have a car.'

Given these morphophonological facts, it is clear that the noun root actually incorporates into the locative element in Mohawk, rather than simply forming a phonological word with it under adjacency at PF. As before, I follow Baker 1988a in claiming that this incorporation is accomplished by head movement in the syntax. This is perfectly consistent with the theory of head movement reviewed in chapter 7; indeed, the same principles that allow the head of a direct object to adjoin to the verb that θ-marks it also allow the head of the object of a P to adjoin to that P. The derived structure of a simple example like *ka-nakt-óku* 'under the bed' is thus (15).

(15)

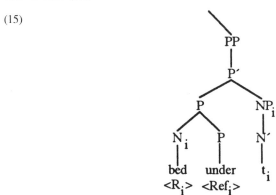

Notice that the moved head adjoins to the left of its host, as usual (see section 1.6); this explains the fact that all of the locative morphemes in Mohawk are suffixes, not prefixes. This movement also satisfies the MVC with respect to the adposition, since its only argument is coindexed with a morpheme in the word containing the adposition. This is parallel to the way that NI into a verb can serve to satisfy the MVC with respect to that verb (see section 7.1.2).

A priori, one would expect that the complement of the P could be morphologically expressed by agreement instead of by NI. This would make Ps entirely comparable to, say, unaccusative Vs, whose internal arguments can, in general, be expressed in either of these two ways. This option is seen most clearly in Nahuatl, where locative notions are expressed by what the grammars call "relational nouns" or "place nouns" *(noms de lieu)*. These can appear combined with noun roots, as in Mohawk:

(16) a. Tēc-pan Ø-ca'. (Launey 1981:118)
      lord-LOC 3sS-be
      'It's at the palace (the lord's place).'

      b. Tepē-ti-cpac   Ø-ca' cē cal-li. (Launey 1981:120)
         mountain-LINK-above 3sS-be one house-NSF
         'There is a house on top of the mountain.'

      c. No-cal-ti-tlan   Ø-ca' cē mīl-li. (Launey 1981:121)
         1sP-house-LINK-beside 3sS-be a field-NSF
         'There is a field beside my house.'

However, locatives also appear without an incorporated noun. In this case, an agreement prefix appears on the locative morpheme that represents the features of the reference object. The agreement morphemes that appear are identical to those found on nouns to indicate the possessor of the noun (Launey 1981):

(17) a. ō   to-pan   quiyāuh. (Launey 1981:119)
      PAST 1pP-LOC rain/PERF
      'It has rained on us.'

      b. No-cpac Ø-ca' quetzal-li. (Launey 1981:120)
         1sP-above 3sS-be feather-NSF.
         'Feathers are on top of me.' (i.e., 'I have feathers on my head.')

      c. No-tlan   xi-mo-tlāli. (Launey 1981:121)
         1sP-beside 2sSIMPER-2REFL-sit
         'Sit beside me.'

The agreement on the locative morpheme in these examples licenses a pro complement. This pro may, in turn, license a dislocated NP, as in (18). Example (18b), in particular, shows that this NP need not form a constituent with the adpositional element; rather, it is (or at least may be) in an adjoined, A-bar position.

(18) a. ī-pan   tēuc-tli. (Launey 1981:119)
      3sP-LOC lord-NSF
      'the lord's place'

      b. ī-pan   ō-ni-calac   in Pedro. (Launey 1981:119)
         3sP-LOC PAST-1sS-enter/PERF IN Pedro
         'I entered Pedro's place.' (Literally: 'I entered his place, Pedro'.)

In contrast to these patterns, there are two patterns that one apparently does not find in Nahuatl. On the one hand, one does not find bare locative morphemes in construction with a fully inflected, independent noun. On the other hand, one does not find locative morphemes with an incorporated noun root and an agreement prefix, both of which represent the reference object of the adposition. In other

words, there is always a one-to-one correspondence between the nominal morphemes on the adposition and the positions in its θ-grid. The unattested examples
would look like (19a) or (19b).

(19) a. *tēuc-tli pan
          lord-NSF LOC
          'the lord's place'

      b. *ī-tēc-pan
          3sP-lord-LOC
          'the lord's place'

This is exactly what our theory of polysynthesis predicts. Example (19a) is ruled
out by the MVC: the NP 'lord' is not visible for θ-role assignment from the
adposition because it is not coindexed with any morpheme on the word containing
the adposition. On the other hand, either noun incorporation or agreement is sufficient to satisfy this requirement by itself. Thus, forms containing both, such as
(19b), are impossible, Nahuatl being a language that favors "economy" of
agreement over "uniformity" of agreement (see section 1.4). Therefore, the possibilities and requirements for expressing the internal argument of a P in Nahuatl
are exactly the same as those involved in expressing the internal argument of a V,
as predicted.[11]

   We already have a suitable analysis for the incorporated forms in (16), and the
agreeing forms in (17) and (18) are also relatively straightforward. The only new
issue concerns where the agreement factor originates. In chapter 5, I argued that
agreement features in polysynthetic languages are generated in the heads of functional categories with Case-assigning features. Adpositions are universally associated with Case-assigning features, so that part of the condition is readily satisfied.
It is less obvious that these Case-assigning features reside in a functional category
dominating the basic PP: Ps are not necessarily associated with any obvious inflectional categories comparable to tense and aspect on verbs or number and definiteness on nouns. On the other hand, it does no obvious harm to say that there is
a functional category dominating P, so I will assume that there is for the sake of
parallelism (see, for example, Koopman 1993 for suggestions along these lines).
The structure of a simple PP with agreement is given in (20).

(20)

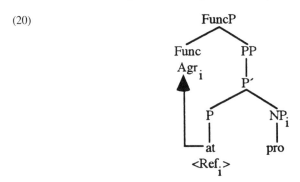

Once the P incorporates into the head of FuncP, the agreement factor can be
coindexed with the reference object, in accordance with the Condition on

Agreement Relations (CAR); the reference object can thus be pro. On the other hand, the complement presumably cannot be an overt NP, because the agreement absorbs the Case associated with the adposition. Thus, when an overt NP does appear, it shows signs of being freely adjoined to some constituent that dominates PP, rather than being in a fixed argument position (see (18b)).

In fact, Mohawk adpositions have the ability to agree with their reference objects as well. This is slightly masked by the fact that when the object of a preposition is animate, the element *ya't* 'body' must appear. This is not particularly surprising, however; the same element shows up when certain verbs that normally take an inanimate object take an animate object instead. Woodbury (1975:ch. 4) analyzes *ya't* in Onondaga as an operator that changes the selectional restrictions of the head and not an incorporated noun root; apart from this, it has no effect on the syntax. Once this is taken into account, the Mohawk examples in (21) are perfectly parallel to the Nahuatl examples in (17) and (18).

(21) a. Owirá'a ye-ya't-ákta   t-ká-yʌ.
        baby   FsS-body-near cis-NsS-lie
        'It is near the baby.'

    b. Okaryahtáne k-yá't-a-ku   ka-yá't-i.
        mosquito   1sS-body-Ø-in ZsS-body-be.in
        'The mosquito is inside me.'

The same theory should, of course, hold for other polysynthetic languages. Unfortunately, the available data are not very informative. The Gunwinjguan languages, Chukchee, Wichita, and Kiowa all have locative suffixes that the grammars treat more or less as ordinary Case endings. Inasmuch as these endings form a morphological word with their NP argument, they do not falsify the MVC. However, there is typically not much positive evidence that the nominal and the adposition combine by syntactic head movement. For example, when an animate noun combines with an adposition in Southern Tiwa, the inflectional noun suffix is retained; this differs from NI into verbs in Southern Tiwa, as well as from NI into V or P in Mohawk, Nahuatl, and Ngandi.

(22) Te-ta'm-ban   seuan-*ide*-'ay. (AGF:304)
      1sS/cO-help-PAST man-SG-to
      'I helped (to) the man.'

Apparently, then, the process by which Ns are combined with Ps is somewhat different from ordinary incorporation, at least in Southern Tiwa. Nor does it seem to be possible for locative elements to agree with their reference object in most of these languages. Thus, they do not give very dramatic evidence either for or against the MVC.

The Mayali locative system is somewhat different from that of the other polysynthetic languages, however, including the other Gunwinjguan languages. First of all, Mayali is the only language in my sample that has locative prefixes, rather than suffixes. An example of this is the general locative prefix *gu*, shown in (23) (from Evans 1991:83).

(23) Ba-ngolu-ngi   ba-rro-ngi   gu-warde.
      3sS-roast-PAST/IMPF 3sS-pound-PAST/IMPF LOC-rock
      'She roasted it on the coals and pounded it on a rock.'

This is a rare counterexample to the generalization that the incorporated head appears to the left of the incorporation host.[12] A still more serious problem is posed by the fact that Evans (1991) describes Mayali as having at least one locative preposition, *gure:*

(24) An-bukka-ng   gure bedda.   (Evans 1991:224)
      3sS/1sO-show-PAST/PERF LOC   them
      'He showed me to them.'

This preposition does not form a single word with its reference object, as it should to satisfy the MVC. However, the problem is not as serious as it seems. *Gure* is clearly related to the locative prefix *gu* in (23). In fact, the two are in complementary distribution: *gu* attaches only to inanimate nouns, whereas *gure* is used when the reference object is human or a pronoun or a clause. Furthermore, Evans suggests (1991:87) that *gure* is a reduction of *gu-red*, where *red* is a noun meaning 'place'; thus, the combination originally meant something like 'at the place, at the camp'. If this is so, we can say that *red* is a dummy noun that incorporates into *gu* to satisfy the MVC whenever direct incorporation of the N would be morphologically ill-formed. According to this proposal, the structure of (24) would be (25).

(25)

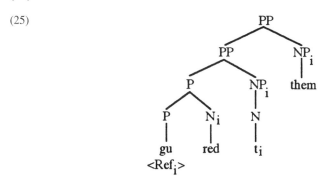

This, then, is perfectly consistent with the MVC; indeed, it is similar to the phenomenon of "classifier incorporation" in the Iroquoian languages. Moreover, there is no equivalent of *gure* in the other Gunwinjguan languages I have consulted; this confirms the suspicion that if *gure* is a preposition at all, it is a recent and marked addition to the grammar of the language.[13]

9.1.3 The Possessor of the Complement

This does not quite exhaust the topic of the internal structure of PPs, however. One further property they have is that when the complement noun is incorporated, the resulting complex may agree with the possessor of the noun. An example from Mohawk is given in (26); (27) shows that the same thing is possible in Nahuatl (Launey 1981:117–118 (see also (16c)).

(26) Shawátis rao-'seré-ht-a-ku   wa'-ke-'nerohkw-íta-'.
     Shawatis MsP-car-NOM-Ø-in FACT-1sS-box-put-PUNC
     'I put the box in Shawatis' car.'

(27) Mo-cal-co   Ø-ca' in no-chichi-uh.
     2sP-house-in 3sS-be IN 1sP-dog-POSS
     'My dog is in your house.'

The agreement in these forms is potentially problematic for my theory. The crucial question is, Where is the agreement factor that expresses the possessor generated? Suppose that it were generated in a functional category such as Det that immediately dominates NP. Then there would be no problem with the fact that the agreement is coindexed with the possessor. However, movement of the N into the P should be blocked by the presence of the intervening functional category, by the Proper Head Movement Generalization. Indeed the whole analysis of complex predicates in chapter 8 is built around the assumption that incorporated elements cannot bring inflectional/functional elements with them. On the other hand, if the agreement factor were generated on the functional category that immediately dominates PP, there is a potential violation of the CAR, because the agreement associated with an argument-taking element (P) is coindexed with something that is not an argument of that head. Thus, whatever one says about the agreement in (26) and (27) seems to run into trouble of one kind or another.

Fortunately, the theory of complex predicates developed in chapter 8 offers a way out. There it was shown that the argument structure associated with an X^0 formed by incorporation need not be that of the head; rather the argument structure of the nonhead can be inherited instead. Suppose we take advantage of this option. Then an example like (26a) could be associated with the structure in (28).

(28)

After the complex preposition incorporates into Func, the agreement factor can be coindexed with the possessor argument, in accordance with the CAR. Since the R argument of 'car' and the Ref argument of 'in' both count as morphologically expressed by virtue of the incorporation, the resulting word passes the MVC. In fact, there is a very close parallelism between these adpositions and the stative verbs analyzed in section 8.4: both allow a kind of "possessor raising" when the head of their argument is incorporated, because the incorporation legitimately expresses their only argument. Thus, they can afford to waive their right of access to the agreement-bearing nodes.

Structure (28) also provides the basis of an account of quirky agreement in Mohawk locative constructions. When a noun incorporates into a P in Nahuatl, there is no trace of agreement on the P. This is not the case in Mohawk; rather, a neuter prefix *ka* or *o* shows up as well. Presumably, this is a kind of default agreement, like the kind found on unaccusative verbs whose sole nominal argument has incorporated (section 5.4). Thus, the difference between Mohawk and Nahuatl is that at least one agreement node needs to be spelled out overtly in Mohawk, whereas Nahuatl allows forms with no agreement whatsoever. The interesting question, then, is whether this dummy agreement is realized as the $+O$ form *o*, or the $-O$ form *ka*. In fact, both are possible in general, with the prefix of the locative complex being the same as the prefix that appears on the N when it is unincorporated and unpossessed. This is illustrated by the contrast between the columns for *kanákta'* 'bed' and *o'neróhkwa'* 'box' in Table 9-1: the forms in the first column all begin with *ka,* whereas those in the second column all begin with *o.* In other words, the locative morpheme has no influence on the $\pm O$ value of the prefix. This fits with the analysis of possessor raising given previously: since the argument structure of the complex P is inherited not from the simple P but rather from the N, it follows that it is the diacritic value associated with the N that determines the form of the agreement prefix. Thus, the analysis of *o-'nerohkóku* 'under the box' is as in (29).

(29)

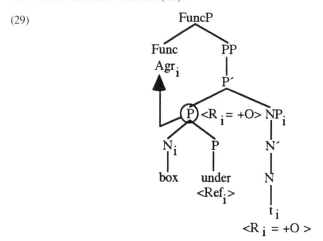

In (29), there is a parallel between the locative morphemes and the purposive morpheme in Mohawk, analyzed in section 8.3: both can attach to a head with any number of arguments, and both leave the quirky agreement features associated with the head unchanged. These properties follow from the fact that neither morpheme needs its own argument structure to be passed upward, so they have no effect on agreement processes.[14] Similarly, locative suffixes in Gunwinjguan languages such as Ngandi and Nunggubuyu do not change the semi-idiosyncratic noun class of the prefixes associated with the noun they attach to (Heath 1978, Heath 1984). (Since most of the other polysynthetic languages do not have overt agreement on nonverbal categories, this issue does not arise in them.)

Thus, the major aspects of PP-internal structure in polysynthetic languages follow straightforwardly from the Polysynthesis Parameter and the other principles we have established.

Before leaving this topic, however, there is one interesting fact that I cannot fully explain, but mention for the sake of descriptive completeness. NI into Ps in Mohawk differs from NI into most other categories in that the trace of the IN apparently cannot license an adjoined NP "double" or a stranded modifier.[15] Thus, examples like (30) are unexpectedly bad.

(30) a. *Thík⋀ o-'neróhkw-a-ku ka-tsikhé't-i.
     that   NsO-box-Ø-in   NsS-candy-be.in
     'The candy is in that box.'

 b. *Ake-'neróhkw-a' o-'neróhkw-a-ku ka-tsikhé't-i.
     1sP-box-NSF   NsO-box-Ø-in   NsS-candy-be.in
     'The candy is in my box.'

 c. *Ka-'sere-ht-a-hútsi   ka-'seré-ht-a-ku   wa'-ke-'nerohkw-íta-'.
     NsS-car-NOM-Ø-be.black NsS-car-NOM-Ø-in FACT-1sS-box-put.in-PUNC
     'I put the box in the black car.'

Related to this is the fact that PPs cannot be the focus of *which*-type questions; nor can they be understood as the heads of internally headed relative clauses:

(31) a. *Ka nikáy⋀ o-'neróhkw-a-ku ka-tsikhé't-i.
     which   NsO-box-Ø-in   NsS-candy-be.in
     'In which box is the candy?'

 b. #Te-yó-'tsu   ne ka-tsiké't-i   o-'neróhkw-a-ku.
     DUP-NsO-dirty NE NsS-candy-be.in NsO-box-Ø-in
     NOT: 'The box that the candy is in is dirty.' (OK only as: 'The candy in the box is dirty.')

The sentences in (31) are ruled out for the same reason that (30a) is ruled out, given that *ka nikáy⋀* 'which' and the null relative operator are of the same category as the demonstrative *thík⋀*. In contrast, INs incorporated into ordinary verbs can perfectly well be doubled by full NPs and bare demonstrative-like elements in Mohawk, as shown in section 7.4.1. They can also be questioned by *ka nikáy⋀* 'which' and can be understood as the heads of IHRCs (see section 4.3). This is true even for stative verbs, which are syntactically the most like Ps; thus (32a) and (32b) contrast with (30a) and (30b).

(32) a. W-ather-owán⋀ thík⋀.
     NsS-basket-big that
     'That is a big basket; that basket is big.'

 b. Thík⋀ raó-[a]ther-e'   w-ather-owán⋀.
     that MsP-basket-NSF NsS-basket-big
     'That basket of his is (a) large (basket).'

Interestingly, the ability to license an external NP is lost in one other situation: when the noun incorporated into the stative verb is possessed. Thus, the examples in (33) are like those in (30) and contrast minimally with those in (32).

(33)   a.   ?*Wak-ather-owánʌ thíkʌ.
            1sO-basket-big   that
            'That is my big basket; that basket of mine is big.'

       b.   *Thíkʌ áther-e' ro-[a]ther-owánʌ.
            that   basket MsO-basket-big.
            'That basket of his is big; that basket is his big basket.'

On the theory developed here, the structures in (33) and (30) have something in common that distinguishes them from all other instances of NI in Mohawk: these are the only constructions in which the argument structure of the noun must be inherited by the complex word for purposes of agreement. For NI into adpositions, this is shown in (28) and (29); for incorporation of a possessed noun into a stative verb, this was shown in section 8.4. In all other cases, including NI of an unpossessed noun into a stative verb, the argument structure of the verb is inherited by the complex verb. Thus, the facts in (30)–(33) follow if we modify the ALC one more time to read as follows:

(34)   *The Adjunct Licensing Condition*(revised)
       An argument-type phrase XP generated in adjoined position is licensed if and only if it forms a chain with an argument Y where the head of Y is:
       (i) a null pronominal, or
       {(ii) a trace *whose θ-grid differs from that of the closest c-commanding head.*}

(The braces around clause (ii) indicate that this type of licensing is allowed in some polysynthetic languages but not others.) This condition is the same as before, except for the italicized material in case (ii). I take it to be a good sign that the theory provides a straightforward distinction between the good cases of NP doubling and the bad ones. On the other hand, the new condition (ii) is entirely ad hoc and not very intuitive. Presumably, it should follow from some deeper and more adequate theory of how adjoined NPs are licensed. Ideally, this same theory would also will explain why it is possible for the trace of an IN to license a dislocated NP in some languages (Mohawk, Mayali, Caddoan) but not others (Nahuatl, Tanoan languages, Chukchee), a fact that was merely stipulated in section 7.4.1. I suspect that the contrasts in this section may be an important clue as to what this deeper theory is, but unfortunately I do not have a complete theory to offer here.[16]

9.2 The External Distribution of PPs

So far, PPs have been considered more or less in isolation, with little regard for how they fit into larger structures. From a theoretical perspective, the fundamental question in this domain is whether a PP could be an argument in a polysynthetic language. In fact, we can anticipate problems with such a construction. If a PP were the argument of a verb, then that argument relationship would have to be morphologically expressed in some way. In general, there are two ways this could be done: the verb could agree with the PP, or the head of the P could incorporate into the verb. Now if the P head incorporated into the verb, the construction would no longer look much like a PP; the adposition would show up as a verbal affix and all that would remain outside of the verb would be its NP complement left behind. In other words, the result would be a kind of applicative construction (Baker 1988a). Applicative constructions are, indeed, found in polysynthetic languages, but I put them aside until the next section. The only way that a PP could be the argument of a verb on the surface, then, is if the verb agrees with the PP.

However, there is good reason to think that agreement with PPs is not possible in general. Informally speaking, it is not clear what agreement form to use for a PP. Agreement in Mohawk is inherently nominal and is categorized by the standard features of person, number, and gender (the so-called Φ-features). Now it makes little sense to say that a PP is first person, or plural, or masculine; hence, there is no agreement form that can match the PP in these features. Of course, the NP object of the P may bear these Φ-features, and it is tempting to try agreeing with those features instead. However, one cannot, in general, ignore the presence of the P in this way; nor will agreement with an NP count as a legitimate expression of a PP argument. Example (35) confirms that direct agreement with the object of a P is generally impossible in Mohawk.

(35)   *Shawatís-hne y-a-*hiy*-atʌnatsher-atʌnyeht-e'.
       Shawatis-LOC TRANS-FACT-1sS/MsO-food-send-PUNC
       'I sent food to Shawatis' place.'

Example (35) can be contrasted with (36), where the same verb in its benefactive form takes what looks like a bare NP argument and agreement is possible:

(36)   O'neróhkwa' y-a-*hiy*-atʌnyéht-ʌ-'   ne Shawátis.
       box   TRANS-FACT-1sS/MsO-send-BEN-PUNC NE Shawatis
       'I sent Shawatis a box.'

These observations can be codified into the general statement in (37).

(37)   Only nominal elements bear Φ-features.[17]

Since PPs are not nominal, they do not have Φ-features and cannot be agreed with. Some kind of default neuter singular form might be used to satisfy the morphological requirement that a verb be inflected, as in English sentences like *Under the tree is a nice place to sit.* However, saying that a verb shows default agreement because its argument is a PP is quite a different thing from saying that the verb actually agrees with a PP. Default agreement would not be coindexed with the PP constituent and therefore could not play a role in satisfying the MVC.

The result of this line of reasoning is that surface PPs should not be arguments in the polysynthetic languages. Rather, overt PPs will be allowed in these languages if and only if they are adjuncts, which are not subject to the MVC. The rest of this section defends the claim that this is a correct conclusion, concentrating for the most part on Mohawk.

9.2.1 The Impossibility of PP Arguments

The strongest motivation for saying that some PPs have the status of arguments in English is simply the fact that there are a few verbs with which the appearance of a PP is obligatory, or very nearly so. This is taken to mean that these verbs are subcategorized for a PP, which, in turn, implies that the PP is an argument of the verb (cf. Chomsky 1981). Thus, the clearest implication of the claim that PPs are not arguments in Mohawk is that they are not obligatory with any verb.

The class of verbs that is most clearly subcategorized for a PP in English is the one that includes *put* and a few other semantically related words:

(38)   I put the pail *(on the table).

Significantly, there is no directly comparable verb in Mohawk. When asked to translate ordinary sentences using *put*, Mohawk speakers produce forms like the following:

(39)   a. Atekhwará-hne wa'-ke-na'ts-a-hrʌ-'.
           table-LOC   FACT-1sS-pail-Ø-put.on-PUNC
           'I put the pail on the table.'

        b. Atekhwara-tsher-óku y-a'-ke-ná'ts-a-yʌ-'.
           table-NOM-under   TRANS-FACT-1sS-pail-Ø-put.down-PUNC
           'I put the pail under the table.'

        c. O-'neróhkw-a-ku y-a'-ke-na'ts-íta-'.
           NsO-box-Ø-in   TRANS-FACT-1sS-pail-put.in-PUNC
           'I put the pail in the box.'

        d. Ka-nhoh-ákta wa'-ke-ná'ts-a-yʌ-'.
           NsS-door-near FACT-1sS-pail-Ø-put.down-PUNC
           'I put the pail near the door.'

Notice that various verb roots are used, depending on the final position and/or posture of the theme. Mohawk has distinct words for 'to put on a raised surface', 'to put on the ground', and 'to put in an enclosed space'. Thus, some information about location is always "conflated" into the verbs of the *put*-class in Mohawk, to use Talmy's (1985) terminology. There is no truly neutral verb meaning 'put' that has the full range of uses of the English verb. Correlated with this is the fact that the locative phrases in (39) are optional. Thus, *yʌ* 'put down, place' can appear without a PP, as in (40).

(40)   Ke-'nerohkw-ʌhaw-í-hne' sok wá'-k-yʌ-'.
        1sS-box-carry-IMPF-PAST then FACT-1sS-put.down-PUNC
        'I was carrying the box, but then I put it down.'

Similarly, *eta* 'put in' may be used without a locative phrase in the last sentence of the exchange in (41), where two people are packing to move.

(41)   A: Kʌ́tho o-'neróhkw-a-ku s-éta   ne akera'-shú'a,
           here   NsO-box-Ø-in   2sS-put.in NE plate-PL

        ok ne kana'tsu-shú'a atekhwará-hne ká-hrʌ-Ø-k.
        but NE pot-PL   table-LOC   NsS-put.on-STAT-CONT
        'Put the plates here in this box, but let the pots stay on the table.'

B: Ohkatiné'e n-ʌ-ka-yér-ha'   kíkʌ owise'-shú'a.
   what   PART-FUT-NsS-do-HAB this glass-PL
   'What will be done with these glasses?'

A: S-éta   ni né'e.
   2sS-put.in also
   Put them in too.

Hrʌ 'put on' and *orok* 'put under, cover' also appear without a locative in similar contexts.[18]

(42) a. . . . Ya-hs-órok   ni né'e
              TRANS-2sS-put.under also
              '. . . Put it under too.'

      b. . . . Í-s-hrʌ   ni né'e.
              Ø-2sS-put.on also
              '. . . Put it on also.'

Thus, verbs of putting do not subcategorize for a locative argument in Mohawk; rather, they have an element of locative meaning conflated within them in the Lexicon. If more information about the location of the putting is desired, then an appropriate locative expression may, of course, be added, but this presumably has the status of an adjunct rather than an argument.

Similar effects are found with verbs of the *go* class. These are also likely candidates for selecting PP arguments in English. *Go* can appear without a PP, but such utterances often sound somewhat elliptical; certainly, it very frequently does appear with a PP, and the idea of location is inherent in its semantics.

(43) John went ?(into the cave).

Indeed, *go* may be thought of as the unaccusative version of *put* in English. Again the verb *go* translates into a variety of verbs in Mohawk, most of which have a locational or directional component of meaning built in. Thus, there are distinct verbs for 'go under', 'go into', and 'go in a general location':

(44) a. Otsinówʌ anitskwara-tsher-óku y-a-ha-[a]t-órok-e'.
         mouse   chair-NOM-under   TRANS-FACT-MsS-SRFL-cover-PUNC
         'The mouse went under the chair.'

      b. Otsinówʌ o-'neróhkw-a-ku y-a-ha-[a]t-íta-'.
         mouse   NsO-box-Ø-in   TRANS-FACT-MsS-SRFL-go.in-PUNC
         'The mouse went into the box.'

      c. Otsinówʌ ka-nhoh-ákta   n-yahá-hr[a]-e-'.
         mouse   NsS-door-near PART-TRANS/FACT-MsS-go-PUNC
         'The mouse went near the door.'

      d. Otsinówʌ atekhwará-hne y-a-ha-ráthʌ-'.
         mouse   table-LOC   TRANS-FACT-MsS-climb-PUNC
         'The mouse went up (climbed) onto the table.'

As before, the PPs appearing with these verbs are optional. For example, the following are complete sentences:

(45)   a. Y-a-k-at-órok-e'.
           TRANS-FACT-1sS-SRFL-cover-PUNC
           'I went underneath.'

       b. Y-Λ-k-at-íta-'.
           TRANS-FUT-1sS-SRFL-go.in-PUNC
           'I will go in (an enclosed space).'

Hence, the PPs in (44) may be taken to be adjuncts.

Finally, the Jackendovian analysis of PPs adopted in section 9.1 implies that copular verbs such as *be* in English must take a locative PP complement. Thus, *be* has a similar argument structure to that of *go,* but it is a stative verb rather than eventive verb. Once again, Mohawk has a variety of copular/locative verbs, each of which includes specialized information about the location and position of the theme:

(46)   a. Sak ka-'seré-ht-a-ku   t-ha-yá't-i.
           Sak NsS-car-NOM-Ø-in CIS-MsS-body-be.in/STAT
           'Sak is over there in the car.'

       b. Uwári ka-wehnó-'ke   í-t-yΛ-[e]-s.
           Mary NsS-island-LOC Ø-CIS-FsS-go/be-HAB
           'Mary is on the island.'

       c. Sak ka-nakt-óku   t-ha-ya't-óru.
           Sak NsS-bed-under CIS-MsS-body-cover/STAT
           'Sak is under the bed.'

Moreover, these verbs can also appear without the independent locative expression:

(47)   a. T-k-yá't-i.
           CIS-1sS-body-be.in
           'I am inside.'

       b. (Ka-rist-á-'ke)   ká-her-e'.
           NsS-iron-Ø-LOC NsS-be.placed-STAT
           'It's on top (of the stove).'

Summarizing so far, we have surveyed three important classes of verbs involving location—transitive *put*-type verbs, intransitive *go*-type verbs, and stative *be*-type verbs. In each domain, Mohawk expresses the location relation primarily by conflation in the Lexicon rather than by subcategorization for a PP. This appears to be a systematic property of the language. My claim, then, is that this is not accidental: Mohawk verbs do not subcategorize for locative PPs because they cannot; PP arguments are incompatible with the polysynthetic nature of the language.

Whether full PPs are ever subcategorized arguments in other polysynthetic languages is hard to judge from the literature, since most grammars do not discuss the θ-grids of individual verbs in any detail. However, the grammars contain sporadic examples that look similar to the situation described for Mohawk. For example, the clearest example of a *put*-type verb in Wichita is *re:hi.* This verb, like its Mohawk cousins, contains information about the final position of the theme (it is lying), and does not require a locative complement:

(48)   Ti-re:s.   (Rood 1976:64)
       IND/3sS-put.lying
       'She laid them down.'

If more information about the position of the theme is desired, a locative morpheme can be compounded with the verb root. Hence, there is little reason to think
that this verb ever takes a true PP complement. Similarly, (49) is an example from
a Ngandi text in which a *put*-type verb appears without a PP or other locative
element.

(49)   . . . gu-burt-jung   njaru-ga-yu-ri. . .   (Heath 1978:192)
       GU-antmound-NSF 1PEXS/GUO-SUB-put.on-PAST/CONT
       'We put the antmound chucks on.'

Only in Chukchee do the references discuss ditransitive verbs that take an NP and
a PP (locative oblique), or intransitive verbs that appear with PPs (Nedjalkov
1976), and it is by no means clear from the sources that the locative oblique
elements are obligatory even in this language. Thus, what evidence is available is
generally consistent with the predictions of the MVC.

The claim that all PPs in polysynthetic languages are adjuncts also predicts that
they should all have more or less the same syntactic behavior. In this respect, the
polysynthetic languages should differ from English, where some PPs are arguments and some are adjuncts. In English, argument PPs are generated as complements to the verb, as in (50a), whereas adjunct PPs are adjoined to some higher
projection, as in (50b).

(50)   a. I [$_{VP}$ put the book on the couch].

       b. I [$_{VP}$ read the book] on the couch.

Moreover, this structural difference could have a variety of syntactic consequences. However, any differences between sentences of these types should be
neutralized in Mohawk. In fact, it is embarrassingly difficult to find clear syntactic
differences between the PPs in (50a) and (50b) even in English. Moreover, some
of the differences that have been proposed in English (such as whether preposition
stranding under movement is possible or extractability from weak islands) cannot
be used in Mohawk for independent reasons. Nevertheless, it is worth pointing out
that all PPs do seem to have the same syntactic behavior in Mohawk, regardless
of whether one is tempted to consider them arguments or adjuncts on the basis of
their English glosses.

One obvious place where one might expect to see a difference between argument PPs and adjunct PPs in Mohawk is in word order. In chapter 2, we saw that
all overt NPs in Mohawk are dislocated, adjoined to the clause. Thus, if Mohawk
had a class of argument PPs that were generated inside the VP, these should
appear inside of all NP expressions—either immediately before the verb or immediately after it. On the other hand, adjunct PPs if they are adjoined to the clause
should be freely ordered with respect to overt NPs. In fact, no such division is
found. The most common and easily elicited position for locative expressions of
all types in Mohawk is immediate preverbal position:

(51) a. Sak atekhwará-hne wa-há-hrʌ-'   ne o'neróhkwa.
          Sak table-LOC   FACT-MsS-put.on-PUNC NE box
          'Sak put the box on the table.'   (argument PP?)

   b. Sak ka-rhá-ku   t-a-huwá-[a]hseht-e'.
       Sak NsS-forest-in CIS-FACT-FsS/MsO-kill-PUNC.
       'Sak was killed in the forest.'   (adjunct PP)

Apparently, this is also true in Nahuatl (Launey 1981:53). However, this is probably to be understood in functional terms rather than structural terms. The immediate preverbal position in Mohawk often has a mild degree of focus associated with
it (cf. Mithun 1987). Since locative adjuncts are by definition optional, the fact
that one appears at all suggests that there is some degree of focus on the location.
This may account for why the preverbal position is so common. However, this is
certainly not the only acceptable position. When (52) is uttered as an answer to
someone asking why a box is on the floor, there is no real focus on 'on the table'
and it can easily appear after the verb as well as before it.

(52) Ne tsi Sak wa-há-hrʌ-'   atekhwará-hne tánu t-úhsʌ'-ne'.
      because Sak FACT-MsS-put-PUNC table-on   and CIS-FACT/NsS/fall-PUNC
      'Because Sak put it on the table and it fell off.'

The same order is acceptable with PPs that are clearly adjuncts:

(53) Sak t-a-huwá-[a]hseht-e'   ka-rhá-ku.
      Sak CIS-FACT-FsS/MsO-kill-PUNC NsS-forest-in
      'Sak was killed in the forest.'

Indeed, both V–PP and PP–V orders can easily be found in texts; (54) gives a
naturally occurring minimal pair from adjacent sentences in the same story
(KO:99–100).

(54) a. . . . y-a-ho-ya't-Áhaw-e'   ne rohsótha tánu'
            TRANS-OPT-MsS/MsO-body-carry-PUNC NE old.man and

            ka-rhá-ku   y-a-hó-htka'w-e'.
            NsS-forest-in TRANS-OPT-MsS/MsO-let.go-PUNC
            '(This man sent his son) to take the old man out and let him go in the
            woods.'

   b. . . . t-a-ho-[a]hsir-a-wÁ'ek-e'   ne rohsótha
            DUP-OPT-MsS/MsO-blanket-Ø-wrap-PUNC NE old.man

            nónʌ y-ʌ-hó-htka'w-e'   ka-rhá-ku.
            when TRANS-FUT-MsS/MsO-let.go-PUNC NsS-forest-in
            '(The man gave his son a blanket) to wrap the old man in when he let him
            go in the woods.'

Moreover, orders in which the locative expression is outside of an overt NP are
judged to be marginally possible. There is no difference in this regard between
those one might be tempted to treat as arguments, as in (55), and those that are
clearly adjuncts, as in (56).

(55) ?Atekhwará-hne kaná'tsu wá'-k-hrʌ-'.
       table-LOC   pail   FACT-1sS-put.on-PUNC
       'I put the pail on the table.'

(56)   ?Ka-rhá-ku Sak t-a-huwá-[a]hseht-e'.
       forest-in   Sak CIS-FACT-FsS/MsO-kill-PUNC
       (Did you hear?) 'Sak was killed in the forest.'

These sentences have the same degree of acceptability if the word order is verb–object–location. Thus, all PPs in Mohawk pattern in the same way with respect to word order considerations. Moreover, after the effects of focus are controlled for, PPs have a degree of freedom of word order that one expects from adjuncts, not arguments. Locative expressions also have reasonably free word order in Nahuatl (Launey 1981) and the Gunwinjguan languages (Evans 1991:302–303).

One other place where one might expect to find differences between argument and adjunct PPs is in disjoint referent effects. Suppose that one creates sentences in which the object of the P is a referential NP and the object of the verb is a pronoun with the same Φ-features. One could then ask whether the pronoun and the NP can be understood as being coreferential. If the PP were an argument of the V, it would be generated within V' and hence c-commanded by the direct object (see (50a)). Thus, coreference should be ruled out by Condition C of Binding Theory. On the other hand, if the PP were an adjunct, it would be generated outside of the smallest VP (see (50b)). This would put it outside of the c-command domain of the direct object, and coreference would not be ruled out by Condition C. However, when the relevant examples are constructed, no difference in the referential possibilities is observed; the coreference in question is consistently ungrammatical. This is true regardless of whether or not the PP could plausibly be considered an argument[19]:

(57)   Sák-hne yu-s-a-hiy-atÁnyeht-e'.
       Sak-LOC TRANS-ITER-FACT-1sS/MsO-send-PUNC
       'I sent *him* back to *Sak's* place.' (disjoint only)

(58)   Sák-hne t-a-huwá-[a]hseht-e'.
       Sak-LOC CIS-FACT-FsS/MsO-kill-PUNC
       'They killed *him* at *Sak's* place.' (disjoint only)

Examples (57) and (58) support the theory inasmuch as no difference between the two classes of PPs is found. However, the judgments given are the ones that would be expected if all PPs were subcategorized arguments, rather than adjuncts. This is hardly plausible. It is much more likely that coreference between a pronominal object and an NP inside an adjunct PP is ungrammatical for some reason other than the standard Condition C. Zubizarreta (1985:256) proposes the following condition, which may be relevant:

(59)   If X is an argument of Z and Y is an adjunct of Z, then X cannot be referentially dependent on Y.

The effects of (59) can be seen in English sentences like those in (60), assuming that the locative PP is an argument of *put*, while the instrumental PP is an adjunct of *carve*.

(60)   a.   ?I put *its* cover in *the box*.

       b.   *I carved *its* handle with *the knife*.

Moreover, a coreferential interpretation is difficult to get in the English gloss of
(58) as well. Thus, if a condition like (59) is correct, the judgments in (57) and
(58) can be explained in a unified way. Again, the prediction that Mohawk will
not have a class of PPs that behave syntactically like arguments is supported, as
is the Polysynthesis Parameter from which this prediction is derived.

9.2.2 The Licensing of Adjunct PPs

Having concluded that most PPs are not licensed as arguments of a predicate but
rather as adjuncts, it is appropriate to say something about PP adjuncts in the
polysynthetic languages. In this I am inhibited by the fact that the licensing conditions on PP adjuncts are not well understood in P&P theory. Nevertheless, a few
worthwhile points can be made.

One thing that is clear is that PPs are not subject to the same licensing condition as NPs. Chapters 3 and 4 showed that NPs in polysynthetic languages are, in
general, licensed only if they are coindexed with an argument position. This is
clearly not the case for PPs; they can be adjoined to virtually any clause, regardless of its internal structure. Thus, one finds minimal contrasts like the following
in Mohawk:

(61)   a. Thíkʌ o-nut-á-'ke   yó-hskats   ne okwire'-shú'a.
          That NsO-hill-Ø-LOC NsO-be.pretty NE tree-PL
          'The trees are pretty on that hill.'

       b. *Thíkʌ onúta', yó-hskats   ne okwire'-shú'a.
           That hill   NsO-be.pretty NE tree-PL
          'As for that hill, the trees are pretty.'

(62)   a. O-'neróhkw-a-ku te-w-a'shár-i.
          NsO-box-Ø-in   CIS-NsS-knife-be.in
          'The knife is in the box.'

       b. *O'neróhkwa' te-w-ashár-i.
           box   CIS-NsS-knife-be.in
          'As for the box, the knife is inside.'

The bare NPs in these examples violate the ALC, the most recent version of which
is (34) in the previous section. However, the corresponding locatives do not violate this condition; they are not "argument-type phrases." I leave open exactly
what principles are involved in the generation of PP adjuncts, simply observing
that there is no evidence that polysynthetic languages are different from other
languages in this respect. For present purposes, the main importance of (61) and
(62) is that they give additional support to the claim that locative expressions are
of a different category from simple NPs; hence, they are subject to different licensing conditions.[20]

Of course, it is still possible that PPs are sometimes coindexed with argument
positions. If a verb formally selects an NP, its argument can satisfy the MVC
either by incorporating or by triggering agreement. A PP adjunct could then, in
principle, be linked to this argument position, just as an NP adjunct can. Indeed,
this seems to be possible, as shown by the following examples in Mohawk:

(63) a. Te-yó-'tsu   ne ka-nakt-óku.
         DUP-NsO-dirty NE NsS-bed-under
         'It's dirty under the bed.'

      b. Wa'-e-rákʌ-st-e'   ne o-'neróhkw-a-ku.
         FACT-FsS-white-CAUS-PUNC NE NsO-box-in
         'She made the inside of the box white.'

      c. (*)Wa'-e-ránye-'   atekhwará-hne.
         FACT-FsS-rub-PUNC table-LOC
         'She scrubbed on the table top.'

In each of these examples, the locative expresses the theme argument of the verb. Similarly, Evans (1991:83) shows that the locative expressions formed by prefixing *gu* to a noun in Mayali can be associated with an argument position as well as being pure adsentential adjuncts.

Curiously, Nahuatl seems to differ from Mohawk and Mayali in this regard. Launey (1981:54–55) shows that locative expressions typically cannot be associated with NP argument positions. Thus, examples such as the following are ungrammatical:

(64) a. *Ca cualli in mexi'-co.
         PRT good IN Mexico-LOC
         'It is nice in Mexico.'

      b. *Ni-qu-itta   in mexi'-co
         1sS-3sO-see IN Mexico-LOC
         'I saw Mexico.'

Instead of (64b), one must say the equivalent of 'In Mexico I saw things,' with an incorporated object N. This seems like a peculiar way for otherwise similar languages to differ.

A hint as to what might be going on here comes from Launey's observation (1981:120–121) that some locative expressions in Nahuatl can appear with the noun suffix *tli*. When this happens, the expressions are related to NP argument positions in the usual way:

(65) a. Ni-qu-itta   in teō-pan-tli.
         1sS-3sO-see IN god-LOC-NSF
         'I saw the church (the place of God).'

      b. Cuix olōltic in tlāl-ti-cpac-tli.
         Q   round IN land-LINK-above-NSF
         'Is the earth (the surface of the land) round?'

      c. Iztāc in cal-tech-tli.
         white IN house-against-NSF.
         'The side of the house is white.'

This suggests that certain locative morphemes are actually ambiguous as to their category: they may be Ps or Ns. When they head PPs, they may be licensed as adjuncts but may not be coindexed with an NP argument position, due to the conflict in category. However, when they head NPs they may be coindexed with an argument position; indeed, they must be in order to be licensed. Which category a given token belongs to is clearly marked in Nahuatl by the presence or absence of the noun suffix.

In fact, there is no real obstacle to extending this analysis to Mohawk and Mayali. Mohawk also has noun suffixes, but these are usually nothing more than a glottal stop following a vowel-final root. Moreover, this glottal stop is usually deleted word finally in Kahnawake Mohawk. Thus, the morphological distinction between an NP and a PP is much less clear in Mohawk. It is perfectly possible then that the locative expressions in (63) are actually NPs, not PPs. This may also explain why I have been unable to construct acceptable examples with *akta* 'near' similar to (63) (meaning something like 'the vicinity of the table is dirty'), and why consultants differ in their reactions to (63c): it is simply an idiosyncratic lexical property of some locative morphemes that they are Ns as well as Ps. If this is so, Nahuatl shows that it is not possible to coindex a PP with an NP argument position after all; rather, true PPs are licensed as adjoined clausal modifiers only. Indeed, this fits well with the results in chapter 2, where it was concluded that clauses cannot be dislocated in the same manner as NPs. Theoretically, this follows from the ALC, since one of the conditions on chain formation is that the two elements in question must match in all features, including category (see section 3.1.5). Another, arguably more important, instance of the same phenomenon is the use of instrumental Case for transitive subjects and dative/allative Case for indirect objects in Chukchee and some of the Gunwinjguan languages, as discussed in section 3.3.3. If I have interpreted the Nahuatl examples correctly, then these elements also must be underspecified as to their category; hence, they can be licensed either as NPs coindexed with an argument position or as PP adjuncts.

9.2.3 The Null Adposition

So far I have claimed that PPs cannot be arguments in polysynthetic languages. However, there is one special case that requires a separate discussion. This is the possibility of a PP headed by an adposition that is lexically null. In section 7.3.3, I argued that a limited number of verbs in the polysynthetic languages select a PP that is headed by a null P. These are verbs that involve a transfer of possession (perhaps in an extended sense) and that have the direction of motion encoded in them. In these circumstances, there is no nonredundant information about the nature of the path to be expressed in the P. Many languages seem to have the option of using a lexically null P in this case. Typical examples of verbs of this type are those meaning 'give', 'show', 'tell', or 'lend' (selecting goals), and 'steal' or 'take from' (selecting sources). One such example is (66). The structure in question is (67), repeated from chapter 7.

(66)   T-a'-khey-athʌnó-tsher-u-'   ne owirá'a.
       CIS-FACT-1sS/FsO-ball-NOM-give-PUNC NE baby
       'I gave the ball to the baby.'

Syntactic evidence for the null P in polysynthetic languages comes primarily from the fact that even though goals often look like simple NPs in these languages, the head of the N can never be incorporated into the verb. In other languages, the null P has the effect of determining which NP in a so-called double object construction

(67)

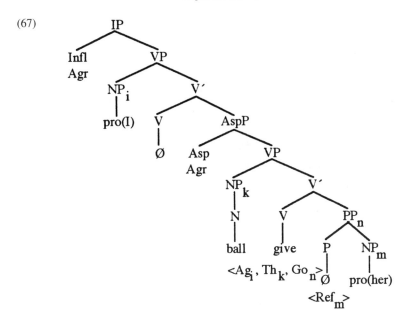

can receive inherent accusative Case from the verb (Baker 1992a). The question now is how this type of PP argument can pass the MVC where all others have failed.

This question breaks down into two parts: How is the argument relationship between $\emptyset_P$ and NP_m morphologically expressed? How is the argument relationship between the verb and the PP morphologically expressed?

Consider first the $\emptyset_P$–NP_m relationship. Here the solution is trivial. The MVC says that an NP can only receive a θ-role from a head X if it is coindexed with a morpheme in the complex word containing X. Normally, this requires either that incorporation take place or that an agreement relationship of some kind be established. However, since the P is null in (66), *there is no word that contains it.* This means that there is no word that must contain a morpheme coindexed with NP_m. In other words, the MVC is satisfied vacuously just in case the θ-assigning head is lexically null. This, then, is one straightforward way in which PPs headed by a null adposition behave differently from other PPs. Since P is probably the only θ-marking category that can be redundant semantically, examples like (66) are the only ones in which the possibility of satisfying the MVC vacuously comes into play.

The proper theoretical treatment of the V–PP relationship is less straightforward. What actually happens is that the triadic verb appears to agree with NP_m. In (66), this shows up as the FsO morphology in the pronominal prefix; the same thing happens with similar verbs in the other polysynthetic languages, as shown in chapter 5. Apparently, this agreement with the complement of the complement of the verb counts as agreement with the complement itself for purposes of satisfying the MVC. However, the verb can only agree with the complement of its PP complement when the P is lexically null; when the P is overtly realized, such agreement is quite impossible, as shown previously in (35). The intuition, then, is that the features of an NP can be reckoned as the features of a PP that contains it if and only if the PP contains nothing other than the NP. This is given a more formal and general expression in (68).[21]

(68)   If X has morphosyntactic features [α] and Y is a category that contains X but no lexical material other than X, then the features [α] can be associated with Y.

Condition (68) implies that the PP node in (67) can have the features feminine and singular (and $+O$); hence, this PP is an exception to the general rule in (37) that only nominal elements bear Φ-features, and it can be agreed with. Thus, the MVC is satisfied if the two agreement factors agree with the goal and agent arguments of the verb after verb raising, while the theme argument is expressed by noun incorporation prior to verb raising, as in (69).

(69)

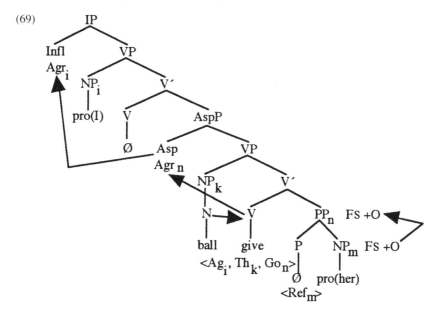

I conclude that null-headed PPs in which the content of P is semantically predictable from properties of its selecting V are the one kind that can exist as arguments in a polysynthetic language—apart from the possibility of incorporation, to which I now turn.

9.3 Applicative Constructions

In the previous section, we saw that PPs with an overt P cannot satisfy the MVC by triggering agreement because of their lack of Φ-features; hence, anything that looks like a PP must be licensed as an adjunct in polysynthetic languages. However, I put aside the possibility that an argument PP could satisfy the MVC by having its head incorporate into the verbal complex. Such a derivation would yield an applicative construction of the type discussed in Marantz 1984, Baker 1988a:ch. 5, and much other work. In fact, applicative constructions are found in most—perhaps all—of the polysynthetic languages. Indeed, examples throughout this book have contained many instances of applicatives, particularly in chapter 5 and section 8.1. However, up to now their internal structure has been ignored. Let us, then, investigate how this gap can be filled in in a way that is consistent with the MVC and that explains the basic properties of the applicative construction.

Applicatives are standardly characterized as constructions in which a derivational morpheme is attached to the verb resulting in the verb taking a new nominal as its surface object. Thus, the applicative form of an intransitive base verb acts like a transitive verb, while the applicative form of a transitive base verb acts like a ditransitive verb. This new "applied" nominal expresses a thematic role that otherwise would have to be expressed obliquely or not at all. This is a rather common phenomenon across languages; the Bantu family, in particular, is famous for its applicatives. A very similar construction is found in Mohawk:

(70) a. Wa-ha-natar-a-kwétar-e'.   (simple transitive)
          FACT-MsS-bread-Ø-cut-PUNC
          'He cut the bread.'

      b. Wa-hake-natar-a-kwétar-ʌ-'   (applicative)
          FACT-MsS/1sO-bread-Ø-cut-ben-PUNC
          'He cut the bread for me.'

The applicative morpheme in (70b) is the suffix ʌ. Like most suffixes in Mohawk, it shows a large amount of semi-idiosyncratic allomorphy; its most common realizations are *'s,* ʌ and ʌ*ni.* The added argument in (70b) (pro-dropped 'me') is interpreted as someone who is favorably affected by the action or state named by the base verb; in other words, it is a benefactive or a goal. In other examples, the argument added by this same morpheme can be interpreted as a person adversely affected by the action or state, as a malefactive or source. Which interpretation is dominant in a given sentence depends on the inherent lexical meaning of the base verb and also to some extent on the context. For example, verbs of creation such as *uni* 'make' easily appear with benefactives, whereas verbs of destruction easily appear with malefactives. It is also common for the added "affected argument" to be understood as the possessor of the theme of the verb root, since an event that changes an object X typically indirectly affects the owner of X (see section 8.1). This range of meanings is very typical of a certain kind of applicative across languages, and hence must be more than accidental homophony. Inspired by Jackendoff (1983), I assume that all of these "affected arguments" are subtypes of a more general proto-role "path." Since the benefactive/goal interpretation is statistically the most common, I follow the literature in calling these benefactive applicative constructions, but this can be confusing because the meaning is sometimes exactly the opposite. The benefactive applicative is the only type found productively in Mohawk and is by far the most common in other polysynthetic languages as well. Thus, I will concentrate almost entirely on it, mentioning other types only in passing.

Building on Marantz 1984, in Baker 1988a I analyzed all applicatives as being derived by incorporation from an abstract source in which the benefactive morpheme was an adposition that θ-marked the affected object. Thus, the structure for examples like (70b) was be taken to be (71).

(71)

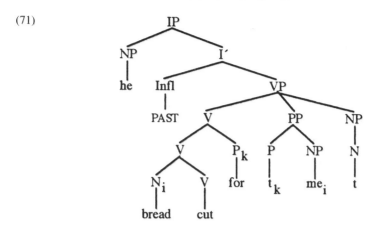

The preposition incorporation (PI) in the structure in (71) was accomplished by head movement and was subject to exactly the same formal principles as the noun incorporation and verb incorporation structures discussed in chapters 7 and 8. Notice that (71) contains a ternary-branching VP, so that both the head of PP and the head of NP can incorporate. However, the essential structure can easily be updated to a Larsonian system that includes a binary branching VP and a higher VP shell containing the agent argument, thereby building on Larson's (1988) account of the well-known binding and word order asymmetries found in double object constructions.

However, there are both theoretical and empirical reasons to think that this analysis is not entirely correct for the polysynthetic languages. The theoretical problem is that (71) is not compatible with the MVC. It was crucial to the account in Baker 1988a that the verb assigned a θ-role to its PP complement; otherwise, PI would be blocked by a kind of adjunct island effect. Meanwhile, the P itself assigned a distinct θ-role "reference object" to its NP complement. Thus, if we annotate the structure in (71) with the relevant argument structures and add two agreement factors (both put in Infl for simplicity) we get (72).

(72)

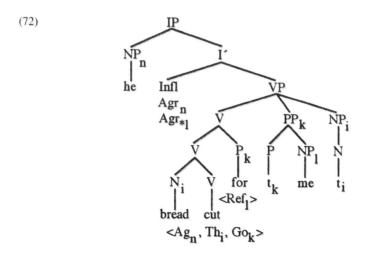

Does the structure in (72) satisfy the MVC? Interpreting the principles strictly, the answer is no. The main verb selects three arguments: the agent, the theme, and the PP goal. The agent can trigger agreement, the PP argument is represented by incorporation of the P, and the theme argument can be expressed either by agreement or by incorporation of the head N into the V. Thus, the MVC is satisfied with respect to the verb. The problem arises with the argument of the incorporated adposition. Since this is not incorporated—and indeed could not incorporate directly into the verb by the Head Movement Constraint (HMC)—it must trigger agreement. However, there cannot be any functional category that hosts agreement features between the PP and the verb; if there were, PI into the verb would be blocked by the Proper Head Movement Generalization (PHMG). Thus, the affected object would have to trigger agreement in one of the functional categories dominating VP. However, the affected object argument is not visible to these agreements, given the CAR (see chapters 5 and 7), which states that an agreement element can only be coindexed with something contained in the unique argument structure of the X^0 it is adjoined to—here the complex verb subsequent to verb raising. This complex verb inherits its argument structure from the verb root; thus, it contains the path role (bearing index k), but crucially not the reference object role (bearing index l). Thus, agreement cannot be coindexed with NP_l in (72). Since NP_l cannot incorporate into the verb and cannot trigger agreement, (72) is ruled out by the MVC. This line of reasoning is very much like the one developed in chapter 8 that (correctly) rules out most instances of possessor raising and causatives of most transitive verbs in the polysynthetic languages. Moreover, adopting more recent assumptions about phrase structure does not affect this reasoning in any significant way. Apparently, then, the system predicts that applicatives cannot be derived by PI in polysynthetic languages, at least by this derivational route.

As an aside, I mention one obvious way to solve the MVC problems surrounding (72) that is ruled out for independent reasons. This is the option of incorporating the argument of the P into P before P incorporates into the verb. This would give the partial syntactic structure in (73) for a hypothetical example meaning 'He cut bread for the baby.'

(73)

The substructure in (73) satisfies the conditions on head movement and gives appropriate morphological representation to both the path argument of 'cut' and the reference object of 'for'. The theme of 'cut' would then have the option of either incorporating or being coindexed with an agreement factor. Either way, the MVC is satisfied, with a final morphological structure like (74).

(74)   [Agr$_m$ [Agr$_k$ [[baby$_n$ for$_i$]   cut]   Asp] tense]
                    <R$_n$><Ref$_n$> <Ag$_m$, Th$_k$, Go$_i$>

Nevertheless, this type of derivation is impossible in Mohawk. There is no benefactive adposition to test this with, but similar examples with locative adpositions would look something like (75).

(75)   a. *Wa'-k-atekhwara-hné-hrΛ-'.
              FACT-1sS-table-LOC-put-PUNC
              'I put it on the table.'

       b. *Wa'-ke-'nerohkw-a-ku-(tsher)-íta-'
              FACT-1sS-box-Ø-in-(NOM)-put.in-PUNC
              'I put it in the box.'

       c. *Wa'-ke-nakt-oku-(tsher-a)-yΛ-'.
              FACT-1sS-bed-under-(NOM-Ø)-lay-PUNC
              'I laid it down under the bed.'

These forms can be ruled out on morphological grounds. The only kind of compound verb that is productively allowed in Mohawk is N–V compounds; even V–V compounds are ruled out, except for a few lexicalized forms. The N–P combination formed by the first X^0 movement is of category P, by standard principles of adjunction. Moreover, the entire N–P–V complex must be classified as a compound, since at least the N and the V are roots. Therefore, the complex verb form in (73) is actually a P–V compound—a type that is not permitted in Mohawk. Derivations of this kind are typically ruled out in other polysynthetic languages as well, perhaps for the same reason. I leave open the question of whether derivations of this type are ever possible or not; if not, then perhaps there is something more fundamentally wrong with the structure in (73).[22] In any case, it is clear that this is not the structure of the applicative construction.

A more empirically oriented concern with a pure PI theory of applicatives comes from the order of morphemes. We have assumed throughout that head movement consistently adjoins the moved element to the left of its landing site. Thus, incorporated nouns always come before the verb stem, and lower verb stems consistently come before a higher predicate such as a causative or desiderative element. Extending this to PI, the applicative morpheme should appear to the left of the verb root, either before the incorporated noun or between the incorporated noun root and the verb stem. Indeed, given the Larsonian assumption that the V and the PP form the innermost constituent, a strong version of the Cycle would favor incorporating the P before the N, leading to the order [noun [ben [verb]]]. This order is never found. Rather, the benefactive applicative morpheme is found in one of two places. In (70), it follows the verb root, coming between that root and the aspect suffix. The same order is found in Nahuatl:

(76)   Ni-quin-xōchi-tēmo-*lia.*   (Andrews 1975:164)
       1sS-3pO-flower-seek-BEN/PRES
       'I seek flowers for them.'

This is also the order of the Bantu applicative, and indeed all of the other languages surveyed in Baker 1988a. In other languages, the applicative morpheme appears as a prefix toward the beginning of the verbal complex. More specifically, it precedes the incorporated noun root and often adverbial material as well, but follows the object agreement prefix. This is the morpheme order found in the Gunwinjguan languages, as in (77) from Mayali, (78) from Ainu, and (79), from Wichita.

(77)   Na-mege daboldabolk bandi-*marne*-ganj-ginje-ng.   (Evans 1991:210)
       I-that   old.people   3pS/3pO-BEN-meat-cook-PAST/PERF
       'They cooked meat for the old people.'

(78)   A-Ø-*ko*-tam-enere.   (Shibatani 1990:69)
       1sS-3sO-APPL-sword-swing
       'I swung the sword at them.'

(79)   I-s-kí-*ic*-ʔasi-reʔe.   (Rood 1976:41)
       IMPER-2sS-1sO-BEN-shoe-make
       'Make me one shoe.'

(Southern Tiwa and Chukchee have no clear-cut applicative morpheme, although in Southern Tiwa it may be absorbed into the agreement prefix.) Perhaps, then, it is actually a good thing that the MVC does not allow a simple PI derivation.

We must look for a new source for applicative constructions. Suppose in this quest that one trusts the morpheme orders. Then there must, in fact, be two distinct sources of applicatives. The applicative in Mohawk and Nahuatl must be a kind of higher predicate that takes a projection of the verb root as a complement; only in this way would it become a suffix. In fact, constructions of this type are independently attested in languages of the world. Typically, the higher predicate is a ditransitive verb such as 'give', which takes the benefactee as its goal argument and a VP as its theme argument. Such constructions are found in Japanese, for example (Zushi 1992):

(80)   John-ga Mary-ni hon-o   kat-te   age-ta.
       John-NOM Mary-DAT book-ACC buy-CONJ give-PAST
       'John gave Mary the favor of buying a book.'

They are also found in South Asian languages. Notice that the meaning of this example is more or less the same as 'John bought a book for Mary'; compare Shibatani (1992), who explicitly draws the parallel between benefactive applicatives and this type of construction in Japanese and Sinhala. Furthermore, in a verb-final language one finds the sequence 'buy–give', so having a verb stem meaning 'give' evolve into a benefactive suffix attached to 'buy' is a very simple historical change.

On the other hand, the applicative morphemes in Gunwinjguan, Ainu, and Wichita appear on the left of the verbal complex. Thus, they must be adjoined material that starts out subordinate to the matrix verb. Indeed, the phenomenon of preposition incorporation is well attested, particularly in verb-final languages (Craig and Hale 1988). Example (81) gives a set of examples from Slave (Rice 1989:770).

(81)   a. Denǫ   ghá ts'a nį?ǫ.
          REFL/mother for hat 3s/gave
          'She gave her mother a hat.'

       b. Ts'a denǫ   ghá-nį?ǫ.
          hat REFL/mother for-3s/gave
          'She gave her mother a hat.'

       c. Ts'a se-ghá-nį?ǫ.
          hat 1sO-for-3s/gave
          'She gave me a hat.'

Since PPs come before the verb in verb-final languages, having a P turn into a prefix is also a small historical step. However, (81b) is unlike the type of PI discussed in Baker 1988a in two respects. First, the incorporated preposition is more or less at the left periphery of the verb. Second, it often forms a kind of morphological constituent with an object agreement, as in (81c). Therefore, the construction often looks more like the cliticization of an oblique pronoun than like compounding or derivational affixation.

In the remainder of this section, I develop these two analyses and show how they avoid the MVC problems associated with the original PI analysis. The resulting syntax of these two types of applicatives turns out to be almost the same in most respects. However, these is a subtle difference in how the two kinds of applicative interact with unaccusative verbs. This confirms that, in fact, two slightly different structures are involved.

9.3.1 Higher-Predicate Applicatives

Let us take the Mohawk type of applicative first, because it is relatively straight-forward. Some additional examples of this morpheme combining with a transitive verb are:

(82)   a. Kʌ́tsu ʌ-ku-yéna-'s-e'.
          fish   FUT-1sS/2sO-catch-BEN-PUNC
          'I will catch fish for you.'

       b. Wa'-khe-tshʌ́ry-a-'s-e'   ne atyá'tawi.
          FACT-1sS/FsO-find-Ø-BEN-PUNC NE dress
          'I found a dress for her.'

In previous chapters, I ignored the applicative morpheme, assuming that the syntax of a verb that had acquired a goal argument from the attachment of the applicative morpheme was the same as that of a simple verb that selected a goal inherently. If this assumption can be justified, then what has been said previously about agreement, noun incorporation, and so on will carry over to these examples with little further comment. Indeed, this result is rather easily achieved with one or two extensions of the theory of complex predicates presented in chapter 8.

The first step is to establish the underlying structure of these examples. By hypothesis, this should be roughly the same as (80) in Japanese. Thus, the applicative morpheme is a three-place predicate that means something like 'give'; it selects an agent, a theme, and a goal. The goal phrase is a PP headed by a null P of the kind discussed in the last section, as is typical for this type of verb. The only unusual thing about the applicative morpheme then is that its theme argument is a VP.[23] Thus, the structure of (70b) is (83).[24]

(83)

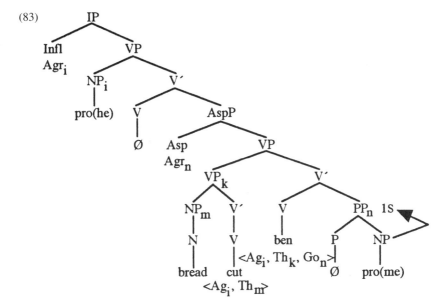

One point that needs to be clarified with respect to the structure in (83) is how the agent θ-role of the embedded verb is handled. This VP is unusual as an argument in that it has an unassigned role at the point where it combines with 'give'. Significantly, however, this unassigned role matches an unassigned agent role of the argument-taking verb. Under these circumstances, I assume that the agent role of the embedded verb can be discharged by θ-role identification with the corresponding role of the higher verb (Higginbotham 1985). Semantically, this means that whatever is the agent of the favor-giving act (here 'he') also will be the agent of the cutting act. This is the correct interpretation.

Given the structure in (83), the surface form can easily be derived. Since there are at most two agreement factors in the construction and at least four arguments (not counting the argument relationship between the null P and its NP object, which satisfies the MVC vacuously), there must be two instances of incorporation. Since only themes are in a position to incorporate, there are no choices here: 'bread' must adjoin to the left of 'cut',[25] and then 'cut' must adjoin to the left of the benefactive morpheme. Next, the triadic argument structure of the benefactive morpheme is chosen as the argument structure of the whole complex, and the complex combines with the functional categories in the usual way. The agreement factors adjoined to Infl and Asp can then be coindexed with the agent and the goal arguments[26] of the benefactive morpheme, respectively, in accordance with the CAR. Because the agent argument of 'cut' is coindexed with the agent argument of the benefactive morpheme, the outer agreement is automatically coindexed with it as well. This results in the morphological structure in (84).

(84) [Agr$_i$ [Agr$_n$ [[bread$_m$ cut$_k$]   Ben]   Asp] tense]
        $<$R$_m$$>$ $<$Ag$_i$, Th$_m$$>$$<Ag_i$, Th$_k$, Go$_n$$>$

This has the correct morpheme order and satisfies the MVC. Indeed, the structure is very much like that of a simple triadic verb such as *u* 'give' or *ni* 'lend'. The reason for the similarity is simply that the benefactive morpheme is itself a triadic verb with the same general lexical properties, and it is the head of the construction. From this it follows that its interactions with agreement and incorporation are essentially the same as those of other triadic verbs, as assumed in chapter 5.

Unergative verbs also take the benefactive applicative suffix productively in Mohawk. A range of examples was given in section 5.2.1, of which (85) is typical.

(85)   Λ-hi-yó'tΛ-hs-e'.   (D&D:427)
       FUT-1sS/MsO-work-BEN-PUNC
       'I will work for him.'

The analysis generalizes easily to this class of examples. The structure of (85) is identical to (83), except that the embedded verb does not take a theme argument in this case. Thus, the verb root is the only element inside the VP argument of the benefactive morpheme, and the NI that was the first step in deriving (84) does not take place. Otherwise, the derivation is identical: the lower verb left adjoins to the benefactive morpheme, morphologically expressing the theme argument of the latter, while the two agreement factors express the shared agent role and the goal role of the benefactive morpheme.

Unaccusative verbs are more interesting. The benefactive applicative morpheme attaches quite productively to verbs of this class also, as shown in section 5.2.1. However, this time there are some restrictions. In particular, the theme argument must either be grammatically neuter or overtly incorporated, while the verb shows only object agreement with the new, affected object. In (86), one set of examples is repeated that illustrates these generalizations.

(86)   a. Sak wa-hó-[a]hs-Λ'-s-e'   ne ówise'.
          Sak FACT-MsO-thing-fall-BEN-PUNC   NE glass
          'The glass fell on Sak.'

       b. *Sak wa-huwa-yá't-Λ'-s-e'   ne owirá'a.
          Sak FACT-FsS/MsO-body-fall-BEN-PUNC NE baby
          'The baby fell on Sak.'

       c. Sak wa-ho-wír-Λ'-s-e'.
          Sak FACT-MsO-baby-fall-BEN-PUNC
          'The baby fell on Sak.'

In fact, only one adjustment is needed to accommodate this class of examples: apparently, the agent argument of the benefactive morpheme is optional. This is expressed in the following lexical entry:

(87)   benefactive: Verb   (syntactic category)
                              hs, 's, Λ, Λni, . . .   (phonological forms)
                              $<$(Ag), Th, Go, e$>$ (argument structure)

Once this is done, (88) is a legitimate underlying structure for (86c).

(88)

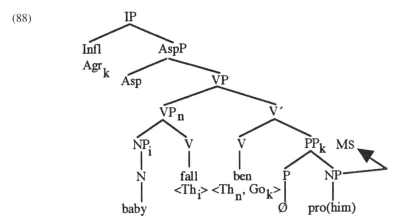

In (88), the benefactive morpheme takes a VP as its theme and a PP with a null P as its goal, as before. This time, however, the lower VP does not have an unassigned agent role associated with it. Hence, the benefactive morpheme can appear in its agentless guise as well.[27] On this analysis, the most literal gloss of (86c) would be something like 'That the baby fell happened to Sak,' where *happen* is a theme–goal verb in English. The principles of agreement and incorporation now take over. Since the matrix verb does not assign an external θ-role, Asp does not have accusative Case, by Burzio's Generalization. Hence, there is only one agreement factor, generated in Infl. This agreement factor must be coindexed with the goal argument of the benefactive morpheme, because that argument is unincorporable. Meanwhile, 'baby' incorporates into 'fall', expressing the theme relationship between them; the resulting complex then incorporates into the benefactive morpheme, expressing the other theme relationship. This derivation satisfies the MVC. Moreover, the agreement in Infl must show up as a $+O$ "object" agreement form, because it is coindexed with an NP that is c-commanded by a co-argument (the SAP), as discussed at length in section 5.4. This, then, accounts for the essential features of examples like (86).

For purposes of this chapter, the most important point to notice about this construction is that the verbal complex cannot agree with the theme argument of the unaccusative root as well as with the goal. Such agreement is impossible for two reasons. First, the unaccusative nature of the construction means that only one agreement factor is available, and this is needed to express the goal argument. Second, since the theme argument is only the argument of the embedded verb, and the matrix verb has arguments that the embedded verb does not share, the theme argument is not accessible to the agreement factors by the CAR. This explains why (86b) is ruled out. Ruled out for the same reason are first and second person combinations such as 'You will fall on me' (spoken, say, to a baby). As we will see, this restriction is a distinctive characteristic of higher-predicate-type applicatives.

Since this analysis is based on the assumption that the benefactive morpheme in Mohawk is a higher predicate, it is reasonable to ask whether there is etymological evidence that it came from a verb historically. In fact, Deering and Delisle

(1976:426) report that some of the allomorphs of the benefactive morpheme seem
to be related to verb roots. The case they specifically cite is that of the ʌni allomorph, which may be related to *ni*, a three-place verb root meaning 'lend'. An
even better case might be the few verbs like 'visit' and 'blame' that take *awi* as
their form of the benefactive in the stative (Deering and Delisle 1976:430); *awi* is
also the suppletive stative form of the ordinary verb *u* 'give'. Conceivably, the ʌ
form of the benefactive is also related to *u* 'give', since there are phonologically
governed [u]–[ʌ] alternations in the language. However, I know of no plausible
source for the *'s* form of the benefactive morpheme, which is the most common.
Overall, then, the similarities between the allomorphs of the benefactive and triadic verb roots are suggestive but not overwhelming.

   Also relevant to this question is the fact that adding the benefactive morpheme
to a stative/adjectival verb produces an interesting change in its inflectional pattern:

(89)   a. Ka-nutar-áksʌ.
           NsS-soup-bad
           'The soup is bad.'

       b. Wa-ho-nutar-áksʌ-'s-e'.
           FACT-MsO-soup-bad-BEN-PUNC
           'The soup went bad on him.'

(90)   a. Ka-nakt-íyo.
           NsS-bed-good
           'The bed is good, it is a nice bed.'

       b. Wa-ha-tshʌ́ri-'   kanúwe' kíkʌ wa-ho-nakt-íyo-hs-e'. (D&D:480)
           FACT-MsS-find-PUNC where   that FACT-MsO-bed-good-BEN-PUNC
           'He found somewhere that was a nice place for him (to sleep).'

Simple stative/adjectival verbs in Mohawk do not take aspect suffixes, because
they do not have an event position in their argument structures (see section 8.4).
However, when benefactive morphology is added to a stative verb, an aspect suffix
becomes necessary. Thus the (b) examples are both in the punctual aspect and the
factual mode. This change would be a strange one if the benefactive morpheme
were an adposition; however, it is exactly what one expects if the benefactive
morpheme is a verb meaning 'give' or 'happen to', since this verb plausibly has
its own e-role (see (87)).

   One of the major motivations for the higher-predicate analysis of the Mohawk
benefactive morpheme is that it explains the gross position of that morpheme
within the complex word—the fact that it appears after the verb root but before
aspect suffixes. In fact, this analysis also explains most of the fine-grained aspects
of morpheme order as well. In Baker 1988a:392–400, I pointed out that benefactive applicative morphemes must follow causative morphemes in many languages
and offered a partial explanation for this fact in Swahili. The same empirical generalization holds in Mohawk. Thus, suppose that one starts with an unaccusative
verb root to which both the causative morpheme and the benefactive morpheme
can attach. When both morphemes are desired, the causative must always combine
with the verb root first, as shown in (91) (cf. Lounsbury 1953:73).

(91) a. Wa'-t-hake-wis-a-hrí'-t-ʌ-'.
      FACT-DUP-MsS/1sO-glass-Ø-break-CAUS-BEN-PUNC
      'He broke my glass; He broke the ice for me.'

    b. *Wa'-t-hake-wis-a-hrí'-s-a-ht-e'.
      FACT-DUP-MsS/1sO-glass-Ø-break-BEN-Ø-CAUS-PUNC
      'He made the glass break for/on me.'

Translating these morpheme ordering facts into hierarchical embedding facts, we see that a causative predicate can be embedded under a benefactive predicate, but not vice versa. This is what we expect. The causative predicate combines with the unaccusative base to form a transitive VP, and transitive VPs are readily embedded under benefactive predicates, as shown in (83). On the other hand, the benefactive predicate combines with the unaccusative base to form a VP that has a theme and a goal argument, as shown in (88). Section 8.2.1 showed that VPs with a theme and a goal cannot be embedded under the causative in Mohawk; there is no way that is consistent with the CAR for agreement to express both the agent of the causative verb and the goal of the embedded VP. This explains the facts in (91). In contrast, any VP that has an agent argument can be embedded under the purposive morpheme (see section 8.3.1). Thus, we correctly predict that the purposive morpheme (unlike the causative) can follow the benefactive morpheme in a derived word structure (see Lounsbury 1953:73 and Deering and Delisle 1976:426–427):

(92) ʌ-hi-'nikhu-'sé-hra-'.
      FUT-1sS/MsO-sew-BEN-PURP-PUNC
      'I'll go there to sew for him.'

In principle, the benefactive morpheme should be able to follow the purposive morpheme as well, but this does not seem to be possible; this aspect of morpheme order I must treat as idiosyncratic.[28] Nevertheless, most of the fine-grained interactions between the benefactive morpheme and other higher-predicate morphemes in Mohawk are as expected. I will leave it to the interested reader to work out the detailed structures of these examples; although complex, they are predictable combinations of the structures already considered.

The other polysynthetic language with a clearly suffixal applicative morpheme is Nahuatl. This should be subject to the same higher-predicate analysis, and the data I have are consistent with this claim. The applicative suffix attaches productively to transitive verbs, deriving a form that acts with respect to agreement and noun incorporation very much like a simple ditransitive verb of the 'give' class[29]; a typical example was given in (76). The applicative also attaches to unergative verbs, as in (93).

(93) Ni-mitz-tza'tzi-lia. (Launey 1981:192)
      1sS-2sO-shout-BEN/PRES
      'I shout to/for you.'

Other, similar examples include verbs meaning 'laugh', 'cry', and 'sing'. The crucial question, however, is how unaccusative verbs work. Here, the evidence is fragmentary. Launey gives no clear examples of *lia* attaching to an unaccusative verb. Andrews (1975:103) gives some examples like the following, which may be relevant:

(94)   tla-nemi-lia
        3INDEF-live-BEN
        'to think about something' (verb stem)

However, he also observes that this is idiomatic and makes the suggestive remark: "Applicatives derived from intransitive verbs frequently have a meaning that shifts idiomatically away from that of the source." Other examples of this type are: *nāhauati* 'to have a loud clear sound', whose applicative means 'to give commands to someone'; *tlaōco-ya* 'to be sad', whose applicative means 'to pity someone'; *cocō-ya* 'to be sick', whose applicative means 'to hate someone'. If we put these aside as lexicalized examples, we can tentatively conclude that applicatives of unaccusative verbs are at least limited in Nahuatl. There are two ways this might play out. One is that productive applicatives of unaccusative verbs are possible in Nahuatl, but they have not been distinguished from unergatives in the sources. In this case, my theory predicts that such applicatives will be subject to the same restrictions as in Mohawk; in particular, the theme argument should not be able to be a first or second person pronoun. The second possibility is that productively formed benefactives of unaccusative verbs are impossible in Nahuatl. If so, this might be explained in terms of the (unexplained) fact that NI into unaccusative verbs seems not to be found in classical Nahuatl; the grammars make no mention of intransitive subject incorporation on a par with transitive object incorporation.[30] Now, noun incorporation into an unaccusative verb is required for that verb to have an applicative, as shown previously. Thus, in languages such as Chichewa and Sesotho, which have higher-predicate applicatives but no NI, benefactive applicatives of unaccusative verbs are systematically ungrammatical (see section 5.4). It may be that special limitations on NI in Nahuatl put it into this class as well.

Nahuatl is also interesting in that the analysis of its applicative just sketched is quite similar to the analysis developed for its causative in section 8.2.3. In particular, both the causative morpheme and the applicative morpheme are triadic 'give'-like verbs that take a VP as their theme argument. The examples in (95) are a near-minimal pair; note that they can be given almost the same literal gloss.

(95)   a. Ni-c-tla-pāqui-lia.   (Andrews 1975:107)
           1sS-3sO-3INDEF-wash-BEN/PRES
           'I wash things for him, I give him washing of things.'

        b. Ni-mitz-tla-pāca-l-tia.   (Andrews 1975:108)
           1sS-2sO-3INDEF-wash-NONACT-CAUS/PRES
           'I have you wash things, I give you washing of things.'

This may make the two analyses seem a bit too close for comfort. In fact, the similarity is arguably a good thing. It has been pointed out in the literature that causatives and benefactives are homophonous in some languages; Indonesian apparently has this property, as do certain Australian languages (Austin, to appear). This makes sense if both causative constructions and benefactive constructions can evolve from complex constructions using the same higher verb. Indeed, Nahuatl itself has similar homophonies. The most productive form of the applicative is *lia* and the most productive form of the causative is *tia,* but there are a few verbs that form causatives by suffixing *lia* (Andrews 1975:93–94, Launey 1981:276), as well as a few that form applicatives by suffixing *tia* (Andrews 1975:106, Launey 1981:194). Possibly these two suffixes even came from the same morpheme (*ia?*) historically; in any case the lexical difference between them is somewhat fuzzy. Rather, the key difference between the causative and the benefactive lies in the treatment of the agent argument of the embedded verb. In the benefactive, the lower agent is identified with the agent argument of the matrix verb, as shown in (83). Thus, in (95a), I give him the favor of *me* washing the clothes. In the caus-ative, there is no such identification; hence, the higher predicate has the effect of introducing a new agent, the causer. In Nahuatl, this difference shows up morpho-logically in that the benefactive morpheme attaches to the simple, active stem, whereas the causative morpheme attaches to the nonactive stem in *l*. The argument of the embedded verb suppressed by this *l* is then understood as the same as the goal argument of the matrix verb. Thus, in (95b), I give you the property of *you* having washed the clothes. This last element of interpretation is not explained directly in my account; I leave open whether it has the status of an extrasyntactic inference, or whether it can be attributed to a theory of thematic control of the kind explored by Edwin Williams.

9.3.2 Adpositional Applicatives

Consider next those polysynthetic languages in which the applicative morpheme is a prefix that appears before the verb root and any incorporated noun. This class includes the Gunwinjguan languages, Ainu and Wichita. In (96), a typical example from Mayali is given, repeated from earlier in this section.

(96) Na-mege daboldabolk bandi-*marne*-ganj-ginje-ng.
      I-that   old.people   3PS/3PO-BEN-meat-cook-PAST/PERF
      'They cooked meat for the old people.'

Since the preverbal position is characteristic of adjoined elements, it is reasonable to think that these are real instances of incorporated adpositions.[31] However, we have already seen that the simple PI derivation of Baker 1988a runs afoul of the MVC. Moreover, the benefactive applicative morpheme consistently shows up outside of any incorporated noun root, rather than inside of it, as we might expect given that the PP forms a closer constituent with the verb than does the theme NP.

There is, however, another way of incorporating the adposition that solves both of these puzzles. Suppose that rather than having its head incorporate directly into the verb, the PP as a whole moves into the specifier of AspP. Nothing blocks such movement, at least if the main verb is transitive or unergative. From this position, the P can incorporate into the head of AspP. This is consistent with the principles governing head movement as presented in chapter 7. The structure of (96) would then be (97).

(97)

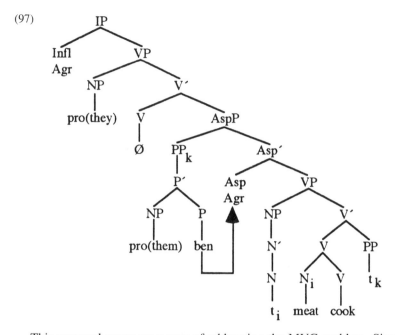

This proposal opens up a way of addressing the MVC problem. Since the verb incorporates into Asp from inside the complement and the P incorporates from inside the specifier, the two processes can happen in either order as far as the principles of movement are concerned. Suppose that the P incorporates first. The CAR says that an agreement factor can be coindexed with a position in the argument structure of the X^0 it is adjoined to. At this point in the derivation, there is no competition with the arguments of the verb. Thus, the agreement factor in Asp can be coindexed with the argument of the adposition. Next, the verb is incorporated into Asp. Now there are two distinct argument structures associated with the complex Asp, so one of them must be chosen to be the argument structure of the whole. We choose the argument structure of the verb, so that its arguments can be identified. Crucially, however, the Agr in Asp retains the index already assigned to it, the one shared with the argument of P. The whole complex then moves through the higher V position and into Infl. The Agr in Infl can now be coindexed with any argument of the complex Asp; in particular, it can be coindexed with the agent argument. The theme and goal arguments of the verb are morphologically expressed by NI and PI, respectively. In this way, the MVC is satisfied. This derivation is summarized in (98), from the point of view of the complex functional head that is formed at each point.

(98) a. $[_{Asp}$ Agr $[Asp]]$ (pre-incorporation)

   b. $[_{Asp}$ Agr$_n$ $[_{Asp}$ ben$_k$ $[Asp]]$ (incorporation of P)
         $<Ref_n>$

   c. $[_{Asp}$ Agr$_n$ $[_{Asp}$ ben$_k$ $[_{Asp}$ $[_V$ meat$_i$ - eat] $[Asp]]]]$ (V-incorporation)
         $<Ref_n>$ $<Ag_m, Th_i, Go_k>$

   d. $[_{Inf_l}$ Agr$_m$ $[_{Asp}$ Agr$_n$ $[_{Asp}$ ben$_k$ $[_{Asp}$ $[_V$meat$_i$ - eat] $[Asp]]]]$ Infl]   (Asp to I raising)
         $<Ref_n>$ $<Ag_m, Th_i, Go_k>$

The crucial point about this derivation is that the adposition has access to the agreement factor in Asp before its argument structure is repressed by combination with the verb. This contrasts with the Baker 1988a type of derivation in which the adposition combined with the verb first; in that case, the choice of which argument structure is carried forward has to be made before anything in either argument structure is agreed with, resulting inevitably in a violation of the MVC.

The derivation in (98) also shows how the observed morpheme order is derived. I have assumed throughout that an Agr is adjoined to Asp if Asp has Case features. Like all adjoined elements, it appears to the left of Asp. I have also assumed that X^0 movement attaches a category to the immediate left of the head of its target, inside of other things that are adjoined to that head (see section 1.6). Thus, the verb root generally appears *between* the aspect morpheme and its associated agreement. These same assumptions entail that the adposition will appear between the two, as in (98b). Then, when it is time for the V to incorporate into Asp, it again adjoins to the left of the head of its target, deriving the order [Agr [P [V [Asp]]]], as in (98c). Moreover, if the head of the theme NP incorporates into the verb, it must do so before the verb moves to Asp, by the "shortest movement" property of the Economy framework (the HMC of earlier work). The verb and the noun thus already form a morphological unit at the time that the verb combines with the adposition. In this way, the correct morpheme ordering is derived.

Although this solution has been implemented with some technical gimmicks,[32] it is worth emphasizing its basic intuition. That intuition is simply that incorporated adpositions often form a kind of morphological constituent with an agreement factor, as in (98b). This is something that can be observed rather directly in verb-final languages with relatively transparent adposition incorporation, such as Slave and certain Caucasian languages (see (81c)). This explains why the applicative morpheme shows up close to the object agreement morpheme, rather than next to the verb root, and why the agreement factor can be coindexed with the argument of the applicative morpheme, satisfying the MVC.

In spite of their rather different underlying structures, the morphosyntax of the adpositional applicative turns out to be very similar to that of the higher-predicate applicative. In both, the full person/number/gender agreement is with the agent and the goal (affected object) of the construction, since these are the arguments that cannot be incorporated. Moreover, the lower agreement in Asp must be the one to agree with the goal NP, because it alone can be in the necessary configuration with the P. Thus, the goal triggers "object" agreement and the agent triggers "subject" agreement. Finally, the possibilities for the theme are limited by the fact that there is no agreement factor available to it. Hence, the theme must be incorporated, either overtly or in the guise of a null cognate object (see section 5.3). Thus, Evans (to appear b) shows that in Mayali animate nouns that do not normally incorporate are coerced into doing so in applicatives such as (99).

(99)   Nga-marne-beywurd-berrebbom.
        1sS/3sO-BEN-son/daughter-promise/PAST/PERF
        'I promised him/her my daughter/son.'

This is very much like what we previously saw in Mohawk. More generally, the theme argument of an applicative has to be third person. In the relatively unusual case where one wants to express, say, a first person theme in Mayali, the applicative construction cannot be used; rather a highly marked prepositional construction is used instead (Evans to appear b):

(100)   Arduk abbard an-berlwo-ng   kuri nanih bininj.
        my   father 3sS/1sO-give.in.marriage-PAST/PERF LOC that   man
        'My father gave me in marriage to that man.'

Apart from this, overt PPs are not possible with triadic verbs. Thus, Mayali applicatives act like Mohawk applicatives in these respects, as we expect. The same is true for the Gunwinjguan languages, Ainu, and Wichita.

This analysis generalizes readily to applicatives formed from unergative verbs. As expected, these behave much like applicatives formed from transitive verbs, except that there is no need to incorporate a theme argument. An example from Mayali is given in (101). (See also Shibatani 1990:65 for Ainu, and Rood 1976:41 for Wichita.)

(101)   A-marne-yime-n. (Evans 1991:211)
        1sS/3sO-BEN-say-NONPAST
        'I will say to her.'

Once again, the situation is more complex with unaccusative verb roots. Recall that applicatives of such verbs are possible in Mohawk, but they are subject to rather tight restrictions. In particular, the theme argument must incorporate, either as a full lexical noun root or as a null cognate object. Examples of this type are possible in Mayali and Ainu as well:

(102)   Ngan-marne-ganj-warre-m-inj. (Evans 1991:211)
        (3sS)/1sO-BEN-meat-bad-INCH-PAST/PUNC
        'The meat went bad on me.'

(103)   Kane   rakko Ø-o-tumi-osma. (Shibatani 1990:63)
        golden otter 3s-APPL-war-begin
        'The war started because of the golden sea otter.'

However, neither Ainu nor the Gunwinjguan languages are limited to this type of example. Indeed, the theme argument of an unaccusative applicative can even be a first or second person pronominal, something that is never possible in Mohawk. Shibatani (1990:66–67) discusses this explicitly, claiming that applicatives can be formed rather freely from unaccusatives in Ainu. Two of his best examples are the following:

(104)   a. A-kor   kotan a-Ø-e-sirepa.
           1sS-have village 1sS-3sO-APPL-arrive
           'I have arrived at my village.'

        b. Sake a-Ø-e-niste.
           wine 1sS-3sO-APPL-be.strong
           'I am strong in (drinking) wine.'

Here, the theme argument is first person, so clearly unincorporable. Similar examples are attested in the Gunwinjguan languages. One from Mayali is the following:

(105) Gan-marne-bebm-i. (Evans 1991:210)
       2sS/1sO-BEN-arrive-PAST/IMPF
       'You came out for me, to get me.'

This example has explicitly transitive agreement morphology, with both agreement factors showing non–third person forms. Nevertheless, the same verb hosts NI of its basic argument, showing that it is (or at least may be) unaccusative[33]:

(106) Ngan-marne-djen-bebme-ng. (Evans 1991:211–212)
       3sS/1sO-BEN-tongue-appear-PAST/PERF
       'Her tongue came out on me; She stuck her tongue out at me.'

Similarly, McKay (1975:265–273) gives examples from Rembarrnga of applicatives derived from intransitive verbs meaning 'stand', 'go', 'enter', 'die', 'arrive', and 'leave'. At least two of these (*pol?* 'arrive', and *manj* 'go') have examples in which their theme is incorporated elsewhere in the grammar, confirming that they are unaccusative. Finally, Rembarrnga and Nunggubuyu allow applicatives to be formed from verb stems that have been detransitivized by the addition of a reflexive suffix (McKay 1975:283, Heath 1984:405–406). Such reflexive formations typically derive unaccusative verbs, and thus are quite impossible in Mohawk unless the theme argument is incorporated.[34]

As Shibatani (1990) points out, these examples are problematic for the theory of PI in Baker 1988a; they also contrast with what one finds in Mohawk and the Bantu languages. However, they fall into place rather easily in the current theory. The reason that examples like (105) are ruled out in Mohawk has to do with Burzio's Generalization: because the verb root does not assign an external θ-role, Asp is not a Case assigner. Therefore, it cannot host an agreement factor, and one of the two agreement factors in (105) is unlicensed. The Mayali/Ainu applicative is crucially different, however, in that an adposition is incorporated into the Asp node early in the derivation. Now, adpositions are Case-assigning categories universally. Thus, it is reasonable to say that once the P has incorporated into Asp, the P–Asp combination has the Case features needed to license an agreement factor after all. This is in accordance with the basic intuition that (object) agreement and the incorporated P are closely associated in these languages. At the crucial point in the derivation, the structure of (105) is therefore something like (107). The rest of the derivation then proceeds very much as in (98). The agreement in Asp sanctioned by the Case of P morphologically expresses the reference object of that P. The verb then incorporates into Asp, combining with P (which expresses the goal role of the verb) and giving its argument structure to the complex as a whole. There are two options available for the theme argument of 'arrive'. On the one hand, it can incorporate into the verb before the verb raises into Asp; in that case Mohawk-like sentences such as (102) and (103) will be derived. However, there is no necessity for the theme to incorporate; rather, the verb can move from Asp on to Infl and have its theme argument coindexed with the agreement factor that is there. This produces examples like (104) and (105), which are impossible in Mohawk. Moreover, it follows from this analysis that the lower "object" agreement factor expresses the benefactive/affected object, whereas the subject agreement factor expresses the theme.[35]

(107)

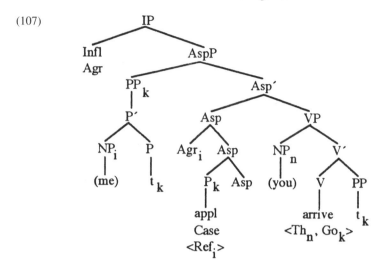

There is one other aspect of the derivation in (107) that still needs to be clarified; this is the very first step—the movement of the PP argument to the specifier of AspP. Although such movement is unproblematic in (97), NP movements comparable to the PP movement in (107) are ruled out, as shown in section 5.4 and Baker 1992c. In particular, (107) seems like a violation of Binding Theory because the trace of the PP is not bound within VP, a complete functional complex that has a distinct subject argument. There seems to be a real difference between PPs and NPs in this respect. Thus, PPs can move past theme NPs and into the subject position in the so-called locative inversion construction[36]:

(108)   a. Someone put a book on the table.

     b. On the table was put a book t.

     c. On the table sits a book t.

In (108a), the theme NP clearly c-commands the locative PP; nevertheless the locative can move past it if the verb is passive, as in (108b) or unaccusative, as in (108c). The same thing can be seen with goal phrases, albeit more marginally:

(109)   a. Susan passed the heirloom ring on to Mary.

     b. To Mary passed the heirloom ring t.

Example (109b) contrasts sharply with *Mary passed the heirloom ring t,* where the goal is expressed as a bare NP, as in dative shift examples. This contrast illustrates clearly the asymmetry between PP complements and NP complements: the former but not the latter can move out of an unaccusative VP.

There are several ways to capture this difference between NPs and PPs theoretically. Perhaps the most appealing involves adopting an intuition used by Cinque (1990:71–73) in a very different context. He observes that NP has a special status among the phrasal categories in that it is the only category whose members are specified as [±pronominal] or [±anaphor]; hence, NPs are the only phrases subject to Binding Theory per se. This seems to be observationally correct: many languages have special NPs that are inherently anaphoric, but languages do not have PPs that are inherently anaphoric in the same sense. (Of course a PP may contain an NP that is an anaphor, but that is a different matter.) This insight has immediate consequences for our situation. The trace left by NP movement to the specifier of AspP may be an anaphor, but the trace left by PP movement to such a position is not—such distinctions are simply not relevant to the PP category. Thus, there is no Binding Theory violation in (107), (108b), (108c), or (109b) after all, and we explain why these sentences are possible.[37] This completes the analysis of adpositional applicatives derived from unaccusative clauses.

In closing, I point out that this account of adposition applicatives is not dependent in any way on the semantics or special lexical properties of the adposition itself. Thus, although my examples have all been animate goals or benefactives, the account generalizes to other path-expressing PPs as well. Indeed, Shibatani (1990:65–66) shows that many kinds of oblique relations can be expressed by the Ainu applicative. For example, the applied object in (110a) is a pure location; in (110b) it is an inanimate goal.

(110)　a.　Poro cise　Ø-Ø-e-horari.　(Shibatani 1990:65)
　　　　　　big　house 3sS-3sO-APPL-live
　　　　　　'He lives in a big house.'

　　　　b.　Kane　rakko riraskitay　a-Ø-e-orawki-re.　(Shibatani 1990:68)
　　　　　　golden otter　high-beam 1sS-3sO-APPL-escape-CAUS
　　　　　　'I let the golden otter escape to the high beam.'

Similarly, the applied object in (103) is a kind of source or cause. Since applicatives in Ainu are formed by adposition incorporation, this range of meaning is not particularly surprising; it more or less recapitulates the range of meanings expressible by path-type PPs in the language.[38] In contrast, the higher-predicate applicative in Mohawk is never used to express pure locational notions. Indeed, the benefactive applicative in such a language is more likely to be homophonous with causative morphology than with a locative applicative, because of its verbal source (see the previous discussion of Nahuatl). Thus, although higher-predicate applicatives and adpositional applicatives look quite similar in many respects, they are not identical in either their syntactic properties or their natural range of meanings.

9.4 Conclusion

At the beginning of this chapter it was mentioned that the existence of the category P is controversial in some of the polysynthetic languages. However, in the course of this chapter we have seen that locative expressions in these languages have a unique cluster of properties that distinguishes them from other categories. These are summarized in (111).

(111)　*Properties of PPs:*
　　　　(i)　They cannot be predicates.
　　　　(ii)　They can be adjuncts licensed independently of any argument position.
　　　　(iii)　They can incorporate the heads of their complements (like a verb).
　　　　(iv)　They take noun-like agreement prefixes (at least in Mohawk and Nahuatl).

This suggests that the locative elements are, in fact, members of a distinct category, not fully reducible to N or V. To the extent that it shares properties with N and V, these can be captured by X-bar theoretic generalizations, possibly making use of Chomsky's features [±V] and [±N]. However, the existence of this category appears to be universal.

However, PPs do have some peculiarities in polysynthetic languages that contribute to the fact that they sometimes have not been recognized as such. I have identified two peculiarities in particular. First, the argument of the P must either agree with the P or incorporate into it, perhaps making the P look like a stative verb or a Case morpheme. Second, PPs with an overt P cannot be arguments of another head because they do not bear Φ-features and thus cannot be agreed with. This has an indirect influence on the class of lexical items that are found in polysynthetic languages, making it impossible for them to have verbs directly comparable to 'put' in English. Indeed, a PP can only be the argument of a verb if the head of the P is lexically null (allowed by only a limited set of verbs, including one type of applicative morpheme), or if the head of the P incorporates into the verb (creating the other type of applicative). In either of these cases, the constituent no longer looks like a PP on the surface. Each of these peculiarities follows in a rather straightforward way from the Polysynthesis Parameter, which places special restrictions on argument relationships.

Notes

1. Certain other locative notions in Mohawk are expressed by elements that are clearly stative verbs, such as *ati* 'at the side of'. These will not be discussed here.

2. Kenneth Hale (personal communication) mentions a possible counterexample: postpositions in Hopi can agree with their "subject." It may be relevant that agreement is with number only in this language.

3. This example may be accepted with a different interpretation, namely "That is the inside of the box." This would be appropriate, for example, if the speaker has a kit to build a doghouse and is pointing to the pieces that will constitute its interior lining. This suggests that locative expressions may under some circumstances be nouns, taking an R-like role in addition to the theme (see section 9.2.2). However, it is clear that this locative never assigns the theme-like role often attributed to it.

4. Rothstein (1983) proposed that XPs were predicates, but that was prior to the VP-internal subject hypothesis. The text proposal is the natural reworking of Rothstein's claim, modified to take this into account.

5. In fact, I believe the same thing can be seen in English, in small clause contexts where there is no copula. Thus, it is relatively difficult for an ordinary locative PP to function as the predicate of a small clause:

(i)

	wash the car.	(VP)
John made me	angry at my mother.	(AP)
	president of the chess club.	(NP)
	*under the bed.	(PP)

Similarly, *I consider Mary in the living room* is awkward. Again, this follows if PPs have no θ-role to assign to a subject, even in English. This analysis entails that in sentences like *I am under the bed* or *Mary is in the living room* the subject gets its θ-role from *be*, rather than from the PP. I believe that this view is not only plausible but independently motivated; however, I will not take the space to go into the matter here.

6. However, *akta* can appear as a bare root if its complement is an internally headed relative clause and thus not incorporable. In this, it is different from the other locative elements.

(i) Tho wa'-k-átyʌ-'   ákta tsi nikáyʌ wa-ha-'sere-ht-a-hnínu-'.
   there FACT-1sS-sit-PUNC near which   FACT-MsS-car-NOM-Ø-buy-PUNC
   'I sat down near the car that he bought.'

7. There is controversy over *'ke,* which can in some cases be analyzed either way (see Michelson 1991a).

8. Generally these "nominalizers" appear on nouns that are historically verbal forms. For example, *atekhwara* 'table' comes from the verb root *ra* 'put' with the incorporated noun root *khw* 'food' and the semireflexive morpheme *at*. Similarly, *'sere* comes from the verb root 'to drag'. (Originally this applied to sledlike vehicles and was later generalized to carriages and then to motor vehicles.) See Deering and Delisle 1976 for a description of the basic facts.

9. The [a] vowels in *a'ke* and *akta* could also be epenthetic, but there is little clear evidence for or against this, because the vowels are followed by two consonants. This means that they attract stress whether they are epenthetic or not, according to the usual rules of Mohawk phonology (see Michelson 1989).

10. This form is morphologically exceptional in taking the *hne* allomorph rather than the *'ke* allomorph, and in the fact that the nominalizer *tsher* is not inserted (see Michelson 1991a). I have included it because it is a convenient form for constructing example sentences.

11. Not all locative morphemes in Nahuatl allow both the (16) structure and the (18) structure. Thus, *c(o)* 'in, on' allows only the NI variant, while *huic* 'against, toward' and *icampa* 'behind' allow only the agreement variant. One way of capturing this morpheme by morpheme variability is to say that Nahuatl does not allow productive N + P compounding. Thus NI into P will be possible if and only if that P is lexically specified as being an affix; *c(o)* is always an affix, *icampa* never is, and *pan* may be an affix optionally. The lexical entries look approximately like (i).

(i) a. *c(o)*   'in, on' <Ref> [N __]
   b. *icampa* 'behind' <Ref>
   c. *pan*   'at'   <Ref> [(N) __]

However, this involves a weakening of the claim in section 1.6 that morphological subcategorization frames are generally predictable in the polysynthetic languages.

12. This exception is probably not an unprincipled one. Mayali also differs from the other Gunwinjguan languages in that the locative morpheme replaces the noun class prefix of the noun, rather than cooccurring with it. This suggests that *gu* is actually a combination of adposition and noun class prefix, with the morphological position of the latter. This is somewhat reminiscent of the way locative morphology interacts with noun class prefixes in some Bantu languages (see, e.g., Bresnan and Kanerva 1989).

13. Mayali also has putative postpositions, such as *ganjdji* 'inside, underneath', *gaddung* '(on) top (of)', and *darngih-djam* 'next to' (Evans 1991:87–88). However, Evans mentions that these elements can also be used as independent adverbials and nominals (e.g., 1991:76). Thus, it is possible that these elements are simple adverbs, with no argument structure at all. If so, the fact that they are not inflected or compounded is perfectly consistent with the MVC.

Another apparent problem for the claim that Ps must incorporate or agree with their reference object comes from Ainu. Shibatani (1990) consistently writes locative Case parti-cles in that language as separate words that follow their NP complements. However, his justification for this is unclear, given that there is, in general, less morphological and phono-logical evidence for when incorporation has taken place in Ainu than in the other polysyn-thetic languages. Shibatani (1990:62–63) raises this issue explicitly in the context of de-termining when a noun is incorporated into the verb and when it is merely adjacent to it (see also section 1.6 for evidence that collocations of a verb with the "auxiliary" *rusuy* 'want' are single words in Ainu, even though Shibatani writes them separately). In the same way, I assume that Ainu Ns really do form complex words with the locative particles. Perhaps more detailed knowledge about the phonology of Ainu could confirm this claim.

14. We might also say that because the locatives are always bound forms, they have no quirky agreement values of their own. This means that the agreement values of the noun must be used. In this the locatives are similar to the purposive morpheme, but different from the stative verbs of 8.4, most of which can be used as independent roots and thus have ±O values of their own.

Notice also that the agreement on the P in (26) has the same form it does on Ns, with the diphthongized vowel [rao], not [ro] as on verbs. This means that P is grouped with N for the purposes of the quasiphonological rules of glide deletion and diphthongization that determine the form of agreement. Similarly, Ps in Nahuatl take N-like possessor agreement forms, rather than V-like object agreement forms. (See note 3 and section 9.2.2 for evidence that locative Ps are often noun-like in some respects.)

15. These examples have only been checked systematically with one primary consul-tant. However, I have not seen examples like (30b) and (30c) in texts, and there is some indication that the other primary consultant also avoids (30a), although that was not a direct focus of inquiry and my fieldnotes are not entirely consistent on this point.

16. Perhaps some notion of "referentiality" is the key. Suppose that an argument posi-tion can only enter into a binding chain if it is referential in some sense. Now pro is always fully referential. Moreover, INs are fully referential in some languages (Mohawk, Mayali), but not in others (Nahuatl, Chukchee). However, it may be that an NP ceases to count as referential when its argument structure is inherited by the complex predicate, because this brings out its latent predicative properties. An account along these lines may be feasible.

17. Although this statement is very generally valid, it is not universal. Thus, in Chi-chewa and some other Bantu languages it is possible for a verb (or other item) to agree with a locative expression in a way that is perfectly parallel to agreement with ordinary NPs. (See Bresnan and Kanerva 1989, Baker 1992a, and Bresnan and Mchombo, to appear, for relevant discussion.) This situation is quite rare, however; I do not know of instances outside the Bantu family.

18. In fact, the context must be constructed with some care for the verbs to be felici-tous without a PP or some kind of locative particle. The location of the putting must be known from the context; otherwise, leaving out the PP is not considered adequately infor-mative. On the other hand, the location must not be a discourse topic; if it is, then a locative pronoun is used. The context in (41) meets these conditions. In fact, the contexts in which the Mohawk verbs can be used seem quite parallel to those in which one can use *put* plus a bare directional particle in English *(I put the book down/in/on)*.

19. Not surprisingly, the object of a preposition must also be disjoint in reference from the subject of the clause.

20. Interestingly, expressions that are morphologically verbs also do not need to be linked to an argument position, even when they are interpreted as nominals. In other words, an "internally headed relative clause" can be used without locative morphology and without being licensed by an NP position. Thus, (i) is like (62a), not (62b).

(i) Ka-'nerohkw-a-hútsi te-w-a'shár-i.
 NsS-box-Ø-black   CIS-NsS-knife-be.in
 'The knife is in the black box.'

This may suggest that IHRCs are bare clauses, not dominated by an NP node—a question left open in section 4.3.2.

21. As stated, (68) is rather stipulative, and it would be highly desirable to deduce it from a more general theory of features and categories. However, to pursue this question properly one would need to have other cases in which one lexical category contained another one with no lexical material, and I know of none offhand; thus, I put this task aside.

22. For example, it might be that P has some characteristics of a functional category, such that the derivation in (73) counts as movement from a lexical category to a functional category and back to a lexical category again, a violation of the PHMG (cf. Li 1990). The one potential case I know of in my language sample is the incorporation of comitative nouns in Rembarrnga, as described by McKay (1975). However, it is not clear that the comitative morpheme is necessarily treated as an adposition in this language. Furthermore, the Rembarrnga construction seems to be historically unstable; it has been reanalyzed as a kind of applicative in Mayali (Evans 1991).

23. Actually, Zushi (1992) assumes that the embedded verb in Japanese heads a full clause, whose subject is a PRO controlled by the matrix subject. Although this structure could be made to work for Mohawk, too, I prefer the VP analysis because it gives a somewhat more natural account of benefactives of unaccusative verbs, where there would be no matrix subject to act as a controller (see later discussion).

24. Structure (83) is very much like the underlying structure that Marantz (1993) attributes to applicatives in Bantu. The one difference is that the benefactee is lower than VP in (83) in accordance with my assumptions about the UTAH and the thematic hierarchy; Marantz reverses the relative order of these two. In Baker 1991b, I explore another possible source for benefactive applicatives cross-linguistically, namely the serial verb construction, as in example (i) from Yoruba.

(i) Ó ra iṣu fún mi.
 he buy yam give me
 'He bought a yam for me.'

This gives more or less the same results as (83) and may, in fact, have some technical advantages. However, I will stick with (83) because it works without the need to explicate how head movement and θ-role assignment take place in serial verb constructions. The task of distinguishing more carefully between these two possible sources for applicative suffixes is left to future research.

25. Alternatively, a null cognate object can incorporate into the lower verb; this produces sentences like those in (82), where the theme nominal does not appear to be incorporated. (See section 5.3 for discussion.)

26. Recall that the null-headed PP acquires Φ-features from the NP it dominates, allowing it to take part in agreement relationships, as discussed above.

27. However, it is not clear why the benefactive morpheme *must* be agentless when it appears with an unaccusative verb. If it did assign an agent θ-role, the result would mean something like 'Mary gave falling of the baby to him.' There is nothing obviously wrong with this meaning; it seems like it could have more or less the same force as the benefactive of a causative verb 'Mary made the baby fall for him.' Nevertheless, forms like (i) are hopelessly impossible in Mohawk and (as far as I know) other languages.

(i) *Uwári wa-huwa-wír-ʌ'-s-e'   ne Sak.
     Mary FACT-FsS/MsO-baby-fall-BEN-PUNC NE Sak

Thus, there may be something missing in the account at this point. Intuitively, what is going on is that the benefactive morpheme and its VP argument must match in their external argument properties; perhaps this result will someday follow from a better understanding of VP complements, which are known to be rather limited across languages.

28. This idiosyncrasy may be due to the fact that the purposive morpheme plays a role in the tense/aspect system of Mohawk (see Postal 1979). This may cause it to appear late in the string, adjacent to the aspect suffix.

29. One complication that does not arise in Mohawk is caused by the animate indefinite object marker *tē* in Nahuatl. This can morphologically express the goal argument, but does not exhaust the object agreement factor. Moreover, when this element is used, the applicative verb shows normal object agreement with the theme of the verb root:

(i) Ni-c-tē-pāqui-lia   (Andrews 1975:107)
     1sS-3sO-3INDEF-wash-BEN/PRES
     'I wash it for someone'

The same agreement pattern occurs if the benefactive argument is expressed by a reflexive morpheme. Given the structure in (83), the lower object is the argument of the lower V but not the higher one. Hence, it should not be able to trigger agreement even if an unused agreement factor were available. This suggests that (83) may not be quite the right structure for benefactive applicatives after all, at least for Nahuatl. Rather, benefactive applicatives are probably derived from a serial verb source like that mentioned in note 24, or a light verb–like source similar to the one used for causatives in section 7.2. Either of these structures would have the property that the theme of the lower verb also counts as the theme of the higher verb, and hence is visible to agreement, explaining (i). However, I will not pursue this because the differences are slight, and I do not have an analysis of *tē* or reflexive morphology in Nahuatl.

30. However, Merlan (1976:183) shows that the subjects of unaccusative verbs may incorporate in the modern dialect she studied.

31. None of the morphemes involved has a very clear etymology that confirms or disconfirms this. Evans (1991:213) gives some possible verbal cognates of *marne* in Mayali; on the other hand, Kenneth Hale (personal communication) believes this element to be adpositional (or perhaps nominal). (The benefactive applicative morpheme in the other Gunwinjguan languages considered here is noncognate *bak*.)

32. In particular, the argument depends crucially on the mechanisms of indices and an ordered derivation, which for the other arguments in this book can be understood merely as expository conveniences. In (98), they are essential because the MVC is satisfied by an index that is inserted in a context that is destroyed in the subsequent derivation.

33. This example happens to have body part incorporation rather than the ordinary NI analyzed in chapter 7; however, Evans shows that the two types of incorporation have the same distribution in Mayali.

34. Nahuatl also allows applicatives to be formed from reflexive verbs. However, the morphosyntax of reflexives is quite different in Nahuatl than in Mohawk or the Gunwinjguan languages. In particular, reflexive morphology is not incompatible with object agreement in Nahuatl. Thus, reflexive verbs are probably not unaccusative in that language.

I do not know if examples like (104) and (105) are possible in Wichita. I did not find any clear examples in Rood 1976, and one could interpret his benefactive-adding rules (1976:37–38) as excluding this case. However, Rood does not explicitly say that such formations are impossible.

35. One might imagine that the PP moves on from the specifier of AspP to the specifier of IP. The P could then incorporate into Infl, making it possible for the Agr in Infl to be coindexed with the reference object. However, this leaves the Asp node without a Case feature, and hence unable to license agreement. Therefore, this cannot be a valid alternative derivation for examples like (104) and (105).

36. See Bresnan and Kanerva 1989 for extensive discussion of a similar construction in Bantu.

37. This analysis leaves open the question of what (if anything) guarantees the locality of PP movement.

Another approach, more in the spirit of the Minimalist framework, would be to eliminate Binding Theory considerations in favor of some version of Relativized Minimality. In these terms, we could capture the same facts by saying that a phrase A can move past a c-commanding position B only if A and B are of different categories. This version leads to a number of technical difficulties, however, which I will not explore here.

Technically, we must also block a PP headed by the null preposition from moving to Spec, AspP; otherwise *[$_{PP}$ Ø *Mary*] *passed the heirloom ring t* should be fine, on a par with (109b). I assume that this has to do nature of the null P itself; presumably it must remain in the minimal domain of the verb that licenses it, just as certain idiom chunks must.

38. Here, as elsewhere in this chapter, I put aside those elements that are often expressed by PPs but that are not paths or locations in any sense. Prominent in this class are instruments and comitatives. Indeed, instrumental and comitative applicatives are not uncommon in the polysynthetic languages: Mohawk has a kind of instrumental construction (or did until quite recently) (see Lounsbury 1953:79–81); Mayali has a comitative construction (Evans 1991, to appear b); Wichita has a so-called portative construction (Rood 1976:64–65); Ainu has instrumental and comitative constructions (Shibatani 1990:66). These often differ from benefactive/locative applicatives in that the "applied object" can be incorporated into the complex verb. This suggests to me that there is actually no preposition involved; rather the relevant applicatives are derived by incorporation from serial verb constructions such as 'John take knife cut bread' and 'John take Mary go to-town' (see Baker 1989 for real examples). However, the syntax of each language is different in this area. Moreover, my Mohawk consultants no longer feel that they control the instrumental applicative construction and are insecure about certain crucial judgments. For these two reasons, I do not pursue this topic here.

10

Embedded Clauses

The last topic I wish to discuss in detail is that of embedded clauses in the poly-synthetic languages. The issues that arise here are partially similar to those dis-cussed in chapter 9. In particular, embedded clauses share with PPs the property of not being NPs. This means that the standard ways of satisfying the Morphologi-cal Visibility Condition—agreement morphology and incorporation—are not well suited to them. From this it follows that argument clauses are more restricted in polysynthetic languages than in languages of other types. This fits well with the fact that polysynthetic languages often have few clear cases of subordinate clauses, as pointed out by Mithun (1984b). However, exactly how languages adapt to this grammatical pressure is rather different for embedded clauses than for PPs, and therefore a separate discussion is warranted. Moreover, there is clear evidence that *some* CP complements are possible in some polysynthetic languages, so one must account for how this can be.

The Polysynthesis Parameter also has implications for the internal structure of embedded clauses. A straightforward consequence of the parameter is that it is impossible to have typical instances of nonfinite complements in a polysynthetic language. This is a property of polysynthetic languages that is known to typolo-gists and functional linguists (Heath 1975, Mithun 1984b, Nichols 1992). More-over, this property interacts with the theory of PRO to imply that the polysynthetic languages will not have control phenomena in anything like the familiar Indo-European sense.

In contrast to the discussion of PPs, this time it is easier to consider the issue of external distribution first.

10.1. The Distribution of Argument Clauses

English and other familiar languages allow embedded clauses (CPs) to appear in virtually any syntactic role: they may be the internal argument of a predicate, the external argument of a predicate, or an adjunct modifier of a predicate. If, however, a CP were to perform one of the first two functions in a polysynthetic language, it would be subject to the MVC. This means that there would have to be a morpheme in the word containing the predicate (e.g., the main verb) that is coindexed with the CP. What kind of morpheme could this be?

One possibility is that it could be an agreement morpheme. However, in chapter 9, I argued that agreement was an inherently nominal phenomenon in most languages. In particular, (1) typically holds.

(1) Only nominal elements bear Φ-features.

Now CPs are not nominal, and in the normal course of affairs they do not bear features of person, number, or gender. It is meaningless to say that a clause is masculine or plural or second person, for example. When one finds a CP subject in a language with subject agreement, the verb generally appears in the third person singular (neuter) form:

(2) That John stole a candy bar *is* disturbing.

However, this does not mean that the CP bears the Φ-features third person, singular, and neuter. Rather, the verb shows up in this form because it has to have some form and these are the default feature values in English. Evidence for this comes from sentences like (3), where the conjoined CP subject ought to be a plural CP if anything is; nevertheless the verb still appears in the singular form.[1]

(3) That John stole a candy bar and that his parents didn't discipline him for it *is* (??are) disturbing.

Thus, although there may be an agreement morpheme on the verb, it is not in a feature-sharing relationship with the CP argument. Thus, I conclude that CPs, like PPs, cannot, in general, satisfy the MVC by way of agreement.

The other way that an argument CP could potentially satisfy the MVC is by having its head incorporate into the word containing the predicate that it is an argument of. In order to explore this possibility, we must face immediately the question of what we mean by the head of a CP. The recent literature on functional categories often distinguishes between the *categorial* head of a phrase and the *semantic* head of a phrase, following Abney (1987). These notions are clearly distinct in the case of a CP. The categorial head of a clause has been taken to be the complementizer (C) since Stowell 1981. On the other hand, the semantic head of a phrase is the head of the lexical category selected (directly or indirectly) by the categorial head; in typical clauses this is a verb. Intuitively, the semantic head is the category that was taken to be the head of the construction before functional categories were introduced into the X-bar structure.

Could incorporation of the categorial head of a CP satisfy the MVC? The answer is presumably no. First of all, it is not clear that such an incorporation is even allowed by Universal Grammar. There are few or no attested cases of a complementizer visibly incorporating into the higher verb with the kinds of consequences that the theory of incorporation would predict.[2] Indeed, it is striking that in languages where complementizers are morphologically bound forms, they almost always show up as affixes on the lower verb, not on the higher. For example, Ngalakan, Wichita, and Kiowa have C-like morphemes that indicate that a clause is subordinate or relative, and these invariably suffix to the embedded verb itself. This fits under a much broader generalization: there are few or no cases of any kind of functional category incorporating into a higher lexical category. This contrasts strikingly with the incorporation of a lexical category into a functional category, which is abundantly attested. Why this asymmetry should exist is not entirely clear, but it looks like movement of a functional head to a lexical one is a kind of "improper movement," just as movement from an A-bar position to an A-position is (cf. Li 1990). Moreover, even if incorporation of the C were possible, it is not clear that it would be sufficient to satisfy the MVC. Intuitively, it could be that not enough of the clause has incorporated to count as a legitimate word-internal representation of the argument; rather, the incorporation of the semantic head might be required. Certainly, this is the case with NP arguments: the MVC is satisfied not when a determiner is incorporated into the verb (if that is ever possible), but rather when the noun root itself is incorporated.

Could, then, the argument CP satisfy the MVC by having the verb that is its semantic head incorporate into the higher verb? This question leads into the kind of problems that were investigated in chapter 8. First, there is the matter of whether such verb incorporation is even possible. The verb cannot move directly from its base position to combine with the higher verb, because this movement would skip at least one and probably several functional head positions (C, Infl, and Asp), in violation of the Head Movement Constraint, a type of economy of derivation. On the other hand, if the verb moved through these functional heads on its way to the higher verb, the last step of the movement will again count as incorporating a functional category (the complex C) into a lexical one. This too seems to be an "improper movement," violating the Proper Head Movement Generalization.[3] Thus, verb incorporation is only possible if there are no functional categories dominating the projection of the embedded verb. In other words, the argument must not be a CP at all, but rather a VP. This is only viable if the matrix verb is a member of the relatively small class of verbs that can select a bare VP complement—the class that Rochette (1988) calls "effective verbs" (causatives, aspectual verbs, modal verbs; see also Li (1990)). Moreover, even within this class there will be limitations due to the Polysynthesis Parameter, as discussed in detail in chapter 8. Therefore, verb incorporation will not be able to express anything like the full range of structures that involve clausal complementation in a language like English.

Putting together the parts of this reasoning, the theory predicts that—barring unforeseen factors—clauses simply cannot be arguments in a polysynthetic language. The following sections show that this prediction is true in part: most polysynthetic languages have fewer CP arguments than languages like English, and some may indeed have none. However, we will also discover some unforeseen factors that allow certain clausal arguments to appear in polysynthetic languages after all.

10.1.1 Clausal Subjects

Let us begin the investigation by looking for CPs that are associated with the external argument role in Mohawk. External argument positions are associated with agent and agent-like θ-roles according to the UTAH. However, CPs refer to propositions, and there is a very limited range of things that a proposition can do. Essentially, one only expects to find CP subjects of verbs with a causative meaning.[4] In English, CPs can be the cause of a psychological state (e.g., with verbs like *anger, bother, annoy, sadden*), or they can be the cause of some other proposition acquiring a certain status (e.g., *prove, show, remind, discredit*). In Baker 1991a, I claimed that comparable verbs could take CP subjects in Mohawk as well, but further investigation suggests that this was a mistake.

Psychological predicates of the relevant type are interesting in Mohawk. They are not as common as they are in English, and many of them are morphologically complex. They appear most readily in intransitive stative or inchoative forms; these, then, can be followed by a clause:

(4) a. Uke-nákw-ʌ-' tsi Sak wa-ho-rasʌ́tho-' ne
       FACT/1sO-anger-get-PUNC that Sak FACT-MsS/MsO-kick-PUNC NE

       érhar.
       dog
       'I got mad that Sak kicked the dog.'

   b. Uke-'nikuhr-áksʌ tsi Sak s-a-huwa-'nhá-hsi-'.
      FACT/1sO-mind-bad that Sak ITER-FACT-FsS/MsO-hire-REV-PUNC.
      'I was sorry that Sak lost his job.'

   c. Wak-atunhár-ʌ tsi s-a-hí-kʌ́-' ne Sak.
      1sO-good.spirits-STAT that ITER-FACT-1sS/MsO-see-PUNC NE Sak
      'I am happy that I saw Sak again.'

Although the literal meanings of these sentences are as given, it is interesting that when a Mohawk speaker is asked to translate an English sentence like "That I saw Sak again made me happy," one often gets a form like (4c) in response. These verbs also have transitive eventive versions, sometimes formed with overt causative morphology. These are used when the cause of the emotion is a person:

(5) a. Wa-hake-nak[w]-úni-'.
       FACT-MsS/1sO-anger-make-PUNC
       'He made me mad.'

   b. Wa-hake-'nikuhr-áksʌ-ht-e'.
      FACT-MsS/1sO-mind-bad-CAUS-PUNC
      'He made me sad.'

   c. ?Wa-hakw-atunhár-a-ht-e'.
      FACT-MsS/1sO-good.spirits-Ø-CAUS-PUNC
      'He made me happy, he cheered me up.'

However, when one replaces the animate subjects in (5) with a clause, the results range from slightly awkward to solidly ungrammatical:

(6) a. Uke-nak[w]-úni-' (ne) tsi Sak wa-ho-rasʌ́tho-' ne
       FACT/NsS/1sO-mad-make-PUNC NE that Sak FACT-MsS/MsO-kick-PUNC NE

       érhar.
       dog
       'It made me mad that Sak kicked the dog.'

    b. ?Uke-'nikuhr-áksʌ-ht-e'   tsi Tyer s-a-huwa-'nhá-hsi-'.
        FACT/NsS/1sO-mind-bad-CAUS-PUNC that Tyer ITER-FACT-FsS/MsO-hire-REV-PUNC
        'It made me sad that Tyer lost his job.'

    c. *Uk-atunhár-a-ht-e'   tsi s-a-hí-kʌ-'
        FACT/NsS/1sO-good.spirits-CAUS-PUNC that ITER-FACT-1sS/MsO-see-PUNC
        ne Sak.
        NE Sak
        'It cheered me up that I saw Sak again.'

The surprising contrast between (6) and the examples in (4) and (5) suggests that Mohawk does not like CP subjects.

The paradigm in (6) can be sharpened when one controls for the possibility that in the relatively acceptable examples the postverbal CP could be a causal adjunct rather than a subject. A complicating factor in Mohawk is that the complementizer system is quite impoverished; that is, complementizers do not tell as much about the role of the CP in the clause as one might hope.[5] For example, the most common way to express a 'because' clause in Mohawk has no word for 'because'; rather the clause is introduced with the particle sequence *ne tsi.* Now, *tsi* is a particle that occurs more or less optionally before clauses of all kinds, both argument and adjunct, and *ne* is a ubiquitous particle in Mohawk, appearing semioptionally before postverbal NPs and other categories. Thus, the difference between an argument clause and a causal adjunct is not very well marked. Since the verbs in (4) are monadic, the clauses are presumably adjuncts, there being no argument role they could plausibly be linked to. Thus, a better gloss for (4a) would be "I got mad *because* Sak kicked the dog." It might well be that the clause in (6a) is a causal adjunct as well.

There are several indications that this is correct, ranging from the anecdotal to the technical. Thus, speakers sometimes translate sentences like (6a) as 'It made me mad because Sak kicked the dog.' They also often spontaneously add the particle *ne* before the clause, creating the *ne tsi* 'because' sequence. Furthermore, the neuter singular subject agreement in (6a) can be replaced with a masculine singular subject agreement understood as referring to 'Sak':

(7)   Wa-*hake*-nak[w]-úni-'   tsi Sak wa-ho-rasátho-'   ne
       FACT-MsS/1sO-mad-make-PUNC that Sak FACT-MsS/MsO-kick-PUNC NE
       érhar.
       dog
       'He made me mad that Sak kicked the dog.'

In (7), the dyadic verb *nakuni* 'make angry' appears with two animate arguments; thus, the clause 'that Sak kicked the dog' must be a pure adjunct in this example. It is quite possible that the same clause has the status of an adjunct in (6a) as well. Finally, it is ungrammatical to move an interrogative phrase out of the postverbal clauses in (6)[6]:

(8)   a. *Úhka we-sa-nak[w]-úni-'   (ne) tsi Sak
          who FACT-NsS/2sO-mad-make-PUNC NE that Sak

wa-shako-rasÁtho-'?
FACT-MsS/FsO-kick-PUNC
'Who did it make you mad that Sak kicked?'

b. *Oh nahótʌ we-sa-nak[w]-úni-'   tsi Uwári
   What   FACT-NsS/2sO-mad-make-PUNC that Mary

wa'-t-yé-ya'k-e'?
FACT-DUP-FsS-break-PUNC
'What did it make you mad that Mary broke?'

Although preverbal CP subjects are quite strong islands in such languages as Italian and English, postverbal (extraposed) subjects are not; they allow argumental *wh*-phrases to be extracted with no more than perhaps a slight awkwardness (see Cinque 1990:ch. 1). Thus, the English glosses of the examples in (8) are quite acceptable. This means that the judgments in (8) are unexpected if the CP can have the status of an extraposed subject in Mohawk. On the other hand, this judgment is expected if these CPs can only have the status of causal adjuncts, since clausal adjuncts are known to be strong islands in Mohawk, as they are in other languages (see section 2.1.5). I conclude that CPs never count as the external argument of a psychological verb in Mohawk.

Verbs of the 'prove/show' class confirm these results. Mohawk does not have many verbs of this type, as might be expected given that they had little exposure to European jurisprudence or Euclidean geometry until recently. The best analog of 'prove' that my consultant could find was *rihw-a-hnir-a-ht,* literally 'to make the matter hard'. With an animate subject, this verb means essentially 'to swear'. She also accepted examples like (9), with what looks like a propositional subject.

(9) Tsi wa-huwa-hwíst-u-'   ne Uwári *(ne'e)
     that FACT-FsS/MsO-money-give-PUNC NE Mary   NE

wa'-ka-rihw-a-hnír-a-ht-e'   ne sa-kára'.
FACT-NsS-matter-Ø-be.hard-Ø-CAUS-PUNC NE 2sP-story
'That Mary gave him money, it proves your story.'

However, this sentence is only possible if there is an emphatic particle *ne'e* 'this, it' before the matrix verb. This particle is presumably the grammatical subject of the verb, leaving the CP as an appositional adjunct. The consultant also spontaneously suggested that one could put *ne tsi* before the clause, making the translation 'Because Mary gave him money, it proves your story.' Finally, extraction out of this putative clausal subject is also completely ungrammatical, even if it appears postverbally:

(10) #Oh nahótʌ ʌ-ka-rihw-a-hnír-a-ht-e'   tsi Uwári
      what   FUT-NsS-matter-Ø-be.hard-Ø-CAUS-PUNC that Mary

wa-huwáy-u-'?
FACT-FsS/MsO-give-PUNC
NOT: 'What will that Mary gave t to him prove it?' (OK as: 'What will prove that Mary gave it to him?')

The same effects are found when one tries to construct examples of CP subjects using the verb *eyarahkw* 'remind'. Again, the available evidence suggests that CP subjects are impossible in Mohawk; the few examples that could be considered as such turn out to be causal adjuncts instead.

Unfortunately, I have no information about the possibility of clausal subjects in other polysynthetic languages (except Nahuatl, where they are possible for reasons to be discussed below). One may be mildly optimistic about the prediction, given that none of the grammars mention that CP subjects are possible; however, the discussions of complementation are often brief and incomplete. However, it is clear that Mohawk at least has a dislike of CP subjects that cannot simply be explained by accidental gaps in the Lexicon of the language. This supports the predictions of the Polysynthesis Parameter.

10.1.2 Clausal Complements

Although CP subjects are a rather marginal phenomenon, CP complements are fundamental to English syntax, and there are a wide variety of verbs that select them. Thus, for linguists trained on the syntax of English, it may seem bizarre that a language could have no CP complements, as this theory predicts. Nevertheless, it is the case that polysynthetic languages use relatively little clausal complementation and employ other constructions to express more or less the same ideas.

The clearest case of a language that may have no complement clauses at all is Nunggubuyu, as argued by Heath (1984:558–559, 582–586). Heath observes that Nunggubuyu has no infinitival or nominalized clauses, no complements with anything like a *that*-complementizer, and no indirect discourse. When verbs that take sentential complements in English are translated into Nunggubuyu, a variety of noncomplement constructions appear. For example, verbs of speech ('say', 'ask', etc.) appear only with direct discourse, quotative constructions (Heath 1980:112):

(11) "Ngawa:-'ni-jara-ng   nga-ya-nggi yuwa-ga:-'la" ni-yama:-'.
    1sS/3sO-coal-smell-PAST 1sS-go-PAST from-there   MsS-do(say)-PAST
    " 'I detected the smell of fire and came here," he said.'

Such quotative clauses are indistinguishable from matrix clauses, are set apart intonationally, and have none of the characteristic properties of embedding. Furthermore, there are few or no dependencies of anaphora or movement where the dependent element is in a quotative expression and the antecedent is in the matrix. Rather, the quotation is a separate linguistic expression from its "matrix." This tendency to use direct quotation carries over even to verbs that express unspoken decisions or other mental acts—verbs like 'decide', 'want' and 'think'. Many other verbs that would take CP complements in English are paraphrased by conjoined or sequenced clauses in Nunggubuyu. For example, where an English speaker might say "I tried to break it off," Nunggubuyu has (Heath 1980:502):

(12) Ngangu-wagiwa:-' lha:lhag, araga   ngijang nga-wurij-banngi-'-nj.
    1sS/3sO-break-PAST nearly   suddenly again   1sS-fail-PAST
    'I nearly broke it (a rifle), but I failed.'

Similarly, the conventional way to say 'He persuaded (ordered, suggested) me to go' in Nunggubuyu is: ' "Go!" he said; "All-right," I said.' In Nunggubuyu, one does not say "They stopped weaving it," but rather the equivalent of "They were weaving it and (then) they finished." There are expressions meaning 'to know', 'to forget' 'to be unaware', but these only take nominal complements, such as 'his name'. In the same way, the verb *nganjbanda* 'to want, to like' appears in texts only with a nominal object. In elicitation, speakers accept utterances like (13).

(13) Ngawu-nganjbandi:-'   nganj-ja:-ri:.
  1sS/3s(ANA)O-want-NONPAST 1sS-go-FUT
  'I want to go.' (Literally: 'I want it, I will go.')

However, even these examples show signs of being a sequence of two independent clauses; for example, to say 'I do not want to go' one must put a separate negative particle in front of each verb. Finally, certain aspectual or modal categories that can be expressed by CP-selecting predicates such as 'begin' or 'be able to' in English are expressed within the tense/mood/aspect inflection system in Nunggubuyu. This, then, gives a good idea of how a language could function with no clausal complementation at all. This may, in fact, be typical of the Gunwinjguan languages. Thus, Merlan (1983:135–142) goes through the various kinds of subordination in Ngalakan, but there is no sign of true clausal complementation in her discussion. Like Nunggubuyu, Ngalakan uses direct quotation in place of indirect quotation (Merlan 1983:151–152), whereas modal categories such as 'try' and 'should' are expressed by a combination of tense/mood inflection and nonverbal particles.[7]

 Mohawk has many of the same characteristics as Nunggubuyu. It also prefers to use quotative constructions in some environments where English would use indirect discourse. In (14), an example with the verb *iru* 'say' is given (KO:130).

(14) Wa-hʌ́-[i]ru-' ne ro-yáner, "Kʌ́'ʌ ka-nyatar-ákta
  FACT-MsS-say-PUNC NE MsO-be.good here NsS-river-near

  ʌ-tewa-ya't-áta-'   kʌkwité-hne t-ʌ-ti-tewa-kó-ha-'."
  FUT-1PINS-body-bury-PUNC spring-LOC DUP-FUT-CIS-1PINS-get-PURP-PUNC
  'The chief said, "Let's bury it (a church-bell) here near the lake; in the spring we will come and get it again." '

Indeed, this is the only use of *iru* that is attested in texts, although in elicitation some speakers hesitantly accept a true embedded clause with *iru*. Mohawk also has a tendency to use a series of conjoined clauses or sequences of clauses in certain cases where English has CP complements (Mithun 1984b). Examples (15) and (16) show this for the verbs *atst* 'use' and *s . . . ahtʌti* 'go home'.

(15) a. Atókwa rá-[a]tst-ha' káwhe ro-hnekír-ʌ.
    spoon MsS-use-HAB coffee MsO-drink-STAT.
    'He is using a spoon to drink the coffee.'

  b. *Nahótʌ atókwa rá-[a]tst-ha' ro-hnekír-ʌ?
    what spoon MsS-use-HAB MsO-drink-STAT.
    'What is he using a spoon to drink?'

(16) a. S-hon-aht́ty-u   s-hon-ather-uny-á-hn-u.
         ITER-MpO-move-STAT ITER-MpO-basket-make-Ø-PURP-STAT
         'They have gone home to make baskets.'

     b. *Nahót⋀ s-hon-aht́ty-u   s-a-hun-uny-á-hn-e'?
         what   ITER-MpO-move-STAT ITER-FACT-MpS-make-PURP-PUNC
         'What have they gone home to make?'

The evidence that these are conjoined clauses of some kind rather than CP complements comes from the (b) sentences, where one tries to extract an interrogative word out of the second clause. This is impossible in these Mohawk examples, although the English translations are grammatical. Presumably, the Mohawk sentences violate the Coordinate Structure Constraint of Ross 1967.

This avoidance of complement clauses is found in other polysynthetic languages as well. The preference for quotative complements with speech verbs is widespread in languages of this type. Moreover, Watkins (1984:239) shows that expressions meaning 'ask' and 'persuade' undergo clause chaining rather than complementation in Kiowa; this is confirmed by the fact that the verbs in question bear switch reference morphology—a characteristic of adjoined clauses but not complement clauses in most languages (Finer 1984, Finer 1985, Bonneau 1992). Another case in point is Alutor, a language closely related to Chukchee. Mel'cuk and Savvina (1978:17–19) give as grammatical the sentence in (17), where a verb of perception takes a clausal complement and shows third person singular agreement with it.

(17) (?*)Qamav-ənak ləʔutkə-nin gənannə kəlgatətkə-na   qura-wwi.
      Qamav-ERG   see-3sS/3sO you/ERG harness-2sS/3PO reindeer
      'Qamav sees you harnessing the reindeer.'

However, in discussing the example they write:

> It should be noted that many speakers of Alutor do not accept or produce sentences like [17]. . . . Perhaps this could be explained by the difficulty of making the verb agree not with an actual noun but with a pure abstraction of a clause. We still believe that such sentences are admissible if only as marginal cases, but we by no means insist on it because of the paucity of our data.

In place of (17), Alutor speakers prefer to have the matrix verb agree with one of the participants of the perceived event, either the subject or the object; the perceived event is then expressed as a full clause or a participial construction:

(18) Qamav-ənak *na*-ləʔutkəni-*gət* gənannə kəlgatətkə-na   qura-wwi.
      Qamav-ERG   3sS-see-2sO   you-ERG harness-2sS/3PO reindeer
      'Qamav sees you harnessing the reindeer.'

(Example (18) is also the typical pattern for perception verbs and causative verbs in Mohawk.) Mel'cuk and Savvina go on to suggest that examples like (18) could plausibly be analyzed as instances of clausal conjunction rather than embedding; if so, the gloss would be something like 'Qamav sees you, (as) you are harnessing the reindeer.' Ideally, this conjecture would be confirmed with data from extraction and the like, but Mel'cuk and Savvina do not pursue the issue further. Nevertheless, it is a consistent theme that polysynthetic languages are uncomfortable with CP arguments.

Saying that CP arguments are disfavored is not the same thing as saying that they are impossible, however. Some clausal complements are clearly possible in Mohawk, for one. Certainly, there are a number of Mohawk verbs that appear naturally with a CP, where the presence of a propositional complement is implied by the verb's lexical semantics. Moreover, syntactic tests show that these clauses are inside the VP and governed by the verb, as shown in section 2.1. For example, the Condition C effect in (19) shows that the embedded clause is c-commanded by the object pro, hence within VP.

(19) Wa-hi-hróri-' tsi Sak ruwa-núhwe'-s.
FACT-1sS/MsO-tell-PUNC that Sak FsS/MsO-like-HAB
'I told *him* that she likes *Sak*.' (disjoint only)

Example (20) shows that interrogative phrases can be extracted from embedded clauses, implying that those complements are properly governed by the verb.

(20) Úhka í-hs-ehr-e' ʌ-yu-[a]tya'tawi-tsher-a-hnínu-'?
Who Ø-2sS-think-IMPF FUT-FsS-dress-NOM-Ø-buy-PUNC
'Who do you think will buy a dress?'

Finally, an interrogative phrase associated with the matrix verb can create a bound variable interpretation for an overt pronoun inside the embedded clause:

(21) Úhka í-hr-ehr-e' Uwári raúha ruwa-núhwe'-s.
who Ø-MsS-think-IMPF Mary him FsS/MsO-like-HAB
'*Who* thinks that Mary likes *him?*' (bound reading marginally OK)

In each of these respects, the CP associated with verbs like *ehr* 'think' and *hrori* 'tell' contrasts with clear cases of adjunct clauses, as shown in chapter 2. Thus, there is excellent evidence that these clauses are not merely some kind of adjunct or clause series; rather, CP complements are possible in Mohawk. Indeed, they are the only kind of phrase that seems to be allowed in argument positions.

How is the MVC satisfied in these cases? The clause clearly does not incorporate, as predicted. Nor does the clause trigger agreement. This is clear in (19), where the two agreement factors are used to express the agent and goal arguments of the three-place verb *hrori* 'tell'. The same thing can be seen for the two-place verb *ehr* 'think' when it is put in the stative form. As mentioned in chapter 5, verbs in the stative use +O "object" agreement forms for their subjects if and only if they do not agree with an object (Postal 1979; see Ormston 1993 for a recent analysis). Now when a verb that takes a CP complement appears in the stative, +O agreement with the subject appears:

(22) Sak *raw*-éhr-u ʌ-ha-'sere-ht-óhare-'.[8]
Sak MsO-think-STAT FUT-MsS-car-NOM-wash-PUNC
'Sak has thought he would wash the car.'

This shows that the matrix verb does not agree with the CP complement, even covertly—again as predicted. Thus, the reasoning that CP complements could not be morphologically expressed by either incorporation or agreement seems to be correct. Either the MVC is wrong, or there is another way to satisfy it that we have not anticipated.

An important clue to what is happening here comes from a morphological fact about verbs that take CP complements in Mohawk. A substantial percentage of these verbs are morphologically complex, containing the N root *rihw*. This root can be used in an independent noun *o-rihw-a'*, glossed as 'matter', 'affair', 'fact', 'news'—a very general word referring to a kind of proposition. It also appears in possessed and locative constructions meaning 'cause' or, in negative contexts, 'fault'. Many Iroquoianists have recognized that this element plays a special role as a kind of classifier for clauses (see especially Woodbury 1975:ch. 4). In some cases, it appears on a verb that otherwise selects NP arguments; the result is a verb that takes a CP:

(23) Sak ro-*rihw*-a-nuhwé'-u   a-ha-'sere-ht-óhare-'.
      Sak MsO-matter-Ø-like-STAT OPT-MsS-car-NOM-wash-PUNC
      'Sak has agreed to wash the car.'

In other cases, the verb root is never synchronically used without *rihw*, as far as I know. Some of the more common combinations are listed in (24).

(24)   *CP-taking verb*   *Literal gloss*   *Free gloss*
                rihw-a-nuhwe'   matter-like   'to agree to S'
                rihw-a-tshʌri   matter-find   'to find out that S'
                rihw-a-yʌta's   matter-acquire   'to decide to S'
                rihw-isak   matter-seek   'to investigate S'
                rihw-a-yo'tv   matter-work   'to plan to S'
                rihw-a-ruk   ???   'to hear that S'
                rihw-a-nutu   ???   'to ask S'

The *rihw* in these examples is formally parallel to other INs. Thus, it is reasonable to suppose that it is this element that morphologically expresses the propositional argument of the verb root for purposes of the MVC.

One might think that these verbs actually select an ordinary NP argument, of which *rihw* is the head. The clause could then be some kind of dislocated adjunct, coindexed with this NP position. This would make sentences like (23) parallel to those in which an incorporated noun is doubled by an overt NP adjunct. The problem with this obvious approach is that the clause does not act like an adjunct syntactically. On the contrary, it behaves exactly like the argument clauses shown in (19)–(21). Thus, the subject of the matrix verb must be disjoint in reference from a name inside the clause:

(25) Y-a'-t-ho-rihw-a-yʌta's-e'   tsi
      TRANS-FACT-DUP-MsO-matter-Ø-acquire-PUNC that

      ʌ-ha-'sere-ht-a-hnínu-'   ne Sak.
      FUT-MsS-car-NOM-Ø-buy-PUNC NE Sak
      '*He* decided that *Sak* would buy the car.' (disjoint only)

Similarly, interrogative phrases can be extracted from the clause:

(26) Ka nikáyʌ y-a'-te-sa-rihw-a-yʌta's-e'
      which   TRANS-FACT-DUP-2sO-matter-Ø-acquire-PUNC

      a-hs-hnínu-'   ne áthere'?
      OPT-2sS-buy-PUNC NE basket
      'Which basket did you decide to buy?'

In short, there are no syntactic differences between CP-selecting verbs that have *rihw* incorporated and those that do not. If, however, the CP in these examples is the internal theme argument of the verb, then it is not clear where the IN *rihw* originates—if, indeed, it is incorporated syntactically.

This paradox can be resolved if one assumes that sentences like (23) and (25) have roughly the same structure as those in (27).

(27)   a. I believe *the claim* that the moon is made of green cheese.

      b. John denied *the allegation* that he was in Tokyo the night of the 23rd.

      c. Mary regrets *the fact* that she lost her scarf.

In these examples, the embedded clause forms a constituent with an appropriate noun. These nouns add little or nothing to the interpretation of the sentences as a whole; if they are omitted the examples mean basically the same thing. However, the constituent as a whole is an NP and not a CP; for example, it needs to receive Case (*It is widely believed (*the claim) that the moon is made of green cheese*). The structure of (23) and (25) can be taken to be the same, except that the head noun of the noun-plus-clause constituent incorporates into the verb.

To evaluate the implications of this proposal for the MVC, we must take a stand on the nature of the relationship between the head noun and the CP in this kind of construction. In fact, the literature is clearer about what the relationship is not than about what it is. First, it is clear that CPs are not adjunct modifiers of the nouns in the normal sense. If they were, then *wh*-movement out of the CPs should be completely impossible: the extraction would violate the Adjunct Island Condition, plus there would be whatever extra degradation comes from having the structure embedded inside an NP. In fact, such clauses are relatively mild islands; extraction of an argument out of them, although awkward, is generally better than extraction out of a relative clause modifier. For example, Chomsky (1986a) discusses the following contrast (diacritics added, consistent with his text):

(28)   a ?*Which book did John meet [$_{NP}$ a child [$_{CP}$ who read t]]?

      b.   ?Which book did John hear [$_{NP}$ a rumor [$_{CP}$ that you had read]]?

On the other hand, there is reason to think that these CPs are not arguments of the head noun either. Stowell (1981:197–203) shows that these constructions have neither the meaning nor the structural properties of head–complement constructions. Thus, deverbal Ns like *claim* and *allegation* in (27) do not have an event nominalization reading, but only a result nominalization reading. As such, they do not θ-mark the proposition, but rather refer themselves to the proposition. Stowell brings this out by showing that the NP and the CP can be linked by equative *be:*

(29)   a. The claim was that the moon is made of green cheese.

      b. The allegation was that John stayed in Tokyo the night of the 23rd.

      c. The fact is that she lost her scarf.

This is not possible when the deverbal noun is a true action nominal (*??Jack's attempt was to finish on time*). Stowell also points out (1981:397–398) that although the complementizer *that* can optionally be omitted in a CP that is the complement of a verb, it can never be omitted in the nominal equivalent:

(30)   a. John believes (that) he will win the race.

b. John's belief *(that) he would win the race (was misguided).

He derives this dissimilarity from the assumption that CPs of this type are not complements of the noun, so the structure needed to license complementizer omission is not present. Stowell (1981:200) concludes that "the relation between the derived nominal and its 'complement' is actually one of apposition, rather than of θ-role assignment."

Stowell's analysis is ideal for explaining the properties of sentences like (23) in Mohawk. The "appositional" relationship between the nominal and the clause is naturally represented by assigning them the same referential index. Together they form a constituent that is the internal argument of the verb root, as shown in (31).

(31)

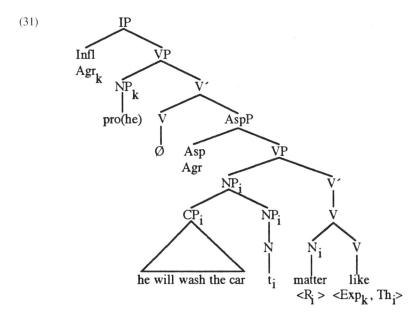

Since both CP and NP are coindexed with the argument position of the verb, neither is an adjunct in the usual sense; rather, the larger NP constituent is in some sense jointly headed by both the CP and the NP. Hence, the head noun *rihw* 'matter' can incorporate into the verb without violating the conditions on movement. By virtue of this incorporation, the internal argument of the verb is coindexed with a morpheme in the word containing the verb; thus, the MVC is satisfied without the use of object agreement. The NI leaves the CP behind inside the verb phrase; the CP is therefore c-commanded by the matrix subject position, explaining the disjoint reference effect in (25). Furthermore, since the CP is governed by the verb and coindexed with its θ-grid, it counts as L-marked in the terminology of Chomsky 1986a; in this respect, the CP is not significantly different from a simple complement clause, explaining why it is not an island for extraction (see (26)).[9] Thus, while there is still a degree of mystery as to the exact nature of the apposition in these N–CP structures,[10] once their existence is admitted by

Universal Grammar the morphological and syntactic properties of examples like (23) can be derived quite straightforwardly.

Now we can return to the general question of how putative CP complements satisfy the MVC in Mohawk. Apparently, a significant percentage of them do so by incorporating the noun *rihw* 'matter', which is in apposition to the CP. What then about those verbs like *ehr* 'think', *hrori* 'tell', *atʌhutsoni* 'want' and others, which take propositional complements but do not incorporate *rihw*? These are syntactically indistinguishable from verbs that take *rihw* as far as anaphora and extraction are concerned. There was also good evidence that the matrix verb does not agree with the CP even covertly, based on the fact that agreement with the subject shifts to the object paradigm in the stative (see (22)). Thus, I claim that examples like (22) have exactly the same structure as (23)/(31), *except that the noun in apposition to the clause is phonologically null.* Although certainly abstract, this claim is not particularly strange, given what we already have said about Mohawk. In particular, in section 5.3 I argued on independent grounds that Mohawk verbs that select an inanimate theme can express that theme as a kind of cognate object. This explained why those arguments that do not need to be associated with an agreement factor in Mohawk are precisely those that are associated with positions from which NI is possible. For some verbs, this incorporated cognate object is overt, in the form of a "dummy N root"; however, in many other verbs it is not overt. Now we see that exactly the same situation occurs with verbs that select a propositional theme: all take a cognate object that may be in apposition to a full clause; for some verbs this is the overt form *rihw,* and for others it is phonologically null. Thus, the structure of (22) is as crudely indicated in (32).

(32) Sak Ms$_k$-Ø$_i$-   think-Asp [$_{NP}$ t$_i$ [$_{CP_i}$ FUT-Ms-car-wash]]
        <R$_i$> <Exp$_k$, Th$_i$>

In conclusion, we have seen that although the prediction that CPs can never be arguments may be true for some polysynthetic languages (such as Nunggubuyu), it is not true for Mohawk. The reasoning used to derive the original prediction was generally sound, but there was an unforeseen factor—CPs can appear in an appositive construction with a noun. This noun can then be incorporated, as a way of morphologically expressing the relevant argument of the verb. When the proposition is the theme of the verb, as in this section, incorporation is possible. If, however, the proposition were the external argument of the verb, such incorporation would not be possible (see section 7.3.5). Thus, the fact that CPs cannot be subjects in Mohawk still follows from the theory.

10.1.3 Nominalization

The fact that what looks like a CP could actually be contained in an NP brings up another way in which the MVC could be satisfied. Mohawk makes use of this possibility so that there will be a noun coindexed with the clause that can be incorporated. However, the containing NP will also presumably bear ordinary person, number, and gender features. Under these conditions, it would be possible for the verb to agree with its propositional argument after all. Thus, CPs could be associated with a full range of argument positions, as long as the CPs showed independent evidence that some kind of nominalization had taken place.

This possibility is attested in Nahuatl, whose complementation patterns are quite different from those of Mohawk and Nunggubuyu. Verbs in Nahuatl clearly show third person singular agreement with their clausal complements, as in (33a) to (33c). The only time such agreement does not show up is if the matrix verb is triadic (see (33d)) or a middle reflexive; in these cases, overt agreement with the theme is impossible by the general principles of agreement in Nahuatl (Launey 1981:292–300, Andrews 1975:209–210).

(33)   a. Ø-*Qu*-i'toa   in Pedro in (ca) Ø-huāllā-z.
          3sS-3sO-say IN Pedro IN PRT 3sS-come-FUT
          'Pedro says that he will come.'

       b. Ni-*c*-mati   in ō-Ø-mic.
          1sS-3sO-know IN PAST-3sS-die/PERF
          'I know that he is dead.'

       c. Ni-*c*-nequi   am-mo-mā-po'pōhua-z-que'.
          1sS-3sO-want 2pS-2REFL-hand-wash-FUT-PL
          'I want you to wash your hands.'

       d. ō-Ø-mitz-ilhui'   in ti-c-chīhua-z.
          PAST-3sS-2sO-tell IN 2sS-3sO-make-FUT
          'He told you to make it.'

Launey (1981:297) also shows that such clauses may function as subjects of transitive verbs, unlike in Mohawk:

(34)   a. Ca Ø-nēch-pāc-tia   in nicān ti-ca'.
          PRT 3sS-1sO-please-CAUS IN here 2sS-be
          'It pleases me that you are here.'

       b. Ca Ø-nēch-tequipachoa in ō-Ø-mic.
          PRT 3sS-1sO-worry   IN PAST-3sS-die/PERF
          'It worries me that he is dead.'

Thus CPs trigger agreement in Nahuatl and therefore can be associated with any grammatical function.

Correlated with this behavior is a small but important difference in the structure of the Nahuatl clause. Although there is no blatant nominalization morphology on the verbs in (33) or (34), most of the clauses are introduced by the particle *in*. This extremely common particle was discussed briefly in section 6.1.2: in some cases, it is used as a bare demonstrative, playing the role of an NP; in others it is article-like, appearing immediately before an NP of any internal structure.

(35)   a. Ca tetl   in. (Launey 1981:45)
          PRT stone IN
          That is a stone.

       b. Ø-Qui-tlazo'tla in Pedro.
          3sS-3sO-like   IN Pedro
          'He/she loves Pedro; Pedro loves him/her.'

In these respects, Nahuatl *in* is exactly like the particle *ne* in Mohawk. However, *ne* in Mohawk does not usually appear before a CP constituent unless that constituent is understood as a headless relative. Argument-like clauses in Mohawk are either bare or they are preceded by the particle *tsi,* which has no nominal use[11]:

(36) Sak í-hr-ehr-e'   (tsi/*ne) ri-núhwe'-s.
      Sak Ø-MsS-think-IMPF that/NE 1sS/MsO-like-HAB
      'Sak thinks (that) I like him.'

This difference suggests that clauses in Nahuatl are in some sense nominal, while clauses in Mohawk are not. Their nominal nature, then, allows clauses to be agreed with in Nahuatl, which, in turn, allows them to be associated with any argument position.

There are two ways in which this suggestion might be implemented. First, using (35a) as a model, one might think that *in* itself is the head noun that the CP is in apposition to.[12] Alternatively, one could say that there is a phonologically null head noun that the CP is in apposition to, and the *in* that precedes it is the article-like pre-NP particle seen in (35b). Probably the second choice is better, because *in* does not appear before every clausal argument in Nahuatl; (33c) is an example where there is no *in,* and yet the matrix verb agrees with its propositional argument anyway. This example motivates the existence of a null noun head in any case. Interestingly, *in* is not obligatory before simple NPs either; it is absent when the NP follows the verb and is in some sense "indefinite" (Launey 1981:38):

(37) a. In cihuātl qu-itta   in calli.
          IN woman 3sS-3sO-see IN house.
          'The woman sees the house.'

      b. Ni-qu-itta   calli.
          1sS-3sO-see house
          'I see houses.'

Example (33c) is similar to (37b) in that the complement of *nequi* 'want' does not refer to a specific event of handwashing, just as *calli* does not refer to a specific house; rather there is some kind of modal or generic quantification over instances of the indicated type. In contrast, the complement of *mati* 'know' in (33b) does refer to a specific event of dying, just as *calli* in (37a) refers to a specific house. Thus, it seems that essentially the same semantic factors condition the presence or absence of *in* before simple NPs and before CPs. The syntactic structure of (33b) is then (38). The structure of the complex constituent representing the proposition is very much like the one in (31) in Mohawk, except that the null N does not incorporate in Nahuatl.

This analysis makes important predictions about the syntax of complementation in Nahuatl. Structure (38) shows the propositional constituent in a dislocated position. Presumably this must be so, because the same nominal features that allow the proposition to enter into an agreement relationship also require it to receive Case when it appears in an argument position. However, the object agreement morphology required by the MVC absorbs the only available Case features. Therefore, the propositional phrase must appear in an adjunct position, just as other

(38)

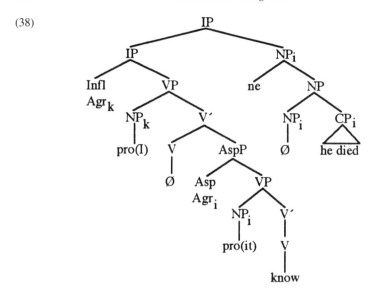

phonologically overt NPs must in polysynthetic languages (see section 2.2). The theory thus predicts that CPs in Nahuatl should behave syntactically like adjunct clauses, even though they fill the functional role of complements. For example, it should be impossible to extract out of embedded clauses in Nahuatl, and, barring connectivity effects, arguments of the matrix verb should not bind NPs inside the embedded clause. In short, the Nahuatl translations of the Mohawk sentences in (19)–(21) should give exactly the opposite pattern of judgments.

Unfortunately, I have no information about whether these predictions are true or not. However, partial support comes from similar facts in Lakhota. Lakhota is distantly related to Mohawk and although it is not a polysynthetic language, it has some nonconfigurational properties. Furthermore, clausal complements in Lakhota are like their Nahuatl analogs in that they take the same determiner-like elements as NPs (Williamson 1984:112–123):

(39)   a. Bill [$_{NP}$ hokšila] *ki*   aphe. (Williamson 1984:29)
          Bill   boy   the hit.
          'Bill hit the boy.'

       b. [$_{CP}$ Wichaša ki hi]   *ki* Mary ableze. (Williamson 1984:117)
              man   the come the Mary notice
          'Mary noticed that the man came.'

Presumably the clause in (39b) also triggers third singular object agreement on the verb, but this is not obvious because such agreement happens to be null in Lakhota. Williamson discusses coreference patterns in Lakhota in some detail. Among other things, she shows that a name within a putative complement clause may be coreferential with the understood subject of the matrix clause. Thus, there is no Condition C violation in (40) (Williamson 1984:214).

(40)   [$_{CP}$ Owayužaža wą hihąni   John ophethų] ki o-Ø-ma-ki-yake.
            tub   a morning John buy   the LOC-3sS-1sO-DAT-tell
       '*He* told me that *John* bought a tub this morning.' (coreference OK)

This confirms that nominalized clauses are in adjunct positions, outside of the c-command domain of other arguments, exactly as predicted. Less exotic evidence that clauses are adjuncts in Lakhota is the fact that they may be freely ordered with respect to other preverbal elements; indeed, the preferred position for them is at the left periphery, as in (39b).[13]

10.1.4 Predicting the Patterns

So far, we have seen that there are two rather different ways in which a polysynthetic language might take advantage of N–CP appositional structures to allow a degree of clausal complementation. First, the appositive N could be incorporated. In that case, there is no agreement with the clause, the clause acts like a complement that is internal to the VP,[14] and CP subjects are impossible; this is the Mohawk pattern. Second, the appositive N could trigger agreement on the verb. In that case, the constituent as a whole takes nominal modifiers, the clause acts like an adjunct, and clauses can be linked to the subject position; this seems to be the Nahuatl pattern, on the basis of the data available. If a language does not take advantage of either of these two options, no clausal arguments are allowed, as may be the case in Nunggubuyu.

Before moving on, it is worthwhile to think about why there is a consistent difference between Nahuatl and Mohawk. One might instead have expected that both languages would allow the agreement construction and the incorporation construction in free variation. Although I cannot answer this question completely, there are other differences between the two languages that seem to play a role here.

First, why are adjoined N–CP constructions allowed in Nahuatl but not Mohawk? There is a difference in the verb paradigms of the two languages that is probably relevant here. Nahuatl clearly has a 3sO agreement morpheme *k(i)* that can be used with inanimate NPs; this is the one that is used in examples like (33). Mohawk, on the other hand, apparently does not have a third person neuter object agreement morpheme; rather, some kind of incorporation is always involved when a transitive verb takes an inanimate object (see section 5.3). The fact that CP complement constructions must involve incorporation of the neuter head noun in Mohawk is thus a special case of this broader generalization.

Next consider why the head of an N–CP construction can be incorporated in Mohawk but not in Nahuatl. In compensation for the gap in its agreement paradigm, Mohawk has the property that dislocated NPs can be licensed by traces of incorporation as well as by ordinary pronominals (see section 7.4.1). This results in the classifier incorporation structures of Mohawk, as well as many cases of what look like stranded modifiers. However, Nahuatl does not have this option: INs are never doubled or modified by external material. The fact that CP complement constructions cannot involve incorporation of the neuter head could be a special case of this broader generalization.

If these remarks are on the right track, then it ought to be possible to make some predictions about which strategy for expressing CP complements (if any) a given polysynthetic language will use on the basis of more basic properties of NI and agreement in that language. Take, for example, Southern Tiwa. This language is similar to Mohawk in that neuter direct objects must incorporate (Allen et al. 1984; see also section 5.3) and INs can be associated with modifying material outside the verb (see section 7.4.1). Therefore, Southern Tiwa should have the Mohawk pattern of complementation and not the Nahuatl pattern. Among other things, this predicts that CPs associated with internal θ-roles will act as though they are in argument positions. This is correct; (41) shows that a nominal inside the CP complement cannot be understood as coreferential with a pronoun in the matrix clause (Donald Frantz, personal communication).

(41)   A-na-kacha-m   hi'a ti-seuan-mu-mi-'i.
       AO\AO-q-know-PRES that 1sS/AO-man-see-PRES-SUB
       '*He* knows that I see *the man*.'   (disjoint only)

The judgments for this sentence are similar to those for (19) and (25) in Mohawk, but different from those for (40) in Lakhota. Moreover, interrogative phrases can be extracted out of CP complements in Southern Tiwa (Donald Frantz, personal communication):

(42)   a. Hiriyu te-na-khīwi-we ti-thā-hi-'i?
          what   1sS-q-try-PRES 1sS/AO-find-FUT-SUB
          'What am I trying to find?'

       b. Hiriyu a-chaybe-ban   a-k'ar-hi-'i?
          what   2sS-tell/PASS-PAST 2sS/AO-eat-FUT-SUB
          'What were you told to eat?'

This is similar to (20) and (26) in Mohawk. The theory also predicts that CPs should not be able to function as subjects in Southern Tiwa. I do not have any information on this point specifically, but suspect that it is true, given the claim of Allen et al. (1984) that inanimate subjects are never possible in Southern Tiwa. Southern Tiwa should differ from Mohawk in the area of agreement, however, since many Southern Tiwa verbs show agreement with the gender class of their IN, whereas Mohawk verbs do not. Assuming that this carries over to Ns that refer to propositions, we expect that many Southern Tiwa verbs that select propositional objects will also show some kind of "object agreement." Frantz (1993a) shows that this is true:

(43)   a. In-na-kacha-m   Ø-heurpe-mi-nap.
          1sO\AO-q-know-PRES AS-sick-PRES-FACT
          'I know that she is sick.'

       b. Ka-na-mahwêhwī-we   ku-p'ahwe-heiami-ba-'i.
          1sS/2sO\AO-q-accuse-PRES 2sS/cO-egg-steal-PAST-SUB
          'I accuse you of stealing eggs.'

Further examples of this are given later in (51). In this respect, Southern Tiwa looks deceptively like Nahuatl, even though its structure is predictably more like Mohawk. Finally, we can ask if the IN referring to the proposition is ever overt in Southern Tiwa. The answer is "maybe." It is striking that a large number of verbs that take clausal arguments in Southern Tiwa also have the prefix element *na* appearing in the same morphological position as an IN would. Thus, it is very tempting to analyze *na* as the Southern Tiwa version of *rihw* 'matter' in Mohawk. However, Donald Frantz (personal communication) says that *na* does not appear on all verbs that take a CP (e.g., see (42b)), and appears on a good number of verbs that do not take a CP; he does not know what it is and simply glosses it "q." Thus, the identification of *na* with the propositional IN must remain highly tentative until there is a better understanding of this mysterious morpheme.

Having successfully predicted the major properties of complementation in Southern Tiwa from more basic properties, one would like to go on and do the same for the other polysynthetic languages. Although I can make the predictions, I have few data for checking them. For example, Chukchee is like Nahuatl in that it has overt agreement with third person neuter objects and does not allow INs to be externally modified; therefore, if it allows complement-like CPs at all, it should be by means of a nominalization strategy rather than incorporation. This seems likely, given the presence of object agreement and the absence of an IN in Mel'cuk and Savvina's example, given earlier in (17), if this is grammatical in Chukchee. (See, also, later discussion of more radical nominalizations in Chukchee.) Ainu also does not allow INs to have external modifiers, and hence should use a nominalizing strategy for CPs. This is consistent with the few data Shibatani (1990) gives on this topic; thus, the propositional argument in (44) is followed by the suffix *i*, which is otherwise a noun-forming derivational affix in the language (Shibatani 1990:32–34).

(44)   Ene ku-kari-*i*   ka ku-(Ø)-erampetek.   (Shibatani 1990:86)
       what 1sS-do-NOMI too 1sS-(3sO)-not.know
       'I did not know what to do.'

Furthermore, the morphology is consistent with the claim that the verb agrees with the propositional argument, as expected in the Nahuatl pattern. On the other hand, this system makes no clear predictions about Wichita: since INs can be doubled in Caddoan (Mithun 1984a) it could use the Mohawk pattern; on the other hand, there is no evidence that neuter objects must incorporate, so the Nahuatl pattern might also be possible.[15] Indeed, it is probably too strong to say that the pattern of complementation in a polysynthetic language is *entirely* predictable from other properties: I know of no good reason why CP complements should be possible in Mohawk but not Nunggubuyu, for example.

10.2. The Internal Structure of Clauses

The last topic to be discussed in this book is the internal structure of embedded clauses. In fact, this is something we already know a good deal about: since the MVC also holds within embedded clauses, everything that has been said about its implications for matrix clauses should apply in this domain as well. Not surprisingly, this is true.

However, it is well known that distinctive phenomena exist in embedded clauses in many languages. One of the most important involves nonfinite complementation. Many verbs in English select for infinitival complements; English also has infinitival adverbial clauses (such as purposives) and infinitival relative clauses. Nevertheless, infinitives can never be matrix verbs in English. Similar remarks hold of gerundive clauses. Furthermore, most of the interesting quirks surrounding complementation in English crucially involve infinitival complements—including obligatory control, raising to subject, and raising to object phenomena. This section shows that nonfinite clauses are impossible in polysynthetic languages for principled reasons. Given this, it is not surprising that control phenomena are not found either. Thus, in polysynthetic languages the statement that "embedded clauses have the same structure as matrix clauses" holds true to a remarkable degree. Indeed, researchers on these languages often point out that literally anything that can be an embedded clause can be used as a matrix clause as well with essentially no readjustments (e.g., Mithun 1984b)—something that is not true of English. This section shows how an important part of this observation follows from the Polysynthesis Parameter.

10.2.1 The Absence of Infinitives

Imagine what would happen if a polysynthetic language had nonfinite verb forms. By definition, this would mean that the Infl node (equivalently, the "Tense" or "Mood" node) is either syntactically inert or missing altogether. However, Infl plays a very important role in our account of polysynthesis: it hosts an agreement factor (see section 5.1). I have argued that agreement can only be adjoined to Case-assigning functional heads; although tensed Infl is a paradigm instance of this category, tenseless Infl is not. Thus, nonfinite clauses also typically lack agreement morphology, at least for the subject. This is seen clearly in many languages both inside and outside the Indo-European family. However, for a polysynthetic language, the effects of not having subject agreement are catastrophic. Any verb that takes an external argument needs to have that argument morphologically expressed in order to satisfy the MVC. However, the head of an external argument cannot be incorporated without violating the conditions on movement (see section 7.3.5). If the external argument cannot be expressed by agreement because of the nonfinite morphology, then there is no way that the structure can satisfy the MVC. Thus, no transitive or unergative verb could ever appear in a nonfinite clause.

In fact, there would be problems even if the verb did not have an external argument, although the reasoning is less direct. Suppose that the verb in a nonfinite clause had only an internal argument. Since the verb has no external argument, its Asp node will not be a Case assigner, by Burzio's Generalization. Thus, there could be no agreement whatsoever in the clause. Since the one argument of the verb is generated in the object position, it can be incorporated, thereby passing the MVC apart from agreement. However, the clause still needs a structural subject, by the Extended Projection Principle of Chomsky 1981. The verb's only argument cannot fulfill this role, because it needs to incorporate from the object position. Hence, the subject position could only be filled by a pleonastic. However, pro is not licensed in the subject position of an infinitive. PRO can appear in this position, but it cannot be a pleonastic (Safir 1985):

(45)　a.　[For there to be five people in the lifeboat] would be a disaster.

　　　b.　*[PRO to be five people in the lifeboat] would be a disaster.

　　　c.　[For it to seem that you are not paying attention] would be inappropriate.

　　　d.　[*PRO to seem that you are not paying attention] would be inappropriate.

Thus, although the MVC could be satisfied when an unaccusative verb appeared in a nonfinite form, the Extended Projection Principle could not. This means that if a polysynthetic language had a nonfinite verb form in its paradigm, transitive, unergative, and unaccusative verbs would not be able to appear in that form. Since virtually all verbs are in one or the other of these classes, I conclude that a polysynthetic language could not have a nonfinite verb form.

This prediction seems to be substantially correct. It is a known generalization in the functional/typological literature that polysynthetic/head-marking languages do not have infinitives (Heath 1975, Mithun 1984b). Moreover, this generalization is supported by the statistical survey of Nichols 1992:152–153. Mohawk, for example, has nothing like an English infinitive. The nearest functional equivalent is what Iroquoianists call the "optative" or "indefinite" form (see Lounsbury 1953:50 and Deering and Delisle 1976:332–333, among others). This form appears in the complement of verbs that correspond to those that take infinitival complements in English:

(46)　a.　K-ate'nyΛt-ha' au-sa-ke-'sere-ht-a-hserúni-'.
　　　　　1sS-try-HAB　　OPT-ITER-1sS-car-NOM-Ø-fix-PUNC
　　　　　'I am trying to fix the car.'

　　　b.　Yah th-a-hs-kwéni-'　　　　　　a-hs-a'ther-úni-'.　(D&D:353)
　　　　　not　CONTR-OPT-2sS-be.able-PUNC OPT-2sS-basket-make-PUNC
　　　　　'You aren't able to make a basket.'

　　　c.　Te-yukwa-[a]tuhwΛtsóni a-yakwá-hser-e'　　　ne　(KO:94)
　　　　　DUP-1pO-want/STAT　　　　OPT-1pS-follow-PUNC NE

　　　　　Ka-yaner-e'-kówa.
　　　　　NsS-good-NSF-big
　　　　　'We want to follow the League of Peace.'

　　　d.　Wa-hi-rihwanútu-'s-e'　　　　Sak y-a-ha-yΛt-a-ko-'.
　　　　　FACT-1sS/MsO-ask-BEN-PUNC Sak TRANS-OPT-MsS-wood-Ø-get-PUNC
　　　　　'I asked Sak to get wood.'

It is also used in purpose clause adjuncts:

(47)　Atekhwará-hne wa'-t-k-yΛtótΛ-'　　　　　ne akera-shú'a
　　　table-LOC　　　FACT-DUP-1sS-stack-PUNC NE dish-PL

　　　ne au-sa-ke-noharé-nyu-'.
　　　NE OPT-ITER-1sS-wash-DIST-PUNC
　　　'I stacked the dishes on the table in order to wash them.'

However, the optative is clearly not the formal equivalent of an infinitive. Thus, the optative forms all have ordinary subject agreement morphemes; indeed, they take exactly the same agreement morphemes as any other verb in the language. Moreover, the optative morpheme itself (typically *a,* with some complications) appears in the same position in the derived word as the ordinary tense/mood markers *wa'* 'factual' and *ʌ-* 'future'. If either this morpheme or the agreement morpheme or both are omitted, the sentences in (46) become hopelessly ungrammatical:

(48)   *K-ate'nyʌt-ha' se-'sere-ht-a-hserúni-'.
        1sS-try-HAB   ITER-car-NOM-Ø-fix-PUNC
        'I am trying to fix the car.'

Finally, optative verbs can be matrix clauses, and they are then interpreted with a modal reading something like 'should' (D&D:310)[16]:

(49)   Kak nu   y-a-yétew-e-'   n-ʌ-yó-karahw-e'.
        some place TRANS-OPT-1PINS-go-PUNC NE-FUT-NsO-get.dark-PUNC
        'We should go someplace tonight.'

I conclude that these optative forms are fully finite; the optative is simply one of the tense/moods of Mohawk, parallel to the factual and the future. Instead of saying in Mohawk 'I decided to buy a car,' one says the equivalent of 'I decided that I should buy a car'; instead of saying 'I tried to fix the car,' one says 'I tried that I should fix the car.'

This result can be generalized somewhat. Not only is the optative not an infinitive, but nothing else in Mohawk is either. Nor does Mohawk have a gerundive verb form, a participial verb form, a verbal noun, or anything else that is less than fully finite.[17] Although verbs in Mohawk typically have many morphemes, stative verbs and imperative verbs can have as few as two: a verb root and an agreement prefix. The agreement prefix is thus the one category that is absolutely obligatory. The MVC explains why this is so.

These facts seems to be quite typical of polysynthetic languages in general. For example, the equivalent of infinitival complementation in Nahuatl is selection for a complement in the future tense. Such verbs take ordinary subject and object agreement and are identical to matrix clauses in the future (Launey 1981:294–295):

(50)   a. ō-n-ilhuī-l-ō-c   in ni-c-chīhua-z.
            PAST-1sS-tell-NONACT-PASS-PERF IN 1sS-3sO-make-FUT
            'I was told to make it.'

       b. Ni-c-nequi   ni-c-chīhua-z.
            1sS-3sO-want 1sS-3sO-make-FUT
            'I want to make it.'

Neither Launey (1981) nor Andrews (1975) mentions any clause type that does not have such agreement. Exactly the same description holds in Southern Tiwa (Frantz 1993a):

(51)   a. Ti-na-khīwī-ban   te-ch'euat-hi-'i.
            1sS/AO-q-try-PAST 1sS-enter-FUT-SUB
            'I tried to go in.'

       b. Ti-na-p'euyam-ban te-pa'khu-kha-hi-'i.
            1sS/AO-q-start-PAST 1sS/cO-bread-bake-FUT-SUB
            'I started to bake bread.'

Frantz (1993a) gives similar patterns for verbs meaning 'help', 'decide', 'let', 'learn', 'be supposed to', 'forget', and 'be hard to' in Southern Tiwa. This also holds true for most of the Gunwinjguan languages. For example, Evans (1991:332–335, 338–342) discusses the lack of infinitival complementation in Mayali; tensed irrealis clauses are used instead:

(52) Nga-djare nga-m-ra-yi   nga-bunjhme-yi. (Evans 1991:341)
     1sS-want 1sS-CIS-come-IRR 1sS-kiss-IRR
     'I wanted to come and kiss her.'

Similarly, Merlan (1983:141) and Heath (1984:558, 1986:395) claim that nonfinite clauses are absent in Ngalakan and Nunggubuyu, respectively. Other grammars of polysynthetic languages are less explicit, but consistent with this claim; for example, there is no hint of any infinitival verb forms in Shibatani's (1990) description of Ainu. In this way, polysynthetic languages differ from languages such as Chichewa, Greenlandic, Alamblak, and Yimas, all of which are languages of considerable morphological complexity that do (arguably) have nonfinite clauses.

10.2.2 Alleged Examples of Infinitives

There are, however, at least two polysynthetic languages that do present possible counterexamples to this claim: Rembarrnga and Chukchee. In Rembarrnga, the putative examples of infinitives are relatively marginal and may result from misanalysis or language contact. However, Chukchee presents a much more formidable challenge, forcing us to clarify certain points that have been left vague in the statement of the MVC.

Rembarrnga is a Gunwinjguan language rather closely related to languages known not to have infinitives. Nevertheless, it has reportedly developed something rather like an infinitive, which may be used in purpose clauses (McKay 1975:318–329). Thus, one finds (53b) in Rembarrnga as well as the more typical form in (53a).

(53) a. Tjurla nga-ma-ngara   kuwa ka-rtom-ma-kan.
       water 1sS/3sO-get-FUT PURP 3sS-drink-FUT-DAT
       'I fetched him some water to drink.'

     b. Tjurla nga-ma-ngara   kuwa rtom-Ø-kan.
       water 1sS/3sO-get-FUT PURP drink-INFIN-DAT
       'I fetched him some water to drink.'

Although the two sentences are essentially synonymous, the purpose clause in (53a) has a verb with full tense and agreement morphology, whereas the embedded verb in (53b) lacks both. Notice, however, that the understood subject of the embedded clause in these examples is third person singular. This turns out to be important; when the understood subject is second person, speakers differ in their judgments:

(54) (*)Tjurla nginj-pak-ma-ngara   kuwa rtom-Ø-kan.
       water 1sS/2sO-BEN-get-FUT PURP drink-INFIN-DAT
       'I'll fetch you some water to drink.'

At least one of McKay's consultants accepted (54), but several others rejected it; they required the verb form to be fully inflected in these circumstances. Indeed, all of McKay's other examples of infinitival purpose clauses have either a third person singular understood subject or a generic/arbitrary understood subject. This suggests that there are at least two different dialects in the speech community. For those speakers who reject (54), we can say that the so-called infinitive forms are actually finite forms in which the 3sS/(3sO) marker happens to be Ø. This would not be particularly unusual; indeed, 3sS/(3sO) is spelled out as Ø in certain tenses in Rembarrnga and other Gunwinjguan languages. The innovation in this dialect is merely one of generalizing this form from the past tenses to the "tenseless" verb. This leaves only the speaker who accepted (54) as a candidate for having a true infinitive. Yet even here there is an alternative interpretation. The infinitival purpose clauses are typically marked with the dative case *kan*. This morpheme is also used to mark purposive noun phrase adjuncts in Rembarrnga, as in (55).

(55) Yara-manj kuwenj-kan.   (McKay 1975:262)
      1pS-went   kangaroo-DAT
      'We went [hunting] for kangaroos.'

This raises the possibility that the verb form in (54) is not an infinitival at all, but rather a nominalized verb. Nominalizations are crucially different from infinitival verbs in that the arguments of the base verb are often suppressed in nominals (Chomsky 1981 and Grimshaw 1990, among many others; see also section 6.2.5). If *rtom* is a nominalization in (54), we can assume that its external θ-role is suppressed; thus, subject agreement is not needed to satisfy the MVC. In this case, the correct gloss for (54) would be 'I got you some water for drinking.' Thus, it seems likely that Rembarrnga does not allow true infinitives after all. Rather, the clauses that look like infinitives are either tensed clauses with an innovative null 3sS agreement form or nominalized verbs, depending on the dialect.[18]

With this encouraging result in hand, I turn to the more difficult case of Chukchee. Chukchee is commonly described as having not only infinitival verb forms, but a variety of gerunds and participles as well. There is relatively little information on these forms available in English, so my discussion must be somewhat tentative; however, some progress can be made. To start with, it is useful to break down the examples into three broad categories: nonfinite verbs that head adsentential modifiers, nonfinite verbs in auxiliary-like constructions, and nonfinite verbs as complements to higher verbs. In fact, only the third category, if it exists, is truly problematic.

Nonfinite adsentential modifiers in Chukchee are actually reminiscent of constructions in Rembarrnga in several ways. They are not discussed systematically in the available literature, but a reasonable number of examples can be picked out from the various articles. Those in (56) are representative of examples in which the verb has the "gerund" suffix, while (57) gives examples with verbs in the "infinitive." In each case, the adverbial clause is italicized.

(56) a. *Rənowərgə-rkəpčew-a* n-ena-npeqetaw-gəm   yara-t.   (Polinskaja and
         smoke.hole-hit-GER   IMPF-1sS-throw.over-1sS house-ABS/PL   Nedjalkov
         'I overthrow houses by merely hitting down their smoke holes.'   1987:253)

b. *Anə 'atča-ma* keyŋ-ən n-uttə-numekew-qin. (Polinskaja and Nedjalkov
well wait-GER bear-ABS IMPF-wood-collect-3sS 1987:252)
'While waiting, the bear was picking up wood.'

c. *∃tləg-ək emič-e* Qergənkaaw ga-qaa-čwentat-len. (Kozinsky et al.
father-LOC be.away-GER Qergynkaaw PASTII-deer-stray-3sS 1988:701)
'While the father was away, Qergynkaaw had some of his deer stray away.'

(57) a. *Pukerəŋo-k* rə-čəp-ew-nin. (Bogoras 1922:785)
arrive-INFIN CAUS-dive-CAUS-3sS/3sO
'When he arrived, he made him dive.'

b. Yič'emittumg-ət ŋew'en-e ine-ret-g'e-t iŋqun (Polinskaja and Nedjalkov
brother-ABS/PL wife-INSTR APASS-bring-3PS in.order.to 1987:255)
ŋaw-kalgotke-k.
wife-boast-INFIN.
'The brothers came with their wives to show the wives to everybody.'

c. 'Etki ine-n'e'ek-w'i gem *r-'etyiw-et-ək.* (Polinskaja and Nedjalkov
badly 1sO-offend-3sS me(ABS) CAUS-argue-CAUS-INFIN 1987:250)
'She offended me by arguing with me.'

d. I'am gət . . .r'otawə-tko-rkən iŋqun muri mə-nə-mŋi-mək (Kozinsky et al.
why you prohibit-ITER-PRES that we IMPF-celebrate-1PS 1988:661)
r'ew-u-k?
whale-catch-INFIN
'Why are you prohibiting that we celebrate the whale-catch?'

The first thing to observe about these forms is that there are some important homophonies. In particular, the so-called infinitival morpheme *k* is identical to the locative Case suffix in Chukchee, and the so-called gerund *(t)e/(t)a* is identical to the ergative/instrumental Case (Bogoras 1922). Moreover, the meaning of the nonfinite construction is generally related to the meaning of the homophonous Case affix. A noun in locative Case is an adjunct that specifies the place or time that an action occurred; a verb root in locative case can refer to an event that identifies when the action of the main verb occurred. Nouns in ergative Case can refer to, among other things, an instrument used to perform the action; similarly, verbs in the ergative case can refer to techniques used to perform the action of the main verb (see especially (56a)). This is similar to what we saw in Rembarrnga, where nonfinite verbs usually take the dative Case suffix, which also attaches to nouns with a similar meaning. Given this, I propose that these Chukchee examples are also nominalizations, where the Case suffix simultaneously acts as the nominalizer and the licensing adposition. This view is consistent with that of Bogoras (1922), who refers to the nonfinite constructions as "verbal nouns." Indeed, he says that such verbal nouns can appear in the allative Case as well, creating a kind of purposive modifier in Chukchee (although not in Koryak) :

(58) *Awkwat-etə* tə-gaičaw-rkən. (Bogaras 1922:784)
leave-ALL 1sS-hasten-PRES
'I make haste to depart.'

Thus, literal translations of the sentences in (56)–(58) would be closer to the following: 'I overthrow houses by striking'; 'At the arrival, he made him dive,' 'I hasten toward departure,' and so on.

Once again, the explanatory virtue of this view is that nominalizations do not necessarily inherit the argument structure of the related verb. Rather, the subject and object arguments associated with the root verb are often left unexpressed, or are expressed only as a kind of adjunct (Grimshaw 1990). If this is so for the examples in (56)–(58), then the fact that the verbal nouns have no agreement on them is not problematic. In support of this hypothesis, notice that *none of these nonfinite forms is associated with an argument in structural Case.* The verbs in (56b), (57a), and (58) are intransitive, with no expressed subject argument; this is then pragmatically understood as the same as some matrix clause participant, as in Rembarrnga. The forms that are derived from transitive verbs either leave the object unexpressed and pragmatically interpreted, as in (57c), or have the object incorporated into the verbal noun form as in (56a), (57b), and (57d). The one example of a subject argument related to a nonfinite form is in locative case, rather than absolutive (see (56c)); this is consistent with the claim that it is an adjunct modifying a nominal head. This apparent inability to take direct Case arguments is exactly what we would expect of nominalizations. Of course, I do not know whether these generalizations hold true for the language as a whole,[19] but if they do then this class of examples is not problematic after all.

The next class of nonfinite verbs to consider are those that appear in auxiliary-like constructions. Nedjalkov (1976:196) discusses alternations like the following:

(59) a. Ǝtləg-ən ləwaw-ə-rkən   maraw-ək ekke-k reen.
         father-ABS cannot-PRES/3sS scold-INFIN son-LOC with
         'The father cannot scold with the son.'

      b. Ǝtləg-e   ləwaw-ə-rkə-nen   rə-maraw-at-ək   ekək.
         father-ERG cannot-Ø-PRES-3sS/3sO CAUS-scold-CAUS-INFIN son(ABS)
         'The father cannot scold the son.'

Along with *ləwaw* 'not be able to', Nedjalkov mentions *paa* 'stop' and *ayəlgaw* 'fear' as being matrix verbs in this construction; Bogoras (1922:785–786) adds *nka* 'to refuse' and (for Koryak) *ŋvo* 'to begin', *plə* 'to finish', and *nkaw* 'to cease'. Elsewhere, Nedjalkov gives the following examples:

(60) a. Tilmə-til riŋe-k   tantenmiaṇt-g'e. (Nedjalkov 1976:192)
         eagle-ABS fly-INFIN try-3sS
         'The eagle tried to fly.'

      b. Ŋewəsqet-ti ləg-eqəlpe uwi-k   moo-g'at. (Kozinsky et al. 1988:681)
         women-ABS/PL quickly   boil.meat-INFIN start-3PS.
         'The women quickly started boiling meat.'

Examples (59a) and (60) look like they have ordinary infinitival complements with subject control. This, however, holds only when the complement infinitive is an intransitive verb. Some strange properties appear when the complement infinitive is a transitive verb, as in (59b). First, there is no object agreement on the infinitive verb where one might expect it; rather, object agreement with the embedded theme shows up on the matrix verb (see also Kozinsky et al. 1988:701, n. 11). Moreover, the Case of the matrix subject shifts from absolutive to ergative. In these respects, the matrix verb is acting like a transitive verb that takes the semantic object of the embedded infinitive as its own object. Thus, the problem that these constructions pose for the MVC is not so much that agreement is absent, but that it seems to be in the wrong location.

I suggest that this phenomenon can be analyzed in terms of the theory of light verb constructions developed in chapter 8. In section 8.3, in particular, I argued that a light verb construction (LVC) analysis was appropriate for certain control-like modal and aspectual verbs such as the purposive morpheme in Mohawk, and the infinitive-selecting predicates in Chukchee seem to be members of the same semantic class. The key principle underlying the analysis was (61).

(61)   If the argument structure of X is nondistinct from the argument structure of Y, then the head chain $\{X_k + Y, t_k\}$ may assign θ-roles as a unit.

This implies that in all languages the lower predicate must incorporate into the higher light verb in order for the two to assign θ-roles jointly. However, (61) leaves open whether this incorporation takes place in the overt syntax or covertly at LF: if incorporation happens at LF, then a "shared" argument will look like a dependent of the lower predicate only for purposes of Case marking and agreement at PF; if incorporation takes place in the syntax, then the same argument will look like a dependent of the light verb at PF. These two constructions can exist side by side in the same language, as shown by the following examples from Urdu, repeated from chapter 8:

(62)   a. Mə̃y [ys k-a   yntyzam]   kər-ūga.
        I   this GEN-MASC arrangement(MASC) make-FUT/1sS
        'I will arrange this.' (Literally: 'I will make its arrangement.')

        b. Mə̃y ne nəmaz   šwru   ki.
        I   ERG prayer(FEM) beginning made(FEM)
        'I began the prayer.'

Notice that in (62a) the theme agrees with the predicate noun 'arrangement', whereas in (62b) it agrees with the light verb 'make'. Example (62b) is thus the case where the predicate noun incorporates into the light verb in the syntax.

There is an apparent problem with this interpretation, however, which I ignored in chapter 8: the noun *šwru* and the verb *ki* do not constitute a morphological unit in (62b). This can be accounted for by appealing to the device of excorporation, introduced by Roberts (1991). In Roberts' proposal, there are at least two ways in which head movement can apply to an X^0 that is itself made up of two or more elements: either the complex category as a whole can move, or only the head of the category can move. These two possibilities are shown schematically in (63). Structure (63a) represents the "normal" case—the only one allowed in Baker 1988a and the one assumed throughout this book. Structure (63b) is the excorporation case, so-called because the complex word formed by one head movement is destroyed by the next one. Whether (63a) or (63b) will take place in any given situation is a function of the lexical properties of the morphemes involved: if Y satisfies a morphological subcategorization feature of X, the two stay together as in (63a); if not, they split as in (63b). Roberts' paradigm case of excorporation is the Germanic verb clusters formed by V-raising; these involve nonvacuous incor-

(63) a.

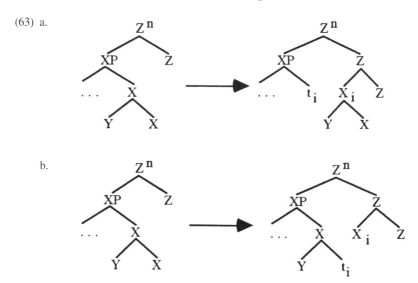

b.

poration, but only the head verb of the cluster moves on to the complementizer position in verb-second contexts. Guasti (1992) shows that essentially the same process takes place in the Romance languages. The Urdu example in (62b) is presumably another such case: the predicate N incorporates into the light verb in the syntax, but the V then excorporates and moves into the functional categories associated with inflection by itself.

With this additional background, we can now analyze examples like (59) and (60) in Chukchee as LVCs, like those analyzed in section 8.3, in which excorporation has taken place. Thus, the structure of (59b) is (64) (here I ignore the NPs adjoined to the clause and the internal structure of the causative verb 'scold').

(64)

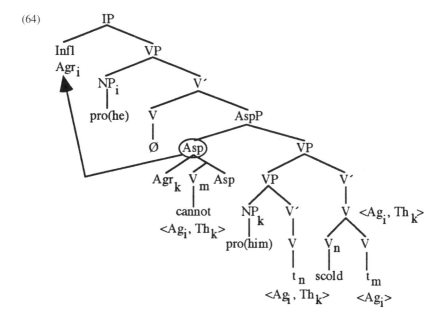

In (64), 'scold' incorporates into 'cannot', the head of the matrix VP. Since the argument structures of the two verbs are nondistinct, they can assign θ-roles as unit. In particular, they jointly assign their agent-like roles to the external argument position. At the same time, a choice is made as to which verb's argument structure will be the argument structure of the whole V–V complex; the argument structure of 'scold' is chosen because it is the larger of the two. So far, this is exactly like the purposive constructions discussed in section 8.3. The difference, however, is that rather than the whole V complex moving to Asp, only the head of that complex does. Crucially, it bears along with it the argument structure of the complex that it represents, $<Ag_i, Th_k>$. The Agr factor in Asp can therefore be coindexed with NP_k, in accordance with the CAR. Subsequently, the Asp complex incorporates into Infl, and the Agr in Infl is coindexed with the Agent argument. This derives the correct form, in which the higher verb is inflected for tense, aspect, and agreement; the lower verb is uninflected; and the agreement factors on the higher verb correspond to the argument structure of the lower verb. We may assume that the analysis of the examples in (59a) and (60) is essentially the same; however, since the lower verb is intransitive, the difference between its argument structure and the argument structure of the higher verb is not striking.

If Chukchee were not a polysynthetic language, the analysis would be complete; however, since it is, we must now face the question of whether this structure satisfies the MVC, which states that a phrase X can receive a θ-role from Y only if X is coindexed with a morpheme in the word containing Y. The crucial question, then, is what is meant by the term "word" in this condition. Throughout this book I have implicitly assumed that it was obvious what a word was. Nevertheless, "word" is a technical concept, and a tricky one at that (see Di Sciullo and Williams 1987 for discussion). If "word" in the statement of the MVC means *morphophonological word,* the domain of lexical phonology, then (64) does not satisfy the MVC: the agreement that expresses NP_k is not on the morphophonological word that contains the verb root that is the ultimate source of NP_k's θ-role (*rəmarawatək* 'to scold'). This is perhaps clearer in an example where the theme argument of the lower verb is an incorporable noun root, rather than a pronoun. Predictably, the noun incorporates into the lower verb before the lower verb incorporates into the higher one, by the HMC. Thus, one finds examples like (65) from Koryak, a language closely related to Chukchee.

(65) Ga-naɛl-in-au   payitt-o-k. (Bogoras 1922:786)
      PAST2–become-PAST2–3pS blackberry-eat-INFIN
      'They came to be eating blackberries.'

Here *o* 'eat' is a transitive verb that selects both an agent and a theme; however, there is no one morphophonological word that contains morphemes related to both. Rather, the infinitival verb includes the incorporated object, while the subject agreement is on the aspectual verb.

Fortunately, we are under no obligation to understand the term "word" in the MVC as "morphophonological word." On the contrary, the morphophonological word is presumably a notion relevant to PF, defined by the nature of that component. On the other hand, the MVC is a condition on θ-role assignment, and as such it is known to hold at LF (see section 2.2). The question then is: What is the relevant notion of "word" in an LF representation? LF is significantly different from PF in that it consists of chains, sequences of distinct positions that act like units. For example, Chomsky and Lasnik (1993) and Chomsky (1992) state that well-formed LF objects are uniform chains. They have in mind NPs, the canonical arguments, but the same logic holds for Vs, the canonical θ-role assigners, given that they also move. Therefore, the proper notion of a word at LF is presumably the word chain: an entity consisting of an X^0 node and all the other X^0 nodes it is related to by movement. This is stated more precisely as follows:

(66) A sequence of positions $\{\alpha_1, \ldots \alpha_n\}$ is a word$_{LF}$ if and only if for all i, such that $1 \leq i < n$:
  (i) α_i is a maximal node of type X^0.
  (ii) α_i contains the antecedent of a trace dominated by α_{i+1}.
  (iii) α_i is associated with the same argument structure as α_{i+1}.

For cases of normal head movement, the difference between the LF word and the PF word is not very important, because the LF word contains one and only one PF word. However, once excorporation is allowed as well as incorporation, the two senses of "word" diverge more noticeably. According to this definition, Infl, Asp, and both V nodes in (64) together count as a single LF word. Thus, when "word" is understood in its proper, LF-oriented sense, (64) and (65) do satisfy the MVC, since each argument is coindexed with a morpheme contained in one of the X^0s of the X^0 chain that θ-marks it.

    In this context, it is natural to ask how widespread the possibility of excorporation is in the polysynthetic languages. In fact, there are a few other constructions that are probably best analyzed in this way. The trademark of such constructions is that the semantic predicate consists of two distinct words, one that is uninflected and one that bears all the agreement morphology. Chukchee is particularly rich in constructions of this type; in addition to the modal/aspectual verbs already discussed, it has auxiliary constructions, where the thematic verb appears in the "gerund" form together with an inflected form of either *it* 'be' or *rət* 'have'. Simple examples are the following (from Bogoras 1922:766, 762):

(67) a. Gumnan činit lu$^\epsilon$-ta   t-re-nt-əŋ-ənet   qaat.
       I/ERG   self see-GER 1sS-FUT-have-FUT-3pO reindeer.
       'I myself shall see the reindeer.'

     b. Loŋ-qamə-tva-ta it-yi$^\epsilon$.
        not-eat-live-GER be-3sS
        'He could not eat it.'

Other constructions of this type are discussed in Nedjalkov 1976, including combinations of negative participle plus auxiliary, psychological predicate plus light verb, and causative verb plus auxiliary (see section 8.2.3 for an example).[20] Similarly, Wichita has a small class of uninflectable adjectives that appear adjacent to an inflected auxiliary verb, as shown in (68) (Rood 1976:12–13).

(68) Né:rhirʔa tac ti-ʔi.
      buffalo   big IND/3sS-be
      'The buffalo is big.'

Finally, Mayali has LVC-like constructions in which an uninflected nominal appears adjacent to an inflected verb; Evans (1991:310) calls such nominals verbal satellites. This is the normal way of borrowing English verbs into Mayali, for example:

(69) Bandi-ga-ni   walkabout.
      3pS/3pO-take-PAST/IMPF walkabout
      'They'd take them walkabout.'

Without going into details, all of these constructions are plausibly instances in which some kind of argument-taking head incorporates into a light verb, followed by excorporation of that verb into the higher functional categories. This shows that the mechanism has some generality in the polysynthetic languages.

Apparently, there are also limits to excorporation, however. Overall, there are two reasons why incorporation takes place in a polysynthetic language: one is to satisfy the MVC (see section 7.1 and elsewhere); the other is to create an LVC interpretation via (61). Interestingly, all the potential cases of excorporation we have seen split apart combinations formed for the second reason. Thus, there is no indication that nouns in Chukchee or any other polysynthetic language can incorporate into the V, satisfy the MVC, and then be split from the V again. It is clear enough what such a structure would look like: a morphologically independent noun would appear linearly adjacent to a fully inflected verb. Moreover, if NI suppressed object agreement, as it does in Mohawk, Nahuatl, and Chukchee, then the semantically transitive verb would be inflected as an intransitive. Structures satisfying this description are, in fact, found in various languages; Mithun (1984a:852) gives a good example from the Mayan language Kanjobal. However, this never seems to happen in a truly polysynthetic language. Thus, I offer the following conjecture:

(70) If a complex X^0 is made up of nonhead A and head B, B can excorporate out of the X^0 only if the combination of A and B was not triggered by the MVC.

If this conjecture holds up under further inquiry, it can be built into the MVC as follows:

(71) *Morphological Visibility Condition* (revised):
      A phrase Z is visible for θ-role assignment from a head Y only if Z is coindexed with a morpheme Z' such that Z' is properly contained in an X^0 node that is part of the word$_{LF}$ containing Y.

The key new phrase here is *properly contained*; this is defined in (72):

(72) An X^0 node properly contains Z if it contains Z and some other morpheme Y, such that Y is not contained in Z and Y is not a trace.

The intuition behind these definitions is that a degree of real morphological union must take place between a morpheme that represents the argument and the morpheme that represents its θ-role assigner. This is perfectly in keeping with the guiding intuition behind the MVC, which is that argument relationships must be expressed by head marking in the polysynthetic languages. This more technical understanding of the MVC then expresses the fact that not only is incorporation often forced, but subsequent excorporation is quite limited.

Concluding this phase of the discussion, we have found ample reason to say that most "infinitives" in Chukchee are not the heads of CP complements at all; rather, they are the fragments of a complex head left behind by excorporation. This is consistent with the MVC once the notion "word" is explicated in the proper way.[21]

Finally, I found three examples of infinitives cited in the Chukchee literature that do not fit with either of the two analyses given so far. These are apparently selected by a predicate ('help', 'pity') and, unlike the adsentential modifiers discussed previously, they do have absolutive NPs associated with them. The examples are given in (73).

(73) a. Morg-ənan gət mət-re-winret-gət *riwl-ək*   *əməl'o*   (Comrie 1979:226–227)
         we-ERG   thou 1pS-FUT-help-2sO move-INFIN all(ABS)
         gečе-yo-t.
         collect-PASS/PART-ABS/PL
         'We will help you to move all the collected items.'

      b. Winren-nin Roltəgərg-ən *ilgətw-ək*   *'in-ət.* . . .   (Kozinsky et al.
         help-3sS/3sO Roltygyrgyn unharness-INFIN wolf-ABS/PL   1988:693)
         'He helped Roltygyrgyn unharness the wolves. . . .'

      c. Kəlgəlogərge-gət *gəm-nan gət*   *pela-k.* (Nedjalkov 1979:243)
         pity-2sS   I-ERG   you-ABS leave-INFIN
         'Pity (me) that I leave you; I am sorry to leave you.'

Comrie uses (73a) to show that object control in Chukchee works as it does in English; Nedjalkov uses (73c) to show that Chukchee consistently has an ergative–absolutive Case pattern even in infinitival clauses. These examples cannot be accounted for in my theory. I am forced to conclude that they are marked structures, perhaps due to the large influx of materials translated from Russian into Chukchee. Indeed, Comrie (1981:34) observes that Russian influence on the aboriginal languages is particularly evident in their clausal subordination systems. In principle, this markedness claim could be tested by way of the prediction that examples like (73) should not be found in older, traditional texts. In fact, I found no examples of absolutive (or ergative) NPs dependent on a nonfinite verb that is not in construction with an auxiliary in the two texts included in Bogoras 1922[22]; nor are there any among the examples of nonfinite verbs that Bogoras cites, which are drawn from a much larger corpus of texts (1922:784–788).

10.2.3 Implications for Control

If polysynthetic languages cannot have nonfinite clauses, it comes as no great surprise that they also cannot have those special syntactic features that are associated with nonfinite clauses. The most important of these is obligatory control.

I begin by reviewing some of the standard properties of obligatory control. Sentences like (74) in English have the property that the understood subject of the embedded clause is coreferential with the subject of the matrix clause.

(74)　a. I tried to fix the car.

　　　b. I decided to buy a house.

　　　c. I want to find my shoe.

　　　d. I promised John to cook dinner.

Similarly, in (75) the subject of the embedded clause is necessarily understood as the object of the matrix clause.

(75)　a. I persuaded John to buy a house.

　　　b. I told John to cook dinner.

This is the control phenomenon. In this respect, some infinitival clauses in English contrast with tensed complements. In tensed clauses, the embedded subject must be overt and can be virtually any NP. If it happens to be a pronoun, then the pronoun can generally be understood as coreferential with the relevant matrix argument or not:

(76)　a. Peter decided that he should buy a house.

　　　b. Peter promised John that he would fix dinner.

　　　c. I persuaded Peter that he should buy a house.

　　　d. I told Peter that he should cook dinner.

In each of these examples, 'he' could in a suitable context refer not to Peter but, say, to Peter's son. In a pro-drop language such as Italian or Spanish, these pronouns could be null. Thus, there is a systematic difference between infinitives with null subjects and tensed clauses.

In the classical GB theory of Chomsky 1981, these facts were accounted for in terms of the empty category PRO. Because of this category's peculiar referential properties (it is a mixture of anaphor and pronoun), it can only appear in ungoverned positions. The subject position of a nonfinite clause is the paradigm instance of such a position—perhaps the only instance. However, the subject position of an infinitive is ungoverned; therefore, no other NP can appear in it, since all other NPs must be either assigned Case under government (phonologically realized NPs) or be governed as part of their licensing conditions (the ECP for traces, identification for pro). Thus, unless the subject position of an infinitive is governed by some element outside the clause, it can only contain PRO. PRO, then, must be assigned an antecedent in accordance with the principles of a special theory of Control (left open by Chomsky). This accounts for (74) and (75). The subject position of tensed clauses, however, is always governed by the combination of finite Infl and agreement; hence, it may not contain PRO. Since nominative Case is assigned, tenses clauses may, however, have any other NP as subject (if other relevant conditions are met). If the subject happens to be a pronoun, it will have the same freedom of reference that is characteristic of pronouns in other positions. This accounts for (76).

Now let us turn to polysynthetic languages. As discussed in the previous section, the MVC implies that all verbs in these languages must have tense/mood and (especially) agreement features. This implies that the subject position is always governed in these languages, which, in turn, implies that PRO will never be possible. Thus, we predict that polysynthetic languages should not have obligatory control paradigms comparable to (74) or (75); in their place, one should find paradigms like (76), where the embedded subject may, but need not, be coreferential with something in the matrix. This is what we find in Mohawk. The results are most striking with such verbs as *try* and *ask,* which take control infinitives but not clauses with *should* in English. The best Mohawk translations of such sentences involve an optative complement, and it is not necessary that the subject of that complement be coreferential with the matrix subject. Thus, the sentences in (77) are perfect in Mohawk, even though they have no natural equivalents in English.

(77) a. Λ-ha-[a]te'nyΛtΛ-' ne a-yako-yéshu-'.
          FUT-MsS-try-PUNC NE OPT-FsO-laugh-PUNC
          'He will try for her to laugh.'

     b. Uwári wa'-khe-rihwanútu's-e' ruwa-yΛ'a
         Mary FACT-1sS/FsO-ask-PUNC her-son
         y-a-ha-yΛt-a-ko-'.
         TRANS-OPT-MsS-wood-Ø-get-PUNC
         'I asked Mary for her son to get wood.'

Even when the embedded subject is a pronominal with the same morphosyntactic features as the matrix subject, a noncoreferential reading is possible:

(78) a. Sak wa-ha-[a]te'nyΛtΛ-' raúha a-ha-nhotúko-'.
          Sak FACT-MsS-try-PUNC him OPT-MsS-open-PUNC
          '*Sak* tried that *he* open it.' (disjoint or coreferent)

     b. Tyer te-ho-[a]tΛhutsóni   raúha a-ha-'wáhr-a-k-e'
         Tyer DUP-MsO-want/STAT him OPT-MsS-meat-Ø-eat-PUNC

         ne kweskwes o'wáhru.
         NE pig   meat
         '*Tyer* wants that *he* eat the pork.' (disjoint or coreferent)

(If the overt pronoun in the lower clause is omitted, then the coreferential reading is the most salient, but the disjoint reading is also possible.) One can use an extraction test to confirm that these CPs are complements, rather than a kind of adjunct; thus the lower subjects in (79) are not controlled, even though an interrogative phrase has moved out of the embedded clause.

(79) a. Ka nikáyΛ kanhóha wa-hs-ate'nyΛtΛ-'   Sak a-ha-nhotúko-'?
          which   door   FACT-2sS-try-PUNC Sak OPT-MsS-open-PUNC
          'Which door did you try for Sak to open?'

     b. Úhka Λ-hs-ate'nyΛ́ytΛ-' a-yako-yéshu-'?
         who FUT-2sS-try-PUNC OPT-FsO-laugh-PUNC
         'Who will you try to make laugh?'

These Mohawk sentences contrast with superficially similar Greek sentences discussed in Terzi 1992 (see later discussion). This same pattern of results holds for other verbs in Mohawk that take optative or future complements and correspond to control verbs in English, including *rihwanutuhs* 'ask', *atΛhutsoni* 'want', *kweni*

'be able to, succeed in', and *rihwayʌta's*, 'decide'.[23] In each case, the subject of
the optative complement may be distinct in reference from the subject and object
of the matrix verb.

There is not a great deal of information concerning this matter in other polysynthetic languages, but what there is generally confirms this theory. Heath (1975)
claimed that head-marking languages with rich gender distinctions like Nunggubuyu do not have control phenomena (see also Heath 1986:582–584). Similarly,
Evans (1991:332–334) makes it reasonably clear that there is no obligatory control
in Mayali; rather, coreference possibilities between arguments of the embedded
clause and those of the matrix are determined by the lexical properties of pronouns, such as their person, number, and gender features. For example, in (52),
the subject of the verb *djare* 'want' agrees with and is the antecedent of the
subject of its complement. However, it is equally possible for the subject of the
embedded clause to be distinct from the subject of the matrix (Evans 1991:342):

(80) Nga-djare gogok   ba-m-ra-yi   bi-bunjhma-yi.
      1sS-want older.brother 3sS-CIS-go-IRR 3sS/3hO-kiss-IRR
      'I wanted my older brother to [come and] kiss her.'

Similarly, the Nahuatl verb *nequi* 'want' takes a control-like future complement
in (50b), but it can equally well take a future complement with a distinct subject
(Launey 1981:295):

(81) Cuix ti-c-nequi   ni-c-chīhua-z?
      Q   2sS-3sO-want   1sS-3sO-make-FUT
      'Do you want me to make it?'

The Southern Tiwa word *khiwi* 'try' can also take a complement with an uncon-
trolled subject (Donald Frantz, personal communication):

(82) Ti-na-khiwi-ban   in-'u-we-'i   Ø-escuela-mia-hi-'i.
      1sS/AO-q-try-PAST   1sO\AO-boy-be-SUB   AS-school-go-FUT-SUB
      'I tried for my son to go to college.'

The only difference between the apparent control cases and the noncontrol cases
is whether the matrix and embedded agreements are identical or not. Other than
this, I claim that the two have exactly the same structure. Moreover, there is an
interesting contrast between these examples and ones in which *nequi* or *khiwi*
incorporates the head of its propositional complement. When incorporation takes
place, a controlled reading is required as discussed in section 8.3, but when there
is no incorporation the verb's complement is not limited in this way.

So far I have assumed the classical GB account of control, where having a
PRO in the subject position is incompatible with agreement. However, other views
of control have been proposed recently, which seek to make PRO less of an exception to the standard principles of NP licensing. Thus, Chomsky and Lasnik (1993)
argue that PRO is both Case-marked and agreed with; in particular, as the "null
NP" it receives a special "null Case" and triggers a unique kind of "null
agreement". This newer theory does not fit very well with data from the polysynthetic languages presented here. In order to explain the fact that Mohawk does not
have obligatory control phenomena, one would have to say one of two things:

either Mohawk happens to not to have a null agreement form, as a kind of paradigmatic gap, or the null agreement that licenses PRO does not count as satisfying the MVC. Neither approach looks very promising. Saying that Mohawk happens not to have a null agreement misses the generalization that none of the polysynthetic languages allow PRO; thus, it is more than an accidental gap. Stipulating that null agreement cannot satisfy the MVC is more viable empirically, but it undercuts the conceptual idea behind Chomsky and Lasnik's proposal. An important part of their motivation for saying that PRO receives null Case is to explain why it can receive a θ-role at LF, given the standard Visibility Condition. Thus, it seems quite ad hoc to say that null Case is adequate to make PRO pass the standard Visibility Condition, but null agreement is not adequate to have PRO pass the Morphological Visibility Condition. Furthermore, it is clear that phonologically null agreement forms do satisfy the MVC with respect to third person singular arguments in many of the polysynthetic languages. Thus, it seems that the older theory, in which PRO was exceptional from the point of view of licensing, has the right character for explaining the fact that PRO cannot appear in a well-defined class of languages.

The theory of PRO and agreement also interacts in an interesting way with current views about clause structure. In particular, the classical GB view becomes more complex once one adopts the VP-internal subject hypothesis and the claim that clauses have more than one functional category. This raises the possibility that PRO could trigger agreement in the specifier position of one functional category and then raise to the specifier position of a higher functional category to escape being governed by the agreement. In fact, Terzi (1992) shows that this possibility is attested in Modern Greek and other Balkan languages. A simple example is given in (83).

(83)   I Maria prospathise na diavasi ena vivlio.   (Terzi 1992:28)
       Mary   tried/3SG   PRT read/3SG one book.
       'Mary tried to read a book.'

Superficially, (83) looks very much like (77a) in Mohawk. The crucial difference is that the lower subject in Greek is obligatorily controlled by the upper one, unlike in Mohawk (with some complications, which Terzi discusses at length). Hence, sentences like (84), where the agreement features on the lower verb are incompatible with those on the higher verb, are ungrammatical.

(84)   *I Maria prospathise na diavasoun ena vivlio.
        Mary   tried-3SG   PRT read-3PL one book.
       'Mary tried for them to read a book.'

Thus, the Greek verb for 'try' shows English-like control facts in spite of the presence of agreement. This suggests that the subject of the complement of verbs like 'try' in Greek must be PRO after all, and its antecedent is determined by Control Theory. Indeed, Terzi gives further evidence for this conclusion. Thus, PRO and agreement are not necessarily incompatible after all.

Given this, can we still explain the fact that control is impossible in a polysynthetic language? If PRO can trigger subject agreement in Greek, it seems that this should, in principle, be possible in a language like Mohawk as well, contrary to what we observe. This gap in the argumentation can be covered as follows: Crucial to Terzi's analysis of (83) in Greek is the existence of the invariant subjunctive particle *na*. Terzi shows that this is not a complementizer, arguing instead that it is of the category "mood" (M) and projects a "mood phrase" (MP). PRO then moves to the specifier of this MP to escape government, as shown in (85).

(85)

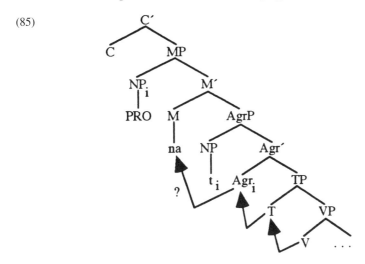

Any account in which PRO must be ungoverned must stipulate which heads count as potential governors. Thus, the fact that PRO is ungoverned in (85) depends not only on its structural position, but also the nature of the heads in its environment. In particular, the M^0 *na* and the null head of C must not be potential governors, or PRO would be ruled out in this position. (Indeed, Terzi shows that with other, phonologically overt complementizers the construction is impossible.) Similarly, in English the null infinitival complementizer and the infinitive marker *to* must not be potential governors. Clearly, it would be desirable to have a universal characterization of which heads are potential governors and which are not. Although I am not aware of any adequate characterization of this in the literature, something like (86) is surely part of the answer.

(86)   A head X is a potential governor (of Y) if X includes an index (shared with Y).

This condition is phrased in such a way that it collapses two relevant cases: lexical heads with θ-marking abilities are always governors (they have indexed θ-grids), and heads bearing agreement features are always governors. Thus, the only categories that may be nongovernors are a subset of the invariant (uninflecting) functional categories, such as Greek *na*, English *to*, and the empty complementizer. Mohawk crucially differs from Greek in that it does not have a particle comparable to *na*. Mohawk might well have an "MP" projection: indeed, the optative morpheme *a* is probably very similar to *na* semantically and may be the head of MP (what I have called IP). The real difference is that the optative is a morphologically bound form that combines with the complex verb. Presumably, this means that the verb raises into the M position in Mohawk, although not in Greek. This complex verb, of course, brings with it both its θ-grid and its agreement morphology; thus, it transforms M into a category with governing potential, by (86). PRO might move into the specifier of MP for all we know in Mohawk, but it will not escape government by doing so, because its potential governor moves to the head of MP.

In fact, none of the polysynthetic languages in my sample have separate mood particles like that of Greek. Presumably, this is not a coincidence. Indeed, the fact that the verb must raise to M can be derived from the MVC under certain assumptions. PRO may have its choice of subject positions to land in, but it must land in an A-position in order to be assigned an interpretation by Control Theory; PRO clearly cannot move to the specifier of a tensed CP to escape government in English, for example. Now if PRO is in an A-position, the position must be "lexically related," in the terminology of Chomsky 1992. Roughly speaking, a position is *L-related* if the head that it is the specifier of discharges some feature inherent to a lexical item. In the case at hand, the specifier of MP is an A-position because M is linked to some feature inherent in V; for concreteness, we may say that M is involved in discharging the "e" position in the θ-grid of V, as tense is in English, according to Higginbotham (1985) (compare section 8.4 and Ormston 1993). However, the genius of polysynthetic languages is that syntactic relationships of this kind must be expressed morphologically. In particular, if M helps bind the e-position, then it is in a thematic relationship with the verb. In this case, the MVC forces M to be associated with a morpheme in the word containing the verb. This is satisfied if and only if the verbal complex raises to M. More generally, any A-position in a polysynthetic language will be governed by a head that attracts the verb almost by definition. Hence, there are no ungoverned positions in a polysynthetic language and PRO is generally barred.

Nevertheless, there is one situation in which polysynthetic languages can and do allow PRO. This is in structures of the type discussed in section 8.3, where a control-type verb incorporates the verbal head of its complement. A typical example is (87) from Nahuatl (compare with (50b)).

(87)   Ni-c-chīhua-z-nequi.
        1sS-3sO-make-FUT-want
        'I want to make it.'

Here, the understood subject of the verb root *chīhua* 'make' does have the typical properties of PRO: it has no overt realization of its own and it is necessarily interpreted as coreferential with the subject of *nequi* 'want', just as in the English gloss. In section 8.3, I used the MVC to explain why the embedded subject in this case could only be PRO: if it were anything else then it would be impossible for the arguments of both verb roots to be morphologically expressed. However, that section had nothing to say about why PRO was possible here without being governed. Now we are in a position to make a tentative proposal about how that can be. Suppose that in (87) PRO raises to the specifier of the MP in the embedded clause, headed by the so-called future morpheme *z*. The embedded verb 'make' necessarily adjoins to M, for the reasons discussed above. However, unlike the examples discussed previously in this section, the verb does not stay there; rather it is forced to move on into the matrix verb, possibly via a null complementizer position.[24] Now it is reasonable to assume that when the verbal complex moves out of M, it takes all of its indices with it. This means that M reverts back to its original status as a nongovernor. Similarly, if there is a C position, it also returns to nongoverning status once the verb moves out of it. The structure of the relevant part of (87) is given in (88).

(88)

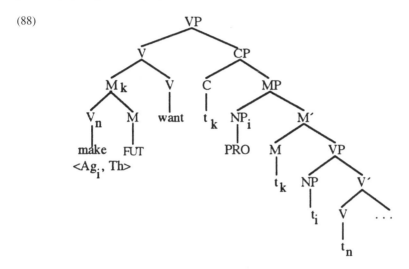

In (88), PRO is ungoverned, as required. Thus, we see that control is found in polysynthetic languages after all—but only if verb incorporation takes place. Once again, it is hard to see how the "null Case" theory of PRO could replicate this result.

10.3 Conclusion

This chapter has shown two important consequences of the Polysynthesis Parameter. First, the conditions under which a clause can count as the argument of a verb are much more restricted in polysynthetic languages than in other languages. In particular, a kind of nominalization is required, which makes use of language-particular resources; if the language has no such resources, then clausal arguments are simply impossible. Moreover, what kind of complementation patterns will result from nominalization seems, for the most part, to be predictable from the basic properties of noun incorporation and agreement in that language.

The second consequence of the Polysynthesis Parameter is that there are fewer types of embedded clauses in polysynthetic languages. In particular, these languages do not have nonfinite clauses such as infinitives, gerunds, or participles. Along with this, it follows that they cannot have the special syntax associated with such clauses; PRO, in particular, is almost nonexistent in polysynthetic languages.[25] The combined effect of these two factors is that all embedded clauses in a polysynthetic language look like they could be matrix clauses and many of them are—the language often preferring a loose type of clause sequencing to true complementation.

Notes

1. This is something of an oversimplification; McCloskey (1991) shows that conjoined CPs in English do trigger plural agreement on the verb when certain semantic conditions are met. However, I take his examples to mean that agreement in English has a semantic component to it, rather than that clauses bear Φ-features.

2. In Baker 1988a, I suggest in passing that Exceptional Case Marking constructions in English may be the result of incorporating C into the governing verb, and this has been developed in interesting ways by David Pesetsky in unpublished work. However, one problem with this approach is that the putative incorporated complementizer is always null. Thus, it is more straightforward to say that the verbs in question simply select an IP directly, as has become standard.

3. Here, however, there are more potential examples attested. In particular, verbs with what seems to be a future tense marker can incorporate into a higher verb in Greenlandic (Woodbury and Sadock 1986), Yaqui (Eloise Jelinek, personal communication), and Nahuatl. The Nahuatl examples will become relevant in section 10.2.2.

4. One type of CP subject often mentioned in the literature appears with intransitive predicates like 'be nice' or 'be true'. However, these predicates are unaccusative verbs, at least in Mohawk, so the CP is a complement underlyingly. Thus, these constructions fall together with those discussed in section 10.1.2.

5. This is also true of other polysynthetic languages; for example, Merlan (1983:135–142) discusses the lack of differentiation among clause types in Ngalakan. To a lesser degree it may also be true of Nahuatl (see Launey 1981:132). If it proves adequately general, this property of polysynthetic languages could be derived from the MVC together with the claim that semantically rich complementizers are of category P, as suggested by Emonds (1985:ch. 6,7). These Ps need to θ-mark their IP or CP complements; however, clauses cannot, in general, become visible for θ-role assignment in languages where the MVC holds, as discussed in the text. Thus, prepositional complementizers are impossible in this class of languages.

6. It is somewhat better to dislocate a referential NP out of these clauses, but still not fully acceptable. Presumably (8b) is worse than (i) because there is no possibility of a resumptive pro with nonreferential interrogative phrases.

(i)   ??ThíkΛ anitskwára uke-nak[w]-úni-'   tsi Uwári
       that   chair   FACT/1sO-mad-make-PUNC that Mary

      wa'-t-yé-ya'k-e'.
      FACT-DUP-FsS-break-PUNC
      'That chair, it made me mad that Mary broke it.'

7. However, Evans' (1991:338–342) discussion of complementation in Mayali presents some evidence that a few verbs take true clausal complements in that language. In particular, verbs meaning 'see', 'make', and 'want' form a single intonational contour with the following verb, do not normally allow an NP to intervene between them and the following verb, and do allow an NP related to the following verb to appear before them (see section 3.1.3 for an example). More detailed comparative work would be needed to establish whether Mayali and Nunggubuyu truly differ in these respects or not, and if so which language is typical of the family.

8. *Ehr* can be translated as 'want' as well as 'think', depending on the mood and aspect of its complement. Either translation would be appropriate here.

9. Indeed, extraction from the CP in Mohawk is perfect, whereas extraction from N–CP constructions in English is mildly deviant (see (28b)). Presumably, this difference fol-

lows from the fact that the N incorporates in Mohawk and not in English; it is a special case of the general fact that incorporation renders the category that launched the movement transparent to many syntactic processes (cf. the Government Transparency Corollary of Baker 1988a, called "pruning" in earlier frameworks). However, I will not go into the nontrivial technical questions that this raises for the theory of Bounding.

10. Clearly "apposition" here is not the same thing as the apposition between NPs found in examples like (i).

(i) Mary saw Rembrandt's best painting, a portrait of Aristotle.

The two NPs in (i) must be separated by a heavy intonation break, unlike the N–CP examples in English. Furthermore, extraction out of the appositive NP is completely impossible:

(ii) *Who did Mary see Rembrandt's best painting, a portrait of t ?

Thus, appositives of this type do act like adjuncts. For some reason, the tighter "cohead" type of apposition assumed in the text seems to be possible only between an NP and a CP. Why this should be so is an intriguing question, but I have nothing to say about it.

11. This is a bit too simple: *ne* can be used sporadically before complement clauses in Mohawk (see Mithun 1984b:504 for an example). However, this is not very common, and I have been unable to find a clear pattern to its usage. It seems to be more common before clauses in the optative mood.

12. A variant of this view would be to say that it is a nominal element that appears in the complementizer position of the CP, thereby creating a CP with nominal features, as proposed for the Germanic languages by Webelhuth (1992). This variant is attractive in that it avoids the awkward N–CP structure; on the other hand, it is not so clear what "CP with nominal features" actually means theoretically.

13. One cannot easily test whether CPs are islands in Lakhota, for the simple reason that constituent questions are not formed by syntactic movement (see Williamson 1984 and Bonneau 1992).

14. Chapter 3 mentioned that clauses in Mohawk must extrapose in some sense, because they appear to the right of right-adjoined NPs. However, this extraposition has no effect on extraction, coreference, and binding. Perhaps it is simply a PF process, motivated for stylistic reasons, such as "heaviness." In any case, I abstract away from it here.

15. In fact, there does not seem to be a consistent treatment of complementation in Wichita. A few verbs take the incorporated element *wakhahr,* which Rood (1976) glosses as 'patient is activity'. This may be comparable to *rihw* in Mohawk. Other verbs take CPs whose verb bears the subordinate suffix, which might have nominal properties. Still other verbs appear with CPs that have neither of these traits. Since agreement with third person arguments is always Ø in Wichita, it gives no clues for sorting out the various alternatives.

16. For at least one consultant, matrix clause optatives are only acceptable if the particle *wahi* is used. On the other hand, Deering and Delisle (1976) make no mention of matrix clause optatives needing such a particle.

17. Conceivably, one should rephrase this to say that Mohawk does have participial verbs but they take agreement morphology, too. This depends on how one defines the traditional notion 'participial verb'. The functional equivalent of an English participle clause in Mohawk is to have a sequence of fully tensed and agreeing verbs under the same intonational contour.

18. McKay also includes a brief and tentative discussion of "jussive complements." These are formally identical to purpose clauses in Rembarrnga, but they are the functional equivalent of infinitival complements to verbs of command in English. They, too, can be

fully inflected or in a bare "infinitival" form. McKay tentatively assumes that jussive complements are, in fact, just another instance of purpose clause adjuncts in the language, although he leaves the matter open. If he is right, then the analysis in the text should extend to this case, too.

19. Comrie (1981:252) cites a counterexample to this generalization, in which the argument of a nonfinite gerund appears in absolutive Case, implying that this is the standard pattern. However, see also the discussion of (73) later in this chapter.

20. The causative construction raises interesting additional problems, because it is not clear how the arguments are to be attributed to the two lexical heads involved. My guess is that it can be analyzed as having a structure similar to that of the Nahuatl causative in section 8.2.3, followed by excorporation of the higher verb; however, it is difficult to tell, because Nedjalkov (1976) gives very limited data and the construction is not discussed in any English-language reference (including, curiously, Bogoras 1922).

It is also interesting to speculate as to why excorporation constructions are more common in Chukchee than in the other polysynthetic languages. A hint comes from considering examples in which the modal verb does not excorporate from the LVC complex. With some modal verbs, the whole complex may move on into Asp and Infl, rather than just the head. Thus, (i) is an alternative realization of (60a).

(i)   Tilmə-til reŋa-tantenmənat-g'e.   (Nedjalkov 1976:192)
      eagle-ABS fly-try-3sS
      'The eagle tried to fly.'

Example (i) is more like the kind of structure found in most other polysynthetic languages (see section 8.3). Now (i) differs from (60) in another way as well: in (60) the predicate verb is marked by the infinitive/locative Case morpheme *k*, whereas there is no equivalent morpheme in (i). Similarly, in the auxiliary construction in (67) the predicate verb is marked with the ergative Case suffix *(t)a*. Apparently, then, a verb root stranded by excorporation must have a Case suffix for some reason. If this observation could be derived from some principle of UG, then the fact that Chukchee has more excorporation constructions than other polysynthetic languages might follow from the obvious fact that Chukchee has the richest Case system of any of the polysynthetic languages.

21. Rood (1976:183) discusses one example of what looks like a controlled infinitive in Wichita, a verb without overt subject agreement embedded under a predicate meaning 'want'. If this is taken at face value, it could perhaps be analyzed like (60) in Chukchee. Unfortunately, Rood does not make it clear how general the phenomenon is. This one example is taken from line 9 of the text analyzed at the end of his grammar (1976:259). This line recapitulates exactly an earlier sentence in the text (line 3, p. 258), except that the matrix subject is shifted from third person to first person. If this is the only example of missing agreement in Rood's corpus, it is possible that it is a speech error caused by the partial repetition.

22. In fact, the large majority of "verbal nouns" in these texts are in auxiliary constructions; the adverbial use of verbal nouns seems to be relatively rare.

23. I am aware of a handful of verbs in Mohawk for which it is relatively difficult for the subject of the embedded clause to be distinct from the subject of the matrix clause. The one I have studied most carefully is *atasawʌ* 'start'. Thus, although (i) is perfect, (ii) is marginal at best.

(i)   Sak t-a-ha-[a]táhsawʌ-'   wa-ha-ks-óhare-'.
      Sak CIS-FACT-MsS-begin-PUNC FACT-MsS-dish-wash-PUNC
      'Sak started washing dishes.'

(ii) (??)Sak t-a-ha-[a]táhsawʌ-'   wa'-e-ks-óhare-'
    Sak CIS-FACT-MsS-begin-PUNC   FACT-FsS-dish-wash-PUNC
    ne shako-yʌ'a.
    NE his-daughter
    'Sak started his daughter washing dishes.'

One consultant accepts such constructions on occasion; others consistently reject them. I assume that this is a semantic effect, which follows from the meaning of *atahsawʌ* in Mohawk (which is in any case not exactly like *start* in English). How this works in detail remains to be clarified. Like *atahsawʌ*, is the aspectual verb meaning 'continue' and *uni* 'make' in its causative sense. (See Ikeda 1991 for further examples and discussion.)

    Donald Frantz (personal communication) says that there are obligatory control verbs in Southern Tiwa, even though 'try' is not one of them. If this is correct, perhaps they, too, are to be explained semantically.

    24. Note that if M is a functional category, this movement violates the PHMG stated in chapter 7. I do not know why this should be tolerated in this case when it is not in others.

    25. Similarly, polysynthetic languages should not have raising to subject or raising to object as it is found in English, since this also requires the presence of an infinitival verb. Indeed, Mohawk has no good instances of raising verbs. Example (i) shows a verb of the type that one might expect to allow raising to subject, but its subject must be a pleonastic; it can never agree with the subject of the lower verb.

(i) Te-yo (*wak)-atʌhutsóh-u ne au-sa-k-ahtʌ́ti-'.   (D&D:334)
    DUP-NsO (1sO)-need-STAT NE OPT-ITER-1sS-leave-PUNC
    'It is necessary that I go home; I need to go home.'

This seems to be a general feature of the language. Similarly, there is no sign of 'raising to object' with epistemic verbs like *ehr* 'believe, think', as shown in (ii).

(ii) Á-k (*hiy)-ehr-e'   ní'i ra-hnʌ́y-es   ne Shawátis.
    OPT-1sS (1sS/MsO)-think-IMPF I   MsS-height-long NE Shawatis
    'I consider Shawatis (to be) tall.'

As far as I can tell, other polysynthetic languages are like Mohawk in this respect. Indeed, quite apart from the issue of infinitives, the NP movement involved in raising would presumably be unable to escape from the [N–CP] apposition structure that all putative CP complements must have in a polysynthetic language.

11

Conclusion: On the Nature
of Parameterization

11.1 Is There a Macroparameter?

This book has explored the idea that there is a class of languages in which the syntax differs from that of languages like English in one essential feature. The grammar of these languages includes the following statement, introduced in chapter 1.[1]

(1) *The Morphological Visibility Condition* (MVC)
     A phrase X is visible for θ-role assignment from a head Y only if it is coindexed with a morpheme in the word containing Y via:
     (i) an agreement relationship, or
     (ii) a movement relationship.

Thus, if one thinks of the syntax of a language as a list of principles that determine the well-formedness of structures ("I-language" in the terms of Chomsky 1986b), then the syntax of polysynthetic languages is extremely similar to that of nonpolysynthetic languages. If, however, one thinks of the syntax of a language as the set of well-formed structures (Chomsky's "E-language"), then the syntax of a polysynthetic language is very different. The reason is that (1) interacts with other principles of grammar to profoundly affect the range of structures permitted. Such a principle, which varies from language to language and has a fundamental impact on the character of the forms generated, I have called a "macroparameter." That such macroparameters exist is my deepest theoretical claim in the present volume.

In classical parameter theory, the evidence for the reality of a parameter was a cluster of (more or less) directly observable properties, such that languages with one setting of the parameter had those properties whereas languages with the other setting did not. This view was somewhat too simple in that it did not adequately take into account the influence of "microparameters"—differences between languages that are localized in the properties of a single lexical item or a class of lexical items. Nevertheless, the logic of the cluster argument is still valid. For this

496

reason, throughout this book I have attempted to study a range of genetically unrelated, areally separate languages to show that they do have the same set of basic properties. The main results that are of typological value are summarized in Table 11–1. In addition to the listing in Table 11-1, the Polysynthesis Parameter also has a number of other effects that cannot be checked using standard sources, such as changing disjoint reference judgments, making NPs islands to extraction, ruling out PP arguments, and restricting control phenomena.

Although Table 11-1 is not quite the perfect array of "yesses" that the theory predicts, I consider it remarkably close to that ideal. Moreover, most of the complications are rather clearly attributable not to defects in the theory but to the presence of microparameters; for example, Chukchee has an unusual NP reflexive with a limited distribution and Southern Tiwa has a causative morpheme with an unusual argument structure. The only column with a significant degree of "noise" in it is the one for Ainu, which has less freedom of word order, interrogative phrases in situ, and unrestricted morphological causatives. It is quite possible that these features can be insightfully analyzed in terms of microparameters, as tentatively suggested in the previous chapters. However, it is also true that these unexpected properties of Ainu are all salient properties of Japanese—the language that surrounded Ainu and placed great cultural pressure on it. Thus, it would not be particularly surprising if one found deviations from the polysynthetic norm precisely here. Indeed, Shibatani (1990:16–17) states that the colloquial dialect should not be considered a polysynthetic language, since phenomena like noun incorporation were no longer productive at that stage (see also Shibatani 1990:61).

Even in the face of this patterning, one can legitimately question whether a single syntactic factor is at work here or several smaller ones. The MVC states that the language in question must consistently use head-marking techniques; this single choice then has an impact over a wide range of constructions. The alternative would be to say that for each type of argument relationship the language makes a separate choice as to whether it will indicate that relationship by head-marking means or not. Thus, the language may or may not have subject agreement, may or may not have object agreement, may or may not have R agreement on nouns, may or may not have noun incorporation, and so on. Mohawk and the other polysynthetic languages could be simply the set of languages that happened to toss 14 coins and get 14 straight heads—a statistical possibility.[2]

This alternative may be correct. It is easy to imagine that further research into extreme head-marking languages will show that the properties in Table 11-1 do not necessarily go together, but rather break up into subclusters or even random patterns, as has happened with many other proposed parameters. As long as some of the empirical discoveries and detailed analyses I have given for Mohawk and the other languages turn out to be more or less true, I will feel that I have not labored in vain. Indeed, the idea of a macroparameter was something that emerged from the study, not something that I brought to it.

Nevertheless, given what is now known, there are two good reasons to believe that a unified interpretation of the MVC is the correct alternative. The first reason comes from recalling how my sample of languages was selected in the first place. I did not simply choose those languages I could find that had a syntax similar to that of Mohawk. Rather, these are representative languages from all and only the

Table 11-1. Major Characteristics of Polysynthetic Languages

Property	Mohawk	Nahuatl	Tanoan	Gunwinjguan	Wichita	Chukchee	Ainu
Syntactic NI	Yes	Yes	Yes	Yes	Yes	Yes	Yes
Object Agr obligatory	Yes	Yes	Yes	Yes	Yes	Yes*	Yes
Free pro-drop	Yes	Yes	Yes	Yes	Yes	Yes	Yes
Free word order	Yes	Yes (favors V-initial)	Yes (favors V-final?)	Yes	Yes	Yes	SOV or OSV
No NP reflexive	Yes	Yes	Yes	Yes	Yes	Yes†	Yes
No true quantifiers	Yes	Yes	Yes	Yes	Unknown	Unknown	Unknown
Obligatory wh-movement	Yes	Yes	Yes	Yes	Yes	Yes	No
N agrees with R argument	Yes	Yes (often Ø)	Maybe (as N suffix)	Yes	(Yes)‡ (always Ø)	In part	(Yes)‡ (always Ø)
No true Determiners	Yes	Yes?	Yes	Yes	Yes	Yes	Yes
N agrees with possessor	Yes	Yes	N/A	Often	N/A	N/A	Yes
Restricted morphocausative	Yes (unacc. Vs only)	Yes (non-active Vs only)	Yes (control plus NI)	Yes (unacc. Vs only)	Yes?	Yes (unacc. Vs only)	No
NI or Agr in PP	Yes	Yes	Yes (Case)	Yes (Case)	Yes (Case)	Yes (Case)	Probable (Case)

CP arguments only if nominal	Yes (NI type)	Yes (N as Comp)	Yes? (NI type)	Yes (no CPs?)	?? (various types)	Probable	Yes (N as Comp)
No infinitive	Yes	Yes	Yes	Yes	Yes	??[§]	Yes

N/A = Test not applicable to the language in question.

*Except perhaps in the innovative "present II" tense (Comrie 1979).

†Chukchee has an NP reflexive, but it is barred from appearing in argument positions.

‡The facts of Wichita and Ainu are consistent with the claim that N agrees with the R argument but provide no positive evidence for that claim, because of Ø morphemes.

§The so-called infinitive is homophonous with a locative Case noun and most examples can be analyzed as nouns or predicates in an LVC.

Table 11-2. Characteristics of Some Nonpolysynthetic Languages

Property	Greenlandic	Lakhota	Slave	Alamblak	Chichewa	Choctaw
Syntactic NI	Yes*	No‡	No (only lexical)	No‡	No	No
Object Agr obligatory	Yes (but not with IO)	Yes	No	No	No	Yes
Free argument dropping	Yes	Yes	When Agr is present	Yes	When Agr is present	Yes
Free word order	SOV (+ OSV, HNPS)§	SOV (limited OSV)	SOV	SOV (+ OSV, HNPS)§	Not if Agr is absent (VO)	SOV
No NP reflexive	No†	Yes	Yes	No†	Yes	No†
No true quantifiers	Yes	Yes	Yes	Yes?	Yes	Yes
Obligatory wh-movement	No	No	No	No	No	No
N agrees with R argument	? (has sg./pl. contrast)	No? (or possibly Ø)	No (or possibly Ø)	Yes	Yes	Yes (Ø-form)
No true determiners	Yes	No	Yes	Yes	Yes	No
N agrees with possessor	Yes	Yes (relative clause?)	Optional	No	No	Yes
Restricted morphocausative	No	N/A	Yes	Yes	No	No

NI or Agr on PP	Yes	Some yes; some no	No	Some yes; some no	No
CP arguments only if nominal	Yes? (V is participial)	Yes (for finite CP)	No	Yes? (no true complements?)	No
No infinitive	No	No	Yes	No	Yes?

Sources: Greenlandic: Fortescue 1984, Woodbury and Sadock 1986, Bittner 1994; Lakhota: Williamson 1984, Boas and Deloria 1941; Slave: Rice 1989; Alamblak: Bruce 1984; Chichewa: Baker 1988a, Bresnan and Mchombo 1987, and others; Choctaw: Broadwell 1990, Davies 1986.

N/A = Test is not applicable to the language in question.

*NI in Greenlandic is syntactic, but it is triggered by affixal verbs only.

†Greenlandic, Alamblak, and Choctaw have reflexive noun roots, but they cannot be agreed with, similar to Chukchee.

‡Alamblak has NI of body parts and noun–verb compounding in subordinate clauses; Lakhota has nonsyntactic noun–verb compounding of various types (de Reuse 1994).

§HNPS stands for heavy NP shift

known families that have noun incorporation that meets a certain standard: they are all and only the languages that have type III or IV noun incorporation in Mithun's (1984a) classification. Thus, the fact that every cell in the first row of Table 11-1 contains a "Yes" is hardly surprising; this is the independent variable of the study. However, the fact that all of the other rows are nearly as uniform is surprising, because they played no role in the selection procedure; they are dependent variables. I find it remarkable that this single criterion picks out a class of languages that is so syntactically homogenous across a rather wide range of phenomena. If there were no such thing as a macroparameter, this would be unexplained.

The second reason for thinking that a single parameter is at work in the polysynthetic languages comes into focus when one considers how other languages pattern with respect to these same features. Table 11-2 summarizes the results of several languages that have considerable morphological complexity within the verb and some head-marking constructions, but do not have noun incorporation of the relevant kind. Indeed, some of them, such as Greenlandic and Alamblak, are excellent examples of languages that are polysynthetic in the traditional, typological sense. (This sample was not chosen using any principled basis; it is simply a sample of languages I happen to know something about.) The important point to notice is that the pattern of properties seen in each of these languages differs from that found in Table 11-1 in several ways, not just in one way. For example, Lakhota is related to both Mohawk and Wichita, yet it differs from them not only in the fact that it does not have productive syntactic noun incorporation: it also has a relatively fixed SOV word order, *wh*–in situ constructions, a determiner system, and infinitival complementation, according to Williamson (1984). Now suppose that Mohawk indeed resulted from tossing 14 straight heads in the setting of its parameters. This is a statistical possibility, but it should be a rare one; simple combinatorics leads us to expect that there should be 14 times as many languages that differ from Mohawk in exactly one feature—languages that tossed 13 heads and one tail in setting their parameters. In other words, there should be something like fourteen times as many "impure polysynthetic languages" as pure ones. This is not what I have found. Rather, languages differ syntactically from the polysynthetic ideal either in several ways (See Table 11-2) or in virtually none (see Table 11-1). This impression is also supported by the much broader but syntactically more superficial study in Nichols 1992. Nichols finds that "languages show a tendency to use either head or dependent marking consistently, though mixtures and splits of various types also occur" (1992:95; see also pp. 76–77). In other words, relatively pure head-marking languages are more common than mixed languages, although simple probabilistic considerations would lead one to expect the opposite if each construction were specified independently.

It goes without saying that this analysis falls short of being a decisive statistical demonstration in several respects. First, Table 11-1 is not quite perfect; Ainu, in particular, and perhaps Chukchee have some unaccounted for properties. Second, my knowledge of the languages in Table 11-2 is relatively superficial, and it is possible that a deeper analysis might dissolve some of the apparent dissimilarities between these languages and the polysynthetic languages. Third, not all of the features in the tables are equally likely. For example, all of the nonpolysynthetic languages surveyed lack nonreferential quantifiers, just like the polysynthetic ones; indeed quantifiers like *everybody* and *nobody* are rather rare from a cross-linguistic perspective. Thus, this feature should perhaps be omitted from the calculations. Finally, the method of sampling languages was haphazard. Thus, it is possible that further investigation will bring to light more "impure polysynthetic" languages. However, even granting all this, the distribution of properties in these tables looks far from random. Rather, it seems that many of these properties do not vary independently, but rather are interrelated by a macroparameter.

More or less the same argument for the existence of macroparameters can be phrased in diachronic terms. Clearly, microparameters are important driving factors in language change. For example, phonological change may operate on a set of pronominal forms in a given language, changing them into morphologically bound agreement markers. This could create a head-marking construction in a previously configurational language. Conversely, phonological change might act so as to reduce agreement markers to the point where they are lost entirely; this could create a configurational construction in a previously pure head-marking language. Such processes are reasonably well understood, but they do not in themselves seem to be a sufficient impetus for language change. Macroparameters fill in what is missing in this respect. They create in the language learner a bias toward a uniform system of grammatical representations.[3] Thus, when a language has, say, acquired a certain critical mass of head-marking constructions through idiosyncratic phonological change, language learners become tempted to believe that the value of (1) is set positively. If this is the case, then new agreement forms must be found in order to complete the paradigms that (1) requires; for example, if there were as yet no agreement morphemes on nouns, those used in the verbal system might be extended into that domain. In this way, the existence of the macroparameter creates a pressure for analogical change. If there were no macroparameter, then there would be no tendency to generalize from one syntactic configuration and one set of idiosyncratic lexical items to another. Under such circumstances, it would take a surprising string of unrelated coincidences for a language of one syntactic type to develop out of a language of another type. Yet this type of change is attested. One good example is the Gunwinjguan languages of Northern Australia. These are quite pure exemplars of the polysynthetic, head-marking type, but Australianists argue that they are historically related to the Pama-Nyungan languages of Southern Australia, many of which are purely dependent marking (Dixon 1980, Blake 1987). Moreover, the reconstructed proto-Australian language is grammatically more like the Pama-Nyungan languages, with the Gunwinjguan languages being the innovators. Thus, it is historically possible for a pure language of one type to become a pure language of another type. The existence of the MVC helps to explain why.[4]

One important point that I have left open is whether the theory should allow for a class of "head-marking nonconfigurational" languages as well as the purely polysynthetic ones. These would be languages in which (1i) holds, but not (1ii). One would expect such languages to be essentially identical to those in Table 11-1 except that they would lack productive syntactic noun incorporation and perhaps certain kinds of complex predicates such as desideratives. In this respect, my decision to focus on languages having noun incorporation was a practical one rather than a principled one; it picks out a natural class of languages of a workable size. If a class of head-marking nonconfigurational languages does, in fact, exist, it will extend considerably the range of the proposals made in this book. Unfortunately, my research is not sufficient to settle this matter one way or another; the languages I have examined at some length are all listed in Table 11-2, because they differ from polysynthetic languages in several ways other than the existence of noun incorporation. If this is true in general, then (1) should be thought of as a single, unified parameter, rather than two related parameters. This is an important area for further research.

Finally, I should emphasize something that is, I hope, already obvious: the languages listed in Table 11-1 are by no means identical syntactically. On the contrary, each language or language family has its own quirks that give it a distinctive flavor. For example, Mohawk has a quirky agreement system that plays an important role in the inflection of both the verbs and nouns; this makes Mohawk an "active" language, unlike most other polysynthetic languages. Nahuatl, on the other hand, has incorporated indefinite nominals *tē* and *tla,* strict transitivity requirements, and much more category-changing morphology than the other polysynthetic languages. The Tanoan languages have particularly complex agreement systems and a large number of incorporating verbs with control properties. Both the Gunwinjguan languages and Chukchee have directional Case morphemes of a kind that are completely absent in the polysynthetic languages of North America. In addition, Chukchee has strong morphological ergativity and a whole set of auxiliary-like constructions. Some languages have many more adverbial prefixes or incorporated modifiers than others. I have no desire to underplay the interest or importance of these differences among the polysynthetic languages; perhaps some of them should even be thought of in parametric terms rather than as "mere" lexical variation. I do, however, claim that they are all different elaborations of a common framework that is induced by the combination of Universal Grammar and a shared setting of the Polysynthesis Parameter.

11.2 Are There Other Macroparameters?

It is not plausible that (1) should be the only macroparameter allowed for by Universal Grammar. Rather, (1) should ultimately be embedded in a more general theory of macroparameters that defines in some insightful way the major typological splits in languages of the world. Although it would be premature to present such a theory now, one can make some tentative remarks about the nature of that theory on the basis of the typological work conducted up to this point.

As discussed in chapter 1, the trend in the field has been toward fragmentation of parameters rather than toward unification. Thus, there are very few proposals for possible macroparameters to be found in the current literature. By far, the most likely candidate is the head-first/head-last parameter. Like the head-marking/dependent-marking distinction introduced by Nichols (1986), which is part of the inspiration behind (1), the head-first/head-last parameter is a technical implementation of a distinction with known typological value (Greenberg 1963). Moreover, there is evidence that head-last languages differ from head-first languages not only in the word orders of their various phrases, but also in a variety of other ways. For example, verb-final languages such as Japanese, Hindi, German, and Turkish typically allow fairly free scrambling of NPs within the VP, something that is much less common in verb-initial languages. Moreover, such languages tend to have overt Case morphology, something which is less common in verb-initial and polysynthetic languages. We have seen that *wh*-movement is generally required in polysynthetic languages; in contrast, interrogative phrases are typically left in situ in pure head-final languages (see Kayne (1995) for a recent analysis of this fact). Furthermore, island phenomena are significantly different in head-final languages if Kayne's (1984) conjectures about directionality of government are substantiated. Schiller (1990) notes that serial verb constructions are much rarer in head-final languages than in head-initial languages. Finally, Craig and Hale (1988) argue that preposition incorporation constructions are favored in head-final languages be-cause the natural word orders automatically put heads in contiguous positions where they are prone to reanalysis; probably the same is true of verb incorporation constructions. If a good number of these claims prove accurate, then the head-first/head-last parameter also has the kind of widespread ramifications throughout the syntax that justify calling it a macroparameter.[5]

In some formulations, the head-first/head-last parameter shares an important feature with the MVC. In particular, Travis (1984) and Koopman (1984) suggest that Case and θ-role assignment are sensitive to directionality. Thus, heads in some languages can only assign Case and/or θ-roles to positions to their left, for example. (Compare also Kayne 1984, which appeals to directionality of govern-ment within a framework where government is a condition for Case and θ-role assignment.) This is nearly equivalent to the statement in (2), which, in turn, is formally parallel to the MVC:

(2)   A phrase X is visible for θ-role assignment from a head Y only if it is coindexed with a position to the left {right} of Y.

We may now state the following conjecture:

(3)   All syntactic differences reduce either to differences in the properties of lexical items *or to visibility conditions.*

By "visibility conditions," I mean a family of statements that define uniform syn-tactic or morphosyntactic conditions that two elements must meet in order to be understood as standing in a primitive interpretive relation. Such visibility condi-tions have the obvious raison d'être that they guarantee a partially systematized relationship between LF and PF. Thus, they help to ensure that meaning is (to a tolerable degree) recoverable from form.

Does this exhaust the range of true parametric variation found across lan-guages? Surely it does not, but it may come closer than one might think. It is certainly not true that all languages fall into one of three classes—head-marking nonconfigurational languages nearly identical to Mohawk, Case-marking head-final languages nearly identical to Japanese, or relatively uninflected head-initial languages nearly identical to English. However, it may be the case that Mohawk,

Japanese, and English come close to defining the boundaries of the space within which language typology takes place. It is not clear that there are other natural language representation systems that do not fit somewhere within the triangle defined by head-first/head-last/adjoined, and the related triangle defined by Case-marked/agreement-marked/uninflected. If not, then we do not need to devise new visibility conditions, but rather need to learn how to "compound" the ones that we have. Such compounded conditions would account for languages with mixed representation systems. For example, Chichewa and the other Bantu languages seem to represent a cross between a head-marking language, with subject agreement, optional object agreement, and adjoined NPs, and a head-first language, with fixed word order and a well-defined verb phrase. Spanish and Italian are also mixtures of this type. On the other hand, Inuktitut, Northern Athapaskan, and Quechua are apparently hybrids of head-marking and head-final languages; they have both verb-final and nonconfigurational tendencies. The idea of crossing a head-first language with a head-final language at first seems absurd, but this may be the case with languages like German that are head-final in their lexical categories but head-initial in many of their functional categories. Other notorious examples of word order mixture that might fit in here are the Kru languages and Chinese (Koopman 1984, Travis 1984).

When I mentioned *compounding* visibility parameters in the previous paragraph, I had in mind a chemical analogy. Compounding parameter values is crucially different from setting visibility parameters independently for each relevant construction;* the latter procedure would produce random mixtures of, say, head marking in a language of a kind that one does not seem to find (see previous discussion). Rather, the allusion to chemical compounding calls to mind the fact that basic elements combine to form new substances only in fixed ratios. Thus, hydrogen combines with oxygen to make water, but only in two-to-one proportions. If one tries to combine oxygen with hydrogen one-to-one, or with twice as much oxygen as hydrogen, no stable compound will result. I suspect that it is the same with visibility conditions: one cannot combine head marking with head first in any random way; rather, there are one or two stable combinations. For example, it is well known that languages may have obligatory subject agreement, optional object agreement, and no agreement on nouns (Chichewa, Slave, Italian); but the mixture of obligatory object agreement and optional subject agreement is never found. The latter would be the linguistic equivalent of HO_2. At present, I do not know how to develop the notion of a "parameter compound" in a meaningful way. Rather, the purpose of this book has been a logically prior one—to give a fuller understanding of one of the elements that is involved in this compounding. A compounding theory may, however, be called for.

11.3 Why Are There Macroparameters?

Finally, I close this book with some speculation on perhaps the curious question of all: why should human language seem to vary so wildly? In P&P terminology, the question is, Why should Universal Grammar be designed in such a way that it includes the possibility of macroparameters? This question has always been present in some form or another, but it emerges in a particularly sharp way in the context of this book.

Thought about linguistic diversity has generally alternated between two extremes. One is the rationalist/Cartesian tradition revived by Chomsky. This tradition holds that language is an expression of universal and innate forms of thought common to the human species. On this view, linguistic variation is relatively superficial, perhaps simply due to impurities of one kind or another. Chomsky, in particular, has recently conjectured that there is, in fact, only one human language in the sense of one computational system, with all apparent differences between languages attributable to the Lexicon (Chomsky 1992). (See chapter 1 for some discussion of the recent history of this idea.)

The other major approach to language and linguistic diversity is the structuralist/anthropological one. This tradition sees language as a cultural phenomenon; hence, languages differ for the same reasons that cultures do. In particular, they may be shaped in important ways by the world view, the patterns of interaction, and the idiosyncratic history of a local group of people. Inasmuch as these cultural factors can be very different, so will languages be. Thus, Sapir and other linguists in the early twentieth century claimed that "language is a human activity that varies without assignable limit" (Sapir 1921) (see Chomsky 1986b:20–21 for other quotations).

The position of this book falls awkwardly between these two alternatives. The overall framework is Chomsky's, built around a rich and detailed notion of Universal Grammar. This framework has been vindicated by the fact that so many principles of syntax that were discovered in the analysis of nonpolysynthetic languages have proven useful in the analysis of polysynthetic languages as well. Indeed, often the same principle (e.g., governing extraction or anaphora) is recognizably at work in a polysynthetic language even though the actual pattern of grammaticality judgments it induces is quite different, as shown in chapter 2. However, UG stops short of fully determining the structure of language. Rather it leaves a few gaps—particularly in the area of visibility conditions—where different solutions to the system of constraints are possible: the head-marking solution, the dependent-marking solution, the configurational solution, and perhaps a handful of others. A priori, this situation seems purposeless and implausible; indeed, I suspect that this is as large a factor in the field's movement away from the notion of a parameter as the empirical problems mentioned in chapter 1.

Since this is a question about the basic structure of linguistic theory, the answer cannot come from linguistic theory itself. Within the current conception of UG it is perfectly possible to imagine a slightly different UG in which the option of quite different linguistic solutions to the system of constraints did not arise. For example, one could imagine that (1) was the universal visibility condition, and not one of a family of visibility conditions. In that case, we would all speak polysynthetic languages. Or, more subtly, one could easily imagine a general notion of "economy" that governed grammar in such a way that one of the visibility conditions was preferred to all the others, thereby blocking them (compare Chomsky 1992). Thus, the answer to the question of deep syntactic diversity is not likely to come from the structure of linguistic theory itself, but rather from some more general force that shapes linguistic theory.

11.3.1 A Biological Explanation

Could there be a biological explanation for syntactic diversity, say in terms of the theory of evolution? This is surely the most natural and familiar place for modern academics to turn. However, in order to phrase the question in these terms we quickly come face to face with some difficult problems about how a Chomsky-style Universal Grammar could have evolved in the first place. Many researchers who have thought about this problem use it as an argument against the Cartesian strains in Chomsky's approach to syntax (Givón 1979:ch. 7, Lieberman 1985, Bickerton 1981, Hattiangadi 1987); Chomsky himself seems to relish the paradox, claiming that it is one of the things that makes linguistics intellectually interesting. Until this issue is faced, we can hardly expect to be able to answer our more specific question in detail. We may, however, consider how this property of UG is likely to fit into logically possible accounts of the evolution of UG, and whether the existence of this property makes such an account look more plausible or less plausible.

The most familiar form of explanation in evolutionary biology is in terms of selectional advantage. A given trait, genetically determined, becomes fixed in a population if it confers on members of that population some advantage in the competition for resources necessary to survival and reproduction. The trait in question here is a UG that leaves room for significant linguistic variation. Would this give its possessors an advantage over, say, a competing population whose UG completely determined the structure of their language? One can begin to imagine scenarios along these lines, but the exercise quickly runs into dead ends. One of the keys to human biological success is supposed to be flexibility and adaptability, which enables survival in a wider range of ecosystems than most other species. Perhaps the flexibility of language is a part of this biological flexibility, which has been such a successful survival strategy. Although this might sound plausible at first, its attraction vanishes with a little more thought. In essence, it would mean that speakers of certain types of languages are more capable of functioning in certain kinds of environments. For example, it would entail that, say, speakers of polysynthetic languages are better suited to Arctic climates, while speakers of head-final languages prosper in tropical climates. This is hardly plausible. I certainly have the sense that as an English speaker I could survive anywhere with suitable training; my vocabulary might have to develop in various areas, but my syntax would not have to change. Nor does this type of account explain the distribution of language types around the globe. The set of probable polysynthetic languages includes Chukchee, spoken on Arctic tundras; Mohawk and Ainu, spoken in Northern temperate forests; Nahuatl, spoken on an arid semitropical plateau; and the Gunwinjguan languages, spoken in a wet-and-dry tropical climate. Thus, there simply is no correlation between ecosystem and typological properties of language, nor has one ever been proposed.[6]

In fact, it seems to me that one could just as well argue that the possibility of syntactic variation makes the human species less likely to survive rather than more likely. When one asks what the selective value of human language itself is, the answer typically focuses on its value in communication: it allows the transfer of detailed knowledge useful to survival (such as how to prepare bitter manioc so that it is edible rather than poisonous), and it makes possible sophisticated cooperative efforts (such as mastodon hunting). These advantages of human language are partially undercut by the possibility of syntactic diversity. The existence of very different languages clearly limits the range of people that one can learn from easily and directly, as well as those with whom one can engage in cooperative ventures. Indeed, linguistic diversity has been a fertile source of misunderstanding in the history of the world. Furthermore, it is often used as a marker to distinguish one group of humans from another so that they can try to kill each other, a dynamic present in both traditional societies and modern ones. From the perspective of sheer survival, macroparameters could be viewed as a design flaw rather than an advantage.[7]

Of course, the adaptive value of a specific trait is only one way of explaining its existence in modern biology; adaptive value does not explain why humans have an appendix, for example (see Hill 1993 for discussion of this point in a linguistic context). Thus, the fact that UG includes the possibility of a few macroparameters might not have any selectional value in itself (or even a modest negative value), but UG as a whole has great selectional value because it makes possible language that is both learnable and has unbounded expressive potential. Thus, macroparameters could get a free ride from the larger system of which they are a part.

This is only an explanation, however, if macroparameters are somehow a necessary concomitant of this type of UG. It is not easy to see why this is the case. Clearly, it is not *logically* necessary that a UG sufficient to make possible a learnable language of unbounded generative capacity should have macroparameters, as mentioned above. It is conceivable that it is *biochemically* necessary for an organic system with a UG to have macroparameters. This would be the case if, say, the enzymes that regulate the building of the knowledge structures of UG also build macroparameters as a side effect for reasons having to do with reaction rates and biochemical mechanisms. For that matter, it is conceivable that it is biochemically necessary that an organic system with an opposable thumb has linguistic macroparameters, for the same kind of reason. However, this form of explanation seems far-fetched and completely without evidence. Indeed, providing such an answer would not only involve enormous biochemical complexities (I suppose), but also a decisive solution to aspects of the mind–body problem.

The third possibility is that it could be *historically* necessary that the organic system with UG also has macroparameters. This would be the case if the mental structures (call them X) that UG evolved out of happened as a matter of fact to have some property (call it P) that was the seed of the macroparameters. Thus, macroparameters would be the natural projection of property P as X turned into UG. Now we crucially come face to face with the main puzzle of evolution from a Chomskian viewpoint: what is X that UG developed out of? It is difficult to give a plausible answer. Probably the most popular one is that X is some kind of conceptual system, perhaps the one used by apes in perception, social cognition, and problem solving. This is approximately the view presented in Bickerton 1990, the work on language evolution that is most knowledgeable about the syntactic issues involved. This view fits well with the research program of the functional linguists, who hold that syntax develops out of cognitive and discourse factors. Formalist that I am, I think that the difficulties in this view are formidable, and the more one knows about the details of syntax the more formidable they seem. Putting this aside, however, the question now is not so much what is X, but what is P? What property could the primate conceptual system have such that once that conceptual system developed into or spun off a language system the result was macroparameters? It is hard to imagine. Conceivably, the parameters of natural language have come historically from some kind of parameters in an older conceptual system. But what independent reason do we have for believing that conceptual systems admit of parameterization of this kind? Is the basic "language of thought" parameterized? This seems unlikely. Moreover, if it were true it would only push the interesting question back one step on the evolutionary scale; we would now have to ask why conceptual systems should allow for this kind of variation.

Finally, it could be that macroparameters are simply the result of a biological accident. It could be that, say, a certain gamma ray happened to hit a certain DNA sequence just so at an opportune point. This could, of course, be true. However, it does not count as an explanation in any intellectually interesting sense. In particular, it fails to relate a salient and important fact of the world (the existence of structural diversity among languages) to any other known facts. In these circumstances, one should at least be open to the possibility of a better explanation in other terms. Indeed, as far as I know, no one has offered an explanation of syntactic diversity in purely biological terms. For example, Bickerton (1990) and Lieberman (1985) are both silent on this issue.[8]

11.3.2 A Sociological Explanation

Could there be a sociological explanation of syntactic diversity? If evolutionary biology cannot explain the existence of macroparameters in terms of humanity's relationship to the physical or biological environment, perhaps the study of culture can explain it in terms of relationships among humans. This view has adherents among anthropological linguists and others influenced by Benjamin Whorf, and it has a certain weight of research behind it. Functionalist approaches to the evolution of language (see e.g., Givón 1979) also fit into this category, inasmuch as the discussion of the evolution of language attributes more influence to societal developments than to strictly biological ones.

Nevertheless, the more one knows about the syntax of polysynthetic languages, the less plausible a sociological explanation looks. If my analysis is on the right track, then what is special about Mohawk is its positive setting of (1), the MVC: all θ-role assigners must contain morphemes that correspond to each θ-role. It is hard to see how this could this be derived from some other feature of Mohawk society or culture. Suppose that we enumerate some of the other distinctive features of traditional Mohawk culture. For example, their kinship system was matrilineal, and a clan system determined permissible marriages. Community life was structured around their longhouse dwellings and villages. Economically, they practiced a relatively efficient version of slash-and-burn agriculture, cultivating corn, beans, and squash; they also hunted, fished, and wove baskets. Religiously, they were broadly speaking animistic; they carved false-face masks, burned tobacco, and had elaborate prayers of thanksgiving. Politically, they were involved in founding the famous league of the Iroquois, in which they were the keepers of the Eastern door. They were renowned as orators and warriors. Does it follow from any of these features of their traditional society that their syntactic constructions should be consistently head marking? Not that I can see. Moreover, most of these features of Mohawk society have changed rather radically over the last 350 years, at least in large parts of the community; nevertheless, the language of the Catholic nuns and high-rise steel workers still has recognizably the same syntax as the language of their predecessors. Thus, there is no evidence that the syntax of the language covaries with independently ascertainable features of the society.

I know of one claim that scholars have seriously debated in this domain, which illustrates the logic of this type of explanation.[9] The claim was that head marking, polysynthetic languages were a feature of small-scale "societies of intimates," where the ratio of shared knowledge to new information is very high compared with that of modern Western culture. (This line of thought is not identical to Givón's (1979:ch. 7), but owes much to his introduction of these notions into discussion about the properties of language.) This type of sociological setting supposedly favors rich pronominal agreement systems, null anaphora, pragmatically determined word order, lack of clearly differentiated subordinate clauses and other features of a "pragmatic mode" of communication—all properties of the polysynthetic languages. This time, a quick survey of the distribution of polysynthetic languages seems encouraging: they are all spoken by native/aboriginal groups scattered throughout North America, Australia, and Asia, and most of the groups are quite small. However, a closer look at the distribution of these languages raises serious problems. Hill (1993:451–452) points out that one of the most complex and socially stratified societies of the Americas was the Aztecs. In fact, fifteenth-century Aztec society was probably the equal of contemporary European society in many of these respects, and the Aztecs politically dominated groups whose languages had almost no head-marking or polysynthetic features, such as the Mixtecs and the Zapotecs.[10] Nevertheless, Nahuatl itself is an excellent example of polysynthesis. Similarly, the League of the Iroquois was the most complex sociopolitical system north of Mesoamerica at the time of contact with Europe, but the Iroquoian language is more polysynthetic than the neighboring Algonquian languages. Hill also calls attention to the fact that the polysynthetic languages of northern Australia developed from a protolanguage similar to the dependent-marking languages spoken in the South (see section 11.1), many of the latter being spoken in excellent examples of "societies of intimates." If so, then there is no uniform direction of linguistic evolution from head marking and polysynthesis to configurationality and/or dependent marking driven by the increase in the size and complexity of society. That the polysynthetic languages are now spoken by small aboriginal groups and not by large nation states is apparently a consequence of the historical fact that the modern nation-state happened to develop in Europe, an area without polysynthetic languages. It is a small world, and there is room for coincidence in the distribution of language types. However, there seems to be little evidence that social organization correlates with language type. Thus, sociological terms also fail to explain the existence of deep syntactic diversity.

11.3.3 A Theological Explanation

If biological and sociological categories are ill-equipped to explain the possibility of syntactic diversity, are there any other candidates? Are there any other forces at work that might play a role in shaping human language capacities?

In fact, many cultures and historical periods have believed that language is not just a biological phenomenon or a social institution; rather, it also has an important *spiritual* component. This naturally takes somewhat different forms in different religious traditions. For example, in the Judeo-Christian tradition, language has its origins in God, rather than in humanity. God (the Son) is himself[11] referred to as "the Word" (Greek *logos*) in the New Testament (especially John 1:1, 14), implying that he is a fundamentally linguistic and rational being and the ultimate source of language and rationality. Indeed, the creation narrative of Genesis 1 portrays God as speaking in the process of creation, before there was anything or anyone else to talk to. This language use by God takes many forms. There are speech act commands that carry creative power: "And God said, 'Let there be light,' and there was light" (Gen. 1:3; also vv. 6, 9, 11, 14, 20, 24). There are acts of naming: "God called the light 'day' and the darkness he called 'night' " (Gen. 1:5; also vv. 8, 10). There are acts of blessing and commission: "God blessed them [fish and birds] and said, 'Be fruitful and increase in number and fill the water in the seas, and let the birds increase on the earth' " (Gen. 1:22). Finally, there is taking counsel with himself concerning the last stage in the creative plan: "Then God said, 'Let us make man in our image, in our likeness, and let them rule. . . .' " (Gen. 1:26). Since God is the quintessential spiritual being, and language has its origins in him, language is therefore a spiritual phenomenon.

In the Judeo-Christian scriptures language is, then, a property of humankind by virtue of the fact that God creates humans "in his own image" (Gen. 1:27). All other animals are called forth out of the ground, implying that they have a physical nature and are subject to the same physical principles as inanimate matter (Gen. 1: 24). The creation of humanity, however, has a second step: "The Lord God formed the man from the dust of the ground and breathed into his nostrils the breath of life, and the man became a living being" (Gen. 2:7). In other words, humanity is given a spiritual nature that is specifically said to be parallel in many respects to God's. Among other things, this means that since God is a linguistic being, so are humans. (The Scriptures do not explicitly state that language is part of the divine nature, but this seems clear from context, and as far as I know has always been understood to be so by the Christian church; see, for example, Bavinck (1977:ch. XII especially p. 200). This fits well with the fact that language is a uniquely human ability, not shared with the animals that we so strongly resemble in terms of our physical nature.) Humanity, then, immediately begins to share in God's linguistic work of naming (Gen. 2:19). Moreover, language becomes a vehicle of communication between God and human, even before it becomes a vehicle of communication between human and human (Gen. 2:18). Indeed, language is integrally bound up with all the dynamics of the early part of Genesis; it plays a role in the divine commands, the commissions, the blessings, the prohibitions, the temptations, the excuses, the fault findings, the confessions, the curses, the predictions, and the promises. In short, language is involved in all the dynamics of the spiritual life as this tradition understands it. The conclusion is clear: language has a spiritual side and is shaped not only by people's relationship to the physical world or to one another, but by their relationship to God and the spiritual world.

This perspective on language is by no means unique to the Judeo-Christian tradition. Indeed, Native American traditions are often strikingly similar in several essential features. Throughout Native America prior to contact with Europe, language was considered powerful and sacred. For example, the Mayan epic *Popol Vuh* describes the creation of birds and animals as the immediate result of an act of speech, strikingly similar in this respect to the Genesis account (Sherzer 1991:264–265). Gill (1991:281) mentions similar beliefs of other Native American people, including the following discussion of the Witotoan tribes, who lived along the Putumayo River between Columbia and Peru:

> The creator deity, Moma, was a major figure in the stories of the Witotoan tribes. . . . The name Moma means "father," and Moma, identified with the moon and perhaps in another form with the sun, is both creator and culture hero. The Witoto considered that "the word" preceded Moma and even gave origin to him. Moma was understood as the personification of the power of the word. As hero, he transmitted this power to the first human beings. For the Witotos, as for many peoples throughout the Americas, the word was identified as a creative force.

This belief is similar to the one expressed in Genesis that language was passed on to humanity by a spiritual being. In this context, it is not surprising that language was considered a vehicle for communication between the human world and the spiritual world. It was considered an essential element in rituals designed to achieve cures from disease, success in hunting, and so on (Sherzer 1991:268). This can be compared to the important role of language in prayer, both liturgical and private, in the Christian tradition. The Iroquois, for example, put great emphasis on oratory and public speaking, which entered into all facets of their traditional religious life, including death, curing, and agricultural ceremonies. "Oratory was a central feature of ritual and kept the Iroquois world spiritually alive and well" (Sherzer 1991:265). Certainly the forms of these beliefs and ritual practices varied widely from group to group. However, underneath the variations is a widespread belief that language is a spiritual phenomenon.

Suppose that these traditions are either more insightful or have better memories, or both, than the dominant modern academic tradition in this respect. Then one might expect spiritual forces to give some insight into the particular shape of language. Thus, we can ask whether there is a *theological* explanation of syntactic diversity.

Strikingly, the problem of syntactic diversity is the one aspect of language for which the Judeo-Christian scriptures provide an explanation. The origins of language itself are only revealed indirectly, as a corollary of creation in the divine nature. Linguistic diversity, however, merits a story of its own—the account of the Tower of Babel (Gen. 11:1, 5–9):

> Now the whole world had one language and a common speech. . . .
> But the Lord came down to see the city and the tower that the men were building. The Lord said, "if as one people speaking the same language they have

begun to do this, then nothing they plan to do will be impossible for them. Come, let us go down and confuse their language so they will not understand each other."

So the Lord scattered them from there over all the earth, and they stopped building the city. That is why it was called Babel—because there the Lord confused the language of the whole world.

However the historical details of the story are to be taken, its basic point is clear: linguistic diversity results from a direct act of God. This act was logically distinct from the act that gave humanity a linguistic nature in the first place. If macroparameters are one of the important mechanisms giving rise to serious linguistic diversity (diversity that cannot be overcome by ordinary lexical learning), then their origin is distinctly spiritual in nature.

Is this account explanatory, as compared, say, to the view that macroparameters were introduced into language by a gamma ray striking a strand of DNA at a key moment?[12] Here the word "explanation" becomes something of a problem: what counts as an explanation is, in part, theory-bound, and we are now beyond the limits of most theoretical frameworks. However, I take the core notion of "explanation" to be an account that attributes more than one body of facts to a single factor in a way that does justice to the nature of those facts and is intuitively satisfying.[13] In this sense, I think that the theological account does have a degree of explanatory force. It does not make any predictions about the distribution of polysynthetic languages across the world, but that is just as well, since such predictions derived from other perspectives proved to be false. However, the Genesis narrative does not present God's creation of linguistic diversity as a capricious or unexplained act. Rather, God acts in response to a particular situation and with a declared motive. In essence, he creates linguistic diversity to make difficult or impossible large-scale and long-term cooperative endeavors. The reason for this (given that God is good) is presumably that such endeavors have an inherent tendency toward evil and destructive manipulation. It is not hard to see why this is so: any such endeavor would command immense power and influence over individuals, almost by definition. Hence, those who crave power and influence for their own purposes (a subset of the evil) will be drawn to the leadership of such endeavors—if, indeed, they were not the founders. As a point of historical fact, all movements that have sought direct political power on a large scale have been unstable and limited in both time and extent. Empires are difficult to build and they all fall apart, often along more or less ethnolinguistic lines. Events in Eastern Europe and Central Asia over the last decade are one recent example of this dynamic. Thus, the theological account is explanatory in the sense that it relates two important bodies of fact (syntactic diversity and the instability of empires) under one theoretical construct: the declared purposes of God.

The theological approach also fits well with the fact, mentioned above, that linguistic diversity seems to decrease rather than increase human chances for survival. From the evolutionary standpoint, this is a potential embarrassment. However, Genesis presents the creation of linguistic diversity as an act of judgment and limitation, meant to afflict humanity and prevent it from reaching certain goals, rather than an act of blessing. And so we often find it to be. This is not to say that the diversity of languages cannot be a good thing from other perspectives;

for example, it clearly facilitates the development of different traditions of poetry and verbal art, thereby enriching the human experience.[14] However, it is hard to imagine this kind of advantage playing a role in the Darwinian struggle for existence. Rather, it can be understood as an act of a good God, whose curses become blessings to those who are willing to submit themselves to him.

In closing, I should say that I do not intend these last few pages to single-handedly convince those who are materialists in theory or practice that there are spiritual forces at work in the world. However, it does seem right that those who are already convinced of this be alert to places where spiritual forces may shed some light on important facts of intellectual interest. Indeed, I have taken much the same approach in my use of the Chomskian Principles and Parameters framework; I have not argued for that framework directly, but have presupposed it and used it to try to shed some light on the material I was analyzing. However, to the degree that this project has been successful, it constitutes an implicit challenge to those who do not agree with important aspects of that framework to either show that they can do better or to incorporate aspects of my framework into their own work. Similarly, I suggest that part of the meaning of the Polysynthesis Parameter is that we are not simply biochemical survival machines or the cells of a social organism; rather, we are spiritual beings that in part transcend those forces. The Polysynthesis Parameter is also a quiet reminder that there are limits to our pride and ambition set at the borders of our ethnolinguistic group.

Notes

1. Slightly different technical formulations were proposed in sections 7.1 and 10.2, but the differences are not important for summary purposes.

2. This possibility was raised most sharply in discussion with Richard Kayne (personal communication).

3. More precisely, macroparameters may create a bias toward grammatical representation systems that are stable compounds (see the next section).

4. This is consistent with the position of Nichols (1992:181), who reports that head marking is a fairly conservative feature of a language family, but may change under areal pressures. The fact that head marking is rather conservative is also explained by the macroparameter. Thus, suppose that phonological changes or some other innovation causes one set of agreement morphemes to be lost in a head-marking language. The MVC then creates pressure to innovate a new set of agreement morphemes for the affected construction, restoring the pure value of the parameter. Thus, children will only tend to change the setting of the macroparameter in the relatively unusual case that other agreement morphemes are lost before the first set is restored.

5. Notice that this still has something of the status of a parameter in Chomsky 1992, even though Chomsky tentatively adopts the claim that all parameters are lexical. Kayne (1995) calls into question the status of this parameter, but I interpret his work not so much as a refutation of the parameter, as an interesting new theory of it.

6. Actually, Bickerton's (1981:290–291) view sounds rather like this one, but I am not sure he would hold it seriously for the large-scale typological differences I am interested in here.

7. The situation is a bit more complicated than this. Evolutionary theorists have shown that a property can become fixed in a species even if it is harmful to the species as

a whole as long as it is beneficial in the short term to individual carriers of the property. Properties that mark social groups so that individuals can distinguish those who are likely to cooperate with them from those who are likely to betray them can be of this type. (I am grateful to Brian Skryms for discussion of these matters.) Linguistic diversity plays this kind of role for humans. Nevertheless, this does not provide a biological explanation for the existence of macroparameters, because superficial phonological and lexical differences can (and often do) perform this kind of marking function just as well.

8. In earlier work, Bickerton (1981:289–292) explicitly attributed language diversity to cultural diversification and not to the "bioprogram" (Universal Grammar) at all.

9. This debate took place at the Wenner-Gren Symposium on "The Role of Theory in Language Description" held at Ocho Rios, Jamaica in November 1987. The case against the claim is summarized by Hill (1993:451–452). Since I do not know whether those involved on the pro side of the debate would still hold that position, I leave them anonymous.

10. See Black 1994 for a description of one of the modern Zapotec dialects.

11. I use masculine pronouns for the Godhead in deference to the usage in the Scriptures of this tradition. This is by no means to imply that anyone believes that God is male in anything like the biological sense.

12. It should, however, be pointed out that these two claims are not logically inconsistent; rather, they could both be true explanations of the same fact at different levels of description.

13. Ideally, it should also predict facts not yet discovered, but this is less crucial because it depends on one's ability to do experiments that will uncover new facts in the relevant domain. In this respect, evolutionary biology, for example, has much less support than Newtonian physics. However, this is not generally counted against evolutionary biology, because for the most part it is understood that it is impossible to do experiments of the usual kind in that domain (see Kitcher 1982:78–81).

14. Indeed, this is arguably the view of the New Testament. Thus, when God undoes the curse of the Tower of Babel, he does not do so by erasing linguistic diversity; instead, he gives his people supernatural ability to cope with linguistic diversity, in the form of the gift of tongues, given along with the Holy Spirit on the day of Pentecost (Acts 2). Thus, the multilingual crowd present "hear[s] them declaring the wonders of God in [their] own tongues" (v. 11)—using, one may imagine, the full potential for verbal art created by those tongues.

Appendix A: Abbreviations

Mohawk Morphemes

The Iroquoian literature has two sets of terms for its morphemes: older works use the terminology of Lounsbury 1953; newer works use a revised terminology. For the most part, this book uses the newer terms, and the abbreviations are based on these newer terms. Where the older terminology is different, the equivalent term is given in the following list to facilitate comparison with the original sources.

Name	Abbreviation	Older Name
benefactive	BEN	dative
causative	CAUS	
cislocative	CIS	
continuative	CONT	
contrastive	CONTR	
decessive	DEC	
distributive	DIST	
duplicative	DUP	dualic
factual	FACT	aorist
future	FUT	
habitual	HAB	serial
imperfective	IMPF	
inchoative	INCH	
instrumental	INSTR	
locative	LOC	
negative	NEG	
nominalizer	NOM	
noun suffix	NSF	
optative	OPT	indefinite
particle	PRT	

Name	*Abbreviation*	*Older Name*
partitive	PART	
past	PAST	former past, remote past
plural	PL	
progressive	PROG	
punctual	PUNC	
purposive	PURP	
question prt	Q	
reflexive	REFL	
repetitive	ITER	iterative
residential	RESID	
reverser	REV	infective
semireflexive	SRFL	
simultaneous	SIM	coincident
stative	STAT	perfective
translocative	TRANS	

Finally, the amount of morphological analysis that I give to a particular form varies somewhat. In particular, derivational morphology on the verb and the internal structure of nouns is often suppressed when it is not relevant to the point at hand; this helps make the literal glosses more readable.

Mohawk Agreement Morphemes

Mohawk maximally distinguishes four genders and three numbers. In addition, there are first and second person forms that distinguish number but not gender, and there is a distinction between first inclusive and first exclusive. Agreement also exists in three series: "subject" (A-class) agreement, "object" (O-class) agreement, and "possessor" agreement. Agreement morphemes are glossed with a complex symbol, where the first number or capital letter indicates the person or gender, the second (small capital) letter indicates the number, and the third (capital) letter indicates the series (and indirectly the grammatical function). The symbols used are:

Person/Gender		*Number*		*Series*	
1	first person	S	singular	S, A	"subject," A-class
2	second person	D	dual	O	"object," O-class
3	third person (general)	P	plural	P	possessor
N	Neuter	IN	inclusive		
M	Masculine	EX	exclusive		
F	Feminine (Indefinite)				
Z	(Feminine) Zoic				

When two agreement factors are included in a portmanteau form (the usual case in Mohawk), they are divided by a slash (/). For example, the gloss "2DS/MsO" indicates a second person (exclusive) dual subject and a masculine singular object. Null agreement morphemes (e.g., for neuter arguments) are not always represented in the glosses.

Possessor agreement forms are the same as object agreement forms, apart from some phonological differences. The terminology can be confusing, because whether a given argument triggers "subject" or "object" agreement is not necessarily determined by its grammatical function or semantic role; however, transitive subjects usually trigger subject agreement and transitive objects always trigger object agreement (see chapter 5 for details). Also, many distinctions are neutralized in parts of the Mohawk paradigm. For example, gender and number distinctions are lost for third person nonsingular object arguments in the presence of anything but a neuter subject. Sometimes the results of this neutralization will be expressed with a gloss like "3O" (third person object, gender and number unspecified); in other cases, I abstract away from these morphological details. (See Postal 1979 for a systematic discussion of the neutralizations found in Mohawk.)

Morphemes in Other Languages

Generally the abbreviations in the glosses of other languages are a compromise between those used in the original sources and the conventions used for Mohawk, as described above. In particular, where morphemes seem quite comparable across languages I have given them uniform names to make comparison easier for the reader; otherwise, the terminology of the original source is maintained.

The following are symbols used in the glosses of agreement morphemes in other languages:

3HO	Third higher object (Mayali)
A, B, C	Noun gender classes in Southern Tiwa
GU, MA, NI, A	Noun gender classes in Ngandi
MANA, WA	Noun gender classes in Nunggubuyu
MU	Noun gender class in Ngalakan
I, II, III, IV	Noun gender classes in Mayali

Other abbreviations used only for languages other than Mohawk are the following:

Name	*Abbreviation*	*Language(s)*
absolutive Case	ABS	Chukchee, Ngandi
accusative Case	ACC	Urdu
aorist	AOR	Wichita
antipassive	APASS	Chukchee
applicative	APPL	Ainu
augment	AUG	Ngandi
conditional	COND	Wichita

Name	Abbreviation	Language(s)
dative Case	DAT	Ngandi
durative	DUR	Wichita
ergative Case	ERG	Chukchee, Ngandi, Urdu
feminine gender	FEM	Urdu
genitive Case	GEN	Gunwinjguan languages
gerund	GER	Chukchee
immediate	IMM	Mayali
imperative	IMPER	Wichita
indicative	IND	Chichewa, Wichita
indefinite	INDEF	Nahuatl, Wichita
infinite	INFIN	Rembarrnga
intransitive	INTR	Sora
irrealis	IRR	Mayali
linking morpheme	LINK	Nahuatl
nonactive stem	NONACT	Nahuatl
nonpast tense	NONPAST	Sora
object marker	OM	Chichewa
participle	PART	Chukchee
passive	PASS	Nahuatl, Southern Tiwa
perfective	PERF	Nahuatl, Wichita, Mayali
pergressive case	PERGR	Nunggubuyu
permanently	PERM	Wichita
portative	PORT	Wichita
possessive	POSS	Chukchee, Wichita
present	PRES	Nahuatl, Ngandi
predicative	PRED	Nahuatl
preverb	PREV	Wichita
progressive	PROG	Japanese
quotative	QUOT	Wichita
reciprocal	RECIP	Ngandi
reduplication	RED	Nahuatl, Ngandi
relative	REL	Nunggubuyu
singular	SG	Southern Tiwa
subject marker	SM	Chichewa
subordinator	SUB	Ngandi, Southern Tiwa, Ngalakan

General Abbreviations

The following are abbreviations used for linguistic theories, theoretical principles or generalizations, syntactic constructions, and specific articles:

AGF	Allen, Gardiner, and Frantz 1984
ALC	Adjunct Licensing Condition
CAR	Condition on Agreement Relations
CED	Condition on Extraction Domains

CLLD	Clitic Left Dislocation
DS&W	Di Sciullo and Williams 1987
ECP	Empty Category Principle (Chomsky 1981)
GB	Government-Binding Theory
HMC	Head Movement Constraint
LVC	Light Verb Construction
MVC	Morphological Visibility Condition
P&P	Principles and Parameters Theory
PHMG	Proper Head Movement Generalization
RG	Relational Grammar
SAP	Structural Agreement Principle
UG	Universal Grammar
UTAH	The Uniformity of Theta Assignment Hypothesis (Baker 1988)

Names of thematic roles are abbreviated as follows:

Agent (= Actor, causer)	Ag
Event	Ev, e
Experiencer	Exp
Goal (= benefactive, recipient)	Go
Possessor	Poss
"Reference" argument	R
Theme (= Patient)	Th
Reference object	Ref

See also appendix C for abbreviations used to identify the source of Mohawk examples taken from published works.

Appendix B: Orthography and Pronunciation

The transcription used for the Mohawk examples is approximately that of Lounsbury 1953 and Postal 1979, except that the glottal stop is represented by ['] (as in the practical orthography) rather than by [ʔ]. Examples from texts or other sources are converted into this system. Most symbols have more or less their expected values, except that [ʌ], the mid central vowel, and [u], the high back vowel, are weakly nasalized. The [r] of Kahnawake Mohawk, reported here, corresponds to [l] in Akwesasne Mohawk and Oneida.

The transcriptions represent a level that is somewhere between a true underlying representation and a surface phonetic representation. Roughly, those phonological processes that would be deemed lexical or cyclic have been applied, whereas those that are word level or postlexical have not. The following general statements will give the reader a good idea of how the examples should be pronounced:

(i) Delete segments written in brackets.

(ii) Voice the obstruents [s, t, k] when they appear before a vowel.

(iii) [t] and [k] are palatalized before [y], both becoming (if initial or intervocalic) [j]; [y] then deletes. Similarly, [s] plus [y] becomes [ts] or [dz]. Some speakers also delete [r] before [y].

(iv) Stressed vowels are usually lengthened in open syllables. ['] deletes after a stressed vowel, producing a falling tone on that vowel. Under certain circumstances, this also applies to [h].

(v) [w] is deleted before [o, u].

(vi) Word final ['] is usually deleted.

Phonologically conditioned allomorphy in Mohawk is relatively complex; I mention only a few of the major processes to help the reader recognize the same morpheme across different examples. First, there are three kinds of epenthesis: insertion of the "joiner" vowel [a] between noun roots and verb roots, and between verb roots and certain "derivational suffixes"; insertion of [e] between inflectional affixes and the stem to break up inadmissible consonant sequences; insertion of the prothetic vowel [i] when needed to bear stress. The first and the last of these I write as separate morphemes, glossed as Ø; epenthetic [e] is written together with the inflectional affix. Stress is generally on the penultimate vowel, but there are complexities about when epenthetic vowels count for stress placement and when they do not. There are several glide–vowel alternations of [i]–[y] and [u]–[w], depending in part on syllable structure. There are also glide dissimilation processes where [y] appears before the back vowels [o, u] and [w] before mid and front vowels. Vowel–vowel sequences are generally avoided, sometimes by insertion of a [y] glide, sometimes by deletion of one vowel, sometimes by peculiar mergers (e.g., [e] + [a] → [u]). For the latter, I write the surface vowel as part of the affix, and put the stem vowel in brackets with the stem. Many masculine agreement prefixes have /hr/ underlyingly, with the /h/ dropping in word-initial position and the /r/ usually dropping in word-medial position. Finally, laryngeal clusters of [h] and ['] are simplified.

Further details about the phonology of Mohawk can be found in most of the grammars listed in the references. Michelson 1989 is a good introduction to issues of stress, epenthesis, vowel length, and syllable structure, and touches on other points as well. The reader should also be warned that the transcriptions are not in all cases accurate enough to be useful for phonological purposes. This is particularly true for laryngeal segments in consonant clusters, which I found difficult to hear reliably and which were the locus of a fair amount of confusion and variation across the consultants.

In other languages, the transcriptions follow the original source with a few exceptions. Chukchee examples from Nedjalkov 1976 have been transliterated from the Cyrillic script into familiar Western symbols following the example of other papers on Chukchee; however, some mistakes may have been made in this regard. Also, examples from Rembarrnga, Ngalakan, Ngandi, and Nunggubuyu have been transliterated into the standard, practical Australian transcription used by Evans (1991) for Mayali. (This practical orthography uses digraphs for consonants with different points of articulation, rather than superscripts and other diacritics: thus, *dh* is a dental stop, *rd* is a retroflex stop, *nj* is a palatal nasal, *ng* is a velar nasal, and so on.) Examples from Classical Nahuatl, in particular, differ substantially from normal transcription practices, following the standard (Spanish-based) orthography for the language.

Appendix C: Sources and Methods

The Mohawk examples in this work come from two types of sources. The majority come from fieldwork done by the author and his team members at Kahnawake, Quebec, from April 1989 to August 1993. I met consultants for one and a half or two hour sessions once or twice a week; thus, a great deal of planning time could be spent in preparation for each hour of fieldwork time. Six consultants were used; the approximate number of fieldwork hours with each are as follows:

Carolee Jacobs	142 hours
Grace Curotte	142 hours
Frank Jacobs, Jr.	32 hours
Georgina Jacobs	8 hours
Dorothy Lazore	3 hours
Margaret Lazore	2 hours

(These figures do not count a substantial amount of time that Adriana Chamorro and Edward Ikeda spent with Carolee Jacobs, Frank Jacobs, Georgina Jacobs, and Doreen Jacobs while doing their Master's thesis research, although the material they collected was included in my database.) I refer to the first two as my primary consultants; every generalization in the book was worked out with one or the other of them in detail, and most were investigated with both of them. The secondary consultants were used to clarify, correct, and confirm paradigms originally developed with the primary consultants. This was found to be the most efficient way to take advantage of each speaker's availability. In this way most of the material has been checked with at least three consultants and in some cases with as many as five. I also experimented with having graduate students who did not know what I was looking for ask questions of consultants I myself had not yet worked with personally; in this way, it was possible to avoid any influence of my expectations or unconscious training of the consultant. Many of the basic findings were replicated in this way. In most cases, the data presented are only a representative subset of the data actually collected; further examples can be obtained by contacting me. Overall, I identified very few systematic differences in judgments among the various consultants, so I have not revealed the source of particular sentences, to protect them from possible criticism. The few areas in which there seems to be non-trivial disagreement are identified in the notes.

A few examples in this work are taken from published texts that I have analyzed. These texts were collected at different times and represent different genres.

Source	Abbreviation	Genre
Hewitt 1903	H	traditional cosmology myth (collected at Grand River)
Prayer Book (1903)	PB	translated Bible passages
Williams 1976a	KO	traditional stories by a variety of authors (a few in the Akwesasne dialect)
Deering and Delisle 1976	D&D	dialogues, short stories, question/answer pairs, other examples
G. Michelson 1976	M	traditional story
Bonvillain and Frances 1980	B&F	traditional story (Akwesasne dialect)
Old Kahnawake (Scott 1991)	OK	reminiscences of various people, translated from English into Mohawk by Carolee Jacobs and Frank Jacobs, Jr.
K. Michelson 1980		Condolence ritual (reelicited based on an original from 1880s)

Except where indicated, the source is in the Kahnawake dialect spoken by my consultants. The influence of these texts was actually greater than it seems, because in the first three years of the project I studied Mohawk texts for a half an hour each day, and many sentences in the elicited fieldwork were based on models found in texts. This was done to ensure that the fieldwork was grounded in reality and to identify areas worthy of investigation. Nevertheless, I have chosen to cite mostly elicited examples because they contain more elegant minimal pairs and a minimum amount of distracting material. Textual examples are cited only where they seem particularly appropriate or where there might be serious question as to what the naturally occurring pattern is.

References

Abasheikh, M. 1979. The grammar of Chimwi:ni causatives. Doctoral dissertation, University of Illinois, Urbana.

Abney, Steven. 1987. The English noun phrase in its sentential aspect. Doctoral dissertation, MIT, Cambridge, Mass.

Aissen, Judith. 1979. *The syntax of causative constructions.* New York: Garland.

Allen, Barbara, Donald Frantz, Donna Gardiner, and David Perlmutter. 1990. Verb agreement, possessor ascension, and multistratal representation in Southern Tiwa. In *Studies in relational grammar 3,* ed. Paul Postal and Brian Joseph, 321–384. Chicago: University of Chicago Press.

Allen, Barbara, Donna Gardiner, and Donald Frantz. 1984. Noun incorporation in Southern Tiwa. *International Journal of American Linguistics* 50:292–311.

Alsina, Alex. 1992. On the argument structure of causatives. *Linguistic Inquiry* 23:517–556.

Alsina, Alex. to appear. A theory of complex predicates: Evidence from causatives in Bantu and Romance. In *Complex predicates,* ed. Alex Alsina, Stanford, Calif.: CSLI.

Alsina, Alex, and Sam Mchombo. 1988. Lexical mapping in the Chichewa applicative construction. Paper presented at the Nineteenth Annual African Linguistics Conference, Boston University, April 1988.

Anderson, Stephen. 1982. Where's morphology? *Linguistic Inquiry* 13:571–612.

Anderson, Stephen. 1992. *A-morphous morphology.* Cambridge: Cambridge University Press.

Andrews, Avery. 1982. The representation of case in Modern Icelandic. In *The mental representation of grammatical relations,* ed. Joan Bresnan, 427–503. Cambridge, Mass.: MIT Press.

Andrews, J. Richard. 1975. *Introduction to Classical Nahuatl.* Austin, Texas: University of Texas Press.

Aoun, Joseph. 1985. *A grammar of anaphora.* Cambridge, Mass.: MIT Press.

Austin, Peter. to appear. Causatives and applicatives in Australian aboriginal languages. In *Theoretical linguistics and Australian aboriginal languages,* ed. Peter Austin and Barry Blake.

Austin, Peter, and Joan Bresnan. 1994. Non-configurationality in Australian aboriginal languages. Ms., La Trobe University and Stanford University, Stanford, Calif.

Bach, Emmon. 1993. On the semantics of polysynthesis. Ms., University of Massachusetts, Amherst.

Baker, Mark. 1985. The Mirror Principle and morphosyntactic explanation. *Linguistic Inquiry* 16:373–415.

Baker, Mark. 1988a. *Incorporation: a theory of grammatical function changing.* Chicago: University of Chicago Press.

Baker, Mark. 1988b. Morphological and syntactic objects: A review of A.M. Di Sciullo and E. Williams, On the definition of word. *Yearbook of Morphology* 1:259–283.

Baker, Mark. 1988c. Morphology and syntax: An interlocking independence. In *Morphology and modularity,* ed. Martin Everaert, Dordrecht: Foris.

Baker, Mark. 1988d. Theta theory and the syntax of applicatives in Chichewa. *Natural Language and Linguistic Theory* 6:353–389.

Baker, Mark. 1989. Object sharing and projection in serial verb constructions. *Linguistic Inquiry* 20:513–553.

Baker, Mark. 1990a. Elements of a typology of applicatives in Bantu. In *Current Approaches to African Linguistics 7,* ed. J. Hutchison and V. Manfredi, 111–124. Dordrecht: Foris.

Baker, Mark. 1990b. Pronominal inflection and the morphology-syntax interface. In *Proceedings of the the 26th annual meeting of the Chicago Linguistics Society.* Chicago Linguistics Society, University of Chicago, Chicago, Ill.

Baker, Mark. 1991a. On some subject/object non-asymmetries in Mohawk. *Natural Language and Linguistic Theory* 9:537–576.

Baker, Mark. 1991b. On the relation of serialization to verb extensions. In *Serial verbs: grammatical, comparative, and cognitive approaches,* ed. Claire Lefebvre, 79–102. Amsterdam: John Benjamins.

Baker, Mark. 1992a. Thematic conditions on syntactic structures: evidence from locative applicatives. In *Thematic structure: its role in grammar,* ed. I. M. Roca, 23–46. Berlin: Foris.

Baker, Mark. 1992b. Unmatched chains and the representation of plural pronouns. *Natural Language Semantics* 1:33–72.

Baker, Mark. 1992c. Why unaccusative verbs cannot dative-shift. In *Proceedings of NELS 23,* 33–47. Graduate Student Linguistic Association, University of Massachusetts, Amherst.

Baker, Mark. to appear a. Complex predicates and agreement in polysynthetic languages. In *Complex predicates,* ed. Alex Alsina. Stanford, Calif.: CSLI.

Baker, Mark. to appear b. On the absence of certain quantifiers in Mohawk. In *Quantification in Natural Languages,* ed. Emond Bach, Eloise Jelinek, Angelika Kratzer, and Barbara Partee. Dordrecht: Kluwer.

Baker, Mark, and Kenneth Hale. 1990. Relativized minimality and pronoun incorporation. *Linguistic Inquiry* 21:289–298.

Baker, Mark, Kyle Johnson, and Ian Roberts. 1989. Passive arguments raised. *Linguistic Inquiry* 20:219–251.

Barbosa, Pilar. 1993. Clitic placement in Old Romance and European Portuguese and the Null Subject Parameter. Ms., MIT, Cambridge, Mass.

Barker, Muhammad. 1967. *A course in Urdu.* Montreal, Que.: McGill University Press.

Barss, Andrew. 1986. Chains and anaphoric dependence: On reconstruction and its implications. Doctoral dissertation, MIT, Cambridge, Mass.

Bavinck, Herman. 1977. *Our reasonable faith.* Grand Rapids, Mich.: Baker Book House.

Belletti, Adriana, and Luigi Rizzi. 1988. Psych-verbs and θ-theory. *Natural Language and Linguistic Theory* 6:291–352.

Benger, Janet. 1990. Morphologically bound pronominals in Mohawk: configurationality within the verb complex. Ms., University of Ottawa, Ottawa, Ont.

Bickerton, Derek. 1981. *Roots of language.* Ann Arbor, Mich.: Karoma Publishers.

Bickerton, Derek. 1990. *Language and species.* Chicago: University of Chicago Press.

Bittner, Maria. 1994. *Case, scope, and binding.* Dordrecht: Kluwer.

Bittner, Maria, and Kenneth Hale. 1994. The structural determination of Case. Ms., MIT and Rutgers University, New Brunswick, NJ.

Bittner, Maria, and Kenneth Hale. to appear. Remarks on definiteness in Warlpiri. In *Quantification in Natural Languages,* ed. Barbara Partee, Emond Bach, Angelika Kratzer, and Eloise Jelinek. Dordrecht: Kluwer.

Black, Cheryl. 1994. Quiegolani Zapotec syntax. Doctoral dissertation, University of California, Santa Cruz.

Blake, Barry. 1987. *Australian aboriginal grammar.* London: Croom Helm.

Boas, Franz 1911. Introduction. In *Handbook of American Indian Languages,* ed. Franz Boas, 1–83. Washington, D.C.: U.S. Government Printing Office.

Boas, Franz, and E. Deloria. 1941. *Dakhota grammar.* Washington, D.C.: U.S. Government Printing Office.

Bogoras, Waldemar. 1922. Chukchee. In *Handbook of American Indian Languages,* ed. Franz Boaz, 631–903. Washington, D.C.: U.S. Government Printing Office.

Bonneau, Jose. 1992. The structure of internally headed relative clauses: implications for configurationality. Doctoral dissertation, McGill University, Montreal, Que.

Bonneau, Jose, and Mihoko Zushi. 1993. Quantifier climbing, clitic climbing, and restructuring in Romance. Paper presented at the Annual Meeting of the Linguistic Society of America, Los Angeles, January 1993.

Bonvillain, Nancy. 1973. *A grammar of Akwesasne Mohawk.* Ottawa, Ont.: National Museum of Man.

Bonvillain, Nancy, and Beatrice Francis. 1980. The bear and the fox, in Akwesasne Mohawk. In *Northern Iroquoian texts,* ed. Marianne Mithun and Hanni Woodbury, 77–95. Chicago: University of Chicago Press.

Borer, Hagit. 1984. *Parametric syntax: case studies in Semitic and Romance languages.* Dordrecht: Foris.

Bresnan, Joan. 1982. Control and complementation. In *The mental representation of grammatical relations,* ed. Joan Bresnan, 282–390. Cambridge, Mass.: MIT Press.

Bresnan, Joan, and Joni Kanerva. 1989. Locative inversion in Chichewa: a case study of factorization in grammar. *Linguistic Inquiry* 20:1–50.

Bresnan, Joan, and Sam Mchombo. 1987. Topic, pronoun, and agreement in Chichewa. *Language* 63:741–782.

Bresnan, Joan, and Sam Mchombo. to appear. The lexical integrity principle: evidence from Bantu. *Natural Language and Linguistic Theory #13.*

Broadwell, George Aaron. 1988. Multiple θ-role assignment in Choctaw. In *Syntax and semantics 21: thematic relations,* ed. Wendy Wilkins, 113–128. San Diego, Calif.: Academic Press.

Broadwell, George A. 1990. Extending the Binding theory: a Muskogean case study. Doctoral dissertation, University of California, Los Angeles.

Bruce, L. 1984. *The Alamblak language of Papua New Guinea (East Sepik).* Canberra: Australian National University.

Burzio, Luigi. 1986. *Italian syntax: a government-binding approach.* Dordrecht: Reidel.

Butt, Miriam. to appear. Complex predicates in Urdu. In *Complex predicates,* ed. Alex Alsina. Stanford, Calif.: CSLI.

Chafe, Wallace. 1967. *Seneca morphology and dictionary.* Washington, D.C.: Smithsonian Institution.

Chafe, Wallace. 1970. *A semantically based sketch of Onondaga.* Baltimore: Waverly Press.

Chamorro, Adriana. 1992. On free word order in Mohawk. Master's thesis, McGill University, Montreal, Que.

Cheng, Lisa. 1991. On the typology of *wh*-questions. Doctoral dissertation, MIT, Cambridge, Mass.

Chomsky, Noam. 1970. Remarks on nominalization. In *Readings in English transformational grammar,* ed. R. Jacobs and P. Rosenbaum, 184–221. Waltham, Mass.: Ginn.

Chomsky, Noam. 1973. Conditions on transformations. In *A festschrift for Morris Halle,* ed. Stephen Anderson and Paul Kiparsky, 232–286. New York: Holt, Rinehart and Winston.

Chomsky, Noam. 1976. Conditions on rules of grammar. *Linguistic Analysis* 2:303–351.

Chomsky, Noam. 1977. On wh-movement. In *Formal Syntax,* ed. Peter Culicover, Thomas Wasow, and Adrian Akmajian, 71–132. New York: Academic Press.

Chomsky, Noam. 1980. On binding. *Linguistic Inquiry* 11:1–46.

Chomsky, Noam. 1981. *Lectures on government and binding.* Dordrecht: Foris.

Chomsky, Noam. 1982. *Some concepts and consequences of the theory of government and binding.* Cambridge, Mass.: MIT Press.

Chomsky, Noam. 1986a. *Barriers.* Cambridge, Mass.: MIT Press.

Chomsky, Noam. 1986b. *Knowledge of language: its nature, origin, and use.* New York: Praeger.

Chomsky, Noam. 1991. Some notes on economy of derivation and representation. In *Principles and parameters in comparative grammer,* ed. Robert Freidin, 417–454. Cambridge, Mass.: MIT Press.

Chomsky, Noam. 1992. A minimalist program for linguistic theory. Ms., MIT, Cambridge, Mass.

Chomsky, Noam, and Howard Lasnik. 1993. The theory of principles and parameters. In *Syntax: an international handbook of contemporary research,* ed. Joachim Jacobs, Arnim von Stechow, Wolfgang Sternefeld, and Theo Vennemann, 506–569. Berlin: Walter de Gruyter.

Cinque, Guglielmo. 1990. *Types of A-bar dependencies.* Cambridge, Mass.: MIT Press.

Cole, Peter. 1987. The structure of internally headed relative clauses. *Natural Language and Linguistic Theory* 5:277–302.

Collins, Chris. 1994. Economy of derivation and the Generalized Proper Binding Condition. *Linguistic Inquiry* 25:45–62.

Comrie, Bernard. 1979. Degrees of ergativity: some Chukchee evidence. In *Ergativity: toward a theory of grammatical relations,* ed. Frans Plank, 219–240. New York: Academic Press.

Comrie, Bernard. 1981. *The languages of the Soviet Union.* Cambridge: Cambridge University Press.

Craig, Colette, and Kenneth Hale. 1988. Relational preverbs in some languages of the Americas. *Language* 64:312–344.

Czepluch, H. 1982. Case theory and the dative construction. *The Linguistic Review* 2:1–38.

Davies, William. 1986. *Choctaw verb agreement and universal grammar.* Dordrecht: Reidel.

Deering, Nora, and Helga Delisle. 1976. *Mohawk: a teaching grammar.* Kahnawake, Que.: Thunderbird Press.

Demuth, Katherine, and Mark Johnson. 1989. Interactions between discourse functions and agreement in Setswana. *Journal of African Languages and Linguistics* 11:22–35.

de Reuse, Willem. 1994. Noun incorporation in Lakhota Siouan. *International Journal of American Linguistics* 60:199–260.

Di Sciullo, Anna Maria, and Edwin Williams. 1987. *On the definition of word.* Cambridge, Mass.: MIT Press.

Dixon, R.M.W. 1980. *The languages of Australia.* Cambridge: Cambridge University Press.

Dobrovie-Sorin, Carmen. 1990. Clitic doubling, wh-movement, and quantification in Romanian. *Linguistic Inquiry* 21:351–397.

Donegan, Patricia, and David Stampe. 1983. Rhythm and the holistic organization of language structure. In *Papers from the parasession on the interplay of phonology, morphology, and syntax,* ed. John Richardson, Mitchell Marks, and Amy Chukerman, 337–353. Chicago: Chicago Linguistics Society.

Dowty, David. 1979. *Word meaning and Montague Grammar.* Dordrecht: Reidel.

Dowty, David. 1991. Thematic proto-roles and argument selection. *Language* 67:547–619.

Durie, Mark. to appear. Grammatical structures in verb serialization. In *Complex predicates,* ed. Alex Alsina. Stanford, Calif.: CSLI.

Emonds, Joseph. 1985. *A unified theory of syntactic categories.* Dordrecht: Foris.

Evans, Nicholas. 1991. *A draft grammar of Mayali.* Ms., University of Melbourne.

Evans, Nicholas. to appear a. A-quantifiers and scope in Mayali. In *Quantification in Natural Languages,* ed. Emmon Bach, Eloise Jelinek, Angelika Kratzer, and Barbara Partee. Dordrecht: Kluwer.

Evans, Nicholas. to appear b. Role or cast? Noun incorporation and complex predicates in Mayali. In *Complex predicates,* ed. Alex Alsina. Stanford, Calif.: CSLI.

Everaert, Martin. 1990. NP-movement "across" secondary objects. In *Grammar in Progress,* ed. Joan Mascaro and Marina Nespor, 125–136. Dordrecht: Foris.

Finer, Daniel. 1984. The formal grammar of switch-reference. Doctoral dissertation, University of Massachusetts, Amherst.

Finer, Daniel. 1985. The syntax of switch reference. *Linguistic Inquiry* 16:35–55.

Foley, William. 1991. *The Yimas language of New Guinea.* Stanford, Calif.: Stanford University Press.

Fortescue, Michael. 1984. *West Greenlandic.* London: Croom Helm.

Frantz, Donald. 1993a. Empty arguments in Southern Tiwa. Ms., University of Lethbridge, Lethbridge, Alberta.

Frantz, Donald. 1993b. Southern Tiwa argument structure. In *Sixth Biennial Conference on Grammatical Relations.* CSLI, Stanford, Calif.

Fukui, Naoki. 1986. A theory of category projection and its applications. Doctoral dissertation, MIT, Cambridge, Mass.

Fukui, Naoki, and Margaret Speas. 1986. Specifiers and projections. In *MIT working papers in linguistics* 8, 128–172. Department of Linguistics and Philosophy, MIT, Cambridge, Mass.

Gibson, Jeanne. 1980. Clause union in Chamorro and in Universal Grammar. Doctoral dissertation, University of California, San Diego.

Gill, Sam. 1991. Religious forms and themes. In *America in 1492,* ed. Alvin Josephy, 277–304. New York: Random House.

Giorgi, Alessandra, and Giuseppe Longobardi. 1991. *The syntax of noun phrases: configuration, parameters and empty categories.* Cambridge: Cambridge University Press.

Givón, Talmy. 1979. *On understanding grammar.* New York: Academic Press.

Greenberg, Joseph. 1963. *Universals of language.* Cambridge, Mass.: MIT Press.

Grimshaw, Jane. 1982. On the lexical representation of Romance reflexive clitics. In *The mental representation of grammatical relations,* ed. Joan Bresnan 87–148. Cambridge, Mass.: MIT Press.

Grimshaw, Jane. 1990. *Argument structure.* Cambridge, Mass.: MIT Press.

Grimshaw, Jane, and Armin Mester. 1988. Light verbs and θ-marking. *Linguistic Inquiry* 19:205–232.

Grimshaw, Jane, and Ralf-Armin Mester. 1985. Complex verb formation in Eskimo. *Natural Language and Linguistic Theory* 3:1–19.

Guasti, Maria Teresa. 1992. Causative and perception verbs. Doctoral dissertation, Université de Genève.

Hale, Kenneth. 1983. Warlpiri and the grammar of nonconfigurational languages. *Natural Language and Linguistic Theory* 1:5–49.

Hale, Kenneth. 1992. Basic word order in two "free word order" languages. In *Pragmatics of word order flexibility,* ed. Doris Payne, 63–82. Amsterdam: John Benjamins.

Hale, Kenneth, and Samuel Jay Keyser. 1992. The syntactic character of thematic structure. In *Thematic structure: its role in grammar,* ed. I.M. Roca, 107–144. Berlin: Foris.

Halle, Morris, and Alec Marantz. 1993. Distributed morphology and the pieces of inflection. In *The view from building 20,* ed. Kenneth Hale and S.J. Keyser, 111–176. Cambridge, Mass.: MIT Press.

Hattiangadi, J.N. 1987. *How is language possible?* La Salle, Ill.: Open Court.

Heath, Jeffrey. 1975. Functional relationships in grammar. *Language* 51:89–104.

Heath, Jeffrey. 1978. *Ngandi grammar, texts, and dictionary.* Canberra: Australian Institute for Aboriginal Studies.

Heath, Jeffrey. 1980. *Nunggubuyu myths and ethnographic texts.* Canberra: Australian Institute of Aboriginal Studies.

Heath, Jeffrey. 1984. *Functional grammar of Nunggubuyu.* Canberra: Australian Institute of Aboriginal Studies.

Heath, Jeffrey. 1986. Syntactic and lexical aspects of nonconfigurationality in Nunggubuyu (Australia). *Natural Language and Linguistic Theory* 4:375–408.

Heim, Irene. 1982. The semantics of definite and indefinite noun phrases. Doctoral dissertation, University of Massachusetts, Amherst.

Heim, Irene, Howard Lasnik, and Robert May. 1991. Reciprocity and plurality. *Linguistic Inquiry* 22:63–102.

Hewitt, J. N. B. 1903. Iroquoian cosmology. In *Annual report of the Bureau of American Ethnography,* 127–339. Washington, D.C.: U.S. Government Printing Office.

Higginbotham, James. 1983. Logical form, binding, and nominals. *Linguistic Inquiry* 14:395–420.

Higginbotham, James. 1985. On semantics. *Linguistic Inquiry* 16:547–594.

Hill, Jane. 1993. Formalism, functionalism, and the discourse of evolution. In *The role of theory in language description,* ed. William Foley, 437–455. Berlin: Mouton de Gruyter.

Hopkins, Alice. 1988. Topics in Mohawk grammar. Doctoral dissertation, City University of New York, N.Y.

Hornstein, Norbert. 1990. *As time goes by.* Cambridge, Mass.: MIT Press.

Huang, C.-T. James. 1982. Logical relations in Chinese and the theory of grammar. Doctoral dissertation, MIT, Cambridge, Mass.

Iatridou, Sabine. 1988. Clitics, anaphors, and a problem of coindexation. *Linguistic Inquiry* 19:698–703.

Iatridou, Sabine. 1991. Clitics and island effects. Ms., MIT, Cambridge, Mass.

Iatridou, Sabine, and David Embick. 1993. *Pro*-hibitions on reference. In *Proceedings of the West Coast Conference on Formal Linguistics 12* Stanford Linguistics Association, Stanford University, Stanford, Calif.

Ikeda, Edward. 1991. Sentential complementation in Mohawk. Master's thesis, McGill University, Montreal, Que.

Jackendoff, Ray. 1974. A deep structure projection rule. *Linguistic Inquiry* 6:53–93.

Jackendoff, Ray. 1983. *Semantics and cognition.* Cambridge, Mass.: MIT Press.

Jackendoff, Ray. 1987. The status of thematic relations in linguistic theory. *Linguistic Inquiry* 18:369–412.

Jaeggli, Osvaldo. 1982. *Topics in Romance syntax.* Dordrecht: Foris.

Jelinek, Eloise. 1984. Empty categories, case, and configurationality. *Natural Language and Linguistic Theory* 2:39–76.

Jelinek, Eloise. 1988. The case split and pronominal arguments in Choctaw. In *Configurationality: the typology of asymmetries,* ed. Lázló Marácz and Pieter Muysken. Dordrecht: Foris.

Jelinek, Eloise. 1989. Argument type in Athabaskan: evidence from noun incorporation. Ms., University of Arizona, Tucson.

Jelinek, Eloise. to appear. Quantification in Straits Salish. In *Quantification in Natural Languages,* ed. Emond Bach, Eloise Jelinek, Angelika Kratzer, and Barbara Partee. Dordrecht: Kluwer.

Kaiatonsera Ionterennaientakwa (Prayer Book). 1903. Montreal, Que.: Archdiocese of Montreal.

Kayne, Richard. 1975. *French syntax: the transformational cycle.* Cambridge, Mass.: MIT Press.

Kayne, Richard. 1984. *Connectedness and binary branching.* Dordrecht: Foris.

Kayne, Richard. 1995. *The antisymmetry of syntax.* Cambridge, Mass.: MIT Press.

Kitagawa, Yoshihisa. 1986. Subjects in Japanese and English. Doctoral dissertation, University of Massachusetts, Amherst.

Kitcher, Philip. 1982. *Abusing science: the case against creationism.* Cambridge, Mass.: MIT Press.

Knecht, Laura. 1985. Subject and object in Turkish. Doctoral dissertation, MIT, Cambridge, Mass.

Koopman, Hilda. 1984. *The syntax of verbs.* Dordrecht: Foris.

Koopman, Hilda. 1993. The structure of Dutch PPs. Ms., University of California, Los Angeles.

Koopman, Hilda, and Dominique Sportiche. 1981. Variables and the bijection principle. *The Linguistic Review* 2:139–160.

Koopman, Hilda, and Dominique Sportiche. 1988. Subjects. Ms., University of California, Los Angeles.

Koruda, S. Y. 1988. Whether we agree or not. In *Papers from the Second International Workshop on Japanese Syntax,* 103–143. CSLI, Stanford, Calif.

Kozinsky, Isaac, Vladimir Nedjalkov, and Maria Polinskaja. 1988. Antipassive in Chukchee: oblique object, object incorporation, zero object. In *Passive and Voice,* ed. Masayoshi Shibatani, 651–706. Amsterdam: John Benjamins.

Kratzer, Angelika. 1989. Stage level and individual level predicates. Ms., University of Massachusetts, Amherst.

Kroeber, Alfred. 1909. Noun incorporation in American languages. *Proceedings of the International Congress of Americanists* 16:569–576.

Kuno, Susumu. 1973. *The structure of the Japanese language.* Cambridge, Mass.: MIT Press.

Lamontagne, Greg, and Lisa Travis. 1987. The syntax of adjacency. In *West Coast Conference on Formal Linguistics 6,* 173–186. Stanford Linguistics Association, Stanford University, Stanford, Calif.

Larson, Richard. 1988. On the double object construction. *Linguistic Inquiry* 19:335–392.

Lasnik, Howard. 1989. *Essays on anaphora.* Dordrecht: Kluwer.

Launey, Michel. 1981. *Introduction à la langue et à la littérature aztèques.* Paris: L'Harmattan.

Lebeaux, David. 1989. Relative clauses, licensing, and the nature of the derivation. Ms., University of Maryland, College Park.

Li, Yafei. 1990. X⁰-binding and verb incorporation. *Linguistic Inquiry* 21:399–426.

Lieber, Rochelle. 1980. On the organization of the lexicon. Doctoral dissertation, MIT, Cambridge, Mass.

Lieber, Rochelle. 1993. *Deconstructing morphology.* Chicago: University of Chicago Press.

Lieberman, Philip. 1985. *The biology and evolution of language.* Cambridge, Mass.: Harvard University Press.

Lounsbury, Floyd. 1953. *Oneida verb morphology.* New Haven, Conn.: Yale University Press.

Machobane, 'Malillo. 1989. Some restrictions on the Sesotho transitivizing morphemes. Doctoral dissertation, McGill University, Montreal, Que.

Mahajan, Anoop. 1990. The A/A' distinction and movement theory. Doctoral dissertation, MIT, Cambridge, Mass.

Marantz, Alec. 1984. *On the nature of grammatical relations.* Cambridge, Mass.: MIT Press.

Marantz, Alec. 1991. Case and licensing. In *The Eighth Eastern States Conference on Linguistics,* 234–253. Linguistics Department, Ohio State University, Columbus, Ohio.

Marantz, Alec. 1993. Implications of asymmetries in double object constructions. In *Aspects of Bantu grammar 1,* ed. Sam Mchombo, 113–150. Stanford, Calif.: CSLI.

McCloskey, James. 1991. *There, it,* and agreement. *Linguistic Inquiry* 22:563–567.

McDaniel, Dana. 1989. Partial and multiple *wh*-movement. *Natural Language and Linguistic Theory* 7:565–604.

McKay, G. R. 1975. Rembarrnga: a language of central Arnhem land. Doctoral dissertation, Australian National University, Canberra.

Mel'cuk, Igor, and Elena Savvina. 1978. *Toward a formal model of Alutor surface syntax: nominative and ergative constructions.* Bloomington, Ind.: Indiana University Linguistics Club.

Merlan, Francesca. 1976. Noun incorporation and discourse reference in Modern Nahautl. *International Journal of American Linguistics* 42:177–191.

Merlan, Francesca. 1983. *Ngalakan grammar, texts and vocabulary.* Canberra: Australian National University.

Merlan, Francesca. 1985. Split intransitivity: functional oppositions in intransitive inflection. In *Grammar inside and outside the clause,* ed. Johanna Nichols and Anthony Woodbury, 324–362. Cambridge: Cambridge University Press.

Michelson, Gunther. 1973. *A thousand words of Mohawk.* Ottawa, Ont.: National Museum of Man.

Michelson, Gunther. 1976. The legend of Teharahsahkwa. *Man in the Northeast* 12:3–13.

Michelson, Karin. 1980. Mohawk text: the edge of the forest revisited. In *Northern Iroquoian texts,* ed. Marianne Mithun and Hanni Woodbury, 26–40. Chicago: University of Chicago Press.

Michelson, Karin. 1989. *Invisibility: vowels without a timing slot in Mohawk.* Albany, N.Y.: State University of New York Press.

Michelson, Karin. 1991a. On, in, under, and near in Oneida. Ms., State University of New York, Buffalo.

Michelson, Karin. 1991b. Possessor stranding in Oneida. *Linguistic Inquiry* 22:756–762.

Michelson, Karin. 1991c. Semantic features of agent and patient core case marking in Oneida. *Buffalo Papers in Linguistics* 91:114–146.

Mithun, Marianne. 1984a. The evolution of noun incorporation. *Language* 60:847–893.

Mithun, Marianne. 1984b. How to avoid subordination. In *Proceedings of the 10th Annual Meeting of the Berkeley Linguistics Society,* 493–509. Berkeley Linguistics Society, University of California, Berkeley.

Mithun, Marianne. 1986a. On the nature of noun incorporation. *Language* 62:32–38.

Mithun, Marianne. 1986b. When zero isn't there. In *Proceedings of the 12th Annual Meeting of the Berkeley Linguistics Society,* 195–211. Berkeley Linguistics Society, University of California, Berkeley.

Mithun, Marianne. 1987. Is basic word order universal? In *Coherence and grounding in discourse,* ed. R. Tomlin, 281–328. Amsterdam: Benjamins.

Mithun, Marianne. 1991. Active/agentive case marking and its motivations. *Language* 67:510–546.

Mithun, Marianne, and Wallace Chafe. 1979. Recapturing the Mohawk language. In *Languages and their status,* ed. Timothy Shopen, 3–34. Cambridge, Mass.: Winthrop.

Mohanan, K.P. 1983. Move NP or lexical rules? Evidence from Malayalam causativization. In *Papers in Lexical-Functional Grammar,* ed. Lori Levin, Malka Rappaport, and Annie Zaenen, 47–112. Bloomington, Ind: Indiana University Linguistics Club.

Mohanan, Tara. 1991. Wordhood and lexicality: noun incorporation in Hindi. Ms., National University of Singapore.

Müller, Gereon, and Wolfgang Sternefeld. 1993. Improper movement and unambiguous binding. *Linguistic Inquiry* 24:461–507.

Munro, Pamela. 1976. *Mojave syntax.* New York: Garland.

Nakamura, Masanori. 1993. An economy account of *wh*-extraction in Tagalog. In *Proceedings of the West Coast Conference on Formal Linguistics 12.* Stanford Linguistics Association, Stanford University, Stanford, Calif.

Nedjalkov, Vladimir. 1976. Diathesen und satzstruktur im Tschuktschischen. In *Satzstruktur und genus verbi,* ed. Ronald Lötsch and Rudolf Ruzicka, 181–211. Berlin: Akademie Verlag.

Nedjalkov, Vladimir. 1979. Degrees of ergativity in Chukchee. In *Ergativity: towards a theory of grammatical relations,* ed. Frans Plank, 241–262. New York: Academic Press.

Nichols, Johanna. 1986. Head-marking and dependent-marking grammar. *Language* 62:56–119.

Nichols, Johanna. 1992. *Linguistic diversity in space and time.* Chicago: University of Chicago Press.

Noonan, Maire. 1992. Case and syntactic geometry. Doctoral dissertation, McGill University, Montreal, Que.

Obenauer, Hans. 1984. On the identification of empty categories. *The Linguistic Review* 4:153–202.

Ormston, Jennifer. 1993. Some aspects of Mohawk: The system of verbal inflectional categories. Master's thesis, McGill University, Montreal, Que.

Parsons, Evangeline, and Margaret Speas. to appear. Quantification and the position of NPs in Navajo. In *Athapaskan syntax,* ed. Eloise Jelinek and Leslie Saxon. Amsterdam: Benjamins.

Perlmutter, David, and Paul Postal. 1984. The 1-advancement exclusiveness law. In *Studies in Relational Grammar 2,* ed. David Perlmutter and Carol Rosen, 81–125. Chicago: University of Chicago Press.

Pesetsky, David. 1987. Wh-in-situ: movement and unselective binding. In *The representation of (in)definiteness,* ed. Eric Reuland and Alice ter Meulen, 98–129. Cambridge, Mass.: MIT Press.

Pica, Pierre. 1987. On the nature of the reflexivization cycle. In *Proceedings of NELS 17,* 483–500. Graduate Student Linguistics Association, University of Massachusetts, Amherst.

Platero, Paul. 1974. The Navajo relative clause. *International Journal of American Linguistics* 40:365–424.

Polinskaja, Maria, and Vladimir Nedjalkov. 1987. Contrasting the absolutive in Chukchee. *Lingua* 71:239–269.

Pollock, Jean-Yves. 1978. Trace theory and French syntax. In *Recent transformational studies in European languages,* ed. S. J. Keyser, 65–112. Cambridge, Mass.: MIT Press.

Pollock, Jean-Yves. 1989. Verb movement, Universal Grammar, and the structure of IP. *Linguistic Inquiry* 20:365–424.

Postal, Paul. 1979. *Some syntactic rules of Mohawk.* New York: Garland.

Rappaport, Malka, and Beth Levin. 1988. What to do with θ-roles. In *Syntax and semantics 21: thematic relations,* ed. Wendy Wilkins, 7–36. San Diego, Calif.: Academic Press.

Reinhart, Tanya. 1976. The syntactic domain of anaphora. Doctoral dissertation, MIT, Cambridge, Mass.

Reinhart, Tanya. 1983a. *Anaphora and semantic interpretation.* Chicago: University of Chicago Press.

Reinhart, Tanya. 1983b. Coreference and bound anaphora: a restatement of the anaphora questions. *Linguistics and Philosophy* 6:47–88.

Reinhart, Tanya. 1987. Specifier and operator binding. In *The representation of (in)definiteness,* ed. Eric Reuland and Alice ter Meulen, 130–167. Cambridge, Mass.: MIT Press.

Reinhart, Tanya, and Eric Reuland. 1991. Anaphors and logophors: an argument structure perspective. In *Long-distance anaphora,* ed. Jan Koster and Eric Reuland, Cambridge: Cambridge University Press.

Rice, Keren. 1989. *A grammar of Slave.* Berlin: Mouton de Gruyter.

Ritter, Elizabeth. 1991. Two functional categories in noun phrases: Evidence form Modern Hebrew. In *Syntax and semantics 25: perspectives on Phrase Structure,* ed. Susan Rothstein, 37–62. San Diego, Calif.: Academic Press.

Rizzi, Luigi. 1982. *Issues in Italian syntax.* Dordrecht: Foris.

Rizzi, Luigi. 1986a. Null objects in Italian and the theory of *pro. Linguistic Inquiry* 17:501–558.

Rizzi, Luigi. 1986b. On the status of subject clitics in Romance. In *Studies in Romance linguistics,* ed. Oswaldo Jaeggli and Carmen Silva-Corvalan, 391–420. Dordrecht: Foris.

Rizzi, Luigi. 1990. *Relativized minimality.* Cambridge, Mass.: MIT Press.

Rizzi, Luigi. 1991. Residual verb second and the Wh-criterion. Ms., Université de Genève.

Roberts, Craige. 1984. On the assignment of indices and their interpretation in binding theory. In *Proceedings of NELS 15,* 362–376. Graduate Student Linguistics Association, University of Massachusetts, Amherst.

Roberts, Ian. 1991. Excorporation and minimality. *Linguistic Inquiry* 22:209–218.

Rochette, Anne. 1988. Semantic and syntactic aspects of Romance sentential complementation. Doctoral dissertation, MIT, Cambridge, Mass.

Roeper, Thomas, and M.E.A. Siegel. 1978. A lexical transformation for verbal compounds. *Linguistic Inquiry* 9:199–260.

Rood, David. 1976. *Wichita grammar.* New York: Garland.

Rosen, Carol. 1990. Rethinking Southern Tiwa: the geometry of triple agreement. *Language* 66:669–713.

Rosen, Sara Thomas. 1989a. Argument structure and complex predicates. Doctoral dissertation, Brandeis University, Waltham, Mass.

Rosen, Sara. 1989b. Two types of noun incorporation: a lexical analysis. *Language* 65:294–317.

Ross, John. 1967. Constraints on variables in syntax. Doctoral dissertation, MIT, Cambridge, Mass.

Rothstein, Susan. 1983. The syntactic forms of predication. Doctoral dissertation, MIT, Cambridge, Mass.

Rouveret, Alain, and Jean-Roger Vergnaud. 1980. Specifying reference to the subject. *Linguistic Inquiry* 11:97–202.

Rudin, Catherine. 1988. On multiple questions and multiple WH fronting. *Natural Language and Linguistic Theory* 6:445–502.

Sadock, Jerrold. 1980. Noun incorporation in Greenlandic. *Language* 56:300–319.

Sadock, Jerrold. 1985. Autolexical syntax: a proposal for the treatment of noun incorporation and similar phenomena. *Natural Language and Linguistic Theory* 3:379–440.

Sadock, Jerrold. 1986. Some notes on noun incorporation. *Language* 62:19–31.

Safir, Kenneth. 1984. Multiple variable binding. *Linguistic Inquiry* 15:603–638.

Safir, Kenneth. 1985. *Syntactic chains.* Cambridge: Cambridge University Press.

Sag, Ivan. 1976. Deletion and logical form. Doctoral dissertation, MIT, Cambridge, Mass.

Saito, Mamoru. 1985. Some asymmetries in Japanese and their theoretical implications. Doctoral dissertation, MIT, Cambridge, Mass.

Saito, Mamoru. 1990. Long distance scrambling in Japanese. Ms., University of Connecticut, Storrs.

Sapir, Edward. 1911. The problem of noun incorporation in American languages. *American Anthropologist* 13:250–282.

Sapir, Edward. 1921. *Language.* New York: Harcourt Brace Jovanovich.

Schiller, Eric. 1990. The typology of serial verb constructions. In *Papers from the 26th Regional Meeting of the Chicago Linguistics Society,* 393–406. Chicago Linguistics Society, University of Chicago, Chicago, Ill.

Scott, Kawennisake Shirley. 1991. *Old Kahnawake: an oral history of Kahnawake.* Kahnawake, Que.: Kanien'kehaka Raotitiohkwa Press.

Selkirk, Elisabeth. 1982. *The syntax of words.* Cambridge, Mass.: MIT Press.

Sherzer, Joel. 1991. A richness of voices. In *America in 1492,* ed. Alvin Josephy, 251–276. New York: Random House.

Shibatani, Masayoshi. 1990. *The languages of Japan.* Cambridge: Cambridge University Press.

Shibatani, Masayoshi. 1992. Applicatives and benefactives: a cognitive account. Ms., Kobe University.

Shlonsky, Ur. 1987. Null and displaced subjects. Doctoral dissertation, MIT, Cambridge, Mass.

Speas, Margaret. 1990. *Phrase structure in natural language.* Dordrecht: Kluwer.

Spencer, Andrew. 1993. Incorporation in Chukchee. Ms., University of Essex.

Sportiche, Dominique. 1985. Remarks on crossover. *Linguistic Inquiry* 16:460–469.

Srivastav, V. 1991. The syntax and semantics of corelatives. *Natural Language and Linguistic Theory* 9:637–686.

Stowell, Timothy. 1981. Origins of phrase structure. Doctoral dissertation, MIT, Cambridge, Mass.

Talmy, Leonard. 1985. Lexicalization patterns. In *Language typology and syntactic description,* ed. Timothy Shopen, 57–149. Cambridge: Cambridge University Press.

Tenny, Carol. 1987. Grammaticalizing aspect and affectedness. Doctoral dissertation, MIT, Cambridge, Mass.

Terzi, Arhonto. 1992. PRO in finite clauses: a study of the inflectional heads of the Balkan languages. Doctoral dissertation, City University of New York, N.Y.

Travis, Lisa. 1984. Parameters and effects of word order variation. Doctoral dissertation, MIT, Cambridge, Mass.

Travis, Lisa. 1988. The syntax of adverbs. In *McGill working papers in linguistics* 280–310. Department of Linguistics, McGill University, Montreal, Que.

Travis, Lisa. 1991. Inner aspect and the structure of VP. Paper presented at NELS 22, University of Delaware, Newark, October 1991.

Tremblay, Mireille. 1990. Possession and datives: binary branching from the lexicon to syntax. Doctoral dissertation, McGill University, Montreal, Que.

Van Valin, Robert. 1985. Case marking and the structure of the Lakhota clause. In *Grammar inside and outside the clause,* ed. Johanna Nichols and Anthony Woodbury. Cambridge: Cambridge University Press.

Van Valin, Robert. 1987. The unaccusative hypothesis versus lexical semantics: syntactic vs semantic approaches to verb classification. In *Proceedings of NELS 17,* 641–662. Graduate Student Linguistics Association, University of Massachusetts, Amherst.

Vendler, Zeno. 1967. *Linguistics in philosophy.* Ithaca, N.Y.: Cornell University Press.

Vitale, Anthony. 1981. *Swahili syntax.* Dordrecht: Foris.

Watanabe, A. 1991. *Wh*-in-situ, subjacency, and chain formation. Ms., MIT, Cambridge, Mass.

Watkins, Laurel J. 1984. *A grammar of Kiowa.* Lincoln: University of Nebraska Press.

Webelhuth, Gert. 1992. *Principles and parameters of syntactic saturation.* New York: Oxford University Press.

Williams, Edwin. 1977. Discourse and logical form. *Linguistic Inquiry* 11:203–238.

Williams, Edwin. 1980. Predication. *Linguistic Inquiry* 11:203–238.

Williams, Edwin. 1981. Argument structure and morphology. *The Linguistic Review* 1:81–114.

Williams, Edwin. 1989. The anaphoric nature of Θ-roles. *Linguistic Inquiry* 20:425–456.

Williams, Marianne Mithun, ed. 1976a. *Kanien'kéha' okara'shón:'a (Mohawk Stories).* Albany, N.Y.: New York State Museum.

Williams, Marianne Mithun. 1976b. *A grammar of Tuscarora.* New York: Garland.

Williamson, Janis. 1984. Studies in Lakhota grammar. Doctoral dissertation, University of California, San Diego.

Williamson, Janis. 1987. An indefiniteness restriction for relative clauses in Lakhota. In *The representation of (in)definiteness,* ed. Eric Reuland and Alice ter Meulen. 168–90. Cambridge, Mass.: MIT Press.

Woodbury, Anthony, and Jerrold Sadock. 1986. Affixal verbs in syntax: a reply to Grimshaw and Mester. *Natural Language and Linguistic Theory* 4:229–244.

Woodbury, Hanni. 1974. Noun incorporation and Onondaga "relative" constructions. In *Papers in Linguistics from the 1972 Conference on Iroquoian Research,* ed. Michael Foster, 1–17. Ottawa, Ont.: National Museum of Man.

Woodbury, Hanni. 1975. Noun incorporation in Onondaga. Doctoral dissertation, Yale University, New Haven, Conn.

Zubizarreta, Maria-Louisa. 1985. The relation between morphophonology and morphosyntax: the case of Romance causatives. *Linguistic Inquiry* 16:247–289.

Zushi, Mihoko. 1992. The syntax of dative constructions in Japanese. Ms., McGill University, Montreal, Que.

Zushi, Mihoko. to appear. Long-distance dependencies. Doctoral dissertation, McGill University, Montreal, Que.

Index

Abasheikh, M., 51
Absorption, of operators, 184n.22
Active agreement systems, 190, 196, 211–24, 234–37, 243n.34. *See also* Agreement: quirky forms of
Adjectival verbs
  in complex predicates, 351, 436
  inflection of, 333n.19, 396n.42, 396n.44
  as main predication, 402, 403
  noun incorporation into, 301, 340–41, 384–87, 389–90, 413–14
Adjectives
  with auxiliaries, 392n.14, 482
  as bare noun phrases, 309
  in discontinuous expressions, 142–43, 276n.14
  possessive phrases as, 262–65
Adjoined noun phrases. *See also* Dislocation
  and Case, 137n.28
  and definiteness, 91n.15, 125–29
  extraction from, 160, 183n.14
  generation of, 92n.25
  licensed by trace of incorporation, 209–10, 311–12, 318, 336n.33, 448n.16
  licensing of, 96–100, 102–13, 132–33, 133n.1, 142–43, 146, 157
  position of, in clause, 90n.5, 113–21, 182n.7
  and quantification, 53–54
  related to PPs, 407, 413–14
  within noun phrases, 94n.33, 274n.22
Adjunct clauses
  and dislocation, 103–4, 105, 115, 135n.11
  and finiteness, 473, 475–78
  as islands for movement, 74, 161, 170, 175, 179
  and negation, 63
  putative clausal subjects as, 456–58, 492n.6
  position of, 44, 80, 84–86
  quantifiers in, 56, 57
  topicalization within, 101, 134n.8

Adjunct Licensing Condition (ALC), 112–13, 142, 414
  coindexing condition on, 123
  phrases not licensed by, 422, 448–49n.20
  and trace of NI, 312–13
  uniqueness condition on, 142–43, 178
Adjunction
  category of phrase adjoined to, 118–20, 136n.18, 136n.20
  of head to head, 29–33, 38n.30, 280, 441
  left-right asymmetries in, 114–18
  of phrase to phrase, 37n.27, 93n.28, 160
Adjuncts, 41–42, 100–102
  and anaphora, 421–22
  extraction of, 134n.10
  incorporation of, 295, 333n.14
  licensing of, 42, 48, 139–40. *See also* Adjoined noun phrases: licensing of; Adjunct Licensing Condition
  PPs as, 414–24
Adpositional phrases
  internal structure of, 405–14
  licensed only as adjuncts, 112, 414–24
  movement of, 444–45, 451n.35, 451n.37
  in polysynthetic languages, 14, 24, 399–400, 442, 445–46
Adpositions
  and agreement, 448n.14
  argument structure of, 400–404, 446n.5
  barred in compounds, 430
  complementizers as, 492n.5
  as functional categories, 449n.22
  incorporation of, 35, 415, 426–29, 431–32, 439–45, 505. *See also* Applicative constructions
  incorporation of nouns into, 252
  lexically null instances of, 297–98, 333n.17, 391n.4, 391n.7, 424–26, 433, 449n.26, 451n.37